Communications in Computer and Information Science

2023

Rationale

The CCIS series is devoted to the publication of proceedings of computer science conferences. Its aim is to efficiently disseminate original research results in informatics in printed and electronic form. While the focus is on publication of peer-reviewed full papers presenting mature work, inclusion of reviewed short papers reporting on work in progress is welcome, too. Besides globally relevant meetings with internationally representative program committees guaranteeing a strict peer-reviewing and paper selection process, conferences run by societies or of high regional or national relevance are also considered for publication.

Topics

The topical scope of CCIS spans the entire spectrum of informatics ranging from foundational topics in the theory of computing to information and communications science and technology and a broad variety of interdisciplinary application fields.

Information for Volume Editors and Authors

Publication in CCIS is free of charge. No royalties are paid, however, we offer registered conference participants temporary free access to the online version of the conference proceedings on SpringerLink (http://link.springer.com) by means of an http referrer from the conference website and/or a number of complimentary printed copies, as specified in the official acceptance email of the event.

CCIS proceedings can be published in time for distribution at conferences or as postproceedings, and delivered in the form of printed books and/or electronically as USBs and/or e-content licenses for accessing proceedings at SpringerLink. Furthermore, CCIS proceedings are included in the CCIS electronic book series hosted in the SpringerLink digital library at http://link.springer.com/bookseries/7899. Conferences publishing in CCIS are allowed to use Online Conference Service (OCS) for managing the whole proceedings lifecycle (from submission and reviewing to preparing for publication) free of charge.

Publication process

The language of publication is exclusively English. Authors publishing in CCIS have to sign the Springer CCIS copyright transfer form, however, they are free to use their material published in CCIS for substantially changed, more elaborate subsequent publications elsewhere. For the preparation of the camera-ready papers/files, authors have to strictly adhere to the Springer CCIS Authors' Instructions and are strongly encouraged to use the CCIS LaTeX style files or templates.

Abstracting/Indexing

CCIS is abstracted/indexed in DBLP, Google Scholar, EI-Compendex, Mathematical Reviews, SCImago, Scopus. CCIS volumes are also submitted for the inclusion in ISI Proceedings.

How to start

To start the evaluation of your proposal for inclusion in the CCIS series, please send an e-mail to ccis@springer.com.

Wenxing Hong · Geetha Kanaparan
Editors

Computer Science and Education

Computer Science and Technology

18th International Conference, ICCSE 2023
Sepang, Malaysia, December 1–7, 2023
Proceedings, Part I

 Springer

Editors
Wenxing Hong ⓘ
Xiamen University
Xiamen, China

Geetha Kanaparan ⓘ
Xiamen University Malaysia
Sepang, Malaysia

ISSN 1865-0929   ISSN 1865-0937 (electronic)
Communications in Computer and Information Science
ISBN 978-981-97-0729-4   ISBN 978-981-97-0730-0 (eBook)
https://doi.org/10.1007/978-981-97-0730-0

This Springer imprint is published by the registered company Springer Nature Singapore Pte Ltd.
The registered company address is: 152 Beach Road, #21-01/04 Gateway East, Singapore 189721, Singapore

Paper in this product is recyclable.

Preface

Welcome to the proceedings of the 18th International Conference on Computer Science & Education (ICCSE 2023), held December 1–7, 2023, at Xiamen University Malaysia in Selangor, Malaysia. We proudly present these volumes encompassing both online and in-person presentations.

Since its inception in 2006, ICCSE has served as a premier international forum for sharing and exploring cutting-edge advances in computer science, education, and allied fields like engineering and advanced technologies. It bridges the gap between industry, research, and academia, fostering dynamic information exchange and collaboration.

Under the theme "Empowering development of high-quality education with digitalization", ICCSE 2023 invited and received 305 submissions in total, culminating in 106 high-quality manuscripts accepted for these proceedings. Each underwent a rigorous double-blind peer-review process (three reviews per submission) by an esteemed international panel consisting of organizing and advisory committee members and renowned experts.

The proceedings are organized into three volumes reflecting the diversity of submissions: Computer Science and Technology, Teaching and Curriculum, and Educational Digitalization. These reflect the latest developments in computing technologies and their educational applications. Volume 1 covers topics like data science, machine learning, and large language models, while Volume 2 delves into curriculum reform, online learning, and MOOCs. Finally, Volume 3 explores digital transformation and new digital technology applications.

ICCSE 2023 had a dynamic technical program, brimming with cutting-edge insights from renowned figures and diverse opportunities for engagement. Three captivating keynote speeches kicked off the conference:

- Xu Rongsheng, from the Chinese Academy of Sciences, delved into the intricate interplay between the internet, China, and cybersecurity, sparking thought-provoking discussions.
- Andrew Ware, of the University of South Wales, shed light on the transformative potential of generative AI in education, inspiring new perspectives on learning and teaching.
- Zhou Aoying, from East China Normal University, navigated the complexities of digital transformation and its impact on smart education, offering practical guidance for navigating the evolving landscape.

Beyond the keynotes, a dedicated workshop titled "Digitalization Capability Level Certification" provided participants with valuable tools and frameworks for assessing and enhancing their digital skills. Additionally, two Best Paper sessions and 11 parallel sessions offered platforms for researchers to showcase their groundbreaking work and engage in stimulating dialogue with peers.

This comprehensive program ensured that every author had the opportunity to present their research to a receptive audience, fostering a vibrant exchange of ideas and fostering meaningful collaborations.

In closing, we express heartfelt gratitude to everyone who made ICCSE 2023 possible. Our thanks go to the program chairs for their program expertise, the publication committee for their meticulous review process, and the local organizing committee led by the School of Computing and Data Science at Xiamen University Malaysia. We hope these proceedings inspire further discourse and collaboration in the ever-evolving world of computer science and education.

December 2023   Geetha Kanaparan
                                                                       Wenxing Hong

Organization

Honorary Chairs

Jonathan Li   University of Waterloo, Canada
Wang Huiqiong   Xiamen University Malaysia, Malaysia
Li Maoqing   Xiamen University, China

General Chairs

Geetha Kanaparan   Xiamen University Malaysia, Malaysia
Hong Wenxing   Xiamen University, China

Organizing Chairs

Miraz Mahdi Hassan   Xiamen University Malaysia, Malaysia
Hu Jie   Zhejiang University, China
Yang Chenhui   Xiamen University, China

Program Chairs

Li Xin   Louisiana State University, USA
Li Chao   Tsinghua University, China
Wang Qing   Tianjin University, China

Publications Chairs

Weng Yang   Sichuan University, China
Yang Fan   Xiamen University, China

Industry Chairs

Ding Yu   Netease Fuxi AI Lab, China
Cui Binyue   Xiamen Digital Twin Information Technology Co,
                         China

Regional Chairs

Lang Haoxiang   Ontario Tech University, Canada
Xia Min   Lancaster University, UK.

Program Committees

Adam Saeid Pirasteh   Xiamen University Malaysia, Malaysia
Ben M. Chen   Chinese University of Hong Kong, Hong Kong
                         SAR, China
Cen Gang   Zhejiang University of Science and Technology,
                         China
Chen Zhibo   Beijing Forestry University, China
Chen Zhiguo   Henan University, China
Ching-Shoei Chiang   Soochow University, Taiwan
Clarence de Silva   University of British Columbia, Canada
Deng Zhigang   University of Houston, USA
Ding Yu   Netease Fuxi AI Lab, China
Dong Zhicheng   Xizang University, China
Farbod Khoshnoud   California State University, Pomona, USA
Geetha Kanaparan   Xiamen University Malaysia, Malaysia
He Li   Software Guide Magazine, China
He Liang   East China Normal University, China
Hiroki Takada   University of Fukui, Japan
Hiromu Ishio   Fukuyama City University, Japan
Hong Wenxing   Xiamen University, China
Wang Huiqiong   Xiamen University Malaysia, Malaysia
Hu Jie   Zhejiang University, China
Huang Jie   Chinese University of Hong Kong, Hong Kong
                         SAR, China
Jiang Qingshan   Shenzhen Institutes of Advanced Technology,
                         CAS, China
Jin Dawei   Zhongnan University of Economics and Law,
                         China

Jonathan Li	University of Waterloo, Canada
Koliya Pulasinghe	Sri Lanka Institute of Information Technology, Sri Lanka
Lang Haoxiang	Ontario Tech University, Canada
Li Chao	Tsinghua University, China
Li Taoshen	Nanning University, China
Li Teng	University of British Columbia, Canada
Li Xiaohong	Tianjin University, China
Li Xin	Texas A & M University, USA
Li Ying	Beihang University, China
Lin Xianke	Ontario Tech University, Canada
Lin Zongli	University of Virginia, USA
Liu Renren	Xiangtan University, China
Liu Tao	Anhui University of Engineering, China
Liu Tenghong	Zhongnan University of Economics and Law, China
Luo Juan	Hunan University, China
Peng Yonghong	Manchester Metropolitan University, UK
Peter Liu	Carleton University, Canada
Qiang Yan	Taiyuan University of Technology, China
Qiao Baojun	Henan University, China
Sena Seneviratne	University of Sydney, Australia
Shao Haidong	Hunan University, China
Shen Xiajiong	Henan University, China
Tom Worthington	Australian National University, Australia
Wang Chunzhi	Hubei University of Technology, China
Wang Jiangqing	South-Central University for Nationalities, China
Wang Ming	Lishui University, China
Wang Ning	Xiamen Huaxia University, China
Wang Qing	Tianjin University, China
Wang Yang	Southwest Petroleum University, China
Wang Ying	Xiamen University, China
Wang Zidong	Brunel University London, UK
Wei Shikui	Beijing Jiaotong University, China
Wen Lifang	China Machine Press, China
Weng Yang	Sichuan University, China
Wu Xinda	Neusoft Institute Guangdong, China
Xi Bin	Xiamen University, China
Xi Chunyan	Computer Education Press, China
Xia Min	Lancaster University, UK
Xiangjian (Sean) He	University of Technology Sydney, Australia

Xiao Huimin	Henan University of Finance and Economics, China
Xie Lihua	Nanyang Technological University, Singapore
Xu Li	Fujian Normal University, China
Xu Zhoubo	Guilin University of Electronic Technology, China
Xue Jingfeng	Beijing Institute of Technology, China
Yang Li	Hubei Second Normal College, China
Yang Mei	Southwest Petroleum University, China
Yu Yuanlong	Fuzhou University, China
Zeng Nianyin	Xiamen University, China
Zhang Dongdong	Tongji University, China
Zhang Yunfei	ViWiStar Technologies Ltd, Canada
Zhao Huan	Hunan University, China
Zheng Li	Tsinghua University, China
Zhou Qifeng	Xiamen University, China
Zhou Wei	Beijing Jiaotong University, China
Zhu Shunzhi	Xiamen University of Technology, China

Additional Reviewers

Aditya Abeysinghe	University of Sydney, Australia
Ahmad Affandi Supli	Xiamen University Malaysia, Malaysia
Akihiro Sugiura	Gifu University of Medical Science, Japan
Al-Fawareh Hejab Ma'azer Khaled	Xiamen University Malaysia, Malaysia
Cen Yuefeng	Zhejiang University of Science & Technology, China
Chen Lina	Zhejiang Normal University, China
Chen Linshu	Hunan University of Science and Technology, China
Chen Zhen	Tsinghua University, China
Ding Qin	Anhui University of Science & Technology, China
Fumiya Kinoshita	Toyama Prefectural University, Japan
Gou Pingzhang	Northwest Normal University, China
Hironari Sugai	University of Fukui, Japan
Huang Tianyu	Beijing Institute of Technology, China
Jiang Huixian	Fujian Normal University, China
Jin Ying	Nanjing University, China
Kenichiro Kutsuna	Thaksin University, Thailand
Lee Sui Ping	Xiamen University Malaysia, Malaysia
Li Ji	Guangdong University of Foreign Studies, China

Contents – Part I

Computer Science and Data Science

Machine Learning and Its Applications

Large Language Model

Data Mining in Social Science

Contents – Part II

Online Learning and MOOCs

Contents – Part III

Frontiers in Educational Digitalization

Computer Science and Data Science

Optimization of Replica Technology with Two-Stages Dynamic Factor in Cloud Environment

Jun Qin[1,2($\boxtimes$)], Ping Zong[2,3], and Yanyan Song[1]

[1] Communication University of China Nanjing, Nanjing 211172, China
[2] Nanjing University of Posts and Telecommunications, Nanjing 210003, China
{qjun,zong}@njupt.edu.cn
[3] Nanjing University of Science and Technology Zijin College, Nanjing 210003, China

Abstract. The replica technology in cloud storage can not only maintain the high availability of the system, but also improve the performance of the system as a whole. Based on the analysis of the shortcomings of the static copy mechanism of the existing Hadoop distributed file system, this paper dynamically adopts different adjustment strategies for files with different heat, and completes the copy factor adjustment through two stages of filtering and adjustment, which can improve the access performance and avoid the waste of storage resources. The experimental results show that the improved replica factor adjustment strategy, reduced the average response time of system jobs and advance the performance of data access.

Keywords: Cloud Environment · Big Data · Replica · Adjustment Factor

1 Introduction

In the distributed cloud storage environment with largescale nodes, the system availability problems caused by natural disasters and improper human operation cannot be ignored [1]. In addition, the cluster is often composed of a large number of cheap machines, and software and hardware failures become the normal behavior [2]. Therefore, the cloud storage system must provide a series of high availability mechanisms to ensure that the availability of the whole system is not affected, High availability (HA) means that the whole system can ensure more than 99% of the available time, which there are certain differences in service availability between different service providers and their services at different levels, so that the unavailable time of services and its adverse effects can be controlled within a reasonable range. The system can continue to provide services in case of node failure. High availability and performance are a very important factor for the further development of cloud storage. The rational use of replica technology can not only maintain high data availability, but also have important application value for reducing access delay and improving system integrity.

Replica technology is an important way to ensure the high availability mechanism of the system. The redundant storage is setting a certain replica factor for data blocks in the cloud storage system. The redundant replicas is distributed on different nodes in the cluster. So the impact of node failure on system services can be reduced. In dynamic replica technology, three main problems need to be solved intensively: replica factor adjustment timing, replica factor adjustment scheme and replica placement strategy.

2 Hadoop Default Replica Policy

Distributed file system HDFS [3] is mainly based on general distributed machine clusters to provide distributed storage services with high reliability, high performance, scalability and strong fault tolerance for the whole system. HDFS adopts a typical master/slave architecture [4], which is mainly composed of NameNode, DataNode and Secondary NameNode is showed in Fig. 1.

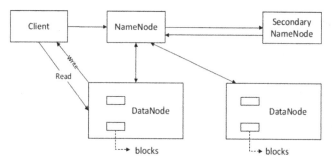

Fig. 1. Main structure diagram of HDFS.

2.1 Default Replica Management Mechanism

At present, the mainstream replica factor management strategies are mainly divided into two kinds: static strategy and dynamic strategy.

The static replica management strategy is a relatively simple replica factor implementation mechanism through the pre-configured replica factor, which cannot adapt to the changes of the system environment due to the lack of flexibility. Too low replica factor will affect the reliability and performance of the system. Too high replica factor will greatly increase the consumption of storage space. Dynamic replica factor strategy can better adapt to the changes of user access frequency, storage space, system bandwidth, system response time and network topology. Dynamically adjusting the replica factor at runtime can adaptively increase, reduce or maintain the number of replicas according to different evaluation indicators, which can often better meet the data access needs of multi-users and heterogeneous storage environment in cloud computing.

2.2 Main Problems and Analysis

The existing distributed file system HDFS adopts the static copy mechanism [5] by default. Especially in the multi-user environment [6] in cloud computing, there are great differences in the access frequency of different files by different users [7]. That is, there are great differences in the access heat of files. If a unified copy factor mechanism is adopted for different files with great differences in access heat, the files with high heat cannot meet the needs of high frequency access because the copy factor is too small [8]. The files with low heat waste storage space because they retain too many copies [9].

Dynamic copy mechanism is an effective solution to the impact of file access response time and network load caused by unequal file access popularity [10]. However, while adopting the dynamic replica factor strategy, it also needs to effectively filter the files to be adjusted. If a unified replica factor dynamic adjustment strategy is adopted for all files, it will bring a large consumption of time and space. At the same time, the replica adjustment strategy also needs to be able to effectively respond to the sudden needs of file access and maintain high data access performance in the case of sudden increase in file heat.

3 Dynamic Replica Factor Adjustment Strategy

Data access in the cloud storage system has the principle of the temporal and spatial locality [11]. The temporal locality refers to the higher probability that data with high access heat in the current time will be re accessed in the future. It reflects that the access of some data in the system has a certain correlation in a certain time period. That is, some files may continue to become hot files in a time period until their access heat gradually decreases.

In the process of cloud storage system performance optimization, due to the large-scale nature of the amount of data stored in the cluster in the cloud storage environment, if a high copy factor is adopted for all files, the system availability and response time can be improved, but the system storage resources will cause a serious waste and bring additional management and maintenance costs to the service provider. Therefore, it is necessary to filter out the hot data in the system according to the locality principle of data access, and then increase the copy factor for this small part of hot data to avoid unified copy factor adjustment. At the same time, for low heat files, the copy factor can be maintained at a low number without affecting the availability, so as to reduce the waste of storage resources.

3.1 Basic Idea of Improved Algorithm

Aiming at the shortcomings of HDFS default static replica strategy in the case of uneven distribution of file access heat, and the problem of unified decision-making and adjustment in the existing dynamic replica strategy, this paper proposes an improved adjustment strategy with two-stages dynamic factor. This strategy not only adjusts the replica factor according to the file access heat, but also considers the priority of different file heat. The adjustment decision of copy factor is made according to two different length time intervals, which can well adapt to the sudden increase of file access heat.

3.2 Improved Dynamic Replica Factor Adjustment Algorithm

The improved dynamic replica factor adjustment algorithm first obtains the set of replica factor files to be adjusted according to the file access heat and replica decision factor value, and then adopts different replica factor adjustment strategies for different files.

Description of Copy Factor File Filtering Algorithm to Be Adjusted

According to the file set F input by the cluster and the sum of the decision-making time interval Δt_1 and Δt_2, the filtering algorithm finally outputs the corresponding high heat file set F_h^1, F_h^2 and low heat file set F_c^1 in the two time intervals respectively. The specific steps of the algorithm are as follows:

Algorithm input: the file set $F = \{f_1, f_2 \dots f_n\}$ in the cluster and the sum of two decision intervals Δt_1 and Δt_2.

Algorithm output: high heat file set F_h^1, F_h^2 and low heat file set F_c^1.

File f_K in t_{now} time access heat FH_k:

$$FH_k = \sum_{t_i = t_{now} - \Delta t}^{t_{now}} (a_k(t_i, t_{i+1}) * decay(t_i, t_{now})) \tag{1}$$

Replica decision factors RD_k for documents f_k:

$$RD_k = \frac{\sum_{t_i = t_{now} - \Delta t}^{t_{now}} (a_k(t_i, t_{i+1}) * decay(t_i, t_{now}))}{br_k * \sum_{j=1}^{n_k} bs_j} \tag{2}$$

Cluster replica decision factor $RD_{cluster}$:

$$RD_{cluster} = \frac{\sum_{k=1}^{n} \left(\sum_{t_i = t_{now} - \Delta t}^{t_{now}} (a_k(t_i, t_{i+1}) * decay(t_i, t_{now})) \right)}{\sum_{k=1}^{n} (br_k * \sum_{j=1}^{n_k} bs_j)} \tag{3}$$

High heat file f_K copy factor dynamic adjustment value DV_k:

$$DV_k = \left\lceil \frac{RD_k - RD_{min}}{RD_{max} - RD_{min}} * \lambda \right\rceil \tag{4}$$

Step 1: According to formula (1), (2) and (3), calculate all files in file set F in sequence $\Delta t1$ and $\Delta t2$ replica decision factor in two decision time intervals RD_k^1 and RD_k^2 (where $\Delta t_1 > \Delta t_2$), and the replica decision factor $RD_{cluster}^1$ and $RD_{cluster}^2$ of the cluster in the two decision time intervals.

Step 2: According to the standards of high heat file and low heat file defined in formula (4), obtain high heat file set F_h^1, F_h^2 in two decision intervals Δt_1 and Δt_2 and low heat file set F_c^1 corresponding to time interval Δt_1, Then from F_h^1 and F_h^2 the intersection F_h^I is obtained.

Step 3: If intersection F_h^I is $\varnothing$, then F_h^1 in a certain proportion γ ($\gamma \in (0,1)$, which can be adjusted according to the actual situation. RD_k^1 is filtered to a certain extent from high to low priority. Some documents with low copy decision-making factor in F_h^1 shall be eliminated. If intersection F_h^I is not $\varnothing$, the documents in F_h^1 will not be filtered in the further.

Step 4: Output the two decision intervals Δt_1 and Δt_2 with the corresponding high heat file set F_h^1, F_h^2 and low heat file set F_c^1, and the algorithm ends.

Description of File Replica Factor Adjustment Algorithm

The adjustment algorithm obtains two decision intervals Δt_1 and Δt_2 with the corresponding high heat file according to the output of the above filtering algorithm.

Set F_h^1, F_h^2 and the set F_c^1 of low heat files in the time interval Δt_1 is dynamically increased arming to the corresponding replica factor for high heat files, meanwhile is dynamically decreased the arming to the corresponding replica factor for low heat files. In order to ensure the reliability of file access in the system, the minimum replica factor is set as $\lambda - 1$. That is the minimum replica factor is 2. The algorithm processing steps of file copy factor adjustment are described as follows:

Step 1: For the high heat file set F_h^1, F_h^2 output by the above filtering algorithm, if the intersection F_h^I of F_h^1 and F_h^2 is $\varnothing$, According to formula (4), the dynamic adjustment value of the replica factor of the files in the file set within the decision-making time interval Δt_1 is calculated successively. For the high heat file set F_h^2, the dynamic adjustment value DV_k^2 of the replica factor will take the dynamic adjustment value λ of the value with the maximum replica decision factor. That is, according to the calculated dynamic adjustment value of the replica factor, adjust the number of existing replica factors to the sum of HDFS default static replica factor λ and dynamic adjustment value of replica factor;

Step 2: If the intersection F_h^I of F_h^1 and F_h^2 is not $\varnothing$, for the files in the set $F_h^1 - F_h^I$, the dynamic adjustment value of the replica factor DV_k^1 of the files in the file set within the decision-making time interval Δt_1 is calculated in turn, and for the files in the set F_h^2, the dynamic adjustment value λ of the replica factor corresponding to the maximum replica decision factor is taken, and then the dynamic adjustment value of the replica factor is calculated according to the dynamic adjustment value of the replica factor to adjust the number of existing replica factors to the sum of HDFS default static replica factor λ and replica factor dynamic adjustment value.

Step 3: For the low heat file set F_c^1 output by the above filtering algorithm, adjust its replica factor as $\lambda - 1$, that is 2.

4 Simulation Verification and Analysis

In order to verify the improvement of the dynamic replica factor adjustment algorithm on the system performance, this paper builds a Hadoop distributed experimental environment in Alibaba cloud environment for simulation experiment verification, and compares and analyzes the impact of the default replica mechanism and the dynamic replica factor adjustment algorithm with two-stages on the average response time of jobs.

Based on the master/slave architecture of Hadoop, a distributed simulation environment is built with the help of Alibaba cloud ECs.

In order to simulate the difference of users' access heat to different files in the cluster, set the access times of files in the cluster to 5, 15, 25, 35, 45, 55, 65, 75, 85 and 100 groups per minute respectively, so as to reflect the change of users' access heat to files. In this experiment, for the determination of high heat files and low heat files, set the parameters is set as (a = 1.2, B = 0.8, Y = 0.8). The decision-making time interval is adjusted as Δt_1 = 45 s, Δt_2 = 5 s. Four groups of files with different sizes (32 MB, 64 MB, 128 MB and 256 MB are set. The comparison of the average response time of system jobs under different access heat is showed in Fig. 2.

By analyzing the relevant results in Fig. 2, it can be seen that when the file access heat is low, the heat of the file has little impact on the dynamic adjustment of the replica factor, and it will not even trigger the dynamic increase or decrease of the replica factor. At the same time, because the algorithm itself needs to consume certain resources and time in the dynamic calculation process, the average job response time of the improved replica factor adjustment mechanism will be longer than that of the default static replica mechanism. That is, the dynamic replica factor adjustment algorithm cannot effectively improve its performance.

With the increasing popularity of file access, the dynamic replica factor adjustment algorithm begins to show some performance advantages. By observing the data results in Fig. 2, it can be seen that when the file access frequency per minute reaches 50–60 times, the dynamic increase of replica factor is triggered. Therefore, for high-popularity files, there will be multiple replicas to provide access services at the same time. So it can effectively reduce the file access competition under high heat concurrent access and shorten the response time of the job. For high heat files, it can timely and dynamically increase the replica factor to meet the continuous or sudden high heat access requirements. As a result it can effectively shorten the average response time of the system job.

Since the access recognition of file D may decline over time, the dynamic replica factor adjustment strategy can also maintain the minimum number of replica factors on the premise of ensuring the basic availability of replicas, reduce the corresponding replica factors according to the attenuation of access recognition, and return to the normal or default number, so as to avoid unnecessary waste of storage space caused by excessive replica factors. At the same time, it also reduces the cost of system consistency maintenance. This improved strategy in this paper can take into account the availability, service performance and rational use of resources as much as possible, and is suitable for the improvement of service performance of multi-users file access in cloud environment.

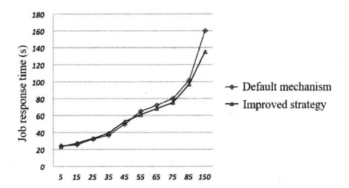

(a) 32MB file job response time changed with access heat

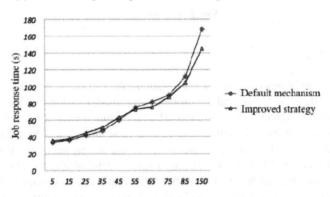

(b) 64MB file job response time changed with access heat

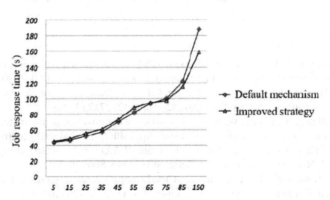

(c) 128MB file job response time changed with access heat

Fig. 2. Comparison of job response time with access heat

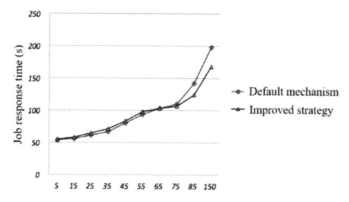

(d) 256MB file job response time changed with access heat

Fig. 2. (*continued*)

5 Conclusion

In view of the limitations of HDFS default static replica strategy in the case of uneven distribution of file access heat, and the problem of unified decision-making and adjustment in the existing dynamic copy strategy when adjusting the replica factor, this paper proposes an improved dynamic replica factor adjustment strategy with two-stages, which not only adjusts the replica factor according to the file access heat, but also considers the priority of different file heat, And the adjustment decision of replica factor is made according to two different length time intervals, which can well adapt to the sudden increase of file access heat, and has good application value. The simulation results also verify the effectiveness of the improved strategy mentioned in this paper.

References

1. Prakash, M., Manikandan, S., Sambit, S., Sanchali, D.: An efficient technique for cloud storage using secured deduplication algorithm. J. Intell. Fuzzy Syst. **41**(02), 2969–2980 (2021)
2. Yanxia, S.U., Qingsheng, W.A.N.G., Yongle, C.H.E.N.: Data sharing of cloud storage based on data segmentation. Comput. Eng. Des. **42**(10), 2742–2747 (2021)
3. Dong, C., Zhang, X., Cheng, W., Shi, J.: Performance optimization of distributed file system based on new type storage devices. J. Comput. Appl. **40**(12), 3594–3603 (2020)
4. Jun, L.I.U., Fangling, L.E.N.G., Shiqi, L.I., Yubin, B.A.O.: A distributed file system based on HDFS. J. Northeastern. Univ. (Nat. Sci.). **40**(06), 795–800 (2019)
5. Dhaya, R., Kanthavel, R., Venusamy, K.: Cloud computing security protocol analysis with parity-based distributed file system. Ann. Oper. Res. **11**(30), 1–20 (2021)
6. Uma, K., Kumar, P., Srinivasu, S.V.N., Nachappa, M.N.: Sqoop usage in Hadoop Distributed File System and Observations to Handle Common Errors. Int. J. Recent Technol. Eng. **9**(04), 452–454 (2020)
7. Elkawkagy, M., Elbeh, H.: High performance hadoop distributed file system. Int. J. Networked Distrib. Comput. (08)3, 119–123 (2020)
8. Wang, B., Wang, K., He, Z., Gao, W., Wei, X.: Optimizing file temperature prediction of Markov based on cuckoo search. Comput Eng. Des. **42**(11), 3121–3127 (2021)

9. Cheng, Z., Wang, L., Cheng, Y., Chen, G., Hu, Q., Li, H.: File access popularity prediction for hierarchical storage for high-energy physic. Comput. Eng. **47**(02), 126–132 (2021)
10. Wang, J., Liu, Y., Yu, C., Wang, M., Liu, X.: Construction of group repairable codes for non-uniform fault protection. J. Beijing Univ. Posts Telecommun. **42**(05), 75–82 (2019)
11. Li, J., Hou, R.: Simulation of information transmission redundancy elimination in big data access. Comput. Simul. **37**(03), 148–151+177 (2020)

Study of Encryption Strategy Based on Multi Owner Attribute

Zhong Zong[✉]

Ping An International Smart City Technology Co., Ltd, No. 123 Shanxi Street, Gulou,
Nanjing 210024, Jiangsu, China
zongzhong@outlook.com

Abstract. The encryption mechanism based on attribute regards a series of attribute sets as the user's identity, associates the ciphertext, private key with attributes and access policies, and uses Boolean expression to represent the access policy to realize fine-grained access control. When the attribute set identifies a user meets the access structure, the user can decrypt the ciphertext with his private key. This paper proposes a multi owner attribute encryption scheme of access structure. The access policies are divided into zoom-in mode and zoom-out mode. In multi owner attribute encryption, multiple owners can jointly control the control strategy of ciphertext, which is suitable for multi author scenarios. The simulation and performance analysis verify the effectiveness and efficiency of the proposed scheme in this paper.

Keywords: Attribute · Multi Owner Structure · Encryption Mechanism · Access Policy

1 Introduction

In the cloud computing environment, the main way to ensure data security is to encrypt data and retrieve ciphertext. The user encrypts the data and stores the ciphertext in the cloud. Even if the ciphertext is leaked by the cloud computing center due to some network attacks or managers' mis operation, it can ensure that the stored message will not be leaked. In searchable encryption, the cloud computing center will use its computing resources to search the ciphertext stored in the center. Users only need to decrypt the ciphertext that meets their requirements, which reduces the computing burden of users.

In traditional encryption and retrieval methods, such as identity encryption algorithm, if the encryptor wants to share some data, the identity encryption algorithm requires the encryptor to know the exact identity of the shared person and use the identity to encrypt the data. The encrypted data is only decrypted by the shared person. However, in the cloud computing scenario, encryptors often want to share data with some specific people who meet some fixed conditions. At this time, encryptors often do not know how many people meet the conditions and what is the identity of each person. Therefore, the encryption algorithm based on identity is not suitable for such application scenarios. How to achieve the access control of encrypted data and retrieval way of cloud storage

W. Hong and G. Kanaparan (Eds.): ICCSE 2023, CCIS 2023, pp. 12–20, 2024.
https://doi.org/10.1007/978-981-97-0730-0_2

data in fine-grained approach have become a key challenge for researchers. Literature [1] proposes an Attributed-based Encryption (ABE) method, which realizes flexible, efficient and fine-grained access control. Therefore, it is well applied to the access and retrieval of encrypted data in cloud computing environment, which is also the basis of further improvement research in this paper.

2 Attribute Encryption Mechanism

Based on the attribute encryption mechanism, the concepts of attribute set and access policy are introduced, and a series of attribute sets are used as the identity of users. When the attributes match the access structure, the ciphertext can be decrypted, which ensures the data confidentiality and realizes fine-grained access control at the same time. The effectiveness, anti-collusion attack and flexible access strategy of ABE mechanism make it in good application prospects in the fields of fine-grained access control [2] (audit log, pay TV system, etc.), directional broadcasting [3], group key management [4] and privacy protection.

The attribute encryption algorithm can be basically divided into two parts: Key Policy Attribute Based Encryption (KP-ABE) [5] and Ciphertext Policy Attribute Based Encryption (CP-ABE) [6]. In the KP-ABE scheme, the private key generation center generates the private key for the user according to the access structure. The user determines the corresponding attribute set for the message, and the ciphertext is related to the attribute set. The user can decrypt the ciphertext whose attribute set meets the access structure corresponding to its private key. In the CP-ABE scheme, the data owner encrypts the data and sets the access structure. The private key is a set of attribute sets [7]. Only the encrypted data of the corresponding attribute set can be decrypted [8].

In the scheme of the encryption based on attribute, the owner of data should be unique. Therefore, determining the access policy and the encrypted data file are only performed by the owner. However, in many application scenarios, the single owner can no longer meet the actual application requirements [9]. In fact, in many application scenarios, multiple owners jointly hold data, and their joint control over the data must be guaranteed [10].

At present, no real multi owner attribute encryption mechanism has been applied in practice. However, privacy control between multi owners is essential in cloud computing. For example, every user in a photo system can participate in determining the access control conditions of photos, but such a mechanism has the problem of privacy conflict. In order to solve the privacy conflict between multiple parties, it is relatively important to evaluate the sensitivity of each conflicting user to the photo, and try to compromise those who have less strict privacy requirements. This idea is a basic scheme that enables multiple owners to realize mutual privacy protection and data sharing. However, in the scheme, a data distributor must be set. Only the distributor who meets the access structure can decide which user can decrypt the original text through the multicast based on the identity. Therefore, there is still no real multi-attribute encryption between the data owner and the other users.

3 Multi Attribute Encryption Mechanism

In the scheme of the encryption based on attribute, the owner of data is unique. In multi owner encryption, the owner is allowed to specify a set of cooperative owners. The cooperative owner can change the access policy of the ciphertext based on the ciphertext encrypted by the owner, so as to ensure the control of the cooperative owner over the data. In addition, in order to prevent possible access policy conflicts when multiple owners jointly determine the access policy, the access policy extension mode and access policy reduction mode can be adopted.

In the traditional encryption based on attribute method, there are four entity attribute institutions, cloud servers, owner and users. The attribute institution generates the public key required by the system and saves the generated master key. When the user enters the system, it determines the attribute set for the user and uses the master key to generate the corresponding private key. The owner encrypts and uploads the ciphertext to Customer Service Provider (CSP). Users use their own private key to decrypt. The process method as shown in Fig. 1.

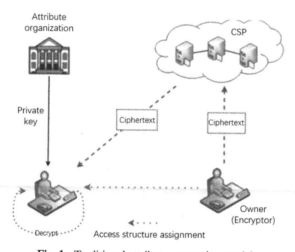

Fig. 1. Traditional attribute encryption model.

Based on the traditional attribute encryption model, the owner is divided into main owner and cooperative owner. The main owner can specify a collaboration owner set, as shown in Fig. 2.

After the designated cooperative owner obtains the cooperative ciphertext of the main owner, it generates an aggregate ciphertext and sends it to CSP. After obtaining the aggregate ciphertext, CSP re-encrypts the initial ciphertext generated by the main owner. CSP uses specific rules to integrate the access structure in the aggregate ciphertext into the access structure of the initial ciphertext, and then get the final ciphertext to ensure the control of each owner over the data.

This paper proposes the access policy reduction mode and access policy expansion mode in order to prevent the conflict of access policies from each owner.

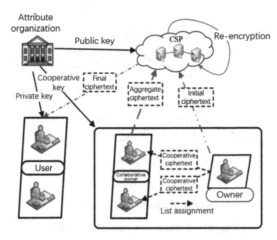

Fig. 2. Multi attribute encryption model.

In the access policy reduction mode, all owners enjoy the same control ability. Decryption can be performed only when the user attributes meet the access policies of all owners. Figure 3 shows the aggregation mode of each owner's access policy when the access policy reduction mode is adopted, in which f0 is the main owner's access policy and f1…N are the access policy of each cooperative owner.

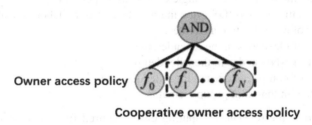

Fig. 3. Access policy reduction mode.

In the access policy extension mode, the access policy of the owner has a higher priority. Only when the user meets the access policy of the owner or the access policy of all cooperative owners, The data can be decrypted. Figure 4 shows the aggregation mode of each owner's access policy when it is the access policy extension mode, in which f0 is the access policy of the main owner and f1…N are the access policy of each cooperative owner.

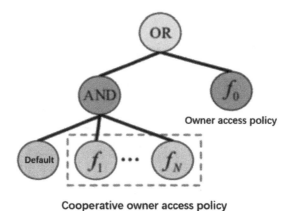

Fig. 4. Access policy extension mode.

4 Simulation Experimental and Performance Analysis

In order to facilitate statistics and expression, this paper focuses on time-consuming operations such as exponential operation and pairing operation. The relevant parameters are defined as follows.

Tpair marks the time required for a single pairing operation.
Texp marks the time required for a single exponential operation.
atts is the user's attribute and IDS is the main collection of collaboration attributes.
n is the number of extended tree attributes.
p is the number of OR nodes in the extended tree.
q is the number of AND nodes in the extended tree.
y is the number of non-page nodes in the extended tree.
|G| represents the bit length of group elements.

Table 1 shows the relevant computing costs required for private key generation, collaborative key generation, encryption, access structure expansion, ciphertext update and decryption in the design scheme above-mentioned.

For the convenience of expression, each non leaf node in the setting scheme has and only has two child nodes. Private key generation and collaborative key generation are independent of the current mode, in which the number of private keys generated from attributes is linear, and the amount of calculation of collaborative key generation is constant. The amount of computation in encryption is related to the current mode. In the access policy reduction mode, the main amount of computation is focused on generating relational ciphertext for the access structure. For attribute nodes, each node needs to perform three exponential operations. For the OR gate, it needs to generate the corresponding C = {CW, i, 1, CW, i, 2} for each child node. Therefore, assuming that each non leaf node in the access tree has only two children, four exponential operations are required. Assuming that each non leaf node in the access tree has only two children, four exponential operations are required. If OR gate has i (i ≤ 2) child nodes, 2i exponential operations are required. For AND gate, since the secret value relation strategy of

Table 1. Comparison of calculation overhead

Stage	Pattern	Computation Overhead
KeyGen		$(2 + |atts|)Texp$
CokeyGen		$Texp$
Encrypt	Access policy reduction mode	$(3n + 4p + 5)Texp$
	Access policy expansion mode	$(3(n + 2) + 4(p + 1))Texp$
Access structure extension	Access policy reduction mode	$2Tpair + (3n + 4p + 5 + 3)$ $Texp$
PolicyApp	Access policy expansion mode	$2Tpair + (3n + 4p + 5 + 2)$ $Texp$
Ciphertext update	Access policy reduction mode	$2NTexp$
	Access policy expansion mode	$NTexp$
Decrypt	Access policy reduction mode	$(2n + 2o + 2q + 1)Tpair$
Decrypt	Access policy expansion mode	$(2n + 2p + 2q + 1)Tpair +$ $Texp$

and gate is changed, no exponential operation or pairing operation is required here. In addition, an exponential operation is required when calculating CK, C0, C1, D2 and C3. Therefore, the final computational overhead is $(3n + 4p + 5)$ Texp. When encryption is an access policy extension mode, users need to generate relational ciphertext for the extended access structure. Compared with the original access structure, the extended access structure has one more attribute node and one more or node. Therefore, in the access policy extension mode, the amount of encryption calculation is $(3 (n + 1) + 4 (P + 1) + 5)$ Texp.

In the access structure extension, both modes need to judge whether the current node is in the collaborative master set. At this time, two pairing operations and one exponential operation are required. At the same time, both modes need to generate $\{CW\}$ w $\in$ f for the extended access policy. The access policy reduction mode needs to generate one more element to generate Di than the access policy extension mode. Therefore, the calculation amount of access policy reduction mode is one unit more than that of access policy extension mode. In the update, if n expansion operations are required, the access policy reduction mode needs to perform n exponential operations on CK and C0; In the access policy extension mode, only CR0, 1, 2 perform n exponential operations. In decryption, specific operations need to be performed on each node in the tree, and two pairing operations are required for attribute nodes. For the OR operation of two child nodes, it needs to be paired with 1. For AND gate nodes, two pairing operations are required. At the same time, in the access policy expansion mode, we need to calculate $(gkranrn + q)1/n$ to get $gkranrn + q$, so it requires more unit of exponential operation than the access policy reduction mode.

The simulation platform built in this paper is: Linux operating system, Intel (R) Pentium (R)/CPU b950/2.10 GHz, 1 GB memory. It provides the implementation of LIBMMAP library function based on CentOS 7. In this section, for the convenience of expression, an access strategy for a specific number of nodes is given: it is assumed that the number of AND gate, OR gate and attribute nodes each account for 1/3 of the summary point.

In the encryption phase, the user selects the access policy expansion mode or access policy reduction mode respectively. From the above performance analysis, it can be seen that the calculation time of encryption is mainly related to the number of nodes in the access policy. Figure 5 shows the time required when the number of nodes is as shown in this figure, when the access policy is the same and the number of cooperative owners is the same. In the access policy expansion mode, for the same tree, it also needs to generate ciphertext for two privileged nodes and the root node. Therefore, the access policy expansion mode takes more time than the access policy reduction mode.

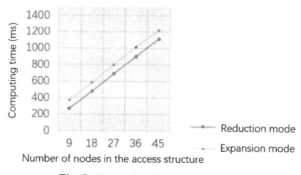

Fig. 5. Encryption time of two modes.

Figure 6 shows the relationship between the calculation time and the number of nodes in the access policy reduction mode and the access policy expansion mode, both in the access structure expansion algorithm. The calculation amount of access policy reduction mode is equivalent to that of access policy extension mode. Therefore, the gap between access policy narrowing mode and access policy extension mode is very small.

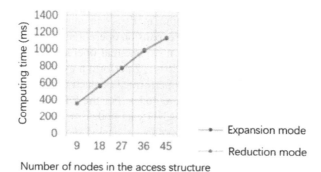

Fig. 6. Time required for access structure expansion.

Finally, Fig. 7 shows the time required for decryption of the scheme, which is longer than that for encryption and access structure expansion. The decryption process requires multiple pairing operations, which is the most time-consuming operation.

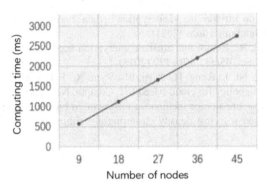

Fig. 7. Time required for decryption.

5   Conclusion

In multi owner attribute encryption, multiple owners can jointly control the control strategy of ciphertext, which is suitable for multi author scenarios. In order to prevent possible access policy conflicts when multiple owners jointly determine the access policy, in the access policy reduction mode, the access policies determined by each owner are at the same level. Users must meet the access policies of all owners before decryption, in the access policy extension mode, the primary owner has higher priority than the cooperative owner. Users can decrypt only when they meet the access policies of the primary owner or all cooperative owners. The design scheme in this paper can not only ensure the security of data stored in the cloud and reduce the computing burden of users, but also better solve the problem of flexible, efficient and fine-grained access control.

References

1. Mollah, M.B., Islam, K.R., Islam, S.S.: Next generation of computing through cloud computing technology. In: IEEE Conference of Electrical & Computer Engineering. Montreal, QC, Canada, pp. 1–6. IEEE (2012)
2. Fan, Y., Wu, X.: Ciphertext-policy attribute-based encryption access control scheme for cloud storage. Appl. Res. Comput. **35**(08), 2412–2416 (2018)
3. You, W., Zhang, L., Ye, Y., Li, H.: Privacy-preserving attribute-based dynamic broadcast encryption mechanism in multi-user communication system. Netinfo Secur. **21**(4), 21–30 (2021)
4. Wei, D., Gao, H.: A ciphtext-policy Attribute-based Encryption scheme supporting arithmetic span program. ACTA Electron. Sinca **48**(10), 1993–2002 (2022)

5. Yang, N., Teng, W., Han, B., Huang, S.: Attribute-based encryption access control scheme of multiple attribute center with constant size ciphertexts. Comput. Eng. Des. **40**(10), 2766–2772 (2019)

6. Chen, L., Li, J., Zhang, Y.: Adaptively secure efficient broadcast encryption with constant-size secret key and ciphertext. Soft Comput. **24**(6), 4589–4606 (2020)

7. Han, X.: Research on attribute-based encryption in data sharing in cloud. Beijing University of Posts and Telecommunications (2021)

8. Tu, Y., Gao, Z., Li, R.: Removable attribute encryption access control algorithm based on CP-ABE. Comput. Sci. **45**(11), 176–179 (2018)

9. Hao, J., Huang, C., Ni, J., Rong, H., Xian, M., Shen, X.: Fine-grained data access control with attribute-hiding policy for cloud-based IoT. Comput. Networks **153**, 1–10 (2018)

10. Gu, B., Ma, J.: A Secure storage method for unstructured big data using revocable attribute encryption combined with fast density clustering algorithm. Comput. Appl. Softw. **38**(5), 337–343 (2021)

Web Accessibility Enhancement for Medical Consultation Platforms

Huike Wang[1] , Chen-Hsiang Yu[2] , and Xiao Yang[1](✉)

[1] Shandong University of Finance and Economics, Jinan 250014, China
20190611817@mail.sdufe.edu.cn, yangxiao@sdufe.edu.cn
[2] Northeastern University, Boston 02115, USA

Abstract. With a rapid evolution of the healthcare domain and COVID outbreak, people start using online consultation platforms to seek treatments. However, the design of medical web pages is complex due to it integrates a lot of information. The goal of this research is to make the Web of medical consultation platforms more accessible for people with visual impairments, especially the elderly. The research was motivated by conducting a survey with 15 elderly people to learn about their needs when visiting the medical web pages. Based on the results, we proposed and designed a new system, TarsiEyes, which not only mined data information from the online platform, but it also provided a new interface integrating results from crawler technology and web customization for accessibility enhancement. The results of the user study with eight users showed that the proposed design significantly enhanced reading speed, reading comprehension and readability of the medical web pages.

Keywords: Online Medical Comments · Sentiment Analysis · The Elderly People · Accessibility Enhancement · Web Customization

1 Introduction

In recent years, with a vigorous development of Internet-based medical industry, many online medical consultation platforms have emerged. Both the number of registered doctors and users of the platform have increased dramatically. As a result, massive online medical data such as comments, rating and number of virtual gifts from the users has exploded [1]. Online medical comments include, but not limited to, evaluation of the doctors' services and medical skills, treatment effects and the patients' medical experience. These types of information can help the users better understand the doctors' information so that they can find a right one to avoid wasting medical resources.

The online medical consultation platforms also have an impact to the traditional model of medical treatment. It not only eliminates a cumbersome procedure of queuing and registration offline, but it also effectively resolves a livelihood issue, named "difficulty of registering and seeing a doctor", which is common in China [1]. Specifically, during the COVID pandemic, online medical consultation platforms allow people to seek medical treatments during the quarantine time. Although this new model of medical treatment has indeed brought great convenience to the public, we found that some

W. Hong and G. Kanaparan (Eds.): ICCSE 2023, CCIS 2023, pp. 21–33, 2024.
https://doi.org/10.1007/978-981-97-0730-0_3

of them violate accessibility guidelines defined by W3C WCAG [2]. For example, some doctors' homepages presented in the consultation platforms have poor color contrast, which violates Guideline 1.4, i.e. Distinguishable. Also, they do not create content that can be presented in different ways without losing information or structure, which violates Guideline 1.3, i.e. Adaptable. Therefore, there is a need to enhance web accessibility of online medical consultation platforms.

Nowadays, there has been extensive work on text analysis and processing for websites with the goal of helping users with special needs. For example, text simplification of websites for users with cognitive difficulties has been studied. Mai Farag Imam et al. [3] designed a system which translated the text on the websites into pictographs to perform text simplification in terms of precision, recall and F-score for people with language deficits. Gert Jan Gelderblom et al. [4] compared parallel corpuses containing simplified texts with original website to identify the better version which can provide an easy-to-read content for reading-impaired people. In terms of interface design, Yu et al. [5, 6] proposed a new transformation method to enhance the readability of web pages for non-native English users. They designed and implemented a new Firefox extension to apply content transformation for public use. Their study found that the proposed content transformation can not only help improve reading comprehension, but it also enhanced the user satisfaction for non-native English readers.

Many researchers found that visually impaired users are easily disturbed by invalid information when browsing the web pages. Suhit Gupta et al. [7] designed a compatibility framework to extract text information interested to the users and applied it to enhance web accessibility. Andrew Arch [8] studied and analyzed the needs of the elderly people who use Internet for accessible web pages. Chen [9] summarized the aging characteristics of the elderly, then made text analysis of Taobao which is one of the most famous online shopping websites in China. They applied the text analysis results (of the original Taobao interface) to the design of shopping interface for the elderly and then proposed a new mobile version of Taobao based on the theory of visual cognition, mainly for the elderly users.

Semi-automated transcoding for accessibility has been studied since the late 90s. Takagi et al. [10] proposed a proxy system which consisted of 5 modules using 3 kinds of annotations to transcoded already-existing Web pages into accessible pages for the blind. Yesilada et al. [11] provided an approach called Dante in which Web pages are annotated with semantic information to make their traversal properties explicit for people with visual impairments. For having an accessibility transcoding in the medical domain, Parmanto et al. [12] developed a multi-modal transcoding system which focused on transcoding full-text biomedical information resources to support mobile devices for healthcare professionals. The proposed system utilizes simplification and summarization techniques to deliver compact information to the mobile user.

At present, there is little research to enhance accessibility of medical consultation platforms for the elderly. In general, medical websites are different from other websites which pages contain a lot of texts, especially the introduction to a doctor and massive comments, and lack of diversified forms of information presentation, which is very difficult to read for the elderly users. Inspired by the ideas of interface design mentioned above, this paper applied text analysis to the web pages of the medical consultation platform to help the elderly easily seek medical information. We used "Good Doctor Online" (www.haodf.com) as an example to demonstrate our idea. This platform is one of the most popular online medical consultation platforms in China.

2 Materials and Methods

2.1 Preliminary Study

To clearly capture the needs of the elderly people when using online medical consultation platform, we conducted a preliminary survey with the elderly who were people with vision loss or suffering from visual diseases. The survey was conducted in Mandarin and there were 15 people participating in it. To make sure participants can feel relaxed all the time, we tried to make the meeting with each participant for less than five minutes.

To obtain the information of what matters when browsing the doctor's homepage, the survey was conducted by using a questionnaire. One question asked the participants to choose 4–5 information items they pay most attention to when looking for doctors online. In the questionnaire, we listed as many items of the medical web page as possible to avoid missing the important one.

Figure 1 shows the statistical results of the survey. The top characteristics are: (1) what diseases the doctor is good at treating, (2) patient comments, (3) service satisfaction, (4) which hospitals and departments the doctors work in, and (5) the frequency of online consultation. In addition, many elderly people hoped that the website can have a function of voice broadcast. In this survey, we also found that the elderly people do not pay much attention to certain kinds of information, such as the papers published by the doctors, the number of virtual gifts sent by the patients (a special feature designed in the website), etc.

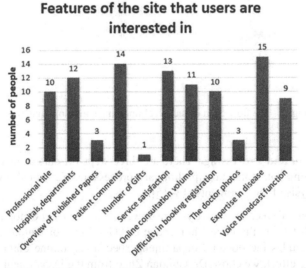

Fig. 1. The statistics of website features that the users are interested in.

Above quotes assured us that the elderly people need a website with a better accessibility for them to find key information from the web pages. Starting from next section, we would like to introduce the design and implementation of the proposed system, TarsiEyes, targeting at addressing found issues.

2.2 System Design and Implementation

Based on the preliminary study, we have some learnings. Firstly, we found that online medical consultation platform was too complex to read for the elderly people. Therefore, we considered to generate customized web pages that keep high frequently selected contents from the preliminary study and remove redundant information. Secondly, the participants said that the amount of comment data on the original web page are too large, and it is difficult to understand users' emotional attitude to the doctors. This kind of comments is important for the users. Based on this comment, we believed data processing and sentiment analysis are needed. Thirdly, the participants commented that it's difficult to obtain key information from the original web pages, and they prefer concise or less-textual presentation to reduce text description. Topic analysis and word clouds are used for comments visualization. All above findings inspired us to design a new system, TarsiEyes, which integrates data processing and visualization to address accessibility issues in medical consultation platforms. In this section, we would like to explain the details of the design (Fig. 2).

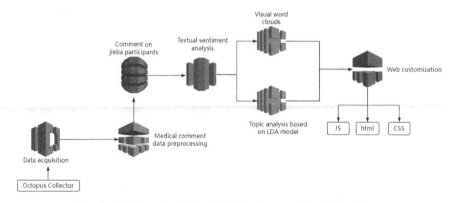

Fig. 2. The flow chart of technical implementation of TarsiEyes.

Data Acquisiton and Processing. There are three steps for data acquisition and processing, including data collection, preliminary processing of medical review data and sentiment analysis of the comments [13–15].

Data Collection. To recreate an easy-to-read web page, we used Octopus Collector to crawl essential data on the doctor homepage of "Good Doctor Online". The crawled information includes the doctor's department, specialties, online comments, etc. To demonstrate the effect, we chose Dr. Guixian Zhao from the Department of Neurology as an example to carry out data acquisition and processing.

Preliminary Processing of Medical Review Data. We found that there are a lot of meaningless or repetitive data in the patients' comments. Data cleaning and preprocessing are necessary for the following operations. Therefore, we ran preliminary processing to the data, including deduplication, mechanical compression and short sentence deletion, etc. Then, to facilitate text simplification, we removed special symbols from massive review data. Because the comments were expressed in Chinese, so we used the technology of Jieba Chinese word segmentation technique [16] to extract text features and customize the word segmentation. After above operations, we generated input text for sentiment analysis.

Sentiment Analysis. Due to massive user comments, it is difficult for people with visual impairments to read each of them and analyze its emotional tendency. To help user s better understand the reputation of the doctor, our proposed system conducted sentiment analysis on patients' comments and provided a graphical representation to the users. The comments were recognized into positive and negative sides, and the proportion of each side was also obtained. We used emotion classification method in Python and scored the emotion of the comments. The emotion score was between 0 and 1. If the score is greater than 0.5, the emotion was considered positive, otherwise it was negative. We used the SnowNLP [19] library for sentiment analysis without retraining the models in our study.

Visualization with Word Clouds. Compared with boring and lengthy text description, our preliminary study with 15 visually impaired people found that they preferred a concise and graphical display. Ostapenko's research [17] suggested that publishing a word cloud as a graphical supplement to a scientific paper can help the readers to understand what basic keywords and terms the author uses directly in the text of the paper. As shown in Fig. 3, We shared the same opinion as [18] and proposed to use word cloud to visually represent the high frequency sentiment words of patient comments.

In the word cloud map, the users can view patients' opinions to the doctor in the form of positive words, such as "patient", "careful", "professional", "responsible", etc. Therefore, the graphical visualization can help the users better understand the level of medical skills and the reputation of the doctor.

Feature Analysis Based on LDA Topic Model. LDA topic model is a well-known unsupervised tool for semantic mining in text [19]. It is a bag-of-words model that treats each document as a word frequency vector and transforms text information into words by choosing a topic mixture θ. We performed LDA topic analysis on two types of comments obtained from sentiment analysis to help understand the potential topic distribution of the patients' comments [13]. Three topics were selected and 10 feature words were extracted. The topics, feature words and their weights generated by LDA topic analysis in positive comments is illustrated as the following (Following is above results translated in English).

(1) 0.033* "experience" + 0.019 * "gratitude" + 0.017 * "patience" + 0.014 * "attitude" + 0.012 * "skills" + 0.012 * "treatment" + 0.012 * "state of an illness" + 0.009 * "diagnosis" + 0.009 * "thanks" + 0.008 * "carefulness"
(2) 0.043 * "experience" + 0.021 * "attitude" + 0.018 * "patience" + 0.017 * "gratitude" + 0.014 * "state of an illness" + 0.013 * "skills" + 0.012 * "treatment" + 0.010 * "thanks" + 0.009 * "diagnosis" + 0.009 * "carefulness"

Fig. 3. The word cloud map of positive comments (in Chinese).

(3) 0.043 * "experience" + 0.027 * "patience" + 0.020 * "state of an illness" + 0.016 * "gratitude" + 0.015 * "skills" + 0.013 * "treatment" + 0.012 * "attitude" + 0.011 * "diagnosis" + 0.010 * "carefulness" + 0.009 * "thanks"

Basically, each topic shows top ten feature words in the comments, and the number before each feature word represents its weights. Obtaining topics from the comments can help the users understand the key content of the massive medical comments.

Page Design. The customized web page was designed to meet Guideline 1 of WCAG 2.0, which was missing in the original web page in "Good Doctor Online" platform. In terms of front end web interface design, our system used HTML5, CSS3 and JavaScript to generate proposed web page [20]. The customized page was created by using natural language processing results from Sect. 4.1 to 4.3. In order to meet Guideline 1.4 of WCAG 2.0, i.e. Distinguishable, the system enlarged the font size, and changed the contrast color to identify the key content, such as doctor expertise and patient comments. Also, in order to meet Guideline 1.3 of WCAG 2.0, i.e. Adaptable, the system provided two forms (the topic groups analyzed by LDA model and word cloud map) to display patients' comment, different < DIV > elements were dynamically created, button IDs were set, and JavaScript was used to control showing or hiding of < DIV > elements. When the user entered the page, the topic groups analyzed by LDA model and word cloud map in the comment column would be hidden. When the user clicked on the button, the corresponding contents would be displayed, and the selected button would turn gray. Considering that the users are visually impaired, an audio button was added to the upper right corner of the page. This feature was created by using VoiceBroadcast function linked to Baidu VoiceBroadcast (https://tts.baidu.com/). The users could click on the button to play or pause audio reading of the text content on the page (Fig. 4).

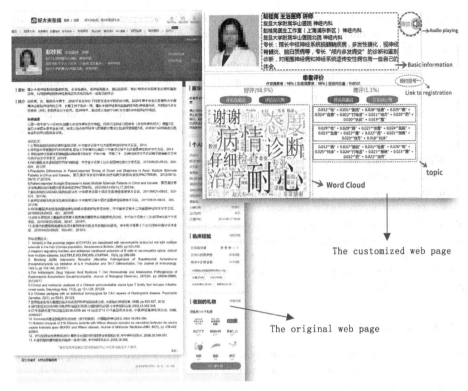

Fig. 4. The comparison of the original web page and the customized web page (in Chinese).

3 User Study and Result

In order to test if the proposed system enhances web accessibility of the medical pages for people with visual impairments, we referenced [21] to design and conduct a user study. Three factors were investigated in our user study, which are reading speed, reading comprehension and user satisfaction.

3.1 Experiment Design and Study

Since our targeted users are the elderly, so we contacted nursing homes for volunteers. There were total eight participants joining the study. All of them have the experiences of surfing on the Internet and they are literate and capable of computer operations. The experiment was conducted in a comfortable and quiet environment with a computer and simulated the scene of using online medical consultation platform at home.

We prepared six web pages for the participants to read. Three of them were original web pages from the "Good Doctor Online" platform and the other three were customized web pages created by TarsiEyes. In addition, we also prepared a pool of questions for the participants to answer after reading web pages. To prevent the learning curve effect, participants were given enough time to rest after reading each web page, and they were randomly and disordered given four pages from prepared pages to read. To counterbalance the reading task, two pages were original web pages from "Good Doctor Online" and the other two were customized web pages. Based on the psychological characteristics of the participants' fear of making mistakes, the purpose of the study was explained before the test. We told the participants in advance that the choice has nothing to do with right or wrong such that the participants could lower their psychological burden and kept relax during the whole study. The participants were told that there was no time limit to read the web page, but we recorded their reading time for subsequent analysis.

When finishing web page reading, the participants were asked to answer both of objective and subjective questions. Objective questions were reading comprehension questions. The comprehension questions were created in advance by the research group. We selected five questions for each web page to examine the participants' understanding of the information on the web page. To avoid the participants knowing the asked questions in advance, the five questions were randomly selected from the prepared question pool. The second type of questions were three subjective questions that measured the participants' overall reading satisfaction, where three questions were scaled from 1 (Very Difficult) to 7 (Very Easy).

3.2   Result Analysis

We analyzed the results of the user study, and three aspects were evaluated, including reading speed, reading comprehension and user satisfaction of the web pages, as shown in Table 1.

Reading Speed. On average, the time of reading original web pages vs. customized pages is 174.19 s (SD = 35.35) and 125.38 s (SD = 31.68) respectively. From Fig. 5 (a), we can see that reading customized web pages is faster than reading original web pages for the elderly [22].

Our research team discussed possible reasons causing this result and concluded three reasons. Firstly, the customized web pages filtered out many unnecessary or less important information from the original web pages, and it's known to all that the shorter texts take shorter time to read. Secondly, the font size of the customized web pages was larger than original one, and the important content was highlighted, which can lower reading burden for the elderly.

Reading Comprehension. To understand the participants' reading comprehension of the web pages, five objective questions were asked after reading each randomly assigned web page, where two pages were original web pages from "Good Doctor Online" platform and the other two pages were customized web pages created by TarsiEyes.

According to the analysis shown in Fig. 5 (b), the average number of correct answers to five comprehension questions is 3.19 (SD = 0.75) vs. 3.81 (SD = 0.83) for reading original and customized web pages respectively. The accuracy of reading comprehension reflects the reader's understanding of the whole page. The results indicated that reading the customized web pages enhanced the reading comprehension for the elderly people.

Table 1. The Descriptive statistical analysis of the results.

Groupa	Type	N	Mean	Std. Deviation	Std. Error Mean	Sig	Sig.(2-tailed)
Speed	The original web pages	16	174.19	35.350	8.838	0.603	0.000280
	The customized web pages	16	125.38	31.684	7.921		
Comprehension	The original web pages	16	3.19	0.750	0.188	0.581	0.033478
	The customized web pages	16	3.81	0.834	0.209		
Integrity	The original web pages	16	5.13	1.088	0.272	0.370	0.164150
	The customized web pages	16	4.63	0.885	0.221		
Readability	The original web pages	16	4.38	0.719	0.180	0.787	0.041204
	The customized web pages	16	4.94	0.772	0.193		
Presentation	The original web pages	16	4.06	1.237	0.309	0.858	0.546768
	The customized web pages	16	4.31	1.078	0.270		

Speed represents reading speed, which is measured in seconds. Comprehension represents reading comprehension, which is measured by the accuracy of answering comprehension questions. Integrity, readability and presentation represent user satisfaction, which were scored on a scale of 1 (very difficult) to 7 (very easy) by users.

User Satisfaction. After reading each page, we also asked three questions to evaluate the participants' subjective feedback, including information integrity, readability and presentation of patients' comments. The results are organized in Fig. 5 (c).

In terms of information integrity, the average scores of the original web pages and the customized web pages are 5.13 (SD = 1.08) and 4.63 (SD = 0.89) respectively. It means that the customized web pages are not as good as original web pages to show a complete information of the doctor. The research team reviewed and discussed possible reasons as the following: The customized web pages only showed the key information by word cloud and feature analysis but not full sentences, and some information, such as papers published by the doctors, the number of gifts, etc., were hidden by the filtering feature, which in turn might affect the participants' perspectives of the doctors.

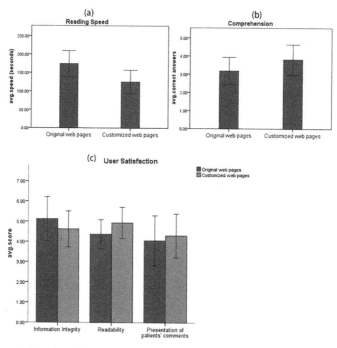

Fig. 5. The analysis of reading speed, reading comprehension, and user satisfaction between original web pages and customized web pages.

The participants gave an average score of 4.38 (SD = 0.72) and 4.94 (SD = 0.77) on the readability of the original and customized web pages respectively. The result indicated that the customized web page significantly enhanced the readability of the web pages and this kind of changes was suitable for the elderly people when they sought medical consultation online.

For the presentation of the patients' comments, the participants gave an average score of 4.06 (SD = 1.24) to the original web pages and 4.31 (SD = 1.08) to the customized web pages. The difference was not significant, but the results still showed that the presentation of patients' comments in the customized web pages were more favored by the elderly users. The original web pages simply put all the users' comments on a web page and the information was very complex. Although this presentation can allow the users to comprehensively understand the patients' attitude to the doctor, it is not a friendly interface for the elderly. However, the customized web pages reduced the reading burden for the targeted users.

Significance Test. Because the sample size of the participants was small and the study tried to understand the participants' performance in two different conditions, so we used T-test to evaluate data and set the confidence level to 95% ($\alpha = 0.05$) [23, 24]. In Table 1, the analysis showed that Sig. Values in Levene's test for equality of variances are all greater than 0.05, and it means all the statistics satisfy homogeneity of variance. We analyzed double-tailed critical P values and found that there was a significant difference between reading original web pages and the customized web pages in reading speed (p = 0.00028 < 0.001), reading comprehension (p = 0.0335 < 0.05) and readability of web pages (p = 0.0412 < 0.05). However, we did not see any significant differences in information integrity (p = 0.1642 > 0.05) and presentation of patients' comments (p = 0.5468 > 0.05).

4 Discussion

Through the survey with the participants, we found that there are many accessibility challenges existing in web pages of medical consultation platforms. For example, the web pages contain a lot of text descriptions, including the introduction to the doctor and massive comment data, and lack of diversified forms of information presentation and have poor color contrast. How to design accessible web pages for the elderly people should be addressed. In this paper, we proposed a new system to address accessibility issues for the elderly.

There are some limitations in this study. Firstly, the number of participants in the study is relatively small. Even though we spent a long time in the recruitment, we were only able to recruit a limited number of qualified participants. Therefore, it would be great to run the same study with more participants to get more insights. Secondly, although the customization improved the participants' reading speed, reading comprehension and the readability of web pages, comparing reading times between the original web pages and customized web pages which have less content does not seem to be a fair comparison, but we believe it is what customization is for, i.e. providing less text for reading. Also, even though the study results are promising, since our system covers more than two features, including topic analysis, word cloud, sentiment analysis, etc., it's not clear which specific feature makes the web pages more accessible. Thirdly, the proposed system for generating customized web pages is still in an early stage and it can only be applicable to certain medical consultation platform at current stage. There is still a space to improve and automate the generation process.

5 Conclusions and Future Work

In this paper, we proposed a new system named TarsiEyes to address the identified issue and presented the result of the user study that comparing reading original web pages and customized web pages. The sample pages are obtained from "Good Doctor Online", which is a popular medical consultation platform in China. There were eight participants joining the study and we were able to see a significant improvement in reading speed, reading comprehension and readability of web pages from the study results.

There are three future directions of this research. Firstly, we will expand the target user groups. In this paper, we were only able to study the customized web pages with the elderly people. There is a need to understand if the proposed interface is also applicable for other user groups. Secondly, since we have limited participants in the study, it would be great to recruit more participants to verify the findings. The study would be further improved to evaluate each specific feature, such as topic analysis, word cloud, etc. Thirdly, according to the study results, there is a space to improve the feeling of information integrity of web pages for the elderly people.

References

1. Fu, Q.: Research on the Development of Internet medical care in China. Wuhan University, 1–57 (2017)
2. Web Content Accessibility Guidelines (WCAG) 2.0. http://www.w3.org/TR/WCAG20/. Accessed 01 Sept 2023
3. Imam, M.F., Aboutabl, A.E., Mohamed, E.H.: Automating text simplification using pictographs for people with language deficits. IJ Inf. Technol. Comput. Sci. **9**(1), 26–34 (2019)
4. Gelderblom, G.J., et al.: Empirical identification of text simplification strategies for reading-impaired people. In: Assistive Technology Research Series, vol. 29 (2011)
5. Yu, C.H., Miller, R.C.: Enhancing web page readability for non-native readers. In: Proceedings of the sIGCHI Conference on Human Factors in Computing Systems (CHI 2010), New York, NY, USA, pp. 2523–2532. Association for Computing Machinery (2010)
6. Yu, C.H., Thom-Santelli, J., Millen, D.: Enhancing blog readability for non-native english readers in the enterprise. In: CHI 2011 Extended Abstracts on Human Factors in Computing Systems (CHI EA 2011), New York, NY, USA, pp. 1765–1770. Association for Computing Machinery (2011)
7. Gupta, S., Kaiser, G.: Extracting content from accessible web pages. In: Proceedings of the 2005 International Cross-Disciplinary Workshop on Web Accessibility (W4A 2005), New York, NY, USA, pp. 26–30. Association for Computing Machinery (2005)
8. Arch, A.: Web accessibility for older users: successes and opportunities (keynote). In: Proceedings of the 2009 International Cross-Disciplinary Conference on Web Accessibililty (W4A 2009) , New York, NY, USA, pp. 1–6. Association for Computing Machinery (2009)
9. Chen, Y.: Research on the Elderly-oriented Design of Shopping Website Based on Visual Cognitive Theory. South China University of Technology, 1–89 (2019)
10. Takagi, H., Asakawa, C.: Transcoding proxy for nonvisual web access. In: Proceedings of the Fourth International ACM Conference on Assistive Technologies (Assets 2000), New York, NY, USA, pp. 164–171. Association for Computing Machinery (2000)
11. Yesilada, Y.Y., Stevens, R., Harper, S., Goble, C.: Evaluating DANTE: semantic transcoding for visually disabled users. ACM Trans. Comput.-Hum. Interact. **14**(3), 14-es (2007)
12. Parmanto, B., Saptono, A., Song, L.: Information summarization and transcoding of biomedical information resources for mobile handheld devices. J. Mob. Multimedia **2**(1), 37–51 (2006)
13. Zhang, G.R., Bao, C., Wang, X.Y., Gu, D.X., Yang, X.J., Li, K.: Text semantic mining and sentiment analysis based on comment data. Inf. Sci. **39**(05), 53–61 (2021)
14. Novotny, R., Vojtas, P., Maruscak, D.: Information extraction from web pages. In: Proceedings of the 2009 IEEE/WIC/ACM International Joint Conference on Web Intelligence and Intelligent Agent Technology - Volume 03 (WI-IAT 2009), Washington, DC, USA, pp. 121–124. IEEE Computer Society (2009)

15. Bahram, S., Sen, D., Amant, R. S.: Prediction of web page accessibility based on structural and textual features. In: Proceedings of the International Cross-Disciplinary Conference on Web Accessibility (W4A 2011), New York, NY, USA, pp. 1–4. Association for Computing Machinery (2011)
16. Jieba Chinese word segmentation. https://github.com/messense/jieba-rs. Accessed 01 Oct 2023
17. Snow NLP library. https://github.com/isnowfy/snownlp. Accessed 01 Oct 2023
18. Ostapenko, R.: "Word cloud" as a graphical supplement to a scientific article. Econ. Consult. **32**(4), 4 (2020)
19. LDA-Topic-Modeling. https://github.com/alejandronotario/LDA-Topic-Modeling. Accessed 01 Oct 2023
20. Hevner, A.R., March, S.T., Park, J., Ram, S., Alan, R.: Design science in information systems research. MIS Quart. **28**(1), 6 (2004)
21. Lau, T.P., King, I.: Bilingual web page and site readability assessment. In: Proceedings of the 15th International Conference on World Wide Web (WWW 2006), New York, NY, USA, pp. 993–994. Association for Computing Machinery (2006)
22. Li, Q., Morris, M.R., Fourney, A., Larson, K., Reinecke, K.Q.: The impact of web browser reader views on reading speed and user experience. In: Proceedings of the 2019 CHI Conference on Human Factors in Computing Systems, New York, NY, USA, pp. 1–12. Association for Computing Machinery (2019)
23. Chen, S.Y., Feng, Z., Yi, X.: A general introduction to adjustment for multiple comparisons. J. Thorac. Dis. **9**(6), 1725 (2017)
24. Chung, J.W., Min, H.J., Kim, J., Park, J.C.: Enhancing readability of web documents by text augmentation for deaf people. In Proceedings of the 3rd International Conference on Web Intelligence, Mining and Semantics (WIMS 2013), New York, NY, USA, pp. 1–10. Association for Computing Machinery (2013)

Philosophy and History from a Cross-Cultural Perspective: Learning Based on the Assassin's Creed

Pengze Chen◉ and Fangting Han(✉) ◉

College of Language and Culture, Northwest A&F University, No. 3, Taicheng Road, Yangling District, Xianyang 712100, Shaanxi, China
clairehft@126.com

Abstract. Gamification and Game-Based Learning is an important studying theme in the field of Computer Science & Education, and Assassin's Creed, a series of historical games, facilitate social education. This paper will first evaluate the historical and educational significance of Assassin's Creed of Assassin's Creed, illustrate that Historical Comparisons, Civilization Diversity and Role-playing are three types of cross-cultural activities working to help education when students playing Assassin's Creed and finally recommend some innovative strategies for Assassin's Creed to improve its social education function while keeping its playability. I hope that more producers can co-operate with scholars to design games with their advanced computer technology to achieve the goal of education.

Keywords: Assassin's Creed · Computer technology · video games · social education · cross-cultural perspective

1   Introduction

Assassin's Creed is a series of computer games produced by Ubisoft Montreal. The summary of their games is "Play your way through history in the award-winning video game series. Assassin's Creed immerses players in the memories of Assassin Ancestors, fighting to protect free will at pivotal moments in human history." Different from other video games, Assassin's Creed allows players to experience philosophy and history while enjoying the entertainment, which leads to a positive social education based on computer technology. From the first Assassin's Creed in the era of the Crusades and Assassin's Creed: Unity whose historical background is set during the French Revolution to Assassin's Creed Origins describing Ancient Egyptian civilization and Assassin's Creed Odyssey based on Homer's Epics and Greek mythology, the series of games show the public its ability to reproduce historical Scenarios. As its slogan goes, "History is your playground."

Thanks to the advanced computer technology of Ubisoft, players have the opportunity to appreciate Assassin's Creed and utilize it academically. Articles from previous scholars will be cited to illustrate the historical and educational significance of Assassin's Creed.

Although the research on Assassin's Creed is very rich, which forms the second part "the historical and educational significance of Assassin's Creed", scholars have not found possibility to explain how students learn philosophy and history in computer games from a cross-cultural perspective. This article will classify three types of cross-cultural activities that influence students' learning: Historical Comparisons, Civilization Diversity and Role-playing.

Finally, some recommendations will be proposed for Assassin's Creed. To work better as a museum or encyclopedia of philosophy and history, it should innovate in some aspects. While keeping its advantage in gameplay and attraction, Assassin's Creed can optimize the voyage of discovery in the sea of knowledge.

2   The Historical and Educational Significance of Assassin's Creed

Assassin's Creed, as a well-known and well-accepted video game, has shown great significance in education. With its realistic restoration of history, it helps students to cultivate certain abilities in the field of education.

2.1   A Realistic Restoration of History

Assassin's Creed has paid attention to historical fact [2]. So all the world it has constructed can be verified. The most famous news about Assassin's Creed is its outstanding contribution to the reconstruction of the Notre Dame de Paris. In 2019 the architecture caught fire, but luckily the government could use the game data in Assassin's Creed: Unity as an archive for the Notre Dame de Paris. From this event people can perceive the realistic buildings in the games [8].

Besides architecture, Ubisoft also focus on details of special norms of different civilization. For examples, in Assassin's Creed Origins, players can appreciate the whole process of mummification near the temple of the Egyptians. The professional first disemboweled the body, and then filled the abdominal cavity with frankincense, cinnamon and other spices, and then stitched the body to cover it with dried natron. Then after 35 days, players would see them wrapped in linen, filled with spices, coated with resin and made into a mummy. For another example, in Assassin's Creed Valhalla, players could see the interesting Viking tradition, duel by verses, which means players should pronounce the next verse to fight back another person's banter. The player can do better only when they are familiar with linguistics and rhythm. Unexpectedly this kind of duel appears often in the game, and sometimes players can even have that with Thor.

It's natural that players could neglect these details, and Assassin's Creed is helpful for players at all levels of knowledge [3]. No matter how encyclopedic or naive the player is, they can always find correspondent experience in the series of games.

2.2   The Abilities it Helps to Cultivate

Students can expect various abilities from Assassin's Creed rather than mere knowledge [1]. Just as the author has said, conception and understanding matter more than historical knowledges. The philosophy and historical events of the ancient times can be perceived again by modern people without limit. The most famous thought of Assassin's Creed is its conspiracy theories, which encourages questioning historical events or great historical figures. It describes many great conquers or officials as hypocritical and dirty men. Though it contains fiction and the personal explanation of history, Assassin's Creed provides us with a thinking model to get insight into seemingly simple cases. Thus the ability to form a dialectical historical view is developed subtly. The facts are important, but the ability to evaluate facts matters more.

Besides training students to be historians, playing Assassin's Creed promotes students becoming more qualified citizens in modern world [4]. In the fictional clash between modern and ancient experiences, students can think their own role in the world, the pattern of the world and the future of the world. Knowing about the past is a good step to know the future, and Assassin's Creed offers opportunities to contact this kind of education at a low cost with advanced computer technology.

2.3   The Practical Applications and Cases in the Field of Education

In recent years many institutes have actually tried to utilize Assassin's Creed academically [1]. Educators think that an immersive experience in video games really helps students to learn philosophy and history, especially when they are asked to make a choice as the protagonists in historical stories. Similar to the time machine that could transport modern people to old times, video games can achieve that goal easily. That's maybe one of the major benefits when computer technology assists independent learning.

Ubisoft also emphasizes its social values in education [2–7]. Along with the Assassin's Creed Origins, teachers can unfold an Egyptian world in front of their students vividly, which is a practical experiment of computer technology applied in the field of education. In Assassin's Creed Odyssey [2], their effort will lead to more cases where Assassin's Creed can guide students to get a sight of ancient times.

3   Three Types of Cross-Cultural Activities When Experiencing Assassin's Creed

An unforgettable experience is provided when players choose to enjoy Assassin's Creed, which paves a way for further understanding of past philosophy and history, because role-playing games as a cross-cultural activity can attract students to the maximum. Then diverse civilizations pictured in Assassin's Creed assure that players can contact traditions, norms and values that they have never imagined in their life, which subtly encourages students to be familiar with unknown knowledge. And finally historical comparisons and profound reflections are possible. Deep thinking and education can be achieved when students compare the present and the past. The above are three types of cross-cultural activities when experiencing Assassin's Creed, and detailed explanation of each will be provided below.

3.1   Experience Role-Playing and Enjoy Vivid History

Previous study pointed out that role-playing is not only good for teachers, but also for their students [9, 10].

Video game is one of the most popular for students to roleplay with computer technology for its low cost and high reduction. Some researchers say that "although graphical realism is not of primary importance in games, it can still offer a rich sensory experience that heightens the player's pleasure" [1]. They pay attention to the realistic experience that Assassin's Creed can bring to their players. The essence of this is actually a kind of role-playing, which means students can acquire a novel identity and make choices in a fictional world as the protagonists. Especially in historical games like Assassin's Creed, students can immerse themselves into the cross-cultural activity. In other words, they "become" other people in history, and understand the past and the present better.

For example, the background of Assassin's Creed 3 is set in the mid to late 18th century on the American continent. Players will play the role of an assassin named Connor, embarking on adventures throughout the United States during the Revolutionary War and experiencing various important events during the Revolution. His father was a white man but his mother was an India, which carries a foreshadowing of what is to follow later on in the story. In the opening stage of Assassin's Creed 3, players will experience Connor's father, and in Chapter 4, they will experience Connor's life when he was raised by the Mohawk tribe (a Native American from New York State). Connor finally stood on the side of the Native Americans, Indians, and opposed British colonizers and tyranny.

In this game, students have the opportunity to live as an Indian and role-playing provide possibility to perceive that period of history from the perspective of Native Americans. In the past years people often studied history based on existing literature describing what had happened and why, and now they have more ways to research from the perspective of ethnic minorities. Actually this marks the progress of civilization. People encourage a more diverse society, support minority groups to speak for themselves, and advocate for people to experience history and culture as their brothers and sisters. Undoubtedly Assassin's Creed has made an example for video games that role-playing can help education.

The truth is the Ubisoft has implemented the concept of role-playing in all works. In the modern plots of Assassin's Creed, the protagonist can experience the memories of their Assassin Ancestors with a special device, Animus. They lay inside the device, after a series of specific operations they can synchronize with ancestral memories. In the memories, they can't kill civilians or they will get out of synchronization, because their Assassin Ancestors had never done that injustice. So Assassin's Creed is essentially a role-playing game, and has played an essential role in broadening its players' horizons.

3.2 Experience Diverse Civilizations and Have Better Cognition

Apparently when students play Assassin's Creed they contact exotic flavors from different civilizations. They bear various cultural identifications and national thoughts that many players have never experienced personally, which generate opportunities for students to deeply understand civilization diversity. For example, in one mission of Assassin's Creed Odyssey when the protagonist rides a horse and follows the mother on the land of Sparta, they will see a Spartan child holding a spear in the wilderness fighting with several wolves. Obviously there's little chance for the child to survive that mortal combat, so the protagonist advices a helping hand. However, the mother disagrees that thought. She says it is a tradition of Spartan warriors to face death-fight from a young age, and only in this way can Sparta have qualified warriors in the future. At this time if the player chooses to walk away, this encounter will end and undoubtedly the child will die, and the player will never know what will happen afterwards. But if the player still determines to save the Spartan child, after the battle with wolves, he will be disappointed because the child was fatally injured. However, when the protagonist sympathizes with that kid and calls for help, the parents of the kid are seemingly cold and uncaring. They say that the child has failed to pass the test, and it's naturally that he can't live as a glorious Spartan warrior in the world. So it's better for him to leave. The protagonist, full of humanistic care, is extremely shocked by this civilization. But then what the child says makes the protagonist accept and understand their culture and spirit. The child thanks the protagonist for saving him bravely, and he confesses to disappointing his parents and the whole nation. Finally, without painful moans emitted the child dies calmly.

Such a case seems contradictory to the philosophy at the present time. In most countries Juvenile Protection Law or Child Protection Law have been established for a long time, and it will be illegal if parents make their kids face mortal dangers. But in different civilization the situation may change. Modern world has been based on the technological and moral revolution since many hundred years ago, but the historical period in which Spartans lived requested them to develop martial or even barbaric national spirit. Overall it's beneficial to contact different civilizations, and sometimes a heavy shock in cognition from foreign countries or old times can urge students to think and become global citizens.

For another example, in Assassin's Creed Origins, the protagonist, Bayek of Siwa, was originally one of the guardians of all Egypt, possessing badges symbolizing duty and the high reputation. But after some years he found a potential cult gradually rise intending to control the entire Egypt. Unfortunately his son was killed by the cult. In order to save common people from the Ptolemy's Rule which was already contaminated by the cult, he had tried to connect with Cleopatra, the Egypt Queen. But finally the queen formed a union with Caesar to satisfy her own interests, and Bayek found it was all a scam. No ruler or conquer really cares for and protect the people. To achieve his lifelong goal, Bayek eventually established his Assassin organization to save common people from tyranny and endow them with precious freedom.

Freedom is something that people have longed for since ancient times, and many civilizations embody this concept. Previous studies also focus on this commonplace of different civilizations [6]. The author in his article supposes that Assassin's Creed is a "counter-hegemonic commemorative play" which produces a lot of thoughts about politics. Politics come from civilizations, and due to objective requirements, inevitably many civilizations have undergone the period when they ignore freedom and the welfare of ordinary people. Through learning these past civilizations with the assistance of advanced computer technology, players would have a better reflection on today's issue and a better understanding of how to build a more civilized world nowadays.

3.3 Make Historical Comparisons and Have Profound Reflection

There was a study to explore the connection between video games and students' historical reflection [5]. Actually the study is essentially related to cross-cultural activities. People can expect them to compare or reflect on something only when they can give students different experience. And inevitably when modern people produce historical games they may add some modern elements to evoke our consciousness to compare.

In Assassin's Creed Valhalla players can experience Nordic Spirit and History. The background of this work is set in the Viking era, which refers to the period from 790 to 1066 AD. During these three hundred years, Vikings who believed in the Nordic polytheism plundered Europe. The term "Vikings" comes from ancient English poetry, meaning pirates, and in modern times, it mostly refers to pirates from northern Europe. The story took place in the 9th century AD. The protagonist, Avril, plundered England along the monsoon. His opponent was Alfred, the first great emperor in English history. This work can help us understand the England in Anglo-Saxon age and what kind of culture has worked to shape today's Britain. Thus comparisons and reflections are possible.

Assassin's Creed Odyssey, for example, could evoke players to compare the status of women in ancient and modern times and thus emphasizing the female power. In the game, as a free mercenary, the player can choose to join Sparta or Athens to get reward from participating in the war. In the game world the player can also find other mercenaries wandering, but many of them are females, who account for 50% of the total amount. Although according to historical research female warriors had been around in ancient world, the proportion of them in the game was an effort Ubisoft has made for the advancement of women and feminism. The meaning of figures is more important when Ubisoft modify history from a modern perspective while the original history remains unchanged.

In Assassin's Creed Odyssey one might encounter the great philosopher Socrates and his unique method to enlighten people's wisdom. Socrates and the player, a renowned mercenary in the game, were friends and to some extent became the latter's life mentor. During their journey Socrates often provided suggestions generously. During the Peloponnesian War, Socrates and the player successively came to the Silver Islands. During his stay on the island, he once posed a dilemma to the player, "Should a rebel army who killed for freedom be punished by law? Can this be considered the extension of 'justice'?" Similarly he also guided the player to think about the conflict between morality and law. In one mission the player needed to save a poor man who was arrested for stealing others' horses. But after the player released him, Socrates would question the player whether the poor man should be punished. If the player thought that he should get away with punishment because he had no other way to support his family, the question from Socrates to the player was "Do you think a person should be punished for killing more people for the sake of someone?" However, if the player thought that even if he was trying to support his family, he should be punished by the law, the question from Socrates to the player was "Do you think a person should be punished for killing someone for the sake of more people?".

In the game his questions are always philosophical and hard to answer. The player can acquaint himself or herself with his repeated rumination on group interests and personal interests, truth and public opinion and whether it is worth dying for the truth. It's a valuable experience for students to communicate with a great philosopher in history.

Socrates accompanied the player the whole journey, and finally he still stuck to his life-long wisdom and belief. After the rebellion overthrew Athens' rule over the archipelago, Socrates joined the local people's celebration and happily talked to the people who were interested in his ideas. During the Great Plague of Athens, Socrates always closely mon-itored the situation of the city and its people. He also witnessed the death of Pericles with his own eyes and decided to stay in Athens to confront the crafty new leader, Cleon. Thanks to Assassin's Creed with the assistance of advanced computer technology, this kind of communication with great ones really educates students nowadays.

4 Recommendations for Assassin's Creed

In the past years, the Assassin's Creed has harvested a wave of positive reviews, and is now preparing for its sequel. However, some still question whether the popularity of this old series can be sustainable. Its playability has been challenged in gaming communities that require diverse experiences and gameplay. To make Assassin's Creed more effective in fulfilling its educational function, three suggestions have thus been proposed.

First, Assassin's Creed should try to innovate itself as a whole. Undoubtedly, Assas-sin's Creed has formed a fixed game process, such as tracking, eavesdropping, infiltrat-ing, assassinations, dialogue selection, etc. Or in the three ancient works, Assassin's Creed Origins, Assassin's Creed Odyssey and Assassin's Creed Valhalla, the Ubisoft encourages players to try a frontal combat. However, the basic concept and gameplay have never changed, which is essential in the rapidly changing gaming community. The Ubisoft should try to avoid excessive repetition in its works.

Second, the combination with newly advanced computer technology, VR, would be promising for Assassin's Creed. VR, or Virtual Reality, is a technology designed to make the user feel immersed in a virtual world. It's a distinctly different feeling than playing a game or navigating a 3D environment on a static 2D monitor, giving a real feeling of presence in the virtual space. This is typically achieved with a VR headset that places one or two displays very close to the user's eyes, whilst tracking the user's position so that it can be translated into the virtual world. Its basic implementation method is mainly based on computer technology, using computers and other devices to create a realistic virtual world with various sensory experiences such as 3D vision, touch, and smell, thus creating an immersive feeling for people in the virtual world. Assassin's Creed can design a set of devices and sites to attract players to participate in a new world, especially in its online museum program. After all, as a series of video games, only by ensuring playability can producers deliver educational content, or otherwise the game will become a boring and empty sermon.

Third, we believe the cooperation of scholars and the Ubisoft would lead to better designs of historical games. Due to the development of computer technology and the gradual maturity of game production technology, students have the opportunity to learn about the past, the world, and themselves through them. A promising future is absolutely opening for video games if they can combine unique playability with social education, and we believe scholars and game-designers can co-operate to realize this future.

5   Conclusion

Assassin's Creed has gained a sound reputation for its playability and unique game concept, and displayed great potential in influencing education considering the historical and educational significance the game brought to education. Role-playing, Civilization Diversity and Historical Comparisons make this game a good channel for students to have better understanding and deeper reflection of history and philosophy. These cross-cultural activities work effectively when a player chooses to spend his time traveling to the ancient times in Assassin's Creed, a good example for computer games. And finally considering the new requirements of the gaming community and the challenge from other games, Assassin's Creed is suggested to make continuous efforts in terms of innovation, combination of VR and cooperation between scholars and game-designers so that it could contribute more to education.

References

1. Adrienne, S.: The tyranny of realism: historical accuracy and politics of representation in Assassin's Creed III. Loading... **9**(14), 4–24 (2015)
2. Politopoulos, A., Mol, A.A., Boom, K.H., Ariese, C.E.: "History is our playground": action and authenticity in assassin's creed: Odyssey. Adv. Archaeol. Pract. **7**(3), 317–323 (2019)
3. Seif El-Nasr, M., Al-Saati, M., Niedenthal, S., Milam, D.: Assassin's creed: a multi-cultural read. Loading... **2**(3) (2008)
4. Lisa, G.: "The Past is Your Playground": the challenges and possibilities of Assassin's Creed: syndicate for social education. Theory Res. Soc. Educ. **45**(1), 145–155 (2017)
5. Lisa, G.: "Assassin's creed reminds us that history is human experience": students' senses of empathy while playing a narrative videogame. Theory Res. Soc. Educ. **47**(1), 108–137 (2019)
6. Hammar, E.L.: Counter-hegemonic commemorative play: marginalized pasts and the politics of memory in the digital game Assassin's Creed: freedom cry. Rethink. Hist. **21**(3), 372–395 (2017)
7. Poiron, P.: Assassin's Creed origins discovery tour: a behind the scenes experience. Near Eastern Archaeol. **84**(1), 79–85 (2021)
8. LUPO, Manzon, B.: Patrimônio cultural e cat´ ástrofe: Os concursos internacionais não-oficiais realizados para a Notre Dame de Paris após o incêndio de 2019. Herança-Journal of History. Heritage Cult. **4**(2), 018–038 (2021)
9. Craciun, D.: Role-playing as a creative method in science education. J. Sci. Arts **10**(1), 175 (2010)
10. Howes, E.V., Cruz, B.C.: Role-playing in science education: An effective strategy for developing multiple perspectives. J. Element. Sci. Educ. **21**(3), 33–46 (2009)

Data Transaction Mode and Its Legal Regulation in the Context of Market-Oriented Allocation of Data Elements

Wei Liu[(✉)] and Xuan Lin

Guangdong University of Finance and Economics, Guangzhou 510320, China
liu_umi@126.com

Abstract. Data is the key factor of production in the development of digital economy while data transaction is the key link of market allocation of data elements. At present, China's data transaction is still facing the realistic dilemma of imperfect legal system of data transaction, difficult data element circulation, underdeveloped data transaction market and unbalanced supply and demand of data transactions. Under the background of market-oriented allocation of data elements and current predicament, it is of great significance to analyze and construct the data transaction model and to carry out targeted legal regulation. This helps to realize the free and safe circulation of data elements and meets the needs of traders in the data element market as well as the needs of legislation and regulation.

Keywords: Marketization of data elements · Data transaction mode · Legal regulation

1 Current Situation and Practical Problems of Data Trading Market

As a new factor of production, data not only has great industrial value but also can be deeply integrated with traditional factors of production such as labor, technology, and land, helping traditional industries to transform to digital development, realizing industrial upgrading and total factor productivity growth [1].

As early as 2015, the Fifth Plenary Session of the 18th CPC Central Committee formally proposed to "implement the national big data strategy". Therefore, to promote the efficient circulation of data resources and make data elements play a greater role in economic development, the Central Committee of the Communist Party of China and the State Council have issued several documents related to the data element market since 2020, officially classifying data as the main production factors alongside the traditional land, technology, labor, capital, etc., and putting forward the direction and key reform tasks of the data element market system construction."Accelerate the cultivation and development of data factor market, establish data resource inventory management

Fund project: this paper is the achievement of the National Ministry of Justice Project "Research on Legal Guarantee of Market-oriented Allocation of Data Elements" (21SFB4015).

mechanism, improve data ownership definition, open sharing, trading, and other standards and measures, and give full play to the value of social data resources". This means that under the background of China's socialist market economy system, the primary task now of the market-oriented reform of data elements is to clarify the transaction rules and build a data market.

In 2022, Guangdong will take "comprehensively promoting the market-oriented allocation reform of data elements, further improving the public data management and operation system, and optimizing the data transaction circulation platform and mechanism" as its annual work point, hoping to build a provincial data transaction spot, build a data transaction platform, to severe the Data Market in Guangdong-Hong Kong-Macao Greater Bay Area as well as improve the data infrastructure system in Greater Bay Area.

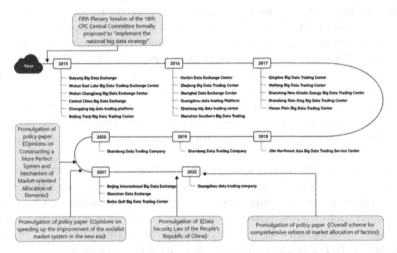

Fig. 1. Policy promulgation and establishment of data platform.

Since the establishment of China's first big data exchange in Guiyang in 2015, there has been a boom in the construction of data exchanges all over the country in the past eight years. Relying on regional advantages, many cities try to set up data exchanges with regional characteristics. For example, on November 25, 2021, Shanghai Data Exchange was unveiled, which conducts comprehensive big data transactions around the world. In March 2022, Guangzhou Data Trading Co., Ltd. was formally established to explore the establishment of a multi-source data fusion application platform. According to the statistics of "White Paper on Big Data" (December 2021) published by the China Institute of Information and Communication, from 2014 to 2017 alone, 23 data trading institutions guided by local governments were set up in China. According to incomplete statistics, there are currently more than 30 big data trading institutions in China (see Fig. 1). The development of the data trading market and the improvement of market system construction are gradually becoming an indispensable and important part of economically developed cities to achieve high-quality development.

However, although the current data trading market seems to be prosperous, it still implies many problems. Take Guiyang Data Exchange as an example. At the beginning of its establishment, the institution estimated that the daily transaction volume in the next 3–5 years would reach 10 billion yuan. However, in the following years, the transaction volume target of Guiyang Data Exchange decreased year by year, from a "daily transaction volume of 10 billion yuan" to "strive to exceed 100 million yuan throughout the year". Other data exchanges and trading platforms also have such problems, as many of them have virtually stopped operating. The "White Paper on Big Data" (published by the China Institute of Information and Communication in December 2021) pointed out that since 2014, most of the data trading institutions built in various places have provided centralized and standardized data trading places and services, in order to eliminate the information gap between the supply and demand sides and promote the formation of a reasonable market-oriented pricing mechanism and reproducible trading system. However, after more than seven years of exploration, the operation and development of local data trading institutions have not achieved the expected results. First, in terms of the number of institutions, most trading institutions have stopped operating or changed their business direction, and the number of data trading institutions that continue to operate is very limited; Second, from the point of view of the business model, the landing business is basically limited to intermediary matching, and a series of value-added services, such as Data ownership confirmation, data valuation, delivery and settlement, data asset management and financial services, which were envisaged at the beginning of the establishment of various institutions, failed to land; Third, from the perspective of business performance, the trading institutions as a whole have low data turnover and insufficient market capacity.

The root of the problem lies in the following two factors. First, most exchanges adopt the Data Matching Trading Mode since its low construction cost. They only serve as a trading intermediary to match buyers and sellers to trade on the platform so that they can collect commissions from it. However, under the realistic situation that the number of data products in the current market is scarce, the demand of customers has not been fully tapped, and the data transaction is inactive, this kind of business model is unsustainable. Secondly, in this trading mode, due to the heterogeneity of data, High-value and low-value data are mixed in the platform trading, diluting the overall value of the data. Due to the replicability of data, the lack of corresponding maintenance measures after the transaction easily leads to the avoidance of data leakage and devaluation. Therefore, in the absence of current data trading standards and legal rules, many data providers prefer to choose the "data black market" or "point-to-point" transactions due to their lower transaction costs.

Based on these situations, the effective use of data resources and the open data ecosystem can fully release the digital value and drive the digital transformation and upgrading of traditional industries and the cultivation and development of new formats. China urgently needs to adopt a data trading mode that can stimulate the role of data elements and activate the data trading market to build the data trading market and speed up the formulation of relevant trading standards and legal rules.

2 Trading Mode of Data Factor Market

2.1 Type of Existing Data Transaction Mode

There are many types of trading patterns in the current data trading market, for example, some scholars divide the trading modes into five categories according to the dominant party of data trading: Data Pipeline (1v1) Mode, Customer-Led Data Mart (Nv1) Mode, Supplier-Led Data Mart (1vn), Data Platform Market (N v M) Mode, Market Maker (N To 1 To M) Mode (see Table 1).

According to the specific content of data transaction, some scholars divide the data transaction mode into the following eight modes: Direct Transaction Data Mode, Data Exchange Mode, Resource Exchange Mode, Member Account Mode, Data Cloud Service Transaction Mode, API Access Mode, Data Transaction Mode Based on Data Protection Technology and Data Platform Transaction Mode of Stakeholders. This classification confuses the difference between the data transaction mode and the specific technical methods adopted in the data transaction, making the classification too detailed, which is not conducive to the research of data transaction mode.

According to the core characteristics of data transactions, the existing data transaction modes can be divided into "Data Individual Transaction Mode", "Data Matching Transaction Mode" and "Data Service Mode".

Data Individual Transaction Mode. Participants in the individual data transaction mode are mainly Data Sellers and Data Customers. In this mode, the two parties determine the transaction content through point-to-point contact and consultation and conduct individual transactions directly, and their data transactions are not reached through a third party. This type of transaction mode includes "Data Pipeline (1v1) Mode", "Customer-Led Data Mart (Nv1) Mode", And "Supplier-Led Data Mart (1vN)". Although the number of participants in the transaction is different, and the dominant party of the transaction is different, they are still "point-to-point" individual transactions when they focus on the transaction itself.

Advantages. The custody of both parties is conducive to the retention of property rights, and the corresponding data services and data products can be customized according to actual needs.

Disadvantage. The transaction is opaque, and the lack of supervision is easy to secretly infringe the rights and interests of third-party data subjects.

Data Matching Transaction Mode. The data matching transaction mode is also called "data mart mode". The main transaction participants are Data exchange, Data Sellers, and Data Customers. In this mode, data trading institutions mainly deal with the raw data of rough processing, without any preprocessing or in-depth information mining analysis of the data, and only collect and integrate data resources to form data packets or data sets for direct sale [2]. Generally, transactions between data suppliers and demanders are centralized in government-led exchanges, and data is transferred from data providers to data demanders through centralized data exchanges.

Advantages. Increase the participation of the government-led data exchange can make the on-floor transactions supervised by the third party, which can effectively protect the rights and interests of data subjects. At the same time, through the centralized matching of exchanges, it is easier for data suppliers and demanders to find matching transaction objects.

Disadvantage. Due to the replicability of data, it is easy to be intercepted when it is traded through a third-party exchange, and there are loopholes in the security of data sets.

Data Transaction Mode. Data service mode is also classified as data value-added service mode by some scholars. The main participants are Data Trading Platforms, Data Sellers, and Data Customers. In this trading model, the data trading organization does not simply match the buyer and the seller, but classifies, cleans, analyzes, models, and visualizes the basic resources of big data according to the needs of the same users, forming customized data products, and then providing them to the demander.

Advantages. It can customize the data resources according to customer requirements, which is more in line with the actual application needs of customers.

Disadvantage. It has higher requirements for data providers. In addition to high-quality data sources, data providers should also have a higher level of data mining and processing, which essentially sets a higher threshold for data providers to enter the market.

All the above-mentioned data trading modes have their characteristics, but their common feature is that they do not have a detailed division of labor among all parties in the market, especially in the data supply link. They often hope that data providers can directly provide directly tradable data sets, data packets, finished data products, and data services. This high demand for a single data provider objectively limits the volume of data trading products in the market. Without sufficient data trading products, the market is bound to be difficult to be active, and the effective circulation of data elements is even more impossible.

Table 1. Schematic Diagram of Data Transaction Mode Classification

Type	Classification of data transaction mode		
	Data transaction mode	participant	characteristic
Traditional mode	Data individual transaction mode	data sellers/data customers	**1v1/1vN/Nv1**
	Data matching transaction mode	data exchange/data sellers/data customers	**N to M**
	Data transaction mode	data trading platforms/data sellers/data customers	**N to 1 to M**
New Pattern	Data division transaction mode	data vendors/data processors/data trading platforms/data customers	**N to 1 to M to C**

2.2 A New Type of Data Transaction Mode: Data Division Transaction Mode

Based on the characteristics of "heterogeneity", "replicability" and "non-exclusivity" of data, we can divide the roles in the data transaction process, distinguish the links between data collection and data processing, encourage non-data industry companies to upload their legally owned data to the data trading platform for trading after data desensitization and data security inspection and expand the sources of high-quality data. And cultivate specialized companies for big data analysis and application, and conduct in-depth mining and processing of data resources in the data market to form rich data products and expand the supply of applied data products in the data market.

Content of Data Division Transaction Mode. Under the data division trading mode, the participants in the transaction mainly include the data provider, data processor, data demander, and data trading platform. Under this kind of transaction, there can be two modes: "data product development mode" around data content and "data service customization mode" around customer demand.

In the data product development mode, the primary data products (data packets) collected and sorted by the data provider are linked to the data trading platform through encryption technology, and the data processor uses its professional knowledge and technology to mine and develops the big data in the data packets, and the same data can form data products with different subdivision directions and functions (enriching the form and quantity of data products). The data processor uploads the processed secondary data products to the platform. Users choose the corresponding data products according to their own application needs (see Fig. 2).

In the data service customization mode, data users publish their requirements for data products in specific application directions on the platform according to their own application needs. The data processor uses its experience accumulation and professional ability in a specific field to purchase the corresponding data packets from the data vendors on the platform according to the needs of users, and carries out corresponding data mining.

Advantages of Data Division Transaction Mode. Compared with the traditional model, the data division trading mode has obvious advantages, which can effectively broaden the source of on-site data, deepen the mining of original data, and enrich the number of on-site data products.

The traditional trading mode is that the data provider collects data, mines, and processes it by itself, and then sells the products to customers through the data exchange or data trading platform. This type of transaction requires a high level of data providers, which not only requires them to have a large amount of original data but also requires them to have the ability of data mining and analysis, which essentially sets a high entry threshold for data providers. As a result, the number of data providers with both data property rights and data mining capabilities is small. Therefore, there is not enough circulation of data trading products in the data trading market, and it is difficult to form market competition. This situation limits the function of the data factor market and makes it unable to achieve institutional goals.

The data division transaction mode divides the role of traditional data business in data collection and processing into two parts, and data collectors can directly list their legally

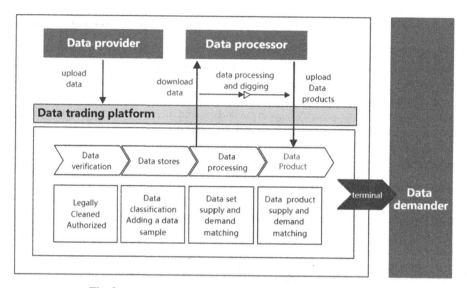

Fig. 2. Schematic diagram of data division transaction mode

collected data, the primary data products after cleaning and anonymization, that is, the legal data packets after security processing, on the data trading platform for sale. By making data samples, subdividing data types, and summarizing the basic characteristics of data packets, data packets can be found and purchased more easily by downstream processors or customers.

Broaden the sources of legal data in the trading market and enrich the data supply. In this trading model, the entry threshold can be relaxed, and outside the specialized data operation companies, ordinary Internet companies are allowed to anonymize the legal data obtained in their daily operations and then put them on the open data trading platform for trading. On the one hand, it can encourage more companies to upload legal data, participate in the data trading market, broaden the data sources of the data trading market, greatly enrich the data types in the data market and increase the total amount of data in production. On the other hand, it provides more trading opportunities and introduces supervision at the same time, which reduces the sale of data by Internet companies through over-the-counter transactions and damages the rights and interests of data subjects [3].

Promote the depth of data mining and enhance the value of data products. Mining primary data products through specialized data processing companies can increase the depth of information mining in data packets and make full use of data. Professional data processors purchase relevant data products for deep processing, produce a variety of data products through modeling, big data analysis, visualization, and other means, and sell them in the corresponding data finished product areas on the platform. The advantage of mining data through professional data processors lies in that data processors specialized in specific fields can dig the value of data information in development packets more deeply, make full use of the information contained in the data, and make their products more in line with customers' needs and bring greater benefits.

Promote the multi-domain development of high-quality data and promote the competition in the data market. Different from other factors of production, the value of data will not decrease because of its use, but will show higher value because of continuous and in-depth mining. The same data may also show different use-values for different users and different fields of use [4]. Based on the replicability of data, the same data packet can also be distributed to multiple data processors to mine and develop data products in different directions, so that the data can be utilized in multiple dimensions, the terminal data products can be enriched, and the full competition in the data trading market can be promoted. Make the data elements flow in production.

By subdividing the links of data transactions, and encouraging more enterprises to invest capital and technology in the links of data processing and mining, a subset of products more suitable for market segments can be produced as trading items, thus promoting large-scale.

3   Legal Regulation of Data Factor Transaction

Although China's national macro policies explicitly encourage big data transactions, laws and regulations that directly regulate big data transactions are still absent. Especially in the absence of a unified data market at present, the trading rules of various exchanges and trading platforms are different, and the data traders can't effectively and centrally control risks, which leads to uncertainty of trading and instability of relief.

Key issues closely related to data transactions, such as the definition of data property rights, the distribution of data ownership, and other basic issues, have not been solved either. Not only has there been no institutional arrangement in legislation, but academic researchers have also failed to reach a consensus on these issues. However, the basic issues such as data ownership are quite complicated. If we wait until we have a full understanding before we construct the data market, we will undoubtedly miss the opportunity for data element development. Therefore, we should hold the view that we should first promote the development and utilization of the data market, and then gradually explore issues such as data ownership. It is the key direction of the current legal regulation of the data factor market to construct the data ownership legal system and the data transaction legal framework through the pilot practice while building the data transaction market.

Data has high timeliness. Only when data is traded to the demander within the limitation period can it realize its expected value. Legislation should promote the efficient circulation of data. At the same time, the data is aggregated, often in the form of scale, and once leaked, it will cause serious consequences. Therefore, when exploring the norms, standards, and management methods of the data trading industry in practice, both efficiency and security should be considered.

3.1   Internal Review of Data Platform

Big data exchange and big data trading platforms undertake two major functions of service and management in the market, that is, the "organizer" of market transactions and the "supervisor" of transactions. When the rules are formulated, the exchange and trading platform should be entrusted with the supervision responsibility, and their own organizational structure should also involve the government, especially when public data sharing is involved in data market transactions.

Compliance Review of Data Transactions. The whole process of the data transaction, the data platform shall conduct a repeated compliance review to ensure that the transaction complies with the provisions of existing laws, and whether it meets the requirements of the Data Security Law of the People's Republic of China, the Personal Information Protection Law of the People's Republic of China and other laws and regulations.

Protection of rights and interests of data subjects. For the data set provided by the upstream data provider, focus on whether its data has been cleaned and desensitized, and obtain the authorization of the data subject. Eliminate illegal data and desensitized substandard data, ensure data quality and safety, and protect the rights and interests of data subjects.

Establish a Data Security Mechanism. The trading platform should have the data security capability, set up a special department for data security, and update the data security technology dynamically. Evaluate the data nature of data providers, data processors, and data consumers in the process of data information transaction and application, and examine whether they have the ability and plan to protect data information.

3.2   External Specification of Data Platform

Legislative aspect. To promote the efficiency of data transactions, we should distinguish the types of tradable data and the scope of non-tradable data as soon as possible, define the boundaries of data transactions, and encourage non-data transaction enterprises to invest their legal data in the data transaction market. Strengthen the legal protection and incentive measures of on-site data transactions [5].

In terms of data security, we should improve the legal framework of data security and prevent data security risks. The legislative department should formulate the Measures for the Administration of Data Transactions as soon as possible according to the pilot situation, strengthen the policy guidance for data transactions, and clarify the management mechanism, concept definition, participation role, and the rights and obligations of each subject of data transactions. At the same time, we should speed up the institutional arrangement of data ownership, and clarify the legal status of data ownership, use rights, management right, and platform right.

Administrative Supervision Aspect. In terms of supervision, it is necessary to clarify the competent department of data transactions, so as to avoid cross-jurisdiction of multiple departments and unclear powers and responsibilities, which will lead to the absence of supervision of data transactions in essence.

Social Participation. Encourage industry associations, research teams, and key enterprises to collaborate to build schemes and standards for data security processing technology, and provide a reference for the evaluation of data transaction security.

4   Peroration

The construction of a data trading mode plays a key role in the data trading market. By subdividing the role of the data trading mode and removing the substantial restrictions on data providers, the data supply sources can be effectively broadened and the data volume in China's data trading market can be effectively increased [6]. At the same time, by refining the division of labor and cultivating professional data analysis and processing enterprises, we can deepen data mining, improve the utilization efficiency of data resources, and enrich the supply of data products. However, lowering the market entry threshold does not mean that the threshold is not needed, regardless of the security of data transactions. The construction of the data trading market should pursue efficiency as well as transaction security and data security. Therefore, it is necessary to build internal and external coordinated data trading legal regulations, improve internal review and external supervision of data trading, and build a multi-dimensional data security system from the aspects of legislation, law enforcement, and social participation.

References

1. LiuHui, X.J.: Analysis on legal governance path of data transaction. Straits Law **24**, 80–88 (2022)
2. Tian, J., Liu, L.: Trading mode, right definition and data factor market cultivation. Reform **7**, 17–26 (2020)
3. Wu, J., Zhang, Y.: Research on the development of data factor trading platform from the perspective of factor market allocation. Credit Inf. **39**(1), 59–66 (2021)
4. Ethan, G.N., Sun, J.: Research and exploration of big data transaction mode based on blockchain. Big Data **7**(4), 37–48 (2021)
5. Li, A.: Construction of legal system for data factor market cultivation. J. Law **42**, 17–28 (2021)
6. Sharla, C., Zhu, X.: Legislative thinking on big data transactions in China. Learn. Pract. **7**, 60–70 (2018)

Study on the Fundamentals of Electrical Engineering Based on Grey Correlation Analysis

Fei Tang[1(✉)], Jian Xu[2], Huamei Qi[2], Qingfen Liao[1], and Junfeng Qi[1]

[1] School of Electrical Engineering and Automation, Wuhan University, Wuhan, China
lncs@springer.com
[2] School of Computer Science and Engineering Center for Teaching and learning development,
Central South University, Changsha, China

Abstract. The fundamentals of electrical engineering is a compulsory course set up by the school of electrical and automation of Wuhan University for undergraduate junior students. As an important platform course of electrical engineering, it has high requirements for students to learn the pre sequence basic courses. Firstly, this paper uses grey correlation analysis to analyze the correlation between the courses of advanced mathematics, circuit theory and electrical engineering of undergraduate students in recent three years and this course. Then the correlation coefficient is obtained and normalized. Finally, it is used as the analysis of new students' learning situation. In this way, we can effectively have a scientific and objective understanding of the basic knowledge of new students and the learning situation of preamble courses.

Keywords: correlation coefficient · electrical engineering · fundamentals of electrical engineering · grey correlation analysis

1 Introduction

The course "Fundamentals of electrical engineering" offered by the school of electrical and automation of Wuhan University is a required professional platform course for undergraduates [1, 2]. It covers the basic teaching contents of many main courses of the former electrical engineering and automation major, such as "power system analysis", "power system overvoltage" and "electrical part of power plant". Through the study of the platform course, the basic courses such as "advanced mathematics" and "College Physics" studied by students majoring in electrical engineering and automation in freshmen and sophomores are connected with the professional basic courses such as circuit, motor and electromagnetic field. And the synthesis and practice are carried out on a unified platform. And in the whole teaching activities, we also need to integrate interactive [3] and heuristic [4] teaching methods.

The content of this course has its own characteristics. It takes the power system as the research object, starting with the components of the power system. Firstly, the basic concept of power system, the load of power system and the main components of power system are introduced. And then the model of power system and the connection modes of power system are gradually established. Then the basic concepts and calculation methods of power flow, short circuit and stability are introduced. It enables students to have a comprehensive understanding of the future work or research object, and enhances their professional identity and professional mission. The students' learning initiative has been greatly improved, and their interest and enthusiasm are very high. However, this course has many basic concepts, many and complex subject formulas, which plays an important connecting role in the whole electrical engineering talent training system. Students' learning difficulty is not small, and they have high requirements for the previous professional courses and basic courses. Based on the grey correlation analysis, this paper summarizes the importance of the previous courses and sorts them. Combined with the examination results of students in recent three years, this paper carries out the closed-loop analysis of learning situation and post teaching evaluation, summarizes and summarizes the relevance of the previous courses to this course, and can be applied to the subsequent teaching.

2 Important Courses of Basic Preface of Electrical Engineering

According to the characteristics of the course "Fundamentals of electrical engineering", the course team cooperates with teachers who have rich teaching experience in different disciplines of the specialty to widely discuss the content of the textbook. Then we constantly adjust and revise the content of the textbook, so as to strengthen the connection with the content of early professional basic courses and subsequent professional courses, and improve the curriculum knowledge structure. Through the scoring and discussion of various experts, the important pilot courses in the preface are summarized as follows: Advanced Mathematics (upper and lower), electrical engineering (upper and lower), and circuit theory (upper and lower).

Advanced mathematics here mainly refers to the part of calculus. The most important thing is the concept and calculation of vector, the solution of differential equation, limit and gradient, etc. It is mainly applied to the mathematical expression of positive sequence, negative sequence and zero sequence networks in the course of fundamentals of electrical engineering, the current and voltage calculation of three-phase alternating current, and the differential equations that need to be used in short-circuit calculation.

The circuit course undertakes the important task of laying a solid foundation of electric network theory for students majoring in electronic information, electrical and automation. It is a bridge for them to transition from basic course learning to professional course learning. Therefore, in the teaching process of theory course, in addition to clarifying the basic concepts, basic laws and basic methods of circuit, we should pay attention to the synthesis of knowledge points and the optimization of analysis methods. We can cultivate students' engineering literacy through examples, discussion and practice. It requires students to have the knowledge of differential equations in Higher Mathematics and electromagnetism in college physics. This knowledge is mainly used to understand the basic concepts and methods of circuit course. The circuit course has its own complete system. After learning, students only need to master the basic theories and methods of the circuit course. As the circuit course is the first professional basic course of electronic information, electrical and automation majors, it plays a very important role in the follow-up courses: analog circuit, Fundamentals of electrical engineering and electrical engineering.

Electrical engineering is a course with electrical machinery as the research object. It is a very important technical basic course of electrical engineering in Colleges and universities of science and engineering. It plays a connecting role between professional basic courses and professional courses. The course of electrical engineering focuses on the steady-state analysis of four models: transformer, DC motor, induction motor and synchronous motor. It mainly introduces its basic principle, basic structure, operation characteristics and main analysis methods. At the same time, it is familiar with and master the basic experimental skills and computer simulation methods of common motor problems. Through the above theoretical knowledge learning and experimental skill training, students will have the ability to analyze and solve motor related problems in engineering practice. This course provides a foundation for the foundation of electrical engineering, which can provide in-depth understanding of transformer and circuit model, the principle and circuit model of synchronous generator, and the analysis of synchronous generator model for power system stability calculation.

3   The Grey Correlation Cluster Analysis Theory

Grey correlation mainly studies the uncertain correlation between various factors [5]. Before grey correlation analysis, we should first find the mapping quantity that can reflect the behavior characteristics of the system, determine the effective factors affecting the system [6], and deal with them appropriately. Then calculate the correlation coefficient and correlation degree between the factors. Finally, it is analyzed according to the calculation results. In essence, this method judges the degree of correlation according to the similarity of the sequence curve of factors.

The relevant definitions of grey correlation analysis theory are given below:

Definition 1: mapping quantity of system behavior characteristics:

$$X_i = (x_i(1), x_i(2), \cdots, x_i(n)), i = 0, 1, 2, \cdots, m \tag{1}$$

Definition 2: Grey Correlation Degree: set x0 as the mapping amount of system characteristics and Xi as the mapping amount of other relevant factors of the system.

$$\gamma(x_0(k), x_i(k)) = \frac{\min\limits_i \min\limits_k |x_0(k) - x_i(k)| + \zeta \max\limits_i \max\limits_k |x_0(k) - x_i(k)|}{|x_0(k) - x_i(k)| + \zeta \max\limits_i \max\limits_k |x_0(k) - x_i(k)|} \tag{2}$$

where $\gamma(x_0(k), x_i(k))$ represents the correlation coefficient between x_i and x_0 at point k, and ζ represents the resolution coefficient, $\zeta \in (0, 1)$.

$$\gamma(X_0, X_i) = \frac{1}{n} \sum_{k=1}^{n} \gamma(x_0(k), x_i(k)) \tag{3}$$

where $\gamma(X_0, X_i)$ represents the gray correlation coefficient between X_i and X_0. And (3) has four characteristics as follows:

11) Normalization, which means neither of the two system behavior mappings can be strictly unrelated.

$$0 < \gamma(X_0, X_i) \le 1$$
$$\gamma(X_0, X_i) = 1 \Leftrightarrow X_0 = X_i \tag{4}$$

21) Overall, indicating the influence of environment on grey correlation:

For $X_i, X_j \in X = \{X_s | s = 0, 1, 2, \cdots, m; m \ge 2\}$, there is as follows:

$$\gamma(X_i, X_j) \ne \gamma(X_j, X_i) \quad (i \ne j) \tag{5}$$

31) Even symmetry, indicating that when there are only two mapping quantities of system behavior feature, pair-wise comparison satisfies the symmetry.

For $X_i, X_j \in X$, there is as follows:

$$\gamma(X_i, X_j) = \gamma(X_j, X_i) \Leftrightarrow X = \{X_i, X_j\} \tag{6}$$

41) Proximity indicates that the quantization of grey correlation degree is constrained.

The $|x_0(k) - x_i(k)|$ smaller, the $\gamma(x_0(k), x_i(k))$ bigger.

4 An Empirical Study of Learning Situation Analysis

According to the above definition, the grey correlation analysis of relevant courses is carried out in combination with the basic preface and synchronous courses of electrical engineering. The specific steps are as follows:

Step 1: define the scores of each student's related pre sequence courses as vectors, and the score sequence of all students in each course as the initial value of a vector:

$$X'_i = X_i / x_i(1) = \left(x'_i(1), x'_i(2), \cdots, x'_i(n)\right)$$
$$i = 0, 1, 2, \cdots, m \tag{7}$$

Step 2: calculate the travel mapping quantity:

$$\begin{cases} \Delta_i(k) = \left|x'_o(k) - x'_i(k)\right| \\ \Delta_i = (\Delta_i(1), \Delta_i(2), \cdots, \Delta_i(n)) \\ i = 0, 1, 2, \cdots, m \end{cases} \tag{8}$$

Step 3: find the maximum difference and minimum difference between two poles:

$$\begin{cases} M = \max_i \max_k \Delta_i(k) \\ m = \min_i \min_k \Delta_i(k) \end{cases} \tag{9}$$

Step 4: calculate the grey correlation coefficient:

$$\gamma_{0i}(k) = \frac{m + \zeta M}{\Delta_i(k) + \zeta M}, \zeta \in (0, 1)$$
$$k = i = 1, 2, \cdots, n; \quad i = 1, 2, \cdots, m \tag{10}$$

Step 5: calculate the grey correlation degree between the course and the basis of electrical engineering:

$$\gamma_{0i} = \frac{1}{n} \sum_{k=1}^{n} \gamma_{0i}(k), \quad i = 1, 2, \cdots, m \tag{11}$$

Step 6: according to the above five steps, calculate the grey correlation degree of the pre sequence courses: Advanced Mathematics (upper and lower), electrical engineering (upper and lower), circuit theory (upper and lower) and basic courses of electrical engineering, and normalize them (Figs. 1, 2, 3, 4, 5 and 6):

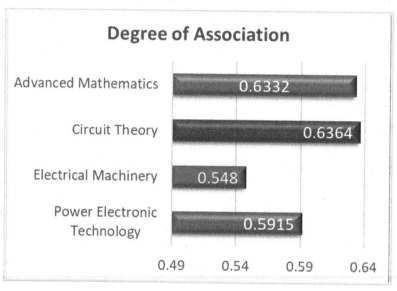

Fig. 1. Degree of association of grade 2017 students' scores

It can be seen that the course of fundamentals of electrical engineering is highly relevant to advanced mathematics and circuit theory, power electronics technology and electrical engineering. The specific analysis is as follows:

(1) Advanced mathematics is the foundation. The course of fundamentals of electrical engineering has three major calculations: power flow calculation, short-circuit calculation and stability calculation, which all use the relevant derivation and differential knowledge of advanced mathematics, especially the solution of differential equations, which is an important premise for solving short-circuit calculation. Through the analysis of test papers in previous years, more than 80% of the points lost in short-circuit calculation are caused by the weak foundation of differential equations;

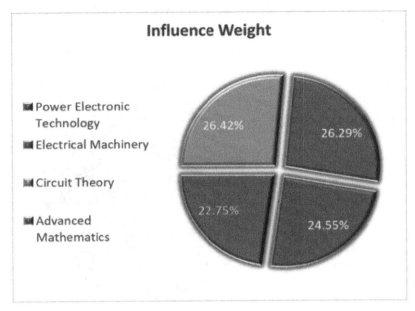

Fig. 2. Influence weight of grade 2017 students' scores

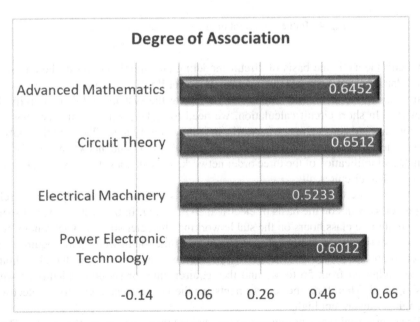

Fig. 3. Degree of association of grade 2018 students' scores

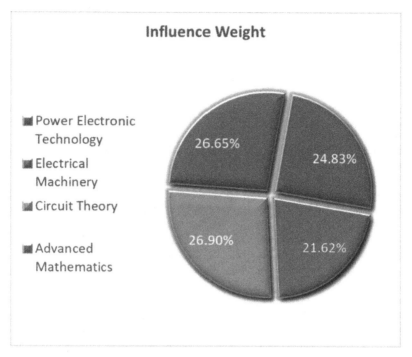

Fig. 4. Influence weight of grade 2018 students' scores

(2) Circuit theory is the basis of circuit modeling and simplification in the course of fundamentals of electrical engineering. In power flow calculation, it is necessary to first determine the circuit extension structure of the system, and then simplify the circuit; In short circuit calculation, we need to make positive sequence, negative sequence and zero sequence networks first and simplify them. Through the analysis of the test papers in previous years, more than 40% of the students will make mistakes in the simplification of the three order network, and can not get the correct Thevenin equivalent circuit at all;

(3) The influence weight of electrical engineering is low, because we adjusted the relevant class hours on the basis of electrical engineering. In the past, we would spend several more class hours on the stable working characteristics of synchronous generator during the stability calculation. At that time, there were more requirements for the pre sequence knowledge of synchronous generator. Later, the class hours were adjusted from 56 to 48, and the requirements for stability calculation were simplified. Therefore, the requirements for the pre sequence mastery of electrical engineering are not high;

(4) Power electronics technology is a course held at the same time as this course. There will be learning task conflict, so it is also analyzed. The relevance here is mainly due to the fact that the course is also difficult, and it is opened at the same time as the basic course of electrical engineering, and the examination also has overlapping time intervals, which puts a certain pressure on students' learning tasks.

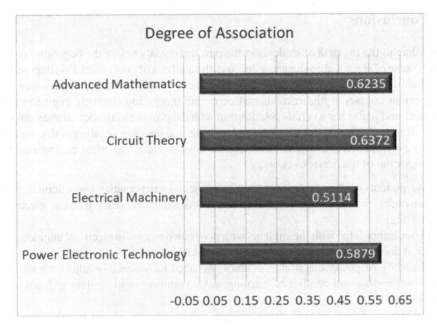

Fig. 5. Degree of association of grade 2019 students' scores

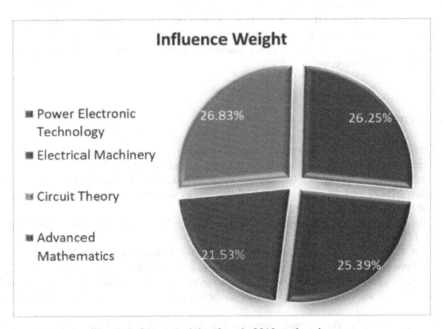

Fig. 6. Influence weight of grade 2019 students' scores

5 Conclusions

According to the big data of students in the past three years before the beginning of the basic course of electrical engineering, through the analysis of grey correlation degree, the correlation degree between the final basic evaluation score of electrical engineering and the previous courses of higher mathematics, circuit theory and electrical engineering is obtained, and it also has a certain relationship with the power electronics courses offered at the same time. Thus, we can analyze and mobilize the learning situation of the students of the newly opened courses, and estimate the basic score of electrical engineering for the proportion of the previous courses:

For the students with poor performance in advanced mathematics and circuit theory, we must seize the time to review, otherwise it will affect the study of basic electrical engineering;
Don't be disappointed with the students with poor performance in electrical engineering. In fact, it doesn't have a great relationship with this course;
For the study of power electronics courses, we need to reasonably adjust the time to avoid overlapping and conflict of learning tasks, resulting in the failure to learn both courses well.

Acknowledgments. This research was supported by the project of Wuhan University graduate credit course construction, "a new electromechanical system dynamics modeling method", the general education course 3.0 project of Wuhan University "Internet creative thinking and user experience", and the specific research project of teachers' teaching development of Wuhan University "Research on the reform of practical teaching system of E-commerce Specialty under the background of 'intelligence +'".

References

1. Zhu, L., Yang, Y., Sun, H.: Practice and Exploration of teaching reform of basic course of electrical Engineering. Metallurgical Educ. China Beijing **S1**, 55–56 (2013)
2. Yin, X., Luo, Y., Zhang, B.: The idea of "Basic electrical Engineering" course construction which ADAPTS to the major training scheme of electrical engineering. J. Electr. Electron. Teach. Nanjing **30**(7), 14–15 (2008)
3. Chen, K., Liao, Z.: Fine particles, thin films and exchange anisotropy. After-school Educ. Chin. **15**, 117–120 (2018)
4. Chen, K., Liao, Z., Shi, H.: The application of heuristic teaching method in the course of Fundamentals of Electrical Engineering. Educ. Modernization **5**(20), 2095–8420 (2018)
5. Deng, J.: Three properties of grey predictive model GM(1,1) -- optimization structure and optimization information amount of grey predictive control. J. Huazhong Inst. Technol. **05**, 1–6
6. Deng, J., Zhou, C.: Title of paper with only first word capitalized. J. Name Stand. Abbr. Inf. Control **4**, 24–27 (1987)

The Network Planning for LSP Protection in PTN

Xin Zhou[✉]

Hubei University of Technology, WuHan, China
zhouxin@hbut.edu.cn

Abstract. PTN (Packet Transport Network) can support end-to-end connections and various services for tenants. It employs Label Switching Path (LSP) technology to serve tenants and utilizes LSP protection to ensure service reliability. However, PTN planning stage is critical and the associated LSP problem is unexplored. We formulate the LSP protection problem as an integer linear programming (ILP) model. The objective is to minimize the utilized bandwidth to serve the given tenant service requests, and satisfy non-same-node and non-same-board constraints. However, the ILP can not achieve an optimal solution within reasonable time. To solve the problem, a fast heuristic algorithm, that is, most request demand ordering (MRDO) is proposed to obtain a sub-optimal solution. The simulation results represent that an optimal solution can be obtained by ILP in small PTN topologies, whereas MRDO achieve a sub-optimal solution in large PTN topologies. The results also indicate that MRDO provides a more efficient solution than a baseline algorithm.

Keywords: PTN · LSP · Protection · ILP

1 Introduction

1.1 A Subsection Sample

PTN (Packet Transport Network) is an optical transport network architecture based on packet switching. It is owned by communication operators and supports end-to-end connections and various services for tenants [1]. PTN employs Label Switching Path (LSP) technology to serve tenants in form of end-to-end connection. PTN provides LSP protection, which means it provides major and backup LSP connections with two distinct routings for each tenant, to assure service reliability, i.e. network connection reliability. The two routing should not share the same node and board, so that if the major routing fails, the backup routing can take over and provide service to tenants [2].

However, in both network planning and operation stages, to provide service for tenants quickly, network operator does not consider the LSP protection [3]. That is, the network operator only provides the major LSP connection, and does not consider the backup LSP connection, or offers a false LSP protection. The false LSP protection is that the two routings of major and backup LSP connections have either same-node or same-board problem. Once the routing of the major LSP connection interrupts, the service will stop and affect the tenant's service experience [3].

For the problem, in the operation stage, some researches provide the routing of backup LSP connection though the solution of top K- shortest path algorithms. The solution tends to adjust some services with a valid LSP protection and affect the service experiment [5–7]. However, the life cycle of a network is first network planning, and then network operation. The network planning is significant, since it not only solves the LSP protection problem, but also uses the minimum network bandwidth to serve the given tenant service requests. Thus, it is an effective to consider LSP problem in network planning rather than network operation.

To address the problem, in this paper, we first build a mathematical model to describe the LSP protection problem. The objective of the problem is to minimize the utilized bandwidth for given tenant service requests, and non-same-node and non-same-board constraints are satisfied. To the best of our knowledge, this is the first work on the LSP protection problem in PTN planning. The model is an integer linear programming (ILP) problem, which is difficult to solve. When the problem scale is small, the optimal solution can be found. However, when the problem scale is large, the optimal solution can not be found in tolerant time. Thus, we resort to fast heuristic algorithms.

The rest of this paper is organized in the following. In Sect. 2, the description of LSP protection problem is introduced. In Sect. 3, the ILP model is presented using mathematical formulations. In Sect. 4, a fast heuristic algorithm is proposed. In Sect. 5, the performance of ILP and the heuristic algorithm are evaluated. The work is concluded in Sect. 6

2 The Problem of LSP Protection

LSP protection is PTN operators assign major and backup LSP connections for every tenant request. In general, the major connection is active and the backup connection is inactive, and the former offers service for tenants. Once the major connection is interrupted, the backup connection is activated and offers service for tenants.

However, the false LSP protection can lead to an invalid protection. The false LSP protection is presented by the routings of the major and backup connections, and can be divided into two categories. First, in source or destination node, their routings share the same board, which is called same-board problem. Second, in intermediate nodes, their routings share the same node, which is called same-node problem. In such case, once outage appears in board of source node or intermediate nodes, the LSP protection is invalid and the tenant service will interrupt. For a valid LSP protection, non-same-node and non-same-board constraints should be satisfied. In the following, false LSP protection is described first, and then valid LSP protection is introduced.

2.1 False LSP Protection

To illustrate LSP protection problem and simplify our analysis, a conceptual PTN topology is considered and shown in Fig. 1. The PTN consists of 5 nodes and 7 bidirectional optical links colored by black. There are two boards in every node. For example, for node E, there are 2 boards indexed by 0 and 1, respectively. To simplify, we assume that every board has one optical port that can be shared by many optical fibers. The optical ports are used to connect optical fibers for two nodes. There are two tenant requests represented by R_{AC} and R_{AE}. Specially, $R_{AC} =< A, C, 1 >$ denotes the source node of tenant request is A, and the destination node is C, and the bandwidth demand is 1 unit of bandwidth.

Subsequent paragraphs, however, are indented. For R_{AE}, the routing of major LSP connection denoted by LSP_{AE_m} is (A_0, D, E_0) colored by blue solid line, while the routing of backup LSP connection denoted by LSP_{AE_b} is (A_1, B, C, D, E_0) colored by blue dotted line. For node A_0, the subscript is the index of board 0. But, the LSP protection for R_{AE} is invalid because either same-board or same-node problem appears. First, the major and backup routings share node D that is an intermediate node, which lead to the same-node problem. Second, at node E that is a destination node, their routings share the same board 0, which lead to the same-board problem.

For R_{AC}, the routing of major LSP connection denoted by LSP_{AC_m} is (A_0, C_0) colored by red solid line. But, the backup LSP connection is missed, which can also give rise to an invalid LSP protection.

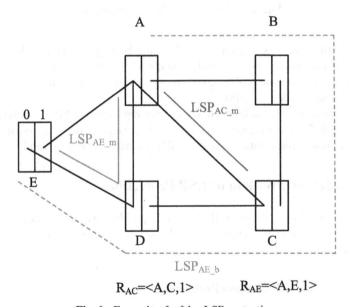

$R_{AC}=<A,C,1>$ $R_{AE}=<A,E,1>$

Fig. 1. Example of a false LSP protection.

2.2 Valid LSP Protection

For the problem of invalid LSP protection in Sect. 2. A, we can solve it as followed. For R_{AE}, , the routing of major LSP connection is modified into (A_0, E_1), as shown in Fig. 2. For node E, the major LSP connection employs board 1, while the backup LSP

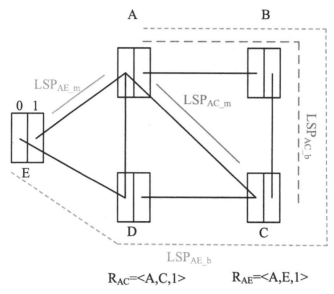

Fig. 2. Example of a valid LSP protection.

connection employs board 0, which solves the same-board problem, i.e., the non-same-board constraint is satisfied. We also find the major LSP connection does not use node D, which solves the same-node problem, i.e., non-same-node constraint is satisfied. Thus, the LSP protection for R_{AE} is valid.

For R_{AC}, we assign the backup LSP connection represented LSP_{AC_b} colored by red dotted line in Fig. 2. Its routing is $(A_{\_1}, B, C_{\_1})$, which satisfies both the non-same-board and non-same-node constraints. Thus, the LSP protection for R_{AC} is valid.

3 ILP Model for Problem of LSP Protection

In this section, we formulate the LSP protection problem as an ILP model. Its objective is to minimize the used bandwidth, and both non-same-node and non-same-board constraints are satisfied.

3.1 Definition of LSP Protection Problem

Define a PTN as $G(N, L, B)$, where N is the set of nodes, L is denoted as the set of bidirectional optical links (i.e., optical fibers), and B is the set of bandwidth on each optical link.

LSP protection problem - given a PTN $G(N, L, B)$, and a predefined set of tenant requests with $|\mathbb{R}|$ requests ($\mathbb{R} = \{R_{sd}, ...\}$), where $R_{sd} = <s, d, T_{sd}>$ means the source node of request is s, and its destination node is d, required by T_{sd} units of bandwidth. How to serve $|\mathbb{R}|$ requests with minimum utilized bandwidth? That is, for every request, assigns both major and backup LSP connections, satisfying both the non-same-board and non-same-node constraints.

3.2 Notations and Variables

- $R_{sd} = <s, d, T_{sd}>$, a tenant request, and $s, d \in N$.
- K, a constant number, is the number of boards in a node.
- ki, an integer variable represents the index of board at node i, and satisfies $0 \leq ki \leq K - 1$.
- $l_{i,j}^{ki,kj}$, a boolean variable. $l_{i,j}^{ki,kj} = 1$ means that there is an optical link between node i and j, through board ki at node i and board kj at node j; $l_{i,j}^{ki,kj} = 0$ otherwise.
- $f_{sd,ij}^{ki,kj}$, a boolean variable, $f_{sd,ij}^{ki,kj} = 1$ means that the LSP connection of tenant request R_{sd} go through link between nodes i and j; $f_{sd,ij}^{ki,kj} = 0$ otherwise.
- c, an integer variable represents the value of utilized bandwidth in every link.

3.3 Objective and Constraints of LSP Protection Problem

More utilized bandwidth on a fiber link leads to increased cost and consumes more power. Therefore, for a given tenant request matrix, the objective of the LSP protection problem is to minimize the used bandwidth among all optical links, as shown in (1). Meanwhile, (2) is used to achieve the maximum utilized bandwidth among all optical links, which is the sum of tenants bandwidth request for every link.

$$Minimine \ c \tag{1}$$

$$\sum_{sd,ki,kj} f_{sd,ij}^{ki,kj} T_{sd} \leq c, \forall i, j \tag{2}$$

subject to the following constraints:

$$f_{sd,ij}^{ki,kj} \leq l_{i,j}^{ki,kj}, \forall i, j \tag{3}$$

Equation (3) means that, the link between nodes i and j is used to support service for R_{sd}, unless the link exists in PTN topology, which is represented by $l_{i,j}^{ki,kj}$.

$$\sum_{d=j,ki,kj} f_{sd,ij}^{ki,kj} T_{sd} \leq 2T_{sd}, \forall s, d \tag{4}$$

$$\sum_{s=i,ki,kj} f_{sd,ij}^{ki,kj} T_{sd} \leq 2T_{sd}, \forall s, d \tag{5}$$

Equation (4) represents that the bandwidth demand for tenant request R_{sd} should be added at node s with a value of $2T_{sd}$, due to major and backup LSP connections; on the contrary, Eq. (5) specifies that the bandwidth demand for R_{sd} should be dropped at node d with a value of $2T_{sd}$.

$$\sum_{s=d,ki,kj} f_{sd,ij}^{ki,kj} T_{sd} \leq 0, \forall i, j \tag{6}$$

Equation (6) makes sure that for every tenant request, no bandwidth is needed at the same nodes.

$$\sum_{ki,kj} f_{sd,ij}^{ki,kj} = \sum_{kj,kt} f_{sd,jt}^{kj,kt}, \forall s, d, j \qquad (7)$$

Equation (7) is bandwidth conservation constraint. For every tenant request at intermediate node j, the bandwidth added is equal to that dropped.

$$\sum_{s=i,ki,kj} f_{sd,ij}^{ki,kj} = 2, \forall s, d \qquad (8)$$

$$\sum_{d=j,kj,kj} f_{sd,ij}^{ki,kj} = 2, \forall s, d \qquad (9)$$

Equations (8) and (9) are the non-same-board constraints. It guarantees that at source or destination node, the major and backup LSP connections must employ two different boards.

$$\sum_{s\neq i,kj,kj} f_{sd,ij}^{ki,kj} = 1, \forall s, d, i \qquad (10)$$

$$\sum_{d\neq j,ki,kj} f_{sd,ij}^{ki,kj} = 1, \forall s, d, j \qquad (11)$$

Equations (10) and (11) are the non-same-node constraints. It ensures that for R_{sd}, every intermediate node can only support a major or a backup LSP connection. That is, it can support a LSP connection, not both major and backup.

4 Heuristic Algorithm

The ILP model can offer an optimal solution through optimal algorithms when PTN scale is small. However, for a large scale PTN, the optimal solution can not be achieved by the ILP model within reasonable time. This is because the optimal algorithms have hugely high complexity in computation. The optimal algorithms, including enumeration and branch-and-bound. When PTN scale increases, the complexity of the optimal algorithms can rapidly increases, since the number of variables and constraints rapidly increases. For our ILP model, PTN size $|N|$ can determine the number of variables and constraints.

To solve the large ILP model, heuristic algorithms are resorted to achieve a sub-optimal solution. Because heuristic algorithms always have low computation complexity, so that the sub-optimal solution can be obtained within tolerable time. For the LSP protection problem, its ILP model is equivalent to a combinatorial optimization problem, so that different orderings of tenant requests can give rise to different solutions. Thus, a heuristic algorithm is presented to address the problem.

4.1 Most Request Demand Ordering Algorithm

In this subsection, most request demand ordering (MRDO) algorithm is proposed. MRDO utilizes an ordering of tenant bandwidth request. These requests are sorted in a queue Q, in a decreasing order with respect to their bandwidth demand (i.e., T_{sd}). The requests are served one-by-one from the top of Q. Specially, large requests (with larger bandwidth demand) are served first. That is, smaller requests at the bottom of Q are served finally, which can balance the load of optical links, leading to the reduction of bandwidth used.

The proposed MRDO algorithm is introduced by Algorithm 1. Sort the requests according to their T_{sd}, in a descending order in Q, and pre-calculate top-K routing for all node pairs. The top-K routing stored in $\mathbb{Q}$, is achieved by the K-shortest path algorithm. The major LSP connection is established by the top routing from $\mathbb{Q}$ and c is updated, which is shown in lines 3–4. For the backup LSP connection, the algorithm iterates $\mathbb{Q}$, until a routing, that satisfies the same-board and same-node constraints, is found. Then, the backup LSP connection is established by the routing from $\mathbb{Q}$ and c is updated, which is described by lines 5–7.

---

1. Sort the tenant requests in the descending order of their bandwidth demands in Q; c is the maximum utilized bandwidth for all links;

2. **while** $Q \neq \varnothing$ **do**

3. pick the top request $R_{sd} = <s, d, T_{sd}>$ in Q, and   store the top-K routing for R_{sd} in list queue $\mathbb{Q}$;

4. assign the major LSP connection using the first routing, and update the maximum utilized bandwidth : $c = c + T_{sd}$; pop the routing;

5.   **while** $\mathbb{Q} \neq \varnothing$ **do**

6.   **if** the top routing satisfies non-same-board and non-same-node constraints **then**
                assign the backup LSP connection using the routing, and update the maximum utilized bandwidth: $c = c + T_{sd}$;

7.   **end while**

8. pop the R_{sd} ;

9. **end while**

---

5 Performance Evaluation

In this section, the ILP model and two fast heuristic algorithms are evaluated, which can result in the optimal and sub-optimal solutions, respectively. CPLEX 12.5 that is a mathematical solver, is employed to implement the ILP model, and Visual Studio 2015 C + + is used to implement the heuristic algorithms. The proposed ILP model and heuristic algorithms are carried by a computer with a 1.80 GHz processor and 16 GB RAM. To enforce the simulations, 5-node and a 14-node PTN topologies are utilized as a small-

and a large network topology, respectively. Two PTN topologies are as shown in Fig. 3, where (a) presents the small network, and (b) presents the large network, and every node has two boards. As we known, the standard PTN topology is a ring. However, due to the demand of improvement in network reliability, mesh networks will be the mainstream network topologies. Thus, two mesh topologies are employed.

The bandwidth demand T_{sd} for each R_{sd} in terms of the number of 100Mbps is randomly generated between 1 and $D=\{4, 8, 12, 16, 20\}$, where D is the maximum bandwidth demand for R_{sd}, and is referred as bandwidth granularity. Here, the maximum bandwidth demand is 2Gbps. Essentially, D denotes the load of PTN, and large values of D specifies high load.

5.1 ILP and Heuristic Algorithms Under a Small Topology

To compare the performances the proposed ILP model and the MRDO algorithm, a random ordering (RO) heuristic algorithm is also evaluated and regarded as a baseline. They are implemented on a 5-node topology with 7 bidirectional optical links, which is depicted in Fig. 3(a). The tenant bandwidth requests are launched and terminated at the 5 PTN nodes, and the minimum bandwidth utilized is employed as the metric.

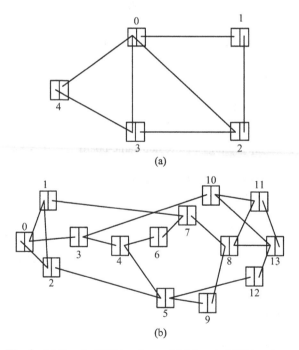

Fig. 3. (a) 5-node PTN topology; (b) 14-node PTN topology.

The minimum utilized bandwidth with varying bandwidth granularity D are considered, and the results are depicted in Fig. 4. The RO heuristic is introduced as the baseline, which sorts the tenant requests in a random ordering with respect to T_{sd}. From Fig. 4, two main trends can be observed.

First, it is clear that bandwidth required increase as long as bandwidth granularity D increases. This is because that the increase in D results in the increase of PTN load, which can consume more network bandwidth.

Second, we can also observe that RO performs badly. The reason is that in RO, some bigger tenant request might be served finally, so that the utilized bandwidth can expand vastly. On the contrary, the bigger requests are served first, then the smaller requests are served finally, which can balance the load of links and reduce the utilized bandwidth. As expected, MRDO gets the better performance, since the bigger requests are served first. Compared to MRDO, the ILP model obtains the optimal solution through an optimal algorithm that is integrated in CPLEX 12.5. When bandwidth granularity D is at a value of 20, the network load is high, and ILP outperforms MDRO and RO by 14.5% and 25%, respectively.

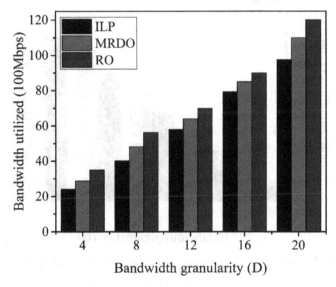

Fig. 4. Bandwidth utilized versus bandwidth granularity in a 5-node topology.

5.2 Heuristic Algorithms in a Large Topology

To evaluate the two heuristic algorithms further, a 14-node network is employed as a large PTN topology, as depicted in Fig. 3(b). The tenant requests are launched and terminated at the 14 nodes. The metric here is also the minimum bandwidth utilized.

Figure 5 exhibits the trend of minimum bandwidth utilized as the bandwidth granularity D increases when the number of tenant requests is fixed. From Fig. 5, on the one hand, we can observe that the bandwidth required by the two heuristic algorithms increase when D increases. This is because that the increase in D means the increase in network load, leading to more bandwidth utilized. On the other hand, MRDO obtains the better sub-optimal solution, and RO performs badly. The reason is that for MRDO, the bigger requests are served first, then the smaller requests are served finally, which can balance the load of links and reduce the utilized bandwidth. From Fig. 5, when $D = 20$, MRDO outperforms RO by up to 12.7%.

The trend of minimum required bandwidth along with the increase in the number of tenant request is considered, and the results are shown in Fig. 6. Here, in the horizontal axis, the number of tenant requests at $2X$ is two times that of $1X$. It can be observed that utilized bandwidth grows as the number of tenant requests increases by setting $D=4$, since the network load increases. MRDO outperforms RO, the reason is same as describe in the above paragraph. It can be clearly seen that when network load is at a value of $3X$, MRDO outperforms RO by up to 14%.

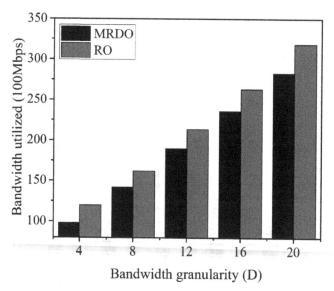

Fig. 5. Bandwidth utilized versus network load in a 14-node topology.

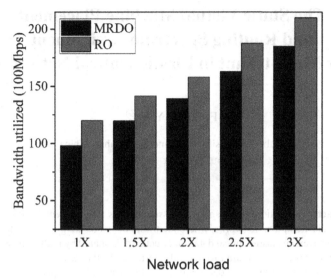

Fig. 6. Bandwidth utilized versus network load in a 14-node topology.

6   Conclusion

In this paper, the LSP protection problem in PTN planning was introduced. The problem was formulated as an ILP model. Its objective is to minimize the utilized bandwidth to serve the given tenant service requests, and satisfy non-same-node and non-same-board constraints. However, the ILP was unable to get an optimal solution within tolerable time. Thus, MRDO algorithm was proposed to achieve a sub-optimal solution, and it was found to outperform a baseline algorithm.

References

1. Razo, M., et al.: The PlaNet-PTN module: a single layer design tool for Packet Transport Network. In: 2009 IEEE 14th International Workshop on Computer Aided Modeling and Design of Communication Links and Networks (2009)
2. Wu, Y., Sun, S., Chen, J.: Strategy for intercommunication of PTN and SDH. In: 2010 2nd IEEE International Conference on Network Infrastructure and Digital Content, pp. 129–133 (2010)
3. Zhang, H., Li, F.: Study of the China PTN industry standard and its key issues. ZTE Commun. **8**(3), 1–4 (2020)
4. Cano-Cano, J., Andújar, F.J., Alfaro, J., Sánchez, L.: QoS provision in hierarchical and non-hierarchical switch architectures. J. Parallel Distrib. Comput. **148**, 10–12 (2021)
5. Zeng, Q.: 4G/5G-oriented PTN network QoS strategy and deployment. Telecommun. Express **11**, 10–15 (2017)
6. Mayr, C., Risso, C., Grampín, E.: Crafting optimal and resilient iBGP-IP/MPLS overlays for transit backbone networks. Opt. Switching Networking 1–2 (2021)
7. Gao, Q., Yin, Y.: Study on some problems of PTN transmission in relay protection services. Power Syst. Protection Control. **44**(8), 57–62 (2016)

The Static Virtual Machine Placement and Routing Spectrum Assignment for Multi-tenant in Elastic Optical Networks

FangPing You[(✉)]

Hubei University of Technology, Wuhan, China
youfp@hbut.edu.cn

Abstract. The static routing spectrum assignment is a fundamental problem in typical elastic optical networks, where the traffic demands are given and stationary. However, an elastic optical data center network is shared by multi-tenant, and hence the traffic demands are varying and determined by the virtual machine (VM) placement of multi-tenant under the given VM demands. In this paper, the problem of virtual machine placement and routing spectrum assignment (VMPRSA) is introduced and the static problem is proved to be NP-Hard. Furthermore, an optimal integer linear programming (ILP) model is formulated, with the target of minimizing the spectrum used to serve all the traffic demands driven by multi-tenant VM placement. Since the ILP model cannot scale to the big networks, a two-tier heuristic algorithm framework is proposed, i.e., the first tier is VM placement and the second is routing spectrum assignment (VMP + RSA). The VM placement of tenants can produce traffic demands, it thus is focused and two VM placement algorithms are proposed, namely random placement (RP) algorithm, and residual node capacity priority (RNCP) algorithm. The simulation results indicate that the ILP model provides the optimal solution, and the RNCP algorithm yields the better sub-optimal solution.

Keywords: Optical · Data centers · Virtual machine placement

1 Introduction

1.1 A Subsection Sample

Data center networks, as the network infrastructures and the platforms for deploying and running many applications of today's business in cloud computing, have attracted significant attentions in recent years [1, 2].

To meet the exponential growth of traffic induced by data-intensive applications, many literatures have begun designing novel network architectures employing off-the-shelf commodity switches. Techniques in these proposals include fat tree and random graph. Furthermore, in contrast to electrical switching, optical switching which possesses huge transmission bandwidth, can benefit data center networks. Many novel optical/electrical hybrid or all optical architectures are presented with the aim to improve

W. Hong and G. Kanaparan (Eds.): ICCSE 2023, CCIS 2023, pp. 72–84, 2024.
https://doi.org/10.1007/978-981-97-0730-0_8

network capacity and scalability [3–6]. Moreover, an advanced modulation technology, orthogonal frequency division multiplexing (OFDM) has been efficiently demonstrated and can implement elastic bandwidth assignment in optical networks [7]. Therefore, we expect that it is necessary for future optical data center networks to employ the modulation technology, which have been demonstrated in papers. We refer the optical data center networks based on OFDM as elastic optical data center networks (EODCNs).

As we known, the problem of resource assignment is investigated by few papers in elastic optical networks recently, including routing and spectrum assignment (RSA) [7], traffic grooming, etc. It seems that the approaches of resource assignment in elastic optical networks can be seamlessly transplanted to EODCNs [8]. However, EODCNs can be shared by multi-tenant in the cloud. The virtual machine (VM) placement can generate traffic demands of all-to-all between VMs for a tenant, since a VM of a tenant should exchange data with all other VMs of the tenant to achieve a complete response to the tenant, which hence poses a novel challenge on resource assignment [9]. Note VMs between different tenants have no correlation and thereby no traffic demand emerges.

In EODCNs, the problem of routing and spectrum assignment has been explored [8]. However, the fundamental problem of placing VMs of multi-tenant and assigning routing spectrum resources, is unexplored. The problem considers each traffic demand driven by VM placement under the given tenants VM demands, while the networks should have the enough node capacity to satisfy the VM placement (in terms of CPU/memory). The problem is defined as virtual machine placement and routing spectrum assignment (VMPRSA) problem.

In this paper, the static VMPRSA problem is studied in EODCNs, with the goal of minimizing the utilized spectrum to serve all the traffic demands determined by VM placement of each tenant. To the best of our knowledge, this is the first time to study static VMPRSA problem in EODCNs. The major contributions of this work are: (i) The VMPRSA problem is formally stated and its NP-hard is proved. (ii) An integer linear programming (ILP) model for the static VMPRSA problem is presented, which can optimally assign the VMs for multi-tenant and the concomitant traffic demands between VMs. (iii) An efficient two-tier heuristic algorithm framework, the first tier is VM placement and the second is routing and spectrum assignment (VMP + RSA), is proposed to solve the VMPRSA problem. (iv) Two VM placement algorithms are proposed, namely random placement (RP) algorithm and residual node capacity priority (RNCP) algorithm. The simulation results indicate that the ILP model achieves the optimal solution, and between the two heuristic algorithms, the RNCP algorithm obtains the better sub-optimal solution.

2   Virtual Machine Placement and Routing Spectrum Assignment

In this section, the overview of traffic demands determined by placing tenant VMs on a set of physical servers (hereinafter referred to servers) is introduced.

2.1   Traffic Demands Driven by VM Placement

A slot is used to refer to one capacity to accommodate a VM placement on servers. A top of rack (ToR) switch has s servers and each server has multiple slots, and each slot can be occupied by any VMs. A scenario where there are m tenants and n slots is considered. For a valid VM placement for multi-tenant, the sum of VM demands (in terms of CPU/memory) of m tenants should be smaller than or equal to n. As shown in Fig. 1, there are 3 tenants, and the sum of VM demands of 3 tenants is 12. The network has 12 slots which can satisfy the VM demands of 3 tenants.

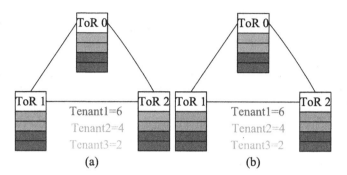

Fig. 1. Two schemes of VM placement.

A tenant demand needs some VMs, and each VM requires the network bandwidth to exchange data to all other VMs. VM placement determines the size of corresponding traffic demands and the switching method (i.e., electrical switching or optical switching) which is reflected into two aspects. On the one hand, if the VMs of a tenant are placed in a ToR switch, VMs send or receive data through electrical switching, which no cross-ToR traffic is produced. However, if the VMs of a tenant are placed into more ToR switches, cross-ToR traffic demands of all-to-all for the tenant would be produced. In this paper, cross-ToR traffic demands of all-to-all (hereinafter referred to traffic demands) using optical switching is focused. Note that the source node and the destination node of traffic demands are in respective of network nodes (i.e., ToR switch), not VMs themselves.

Then, how to quantify each traffic demand for a tenant is explained. When a tenant requires $m + n$ VMs, assume that m VMs are placed into a ToR switch and n VMs are placed into another ToR switch, therefore each ToR switch require m units of bandwidth and n units of bandwidth to send or receive data, respectively. If a ToR switch communicates with the other, the bandwidth will be limited to $\min(m, n)$ units. As shown in Fig. 1(a) which illustrates a scheme of VM placement, tenant 1 requires 6 VMs placed into 3 ToR switches, and each ToR switch has 2 VMs, therefore each ToR switch will require 2 units of bandwidth to exchange data. The communication bandwidth among ToR 0, ToR 1 and ToR 2 switches will be bounded to $\min(2, 2) = 2$ units; for tenant 2, the bandwidth between ToR 0 and ToR 1 is $\min(1, 2) = 1$ unit. In Fig. 1 (b), for tenant 3, all the VMs are placed in ToR 0, thus no traffic is yielded.

2.2 Virtual Machine Placement and Routing Spectrum Assignment

In this subsection, the static VMPRSA problem is formally stated in EODCNs. Define a network as $G(N, C, E, S)$, where N represents the set of nodes, $C =$

$\{C_0, C_1, ..., C_{|N|-1}\}$ is the set of capacity of nodes in N, E is the set of bidirectional fiber links between nodes in N, and S represents the set of spectrum slots on each fiber. The network node set has N nodes, it thus has $\sum_{i=0}^{|N|-1} C_i$ node capacity at all.

Definition. Static VMPRSA problem - given a network $G(N, C, E, S)$, and a pre-defined set of tenant demands (i.e., CPU/memory demands) with $|T|$ tenants ($T = \{T_0, T_1, ..., T_{|T|-1}\}$), where T_k represents that tenant k request T_k CPU/memory units, and satisfies $\sum_{k=0}^{|T|-1} T_k \leq \sum_{i=0}^{|N|-1} C_i$. Integer variable $Allo_i^k$ represents that the size of VMs are placed in node i for tenant k. The traffic demand of any two nodes for tenant k is $min(Allo_i^k, Allo_j^k)$. It is possible to establish each spectrum path in tenant k traffic demands and all tenants traffic demands using consecutive spectrum slots, and satisfy spectrum continuity constraint?

Theorem. The Static VMPRSA problem is NP-hard.

Proof. The typical RSA problem in elastic optical network is a special instance of the VMPRSA problem, in which traffic demands are fixed and no node capacity is considered [7]. Since the RSA problem alone is NP-hard, our claim holds.

3 ILP Model

In this section, an ILP mathematical model is formulated with the objective of minimizing the spectrum used to serve the multi-tenant demands, while the node capacity should satisfy the VM placement.

3.1 Notations and Variables

- T, the set of tenant demands, the element T_k represents the size of VM demands for tenant k;
- C_i, the capacity of node i, and each node has the same capacity for simplification;
- $Traf_{i,j}^k$, a decision integer variable that represents the traffic demand of tenant k between node i and j;
- $F_{i,j,m,n}^{w,k}$, a boolean variable, is equal to 1, if there is a spectrum path using spectrum slots w to satisfy the traffic demand of tenant k between node-pair (i, j) going from node m to node n, and 0 otherwise;
- M, an integer variable represents the maximum utilized spectrum slots for all the tenant traffic demands in the network. For a valid assignment, $|S|$ should always be bigger than or equal to M.

3.2 Objective and Constraints of the VMPRSA Problem

Since more spectrum slots used on a fiber signify more cost on the fiber and further need more corresponding switching equipment and power consumption, the objective of this model is to minimize the maximum spectrum slots utilized among all the fibers to serve all tenants traffic demands. Such traffic demands are determined by VM placement which should be satisfied by the node capacity. To simply our model, the guard-bandwidth between optical routing is not considered. Equation (1) is employed to represent object function.

$$Minimine\ M \tag{1}$$

subject to the following constraints:

$$Allo_i^k \leq T_k, \forall i, k \tag{2}$$

$$\sum_i Allo_i^k \leq T_k, \forall k \tag{3}$$

Equations (2) is VM placement constraints for tenants. It denotes that the size of VM placement for each tenant in each node can not exceed the tenant demand T_k, while the sum of such size in all nodes should equal T_k, which is guaranteed by (3).

$$\sum_k Allo_i^k \leq C_i, \forall i \tag{4}$$

Each node can be shared by multi-tenant, thus capacity provided by each node for multi-tenant VM placement does not exceed the node capacity, as shown in (4).

$$Traf_{i,j}^k = \min(Allo_i^k, Allo_j^k), \forall i, j, k \tag{5}$$

The traffic demand between any two nodes for each tenant is determined by the smaller size of tenant VM placement, as shown in (5).

$$F_{i,j,m,n}^{w,k} * w \leq M, \forall i, j, m, n, w, k \tag{6}$$

Cost function is shown in (6), which obtains the maximum utilized spectrum slots on each fiber.

$$\sum_{w,j=n,m} F_{i,j,m,n}^{w,k} = Traf_{i,j}^k, \forall i, j, k \tag{7}$$

$$\sum_{w,i=m,n} F_{i,j,m,n}^{w,k} = Traf_{i,j}^k, \forall i, j, k \tag{8}$$

$$\sum_{w,i=j} F_{i,j,m,n}^{w,k} = 0, \forall m, n, k \tag{9}$$

The traffic demand between node i and node j for tenant k should be exactly added at node i and dropped at node j, which are guaranteed by (7) and (8), respectively. Equation (9) makes sure that no traffic is required at the same node.

$$\sum_{i,j} F_{i,j,m,n}^{w,k} \leq 1, \forall m, n, k, w \tag{10}$$

One spectrum slot can only be used for satisfying one traffic demand for multi-tenant, which is specified by (10).

$$\sum_{w,j\neq n,m} F_{i,j,m,n}^{w,k} - \sum_{w,i\neq n,p} F_{i,j,n,p}^{w,k} = 0, \forall i,j,n,k \tag{11}$$

The spectrum continuity constraint guarantees that the spectrum path of a traffic demand should use the same spectrum through its routing path, which is shown in (11).

$$(F_{i,j,m,n}^{w,k} - F_{i,j,m,n}^{w,k+1}) * (-B) \geq$$
$$\sum_{\overline{w}\in\{w+2,Cap\}} F_{i,j,m,n}^{\overline{w},k}, \forall i,j,m,n,w,k \tag{12}$$

$$(F_{i,j,m,n}^{w,k} - 1)*B + Traf_{i,j}^{k} \leq$$
$$\sum_{\overline{w}\in\{1,Cap\}} F_{i,j,m,n}^{\overline{w},k}, \forall i,j,m,n,w,k \tag{13}$$

The spectrum consecutiveness constraint is shown in (12), which means that if $F_{i,j,m,n}^{w,k}=1$ and $F_{i,j,m,n}^{w+1,k}=0$, all the spectrum higher than $w+1$ will not be used for the spectrum path of node-pair (i,j) for tenant k on link $m-n$. Equation (13) guarantees that size of consecutive spectrum is $Traf_{i,j}^{k}$ if $F_{i,j,m,n}^{w,k}=1$. In above both equations, a large number B is introduced to realize the if-then relationship.

4   Heuristic Algorithm

The proposed ILP model is NP-hard and is tractable only when the problem size (e.g., the number of tenants, network topology) is small. For a large scale problem, heuristic algorithms are resorted to obtain sub-optimal solutions within reasonable time.

4.1   Two-Tier Algorithm Framework

Since the traffic demands of a tenant are driven by VM placement of the tenant, a two-tier heuristic algorithm framework is proposed to apply the problem.

The two-tier algorithm framework is consisted of VM placement and routing spectrum assignment (VMP + RSA), as shown in **Algorithm 1**. The first tier is VM placement of multi-tenant VM demands, which can produce the corresponding traffic demands and is shown on line 1, and the second tier is to execute RSA algorithm to server all the traffic demands, which is illustrated in the algorithm from line 2 to the end of it.

Since the objective of heuristic algorithms is dominated by the traffic demands of multi-tenant, which are determined by VM placement of multi-tenant, we mainly focus on the VM placement algorithms. The same RSA algorithm is employed to evaluate the network performance of different VM placement algorithms. The key idea of RSA algorithm is the bigger traffic demand with the higher priority, and each traffic demand choose the lowest starting spectrum from K paths which use the K-shortest path algorithm.

Algorithm 1 VMP+RSA algorithm framework

---

1. **VMs placement algorithm**

   Input: $G(N, C, E, S), T_k, C_i, i \in N, TenTraf = \varnothing$

   Output: $TenTraf = \{Traf_{i,j}^k\}, W = 0$

2. **RSA algorithm**

   Input: $TenTraf = \{Traf_{i,j}^k\}, W = 0$

   Output: W

3. Sort traffic demands of all tenants according to their sizes $Traf_{i,j}^k$ in descending order in a queue Q

4. **while** $Q \neq \varnothing$ **do**

5.   Pick the top traffic demand of (i, j) pair in the Q, and search the lowest available starting spectrum m among all K paths;

6.   Select the path with the lowest starting spectrum m within K paths, and assign the spectrum for it. If several paths have the same m, select the first;

7. $M = Traf_{i,j}^k + m$

8.   **If** $W < M$ **then**

9. $W = M$

10.   **end if**

11.   Delete the top traffic demand of (i, j) pair from the queue Q, and update the network state;

12. **end while**

4.2 Random Placement

For the problem of VM placement, a naive approach is random placement (RP) algorithm, i.e., for a tenant VM demand, one node or more nodes are randomly chosen to accommodate all the VMs for the tenant. A tenant demand with more VMs has high priority, since which can avoid the tenant VMs allocated into different nodes to minimize the number of cross-ToR traffic demands. Furthermore, to achieve the goal, each node should accommodate VMs for a tenant with the maximum node residual capacity. Specially, If $T_k \geq C_i$, then $T_k = T_k - C_i$ and $C_i = 0$. Else, $T_k = 0$ and $C_i = C_i - T_k$. From the algorithm, the next tenant VMs will not be allocated until the current tenant VMs have been allocated.

4.3 Residual Node Capacity Priority

However, the bigger traffic demands (in size) could be produced by the RP algorithm due to the randomness of VM placement. In EODCNs, the spectrum can not be evenly utilized by bigger traffic demands, which can make utilized spectrum bigger. Therefore, we should lower the size of traffic demands, which can result in the reduction of average size of traffic demands. As we known, when VMs of a tenant are allocated into more than one node, the traffic demands will appear, and their sizes are determined by the smaller size of VM placement between two nodes. Therefore, residual node capacity priority (RNCP) algorithm is proposed. The key idea of the algorithm is to place all the VMs of a tenant to a node as much as possible, and no traffic demand is yielded; when no node can not accommodate all the VMs for a tenant, a node with the largest residual capacity is employed to accommodate VMs as much as possible and pick a node with smallest residual capacity to accommodate the residual VMs.

5 Performance Evaluation

In this section, the optimal result of the proposed ILP model and sub-optimal results of the two heuristic algorithms are evaluated. The ILP model and the two heuristic algorithms are enforced by using the CPLEX 12.5 and Visual Studio 2015 C++ simulation platform, respectively. Without loss of generality, 5-node and fat-tree networks are employed as EODCNs topology to implement our simulations, as shown in Fig. 2. A ToR switch is represented by a node of network, and servers are omitted for simplification. Traffic demands are launched and terminated by network nodes.

Assume that the width of a spectrum slot is 12.5 GHZ and the guard bandwidth is not considered. For a valid placement, a network has $\sum_{i=0}^{|N|-1} C_i$ capacity and can accommodate $|T|$ tenants. Suppose that a tenant VM demand is a random integer, and $|T|$ random integers whose sum is equal to $\sum_{i=0}^{|N|-1} C_i$, can contribute to certain standard variance. Random integers with the same standard variance should be considered for fairness by changing $|T|$. However, it is very difficult to generate random integers with given standard variance. Therefore, predefine that each tenant has the same VM demand with the same standard variance (i.e., 0 standard variance) for simplification. Furthermore, since the traffic demands are symmetric, we only consider the unidirectional traffic demands.

5.1 ILP and Heuristic Algorithms Under a Small Topology

To compare the performance of the ILP model with the heuristic algorithms, they are enforced on a 5-node network with six bidirectional links as shown in Fig. 2(a). The metrics here include spectrum utilized to sever all the traffic demands, and average size of traffic demand.

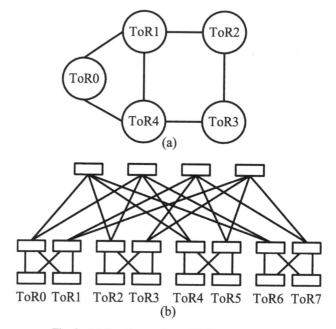

Fig. 2. (a) 5-node topology; (b) fat-tree topology.

The spectrum required to serve all the traffic demands driven by VM placement as $|T|$ increases is investigated and the results are shown in Fig. 3. In the network, each node has the same capacity with 12 slots, the network thus has a capacity of 60 slots. It is clearly that the spectrum required decreases along with the increasing $|T|$. This is because each tenant VM demand T_k decreases along with the increase in $|T|$, which can produce smaller traffic demands and thus lower the utilized spectrum. The ILP model gets the best solution compared with the two heuristic algorithms. RNCP is better than RP. This is because RNCP tends to consider the node with residual capacity, leading to a smaller size of these traffic demand. Please note that no spectrum is required when $|T|=5$ with $T_k=12$ for each tenant, since each node can exactly accommodate a tenant VMs, which produces no traffic demand for any tenants. It can be clearly seen that when $|T|=2$, ILP outperforms RNCP and RP by up to 42.8% and 71.4%, respectively.

The average size of traffic demands driven by VM placement is studied by changing $|T|$ and the results are represented by Fig. 4. The main trend is decreasing due to the degradation of T_k. It is obvious that the ILP model gets the smallest value. RNCP is better than RP, because the former takes the residual node capacity into account when carry out multi-placement for a tenant VMs, while the RP algorithm considers the random node. When $|T|=2$, ILP is better than RNCP and RP by up to 40% and 60%, respectively.

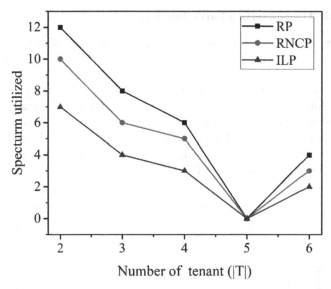

Fig. 3. Spectrum utilized versus number of tenant in a 5-node topology.

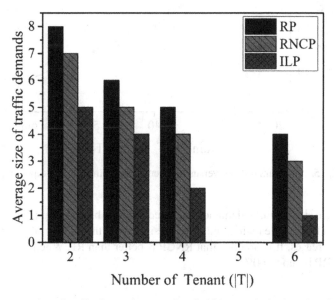

Fig. 4. Average size of traffic demands versus bandwidth granularity in a 5-node topology.

5.2 Heuristic Algorithms in a Large Topology

The fat-tree network with 8 nodes is used as EODCNs topology shown in Fig. 2(b). In the network, each node has the same capacity with 140 slots, the network thus has a capacity of 1120 slots.

The spectrum utilized to server all the traffic demands driven by VM placement as $|T|$ increases is exhibited by Fig. 5. The main tread is declining, since more tenants VMs can be fully placed into a node. The RNCP algorithm obtains the better sub-optimal solution, because it considers the residual node capacity when carry out multi-placement for a tenant VMs, leading to the small traffic demands. When the number of tenant $|T|$ is 60, RNCP outperforms RP by up to 38.4%.

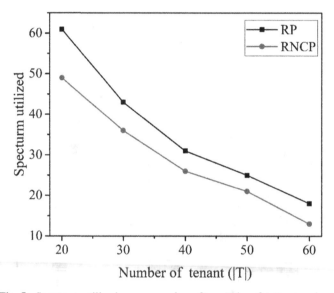

Fig. 5. Spectrum utilized versus number of tenant in a fat-tree topology.

The average size of traffic demands is also considered by different $|T|$ and the results are depicted in Fig. 6. The main trend is decreasing, since the number of tenants increase and the T_k decreases. It is obvious that RNCP is better than RP. When $|T|= 60$, RNCP outperforms RP by up to 60%.

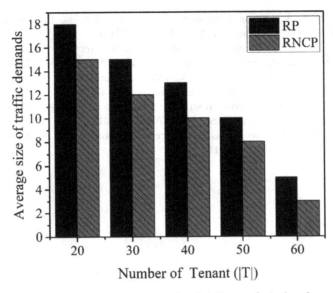

Fig. 6. Average size of traffic demands versus bandwidth granularity in a fat-tree topology.

6 Conclusion

In this paper, the static virtual machine placement and routing spectrum assignment (VMPRSA) problem is investigated in EODCNs. The target of the problem is to minimize the utilized spectrum to serve all the traffic demands driven by VM placement of multitenant, while the network should have enough node capacity to satisfy the VM placement. The VMPRSA problem is formally stated and its NP-hard is proved. An ILP model is presented to solve the problem. Since the ILP model can not scale to a big network, a two-tier heuristic algorithm framework is proposed to apply the problem, i.e., the first tier is VM placement and the second tier is routing and spectrum assignment (VMP + RSA). Two VM placement algorithms are proposed, the RP algorithm and the RNCP algorithm. The simulation results show that the ILP model provides the optimal solution, and the RNCP algorithm achieves the better sub-optimal solution. The dynamic VMPRSA problem will be studied in future work.

References

1. Al-Fares, M., et al.: A scalable, commodity data center network architecture. ACM SIGCOMM Comput. Commun. Rev. **38**(4), 63–74 (2008)
2. Singla, A., et al.: Proteus: a topology malleable data center network. In: The 9th USENIX Symposium on Networked Systems Design and Implementation, pp. 225–238 (2010)
3. Farrington, N., et al.: Helios: a hybrid electrical/optical switch architecture for modular data centers. ACM SIGCOMM Comput. Commun. Rev. **41**(4), 339–350 (2011)
4. Wang, G., et al.: C-Through: part-time optics in data centers. ACM SIGCOMM Comput. Commun. Rev. **41**(4), 327–338 (2011)

5. Porter, G., et al.: Integrating microsecond circuit switching into the data center. ACM SIGCOMM Comput. Commun. Rev. **43**(3), 447–458 (2013)
6. Chen, K., et al.: OSA: an optical switching architecture for data center networks with unprecedented flexibility. IEEE/ACM Trans. Networking **22**(2), 498–511 (2014)
7. Jinno, M., et al.: Spectrum-efficient and scalable elastic optical path network: architecture, benefits, and enabling technologies. IEEE Commun. Mag. **47**(11), 66–73 (2009)
8. Liu, A., Sun, Y., Ji, Y.: Bandwidth reservation for tenants in reconfigurable optical OFDM datacenter networks. IEEE Photonics J. **10**(5), 7906616 (2018)
9. Ballani, H., et al.: Towards predictable datacenter networks. ACM SIGCOMM Comput. Commun. Rev. **41**(4), 242–253 (2011)

Machine Learning and Its Applications

CTAN: Collaborative Tag-Aware Attentive Network for Recommendation

Wenxing Hong[✉], Zhuomin Li, Xiang Li, and Jiacheng Zhu

Xiamen University, Xiamen 361102, China
hwx@xmu.edu.cn

Abstract. Graph-based methods are one of the effective means to solve the data sparsity and cold start problems. They can not only ensure the accuracy of the recommendation results but also have a certain degree of interpretability. However, it is worth mentioning that existing Tag-aware Recommendation Systems (TRS) rely on tag-aware features for recommendations, which is insufficient to alleviate the problems of sparsity, ambiguity, and redundancy brought about by tags, thereby hindering the recommendation performance. Therefore, an end-to-end framework is proposed in this paper. Firstly, a Collaborative Tag Graph (CTG) is designed to handle the problem of extracting heterogeneous semantic information. Secondly, an attention mechanism-based Graph Neural Network (GNN) is introduced to distinguish the importance of neighboring nodes, utilizing the information propagation mechanism of GNN to update node representations. Moreover, a dual interaction aggregator is used to aggregate the neighboring nodes and self-node characteristics. Experiments on three benchmark datasets demonstrate that CTAN outperforms the state-of-the art methods consistently.

Keywords: Graph neural network · Tag-aware · Recommendation

1 Introduction

With the advent of the Internet era, information has exploded exponentially, and recommendation systems have become powerful tools for dealing with information overload. Early recommendation systems were based on matrix factorization methods collaborative filtering , which expressed user-item interaction history as a matrix and aimed to predict a user's preference for any other item by learning user and item representations, i.e., predicting the probability of interaction between a user and an item that has not been interacted with before. These include user-based collaborative filtering, which finds the K users most similar to a certain user based on user similarity and calculates the dot product of the preference scores and similarity of these K users with item i, recommending the top N items with high scores to the user. Item-based collaborative filtering also

Supported by Industry and Information Technology Ministry Industrial Promotion Center Project, Intelligent Analysis Engine for Industrialization of Innovation Achievements in the Manufacturing Industry.

uses similar ideas, but they have cold start problems in practical application scenarios. Although this method can learn the nonlinear characteristics between users and items well, the recommended results still lack good interpretability. Tag-based recommendation systems can be used to solve the cold start problem of recommendation systems, i.e., new users can choose to follow tags of interest after downloading the app, and the system automatically filters and pushes recommendations to improve the quality of recommendations. However, due to the sparsity of tag data, existing tag-based recommendation systems have ambiguity and redundancy problems and do not integrate well with contextual semantic information, such as different meanings expressed by the same word or the same meaning expressed by different words, which cannot be well identified.

With the emergence of representation learning frameworks, the mainstream paradigm of recommendation algorithms has gradually shifted from neighborhood methods to representation learning methods. This method attempts to encode users-items as continuous vectors (i.e. embedding representations) in a shared space. Graph-based algorithms are also one of these methods, considering the information in recommendation systems from the structure of the graph. Essentially, most of the data in recommendation systems are graph data, and typical user-item interaction data can be represented by a bipartite graph between users and items. Social networks among users and knowledge graphs of items and their related attributes can also be constructed as graphs. Graph learning provides a unified framework for modeling rich heterogeneous data in recommendation systems.

In this paper, we propose a Collaborative Tag-aware Attentive Network for Recommendation(CTAN-Rec), an end-to-end framework to capture the potential semantic information between user interests and items, using a heterogeneous graph network to construct a triplet of users, items, and labels, and using the TransR method to construct a Collaborative Tag Graph (CTG), and optimizing the graph embedding representation using a regularizer, using attention mechanisms to distinguish the contribution degree of neighboring nodes, using GNN information propagation to continuously update node representations, fully mining high-order connections of nodes, and using dual interaction aggregators to aggregate neighboring node and self-node characteristics, obtaining representations of items and nodes, and providing accurate recommendation results.

Our contributions in this paper are summarized as follows:

We utilized the transR embedding method to construct the User-Item-Tag Graph (UITG), enriching the attribute representation of users and projects to address the issues of sparse and redundant tag data.

We introduced an attention mechanism to differentiate the importance of different neighboring nodes, effectively utilizing collaborative signals and tag semantic information.

We utilized the information propagation mechanism of GNN to fully explore the high-order connections of nodes and used a dual interaction aggregator to aggregate neighboring nodes and obtain user and project representations.

We conducted experiments on three public datasets and the recommended results were superior to the current baseline models.

2   Related Work

2.1   Tag-Aware Recommendation

Tags are descriptive keywords or phrases used to describe the characteristics, attributes, or themes of an item. Tags are typically added by users themselves, but can also be generated by the system. The characteristics of tags are that they are simple, easy to understand, easy to add and manage, and therefore have been widely used in recommendation systems. There are two main types of tag-aware recommendation algorithms: tag-aware similarity and tag-aware classification. Tag-aware similarity uses the similarity between tags to calculate the similarity between items for recommendation. The advantage of tag-based similarity is that it is simple and easy to implement, but the disadvantage is that it cannot handle the semantic relationships between tags. Tag-based classification divides tags into different categories and uses the relationships between categories to calculate the similarity between items for recommendation. Common algorithms include topic model-based recommendation algorithms, social network-based recommendation algorithms, etc. The advantage of tag-based classification is that it can handle the semantic relationships between tags, but the disadvantage is that it requires complex calculations and model training.

2.2   Graph-Based Representation

In recent years, researchers have developed various graph construction methods by combining neural networks with representation learning frameworks to better improve models and programming practices for utilizing graph-structured data. Graph construction is the first step in utilizing graph representation learning for modeling, and taking recommendation systems as an example, to effectively construct graphs that integrate collaboration signals and semantic information from external knowledge graphs in user-item interactions. Currently, the general direction of graph embedding is node embedding, which includes three mainstream methods: matrix factorization, random walk, and graph convolutional network methods.

Matrix factorization method: Graph structure information is represented using adjacency matrix or co-occurrence matrix of nodes (adjacency matrix with node weights on diagonal), to measure similarity between all nodes. The adjacency matrix is decomposed to learn low-dimensional embedding representation of nodes. Representative methods include Laplacian Eigenmaps [2] and Cauchy graph embedding [3].

3   Method

3.1   Problem Formulation

Definition 1: The recommendation problem with fusion of tag-aware graph attention can be formulated as follows: Given the user-item interaction matrix Y and the tag graph G, the objective is to predict whether the user u has potential interest in the item v that has not been interacted with before. Our goal is to learn a prediction function.

$$\hat{y}_{uv} = F(u, i \mid \Theta, Y, G) \tag{1}$$

where Θ represents the parameters of the model , G represents the triadic graph of the relationships among users, items, and tags,and Y represents the interaction matrix.

Definition 2: Collaborative Tag Graph (CTG): CTG is defined as an undirected weighted graph $G = (V, E, W)$, where $g = (u, i, t)$. V is represented as three types of nodes: users, items, and tags. E is represented as edges that include three types of relationships: 1) $edge =< u, i, 1 >$ reflects the interaction relationship between users and items; 2) $edge =< u, t, w >$ reflects the tagging relationship between users and tags, where w represents the frequency of users using tag t; 3) $edge =< i, t, w >$ reflects the passive tagging relationship between items and tags, where w represents the frequency of item i being tagged with tag t.

3.2 Collaborative Tag-Aware Attentive Network for Recommendation

This section introduces our proposed CTAN model, which utilizes high-order relationships in an end-to-end manner. Figure 1 illustrates the model framework, which consists of four main parts: 1) embedding layer, which parameterizes each node into a vector using the structure of CTG; 2) information propagation layer, which recursively propagates embeddings from neighboring nodes to update their representations and learns the weights of each neighbor in the propagation process using attention mechanism; 3) aggregation layer, which aggregates the representations of neighbors and self and connects the representations of each layer to form the final node representation; and 4) prediction layer, which computes the dot product of the final representations of users and items to output the predicted matching score.

Graph embedding representation methods usually use a distance function to minimize the loss. In order to train the transR method, we define the loss function.

$$L_{TG} = \sum_{(u,t,i) \in G} -\ln \sigma(g(u, t, i), -g(u, t, i^{'})) \tag{2}$$

CTG Embedding Layer. The purpose of the CTG embedding layer is to obtain the initial representation of user and project nodes. The purpose of constructing the collaborative tagging graph is to predict the relationship between two given entities, i.e., link prediction. For a given user, project, and tag, we use the embedding representation method of transR [9] to construct the CTG in the

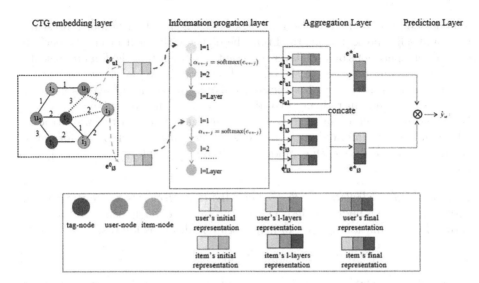

Fig. 1. An overview of the proposed framework. 1) CTG embedding layer, which parameters each node into a vector by utilizing the structure of CTG; 2) information propagation layer, which recursively updates node representations by propagating embeddings from adjacent nodes and leveraging attention mechanism to learn weights of each neighbor in the propagation process; 3) aggregation layer, which aggregates neighbor representations and self-representations and connects them as the final node representation; 4) prediction layer, which computes the predicted match score by performing point-wise operations on the final user and item representations.

vector space. Specifically, the triplet data (u, t, i) is learned for each entity and relationship through an optimizer. The rationality score calculation for a given triplet is defined as follows:

$$g(u, t, i) = \| W_r e_u + e_t - W_r e_i \|_2^2 \tag{3}$$

Where $e_u, e_i, e_t \in R^d$ represent the embedded representation of user, item, and tag respectively.

Among them, $(u, t, i^{'})$ is a randomly replaced triplet constructed from the triplet (u, t, i) in the set, where the label can be regarded as the relationship between the user and the item, and CTG is constructed by predicting the link. σ is a non-linear activation function (such as sigmoid), which serves as a regularizer to model the user, item, and tag triplets, and obtain the initial representation.

Information Propagation Layer. The information propagation layer is the core component of the entire CTAN framework, which is based on the framework of graph convolutional networks and explores multi-hop relationships between entities to encode representations of users and projects. When integrating neighbor representations, we use attention mechanisms to distinguish the importance of nodes and use dual interaction aggregators to aggregate neighbor representations and self-representations to obtain the nodes of the next layer. We perform connection operations on each layer representation to obtain the final representations of users and projects. In the information propagation layer, we fully utilize the information in the graph structure, but due to the use of attention mechanisms, we do not introduce noisy data that can cause overfitting problems. By using dual interaction aggregators to aggregate information, we introduce additional feature interactions to improve representation learning performance. Next, we will introduce each component in detail in the information propagation layer.

Neighbor Node Calculation with Fusion Attention Mechanism. Considering an entity e_j, we use a node e_{Nv} in CTG to represent the neighboring nodes of this entity. The calculation method of neighboring nodes is as follows:

$$e_{N_v} = \sum a_{v \leftarrow j} e_j \qquad (4)$$

The weight of a neighboring node $\alpha_{v \leftarrow j}$ is obtained through a relational attention score, defined as follows:

$$\alpha_{v \leftarrow j} = (W_r e_j)^T \tanh(W_r e_u + e_t) \qquad (5)$$

Bidirectional Feature Interaction Aggregator. After obtaining the representation of each neighboring node, we use an attention mechanism to assign weights to each neighboring node and then sum them up to obtain the aggregated representation of the neighbors, denoted as e_{Nv}. Next, we need to aggregate the neighboring nodes with the self node to obtain the representation of the next layer. Here, we consider two types of feature interactions between neighboring nodes and self nodes. The bidirectional interaction aggregator is defined as follows:

$$e_i^l = Leaky\,\mathrm{Re}\,LU\left(W_1\left(e_i^{l-1} + e_{N(i)}^{l-1}\right) + W_2\left(e_i^{l-1} \Theta e_{N(i)}^{l-1}\right)\right) \qquad (6)$$

Recursively, the next layer entity is:

$$e_\nu^l = f_{Bi-\text{Interaction}}\left(e_\nu^{l-1}, e_N^{l-1}\right) \qquad (7)$$

After executing L layers, we obtain L representations for both the user node u and the item node v. We concatenate these L representations and perform a connection operation to obtain the final representation.

$$e_u^* = e_u^0 \| \dots \| e_u^l \qquad (8)$$

$$e_i^* = e_i^0 \| \dots \| e_i^l \qquad (9)$$

Where,$\|$ denotes the concatenation operation. The initial embedding representation is enriched through the execution of embedding propagation operations, where L can be used to adjust the number of propagation layers. The depth of the model can be adjusted by L to explore the impact of higher-order connections on user-item representations.

Preference Score Prediction. Through the information propagation layer based on graph convolutional networks, we obtained the final representations of users and projects, and used dot product operation to predict their ultimate matching scores.

$$\hat{y}_{ui} = e_u^{*T} e_i^* \tag{10}$$

Model Optimization. In order to optimize the final recommendation results, we use pairwise BPR [10] loss to optimize the prediction model, which assumes that the observed user-item interaction scores have a higher matching score than the unobserved data. The BPR loss function is defined as follows:

$$L_{BPR} = \sum - \ln \sigma \left(\hat{y}_{ui} - y_{ui} \right) \tag{11}$$

Combining the loss of CTG embedding layer, we define the loss function of the entire model as follows:

$$L_{CTAN} = L_{BPR} + L_{TG} + \lambda \|\Theta\|_2^2 \tag{12}$$

Where λ and θ are the hyperparameters of the regularization term. The entire model algorithm for the CTAN is defined as follows:

Algorithm 1: CTAN Algorithm

Input: User project interaction matrix G1, tag diagram G2, Number of training iterations epoch, batch input data size batchsize

Output: Recommended results

1 $step \leftarrow 0 \ l \leftarrow 0$;
2 **while** $step \leq \ epoch$ **do**
3 $\quad e_u + e_t \approx e_i$
4 $\quad g(u,t,i) = \|W_r e_u + e_t - W_r e_i\|_2^2$
5 $\quad L_{TG} = \sum_{(u,t,i) \in G} - \ln \sigma \left(g\left(u,t,i'\right) - g(u,t,i) \right)$
6 $\quad$ **for** $l \leq \ L$ **do**
7 $\quad\quad e_{N_v} = \sum \alpha_{v \leftarrow j} e_j$
8 $\quad\quad \alpha_{v \leftarrow j} = softmax \left(e_{v \leftarrow j} \right)$
9 $\quad\quad e_v^l = f_{Bi- \ \text{Interaction}} \left(e_v^{l-1}, e_{N_v}^{l-1} \right)$
10 $\quad\quad e_u^* = e_u^0 \| \ldots \| e_u^l$
11 $\quad\quad e_i^* = e_i^0 \| \ldots \| e_i^l$
12 $\quad$ **end**
13 $\quad \hat{y}_{ui} = e_u^{*T} e_i^*$
14 $\quad$ Update;
15 $\quad L_{BPR} = \sum - \ln \sigma \left(\hat{y}_{ui} - y_{ui} \right)$
16 $\quad L_{CTAN} = L_{BPR} + L_{TG} + \lambda \|\Theta\|_2^2$
17 $\quad step + +$;
18 **end**

---

4   Experiment Setup

4.1   Dataset

We used three datasets that are widely used in recommendation systems, and their descriptions are as follows:

Last.FM[1]: The dataset contains music listening information from 2000 users and artist attributes from the Last.fm online music system. This dataset is widely used in sequence recommendation, social recommendation, and knowledge graph-based recommendation.

MovieLens-100k[2]: The dataset is widely adopted as a benchmark dataset for user-item collaborative filtering tasks and knowledge graph-based recommendation.

Delicious[3]: The dataset contains social network, bookmark, and tag information, which is commonly used for information heterogeneity and fusion in recommendation systems.

The statistical information of the datasets is shown in Table 1:

Table 1. Statistics of the datasets

	Last.FM[1]	Movielen-100k [2]	Delicious [3]
#user	1845	1651	1843
#item	12212	5381	65877
#tag	2305	1586	3508

Baseline models: In order to validate the effectiveness of our proposed TGAT model, we compared it with knowledge graph-based models, collaborative filtering-based models, and meta-path-based models. The description of the baseline models is as follows:

KGCN [11]: An advanced information propagation-based model that aggregates neighbor information and knowledge graph semantic information through an extended GCN method to mine user latent information.

KGAT [12]: Also a recent propagation-based model, it combines UIG and KG as a homogeneous unified graph of CKG. Compared with KGCN, KGAT uses attention mechanism to distinguish the importance of neighbor nodes in CKG during the propagation process.

CKAN [13]: It employs a heterogeneous propagation approach to encode collaborative indicators and knowledge information, leveraging a knowledge-aware attention mechanism to differentiate the contributions of distinct neighboring nodes.

RippleNet [14]: A method similar to memory networks, it propagates user preferences on KG. Displayed equations are centered and set on a separate line.

---

[1] https://grouplens.org/datasets/hetrec-2011/.

[2] https://grouplens.org/datasets/movielens/100k/.

[3] http://www.dai-labor.de/en/competence_centers/irml/datasets/.

4.2   Evaluation Metrics

We use the following commonly used evaluation metrics to evaluate performance: AUC, the area under the ROC curve, commonly used in binary classification problems. AUC refers to the probability that the model ranks a clicked item higher than an unclicked item. When implicit feedback estimation is considered as a binary classification problem, AUC is widely used for performance evaluation. The overall AUC is the average of all users. The following evaluation metrics exhibit higher values indicating superior model performance.

$$AUC(u) = \frac{\sum_{i \in \hat{f}(u)} \sum_{j \in IT(u)} I\left(\hat{r}_i > r_j\right)}{|T(u)||I \backslash T(u)|} \tag{13}$$

$$\text{Precision } @K(u) = \frac{\left|R^K(u) \cap T(u)\right|}{K} \tag{14}$$

$$\text{Recall@K(u)} = \frac{\left|R^K(u) \cap T(u)\right|}{|T(u)|} \tag{15}$$

$$F1@K(u) = \frac{2 \times \text{Precision } @K(u) \times \text{Recall@K } (u)}{\text{Precision@K } (u) + \text{Recall@K } (u)} \tag{16}$$

4.3   Implementation Detail

The hyperparameters of the models should be set identical to ensure a fair comparison. The values of 4 hyperparameters, such as propagation layers, learning rate, batch size, and random dropout, are implemented as shown in Table 2, while the remaining hyperparameters are set to common values in the experiment.".

Table 2. Hyperparameter setting

Hyperparameter	value
Propagation layers	{1,2,3}
Learning tate	{0.001,0.0001}
Batch size	{128,256}
Dropout	{0.1,0.2,0.3}

5   Result

5.1   Performance Evaluation

We chose the methods described in Sect. 4 as the baseline model and carefully adjusted them to achieve optimal performance. We independently repeated each experiment 10 times and reported the average performance. The experimental results are shown in Table 3.

Table 3. Performance evaluation

Methods	Last.fm		Movielens		Delicious	
	AUC	F1	AUC	F1	AUC	F1
KGCN	0.802	0.708	0.974	0.930	0.845	0.774
KGAT	0.829	0.742	0.976	0.928	0.846	0.785
CKAN	0.832	0.765	0.975	0.929	0.874	0.802
RippleNet	0.776	0.710	0.976	0.927	0.863	0.783
CTAN	**0.842**	**0.779**	**0.977**	**0.932**	**0.880**	**0.812**

Analysis of Experimental Results: Table 3 summarizes the performance comparison of different methods, and it can be visually observed from Fig. 2 that our method has achieved good performance in all three datasets, which proves the effectiveness of the method.

5.2 Ablation Study

Impact of Aggregation Functions. To demonstrate the effectiveness of the Bi-Interaction Aggregation Function, we replaced different aggregation functions in the aggregation layer, including the Sum Aggregator (agg-sum), Average Aggregator (agg-avg), Concatenation Aggregator (agg-concat), Max Pooling Aggregator (agg-pool), GCN Aggregator, and GraphSAGE Aggregator. The experimental results are shown in Table 4.

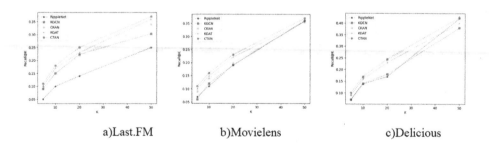

a)Last.FM   b)Movielens   c)Delicious

Fig. 2. The result of Recall@K in top-K recommendation.

Table 4. Effects of aggregation functions.

	Last.fm		Movielens		Delicious	
Aggregators	AUC	F1	AUC	F1	AUC	F1
Agg-sum	0.820	0.753	0.966	0.924	0.870	0.808
Agg-avg	0.833	0.765	0.964	0.923	0.865	0.804
Agg-concat	0.815	0.760	0.970	0.930	0.872	0.809
Agg-pool	0.830	0.762	0.965	0.924	0.863	0.802
Agg-GCN	0.831	0.765	0.972	0.927	0.872	0.809
Agg-Grapgsage	0.826	0.760	0.969	0.926	0.869	0.808
Bi-Interaction	**0.842**	**0.779**	**0.977**	**0.932**	**0.880**	**0.812**

From the experimental results, it can be seen that the bidirectional inter-action aggregator consistently outperforms other aggregators when conducting experiments on different datasets, as it incorporates additional feature interactions, highlighting the importance of self-network and entity representation in performing information aggregation and propagation.

Impact of Embedding Methods and Attention Mechanisms. To verify the effectiveness of the TransR embedding method and attention mechanism, we removed these two modules from the framework to examine whether the overall performance of the model was affected. The experimental results are shown in Table 5.

Table 5. Quantitative comparison between different methods and attention mechanisms

	Last.fm			Movielens			Delicious		
	AUC	F1	TimeCost(second)	AUC	F1	TimeCost(second)	AUC	F1	TimeCost(second)
w/o CTG	0.816	0.771	814.1748	0.975	0.927	1669.8721	0.876	0.808	736.0379
w/o Att	0.842	0.780	827.8724	0.977	0.931	1788.8469	0.881	0.812	744.0569
CTAN	0.822	0.778	833.636	0.972	0.929	1869.4307	0.876	0.810	752.0468

5.3   Parameter Experiment

Effect of Model Complexity. By varying the number of layers L in CTAN, we found that increasing the depth of CTAN significantly improves its performance. Clearly, CTAN-2 and CTAN-3 consistently outperform CTAN-1 on all datasets. These improvements are attributed to the effective modeling of higher-order relationships between users, projects, and entities. Further adding a layer to CTAN-3, we observed only marginal improvement in CTAN-4. This suggests that considering third-order relationships between entities may be sufficient to capture collaborative signals. Experimental results are shown in Table 6.

Table 6. Impact of Model Depth.

Layers	Last.fm		Movielens		Delicious	
	AUC	F1	AUC	F1	AUC	F1
CTAN-1	0.827	0.757	0.956	0.929	0.876	0.809
CTAN-2	0.830	0.765	0.976	0.930	0.879	0.810
CTAN-3	**0.842**	**0.779**	**0.977**	**0.932**	**0.880**	**0.812**
CTAN-4	0.841	0.780	0.977	0.931	0.881	0.812

Impact of Embedding Dimension. Finally, the influence of embedding dimension d on CTAN performance was investigated. The results in the table are quite intuitive: increasing d initially improves performance, as larger d can encode more user and entity information, while excessively large d suffers from the adverse effects of overfitting. The experimental results are shown in Table 7.

Table 7. Impact of Embedding Dimension.

Dimension	Last.fm		Movielens		Delicious	
	AUC	F1	AUC	F1	AUC	F1
64	0.832	0.771	0.975	0.927	0.876	0.808
128	**0.842**	**0.780**	**0.977**	**0.931**	**0.881**	**0.812**
256	0.822	0.778	0.972	0.929	0.876	0.810

6   Conclusion and Future Work

In this paper, we present an end-to-end approach graph attention recommendation framework (CTAN-Rec) that captures the latent semantic information between user interests and items, aiming to address the cold-start and data sparsity issues in recommendation systems. The system describes complex systems using a heterogeneous graph network, introduces a collaborative tag graph (CTG), and optimizes graph embedding representations using a regularizer. The attention mechanism distinguishes the contribution levels of neighboring nodes, and the information propagation of GNN continuously updates node representations. The dual interaction aggregator aggregates the characteristics of neighboring nodes and self-nodes. The experiment is conducted on three datasets, achieving good recommendation results. Of course, this method also has some limitations, such as the requirement for a matched user, item, and tag dataset, and a large amount of labeled data. In future work, more heterogeneous information will be integrated to further enrich the representation of users and projects, such as introducing external knowledge graphs and user social network graphs to further improve the performance of the recommendation system.

References

1. He, X., Chua, T.S.: Neural factorization machines for sparse predictive analytics. In SIGIR.355-364(2017
2. Shang, T.T., Jia, Y.C., Wen, Y., et al.: Laplacian Eigenmaps-Based Polarimetric Dimensionality Reduction for SAR Image Classification. IEEE Trans. Geosci. Remote Sens. **50**(1), 170–179 (2011)
3. Luo, D., Nie, F., Huang, H., et al.: Cauchy graph embedding. International Conference on Machine Learning. Omnipress. (2011)
4. Aditya, G., Leskovec, J. : Node2vec. Proceedings of the 22nd ACM SIGKDD International Conference on Knowledge Discovery and Data Mining, Aug. Crossref, (2016). https://doi.org/10.1145/2939672.2939754
5. Bryan, P., et al.: DeepWalk. Proceedings of the 20th ACM SIGKDD International Conference on Knowledge Discovery and Data Mining, Aug. Crossref, (2014). https://doi.org/10.1145/2623330.2623732
6. Kipf, T.N., Welling, M.: Semi-Supervised classification with graph convolutional networks. In ICRL. (2017)
7. Hamilton, W.L., Ying, Z., Leskovec, J.: Inductive representation learning on large graphs. In NeurIPS. 1025–1035(2017)
8. Velikovi, P., Cucurull, G., Casanova, A, et al.: Graph Attention Networks. (2017)
9. Wang, Q., Mao, Z., Wang, B., Guo, Li.: Knowledge graph embedding: a survey of approaches and applications. IEEE Trans. Knowl. Data Eng. 2724–2743 (2017)
10. Rendle, S., Freudenthaler, C., Gantner, Z., Thieme, L.S.: BPR: Bayesian personalized ranking from implicit feedback. In UAI. 452–461(2009)
11. Wang, H., Zhao, X., Xie, X., Li., W., Guo, M.: Knowledge graph convolutional networks for recommender systems.In the 28th International Conference on World Wide Web. ACM. 3307–3313(2019)
12. Wang, X., He, X., Cao, Yi., Liu, M., Chua, T.S.: KGAT: Knowledge graph attention network for recommendation. In SIGKDD, pp. 950–958(2019)
13. Wang, Z., Lin, G., Tan, H., Chen, Q ., Liu. Xi.: CKAN: collaborative knowledge-aware attentive network for recommender systems. In: Proceedings of the 43rd International ACM SIGIR Conference on Research and Development in Information Retrieval (SIGIR '20). Association for Computing Machinery, New York, NY, USA, pp. 219–228(2020). https://doi.org/10.1145/3397271.3401141
14. Wang, H., Zhang, F., Wang, J., Zhao, M., Li, Xing, Xi, Guo, M.: RippleNet: Propagating User Preferences on the Knowledge Graph for Recommender Systems. In Proceedings of the 27th ACM International Conference on Information and Knowledge Management. ACM. (2018)

Research of Network Intrusion Detection Based on Improved Seagull Optimization Algorithm with Deep Learning

Hai Lan[⊠]

Wuhan FiberHome Information Integration Technologies Co., Ltd., Wuhan, China
lanhai@fiberhome.com

Abstract. In this paper, we study a network intrusion detection method based on deep learning combined with improved seagull optimization algorithm, which extracts the information traces inevitably generated during network intrusion by deep neural network and optimizes the parameters of deep neural network model by improved seagull optimization algorithm, so as to build an efficient network intrusion detection model. The traditional seagull optimization algorithm is improved and applied to the deep learning model hyperparameter optimization. For the shortcomings of the traditional seagull optimization algorithm with strong randomness of population initialization and easy to produce extreme individuals, a reverse learning method is presented to the initialization of the group. And a nonlinear convergence factor is used to enhance the convergence speed, thus improving the performance of the seagull optimization algorithm. The improved algorithm was demonstrated by using standard test functions, and the improved algorithm was used for parameter optimization of the deep learning model. To address the shortcomings of classical rule-based, host behavior analysis, and machine learning network traffic classification methods in performing network intrusion detection with less attention to the temporal correlation characteristics of samples, we propose to apply deep learning techniques to network intrusion detection, and design a network intrusion detection method based on gated cyclic units and multilayer perceptron, and also apply the improved seagull optimization algorithm to the method optimization of hyperparameters in the model, thus improving the performance of the model and achieving better network intrusion detection results on the NSK-KDD dataset.

Keywords: Network intrusion detection · seagull optimization algorithm (SOA) · deep learning · gated recurrent unit (GRU)

1 Introduction

In terms of research content in the field of network security, network intrusion detection is a very important issue that needs extensive attention, and it is also a prerequisite for ensuring network security. On the one hand, it is necessary for companies, enterprises and individuals to detect network intrusions to prevent possible network intrusions.

Losses due to damage to network equipment. On the other hand, cyberspace is also the sovereign space of a country, which is open and inviolable at the same time. Sovereign countries first need to realize the detection of network intrusion from a macro level, and grasp the trend of network intrusion crimes. Timely discover network intrusions that affect national security and social and public interests, and have countermeasures in the face of attacks such as network intrusions, so as to avoid cyberspace becoming an "extra-legal place" and safeguard network sovereignty [4].

However, the rapid development of the Internet also means that the network structure is more complex and the network traffic continues to grow, which means that network intrusion detection faces more and greater challenges. Faced with the current situation, some traditional network intrusion detection technologies have become inadequate, and their shortcomings are mainly concentrated in the following points: First, in the era of big data, the amount of intrusion data is large, and traditional network intrusion detection technologies face such situations. Unable to handle and cope. Second, with the continuous advancement of Internet technology, the attack methods emerge in an endless stream, and traditional rule matching and host-based network intrusion detection methods are difficult to deal with. Third, some new attack methods continue to emerge, which also leads to the problem of imbalance between old and new intrusion data, and traditional network intrusion detection algorithms are inefficient. It is because of these drawbacks that the traditional network intrusion detection technology is difficult to withstand the current network intrusion, so the existing technology needs to be innovated, and deep learning is a method that can change this situation. Deep learning is one of the hotspots of research in recent years. This technology has been applied to many fields, especially in the fields of Computer Vision (CV) and Natural Language Processing (NLP) [5]. For network intrusion detection, deep learning is more intelligent. It can automatically learn to extract and store the spatiotemporal features of data, and continuously learn and strengthen in the process of model building and training. In terms of process, deep learning is an end-to-end process. Learning, data collection, input, processing, and output are systematic, convenient and fast. Therefore, it is a reasonable and effective method to apply depth to network intrusion detection. It is necessary and practical to study how to use deep learning technology for network intrusion detection.

The research on network intrusion detection can be traced back to the 1980s. In 1980, Anderson put forward a famous computer security threat model in a technical report titled "Computer Security Threat Monitoring and Monitoring", and this threat is today's intrusion in a broad sense [1]. In the technical report, intrusion is classified into three types: external intrusion, internal penetration and abuse, and expounds the method of tracking these intrusion activities through audit data, creating a precedent for network intrusion detection. The design and development of intrusion detection system (IDS) by later generations basically take this security threat model as the basic starting point. In 1987, Denning proposed a model of a general intrusion detection system, which brought intrusion detection system theory to the computer network security system [6]. The model proposed by Denning divides intrusion detection into six parts: subject, object, audit record, activity filing, exception record, and activity rule. This model is also considered to be the first substantial intrusion detection system prototype. On the basis of this model, the research on intrusion detection has also begun to be widely carried out. It is worth mentioning that in 1990, Heberlein and others from The University of California Davis put forward the concept of Network Security Monitor (NSM). NSM system takes network traffic packets as the information source to detect intrusion for the first time, which is also the first time that network-based intrusion detection system is proposed [7], which also affects the development of subsequent intrusion detection technology. After that, as a rising star, compared with the original method based on rule matching and host analysis, network-based intrusion detection technology has become more and more sought after. In terms of the difference in several ways, the host-based intrusion detection system collects the required data from its host device, and uses computer log files as important analysis data. Compare and analyze to achieve the effect of detection. The advantages of the host-based intrusion detection system are that the equipment loss and personnel operation cost are low, and the false alarm rate is relatively low. Limited and complex. The network-based intrusion detection system is inseparable from the data packets communicated by network devices. It realizes the determination of network intrusion behaviors by collecting, encoding, decoding, and analyzing network data packets, which is more flexible and convenient. The method based on rule matching requires the establishment and update of a rule database, which is inefficient and has been gradually eliminated (Fig. 1).

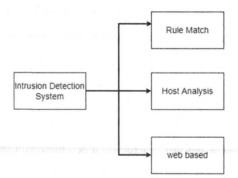

Fig. 1. Intrusion detection system classification

With the development of The Times and technological progress, machine learning technology has attracted the attention of many scholars, and a large number of scholars have participated in the research on how to apply machine learning to network intrusion detection. Traditional machine learning methods have been widely used in network intrusion detection [8, 9]. The intrusion detection system designed by Saleh et al. is a mixture of machine learning methods, which is real-time and can solve multiple classification problems. In data processing, dimensionality reduction is an important operation, this system uses the basis feature selection (NBFS) technology to first process the data samples, and then eliminates the samples with high dispersion through the optimized support vector machine (OSVM). Finally, PKNN (the improved version of classical KNN) is used to detect attacks. Experiments were carried out on classic KDD 99, NSL-KDD and Kyoto2006 + data sets to demonstrate the real-time performance of detection and achieve good detection results [10]. In literature [11], support vector machine (SVM) integrated with compressed sampling is used for intrusion detection, and compression sampling method is used for network data flow processing. A SVM-based model is established to output results, and good experimental results have been achieved in training efficiency and detection speed. Literature [12] proposed an ingenious data processing method, which used Fisher discriminant ratio (FDR) method for feature extraction and denoising. In the subsequent processing, Probabilistic self-organizing Maps (PSOM) was used for modeling to preserve the characteristics of data, which achieved a good effect on classification accuracy. The training time of classifier is also an indicator worthy of attention. Al-Yaseen et al. constructed a multi-level model to improve the training efficiency and the performance of the model. First of all, in terms of data processing, the improved K-means algorithm is used to purify and sample the original training set. Starting from the specific data itself, the optimized data training efficiency is greatly improved. In the final result output stage of the model, the combination of extreme learning machine (ELM) and support vector machine was used to carry out multi-classification, and the classical KDD99 data set was used for experimental evaluation, and the accuracy rate reached 95.75% [13]. See from the above research achievements of many, in machine learning method is applied to solve the problem of network intrusion, scholars generally will first some efficient methods on data processing (e.g., sampling), and then by machine learning methods to realize the feature extraction, build the model for classification or prediction and the final result output. In the selection of models, we can either stack the basic models, or improve the basic model, or combine the two. The ultimate goal is nothing more than to build an efficient model. However, today's network attack traffic keeps increasing, data dimensions keep increasing, attack methods keep innovating, and the seriousness of data imbalance becomes increasingly prominent. Traditional machine learning methods are also unable to cope with these complex situations. First of all, it is the feature extraction. Manual plays an important role in the process of feature extraction, but it is difficult for manual to explore the internal features of data. It mainly relies on experience to operate, unable to distinguish the correlation of data and temporal and spatial characteristics well, and difficult to explore the internal connections and rules of data. Moreover, from the perspective of data volume, such methods are obviously inefficient in the face of big data. Therefore, the intrusion detection technology of traditional machine learning method is faced with many difficulties, and new technology and new ideas are in urgent need of development.

2 Network Intrusion Detection Method Based on Improved Seagull Optimization Algorithm and Gated Recurrent Unit

2.1 Improved Seagull Optimization Algorithm

2.1.1 Inverse Learning and Nonlinear Convergence Factors

When the traditional seagull algorithm is used for optimization, the initial seagull group has strong randomness, the optimization efficiency is low, and it is easy to fall into the local optimum. Because when the traditional seagull optimization algorithm is initialized, the population individuals are randomly generated, and some extreme individuals are prone to appear, thus affecting the initialization quality of the population, which has a certain negative impact on the performance of the algorithm. The method based on reverse learning can improve the quality of the initialized population.

The concept of reverse exists not only in each of our consciousness, but also plays a special role in the natural world and exists in different ways. For example, opposite particles in high-energy physics, antonyms in language and literature, absolute or relative complement, dual variables in mathematics, subject and object in philosophy, etc. The basic reverse concept first appeared in the ancient Chinese symbol of yin and yang, which embodies the dualistic concept that black is yin and white is yang. In addition, the natural pattern in Greek classical philosophy is also closely related to the reverse, such as fire to water, heat to cold, dry to wet, earth to air, and many entities or situations can be described by the concept of reverse.

In fact, the interpretation of different entities can be made easier using the reverse concept. And paired oppositions like east, west, south, and north cannot be defined individually, only when they are used together can they be explained to each other. Therefore, Tizhoosh is inspired by the concept of reverse in the real world, and proposes the concept of reverse in computation, that is, reverse-based learning, referred to as reverse learning [18].

In ISOA, the population position initialization process based on the reverse learning method is expressed as follows (N represents the population size of seagulls, and t is the current number of iterations):

(1) Randomly initialize the population:

$$P(t = 0) = \{x_{m,n}\}1, 2, \ldots, N; \quad n = 1, 2, \ldots N \tag{1}$$

(2) Calculate the reverse population through the formula:

$$P'(t = 0) = \{x'_{m,n}\}, \quad x'_{m,n} = x_{min,n} + x_{max,n} - x_{m,n} \tag{2}$$

Calculate the reverse population, where $x_{min,n}$ and $x_{max,n}$ are the worst and best individuals, respectively.

(3) Select the top N good individuals: select the top N individuals with the best fitness from the set $\{P(t = 0)\} \cup \{P'(t = 0)\}$ as the initialization population.

As mentioned above, we obtained the initialization population with higher fitness through the reverse learning method. In the iterative process of the algorithm, the movement tendency of the individual population significantly affects the convergence speed of the algorithm. From formula (2), it is not difficult to see that in the traditional seagull optimization algorithm, the convergence factor changes linearly, which leads to poor performance and low efficiency in the later stage of the algorithm. This paper proposes a new convergence factor formula, which is described as follows:

$$A = f_c\left(1 - \frac{1}{e - 1} \times \left(\frac{t}{e^{Max_{iteration}}} - 1\right)\right) \tag{3}$$

In the above formula, f_c represents the initial convergence value (usually we set it to 2), t represents the number of iterations of the current population, and $Max_{iteration}$

represents the maximum number of iterations of the population we set. After applying this formula, the seagull optimization algorithm has slow convergence in the early stage and fast convergence in the later stage, so that the global search ability in the early stage and the convergence ability in the later stage can be improved while maintaining the diversity of the population.

In the next two sections, we will show the above-mentioned Improved Seagull Optimization Algorithm (ISOA) process, and verify the performance of our improved algorithm through comparative experiments.

2.1.2 Improved Seagull Optimization Algorithm Flow

The improved Seagull Optimization Algorithm (ISOA) proposed in this paper adopts the population initialization strategy of reverse learning and nonlinear convergence factor to improve the convergence speed and global optimization ability of the algorithm. The steps of the improved ISOA algorithm are as follows:

(1) Population initialization. First, set the population size, the limit of the number of iterations of the algorithm, the movement range of the population, the initial value of the convergence factor, and the movement constants u, v.
(2) Generate a reverse population and select the best. Use the reverse learning algorithm to generate the reverse population, calculate the fitness value of each individual seagull, find the optimal value (optimal seagull position) of the entire population, and eliminate the last 50% of the individuals.
(3) Iterative optimization. Within the set iteration range, according to formulas (5)–(10), calculate the position to which the individual will move, and use formulas (2) and (3) to avoid individual collision and continuous shrinkage.
(4) Update the population. Calculate the fitness value of the new position of the individual, and determine whether the individual needs to move through the comparison, so as to update the population position and update the best individual (position).
(5) Repeat the process of (3) and (4) until the iteration ends.
(6) Output the best individual (position), fitness value and iterative process record of the seagull population, and the algorithm ends.

The corresponding flowchart is as follows:

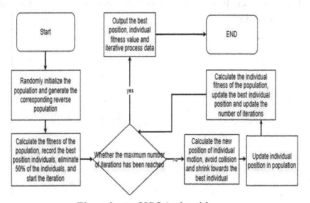

Flow chart of ISOA algorithm

2.1.3   Network Intrusion Detection Method Based on ISOA and GRU

In order to build a deep neural network model for network intrusion detection, GRU, MLP and other components can be regarded as independent modules of the network, and multiple modules are in a cascade relationship. By combining these modules, the overall structure of our proposed intrusion detection model is shown in the following figure.

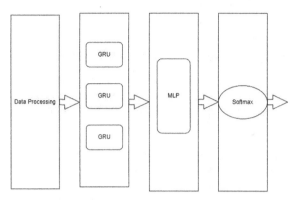

Schematic diagram of model structure

The system consists of data processing module, GRU module, MLP module and output module. The data processing module processes the data into normalized values suitable for input to the neural network without changing the dimension of the data. The setting of some parameters of the model is optimized by the ISOA algorithm. By setting some parameters of the model as the activity range of the population in the ISOA algorithm, and using the loss function in the model as the population fitness calculation formula, the parameters are encoded and set as individual. First, set the parameters and initialize the population, and then access the training module. After obtaining the training fitness, use ISOA to update the individual. The update process will retain the best parameters for comparison. When the number of iterations reaches the limit or the fitness threshold appears during the training process, we will end the process and output the best parameter combination. In order to improve the efficiency of optimization, we only take 20% of the data sets in NSL-KDD as training data to optimize parameters. The overall process is as follows:

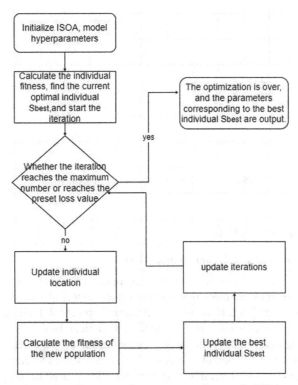

Schematic diagram of parameter flow of ISOA optimization model

The GRU module is composed of one or more layers of GRUs. For the input data, it is mainly used to extract and store features, and is the core part of the system. The MLP module is an n-layer perceptron model, which mainly performs nonlinear mapping on the output information of the GRU again to realize classification decisions. The output module uses Softmax regression to normalize the final classification probability output. In order to improve the phenomenon of model overfitting, we use the dropout algorithm. As shown in Fig. 8, dropout is an important layer in the actual experimental processing. The method is to discard some neurons. The proportion of discarding depends on the experimental experience. Numerically speaking, it is a proportional value. During the training process, A discarded node means that the value of the node is 0. The training of each batch is repeated, and after some neurons are randomly discarded, the interaction between neurons will be alleviated, preventing model overfitting and improving model performance.

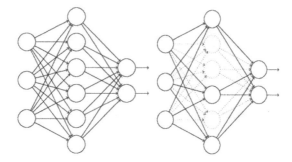

Schematic diagram of dropout process

2.2　Experiment and Analysis

2.2.1　Data Processing and Experimental Design

Since the proposed detection system can only accept numerical input, it is first necessary to convert the different categories in the dataset into numerical data that can be input into the neural network. In each record, only 3 features (protocol_type, service and flag) are symbolic features that need to be converted to numerical data. This is achieved here with 1 to N encoding. Similarly, the classification results are represented by numbers 0~4, as shown in Table 1. Then all the numerical features need to be normalized, that is, scaled between 0 and 1. Here, min-max normalization is used to complete the linear scaling, and the formula is shown in formula (4).

$$f' = \frac{f - min_j}{max_j - min_j} \tag{4}$$

f represents the original value of the feature, and f' represents the normalized feature value. $max_j - min_j$ are the maximum and minimum values of the j th feature.

Table 1. Label value conversion

Label	Numerical encoding
NORMAL	0
DOS	1
R2L	2
U2R	3
PROBING	4

The software and hardware environment of the experiment is still the same as that described in Sect. 2, and the framework is used to facilitate us to quickly build the model. The process of data processing is also a part of our intrusion detection system. After processing, the data will be sent to our model for training, and the final result will be output. In the model part, the GRU module and the MLP module are undoubtedly the most important. We will use the ISOA optimization combination model method named ISOA + GRU + MLP model. In the model comparison part, we use separate MLP, GRU models, and GRU + MLP combined models to conduct experiments.

Among them, starting from our experimental experience, the ISOA + GRU + MLP model hyperparameter optimization includes: batch size, learning rate, number of MLP layers, and number of MLP hidden layer units. The range of batch size we set is [10, 50]; the range of learning rate is [0.005, 0.2]; the range of MLP layers is [1, 5]; the range of MLP hidden layer units is [32, 128]. After the optimization process described in the previous section is optimized, the values are as follows (Table 2):

Table 2. Model Hyperparameter Settings

Hyperparameter	Value
Batch size	30
Learning rate	0.01
Number of MLP layers	3
Number of MLP hidden layer units	65

2.2.2 Experimental Results and Analysis

In order to objectively evaluate the performance of the method proposed in this chapter, we take 80% of the data set as the training set and 20% as the test set, the number of runs is 20 times, and the results are averaged. The experimental results are as follows:

Table 3. Test results of different models

Dataset	Algorithm model	Average accuracy(ACC)	Best accuracy (BACC)	Detection rate(DR)	False alarm rate (FAR)
NSL-KDD	MLP	91.79%	93.34%	90.31%	4.36%
	GRU	94.91%	96.46%	90.75%	9.35%
	GRU + MLP	96.13%	98.35%	95.41%	3.09%
	ISOA + GRU + MLP	**97.59%**	**98.61%**	**97.94%**	**2.01%**

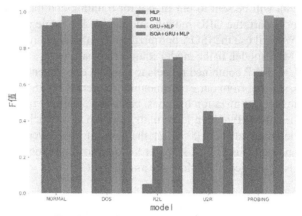

F-value results on NSL-KDD dataset

As can be seen from the results in Table 3, in the NSL-KDD dataset, the results of ISOA + GRU + MLP are the best. In terms of average accuracy, the performance rankings of the models are: ISOA + GRU + MLP > GRU + MLP > GRU > MLP, the average accuracy of ISOA + GRU + MLP reached 97.59%, the best accuracy reached 98.61%, the average accuracy was 1.46% higher than that of GRU + MLP, and the detection rate was also the highest among the five models. The false alarm rate is as low as 2.01%, which proves that the model we designed has excellent performance. As can be seen from Fig. 9, in terms of attack types, the comparison of detection rate and F value shows that the detection effect of DOS attacks and PROBING attacks is significantly better than that of R2L and U2R attacks.

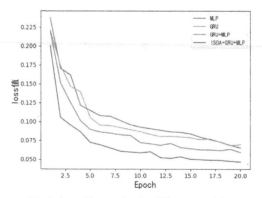

Variation of loss value in different models

Figure 10 shows the variation curve of the experimental average loss value, and compares the convergence of different algorithms. It can be seen that the ISOA + Gru + MLP model proposed by us has fast convergence speed and lower loss value. Combined with the previous results, we can see that using the ISOA + Gru + MLP model not only has advantages in accuracy, but also has a fast convergence speed.

3 Conclusion

In this chapter, a network intrusion detection method based on the improved seagull optimization algorithm and gated recurrent unit is proposed, and the system framework of the network intrusion detection method based on the improved seagull optimization algorithm and the gated recurrent unit is described in detail. We combine a recurrent neural network with a gated recurrent unit and a multi-layer perceptron to construct an intrusion detection system based on a deep neural network, and use the deep learning method to train, and achieve good intrusion detection performance. In the experimental part, the commonly used network intrusion detection data sets are firstly introduced, the advantages of the data characteristics of the NSL-KDD data set are highlighted, and the various evaluation indicators and key points of the experiment are described in detail. The experimental comparison of various combinations shows that the ISOA optimization GRU and MLP proposed in this paper have the best combination performance, excellent performance indicators, and the highest detection accuracy rate of 98.61%, especially in the DOS attack type the average accuracy rate reached 99.17%.

Acknowledgment. This work is funded by the National Natural Science Foundation of China under Grant No. 61772180, the Key R & D plan of Hubei Province (2020BHB004, 2020BAB012).

References

1. Anderson, J.P.: Computer security threat monitoring and surveillance. Technical report, James P. Anderson Company (1980)
2. Sherstinsky, A.: Fundamentals of recurrent neural network (RNN) and long short-term memory (LSTM) network. Physica D **404**, 132306 (2020)
3. Chung, J., Gulcehre, C., Cho, K.H., et al.: Empirical evaluation of gated recurrent neural networks on sequence modeling. arXiv preprint arXiv:1412.3555 (2014)
4. Hong, Y., Goodnight, G.T.: How to think about cyber sovereignty: the case of China. Chin. J. Commun. **13**(1), 8–26 (2020)
5. Coşkun, M., Yildirim, Ö., Ayşegül, U., et al.: An overview of popular deep learning methods. Eur. J. Tech. (EJT) **7**(2), 165–176 (2017)
6. Denning, D.E.: An intrusion-detection model. IEEE Trans. Software Eng. **2**, 222–232 (1987)
7. Heberlein, L.T., Dias, G.V., Levitt, K.N., et al.: A network security monitor. Lawrence Livermore National Lab., CA (USA); California Univ., Davis, CA (USA). Dept. of Electrical Engineering and Computer Science (1989)
8. Sommer, R., Paxson, V.: Outside the closed world: on using machine learning for network intrusion detection. In: 2010 IEEE Symposium on Security and Privacy, pp. 305–316. IEEE (2010)
9. Song, W., Beshley, M., Przystupa, K., et al.: A software deep packet inspection system for network traffic analysis and anomaly detection. Sensors **20**(6), 1637 (2020)
10. Saleh, A.I., Talaat, F.M., Labib, L.M.: A hybrid intrusion detection system (HIDS) based on prioritized k-nearest neighbors and optimized SVM classifiers. Artif. Intell. Rev. **51**(3), 403–443 (2019)
11. Chen, S., Peng, M., Xiong, H., Yu, X.: SVM intrusion detection model based on compressed sampling. J. Electr. Comput. Eng. **2016**, 1–6 (2016)

12. De La Hoz, E., Ortiz, A., Ortega, J., Prieto, B.: PCA filtering and probabilistic SOM for network intrusion detection. Neurocomputing **164**, 71–81 (2015)
13. Xu, H., Przystupa, K., Fang, C., Marciniak, A., et al.: A combination strategy of feature selection based on an integrated optimization algorithm and weighted k-nearest neighbor to improve the performance of network intrusion detection. Electronics **9**(8), 1206 (2020)

Improved Dragonfly Algorithm Based on Mixed Strategy

Shenyang Xia[✉] and Xing Liu

CCCC Second Highway Consultants Co. Ltd., Wuhan 430056, China
xiasy@cccc.com

Abstract. With the rapid development of today, the swarm intelligence optimization algorithm is very popular and has been used in many fields. Dragonfly algorithm (DA) is one of the optimization algorithms, which has been used in some aspects. But it still has some shortcomings, such as slow convergence speed and search precision, and it is also prone to fall into local optimal solutions. Aiming at the shortcomings of the original dragonfly algorithm, a mixed strategy improved dragonfly algorithm (MSDA) is proposed. The algorithm introduces some improvement strategies. Firstly, initialize the population with the Sobol sequence. This allows the algorithm to obtain a better initial population, improve the quality of initial solution. Secondly, inertia weight improvement, use a nonlinear decreasing inertia weight. The modification of inertia weight makes the algorithm better adapt to the convergence process. Then using Cauchy mutation to increase the diversity of the population, improve the global search ability of the algorithm, and increase the search space. Finally, a random learning strategy is added. The random learning strategy enhances the diversity of the population, effectively improve the global optimization performance of the algorithm. The experiment is tested by eight standard test functions, results show that MSDA is better than the original DA algorithm in terms of convergence speed, solution accuracy and stability.

Keywords: Optimization · Swarm intelligence · Dragonfly algorithm

1 Introduction

In nature, if every creature wants to survive, they must have their own ability to survive. Under the screening of nature, only the unique survival ability that can adapt to nature can be preserved. Nowadays, people can observe the ability of various animals in nature, get inspiration from it, and come up with many new ideas that can solve practical optimization problems. This is the origin of the swarm intelligence optimization algorithm. The swarm intelligence optimization algorithm is an evolutionary algorithm based on random search. It mainly simulates the group behavior of insects, beasts, birds and fish. The main behavior of these groups is to forage and avoid enemies. Look for food and constantly exchange food information, so that those animals can find more food faster and avoid the enemy's attack. Studying these swarm behaviors and abstracting an algorithm is the swarm intelligence algorithm.

© The Author(s), under exclusive license to Springer Nature Singapore Pte Ltd. 2024
W. Hong and G. Kanaparan (Eds.): ICCSE 2023, CCIS 2023, pp. 113–124, 2024.
https://doi.org/10.1007/978-981-97-0730-0_11

The swarm intelligence optimization algorithm is an approximate optimization algorithm, which has aroused great interest of many researchers in computer science, engineering, medicine and other fields [1, 2]. This is because these algorithms can solve various complex optimization problems in a relatively short period of time. Since some complex tasks cannot be solved in a short period of time. And at the same time swarm intelligence optimization algorithms are simple, flexible and robust [3].

Dragonfly Algorithm (DA) is a new swarm intelligence optimization algorithm proposed by scholar Seyedali Mirjalili in 2015. Dragonflies are a relatively primitive and relatively few species of insects. There are about 5000 species in the world. They are carnivorous insects. They prey on a variety of agricultural, forestry and animal husbandry pests such as flies, mosquitoes, leafhoppers, horseflies and small butterfly moths. Dragonflies are a class of important natural enemy insects that are beneficial to humans. The main inspiration of the DA algorithm comes from the static and dynamic flocking behavior of dragonflies in nature, that is the behavior of foraging groups and the behavior of migratory groups. The algorithm is simple in principle, easy to understand and easy to implement, has strong search ability, and has been widely studied and discussed by scholars from many countries. The Dragonfly algorithm has been well applied and is currently used to solve various optimization problems, such as image processing, medicine, computer science, engineering, etc. And the dragonfly algorithm has shown excellent performance in these optimization problems. But the algorithm still has some common defects, such as low accuracy, premature convergence, and insufficient global search ability.

In view of the above shortcomings of the Dragonfly algorithm, this paper improves it and proposes an improved Dragonfly algorithm based on mixed strategy (Mixed Strategy Improved Dragonfly Algorithm, MSDA). At the beginning of the algorithm, the Sobol sequence is used to initialize the population to make the distribution in the initial solution space more uniform. This allows the algorithm to obtain a better initial population, improve the quality of initial solution. Then, the global search force and local development force are improved by nonlinearly decreasing inertia weight. The modification of inertia weight makes the algorithm better adapt to the convergence process. Using Cauchy mutation to increase the diversity of the population, improve the global search ability of the algorithm, and increase the search space. And the position of the individual is adjusted by a random learning strategy. The random learning strategy enhances the diversity of the population, effectively improve the global optimization performance of the algorithm. Through the test experiments of 8 benchmark functions. The experimental results show that compared with the original Dragonfly algorithm and some other algorithms, this algorithm has better search power in global search and local development, and has a certain improvement in performance.

2 Related Work

The source of inspiration for the dragonfly algorithm is the behavior of dragonflies in nature. Dragonflies use these behaviors to ensure their own survival, which is a simulation of dragonflies in nature. Dragonflies have social behaviors among individuals. Different from the hierarchical social behaviors of insects such as bees and ants, each individual dragonfly has corresponding activities for its survival. The biggest problem in its survival is the source of food and the avoidance of natural enemies. Under the above conditions, individual dragonflies will follow the society in which they live. Behavior, keeping moving while searching for food and avoiding predators.

In the dragonfly optimization algorithm, dragonfly individual behaviors are mainly described as 5 kinds, they are:

1) Separation behavior. It is a behavior that avoids collision between individual, Each individual in the group tends to maintain the same speed of movement;
2) Alignment behavior. It is the behavior of maintaining speed consistency between adjacent individuals;
3) Cohesion behavior. That is the behavior of individuals moving toward the average position of adjacent individuals;
4) Foraging behavior is that the individual is attracted by the food source;
5) Enemy avoidance behavior is the behavior of the individual to avoid natural enemies. Each behavior has its corresponding weight.

The behaviors of foraging behavior and enemy avoidance behavior are mainly included in the static group behavior. In static group behavior, there is a change in step size, while dragonflies in small groups are in a state of local movement. Dynamic flock behavior is when large numbers of dragonflies come together to make long-distance migrations in the same direction. In the dynamic group behavior, there are three main behaviors: separation behavior, alignment behavior and cohesion behavior. They fly in the same direction, which is also a major feature of dynamic group behavior. Each dragonfly in the group is equivalent to the solution of the search space (Fig. 1).

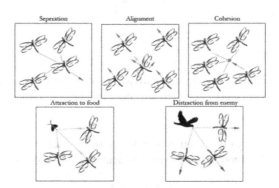

Fig. 1. Inception V1 structure

These five behaviors are the most basic and the most important. Each of these behaviors is essential, and if one of them is missing, the dragonflies will not be able to survive. Dragonflies survive under the above behavior. This is their unique survivability, with which they have survived nature's long sifting. Similar to most swarm intelligence optimization algorithms, the dragonfly optimization algorithm imitates the behavior of individual dragonflies in nature. The Dragonfly algorithm mathematically describes the above five behaviors. The specific mathematical description is as follows:

- Separation

Separation behavior is also known as collision avoidance behavior, it represents the degree of separation, refers to the avoidance behavior between adjacent individuals, and the mathematical expression is as follows:

$$S_i = -\sum_{j=1}^{N} X - X_j \tag{1}$$

Here X represents the position of the current individual, and X_j represents the position of the j-th adjacent individual. N represents the number of adjacent individuals.

- Alignment

The alignment behavior, it represents the degree of alignment. The behavior of individuals tending to the same speed, and the mathematical expression is as follows:

$$A_i = \frac{\sum_{j=1}^{N} V_j}{N} \tag{2}$$

Among them, V_j represents the velocity of the j-th adjacent individual.

- Cohesion

Aggregation behavior, it represents the degree of cohesion, refers to the behavior of individuals tending towards the center of the population, and the mathematical expression is as follows:

$$C_i = \frac{\sum_{j=1}^{N} X_j}{N} - X \tag{3}$$

where X is the position of the current individual, N is the total number of adjacent individuals, and X_j represents the position of the j-th adjacent individual.

- Foraging

Foraging behavior, that is, the attraction degree of food, dragonflies are attracted by food and move towards food, and the mathematical expression is as follows:

$$F_i = X^+ - X \tag{4}$$

where X is the current location of the individual and X^+ is the location of the food. The location of the food is selected from the currently found optimal solution.

- Enemy avoidance

The avoidance behavior of enemies, that is, the repelling force of enemies, the behavior of dragonflies away from enemies when threatened by enemies, and the mathematical expression is as follows:

$$E_i = X^- + X \tag{5}$$

where X is the current location of the individual and X^- is the location of the enemy. The location of the enemy is selected from the worst solution found so far.

Dragonflies are developed according to the above five behaviors, and the step size update formula of the offspring dragonflies is as follows:

$$\Delta Xt + 1 = (sSi + aAi + cCi + fFi + eEi) + \omega \Delta Xt \tag{6}$$

Among them, s, a, c, f, and e represent the weights of separation, alignment, cohesion, foraging, and enemy, respectively, and ω represent the inertia weight, and S, A, C, F, and E represent the degree of the above five behaviors. The t is the current number of iterations. The position of the next offspring dragonfly individual is expressed by the following formula:

$$Xt + 1 = Xt + \Delta Xt + 1 \tag{7}$$

In order to judge whether there are adjacent individuals around the dragonfly, draw a circle with radius r around the dragonfly individual as the search radius of the dragonfly. Individuals in the circle are considered adjacent. As the number of iterations increases, the search radius of the dragonfly is also updated. The update formula of the search radius is as follows:

$$r = \frac{a-b}{4} + 2(a-b)\frac{t}{t\max} \tag{8}$$

Among them, r is the search radius of dragonfly, t is the current number of iterations, $t_{\max}$ is the maximum number of iterations, and a and b are the upper and lower limits of the search range, respectively. If there are no adjacent individuals around the dragonfly, perform the Levy flight behavior of random walk:

$$X_{t+1} = X_t + \text{Levy}(d) \times X_t \tag{9}$$

where t represents the number of iterations of the current iteration, and d represents the dimension of the current position vector. Levy flight is a random walk strategy, where each step can be displaced in any direction and by any length. Many creatures in nature have similar laws in their activities, and their Levy function is:

$$\text{Levy}(x) = 0.01 \times \frac{r1 \times \sigma}{|r2|^{1/\beta}} \tag{10}$$

where r_1 and r_2 is a random number in the range [0,1], β is a constant (equal to 1.5 in the original dragonfly algorithm), and σ is expressed as:

$$\sigma = \left(\frac{\Gamma(1+\beta) \times \sin(\frac{\pi\beta}{2})}{\Gamma(\frac{1+\beta}{2}) \times \beta \times 2^{(\beta-1)/2}} \right)^{1/\beta} \tag{11}$$

3 Mixed Strategy Improved Dragonfly Algorithm

3.1 Initialization Population Based on Sobol Sequence

In many swarm intelligence optimization algorithms, the state of the initial distribution of the population will affect the performance of the next algorithm, and the same is true of the Dragonfly algorithm. In the original DA algorithm, in the initialization phase of the algorithm, the random generation of the initialization population is used. However, the distribution of randomly generated population states is relatively uneven and cannot cover every great point well, which will affect the subsequent performance of the algorithm. In order to improve this defect, this paper discards the original random initialization population, and adopts the initialization population based on Sobol sequence. The Sobol sequence is a low variance and random sequence with good distribution uniformity, which can generate a relatively uniform distribution in the probability space, resulting in non-repetitive and uniform points. The figure below compares the original random number distribution of DA with the spatial distribution of random numbers generated by the Sobol sequence. In the case of population number N = 500, the randomly generated initialization population and the population distribution map generated by Sobol sequence. It can be seen that the population distribution obtained by the Sobol sequence is more uniform and the coverage of the solution space is more complete (Fig. 2).

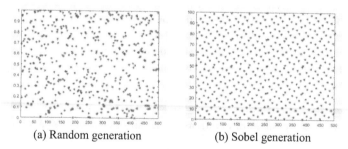

(a) Random generation   (b) Sobel generation

Fig. 2. Random generation sequence and Sobel generation sequence

3.2 Nonlinearly Decreasing Inertia Weights

Inertial weights are used to simulate inertia in real-world physics, enabling objects to maintain their original speed and continue to fly. In the swarm intelligence optimization algorithm, the algorithm should change the corresponding inertia weight at different times to make the algorithm more adaptable to the current changing state. In the original DA algorithm, a linearly decreasing inertia weight is used, and the calculation formula of the inertia weight is as follows:

$$w = 0.9 - \frac{(0.9 - 0.4)t}{t \max} \tag{12}$$

In this formula, t_{max} is the maximum number of iterations, t is the number of iterations in the current iteration. 0.9 and 0.4 represent the upper and lower bounds of the inertia weight, respectively.

Since the original DA uses a linearly decreasing inertia weight, and the search process of the algorithm is not linear, in the later stage of the search, the inertia weight decreases too fast, and the search ability and development ability of the algorithm are not utilized accordingly. Therefore, this paper changes the linear decrease of the original DA algorithm to nonlinear, and uses the following formula to express:

$$W = fc - fc \times (2 \times (t/t\max) \exp(h) - ((t/t\max)^2)) \tag{13}$$

where fc and h are the upper limit of the inertia weight and the lower limit of the inertia weight, $fc = 0.9$, $h = 0.4$, t_{max} is the maximum number of iterations, and t is the number of iterations at the current time. The curve of the above formula is represented by the following figure (Fig. 3):

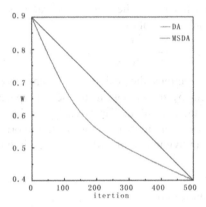

Fig. 3. Modified inertia weight curve

3.3 Random Learning Strategy

In order to enrich the population information and increase the information sharing between individuals among the populations, this paper adds a random learning strategy to the original DA. Randomly select an individual x from the population, and a different individual x_p, and determine the better individual by comparing the fitness values of the two. Adjust the position of individuals by learning from better individuals.

$$xnew = \begin{cases} x + rand(0, 1) \times (x - xp), f(xp) < f(x) \\ x + rand(0, 1) \times (xp - x), f(xp) \geq f(x) \end{cases} \tag{14}$$

The learning factor rand(0,1) is a random number between 0 and 1, which represents the learning difference of different individuals. After learning, if $f(x_p) < f(x)$, accept the new individual X_{new} and replace the original individual, otherwise reject the new individual X_{new}. This strategy increases the information sharing between individuals, increases the diversity of the population, and can effectively improve the global search ability.

3.4 Cauchy Mutation Strategy

Using Cauchy mutation to increase the diversity of the population, improve the global search ability of the algorithm, and increase the search space. The peak value of the Cauchy distribution function at the origin is small, but the distribution at both ends is relatively long, which can generate greater disturbance to the current individual, making it easier for the algorithm to jump out of the local optimal solution and enhancing the global search ability of the algorithm. In this paper, the following Cauchy variation formula is used to update the position of the current optimal individual:

$$x_{newbest} = x_{best} + x_{best} \times Cauchy(0, 1) \tag{15}$$

where $x_{newbest}$ is the new value obtained after the current optimal value is disturbed by Cauchy mutation. Cauchy(0,1) is the Cauchy operator, and the standard Cauchy distribution function formula is as follows:

$$f(x) = \frac{1}{\pi \times (x^2 + 1)}, x \in (-\infty, +\infty) \tag{16}$$

Compared with other functions, the peak of the Cauchy distribution is lower, which can shorten the time spent by individuals in the search space, thereby speeding up the convergence speed of the algorithm. The extension of the two ends of the Cauchy distribution can generate random numbers farther from the origin, which can generate strong disturbance to the individual, so that the disturbed individual has the ability to quickly avoid local traps.

3.5 Algorithm Implementation

After the above improvements, the algorithm flow of this paper is as follows:

Step 1: Initialization algorithm, dragonfly population size N, maximum iteration number MIT, problem dimension D, neighborhood radius r, step vector Δx;
Step 2: Use Sobol sequence to generate initialization population, and set $t = 1$;
Step 3: Calculate the moderate value of each individual;
Step 4: Adjust the individual position through the random learning strategy of Eq. (14);
Step 5: Update the behavior weights s, a, c, f, e;
Step 6: Use the nonlinear decreasing strategy of Eq. (13) to update the inertia weight;
Step 7: Calculate S, A, C, F, E;
Step 8: Update the neighborhood radius r, if there are adjacent individuals, use Eq. (9), (10) Update the step vector, otherwise use the Levy flight to update the position vector;
Step 9: Perturbation of individuals using the Cauchy mutation strategy;
Step 10: The number of iterations is increased by one. If the maximum number of iterations is reached, the optimal solution will be output, otherwise, it will return to Step 3.

The above algorithm flow can be represented by the following chart (Fig. 4):

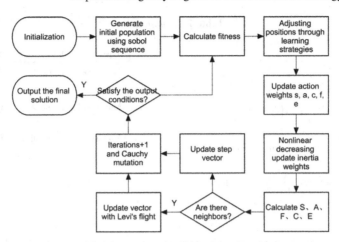

Fig. 4. MSDA algorithm flow chart

4 Experiment

In the experiment, this paper introduces the original Dragonfly Algorithm (DA), Grasshopper Optimization Algorithm (GOA), Particle Swarm Optimization algorithm (PSO), and this algorithm (MSDA) for comparative experiments. The settings of the comparative experiments are as follows: the population size N = 30, the maximum number of iterations MIT = 500, and the dimensions are all set to 30.

In order to verify the improvement effect of the MSDA algorithm, four different standard single-peak test functions and four different standard multi-peak test functions are used for verification tests. The specific function types and attributes are shown in the following table (Table 1):

Table 1. List of test functions

Test functions	Type	Range	Min	Dim
$F1(x) = \sum_{i=1}^{n} xi^2$	Unimodel	$[-100,100]$	0	30
$F2(x) = \sum_{i=1}^{n} |xi| + \prod_{i=1}^{n} |xi|$	Unimodel	$[-10,10]$	0	30
$F3(x) = \sum_{i=1}^{n} \left(\sum_{j-1}^{i} xj\right)^2$	Unimodel	$[-100,100]$	0	30
$F4(x) = \max i\{|xi|, 1 \le i \le n\}$	Unimodel	$[-100,100]$	0	30
$F_5(x) = \sum_{i=1}^{n} \left[x_i^2 - 10\cos(2\pi x_i) + 10\right]$	Multimodel	$[-5.12,5.12]$	0	30

(continued)

Table 1. (*continued*)

Test functions	Type	Range	Min	Dim
$F_6(x) = -20\exp\left(-0.2\sqrt{\frac{1}{n}\sum_{i=1}^{n}x_i^2}\right) - \exp\left(\frac{1}{n}\sum_{i=1}^{n}\cos(2\pi x_i)\right) + 20 + e$	Multimodel	$[-32,32]$	0	30
$F_7(x) = \frac{1}{4000}\sum_{i=1}^{n}x_i^2 - \prod_{i=1}^{n}\cos\left(\frac{x_i}{\sqrt{i}}\right) + 1$	Multimodel	$[-600,600]$	0	30
$F_8(x) = 0.1\left\{\sin^2(3\pi x_1) + \sum_{i=1}^{n}(x_i-1)^2\left[1+\sin^2(3\pi x_i+1)\right]\right.$ $\left. +(x_n-1)^2\left[1+\sin^2(2\pi x_n)\right]\right\} + \sum_{i=1}^{n}u(x_i, 5, 100, 4)$	Multimodel	$[-50,50]$	0	30

The experimental operating environment of this paper is the 64-bit Windows 7. The processor is Intel Core i5-3230M CPU @ 2.60GHz, and the host has 8 GB of installed memory. The simulation software used for the test is MATLAB R2016b.

In order to obtain a more average result in the experiment and reduce the influence of the randomness of the experiment, this experiment will run each test function 10 times independently, and compare the optimal solution, worst solution, mean and std to evaluate the algorithm. The experimental results are shown in following table (Table 2):

Table 2. Experimental structures for different network structures

TF	algorithm	Best	Worst	Mean	Std
F_1	PSO	1.336E−03	27.783	4.348	6.683
	GOA	4.82E−08	4.662E−07	1.266E−07	1.326E−07
	DA	1.993E−05	83.363	7.655	20.803
	MSDA	0	0	0	0
F_2	PSO	4.615E−01	1.2053	7.474E−01	3.675E−01
	GOA	0.021	1.225	0.441	0.402
	DA	0.0271	15.773	6.822	5.237
	MSDA	0	0.0183	0.00183	0.00579
F_3	PSO	5.325E−02	17.335	3.175	5.115
	GOA	82.825	7.242E+03	494.525	1.532E+03
	DA	72.114	793.824	374.258	2.893E + 03
	MSDA	0	0.0943	0.0311	0.0661
F_4	PSO	4.404E−02	1.522	0.952	0.237

(*continued*)

Table 2. (*continued*)

TF	algorithm	Best	Worst	Mean	Std
	GOA	0.469	6.993	2.524	1.211
	DA	0.329	10.593	7.415	3.661
	MSDA	0	0.0251	4.681E−02	9.491E−02
F_5	PSO	37.441	172.249	93.663	23.331
	GOA	21.632	210.367	77.155	21.215
	DA	26.664	29.549	27.972	1.445
	MSDA	0	34.175E−02	7.901E−03	1.321E−02
F_6	PSO	1.543E−03	2.522	9.145E−01	6.122E−01
	GOA	0.007	3.151	1.515	0.853
	DA	3.788	17.843	10.425	5.892
	MSDA	7.994E−15	4.361E−02	5.922E−10	4.992E−10
F_7	PSO	5.263E−02	9.253E−01	3.153E−01	2.954E−01
	GOA	0.037	0.525	0.210	0.052
	DA	1.225	79.385	9.636	17.395
	MSDA	0	1.083E−03	2.092E−04	1.162E−04
F_8	PSO	5.623	9.453	7.633	1.736
	GOA	3.646E−04	0.151	0.052	0.092
	DA	4.663	1.983E+06	6.935E+04	5.364E+05
	MSDA	0.293	0.994	0.468	0.295

To sum up, the MSDA algorithm has obtained better results than other comparison algorithms in both the single-peak test function and the multi-peak test function, and can obtain better solutions under the same conditions.

5 Conclusion

DA has been successfully used in some fields, proving its strength. Compared with other optimization algorithms, it has the characteristics of less parameters, simple control and easy enhancement. But it still has some shortcomings, such as slow convergence speed and search precision, and it is also prone to fall into local optimal solutions. In order to solve these problems, this paper does some work. On the basis of the original dragonfly algorithm, this paper mixes a variety of improved strategies, and proposes an improved dragonfly algorithm MSDA with a mixed strategy. The algorithm introduces some improvement strategies. First, initialize the population with the Sobol sequence. In this way, the algorithm can obtain a better initial population and improve the quality of the initial solution. Secondly, the inertia weight is improved, and the nonlinear decreasing inertia weight is adopted. The modification of inertia weights makes the algorithm better adapt to the convergence process. Then use the Cauchy mutation to increase the diversity of the population, improve the global search ability of the algorithm, and increase the search space. Finally, a random learning strategy is added. The random learning strategy enhances the diversity of the population and effectively improves the global optimization performance of the algorithm. Simulation experiments prove that its performance has a certain improvement compared with the original DA algorithm. The next research direction is towards combining the MSDA algorithm with optimization problems in other domains.

Acknowledgment. This work is funded by the National Natural Science Foundation of China under Grant No. 61772180, the Key R & D plan of Hubei Province (2020BHB004, 2020BAB012).

References

1. Chen, X., et al.: Forecasting short-term electric load using extreme learning machine with improved tree seed algorithm based on Lévy flight. Eksploatacjai Niezawodnosc Maintenance Reliability **24**(1), 153–162 (2022)
2. Sun, S., Przystupa, K., Wei, M., Yu, H., Ye, Z., Kochan, O.: Fast bearing fault diagnosis of rolling element using Lévy Moth-Flame optimization algorithm and Naive Bayes. Eksploatacjai Niezawodnosc Maintenance Reliability **22**(4), 730–740 (2020)
3. Xu, H., Przystupa, K., Fang, C., Marciniak, A., Kochan, O., Beshley, M.: A combination strategy of feature selection based on an integrated optimization algorithm and weighted k-nearest neighbor to improve the performance of network intrusion detection. Electronics **9**(8), 1206 (2020)
4. Mirjalili, S.: Dragonfly algorithm: a new meta-heuristic optimization technique for solving single-objective, discrete, and multi-objective problems. Neural Comput. Appl. **27**(4), 1053–1073 (2015). https://doi.org/10.1007/s00521-015-1920-1
5. Tharwat, A., Gabel, T., Hassanien, A.E.: Parameter optimization of support vector machine using dragonfly algorithm. In: Hassanien, A.E., Shaalan, K., Gaber, T., Tolba, M.F. (eds.) AISI 2017. AISC, vol. 639, pp. 309–319. Springer, Cham (2018). https://doi.org/10.1007/978-3-319-64861-3_29
6. Abdel-Basset, M., Luo, Q., Miao, F., Zhou, Y.: Solving 0–1 knapsack problems by binary dragonfly algorithm. In: Huang, D.-S., Hussain, A., Han, K., Gromiha, M.M. (eds.) ICIC 2017. LNCS (LNAI), vol. 10363, pp. 491–502. Springer, Cham (2017). https://doi.org/10.1007/978-3-319-63315-2_43
7. Russell, R.W., May, M.L., Soltesz, K.L., et al.: Massive swarm migrations of dragonflies (Odonata) in eastern North America. Am. Midl. Nat. **140**(2), 325–342 (1998)

Deep Learning Based Network Intrusion Detection

Jun Yu[✉], Jiwei Hu, and Yong Zeng

Wuhan Fiberhome Technical Services Co., Ltd., Wuhan, China
yujun@fiberhome.com

Abstract. With the advancement of the times, the network has become an important part of people's daily life, and its connection with our daily life of clothing, food, housing, transportation, medical education has become increasingly close. However, while the network brings us a richer and faster life, the network security problem is also becoming more and more prominent. Network security risks are posing new challenges to the economy, politics, ecology, national security, science and technology development and other fields, and the network security problem has received wide attention, and network intrusion detection, as an important part of the network security field, needs more attention from us. To further improve the performance of feature extraction for network intrusion data, a combined model based on convolutional neural networks and long short-term memory units is proposed for the problems of gradient disappearance and gradient explosion of ordinary neural networks, and also the improved seagull optimization algorithm is applied to the optimization of the model parameters, and Batch Normalization and Adam optimizer, thus constructing an efficient model.

Keywords: network intrusion detection · convolutional neural network (CNN) · long short-term memory (LSTM)

1 Introduction

While the network has brought us a richer and more convenient life, its security problems have become increasingly prominent. The risk of network security is posing new challenges to politics, economy, culture, national defense, ecology and other fields [1]. Therefore, it has become an urgent problem to improve the reliability of information, purify the network security environment, maintain the computer system from damage and improve the security and reliability of the network.

With the development of the times and the progress of technology, machine learning technology has attracted the attention of many scholars, and a large number of scholars have participated in the research on how to apply machine learning to network intrusion detection. Traditional machine learning methods have been widely used in network intrusion detection [3]. The intrusion detection system designed by Saleh et al. Combines many machine learning methods, has strong real-time performance, and can solve multi classification problems. Dimensionality reduction is an important operation in data processing. This system uses the basic feature selection (NBFS) technology to process the data samples, and then eliminates the samples with high dispersion through the optimized support vector machine (OSVM). Finally, PKNN (an improved version of the classic KNN) is used to detect the attack, and experiments are carried out on the classic KDD 99, NSL-KDD and kyoto2006 + data sets. It shows the real-time performance of detection and achieves good detection effect [6–8]. Literature [9] uses support vector machine (SVM) combined with compressed sampling for intrusion detection. Compressed sampling method is adopted for the processing of network data stream. A model based on SVM is established to output the results, and good experimental results are achieved in training efficiency and detection speed. Reference [10] proposed a clever data processing method, which uses Fisher discriminant ratio (FDR) method for feature extraction and denoising. In the subsequent processing, in order to preserve the characteristics of the data, the probabilistic self-organizing maps (PSOM) is used for modeling, which has achieved good results in the classification accuracy. The training time of classifier is also an indicator worthy of attention. Al-Yaseen and others constructed a multi-level model in order to improve the training efficiency and the performance of the model. Firstly, in terms of data processing, the improved k-means algorithm is used to purify and sample the original training set. Starting from the specific data itself, the training efficiency of the optimized data is greatly improved. In the final result output stage of the model, it uses the combination of limit learning machine (ELM) and support vector machine to carry out multi classification, and uses the classic KDD99 data set for experimental evaluation. In terms of the accuracy index, its effect reaches 95.75% [11]. From the above research results, it can be seen that when applying machine learning methods to solve the problem of network intrusion, scholars generally first use some efficient methods in data processing (such as sampling), and then use machine learning methods to extract features, construct modeling to realize classification or prediction, and output the final results. In terms of model selection, we can not only stack the basic models, but also adopt the strategy of improving the basic models. Of course, we can also combine the two, and its ultimate goal is to build an efficient model. However, today's network attack traffic is growing, the data dimension is increasing, the attack methods are constantly changing, and the severity of data imbalance is becoming more and more prominent. The traditional machine learning methods are also unable to resist these complex situations. First of all, its deficiency is the extraction of features. Manual extraction plays an important role in the process of extracting features. However, it is difficult to explore the internal features of data manually, which mainly depends on experience. It is unable to well distinguish the correlation and temporal and spatial characteristics of data, and it is difficult to explore the internal relations and laws of data. Furthermore, from the perspective of data volume, such methods are obviously inefficient in the face of big data. Therefore, the intrusion detection technology of traditional machine learning method is facing many difficulties, and new technologies and ideas need to be developed urgently.

2   Related Work

Long short term memory (LSTM) was proposed by Hochreiter [2] and others to better realize these functions. Each LSTM unit includes a memory cell, an input gate, a forget gate and an output gate. The typical structure is shown in the (Fig. 1).

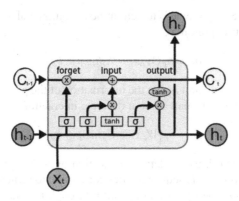

Fig. 1. Typical structure diagram of LSTM

The unit state determines the selection and updating of input data [3]. The updating of time correlation helps to classify and predict time series signals. Its principle and description are as follows:

Corresponding to the structure in the figure, the learnable weights of LSTM are input weights, recursive weights and bias. Matrices W, R and B are series of input weights, recursive weights and deviations of each component, respectively. The connection formula of these matrices is as follows:

$$W = \begin{bmatrix} W_i \\ W_f \\ W_g \\ W_o \end{bmatrix}, \quad R = \begin{bmatrix} R_i \\ R_f \\ R_g \\ R_o \end{bmatrix}, \quad b = \begin{bmatrix} b_i \\ b_f \\ b_g \\ b_o \end{bmatrix} \tag{1}$$

The cell state expression for time t is as follows:

$$h_t = o_t \otimes \sigma_c(c_t) \tag{2}$$

where σ_c represents the activation function. Generally, the LSTM layer function uses the hyperbolic tangent function (tanh) as the activation function, where $\otimes$ represents the element product of the vector.

Although the structure of forgetting gate in the structural diagram is concise, it plays a decisive role in discarding the input information. The expression is as follows:

$$f_t = \sigma_g \left(W_f x_t + R_f h_{t-1} + b_f \right) \tag{3}$$

where f_t represents the forgetting threshold, h_{t-1} is the last output information, and x_t is the input data information. The input data saves the useful data and forgets the useless data through the activation function σ_g.

The function of the input gate is to handle the input of the current sequence position, and its expression is as follows:

$$i_t = \sigma_g \left(W_i x_t + R_i h_{t-1} + b_i \right) \tag{4}$$

The function of the output gate is to determine the output value, which also depends on its state unit, and its expression is:

$$o_t = \sigma_g(W_o x_t + R_i h_{t-1} + b_o) \tag{5}$$

The function of the state unit is that the information of the past time runs directly on the whole chain, with only a small amount of linear interaction. Its expression is:

$$g_t = \sigma_c(W_g x_t + R_g h_{t-1} + b_g) \tag{6}$$

The process of network traffic data classification by LSTM is roughly as follows: first, convert the network traffic sequence after conversion to standardization into F and input it to the state unit, then filter and update F through the state unit to form a new state F1, the softmax classifier acts on the data output corresponding to the state in the previous stage, and finally output the training results.

3   Network Intrusion Detection Method Based on CNN and LSTM

The design of the model structure has a decisive impact on the experimental results. If pooling and convolution stacking are used in the classical convolutional neural network (CNN), it is easy to cause over fitting, and the extracted features are not necessarily representative and are very limited. In view of the above problems, this chapter adopts the method of CNN and long-term and short-term memory unit (LSTM) neural network, starts with the data characteristics, uses the time-series correlation of the detection data, adopts LSTM unit, compresses the network parameters and reduces the amount of calculation through CNN, and better extracts the temporal and spatial characteristics of the data and retains the correlation between the data through the combination of nonlinear modules. The super parameters of the ISOA optimization model are used, and the ReLU function is used as the activation function to make the neurons more robust, reduce the risk of over fitting, and build an efficient model.

The setting of model parameters is optimized through ISOA, and the optimization process is consistent with the previous chapter. Here we focus on the model structure of this chapter, which is shown in the figure below. The model processing steps are as follows: the first step is data preprocessing. The original NSL-KDD data sample contains 41 features. We expand it to multi-dimensional by transposing the matrix, and then input it to the convolutional neural network in the subsequent module for processing. The second step is feature extraction. The main process of feature extraction is shown in the figure below. Each small module plays a different role. Convolution and Max pooling play the role of feature purification. In the model, conv is convolution operation, and then the maximum pooling operation is carried out. The feature is down sampled to a certain size (according to the setting of convolution kernel) as the input of the next step. Batch normalization is mainly used to adjust the data relationship and reduce the impact of data covariance offset. On the whole, batch normalization, activation function and dropout algorithm are nested in each convolution layer, cooperate with each other and constantly adjust and optimize. Of course, the model of this step is stackable, and the number of stacking layers and settings depend on parameter optimization and experimental experience. Step 3: LSTM layer. The convolution and pooling in the previous stage are aimed at the spatial characteristics of the input data, which can maintain the internal feature correlation of the data. However, as we mentioned earlier, the input data has a great correlation in time sequence, and the adoption of LSTM gives the whole further feature extraction ability, fully exploring the main internal space-time correlation of the data. The fourth step is classified output. Finally, through the full connection layer connection, the data dimension transformation is completed, and the softmax classifier is used to detect different attack types and identify normal traffic, so as to complete the output of multi classification results (Fig. 2).

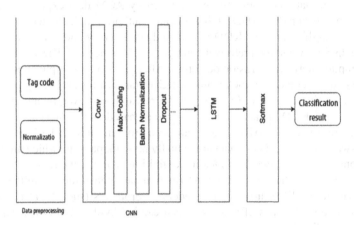

Fig. 2. Structure diagram of CNN + LSTM intrusion detection model

The CNN + LSTM network intrusion detection model proposed in this section takes advantage of the advantages of CNN spatial feature extraction and LSTM time series feature extraction. The combination of the two can fully extract the features of the data. In the parameter setting of the model, we use ISOA to optimize the parameters of the model, so that the parameter setting of the model is more reasonable and the performance of the model is stronger. In terms of the overall steps, after optimizing and setting the parameters, we first preprocess the data, including the conversion of label symbols and normalization processing, and then convert the processed data into the data type received by the neural network and send it to the network model for repeated iterative training. In each round of training, the same amount of data will be randomly selected and put into our model for training. The local features will be extracted and stored through the convolution layer, and then further feature filtering and dimensionality reduction will be carried out in the pooling layer. Then, the BN algorithm and Adam optimizer are used to update the data distribution and network weight, and dropout is used to reduce the impact of over fitting. The whole process can be combined and stacked. The basic features of the original data are continuously extracted and transformed under the action of CNN, LSTM and many optimization methods, forming higher-level abstract features, retaining the temporal and spatial correlation of the data, and feature extraction is more sufficient. The final category judgment is output through the softmax layer, the overall loss value will be calculated, and can be iteratively optimized through back propagation.

The weight and bias of network parameters at each layer are constantly updated, the loss value is continuously reduced, the model is more robust, and the effect obtained in the test set is better.

4 Experiment and Analysis

4.1 Data Sets

International Knowledge Discovery and Data Mining Competition (KDD cup) is the highest level international competition organized by ACM data exploration and data discovery expert group (SIGKDD). It has absolute authority in the field of data retrieval research. The English name of KDD is knowledge discovery and data mining, that is, knowledge discovery and data retrieval competition. The theme of KDD competition in 1999 is computer network intrusion detection. After years of development and verification, KDD99 data set has become an authoritative standard for evaluating performance in network intrusion detection. Many scientific research and experiments use KDD99 as dataset [4]. The KDD99 data set was constructed based on the data captured by MIT Lincoln Laboratory in the DARPA ' 98 evaluation program. It includes 7-week training data and 2-week test data. These data are actually network packets, which are related to network connection. A network connection definition is: the sequence of a TCP packet from the beginning to the end, and the information data transmitted from the source IP address to the target IP address under predefined protocols (such as TCP and UDP). These data include 39 types of attacks, which can be divided into four categories, as described below (Table 1):

Table 1. Dataset attack type

Type of attack	Annotation
DOS	Denial of service, the purpose of which is to prevent users from accessing services normally, such as smurf flood, ping flood, syn flood, teardrop attacks, http halfconnect, dns flood, etc.
R2L	Unauthorized remote access, such as guessing password, ftp write, imap, multihop, phf, worm, etc.
U2R	Unauthorized access to local administrator privileges, such as buffer overflow, perl, load module, root kit, sql attack, etc.
PROBING	Monitoring or other probing activities such as portsweep, ipsweep, satan, mscan, saint, etc.

The KDD99 dataset consists of a total of 5 million records, each of which has 41 features, examples of which are as follows (Table 2):

Among them, the first 41 features can be divided into four types of attributes, and the last one is label. There are 42 attributes in total. The basic contents of various attributes are as follows: 1. Basic features of TCP connection (features 1–9, 9 in total). These

Table 2. Sample dataset

Number	Sample
1	0,tcp,http,SF,215,45076,0,0,0,0,0,1,0,0,0,0,0,0,0,0,0,1,1,0,0,0,0.00,0.00,0.00,1.00,0.00,0.00,0.00,0.00,0.00,0.00,0.00,0.00,normal
2	0, tcp, private, REJ, 0, 0, 0, 0, 0, 0, 0, 0, 0, 0, 0, 0, 0, 0, 0, 0, 38, 1, 0.00, 0.00, 1.00, 1.00, 0.03, 0.55, 0.00, 208, 1, 0.00, 0.11, 0.18, 0.00, 0.01, 0.00, 0.42, 1.00, portsweep
3	2, tcp, smtp, SF, 1684, 363, 0, 0, 0, 0, 1, 0, 0, 0, 0, 0, 0, 0, 0, 0, 0, 1, 1, 0.00, 0.00, 0.00, 0.00, 1.00, 0.00, 0.00, 104, 66, 0.63, 0.03, 0.01, 0.00, 0.00, 0.00, 0.00, 0.00, normal
4	0, tcp, smtp, SF, 787, 329, 0, 0, 0, 0, 1, 0, 0, 0, 0, 0, 0, 0, 0, 0, 0, 1, 1, 0.00, 0.00, 0.00, 0.00, 1.00, 0.00, 0.00, 76, 117, 0.49, 0.08, 0.01, 0.02, 0.00, 0.00, 0.00, 0.00, normal

attributes include the protocol type of the current connection (TCP / UDP / ICMP), the network service type of the destination host, the number of urgent packets, the connection duration, the number of bytes from the source host to the destination host, the status bit indicating whether the connection is normal or not, etc. they are an accurate description of a TCP connection. 2. The content characteristics of TCP connection (No. 10 ~ 22 features, 13 kinds in total). For attacks such as r2l and u2r, due to the particularity of their attacks, they are not frequently recorded in the system like DoS attacks, so their characteristics look no different from normal TCP connection, which is also the main factor for the imbalance of this data set. In order to ensure that such attacks can be detected, the experimenters of KDD99 only extract some feature content from the data content, such as the number of unsuccessful login verification and the frequency of root user access. It is only possible to reflect the intrusion behavior, but it may not be able to detect it accurately. 3. The statistical characteristics of network traffic on time series (No. 23 ~ 31 features, a total of 9 kinds) express the temporal correlation of various attack modes. Therefore, a period of time between connections can be divided into independent time slices, so as to calculate the relationship between current connections and connections in earlier time slices. This is also an important reason for us to adopt the cyclic neural network model that can make use of time correlation. 4. Host based network traffic statistics (features 32–41, 10 in total), that is, the aforementioned time slice based traffic statistics, is the relationship statistics between the current connection and the previous time slice connection. The fixed time period in the data set is 2 s.

In 2009, Tavalllaee et al. proposed a revised version of the KDD99 dataset and named it NSL-KDD [4]. The NSL-KDD dataset overcomes some shortcomings of the KDD99 dataset. For example, NSL-KDD deletes some of the duplicate records in KDD99, reducing the impact of some frequent records on the experimental results; the number of entries in the dataset It has been simplified, and a relatively uniform dataset of different proportions is artificially selected, which improves the comparison and fairness of the research results. The filtered records contain different classification difficulty levels, and the number is more balanced, which makes the evaluation more effective and fair. The total number of records is kept within a reasonable size, allowing the algorithm to be applied to the entire dataset, rather than a randomly selected small subset, thus making it easier to compare different studies.

In this paper, the experimental part will use the improved data set NSL-KDD to evaluate the actual performance of the system. We use the most commonly used data files to test, so as to maintain the fairness of the comparison as much as possible.

4.2 Experimental Results and Analysis

In order to objectively evaluate the performance of the model, after sorting out the data of NSL-KDD data set, we randomly selected 80% of the data as the training set and the remaining 20% of the data as the test set. The number of runs is 20, and the experimental results are as follows (Table 3):

It can be seen from the above results that in the NSL-KDD data set, the result of ISOA + CNN + LSTM is the best. In terms of average accuracy, the performance ranking of the model is as follows: ISOA + CNN + LSTM > CNN + LSTM > CNN > LSTM. Among them, the average accuracy of ISOA + CNN + LSTM is 98.43%,

Table 3. The experimental results

Dataset	Experimental results of nsl-kdd dataset				
	Algorithm model	Average accuracy(ACC)	Best accuracy (BACC)	Detection rate(DR)	False alarm rate (FAR)
	LSTM	94.68%	96.19%	91.08%	6.58%
NSL-KDD	CNN	96.53%	97.64%	94.22%	3.90%
	CNN + LSTM	97.92%	98.47%	96.36%	4.05%
	ISOA + CNN + LSTM	98.43%	99.17%	98.74%	1.49%

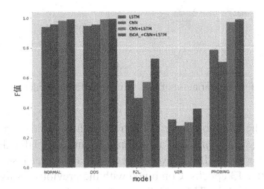

Fig. 3. NSL-KDD dataset F value result

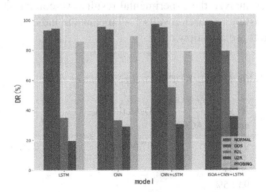

Fig. 4. NSL-KDD dataset DR value result

the best accuracy is 99.17%, the average accuracy is nearly 0.51% higher than CNN + LSTM, and 0.84% higher than the ISOA + Gru + MLP method proposed in Sect. 3, The detection rate is also the highest among these models, and the false alarm rate is as low as 1.49%, which is the lowest among the models proposed in Sects. 3 and 4, which also proves that the model we designed has excellent performance. As can be seen from Figs. 3 and 4, in terms of attack types, the comparison of F values shows that the detection effect of DoS attack and pro attack is significantly better than that of R2l and U2r attack. Through analysis, this is also in line with the characteristics of uneven data in our NSL-KDD data set (Fig. 5).

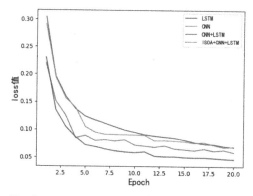

Fig. 5. Variation of loss value in different models

Figure 3 shows the variation curve of the average loss value of the experiment, and compares the convergence of different algorithms. It can be seen that the proposed ISOA + CNN + LSTM model has fast convergence speed and lower loss value. The model converges almost after 13 epochs. Combined with the previous results, we can see that using the ISOA + CNN + LSTM model not only has advantages in accuracy, but also has significantly faster convergence speed.

In order to better analyze the experimental results, we compared the experimental results with some existing research results ("–" means the indicator is not explained in the paper). The results are as follows:

Table 4. NSL-KDD dataset performance comparison

Model	Average accuracy(ACC)	Detection rate(DR)	False alarm rate (FAR)
VELM [12]	97.58%	97.69%	2.22%
DBN + SVM [13]	92.87%	–	–
SVM + ELM [14]	94.85%	–	–
LSTM + MLP [14]	96.41%	97.33%	3.24%
ISOA + GRU + MLP(this article)	97.59%	97.94%	2.01%
ISOA + CNN + LSTM(this article)	98.43%	98.74%	1.49%

It can be seen from Table 4 that ISOA + CNN + LSTM performs well on NSL-KDD data set, achieving the lowest false alarm rate (FPR): 1.49% and the highest accuracy (ACC): 98.43%.

It is worth noting that the above comparison is only a reference rather than an absolute distinction between advantages and disadvantages. In fact, different network intrusion detection methods respond differently to different kinds of intrusion, so it is difficult to find a method that can achieve the best performance in any case. In addition, due to slight differences in evaluation methods, such as different processing methods of data sets and different random sampling, the final results will also be different. Nevertheless, compared with other recent works, our proposed method still has clear advantages in accuracy, detection rate, convergence speed and so on.

5 Conclusion

In order to better extract the temporal and spatial characteristics of the data set, this chapter uses the combined model based on ISOA, CNN and LSTM to detect network intrusion. Firstly, the appropriate model parameter setting is obtained through ISOA, and then in the process of model training, make full use of the locality and spatial correlation of data features, use convolution neural network to extract and filter features, retain the main features of data and eliminate redundant information, so as to reduce the amount of data calculation and avoid over fitting. Then the LSTM layer is added. Using the characteristics of mining and using the temporal correlation of data, LSTM further extracts the high-level abstract features in the data, modifies the distribution of data and updates the weight of the network through BN and Adam algorithms, and continuously optimizes the iterative model through back propagation, so as to train the model more powerful. Finally, the NSL-KDD data set is used to verify the performance of our combined model. The comparative experiment shows that the detection model proposed in this chapter has excellent performance indicators in the experimental process, in which the highest detection accuracy is 99.17% and the average accuracy is 98.43%, which has obvious advantages over other research methods in recent years.

Acknowledgment. This work is funded by the National Natural Science Foundation of China under Grant No. 61772180, the Key R & D plan of Hubei Province(2020BHB004, 2020BAB012).

References

1. Ots, K.: Network Security Azure Security Handbook, pp. 59–76. Apress, Berkeley, CA (2021)
2. Hochreiter, S., Schmidhuber, J.: Long short-term memory. Neural Comput. 9(8), 1735–1780 (1997)
3. Xiong, G., Przystupa, K., Teng, Y., et al.: Online measurement error detection for the electronictransformer in a smart grid. Energies 14(12), 3551 (2021)
4. Sommer, R., Paxson, V.: Outside the closed world: on using machine learning for network intrusion detection. In: 2010 IEEE Symposium on Security and Privacy, pp. 305–316. IEEE (2010)

5. Xu, H., Przystupa, K., Fang, C., Marciniak, A., et al.: A combination strategy of feature selection based on an integrated optimization algorithm and weighted k-nearest neighbor to improve the performance of network intrusion detection. Electronics **9**(8), 1206 (2020)
6. Song, W., Beshley, M., Przystupa, K., et al.: A software deep packet inspection system for network traffic analysis and anomaly detection. Sensors **20**(6), 1637 (2020)
7. Kayacik, H.G., Zincir-Heywood, A.N., Heywood, M.I.: Selecting features for intrusion detection: a feature relevance analysis on KDD 99 intrusion detection datasets. In: Proceedings of the Third Annual Conference on Privacy, Security and Trust, vol. 94, pp. 1723–1722 (2005)
8. Saleh, A.I., Talaat, F.M., Labib, L.M.: A hybrid intrusion detection system (HIDS) based on prioritized k-nearest neighbors and optimized SVM classifiers. Artif. Intell. Rev. **51**(3), 403–443 (2019)
9. Chen, S., Peng, M., Xiong, H., Yu, X.: SVM intrusion detection model based on compressed sampling. J. Electr. Comput. Eng. **2016**, 1–6 (2016)
10. De La Hoz, E., Ortiz, A., Ortega, J., Prieto, B.: PCA filtering and probabilistic SOM for network intrusion detection. Neurocomputing **164**, 71–81 (2015)
11. Al-Yaseen, W.L., Othman, Z.A., Nazri, M.Z.A.: Multi-level hybrid support vector machine and extreme learning machine based on modified K-means for intrusion detection system. Expert Syst. Appl. **67**, 296–303 (2017)
12. Xu, C., Shen, J., Du, X., Zhang, F.: An intrusion detection system using a deep neural network with gated recurrent units. IEEE Access **6**, 48697–48707 (2018)
13. Shen, Y., Zheng, K., Wu, C., et al.: An ensemble method based on selection using bat algorithm for intrusion detection. Comput. J. **61**(4), 526–538 (2018)
14. Kun-peng, Y.: An intrusion detection model based on deep belief networks. Mod. Comput. **02**, 10–14 (2015)

An Optimization Algorithm Based on Levy's Flight Improvement

Ming Wei[(⊠)] and Zhengguo Li

Wuhan Fiberhome Technical Services Co., Ltd., Wuhan, China
weiming@fiberhome.com

Abstract. Aiming at the difficulties of automatic parameter optimization encountered in the development of network traffic forecasting systems, this paper, combined with recent research results of enhanced learning and evolutionary computing, A set of schemes based on improved Q-Learning strategy and Levy's Flight combined with lightning optimization algorithm are proposed. Automatically search for optimal parameters in the data preprocessing stage of network traffic prediction and the deep learning model training stage.

An optimization algorithm for the lightning attachment process based on Levy's Flight improvement (Levy-LAPO) is proposed. Through the overall driving ability of Levy's Flight, solved the problem of slow convergence. This paper compares the improved algorithm with the classic algorithm on standard functions and real data sets to verify the superiority of the improved algorithm.

Keywords: Evolutionary computing · Lightning attachment process · Optimization algorithm · Levy's Flight

1 Introduction

In recent years, with the data volume and dimension of network traffic becoming deeper and deeper, relevant scientific researchers have taken root in the field of network traffic prediction for a long time, and have also made many considerable achievements. At the beginning of the research, due to the weak theoretical basis, the network traffic load was mainly predicted by experience and industry experts in the network field at that time, but the prediction error was large. After a period of research, experts and scholars at home and abroad began to use more scientific methods to predict the network traffic load in multiple dimensions in order to improve the prediction accuracy. At this stage, the main prediction method is the mathematical model method. The core idea of the mathematical model method is mathematical statistics, such as time series method [1] and regression analysis method [2, 3]. These two methods are typical mathematical model methods; In order to deal with the high latitude disaster of data, combined with the recently popular reinforcement learning, the data is comprehensively preprocessed, and then optimize the model.

In the prediction field of optimization algorithms such as evolutionary algorithms, as early as the 1970s, researchers proposed the time series method, which can predict

W. Hong and G. Kanaparan (Eds.): ICCSE 2023, CCIS 2023, pp. 137–146, 2024.
https://doi.org/10.1007/978-981-97-0730-0_13

the future load by establishing the load prediction model of sequential data traffic. If the network environment is in normal operation and the factors change little, the prediction effect of time series method is still ideal. If the number and demand of the network fluctuate greatly, the prediction effect is not ideal. Time series methods mainly include Auto Regressive model (AR) [4], Moving Average model (MA) [5], Auto Regressive Moving Average model (ARMA) [6–8], Auto regressive Integrated Moving Average model (ARIMA) [9], Kalman filtering [10], State estimation, Box- Jenkins [11] model, etc. In 1999, at the University of Washington in the United States, artificial neural network was first applied to network traffic load forecasting, which was proposed by D.C.Park and others. This marks the transition of load forecasting theory and method of network traffic from traditional statistical principle to artificial intelligence. The artificial neural network method is applied to practical engineering, and the prediction results are also more accurate. Machine learning based methods are divided into unsupervised learning and supervised machine learning [12]. In 2004, McGregor et al. Took packet length, packet interval time and stream duration as the statistical characteristics of traffic data and used expectation maximization algorithm EM [13] (expectation maximization algorithm) for unsupervised training and learning; In 2005, Zander et al. Used an unsupervised Bayesian classifier [14] to calculate the eigenvalues of the flow; In 2007, Erman et al. Proposed a solution for the classification of network core traffic, using the method of k-means clustering [15]; Under the supervised machine learning method, Murthy proposed a decision tree model in 1998 [16]; In addition, the support vector machine [17] proposed in 1995 carries out data flow prediction and analysis through nonlinear transformation and structural risk minimization principle; In 2006, Park et al. Proposed a feature selection technology based on genetic algorithm [18]. The experiment is to compare the decision tree classifier [19] with the classifier based on Naive Bayes by using the characteristics of data flow; Semi-supervised machine learning method was also used in traffic field earlier; In 2011, Xiangli et al. Used a semi-supervised support vector machine [20] (SVM) method for traffic research.

The classic Lightning search algorithm [21] (LSA) and Lightning attachment process optimizer (LAPO) are popular evolutionary algorithms in recent years. Compared with the classic PSO, DSA, HAS and other algorithms, they have the characteristics of simple structure, fast convergence speed and strong optimization ability.

Classical evolutionary algorithms are prone to fall into local optimal solutions, high computational complexity and weak convergence. Especially on the premise of using artificial intelligence model based on neural network as fitness function, because there are many circular nested structures in evolutionary algorithms, they often consume a lot of time and computational resources in fitness calculation.

2 Related Works

2.1 Levy's Flight Theory

In nature, many animals go back to look for food, but they are in many uncertain environments. Therefore, Levi flight is a foraging strategy of simulated animals. This form of search strategy relies on two ways: short-distance exploratory jumping and occasional long-distance walking. Among them, Short distance jumping can ensure that animals can search carefully in a small range around themselves in the process of foraging, while another occasional long-distance jumping can ensure that animals can jump out of the current situation and enter another area to search in a wider range, which can prevent local optimization, improve the speed of gradient descent iteration and prevent failure to find the best. The advantage of Levy's algorithm is that it can further improve the global search speed [22]. The experimental results of this paper and the performance of the algorithm can be well improved.

2.2 Levy's Flight Mathematical Representation

The expression (1) of Levy's Flight position update is as follows:

$$x_i^{(t+1)} = x_i^{(t)} + \alpha \oplus Levy(\lambda) i = 1, 2, \ldots, n \tag{1}$$

Among: $x_i^{(t)}$ is the position of x_i in generation t; $\oplus$ is point-to-point multiplication; α represents the control amount of step size; Levy(λ) is A random search path and satisfies formula (2) below:

$$Levy \sim u = t^{-\lambda} 1 < \lambda \le 3 \tag{2}$$

Levy's flight is a random step size, and the step size conforms to Levy's characteristic distribution function. Due to the complexity of its own distribution function, Mantegna algorithm is used to simulate and express the mathematical relationship. The calculation formula of step size s is (3):

$$s = \frac{\mu}{|v|^{1/\beta}} \tag{3}$$

where u and v are normal distribution, and the definition formula is expressed as (4) and (5) respectively:

$$\mu \sim N(0, \sigma_\mu^2) \tag{4}$$

$$v \sim N(0, \sigma_v^2) \tag{5}$$

where σ_μ is expressed by formula (6):

$$\sigma_\mu = \left\{ \frac{\Gamma(1 + \beta) sin(\frac{\pi \beta}{2})}{\Gamma\left[\frac{1+\beta}{2}\right] \beta 2^{\frac{(\beta-1)}{2}}} \right\}^{1/\beta} \tag{6}$$

β in the above formula usually takes the constant 1.5.

It can be found from the literature records of many other researchers that Levy's Flight can improve the global search efficiency for parameters in an uncertain environment. Figure 1 below shows the difference between the walking path based on Levy's Flight and random walking, which can well compare the characteristics of Levi's Flight. As shown in the figure below, when Levy's Flight and random walking are 300 steps, It can be proved that Levy's Flight has a wider search ability, so it can expand the scope of search and optimization. Combining this strategy with the lightning connection process optimization algorithm can make up for the shortcomings of the lightning connection process optimization algorithm, improve the vitality and jumping power of the original algorithm, so as to improve the iteration rate of the overall optimization process of the algorithm and reduce the redundant and time-consuming process.

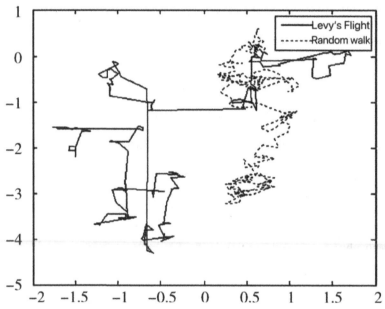

Fig. 1. Comparison of characteristics between Levy's Flight and random flight in optimization process

3 Lightning Connection Process Optimization Algorithm Combined with Levy's Flight

3.1 Algorithm Design Idea

In the classical optimization algorithm of lightning connection process, because the algorithm itself has the characteristics of less parameters, simple structure and strong optimization ability, but when using the deep learning model as the fitness function, the calculation complexity is high, and the optimization process has some redundancy. In order to deal with the problem of high data dimension or multimodal optimization, it will show the disadvantage of poor ability, improve its iteration rate and make up for the shortcomings, the overall design of Levy-LAPO algorithm model is as follows.

Firstly, in the original standard lightning connection process optimization algorithm, LAPO algorithm finds the candidate connection points between the cloud and the ground by initializing the search population and combining the decision variables. The random distribution function model is established through the lightning emission points to solve the optimization problem. In the initial iteration process, the objective function is calculated for all test points and regarded as the electric field of these test points: define a test point:

$$X^i_{testpoint} = X^i_{min} + \left(X^i_{max} - X^i_{min}\right) * rand \tag{7}$$

In this paper, Levy-LAPO algorithm improved by Levy's Flight is adopted. Instead of directly using Levy Flight to enter the next generation of iterations, Levy Flight is directly used to update and jump in position, so that the discharge body can be directly searched and searched across regions.

In the follow-up experiments, the ways to further carry out Levy's Flight on the iterative position of the discharge body are as follows: (1) carry out Levy's flight directly; (2) Firstly, set a threshold to judge whether the iterative position of the lightning observation point has not been updated for a long time, and whether it has fallen into a local optimal area. If it is judged that the iterative space has not been updated for a long time, then carry out Levy's Flight on the position of the discharge body, jump out of the current area by jumping, and search the next space, otherwise Levy's Flight is not required, In other words, it has a choice to fly Levy's. Through the comparison of the two methods in the follow-up experiment, it is concluded that although the experimental effect of scheme 1 is better than that of scheme 2, the time complexity and training process time are much longer than that of scheme 2 due to the addition of Levy's Flight in the whole process of a, so there will be great disadvantages in the practical application of this scheme. Therefore, scheme 2 is adopted in the follow-up experiment in this paper.

3.2 Algorithm Steps and Flow Chart of Levy-LAPO

Levy-LAPO algorithm first defines a lightning candidate point group, selects a test observation point Test point, and then marks the number of jumps of potential test points that have not been iterated as $q_i (i = 1, 2, \ldots, n)$, indicating the number of iterations in which lightning random test points have not reached a better position.

A threshold can be defined to make the non-downward discharge iterative optimization times q_i of random test point p_i^s reach 10 times, then p^s can jump out of the current optimization space by Levy's Flight position update formula, where $x_i^{(t+1)}$ represents the position update of the discharge body after iteration through Levy's Flight. $x_i^{(t)}$ represents the iterative position of lightning test points before Levy's Flight, and $\oplus$ represents the point-to-point multiplication. α represents the control amount of step size; $Levy(\lambda)$ is a random search path. However, in the optimization results, we make trade-offs according to the fitness values before and after, and then compare the positions of $x_i^{(t+1)}$ and $x_i^{(t)}$. If the position after Levy's Flight is better than that before Levy's Flight, the position of $x_i^{(t+1)}$ is used, and the optimal position before Levy's Flight is used conversely.

Levy-LAPO algorithm steps:

(1) Initialization algorithm running parameters: Population size N, Maximum number of iterations Max_{iter}, Maximum channel time T and Step pilot tip energy E_{sl};

(2) Execute the aggregation model under charge branching, randomly generate the seed group of initial jump points, calculate the value of objective function and evaluate the position of test point as Test point;

(3) Enter the main cycle, update the charge branch to determine the best and worst leader;

(4) If the maximum channel time t is satisfied, the channel with the worst fitness value is eliminated and the channel time is reset, otherwise enter the next step;

(5) Update the location of lightning jump point and energy lightning emission point;

(6) Levy's Flight, judge whether the position of the discharge body fails to iterate energy for more than ten times. If so, use the formula $x_i^{(t+1)} = x_i^{(t)} + \alpha \oplus Levy(\lambda)$, Levy's Flight to update the position of the current guiding lightning radiation point. After Levy's Flight, update the optimal individual p-best and global optimal g-best according to steps (4), (5) and (6).

(7) The algorithm terminates. If the final iteration end condition is met, stop the algorithm search, otherwise continue to return to step (5) and continue to find the optimal Lightning Radiation position.

(8) Performance evaluation, evaluation of the best fitness test point as Test point;

The flow chart of parameter optimization algorithm based on Levy-LAPO is shown in Fig. 2 below:

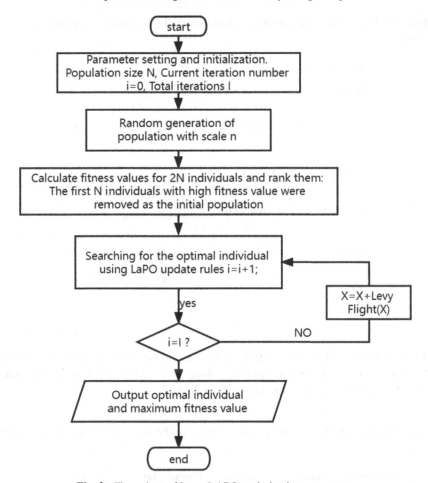

Fig. 2. Flow chart of Levy-LAPO optimization parameters

4   Experiment

In order to verify that the global iteration speed of the improved lightning connection process optimization algorithm combined with Levy's Flight strategy has indeed increased to a certain extent. This section tests the improved lightning search evolutionary algorithm through five classical benchmark functions. These five benchmark functions are unimodal functions. The basic attributes and formulas of the five unimodal functions are shown in Table 1. Because the prediction experiment studied in this paper only needs to find the minimum value. In this round of simulation function experiment, the experimental environment adopted is Win10 operating system, Intel Core i7 processor 2.66 Hz, 16G memory, and the experimental environment is written in Python programming language.

Table 1. The basic properties and specific formulas of the five selected unimodal reference functions

Serial number	Function name	Search scope	Function	Minimum value
F1	Sphere	[0,100]	$f_1(x) = \sum_{i=1}^{n} x_i^2$	0
F2	Sum Different	[−100,100]	$f_2(x) = \sum_{i=1}^{n} (\sum_{j=1}^{i} x_j)^2$	0
F3	Schewel	[−10,10]	$f_3(x) = \sum_{i=1}^{n} |x_i| + \prod |x_i|$	0
F4	Booth	[−100,100]	$f_4(x) = \max\{|x_i|, 1 \le i \le n\}$	0
F5	Beale	[−30,30]	$f_5(x) = \sum_{i=1}^{n-1} [100(x_{i+1} - x_i^2)^2 + (x_i - 1)^2]$	0

In the experiment, the classical lightning connection process algorithm is compared with the lightning connection algorithm combined with Levy's Flight proposed in this chapter. The experimental results are shown in Table 2.

Table 2. The basic properties and specific formulas of the five selected unimodal reference functions:

Function serial number	Dimension	Algorithm	Optimal value	Average value	Variance
F1	2	LAPO	5.75E−25	2.54E−21	5.41E−21
		Levy-LAPO	2.69E−26	9.09E−23	1.34E−22
F2	2	LAPO	2.17E−12	6.02E−09	2.40E−08
		Levy-LAPO	1.70E−13	6.63E−10	1.83E−09
F3	2	LAPO	0.00490267	0.00179973	0.00347591
		Levy-LAPO	1.02E−07	0.002051	0.00173045
F4	2	LAPO	4.02E−13	3.96E−11	2.13E−10
		Levy-LAPO	7.23E−16	6.14E−12	1.61E−11
F5	2	LAPO	4.58E−06	1.28E−06	1.63E−06
		Levy-LAPO	3.76E−08	1.11E−06	1.49E−06

The experimental results show that the optimization results of the two algorithms are similar in the optimal value, average value and variance. Specifically, Levy-LAPO has a weak advantage in the four standard functions of F1, F2, F3 and F4, and the results of the two algorithms are close in the standard function of F5 and F9. It can be said that in the optimization search ability of unimodal function, the optimization performance of Levy-LAPO is similar to that of classical LAPO algorithm, and the gap between them is within the error range, but Levy-LAPO algorithm should have a better convergence speed.

5 Summary of This Chapter

Lightning connection process optimization algorithm is a new intelligent optimization algorithm in recent years. It has the characteristics of less parameters, simple structure and strong optimization ability. However, when using the deep learning model as the fitness function, the computational complexity is high, and the optimization process has some redundancy. In order to solve this problem, this chapter proposes an optimization algorithm combining Levy's Flight and lightning connection process, which uses the large step random walk of Levy's Flight to improve the optimization efficiency.

References

1. Yang, H.M., Pan, Z.S., Bai, W.: Review of time series prediction methods. Comp. Sci. **46**(01), 21–28 (2019)
2. You, S.B., Yan, Y.: Stepwise regression analysis and its application. Stat. Decis. Making **14**, 31–35 (2017)
3. Yeromenko, V., Kochan, O.: The conditional least squares method for thermocouples error modeling. In: 2013 IEEE 7th International Conference on Intelligent Data Acquisition and Advanced Computing Systems (IDAACS), vol. 1, pp. 157–162. IEEE (2013)
4. Xu, H.J.: Research on global least squares analysis of autoregressive AR model. Donghua University of Technology (2012)
5. Rahal, R.: Moving average model for daily euro index in Europe with genetic algorithms and comparing it with box-Jenkins model. Int. J. Math. Stat. **19**(2) (2018)
6. Ye, G.Y., Luo, Y.H., Liu, Y., et al.: Research on power system load forecasting method based on ARMA model. Inform. Technol. (06), 74–76 (2002)
7. Chen, X., Przystupa, K., Ye, Z., Chen, F.: Forecasting short-term electric load using extreme learning machine with improved tree seed algorithm based on levy flight. Eksploatacja i Niezawodnosc-Maintenance and Reliability **24**(1), 153–162 (2022)
8. Zou, B.X., Liu, Q.: Network traffic prediction based on ARMA model. Comput. Res. Develop. (12), 1645–1652 (2002)
9. Han, C., Song, S., Wang, C.H.: Real time adaptive prediction of short-term traffic flow based on ARIMA model. J. Syst. Simul. (07), 1530–1532+1535 (2004)
10. Peng, D.C.: Basic principle and application of Kalman filter. Softw. Guide **8**(11), 32–34 (2009)
11. Yang, H.Z., Zhang, Y.: Comparison between box Jenkins model deviation compensation method and other identification methods. Control Theo. Appl. (02), 215–222 (2007)
12. Pinto, A., et al.: Combining unsupervised and supervised learning for predicting the final stroke lesion. Med. Image Anal. **69**, 101888 (2021). https://doi.org/10.1016/j.media.2020.101888
13. Mader, W., Linke, Y., Mader, M., et al.: A numerically efficient implementation of the expectation maximization algorithm for state space models. Appl. Math. Comput. **241**, 222 (2014)

14. Karthika, S., Sairam, N.: A Naïve Bayesian classifier for educational qualification. Indian J. Sci. Technol. **8**(16) (2015)
15. Lailiyah, S., Hafiyusholeh, M.: PERBANDINGAN ANTARA METODE K-MEANS CLUSTERING DENGAN GATH-GEVA CLUSTERING. Mantik: Jurnal Matematika **1**(2), 26 (2016)
16. AlSaaidah, B., Al-Nuaimy, W., Al-Hadidi, M.R., Young, I.: Zebrafish larvae classification based on decision tree model: a comparative analysis. Adv. Sci. Technol. Eng. Syst. J. **3**(4), 347–353 (2018). https://doi.org/10.25046/aj030435
17. Chau, G., Kemper, G.: One channel subvocal speech phrases recognition using cumulative residual entropy and support vector machines. IEEE Latin Am. Trans. **13**(7) (2015)
18. Wang, H.X., Cao, B.: Effectiveness test of China's stock market based on genetic programming. Comp. Sci. **43**(S1), 538–541 (2016)
19. Abraham, S.K., Sugumaran, V., Amarnath, M.: Acoustic signal based condition monitoring of gearbox using wavelets and decision tree classifier. Indian J. Sci. Technol. **9**(33) (2016)
20. Sun, X., Young, J., Liu, J.H., et al.: Predicting pork color scores using computer vision and support vector machine technology. Meat Muscle Biol. **2**(1) (2018)
21. Shareef, H., Ibrahim, A.A., Mutlag, A.H.: Lightning search algorithm. Appl. Soft Comput. **36**, 315 (2015)
22. Sun, S., Przystupa, K., Wei, M., Yu, H., Ye, Z., Kochan, O.: Fast bearing fault diagnosis of rolling element using Lévy Moth-Flame optimization algorithm and Naive Bayes. Eksploatacja i Niezawodnosc – Maintenance and Reliability **22**(4), 730–740 (2020)

Image Classification Based on Improved Unsupervised Clustering Algorithm

Yichao Wang[1]($\boxtimes$), Chunzhi Wang[2], and Lingyu Yan[2]

[1] School of Computer Science and Technology, HanKou University, Wuhan, China
echarwang@163.com
[2] School of Computer Science, Hubei University of Technology, Wuhan, China
yanlingyu@hbut.edu.cn

Abstract. This paper proposes a k-means model based on density weighting, which is applied to the field of image classification and fused with deep neural network to train pseudo-labels. While clustering the learning features of the residual network, the network parameters are updated to achieve. The clustering performance of pseudo-labeled datasets is improved to solve the problem of scarcity of labeled data.

Keywords: K-means · Image Classification · Deep Neural networks · Clustering Algorithm

1 Introduction

The rapid development of information technology has brought a large amount of unlabeled data, many research subjects have shifted from all labeled data to only a small amount of labeled or unlabeled data, and research methods have shifted from supervised learning to unsupervised learning, which has more practical significance for image processing tasks. Clustering is an important unsupervised learning method that is widely used in machine learning and data mining. Clustering results depend on the clustering algorithm and the feature representation of the data. In the traditional supervised learning task, when the labeling data is insufficient, the generalization ability of the learning model is not strong and cannot meet the requirements of reality. In this technical context, deep clustering as a new unsupervised technology has been proposed, so as to achieve a new clustering method for large-scale end-to-end convolutional networks for a labelless unsupervised network model training, provided that there is a large amount of labeled data to prevent model overfitting, however, manual labeling data is a time-consuming, laborintensive, cost-consuming process, in order to better use existing unlabeled images, clustering and unsupervised learning has attracted great attention and interest from the academic community.

W. Hong and G. Kanaparan (Eds.): ICCSE 2023, CCIS 2023, pp. 147–161, 2024.
https://doi.org/10.1007/978-981-97-0730-0_14

2 An Unsupervised Classification Model Based on Improved Kmeans Clustering Algorithm

2.1 Unsupervised Clustering Algorithm

The K-means algorithm is one of the most commonly used traditional clustering algorithms, which divides a given sample dataset into K user-specified classes. K sample data are randomly selected as the initial cluster center from N sample data, while for other data samples, they are assigned to the class with the highest or closest similarity based on their similarity or distance from the selected cluster center point. Then, calculate the average of the sample data in each class to update the cluster center point, repeating the process until the standard function J begins to converge.

$$J = \sum_{i=1}^{k} \sum_{j=1}^{n_k} (C_i - X_j)^2 \tag{1}$$

where: J denotes the sum of the average errors of the data sample objects in all classes, C_i denotes the cluster centers in the i-th class, X_j denotes the sample objects in the j-th class.

K-means algorithm steps:

Algorithm input: Sample dataset X, $X = \{X_m\}_{m=1}^{n}$, number of clusters K.

Algorithm output: Clustering represents set C, $C = \{C_i\}_{i=1}^{k}$.

Step1: From dataset X, arbitrarily select K sample data objects as the center of the initial cluster cluster.

Step2: Calculate the distance from xm of each sample in the sample dataset to the center point of the cluster ci using the formula $dis(x_m, c_i) = \sqrt{(x_m - c_i)^2}$.

Step3: Find the minimum distance from each data object xm to the cluster center ci min_dis (xm, ci), and classify the data object xm into the same class as ci, that $C_i = \{x_m : dis(X_m - C_i) < dis(X_m - C_j)\}$.

Step4: Calculates the mean of objects in the same class, updates the cluster center.

Step5: Repeat steps Step2-Step4 until all cluster centers no longer change or the maximum number of runs is reached.

The flow chart of the K-means algorithm is as follows (Fig. 1):

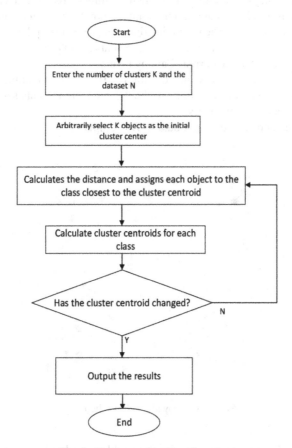

Fig. 1. K-means algorithm flowchart

2.2 Canopy Algorithm

The Canopy algorithm is an unsupervised preclustering algorithm introduced by Andrew McCallum, Kamal Nigam, and Lyle Ungar in 2000 [1], and is often used as a preprocessing step for the K-means algorithm. As shown in Fig. 2, the Canopy algorithm sets two distance thresholds T1 and T2, randomly selects the initial cluster center, and calculates the Euclidean distance between the sample and the initial center. Classify samples into corresponding clusters based on thresholds. Finally, the clustered dataset is divided into n clusters. The clustering of the dataset is completed by taking the cluster number and cluster center of the canopy algorithm as the input parameters of the K-means algorithm.

The steps of the Canopy algorithm are as follows:

Step 1: Given a dataset and quantify it, then set thresholds T1 and T2 (T1 > T2).

Step 2: Randomly select a data sample point S from the data set D, and calculate the Euclidean distance d between the remaining data sample points in the data set D and the sample point S respectively. If there is d < T1, the data samples that meet the conditions will be Points are added to the current Canopy layer.

Step 3: Then compare the distance d with T2. If there is a condition d < T2, the sample points that satisfy the condition will be deleted from the data set D, so they will not be added to other Canopy layers.

Step 4: Repeat steps 2 and 3 until dataset D is empty.

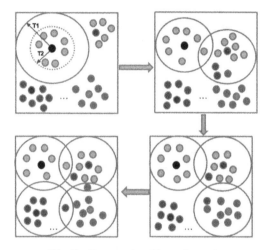

Fig. 2. Canopy algorithm schematic

In the classic Canopy algorithm, the threshold is randomly selected in the algorithm, which has a great impact on the clustering results. In this section, the maximum weight product method is proposed to determine the optimal number of clusters, which reduces the instability caused by randomness and improves the clustering accuracy. The maximum weight product method is shown in Fig. 3:

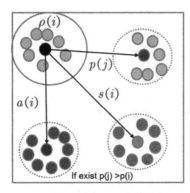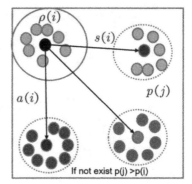

Fig. 3. Maximum weight

$\rho(i)$ denotes the density value of the sample element i in the data set D, s_i denotes the cluster distance, the schematic diagram of obtaining the maximum weight of the best cluster center is shown in Fig. 4:

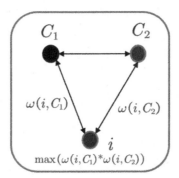

Fig. 4. Schematic diagram of the maximum weights of the largest cluster centers

2.3 Improved K-Means Algorithm Based on Density-Weighted Canopy Algorithm

This paper proposes an improved K-means algorithm based on the idea of density weighting. This paper proposes a density weighting method to solve this problem. In addition, the number of clusters and the initial cluster centers obtained by the density-weighted Canopy algorithm are used as input parameters of the k-means algorithm to complete the calculation of the clusters of the dataset.The improved algorithm flow is as follows (Fig. 5):

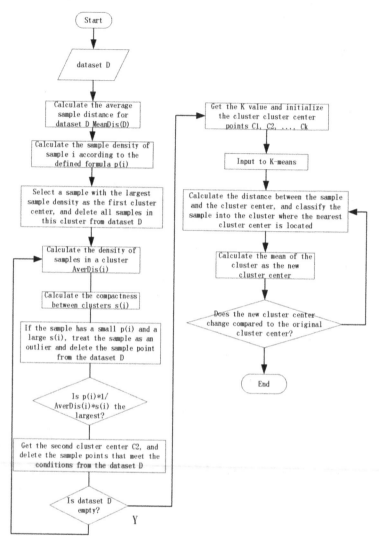

Fig. 5. Improved algorithm flowchart

3   Image Classification Combined with Residual Network Resnet Models

3.1   Unsupervised Classification Model Design

For the traditional deep convolutional neural network, $f_{\theta*}$ denotes the mapping of the residual network from the original dataset image to a specific dimensional vector space, where θ is corresponding parameter set, map this parameter set to the image of the ImageNet dataset, you can get the feature vector of the image information in the dataset for characterization learning,for the N images in the training set $X = \{x_1, x_1, x_1, .., x_n\}$, we hope to find a parameter θ^*, so that mapping f_{θ^*} produces better visual general features, each image x_n is associated with a label y_n in $\{0, 1\}^k$, and then the parameterized classifier g_w predicts which of the image rate belongs to the correct label based on the visual feature $f_\theta(x_n)$, so the loss function at this time can be denotes by (2) and (3):

$$L = \frac{1}{N} {}^{\min}_{\theta, w} \delta(g_w(f_\theta(x_n)), y_n) \tag{2}$$

$$\delta = -\frac{1}{N} \sum_{n=1}^{N} \log(p_n, I_n) \tag{3}$$

p_n denotes the prediction probability that the sample belongs to each class, I_n denotes the true class of the sample data. The unsupervised classification model is optimized based on the loss function in the process of minimizing network training, and the accuracy of the model is inversely proportional to the size of the loss function.

Based on the improved k-means algorithm, the feature $f_\theta(x_n)$ generated by the residual network is used as the input of the clustering algorithm, and the generated feature matrix vector is subjected to dimension reduction processing. Finally, the clustering algorithm divides them into k categories according to the corresponding geometric criteria. Formula (4) minimizes it, and jointly learns the cluster center matrix and the clustering result of each image.

$$p = \min_{c \in R^{d \times k}} \frac{1}{N} \sum_{n=1}^{N} \min_{y_n \in \{0, 1\}^k} \left\| f_\theta(x_n) - Cy_n \right\|_2^2 \tag{4}$$

The results of clustering are used as pseudo-labels to optimize the cluster loss function, and the classifier parameters and mapping parameters are learned together to achieve the ultimate goal of updating the network parameters.

4 Simulation

4.1 Experimental Dataset

The datasets used in the experiments are cifar-10, ImageNet and Pascal VOC2007, of which the first two are datasets for image classification tasks, and the Pascal-VOC dataset is a target detection dataset.

4.2 Evaluation Indicators

This paper uses Accuracy (ACC) and Normalized Mutual Information (NMI) to measure the suitability of clustering results for unsupervised classification. If the total number of data sets is N, the real label mapped by each data is h_i, and the class label obtained by the unsupervised model is g_i, then the function $map(g_i)$ that maps the class label obtained by unsupervised learning to the real label can be obtained, and the accuracy rate The ACC formula is as follows:

$$ACC = \frac{\sum_{i=1}^{n} \delta(h_i, map(g_i))}{N} \tag{5}$$

δ is a mapping association function that calculates the matching degree of hi and $map(g_i)$, and its function expression is:

$$\delta = \begin{cases} 0, h_i = map(g_i) \\ 1, h_i \neq map(g_i) \end{cases} \tag{6}$$

In addition, this paper measures the information shared between two different assignments A and B between the same data sample by normalized mutual information (NMI), which is defined as formula (7):

$$NMI(A; B) = \frac{I(A; B)}{\sqrt{H(A)H(B)}} \tag{7}$$

I donotes mutual information and H denotes entropy, this performance measure can be applied to any cluster assignment between clusters or ground truth labels.The value of NMI varies continuously between 0 and 1. If the two clusters A and B are completely independent and identically distributed, it means that the NMI = 0. If the similarity between the two clusters is higher, it means that the value of the NMI is larger, but it is always less than 1.

Considering this the research is a multi-classification problem. In order to evaluate the unsupervised classification model more objectively and fairly, it is necessary to use a unified parameter index to evaluate the model. Before introducing the evaluation index, first give the concept of confusion matrix as shown in the Table 1:

Table 1. Confusion matrix

Classification result Reality	True	False
True	TP	FN
False	FP	TN

Based on the confusion matrix, this paper aims at image classification. The evaluation indicators mainly use Precision and Average Precision (AP) to judge the accuracy of the experimental classification results, which are defined as follows:

$$P = \frac{TP}{TP + FP} \tag{8}$$

Precision (P) refers to the ratio of the number of correctly classified positive samples to the number of all classified positive samples, and its calculation formula is as follows:

$$mAP = \frac{1}{C} \sum_{q \in C} AP(q) \tag{9}$$

4.3 Experimental Results and Analysis

In this paper, the unsupervised pre-training model on ImageNet is transferred to the PascalVOC dataset, and multilabel classification is realized by fine-tuning. The following figure shows the schematic diagram of the bottom entropy classification result (Fig. 6).

Fig. 6. Bottom entropy classification result visualization

In this paper, the feature map visualization of the convolutional layers of Conv1 to Conv5 is carried out to verify that the improved algorithm can promote the feature extractor of the residual network. After each Conv_x, the visualization operation of the feature map is carried out. This paper Select the first 12 feature maps for visualization. This article randomly selects an original image, the original image is shown in Fig. 7, and the effect image is shown in Figs. 8, 9, 10, 11 and 12.

Fig. 7. Original image

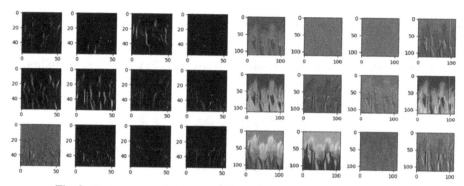

Fig. 8. Feature comparison map of Conv1_x before and after improvement

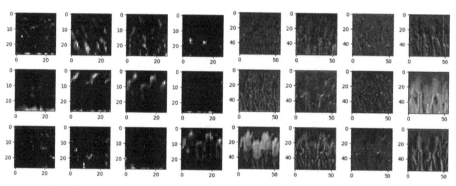

Fig. 9. Feature comparison map of Conv2_x before and after improvement

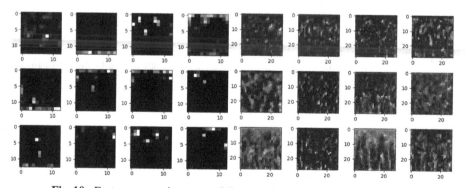

Fig. 10. Feature comparison map of Conv3_x before and after improvement

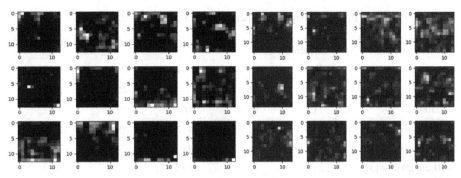

Fig. 11. Feature comparison map of Conv4_x before and after improvement

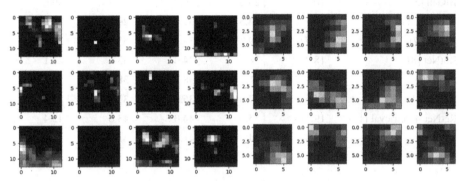

Fig. 12. Feature comparison map of Conv5_x before and after improvement

It can be seen from the figure that as the depth of the convolution layer deepens from Conv1_x to Conv5_x, the features of the image extracted by the convolution filter also become abstract. By comparing the five left and right pictures, we can see that the five pictures on the right show The ability of the convolutional layer to extract features from the image is obviously better than the ability of the convolutional filters of the five images on the left to extract features from the image. It can be seen that the improved k-means algorithm proposed in this paper is effective for the convolutional filters. To a certain positive effect, the ability to extract feature information is improved, so it also reflects that the algorithm can improve the prediction ability of classification.

From Table 2, we can see that on the ImageNet dataset, the features extracted by the network model in this paper have excellent performance values from Conv3_x to Conv5_x through the linear detection classifier., but as the convolutional layer deepens, this gap narrows.

The unsupervised pre-training model on ImageNet is transferred to the PASCAL VOC2007 dataset, and multi-label classification is performed by fine-tuning. The pre-training parameters are set as follows: batchsize is 256, learning rate lr is 0.001, weight decay is set to 1, using 4 GPUs are used for pre-training, and the experimental results are as follows (Figs. 13 and 14):

Table 2. ImageNet's linear detection evaluation table

Methods	ImageNet				
	Conv1_x	Conv2_x	Conv3_x	Conv4_x	Con5_x
ImageNet labels	19.3	36.3	44.2	48.3	50.5
Random	11.6	17.1	16.9	16.3	14.1
DeepCluster [2]	13.4	32.3	41.0	39.6	38.2
SelfLabel3kx1 [3]	---	---	43.0	44.7	40.9
SelfLabel3kx10 [3]	22.5	37.4	44.7	47.1	44.1
Contenxt [4]	15.3	35.2	43.5	45.6	46.7
BiGan [5]	16.2	23.3	30.2	31.7	29.6
Split-brain [6]	17.7	24.5	31.0	29.9	28.0
Jigsaw [7]	17.7	29.3	35.4	35.2	32.8
RotNet [8]	18.2	28.8	34.0	33.9	27.1
AND [9]	18.8	31.7	38.7	38.2	36.5
AET [10]	15.6	27.0	35.9	39.7	37.9
RetNet + retrieval [11]	19.3	35.0	44.0	43.6	42.4
UIC(ours)	12.8	34.3	41.6	41.5	45.3

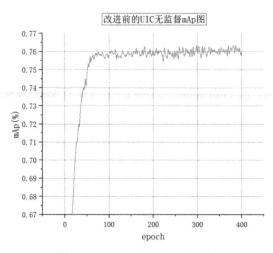

Fig. 13. mAp accuracy map of the unsupervised model before improvement on the VOC dataset.

It can be seen from the figure that when the model is trained for 100 epochs, the model begins to converge. Driven by the pre-trained model, the average classification accuracy mAp of the unsupervised classification model on the PascalVOC2007 validation set

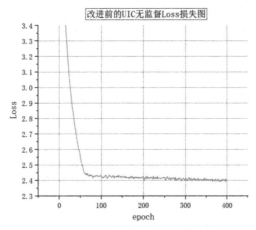

Fig. 14. Loss plot of the unsupervised model before improvement on the PASCAL VOC dataset

is 76.3%, and the unsupervised classification on the PascalVOC2007 training set. The training loss is close to 2.4.

The improved unsupervised clustering algorithm is applied to the unsupervised image classification model. The pre-trained model is used. The batichsize is set to 256, the learning rate lr is set to 0.001, the weight decay is set to 1, and the number of epoch training iterations is set to 400, the mAp obtained by the improved unsupervised classification model trained on the VOC2007 validation set and the loss loss map trained by the pre-training model are as follows (Figs. 15 and 16):

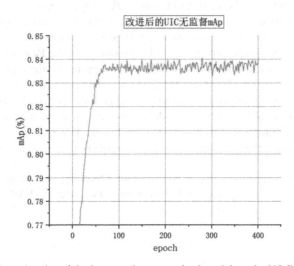

Fig. 15. mAp plot of the improved unsupervised model on the VOC dataset.

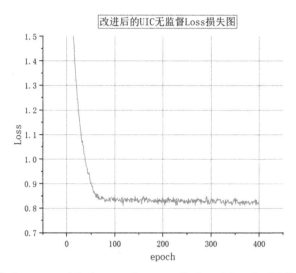

Fig. 16. Loss map of the improved unsupervised model on the VOC dataset

It can be seen from the figure that the model tends to converge after 100 epochs. Recently, under the iteration of 400 epochs, the final model classification accuracy mAp value is 83.9%, and the improved loss loss graph is also close to about 0.8.

5   Conclusion

Based on the unsupervised classification model, this paper improves the unsupervised clustering algorithm, and combines the residual network to obtain an improved unsupervised image classification model, which is trained on the ImageNet dataset without labels, and the learned feature representation Ability to transfer to the Pascal VOC dataset for multi-label classification, fine-tune based on the pre-trained model on the VOC dataset to verify the accuracy of the PASCAL VOC2007 validation set, mAP values of the unsupervised classification model before improvement and unsupervised classification after improvement The mAP values of the model on the validation set are 76.3% and 83.9%, respectively, indicating that the improved algorithm proposed in this paper has certain feasibility to improve the performance of the unsupervised classification model.

Acknowledgment. This work is funded by the National Natural Science Found ation of China under Grant No. 61772180, the Key R & D plan of Hubei Province(2020BAB012).

References

1. Mccallum, A., Nigam, K., Ungar, L.: Efficient clustering of high-dimensional data sets with application to reference matching. In: Proceeding of the Sixth ACM SIGKDD International Conference on Knowledge Discovery and Data Mining, pp. 494–499 (2000).https://doi.org/10.1145/347090.347123

2. Caron, M., Bojanowski, P., Joulin, A., Douze, M.: Deep clustering for unsupervised learning of visual features (2018)
3. Asano, Y., Rupprecht, C., Vedaldi, A.: Selflabelling via simultaneous clustering and representation learning (2020)
4. Doersch, C., Gupta, A., Efros, A.: Unsupervised visual representation learning by context prediction (2015). https://doi.org/10.1109/ICCV.2015.167
5. Donahue, J., Krähenbühl, P., Darrell, T.: Adversarial feature learning (2016)
6. Zhang, R., Isola, P., Efros, A.: Split-brain autoencoders : unsupervised learning by cross-channel prediction, 645–654 (2017). https://doi.org/10.1109/CVPR.2017.76
7. Noroozi, M., Favaro, P.: Unsupervised learning of visual representations by solving Jigsaw puzzles (2016)
8. Gidaris, S., Singh, P., Komodakis, N.: Unsupervised representation learning by predicting image rotations (2018)
9. Huang, J., Dong, Q., Gong, S., Zhu, X.: Unsupervised deep learning by neighbourhood discovery (2019)
10. Zhang, L., Qi, G.-J., Wang, L., Luo, J.: AET vs AED: unsupervised representation learning by auto- encoding transformations rather than data, 2542-2550 (2019). https://doi.org/10.1109/CVPR.2019.00265
11. Feng, Z., Xu, C., Tao, D.: Self-supervised representation learning by rotation feature decoupling (2019)

Partial Attention-Based Direction-Aware Vehicle Re-identification

Yujie Zhou, Caihong Yuan[✉], Chenshuang Su, Mingdong Zou, Xiaoke Zhu, and Wenjuan Liang

School of Computer and Information Engineering, Henan University Henan Engineering Research Center of Intelligent Technology and Application, Henan Province Spatial Information Processing Engineering Technology Research Center, Kaifeng, China
yuanch@henu.edu.cn, whuzxk@whu.edu.cn, 10120085@vip.henu.edu.cn

Abstract. With the rapid development of urban transportation, vehicle re-identification has become a focal point in traffic management and vehicle tracking problems. In order to address the problem of small inter-class similarity among vehicles, previous studies utilize vehicle parsing models to extract local features. Therefore, we introduce the Squeeze-and-Excitation attention mechanism to extract important discriminative information from these local features. Furthermore, we propose a local co-occurrence attention mechanism to represent the proportion of common parts feature matching. To address the issue of large intra-class differences caused by vehicle direction change, we propose a lightweight and effective direction weighted fusion strategy. Experiments on two large datasets show that the proposed algorithm performs competitively.

Keywords: Attention mechanism · Discriminative local feature · Feature alignment

1 Introduction

Vehicle Re-identification (ReID) is an image retrieval problem that aims to find the most similar images in the gallery captured in another camera views. This task plays an important role in intelligent transportation and city surveillance systems [3,23]. For example, the police may quickly lock the suspect's motion trajectory through vehicle re-identification. However, due to the similar color and type, or the same brand, different vehicles may have similar appearance. And affected by different illumination, different vehicle direction, etc. , the same vehicle may look very different in different camera views.

Some previous works learn global feature [1,2,6,13,22,25], but it is difficult to distinguish vehicles solely based on global features. Different vehicles with similar appearances need to be distinguished by subtle differences in local features. Therefore, some works learn both global and local feature. For example, Zhao et al. [20] extracts local features by designing a gradually expanding circular ROI

W. Hong and G. Kanaparan (Eds.): ICCSE 2023, CCIS 2023, pp. 162–172, 2024.
https://doi.org/10.1007/978-981-97-0730-0_15

projection. Liu et al. [11] obtains local features by horizontal splitting the feature map. But simple division of vehicles can result in misalignment issues. Therefore, vehicle ReID must learn vehicle component to capture subtle differences. He et al. [4] uses vehicle predefined regions to learn more discriminative regions. However, this method neglects that discriminative differences between vehicles may appear in any part of the vehicle. Zhang et al. [19] extracts vehicle components using object detection model. This method could achieve more accurate locate information. However, these local features are just simply separated from the global, which may reduce to a suboptimal performance. Therefore, we first use vehicle parsing model to parse the vehicle into four different views (front, back, top, and side), and then introduce the Squeeze-and-Excitation attention mechanism(SE) to learn the important information in the local features. Furthermore, we propose a local co-occurrence attention mechanism(LCA) to discover the proportion of co-occurring parts of two instances, for automatically the importance of each part features, and helping to overcome the challenge of the small differences of similar vehicles in different viewpoints.

Vehicle direction change is a very large challenge, which could make the same vehicle look very different. But vehicle ReID with direction changing is not well studies. For example, Zhu et al. [24] replaces the vehicle ID of a network model with a direction ID to identify the direction. Tang et al. [16] determines the direction through a pose estimation model. Teng et al. [17] designs a multi-view branch network that uses CNN as a viewpoint classifier, each branch learning features specific to a particular viewpoint. Although this method has achieved some success, its disadvantage is that multiple models are complex, training is difficult, and the important information of local features is not fully mined. Some works do not use directional classification model to determine the direction of vehicles. Zhu et al. [22] uses different directional pooling layers to compress the feature maps into horizontal, vertical, diagonal, and anti-diagonal directional feature maps respectively. Finally, these feature maps are spatially normalized and concatenated into four directional deep learning features. Chu et al. [2] divides feature space into similar perspectives and different perspectives, and learns two constraints to improve recognition accuracy. The disadvantages of these methods is neglect the learning of local features. However our method combines global features with local features, fully exploring the important information of local features. We propose a lightweight and effective direction weighted fusion strategy (DF). This strategy determines the similarity of vehicle directions through four components, and automatically adjusts the distance of image features based on their similarity, so as to improve recognition accuracy.

We evaluated our approach on two widely used large vehicle datasets, VehicleID and VeRi776. The experimental results show that our method is competitive. The main contributions of this work can be summarized as follows:

1) We propose a local co-occurrence attention mechanism, which aims to improve the alignment of local features by focusing on the proportion of common parts that appear in two images.
2) We introduce the SE attention mechanism to learn subtle differences in features with greater robustness.
3) We design a direction weighted fusion that determines the vehicle's direction based on its components. This helps to mitigate the re-identification deviation caused by changes in viewpoint.

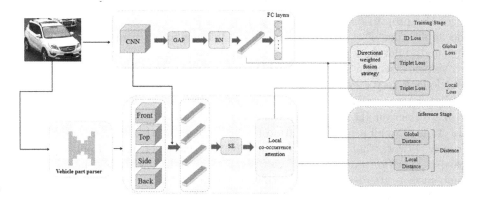

Fig. 1. An overview of the proposed system. It consists of two blocks for global and local feature learning, respectively. "GAP" denotes global average pooling, "BN" denotes batch normalization, and "FC layers" denotes fully connected layers.

2 Methodology

In Sect. 2.1, we show the basic architecture of this paper. In Sect. 2.2, SE attention mechanism is introduced. In Sect. 2.3, local co-occurrence attention mechanism is introduced. Finally, we will introduce the direction weighted fusion strategy in Sect. 2.4.

2.1 Network Architecture

Our network architecture is shown in Fig. 1.

Backbone. We use ResNet50 [5], pre-trained on the ImageNet [15] dataset, as our feature extractor. As shown in Fig. 1, the feature extractor network has two output branches. The first branch is the global branch, which is used to obtain a feature map of the overall appearance of the vehicle. Another branch is the local branch, which obtains local features through vehicle part parser.

2.2 Squeeze-and-Excitation Attention Mechanism

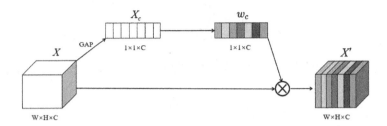

Fig. 2. The structure of SE attention mechanism.

SE attention mechanism is introduced into local branch to enhance the features with a high discriminative degree and suppress the interference of features with a low discriminative degree. This enhancement aims to improve the network's capacity to learn subtle differences. The structure of SE attention module is illustrated in Fig. 2.

The input feature map X is first compressed along the spatial dimension using a global average pooling layer. Then, two FC layers are used to calculate the weight for each feature channel. Finally, the learned features weights w_c of each channel are multiplied by X to obtain a new feature map X'. The SE attention mechanism is formulated as follows.

$$X_c = GAP(X) = \frac{1}{H \times W} \sum_i^H \sum_j^W X(i,j) \tag{1}$$

$$w_c = \sigma_2(w_2 \sigma_1(w_1 X_c)) \tag{2}$$

$$X' = w_c \bullet X \tag{3}$$

GAP is the global average pooling, w_1 and w_1 are the weight parameters of the two fully connected layers, and σ_1 and σ_2 are the ReLU and Sigmoid activation functions, respectively.

2.3 Local Co-occurrence Attention Mechanism

The local branch is designed with local co-occurrence attention to achieve local features alignment, avoiding the features mismatch problem.

Firstly, We use ResNet50 to obtain a $16 \times 16 \times 2048$ feature map F. Secondly, we pool vehicle parsing mask to 16×16 by max pooling, which is defined as $\{M_i | i \in \{1,2,3,4\}\}$. Thirdly, We multiply F with the mask to obtain local features $\{f_i | i \in \{1,2,3,4\}\}$. They represent the front, back, side, and top views of the car.

Given two images p, q and their masks M_i^p and M_i^q, we calculate the visible scores v_i^p and v_i^q for each part, which represent the size of each region of the part. The visible score v_i is defined as

$$v_i = \sum_{j,k=1}^{16} M_i(j,k) \tag{4}$$

We compute the matching score $C_i^{p,q}$ as follows.

$$C_i^{p,q} = \frac{\frac{v_i^p v_i^q}{|v_i^p - v_i^q|}}{\sum_{i=1}^{N} \frac{v_i^p v_i^q}{|v_i^p - v_i^q|}} \tag{5}$$

where $C_i^{p,q}$ measures the matching scores of each corresponding component of the two images. N is the number of local features. Then, the distance of local features $\hat{D}_l^{p,q}$ between the two vehicles is calculated as

$$\hat{D}_l^{p,q} = \sum_{i=1}^{N} C_i^{p,q} D\left(f_i^p, f_i^q\right) \tag{6}$$

where D denotes the Euclidean distance. If there are missing parts of the vehicle, the corresponding area visible score will be relatively small, resulting in a low matching score. A higher matching score indicates a larger proportion of the matched area. In this paper, we optimize the network by constructing ID loss and triplet loss for global feature, as well as triplet loss for local features. The triplet loss of local features is calculated as.

$$L_{triplet}^l = max(\hat{D}_l^{ap} - \hat{D}_l^{an} + \gamma, 0) \tag{7}$$

2.4   Direction Weighted Fusion Strategy

To correct the bias caused by the viewpoint and to better expand the role of local features, we propose a direction weighted fusion strategy.

$w^{p,q}$ denotes the direction similarity between two vehicle images and is defined as follows.

$$w^{p,q} = \frac{\sum_{i=1}^{N} f\left(\frac{v_i^p}{v_i^q}\right)}{\sigma} \tag{8}$$

$$f(x) = \begin{cases} \frac{1}{x} & \text{if } x > 1 \\ x & \text{otherwise} \end{cases} \tag{9}$$

The larger the direction similarity w^{pq} is, the closer the two vehicles are. For Eq. (8), we experimentally conclude that it works best when $\sigma = 6$. Then, the global feature distance between the two vehicles is calculated D as following,

$$\hat{D}_g^{p,q} = w^{p,q} D\left(f^p, f^q\right) \tag{10}$$

The triplet loss of the global feature is computed from the distance of the above global feature as:

$$L^g_{triplet} = max(\hat{D}^{ap}_g - \hat{D}^{an}_g + \gamma, 0) \tag{11}$$

Finally, the total loss in this paper contains the following loss functions:

$$L = L^g_{id} + L^g_{triplet} + L^l_{triplet} \tag{12}$$

3   Experiments

3.1   Datasets

We evaluate our model on two popular vehicle datasets, including VeRi776 and VehicleID.

VeRi776 [12] is the benchmark dataset for the vehicle task. It consists of about 50,000 images of 776 vehicles captured by 20 cameras with different viewpoints. The training set contains 576 vehicles and the test set contains another 200 vehicles.

VehicleID [9] is a large-scale vehicle re-identification benchmark dataset. It contains a total of 221,763 images of about 26,267 vehicles. The images in the dataset are taken in either front or back view. Three test sets, small, medium, and large, are extracted based on size of the test set. In the inference phase, one image is randomly selected for each car as a gallery set, and other images are used as query images.

3.2   Implementation Details

We train models for 120 epochs with warm-up strategy. The initial learning rate is 3.5e-5 and increases to 3.5e-4 after the 10th calendar element. We first fill the image boundary with 10 pixels and then randomly crop it to 256×256. We also augment the data by random erasure using Adam as the optimizer.

To evaluate our method, we first compute the Euclidean distance $\hat{D}_{gloabal}$ between global features. Then, we compute the distance $\hat{D}_{local}$ between the local features defined in Eq. 6. The final distance between the query set and the gallery set is computed as $\lambda_1 \hat{D}_{gloabal} + \lambda_2 \hat{D}_{local}$. Here, we set $\lambda_1 = 1$ and $\lambda_2 = 0.5$.

3.3   Experiments on VeRi776 Dataset

We evaluate our method on the VeRi776 dataset. Table 1 shows the performance comparison between our proposed method and other methods. In the Baseline method, LCA, SE attention, and DF are removed. From the results, it can be seen that recent mainstream vehicle ReId methods combine the learning of global and local features, which greatly improves their effectiveness on the VeRi776 dataset. Compared with the baseline, our method improves by 4.1% on mAP, and 1.8 % on CMC@1. Other than that, our method improves both mAP and CMC@1 over the other methods, and CMC@5 improves over the majority of other methods.

Table 1. The mAP, CMC@1 and CMC@5 on VeRi776

Method	mAp	CMC@1	CMC@5
FACT [12]	0.185	0.510	0.735
OIFE [18]	0.480	0.894	-
VAMI [21]	0.501	0.770	0.908
PROVID [13]	0.534	0.816	0.951
EALN [14]	0.574	0.844	0.941
AAVER [7]	0.612	0.890	0.947
RAM [10]	0.615	0.886	0.940
VANET [2]	0.663	0.897	0.959
PAMTRI [16]	0.718	0.929	0.970
PRN [4]	0.743	0.943	**0.989**
PGAN [19]	0.793	0.965	0.983
SAVER [8]	0.796	0.964	0.986
Baseline	0.759	0.948	0.978
Ours	**0.800**	**0.966**	0.982

3.4   Experiments on VehicleID Dataset

We compare the scores of CMC@1 and CMC@5 on this dataset because there is only one ground truth for each query vehicle. Table 2 gives the comparison results for three different sizes of test datasets. In the Baseline method, LCA, SE attention, and DF are removed. We observed that, when the scale is small, our method improves the CMC@1 by 1.3% compared to the baseline. At a medium scale, our approach achieves 6% and 4% improvement over baseline at CMC@1 and CMC@5, respectively. At a large scale, our approach improved 7.7% and 6.1% over baseline at CMC@1 and CMC@5, respectively. Compared to other methods, our method is superior to the majority of other methods. The above comparison result proves that our method is effective in not only improving retrieval accuracy but also enhancing the capacity to identify more challenging samples.

4   Ablation Study

4.1   The Effects of Key Components

In this section, we perform ablation experiments to evaluate the contribution of each part. LCA is the local co-occurrence attention mechanism, SE is the SE attention mechanism added to local branches, and DF is the direction weighted fusion strategy. The baseline is to remove LCA, SE attention mechanism, and DF. The effectiveness of each part is shown in Table 3.

Table 2. The CMC@1 and CMC@5 on VehicleID

Method	small		medium		large	
	@1	@5	@1	@5	@1	@5
OIFE [18]	–	–	–	–	0.670	0.829
VAMI [21]	0.631	0.833	0.529	0.751	0.473	0.703
AAVER [7]	0.747	0.938	0.686	0.900	0.635	0.856
EALN [14]	0.751	0.881	0.718	0.839	0.693	0.814
RAM [10]	0.752	0.915	0.723	0.870	0.677	0.845
PRN [4]	0.784	0.923	0.750	0.883	0.742	0.864
SAVER [8]	0.799	0.952	0.776	0.911	0.753	0.883
PGAN [19]	–	–	–	–	0.778	0.921
VANET [2]	**0.881**	**0.972**	0.831	0.951	0.803	0.929
Baseline	0.821	0.962	0.779	0.927	0.758	0.904
Ouers	0.834	0.964	**0.839**	**0.967**	**0.835**	**0.965**

Table 3. Ablation study about each part on VeRi776

settings	mAP	CMC@1	CMC@5
Baseline	0.759	0.948	0.978
+LCA	0.794	0.956	0.979
+SE	0.794	0.964	0.979
+LCA+SE	0.796	0.958	**0.985**
+LCA+SE+DF	**0.800**	**0.966**	0.982

Compared to the baseline, the separate local co-occurrence attention mechanism and the addition of the SE attention mechanism both increased mAP by 3.5%. When learning features together with local co-occurrence attention and SE attention, the mAP accuracy increased by 3.7% and CMC@1 by 1%. On the basis of the above results, adding DF, the map increased by 0.4% and CMC@1 increased by 0.8%. The result indicates that the designed parts can effectively identify discriminative features and improve the accuracy of recognition.

5   Qualitative Analysis

Figure 3 shows the qualitative results of our method on the VeRi776 dataset, where the top 5 predictions are contained in the corresponding query image. Our method is better able to retrieve the correct image when the query image is in a different viewpoint from the target image. Also our method recognizes the correct image when the image appears to be occluded. This shows that our proposed method can better match local features and reduce the effect of viewpoint on recognition compared to the baseline.

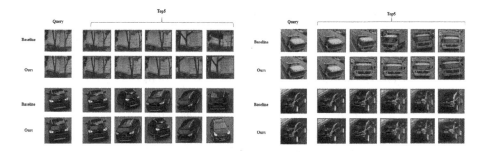

Fig. 3. Visualization of the ranking list on VeRi776. The images in the first column are query images. The remaining images are retrieved from the top 5 ranking results. The correctly retrieved images are indicated by a green border, while false instances are indicated by a red border. (Color figure online)

6   Conclusion

In this article, we propose a new features learning framework. This framework combines global features and local features based on vehicle parsers for joint learning. The Squeeze-and-Excitation attention mechanism is introduced to extract distinctive local features. For the matching of local features, local co-occurrence attention mechanism is designed to better measure the matching of vehicle parts. To reduce the impact of orientation on recognition accuracy, we propose a direction weighted fusion strategy. We evaluate our method on two large-scale vehicle ReID datasets. Experimental results demonstrate the effectiveness of our method.

Acknowledgment. This work was supported by the Young Scientists Fund of the National Natural Science Foundation of China (No. 62006070), and partly supported by Key Scientific and Technological Project of Henan Province of China (Nos. 222102210197,222102210204,232102211013 and 222102210238).

References

1. Chen, X., Sui, H., Fang, J., Feng, W., Zhou, M.: Vehicle re-identification using distance-based global and partial multi-regional feature learning. IEEE Trans. Intell. Transp. Syst. **22**(2), 1276–1286 (2021). https://doi.org/10.1109/TITS.2020. 2968517
2. Chu, R., Sun, Y., Li, Y., Liu, Z., Zhang, C., Wei, Y.: Vehicle re-identification with viewpoint-aware metric learning. In: 2019 IEEE/CVF International Conference on Computer Vision (ICCV), pp. 8281–8290 (2019). https://doi.org/10.1109/ICCV. 2019.00837
3. Guo, H., Zhao, C., Liu, Z., Wang, J., Lu, H.: Learning coarse-to-fine structured feature embedding for vehicle re-identification. In: Proceedings of the Thirty-Second AAAI Conference on Artificial Intelligence and Thirtieth Innovative Applications of Artificial Intelligence Conference and Eighth AAAI Symposium on Educational Advances in Artificial Intelligence. AAAI'18/IAAI'18/EAAI'18, AAAI Press (2018)

4. He, B., Li, J., Zhao, Y., Tian, Y.: Part-regularized near-duplicate vehicle re-identification. In: 2019 IEEE/CVF Conference on Computer Vision and Pattern Recognition (CVPR), pp. 3992–4000 (2019). https://doi.org/10.1109/CVPR.2019.00412

5. He, K., Zhang, X., Ren, S., Sun, J.: Deep residual learning for image recognition. In: 2016 IEEE Conference on Computer Vision and Pattern Recognition (CVPR), pp. 770–778 (2016). https://doi.org/10.1109/CVPR.2016.90

6. Huynh, S.V., Nguyen, N.H., Nguyen, N.T., Nguyen, Q.V., Huynh, C., Nguyen, C.: A strong baseline for vehicle re-identification. In: 2021 IEEE/CVF Conference on Computer Vision and Pattern Recognition Workshops (CVPRW), pp. 4142–4149 (2021). https://doi.org/10.1109/CVPRW53098.2021.00468

7. Khorramshahi, P., Kumar, A., Peri, N., Rambhatla, S.S., Chen, J.C., Chellappa, R.: A dual-path model with adaptive attention for vehicle re-identification. In: 2019 IEEE/CVF International Conference on Computer Vision (ICCV), pp. 6131–6140 (2019). https://doi.org/10.1109/ICCV.2019.00623

8. Khorramshahi, P., Peri, N., Chen, J.c., Chellappa, R.: The devil is in the details: self-supervised attention for vehicle re-identification. In: Computer Vision - ECCV 2020, pp. 369–386 (2020)

9. Liu, H., Tian, Y., Wang, Y., Pang, L., Huang, T.: Deep relative distance learning: tell the difference between similar vehicles. In: 2016 IEEE Conference on Computer Vision and Pattern Recognition (CVPR), pp. 2167–2175 (2016). https://doi.org/10.1109/CVPR.2016.238

10. Liu, X., Zhang, S., Huang, Q., Gao, W.: Ram: a region-aware deep model for vehicle re-identification. In: 2018 IEEE International Conference on Multimedia and Expo (ICME), pp. 1–6 (2018). https://doi.org/10.1109/ICME.2018.8486589

11. Liu, X., Zhang, S., Wang, X., Hong, R., Tian, Q.: Group-group loss-based global-regional feature learning for vehicle re-identification. IEEE Trans. Image Process. **29**, 2638–2652 (2020). https://doi.org/10.1109/TIP.2019.2950796

12. Liu, X., Liu, W., Ma, H., Fu, H.: Large-scale vehicle re-identification in urban surveillance videos. In: 2016 IEEE International Conference on Multimedia and Expo (ICME), pp. 1–6 (2016). https://doi.org/10.1109/ICME.2016.7553002

13. Liu, X., Liu, W., Mei, T., Ma, H.: PROVID: progressive and multimodal vehicle reidentification for large-scale urban surveillance. IEEE Trans. Multimedia **20**(3), 645–658 (2018). https://doi.org/10.1109/TMM.2017.2751966

14. Lou, Y., Bai, Y., Liu, J., Wang, S., Duan, L.Y.: Embedding adversarial learning for vehicle re-identification. IEEE Trans. Image Process. **28**(8), 3794–3807 (2019). https://doi.org/10.1109/TIP.2019.2902112

15. Russakovsky, O., et al.: ImageNet large scale visual recognition challenge. Int. J. Comput. Vis. (IJCV) **115**(3), 211–252 (2015). https://doi.org/10.1007/s11263-015-0816-y

16. Tang, Z., et al.: PAMTRI: pose-aware multi-task learning for vehicle re-identification using highly randomized synthetic data. In: 2019 IEEE/CVF International Conference on Computer Vision (ICCV), pp. 211–220 (2019). https://doi.org/10.1109/ICCV.2019.00030

17. Teng, S., Zhang, S., Huang, Q., Sebe, N.: Multi-view spatial attention embedding for vehicle re-identification. IEEE Trans. Circuits Syst. Video Technol. **31**(2), 816–827 (2021). https://doi.org/10.1109/TCSVT.2020.2980283

18. Wang, Z., et al.: Orientation invariant feature embedding and spatial temporal regularization for vehicle re-identification. In: 2017 IEEE International Conference on Computer Vision (ICCV), pp. 379–387 (2017). https://doi.org/10.1109/ICCV.2017.49

19. Zhang, X., Zhang, R., Cao, J., Gong, D., You, M., Shen, C.: Part-guided attention learning for vehicle re-identification. ArXiv abs/1909.06023 (2019)
20. Zhao, J., Zhao, Y., Li, J., Yan, K., Tian, Y.: Heterogeneous relational complement for vehicle re-identification. In: 2021 IEEE/CVF International Conference on Computer Vision (ICCV), pp. 205–214 (2021). https://doi.org/10.1109/ICCV48922.2021.00027
21. Zhouy, Y., Shao, L.: Viewpoint-aware attentive multi-view inference for vehicle re-identification. In: 2018 IEEE/CVF Conference on Computer Vision and Pattern Recognition, pp. 6489–6498 (2018). https://doi.org/10.1109/CVPR.2018.00679
22. Zhu, J., Zeng, H., Huang, J., Liao, S., Lei, Z., Cai, C., Zheng, L.: Vehicle re-identification using quadruple directional deep learning features. IEEE Trans. Intell. Transp. Syst. **21**(1), 410–420 (2020). https://doi.org/10.1109/TITS.2019.2901312
23. Zhu, W., Hu, R., Wang, Z., Li, D., Gao, X.: Tell the truth from the front: anti-disguise vehicle re-identification. In: 2020 IEEE International Conference on Multimedia and Expo (ICME), pp. 1–6 (2020). https://doi.org/10.1109/ICME46284.2020.9102939
24. Zhu, X., Luo, Z., Fu, P., Ji, X.: VOC-ReLD: vehicle re-identification based on vehicle-orientation-camera. In: 2020 IEEE/CVF Conference on Computer Vision and Pattern Recognition Workshops (CVPRW), pp. 2566–2573 (2020). https://doi.org/10.1109/CVPRW50498.2020.00309
25. Zhuge, C., Peng, Y., Li, Y., Ai, J., Chen, J.: Attribute-guided feature extraction and augmentation robust learning for vehicle re-identification. In: 2020 IEEE/CVF Conference on Computer Vision and Pattern Recognition Workshops (CVPRW), pp. 2632–2637 (2020). https://doi.org/10.1109/CVPRW50498.2020.00317

A Deep Learning-Based Method for Classroom Crowd Counting and Localization

Qin Ding[1] 🄳 and Chunyan Yu[2(✉)] 🄳

[1] Anhui University of Science and Technology, Anhui, China
[2] Chuzhou University, Anhui, China
yuchy@chzu.edu.cn

Abstract. In order to count the students' seating distribution and attendance in offline classroom, which is a better response to the students' learning and teaching situation. Based on the deep learning method, we propose a crowd localization and counting model for students' seating area in offline classroom. Firstly, we choose YOLOv8 to improve it, adding the SENet attention module after the backbone network reinforce the role of important channels and speed up model learning, designing a simple and efficient feature fusion method, using the anchor size and the number of detected heads which are more suitable for classroom scenarios and compute the overall loss of the model by using the loss of confidence and the loss of regression of prediction frames. Enhancement methods with Mosaic and cutout data to increase the generalization ability of the model. The improved network achieved 95.405% precision, 92.808% recall and 96.159% mAP on SCUT-HEAD Dataset and C University Dataset.

Keywords: Crowd Localization · Crowd Counting · Seating Distribution

1 Introduction

In all kinds of teaching activities, face-to-face offline teaching is still the most dominant form of teaching, and student attendance and seat distribution better reflect the learning situation of students and the teaching situation of teachers. However, in this scenario, both the answering and software check-in methods will take up the classroom time and affect the teacher's teaching. Therefore, utilizing surveillance video in the classroom is an effective and convenient way to take attendance. In addition, this method can quickly and significantly mark the position of students in the classroom, and obtain the seating distribution of students, and many studies have shown that classroom seating distribution has a great relationship with students' motivation in class, participation [1], interaction intensity [2] and so on.

Classroom crowd estimation under camera has the following challenges: (1) The size of head scale varies, the target sitting in the front row close to the camera is larger, while the head scale of students in the back row is very small, and it is often easy to miss or misdetect the target during detection. (2) High level of shelter, the distribution of students in the classroom environment is relatively dense, and high occlusion is easy to occur

W. Hong and G. Kanaparan (Eds.): ICCSE 2023, CCIS 2023, pp. 173–184, 2024.
https://doi.org/10.1007/978-981-97-0730-0_16

due to the inconsistency of each student's movements such as raising and lowering their heads. Highly overlapping targets have similar features and are difficult to distinguish during detection. (3) Blurred images, affected by hardware equipment, the cameras in most universities do not have high pixels. Especially for students sitting at the back position, the camera can only illuminate the outline of the human head, which is difficult to judge even with the naked eye in scenes with darker background environment such as desks.

Combining the existing methods and the above problems, the main work and contributions of this paper are as follows: (1) Designing a new feature fusion method, which can accelerate the model convergence speed and improve the model accuracy. (2) Proposing a crowd estimation model for classroom environments, which is used to detect the number and location of students in the classroom to assist teachers in attendance and teaching analysis.

2   Related Work

Deep learning based methods for crowd estimation can be categorized into two types: detection-based methods and map-based methods.

2.1   Detection-Based Methods

The detection method of crowd estimation is the application of target detection on heads. The method first detects the each head in the image and then counts it. In recent years, [3] employs a multi-column architecture with top-down feature modulation, which allows the network to jointly process multi-scale information, facilitating the network's ability to accurately locate people's heads. In particular, the bounding box of each head can be predicted with only point labeling information. Since the YOLO model is a target detection model for a wide range of applicable scenarios, many people choose to improve the YOLO model for head detection e.g., [4] used a modified yolov4 model for head detection and counting, which prevent the occurrence of missed detection by attenuating the score of adjacent detection frames. [5] proposed a self-training method that uses point annotations to directly supervise object centroids which makes data annotation faster. However, the method has high sensitivity to the annotation point density and is more suitable for scenes with uniform target distribution.

2.2   Map-Based Methods

The map-based methods refers to the transformation of the head estimation problem into a density map estimation problem. This method does not need to detect each person explicitly. [6] calculates the loss of pairs of density maps at different scales to achieve multi-scale head estimation, and fuses the density maps at different scales to improve the accuracy and stability of head estimation. Apart from this, a multi-task learning approach is used to obtain both the number and location information of the headcounts, which leads to a more comprehensive understanding of the crowd distribution. [7] introduces a deep prior to improve the accuracy of crowd localization and counting. The depth prior can provide additional information about the size and location of heads, thus helping the model to better understand the crowd scene. At the same time the method relies on depth information to assist in the localization and counting of heads. This means that without reliable depth information, the method may not be able to accurately localize and count heads. This limits its applicability on certain scenarios or devices. In [8], a topological constraint is proposed to address topological errors in crowd localization, and to enforce the constraint, a novel persistence loss based on persistent homotopy theory is proposed.

The existing deep learning based crowd estimation algorithms are improved to address the problems of existing methods and crowd estimation in classroom environments. The main improvements are (1) using smaller and denser anchors to alleviate the problem of model miss-detection and mis-detection on small targets, occlusion, and fuzzy problems. (2) Use bilateral three-path fusion of information from deep semantic features, shallow texture features, and mid-level features, and use anchor of two scales and three aspect ratios to detect heads of different scales and poses. (3) Add the SENet module after feature extraction to allow the model to focus on the features of the important channels to speed up learning and improve model accuracy.

3 Proposed Method

In order to solve the problem of high occlusion, multi-scale and low resolution problem of targets in classroom environment, this paper uses deep learning method to detect the number and location of students. The network structure in this paper refers to the feature extraction method of YOLOv8 and uses the SENet attention mechanism to strengthen the role of important features and weaken the role of background features. A bilateral three-path aggregation network is designed for feature fusion, fusing features from different sensory fields, and two detection heads are used to detect multi-scale targets in the classroom scene. The overall network structure is shown in Fig. 1.

The model firstly resizes the incoming image to 640*640 using non-distortion way, and then downsamples the image once, after which the image features are extracted using four C2F and downsampling operations, in which we obtain feature maps of three scales, i.e. $S_1 = 1/8$, $S_2 = 1/16$, and $S_3 = 1/32$ of the original image size. The C2F structure is a feature extraction module with residual structure in YOLOv8, which ensures lightweight while obtaining richer gradient flow information. Then, using the SENet module to respectively preprocess the S_1, S_2, S_3 features layers to enhance the important feature channels, and obtain the E_1, E_2, E_3 which are the same size as the input. The E_1, E_2, and E_3 feature layers are then fused using a bilateral three-path aggregation network. Finally, we get 20×20 size feature layer and 80×80 size feature layer, and use these two feature layers for head detection, the large feature layer is used mainly to detect small scale targets that are far away from the camera and the small feature layer is used mainly to detect large targets that are close to the camera.

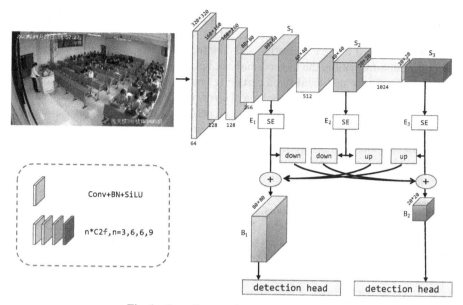

Fig. 1. Overall network architecture design

3.1 SENet Module

Since the model obtains a large number of features in the feature extraction stage, some features have important contributions to the model goal, while some features have smaller contributions, so before feature fusion, the SENet [9] module is added after each of the S_1, S_2, S_3 feature maps respectively, to speed up the model learning speed and to increase the detection accuracy. SENet is a lightweight network that considers the relationship between feature channels and automatically acquires the importance of each feature channel by learning to enhance the features that are important to the current task or suppress the unimportant features. SENet realizes the above functions by Squeeze module and Exciation module. The structure of SENet module is shown in Fig. 2.

The SENet module use global pooling for the three scales of the feature special to get $1 \times 1 \times 256$, $1 \times 1 \times 512$, and $1 \times 1 \times 1024$ feature layers, respectively, and then goes through a fully-connected layer to reduce the c channels of the model to c/r channels to reduce the amount of computation, using the ReLU activation function, and the second fully-connected layer serves to recover the number of channels, and the Sigmoid function is used to limit the range of values between 0 and 1, which is equivalent to the weights of the feature layer. Finally, the weights are multiplied with the original feature layer to get the new feature layer.

3.2 Feature Fusion Module for Bilateral Three-Path Module

Bilateral three-path aggregation module is uesd to fuse the global and local information of different sensory fields on the shallow, middle and deep networks. Firstly, the E_3 feature layer is up-sampled by 4 times and the E_2 feature layer is up-sampled by 2 times,

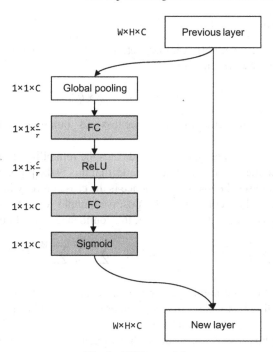

Fig. 2. SENet module

and the two obtained feature layers are fused with the E_1 feature layer to obtain B_1 feature layer of 80×80 size, which fuses the information of each layer. Then the E_1 feature layer is downsampled by 4 times, the feature layer of E_2 is downsampled by 2 times, and the obtained result is fused with the E_3 feature layer to obtain B_2 feature layer of 20×20 size, which fuses the information of each layer. The feature fusion module for bilateral three-path is shown in the Fig. 3.

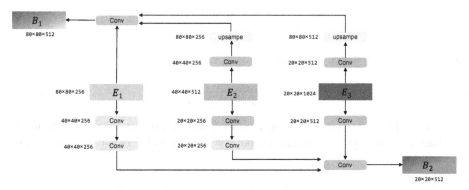

Fig. 3. Feature fusion module for bilateral three-path module. The convolution of the gray squares indicates downsampling, and the convolution of the blue squares indicates channel count adjustment.

3.3 Loss Function

The loss function of this network is jointly determined by confidence loss and bounding box loss, the loss function formula is

$$Loss = \alpha * bbox_{loss} + \beta * obj_{loss} \tag{1}$$

where α and β are the proportion of confidence loss and bounding box loss, respectively, 1 and 0.1.

The confidence of each bounding box indicates the reliability of this bounding box, the larger the value means that the model thinks that this is the probability of the target is larger. The model uses the loss of confidence is the cross-entropy loss, the confidence loss of the bounding box consists of the positive sample loss of confidence and the negative sample loss of confidence together, the confidence of the bounding box is

$$obj_{loss} = \sum_{i=0}^{K*K} \sum_{j=0}^{M} I_{ij}^{obj}[log(C_i)] + \sum_{i=0}^{K*K} \sum_{j=0}^{M} I_{ij}^{noobj}[log(C_i)] \tag{2}$$

k is the grid size, M is the number of predefined anchors for each grid, I_{ij}^{obj} indicates whether the bounding box is a positive sample or not, when it is a positive sample, the change of value takes 1, otherwise it is 0.

The bounding box loss is a measure of how much the predicted box overlaps with the real box in target detection, the bounding box loss used in this paper is CIoU [10]. It is given by the formula

$$bbox_{loss} = \sum_{i=0}^{K*K} \sum_{j=0}^{M} I_{ij}^{obj} L_{CIoU} \tag{3}$$

$$L_{CIoU} 1 - IoU + \frac{\rho^2(b, \widehat{b})}{c^2} + \alpha v \tag{4}$$

v is used to measure the consistency of the aspect ratio and it is expressed as

$$v = \frac{4}{\pi^2}(arctan\frac{\widehat{w}}{\widehat{h}} - arctan\frac{w}{h})^2 \tag{5}$$

α is the weight parameter, which has the expression

$$\alpha = \frac{v}{(1 - IoU) + v} \tag{6}$$

CIoU considers the distance and aspect ratio similarity between target and anchor on the basis of traditional IoU, which is more consistent with the target frame regression mechanism.

4 Experiment

4.1 Experimental Environment and Parameter Settings

Three anchors with different aspect ratios are set for each detector head to detect heads with different postures, and the preset anchor sizes for the two detector heads are [12,12, 14,17, 22,33] and [22,22, 25,32, 35,52]. Momentum is set to 0.937 and the number of iteration rounds is set to 200. The initial learning rate is 0.01, and the learning rate is dynamically adjusted during training based on the loss value of the model and the performance of the validation set. When the loss value of the model decreases or the performance of the validation set improves, the learning rate will decrease accordingly; while when the loss value of the model increases or the performance of the validation set decreases, the learning rate will increase accordingly. This allows the model to converge more stably and efficiently during the training process.

4.2 Experimental Dataset and Preprocessing

The data used in this experiment are (1) SCUT-HEAD Dataset [11], which contains two parts, PartA and PartB, with a total of 4342 images, PartA has a total of 2,000 camera data of a university, and PartB has 2342 images of students. (2) Surveillance data of 48 sections of eight classes in the last semester of 2023 in C University. For each class, 12 frames of images are extracted at regular intervals during class time, resulting in a cumulative total of 572 images. Consequently, the experiment utilizes a combined dataset of 4,914 images.

The SCUT-HEAD dataset encompasses a wide range of authentic student classroom scenarios, including diverse classroom surveillance camera data from different class-rooms and time periods, as well as online classroom images from various contexts. The dataset exhibits a varied distribution of target quantities, ranging from 0 to 162, and encompasses images of varying sizes, ranging from 228×166 to 6280×4710 pixels. Notably, the image size distribution demonstrates a balanced representation across the dataset. Additionally, the C University dataset specifically focuses on classroom surveil-lance camera data from C University, with each image uniformly sized at 1920×1080 pixels. These comprehensive datasets effectively capture the complexities of real-world student classroom environments, encompassing diverse angles, crowd densities, lighting conditions, resolutions, and classroom settings. This rich and diverse collection of data serves as a valuable resource for academic research and analysis in the field.

In this experiment, Mosaic [12] and cutout [13] method data enhancement methods are used to increase the generalization ability of the model.

Mosaic is a data enhancement technique commonly used in target detection tasks. It generates new training samples by stitching several different images together. Specif-ically, the Mosaic data enhancement method stitches together four randomly selected images in a certain ratio to form a new synthetic image. At the same time, the correspond-ing target frames need to be adjusted and transformed accordingly. In this way, more diverse and complex training samples can be generated by the Mosaic data enhance-ment method, which provides more perspective and background changes and enhances the generalization ability of the model. Mosaic data enhancement makes the training samples have more diversity and complexity, provides more background information, and enhances the generalization ability of the model. This helps the model to better adapt to various scenarios and changes.

The Cutout data enhancement method is a simulated random occlusion data enhancement method that improves the generalization ability of the model by cutting out random rectangular regions in the image during the training process. Specifically, Cutout randomly selects some pixels in the image and sets them to zero. There exists a 50% probability that the erased rectangular region is not exactly in the original image. The Cutout method does not have non-informative pixels during training and does not require the generation of additional images to increase the size of the training set as compared to traditional data enhancement methods. Therefore no extra cost is incurred during training. The results of training using Mosaic and Cutout methods are shown in Fig. 4.

Fig. 4. Mosaic and Cutout. Using the Mosaic data enhancement method, four plots are randomly cropped and put together into a single plot, and the different colored and sized squares in the plot are the effect of Cutout data enhancement.

4.3 Experimental Results and Comparison

The experiments in this paper use precision, recall, regression frame loss, confidence loss and mAP to measure the model detection performance.

Precision: the proportion of correctly detected samples to the total detected samples, the formula is

$$P = \frac{TP}{TP + FP} \tag{7}$$

Recall: the proportion of samples predicted to be positive to the actual positive samples, the formula is

$$R = \frac{TP}{TP + FN} \tag{8}$$

mAP: AP is the average value of accuracy under equal interval recall rate, describing the overall situation of accuracy under different recall rates, which is used to react to the global performance of the model. The larger the value of AP, the higher the model accuracy, mAP is the average value of accuracy for each category, there is only one category in this paper, so AP is the same as mAP, and the formula is

$$AP = \int_0^1 P(R)dR \tag{9}$$

$$mAP = \frac{\Sigma AP}{n} \tag{10}$$

The regression frame loss, confidence loss formulas are shown in (2) and (3).

In order to find the most suitable size of detection head for the classroom scenario, we did a comparison test using three different combinations of heads. The detection effect of three different scale combinations of detection heads are shown in Table 1.

Table 1. Comparison of the precision and recall of different sizes of detection head.

Size of detection heads	Precision	Recall
40 × 40 and 80 × 80	95.102	91.243
20 × 20 and 40 × 40	93.635	75.147
20 × 20 and 80 × 80	**95.405**	**92.808**

As shown in the table, the best results in terms of precision and recall were achieved using the 20 × 20 and 80 × 80 sized detection heads. From Fig. 5, it can be seen that the 40 × 40 and 80 × 80 detection heads repeat the detection of large scale heads close to the camera, while the 20 × 20 and 40 × 40 detection heads miss many small targets.

Figure 6 shows the variation of regression frame loss and confidence loss for the training and test sets. The bbox loos and confidence loss decreases rapidly in the first 50 rounds, then the training set loss decreases slowly but still into a decreasing trend in the following 150 rounds, but the test set has converged to a straight line with no decreasing trend.

Through the above comparative experiments with different detection head sizes, we have obtained best precision and recall after 200 rounds respectively. The comparison

Fig. 5. The prediction effect of different detection head sizes. The left picture is the prediction effect after 200 rounds of model training corresponding to 40 × 40 and 80 × 80 sized detection heads, the middle picture is the prediction effect after 200 rounds of model training corresponding to 20 × 20 and 40 × 40 sized detection heads. The figure on the right is the prediction effect after 200 rounds of model training corresponding to 40 × 40 and 80 × 80 sized detection heads. These three models are identical except for the different detection head sizes.

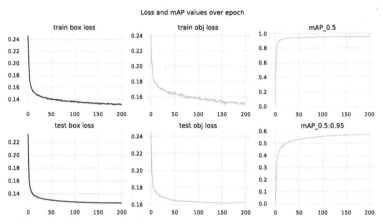

Fig. 6. LOSS and mAP over epoch. The left two plots show the bbox loss for the training and test sets, the center shows the confidence loss for the training and test sets, the top right plot shows the IoU of 0.5 is the mAP value, and the bottom right is the mean value of the mAP when the IoU is from 0.5 to 0.95, with an interval of 0.5.

Table 2. Comparison of precision and recall between our model and YOLOv8 model.

Method	Precision	Recall
YOLOv8	93.429	90.361
Ours	**95.405**	**92.808**

of precision and recall results between our model and YOLOv8 after 200 rounds are shown in Table 2.

Our model has nearly 2% higher precision and 2.5% higher recall than YOLOv8. Since the seat of each person is basically unchanged during a lesson, more C University lesson data can be collected in the future, and for the image frames of the same lesson, we can assist each other's training to further solve the omission detection caused by the occlusion problem.

Through our model, we have successfully extracted the number and spatial coordinates of students at different time intervals within each class. In the subsequent analysis, we aim to calculate the average distance of students from the podium, assess the dispersion of student positions, and investigate potential variations in student engagement across different grades, universitys, and course types. Additionally, we intend to explore the relationship between student motivation and academic performance, leveraging our approach to address the inherent perspective challenges present in the images. Furthermore, we plan to employ tracking algorithms to monitor and analyze the movements of teachers within the classroom, examining their walking routes and the seating arrangements of students in proximity to these routes. This comprehensive analysis will provide valuable insights into classroom dynamics and contribute to a deeper understanding of student-teacher interactions.

5   Conclusion

In order to solve the problem of statistical crowd estimation in the classroom, a model for multi-scale feature fusion based on YOLO algorithm is proposed. Firstly, the backbone network of yolov8 was fine-tuned, and the SEnet module was used to improve the quality of the feature extraction before the special fusion. Then, we replaced the PANnet fusion in the YOLO model by using a bilateral three-path aggregation network. Confidence loss and bounding box regression loss were used to jointly calculate the model loss, and according to the needs of the scene, the anchor and detection head were designed to meet the needs of the classroom scene to detect targets of different scales. Finally, Mosaic and Cutout data enhancement methods were used to increase the generalization ability of the model and the detection ability of occluded targets.

Acknowledgements. The work was supported by science and technology innovation 2030— major project of "New Generation Artificial Intelligence" (2022ZD0115905), the Key Project of Chuzhou University (2022XJZD13) and Anhui University of Science and Technology Graduate Innovation Projects (2023cx2130).

References

1. Yang, X., Zhou, X., Hu, J.: Students' preferences for seating arrangements and their engagement in cooperative learning activities in University English blended learning classrooms in higher education. High. Educ. Res. Dev. **41**(4), 1356–1371 (2022)
2. Juhaňák, L., Cigán, J.: Effects of seating arrangement on students' interaction in group reflective practice. J. Exp. Educ. **91**(2), 249–277 (2023)
3. Sam, D.B., Peri, S.V., Sundararaman, M.N., Kamath, A., Radhakrishnan, V.B.: Locate, size and count: accurately resolving people in dense crowds via detection. In: IEEE Transactions on Pattern Analysis and Machine Intelligence, pp. 2739–2751. IEEE (2020)
4. Zhang, Z., Xia, S., Cai, Y., Yang, C., Zeng, S.: A Soft-YoloV4 for high-performance head detection and counting. Mathematics **9**(23), 3096 (2021)

5. Wang, Y., Hou, J., Hou, X.: A self-training approach for point-supervised object detection and counting in crowds. In: Transactions on Image Processing, pp. 2876–2887. IEEE (2020)
6. Zand, M., Damirchi, H., Farley, A., Molahasani, M., Greenspan, M., Etemad, A.: Multiscale crowd counting and localization by multitask point supervision. In: International Conference on Acoustics, Speech and Signal Processing, pp. 1820–1824. IEEE (2022)
7. Lian, D., Chen, X., Li, J., Luo, W., Gao, S.: Locating and counting heads in crowds with a depth prior. In: Transactions on Pattern Analysis and Machine Intelligence, pp. 9056–9072. IEEE (2021)
8. Abousamra, S., Hoai, M., Samaras, D., Chen, C.: Localization in the crowd with topological constraints. ArXiv, abs/2012.12482 (2020)
9. Hu, J., Shen, L., Sun, G.: Squeeze-and-Excitation Networks. In: 2018 Conference on Computer Vision and Pattern Recognition, pp. 7132–7141. IEEE/CVF (2018)
10. Zheng, Z., et al.: Enhancing geometric factors in model learning and inference for object detection and instance segmentation. In: Transactions on Cybernetics, pp. 8574–8586. IEEE (2021)
11. Peng, D., Sun, Z., Chen, Z., Cai, Z., Xie, L., Jin, L.: Detecting heads using feature refine net and cascaded multiscale architecture. In: International Conference on Pattern Recognition (ICPR), pp. 2528–2533. IEEE (2018)
12. Bochkovskiy, A., Wang, C., Liao, H.M.: YOLOv4: optimal speed and accuracy of object detection. ArXiv, abs/2004.10934 (2020)
13. Devries, T., Taylor, G.W.: Improved Regularization of convolutional neural networks with cutout. ArXiv, abs/1708.04552 (2017)

Use of Computer Vision to Authenticate Retail Invoices with the Convolution-Neural Networks

Aditya Abeysinghe[1], Arundathie Abeysinghe[2], and Sena Seneviratne[3](✉) (iD)

[1] Virtusa Pvt. Ltd., 752 Dr Danister De Silva Mawatha, Colombo 9, Sri Lanka
`arabeysinghe@virtusa.com`
[2] SriLankan Airlines, Colombo, Sri Lanka
[3] Sydney University, Sydney, Australia
`ssen2304@uni.sydney.edu.au`

Abstract. Digital signatures are a new trend when signing electronic documents in shopping cart platforms. The mundane process involves a login application where a user is authenticated using login credentials and then proceeding to a cart application to produce invoices. In this process, a user is required to authenticate invoices created using a digital signature by using a text input. However, intruders could easily impersonate the user by login to the application and creating a digital signature whereby the authorized user is responsible for invoices created. This impersonation process has caused several breaches in the confidentiality of data. Therefore, this research proposes a system that uses the webcam image of a user in the invoice producing process. The image gathered is validated as a human using a convolutional neural network and then a watermark is created using the system's date and added to the invoice instead of the current digital signature mechanism. Results demonstrated that the performance of invoice creation was high and less CPU and time was required under high brightness.

Keywords: Human-Computer Interaction · Digital authentication · Computer Vision · Face recognition · Convolutional Neural Networks

1 Introduction

E-Commerce has been the new trend in consumer purchases worldwide. Early E-Commerce platforms were maintained with web apps and over the last decade. These applications have diversified into web apps, mobile apps and desktop apps. Most E-Commerce companies expose data providers including API endpoints with which these app types interact. As the same backend is used using these APIs, a user can simply login to the website application, select items to buy and use a mobile app to make purchases. Desktop applications are a new arena in the technology domain. The advantage of desktop apps is that these do not specify a URL (Uniform Resource Locator) and is more secure compared with that of web applications.

Security of these E-Commerce applications are ensured by encrypted communication with the central server and using hashing mechanisms for authentication. A user

W. Hong and G. Kanaparan (Eds.): ICCSE 2023, CCIS 2023, pp. 185–193, 2024.
https://doi.org/10.1007/978-981-97-0730-0_17

authenticated is granted privileges based on their authorization level and can make purchases given their valid transaction details. However, intruders could impersonate users and hack into systems commonly using techniques such as SQL (Structured Query Language) injection or brute force attacks. Desktop applications are somewhat secure as they are difficult to be accessed remotely. However, they are prone to risks of intrusion given current malware methods, which include backdoors or Trojan horses, can place scripts or files that provide access to a remote machine once connected to the internet.

In any E-Commerce application, sessions are maintained to specify which user integrates with the system. Once intrusion is made to the system, the impersonator could use this caveat to create an invoice as if the legitimate user created it. The legitimate user is charged and scams could be made to recover information submitted by this third-party. Therefore, there exists a need for proper authentication not only during the initial login stage but also during the invoice preparation stage to properly specify which user interacts with the system. Traditional approach to sign a document electronically is using a digital signature of the user. However, if the digital signature were hacked by the intruder, authentication could be easily made to create a valid request to generate an invoice. Therefore, an alternative, such as with biometric characteristics, is required to validate the request [1]. Therefore, this research proposes a system that requires a webcam image along with a watermark as a digital authentication mechanism in invoice creation to properly authenticate the user submitting the request for purchase.

2   Literature Review

Several researches in the domain of biometric authentication have been performed to enhance security of different platforms. For example, Trusted Platform Module (TPM) has been popular as an external device used for authentication. However, [2–4] reported a security breach of a TPM module that resulted in expose of encryption keys. Another research [4] proposed the use of TPM for strong authentication. The main issue with this technique is the requirement of use of additional hardware for the authentication system.

Moreover, [5] demonstrated the use of iris-based authentication to validate login to an E-commerce application. This research suggested use of encrypted iris image that will be validated by an existing value at a credit card agency system where the E-Commerce application is used as the middleware. Issues with this system proposed include its high complexity in computation due to its use of Principal Components Analysis (PCA), use of encryption and decryption, unresponsive client side if the credit card system is shut down by intrusion, and scalability issues in distribution of public keys.

Multi-modal techniques are currently used as a performance enhancer in biometric authentication systems [6]. For example, [7] used a genetic algorithm and an artificial neural network combination to combine recognition of human interaction with a system. The system developed was able to achieve a very high true positive rate. Main drawbacks in this research include the use of an external device to capture user images far from a computer screen, large time taken to classify humans due to use of multiple algorithms and the use of a database.

[2, 8] Demonstrated several key biometric authentication mechanisms for a cloud-based solution. Encryption mechanisms were also researched in [9] where a "user-centric" model was developed. However, this method typically inclines away from the system under development as a server-based environment needs to be used to process user templates.

It can be seen from the above review that several techniques have been used for biometric authentication. Main problems with existing techniques are high time and computational power used, use of remote servers that increases processing latencies, and use of complex encryption techniques. This motivates us to find solutions to these issues in existing methods to ensure that biometric authentication can be performed with less time and computation. Our aim is to reduce time and computation that is required to authenticate a user while ensuring confidentiality.

3   Methodology

The proposed architecture for the system is illustrated in Fig. 1. As shown, the proposed system[1] will connect to a MSSQL database to store and retrieve data for products and users. A user needs to load the application and sign in to view products they can purchase. When a user navigates to a product listing, the user can set the quantity and add products to a cart where these entries will be saved in the database with product and user data.

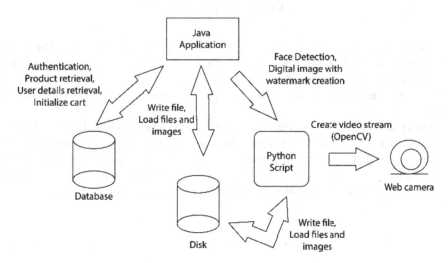

Fig. 1. The system's architecture

---

[1] https://github.com/aditya1962/BuyGrand.

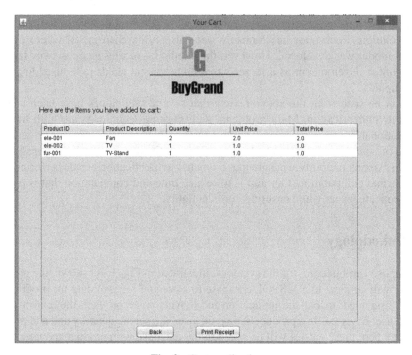

Fig. 2. Cart application

The user can view their cart generated once all transactions are completed. Data from the database will be loaded to the cart as shown in Fig. 2 and the user can go back and change their preferences in product frame and reload the cart. Once the user is satisfied with product purchases, the user can opt to print an invoice generated by the system based on cart data.

The system proposed uses a face detection mechanism as shown in Fig. 1 to authenticate the user. Algorithm 1 shows the steps used to create a video stream using the OpenCV package for python using user's webcam. This will open a video stream and the user can press the space key to capture video frames and press the escape key to quit the stream. Captured video frames will be stored in the project for processing.

Algorithm 1 Face detection and digital signature creation

Get video input from webcamera
counter = 0
while True:
    initialize frames from the camera's read
    show the current frame to the user
    if the returning value is false break the loop
    if escape (esc) key is pressed end capturing frames and end video
    else if space button is pressed:
        create image file
        write to disk
        counter += 1
Release resources
img_value = counter-1
Get image name of the last image from image_value
Read last image
Check the number of detected faces
if 1 face is detected:
    write the digital signature to the image
    open the image to write data
    write current date and time to the image
    save image as a new image to disk

Once the user quits the stream, the script will obtain the last image captured and pass to a CNN (Convolution Neural Network). The CNN is based on the dlib package and uses a pre-trained model to train the model in the form of a data file. Then rectangular objects are drawn around faces detected in the image. The model created in this system will follow only if a face is detected, i.e. if no face or more than one face is detected an exception will be displayed to the user.

The final process involves the watermark composed of the system date at the time of compilation. For this process, the PIL package was used to read the image and draw text on it. A type face was used with a font size, colour and location to display. Finally, the image was resized and saved to disk to be used for generating the invoice.

The invoice generation process is done within the JFrame application with the use of the iText PDF library. The invoice created will use the logo of the brand, a sample letter head and the user to be addressed as illustrated in Fig. 3.

BuyGrand

BuyGrand
12/A, First Road, Park Drive, Sri Lanka
sales@buygrand.com

2019/10/09 20:02:10

Dear abc,
Here is the receipt for items you ordered:

Product ID	Product Description	Quantity	Unit Price	Total Price
ele-001	Fan	2	2.0	2.0
ele-002	TV	1	1.0	1.0
fur-001	TV-Stand	1	1.0	1.0
			Sub Total:	4.0

The following is a generated digital signature of the user. No sign in required.

Fig. 3. A sample invoice created using the application

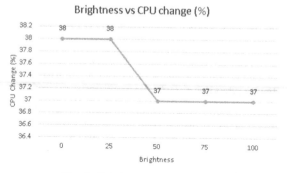

Fig. 4. Brightness vs CPU change

A table will be displayed containing cart information along with the sub total for products. Finally, the digital signature composed of the user image and the watermark is written to the file and the file is opened digital signature composed of the user image and the watermark is written to the file and file is open.

The confidence score was measured for different brightness levels of the background. This was achieved by either changing the brightness of the background of the room or changing the brightness level of the computer the user was using the application.

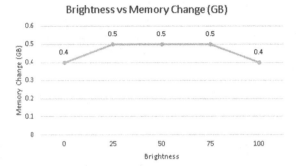

Fig. 5. Brightness vs memory change

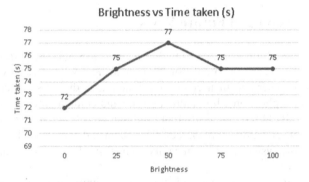

Fig. 6. Brightness vs detection time

4 Results and Discussion

As discussed above, the brightness of the screen of the computer used by the user was changed and the confidence level, time of execution, CPU usage change and memory change was tabulated to identify relationships. Figures 4, 5 and 6 illustrate these variations measured at 0 brightness, moderately low brightness (25%), mid brightness (50%), moderately high brightness (75%) and highest brightness (100%). The brightness was changed from the control panel of the computer and a balanced power plan. The machine under testing used an Intel ® Core ™ 2 Duo CPU at a maximum speed of 2.00 GHz and 2.0 GB DDR2 RAM for execution.

As seen in Fig. 7, higher confidence was seen in video streams filmed under high brightness. The execution time, CPU usage and the RAM usage were comparably low for high brightness streams. Total execution time was around 2.5 min including creating the watermarked image and the PDF file.

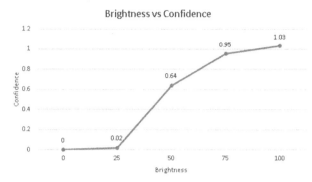

Fig. 7. Brightness vs confidence

5　The Conclusion and Future Works

In this research, a platform was created with.Net, Java, MSSQL and python. The objective was to create a watermark image of the user using a video stream captured from the webcam of the user and then embed the image as a digital signature in invoices created using the application while reducing time and computation required. The system was successfully tested under different brightness levels and a positive relationship was observed between hardware resources, time taken and confidence level with brightness. Therefore, the system could achieve its optimal predictions for higher brightness executions.

The main limitation of this system is that it is not immune to spoofing techniques. Therefore, an impersonator could provide an image of a user or display a video of a user in front of the webcam to create a digital watermarked image. However, though theoretically possible, the authentication level of such an attempt is limited given its artificial approach.

The system under research used digital authentication only during the creation of invoices. The system could be extended as a medium for authentication during the logging process as an alternative to username-password based authentication.

References

1. Phillips, P.J., Martin, A., Wilson, C.L., Przybocki, M.: An introduction evaluating biometric systems. Computer **33**, 56–63 (2000)
2. Al-Assam, H., Hassan, W., Zeadally, S.: Automated biometric authentication with cloud computing. Biometric-Based Phys. Cybersecurity Syst., 455–475 (2019)
3. Hacker extracts crypto key from TPM chip - The H Security: News and Features (2010, 2019-10-08). http://www.h-online.com/security/news/item/Hacker-extracts-crypto-key-from-TPM-chip-927077.html
4. Latze, C., Ultes-Nitsche, U.: Stronger Authentication in E-Commerce - How to protect even naïve Users against Phishing, Pharming, and MITM attacks. In: Presented at the IASTED International Conference on Communication Systems, Networks, and Applications (CSNA 2007) (2007)

5. Vangala, R., Sasi, S.: Biometric authentication for e-commerce transaction. In: Presented at the IEEE International Workshop on Imaging Systems and Techniques (IST) (2004)
6. Conti, V., Militello, C., Sorbello, F., Vitabile, S.: A frequency-based approach for features fusion in fingerprint and iris multimodal biometric identification systems. IEEE Trans. Syst. Man, Cybern. Part C (Appl. Rev.) **40**, 384–395 (2010)
7. Priya, S., Mukesh, R.: Multimodal biometric authentication using back propagation artificial neural network. Int. J. Simul.: Syst. Sci. Technol. (IJSSST) **19**, 1–8 (2019)
8. O'Gorman, L.: Comparing passwords, tokens, and biometrics for user authentication. Proc. IEEE **91**, 2021–2040 (2003)
9. Zhou, K., Ren, J.: PassBio: privacy-preserving user-centric biometric authentication. IEEE Trans. Inf. Forensics Secur. **13**, 3050–3063 (2018)

Automated Analysis of Chemistry Experiment Videos: New Challenges for Video Understanding

Zhichao Zheng[(⊠)], Benhua Wang, Ziwen Wang, Yi Chen, Junsheng Zhou, and Li Kong

Nanjing Normal University, Wenyuan Road No.1, Nanjing, China
{zhengzhichao,wangzw,cs_chenyi,zhoujs}@njnu.edu.cn,
kongli@nnu.edu.cn

Abstract. Compared to static declarative knowledge, procedural knowledge is challenging to assess effectively in education due to its nature of dynamic and complex. However, it serves as a crucial source for essential abilities of students. Can artificial intelligence assist in evaluating procedural knowledge? To explore this question, we focus on the scenario of middle-school chemistry experiments and attempt to use video understanding technology to aid teachers in assessing procedural knowledge of chemistry experiments. Nevertheless, our preliminary findings reveal that chemistry experiment videos differ from typical instructional videos used in research, presenting unique characteristics and complexities. Thus, we pose a new challenge, offering novel research questions for the field of video understanding and a new perspective for leveraging artificial intelligence in modern education.

Keywords: Chemistry Experiment · Automatic Video Analysis · Procedural Knowledge · Educational Reform

1 Introduction

1.1 Declarative Knowledge and Procedural Knowledge

Education plays a pivotal role in the human society [1]. Fundamentally, education is designed to nurture and develop the knowledge, skills, values and ethics of an individual which help them adapt to the society. Although the definition and objectives of education may vary across cultures and regions, the forms of knowledge transmitted through education remain consistent: declarative knowledge and procedural knowledge, both of which play essential roles in the educational process [2]. **Declarative knowledge** pertains to 'what' one knows, encompassing facts, information, data, and other explicit content that can typically be articulated, described, and conveyed. Declarative knowledge is static and objective, allowing it to be assessed in a straightforward manner through methods like exams, quizzes, and written assessments. In contrast, **procedural knowledge** emphasizes 'how' one knows, encompassing skills, capabilities and the

© The Author(s), under exclusive license to Springer Nature Singapore Pte Ltd. 2024
W. Hong and G. Kanaparan (Eds.): ICCSE 2023, CCIS 2023, pp. 194–201, 2024.
https://doi.org/10.1007/978-981-97-0730-0_18

application of knowledge in real-world contexts. This type of knowledge is inherently more dynamic and context-dependent. For example, 'the rules of basketball' represent declarative knowledge, clearly defined and communicable through written documents. On the other hand, 'playing basketball' is considered as procedural knowledge, involving not only knowledge of the rules but also their practical application in real game-play. Hence, declarative knowledge provides the foundation, and procedural knowledge transforms theoretical understanding into practical action. However, the complexity of procedural knowledge makes it challenging to evaluate using traditional testing and assessment methodologies [3].

1.2 Evaluation of Procedural Knowledge

In secondary education, experimental teaching plays a crucial role in imparting procedural knowledge. These experiments not only serve as extensions of classroom teaching but also kindle curiosity of students and boost their scientific literacy. Through practice experimentation, students not only understand declarative knowledge but also gradually master procedural knowledge. However, owing to traditional teaching methods, the evaluation of experimental teaching often relies on manual assessment. This involves using video recording systems to capture students' experimental procedures, which are then reviewed and evaluated by teachers [4]. Nevertheless, this approach places a significant time burden on teachers, compelling them to prioritize the quality of classroom teaching over the acquisition of procedural knowledge. As a result, student may excel in exams but encounter challenges when applying their knowledge to solve problem in real-world.

In recent years, the field of Artificial Intelligence (AI) has experienced rapid development. AI technologies have been progressively applied across diverse industries and domains, leading to substantial changes. In conclusion, AI has emerged as an important factor steering a new wave of technological revolution. This leads us to a question: *Can AI bring changes to modern education by assisting in the evaluation of procedural knowledge?*

We firmly believe the answer is 'Yes'. Although it is still a long way from fully implement AI for the automatic evaluation of procedural knowledge, we can make significant improvements using the existing technologies. With the assistance of video understanding technologies, we can use video understanding models to automatically analyze the video and generate high-level semantic information, including descriptions of students' activities, video clips of complete activities, and video keyframes for evaluation. Teachers can then access this abstract information and quickly navigate to areas of interest. Consequently, teachers are liberated from time-consuming and repetitive video review tasks, reducing hours to mere minutes or even seconds. This allows them to redirect their focus toward evaluating students' learning process of procedural knowledge, which further improves the quality of modern education and comprehensive ability of students. In conclusion, we believe AI has the potential to bring positive changes to the field of education, making it more efficient and intelligent.

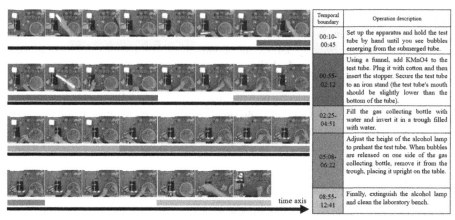

Temporal boundary	Operation description
00:10-00:45	Set up the apparatus and hold the test tube by hand until you see bubbles emerging from the submerged tube.
00:55-02:12	Using a funnel, add KMnO4 to the test tube. Plug it with cotton and then insert the stopper. Secure the test tube to an iron stand (the test tube's mouth should be slightly lower than the bottom of the tube).
02:25-04:51	Fill the gas collecting bottle with water and invert it in a trough filled with water.
05:08-06:22	Adjust the height of the alcohol lamp to preheat the test tube. When bubbles are released on one side of the gas collecting bottle, remove it from the trough, placing it upright on the table.
08:55-12:41	Finally, extinguish the alcohol lamp and clean the laboratory bench.

(a) Visual cues of chemical experiment   (b) Text description of chemical experiment

Fig. 1. A simplified example of chemical experiment video on the Preparation of Oxygen from KMnO4. (a) represents visual changes over time, while (b) provided a text description of experiment. In this context, colors indicate the correspondence between visual cues and text descriptions. Hence, different colors represent distinct annotations. Visual cues with no color indicate that they are 'background' and do not correspond to any specific operation.

2   Chemistry Experimental Video Dataset

To validate our ideas, our team has developed a Chemistry Experimental Videos dataset (CEV). This dataset was created in a simulation environment where students with a foundation in chemistry conducted oxygen preparation experiments without a script. An overhead camera system recorded the entire experimental process. We then invited experts in the field of chemistry to annotate videos at the frame-level. We have collected approximately 200 videos, and an example of chemistry experimental video is shown in Fig. 1.

With CEV, we can train a video understanding model to perform various tasks, such as extracting key frames from the video, generating video descriptions, segmenting the video temporally, and detecting abnormal operations. This abstract information allows teachers to quickly understand the process and identify any issues in the experimental videos. Considering Temporal Action Segmentation (TAS) is a foundational task in video understanding, we conduct an TAS experiments on CEV. However, we found that the state-of-the-art models show worse performance compared to their superior performance on benchmark video datasets. We conducted an in-depth analysis of the characteristics of CEV and have confirmed that **it presents a new challenge**.

3   The Analysis of Chemistry Experimental Videos

Due to the fact that chemistry experiment videos capture the entire process of students completing experiments, we can view these videos as if the students are providing us with step-by-step instructions on how to produce oxygen. In the field of video understanding, such videos are classified as instructional videos [16], as they deliver specific guidance, educational content, or explanations to the audience. Hence, we compare CEV with other instructional video datasets as shown in Table 1.

From Table 1, it is evident that most existing instructional video datasets fall into the categories of cooking tasks and daily life tasks. Daily life tasks are generally simple, comprising only a few actions with straightforward goals. Cooking video is similar to chemistry experimental video. Cooking videos share some similarities with chemistry experimental videos because both of them should adhere to the guides. However, in cooking video, the average video length and average segment number is far fewer than experimental video. The complexity of experimental operations, which may require multiple actions for safety reasons, results in experimental videos being more intricate and challenging. Moreover, the existing instructional datasets cannot adequately support the application of video understanding models in secondary education.

Table 1. Differences between CEV and other instructional video datasets. AVL represents the average video length, and ASN is the average segment number.

Dataset	Samples	AVL	ASN	Video context
YouCook [5]	88	1.59 min	–	Cooking activities according to recipes
50Salads [6]	50	6.4 min	19.32	Making salads according to recipes
Breakfast [7]	1,989	2.32 min	4.25	Making breakfast according to recipes
JIGSAWS [8]	206	0.76 min	8.27	Surgical activities
5 tasks [9]	150	2 min	–	Daily life tasks like making coffee
YouCook2 [10]	2,000	5.28 min	6.91	Cooking activities according to recipes
E-KITCHENS [11]	432	7.64 min	–	Cooking and kitchen activities
E-Skills [12]	216	1.44 min	–	Human activities and actions like repair tasks and sports
CrossTask [13]	4,700	4.8 min	–	Human activities and actions like cooking, cleaning house and hiking
BEST [14]	500	3.12 min	–	Cooking activities ranging from simple food preparation to more complex cooking
HowTo100M [15]	1.22M	6.61 min	–	Human activities like chopping vegetables and assembling
COIN [16]	11,827	2.42 min	3.92	Daily life tasks like installing wheels and changing light bulbs
CEV	192	26.9 min	41.41	Students conduct a series of activities and complex actions to achieve an experimental goal

In summary, we have identified several key characteristics of chemical experiment videos:

Variable Temporal Lengths. In real chemical experiments, the duration of time that students conduct a complete procedure varies widely due to the complex steps involved in chemical experiments and differences in individual experimental abilities. For example, some students may take about 1 min to assemble the test tube, while others may take around 5 min. Unlike other instructional videos with shorter durations, chemical videos exhibit larger variations in temporal length. This requires a model with an adaptive temporal receptive field to effectively model the temporal relationships.

Lacking Enough Visual Cues. For cook task, the action of 'cut onion' and 'cut carrot' can be distinguished by the difference in morphology between onions and carrots. However, in chemical experiment, most of the objects for student interaction are transparent glass instruments, which might not provide strong visual cues for different procedure, making it challenging for models to identify specific apparatus or reactions. Hence, this requires a model has a stronger ability to understanding the behavior of student and combining the purpose of the steps and a small number of visual cues for temporal reasoning.

Perception of Fine-Grained Changes. Understanding the success or failure of a chemistry experiment often depends on sensitivity to subtle temporal and spatial changes. For example, after the experiment is completed, the first step is removing the catheter from the water, and then turn off the alcohol lamp. If these actions are reversed, the catheter may burst due to water backflow. In such cases, the model needs to perceive these differences and alert the teacher to potentially hazardous operations. Hence, models must have the ability to detect these fine-grained changes to correctly interpret the experimental process.

Incomplete or Ambiguous Information. In cooking and daily life video, tasks are relatively simple, and individuals can usually perform them correctly. However, in real experiments, students may forget specific actions, conduct operations in an incorrect order or repeat certain experimental procedures, resulting in more incomplete or ambiguous information. Model must be capable of recognizing and understanding such ambiguous or unclear procedures. Additionally, model need to be error-tolerant and adaptable to account for variations in the experimental process.

These are just a few of the dataset's characteristics and challenges. We believe that more challenges will be revealed with a more detailed analysis. Therefore, automatically analysis Chemistry Experiment Videos task presents a new challenge, imposing higher demands on current video understanding models, and providing a new bridge that connects the real-world applications with video understanding technologies.

4   The Results on Temporal Action Segmentation

In the field of video understanding, Temporal Action Segmentation (TAS) is a foundational task aims to segment temporally untrimmed video sequences on time [17]. TAS plays a significant role in understanding human-to-human interaction and relations. We consider annotations as action labels and employ two state-of-the-art fully supervised models on CEV. We evaluate these models using three commonly adopted metrics: Frame-wise accuracy (Acc), Edit score (Edit), and F1-scores. Acc represents the fraction of the model's correct predictions and is widely used for action segmentation evaluation. However, Acc may be misleading when two models achieve similar accuracy but have significant qualitative differences. In contrast, F1-scores and Edit are evaluation metrics based on segment quality and penalize over-segmentation errors. The results are presented in Table 2.

Table 2. Results of the temporal segmentation models on CEV.

	Acc	Edit	F1@10	F1@25	F1@50
ASFormer [18]	53.09%	36.52%	32.08%	23.59%	10.38%
UVAST [19]	51.03%	62.34%	34.75%	27.43%	12.60%

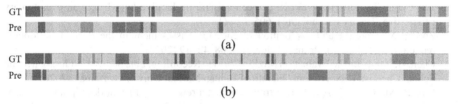

(a)

(b)

Fig. 2. Visualization of the ground truth labels and the corresponding prediction results of UVAST.

These two models show superior performance on benchmark dataset, but have poor performance on CEV. We also visualize the predicted and ground truth segmentations of UVAST on CEV in Fig. 2. We can see that UVAST suffers the over-segmentation problem and cannot capture the temporal relations in the chemical experiment videos. Hence, this discrepancy suggests that chemical experiment videos exhibit variations and complexities, including longer time sequences, more intricate action and activities, and finer-grained changes. Models that excel with benchmark datasets may struggle with this heightened complexity.

Consequently, addressing this newly raised challenge necessitates the design of superior models capable of tackling more complex real-world problems, rather than merely incrementally improving performance on benchmark datasets. We firmly believe that this is a pivotal step in leveraging video understanding technology to drive reform in the modern education.

5   Conclusion

In this paper, we introduce a novel problem: the automated analysis of chemistry experiment videos. This problem introduces a significant challenge to the field of video understanding. We then conduct an in-depth analysis of the characteristics of chemistry experiment videos and provide a preliminary result on temporal action segmentation using

CEV. These findings collectively highlight the need for a more robust model to tackle this challenge. Such a model should encompass enhanced temporal modeling capabilities, improved granularity perception, and stronger comprehension of temporal behaviors. In the future, our plan includes offering more detailed dataset descriptions and developing advanced video understanding models, and advancing AI technology in the realm of education.

Acknowledgements. This work was supported in part by the National Natural Science Foundation of China under Grant No.62377029 and the Natural Science Research of Jiangsu Higher Education Institutions of China under Grant No.22KJB520021, No.22KJB520020.

References

1. Chankseliani, M., Qoraboyev, I., et al.: Higher education contributing to local, national, and global development: new empirical and conceptual insights. High. Educ. **81**(1), 109–127 (2021)
2. Ten Berge, T., Van Hezewijk, R.: Procedural and declarative knowledge: an evolutionary perspective. Theory Psychol. **9**(5), 605–624 (1999)
3. Zhong, X.: Practice and exploration of formative assessment in the context of 'double reduction' (in Chinese). Primary Educ. Res. **08**, 42–49 (2023)
4. Chen, H.: Study on the Evaluation Mode of "Video Recording, Late Scoring" in Junior Middle School Chemistry Experiment Operation. Hainan Normal University, Hainan (2020)
5. Das, P., Xu, C., et al: A thousand frames in just a few words: lingual description of videos through latent topics and sparse object stitching. In: IEEE Conference on Computer Vision and Pattern Recognition, pp. 2634–2641. IEEE, Piscataway (2013)
6. Stein, S., McKenna, S.J.: Combining embedded accelerometers with computer vision for recognizing food preparation activities. In: ACM International Joint Conference on Pervasive and Ubiquitous Computing, pp. 729–738. ACM, New York (2013)
7. Kuehne, H., Arslan, A., Serre, T.: The language of actions: recovering the syntax and semantics of goal-directed human activities. In: IEEE Conference on Computer Vision and Pattern Recognition, pp. 780–787. IEEE, Piscataway (2014)
8. Gao, Y., Vedula, S.S., et al.: JHU-ISI gesture and skillassessment working set (JIGSAWS): a surgical activity dataset for human motion modeling. In: MICCAI Workshop, vol. 3, pp. 3 (2014)
9. Alayrac, J.B., Bojanowski, P., et al: Unsupervised learning from narrated instruction videos. In: IEEE Conference on Computer Vision and Pattern Recognition, pp. 4575–4583. IEEE, Piscataway (2016)
10. Zhou, L., Xu, C., Corso, J.: Towards automatic learning of procedures from web instructional videos. In: AAAI Conference on Artificial Intelligence, vol. 32, pp. 7590–7598. AAAI, Mento Park (2018)
11. Damen, D., et al.: Scaling Egocentric Vision: The Dataset. In: Ferrari, V., Hebert, M., Sminchisescu, C., Weiss, Y. (eds.) ECCV 2018. LNCS, vol. 11208, pp. 753–771. Springer, Cham (2018). https://doi.org/10.1007/978-3-030-01225-0_44
12. Doughty, H., Damen, D., et al: Who's better? who's best? Pairwise deep ranking for skill determination. In: IEEE Conference on Computer Vision and Pattern Recognition, pp. 6057–6066. IEEE, Piscataway (2018)
13. Zhukov, D., Alayrac, J.B., et al: Cross-task weakly supervised learning from instructional videos. In: IEEE Conference on Computer Vision and Pattern Recognition, pp. 3537–3545. IEEE, Piscataway (2019)

14. Doughty, H., Mayol-Cuevas, W., et al: The pros and cons: rank-aware temporal attention for skill determination in long videos. In: IEEE Conference on Computer Vision and Pattern Recognition, pp. 7862–7871. IEEE, Piscataway (2019)

15. Miech, A., Zhukov, D., et al: HowTo100M: learning a text-video embedding by watching hundred million narrated video clips. In: International Conference on Computer Vision, pp. 2630–2640. IEEE, Piscataway (2019)

16. Tang, Y., Lu, J., Zhou, J.: Comprehensive instructional video analysis: the COIN dataset and performance evaluation. IEEE Trans. Pattern Anal. Mach. Intell. **43**(9), 3138–3153 (2020)

17. Ding, G., Sener, F., Yao, A.: Temporal action segmentation: an analysis of modern technique. arXiv preprint arXiv:2210.10352 (2022)

18. Yi, F., Wen, H., Jiang, T.: Asformer: transformer for action segmentation. arXiv preprint arXiv:2110.08568 (2021)

19. Behrmann, N., Golestaneh, S.A., et al.: Unified fully and timestamp supervised temporal action segmentation via sequence-to-sequence translation. In: Avidan, S., Brostow, G., Cissé, M., Farinella, G.M., Hassner, T. (eds.) Computer Vision – ECCV 2022. ECCV 2022. Lecture Notes in Computer Science, vol. 13695, pp. 52–68. Springer, Heidelberg (2022). https://doi.org/10.1007/978-3-031-19833-5_4

Exploiting Adaptive Adversarial Transfer Network for Cross Domain Teacher's Speech Emotion Recognition

Ting Cai, Shengsong Wang, Yu Xiong$^{(\boxtimes)}$, and Xin Zhong

Research Center for Artificial Intelligence and Smart, Education, Chongqing University of Posts and, Telecommunications, Chongqing 400065, China
`xiongyu@cqupt.edu.cn`

Abstract. The speech of teachers in classroom teaching contains their teaching emotions, which have a direct impact on the quality of classroom teaching and the learning effectiveness of students. Therefore, emotional recognition of teacher's speech will help improve their self-awareness and provide scientific support for improving teaching methods. However, in real-world scenarios, many data are unlabeled, especially in the emerging field of smart education, which lacks high-quality teacher speech datasets. Thus, a cross domain teacher' speech emotion recognition model based on adaptive adversarial transfer networks is proposed, which dynamically evaluates the relative importance of global and local distributions using adaptive adversarial modules and automatically assigns weights to both. The common features of the source and target domains were obtained to complete cross domain speech emotion recognition for teacher classroom teaching. Finally, the experiment showed that the classification accuracy of the proposed model reached 75.3%, significantly higher than other cross domain recognition models.

Keywords: Teacher's Speech Emotion Recognition · Transfer Learning · Adaptive Adversarial Network · Big Data of Education

1 Introduction

With the gradual implementation of smart education classrooms, a large amount of educational data has been generated, such as teacher lecture audio materials. By utilizing these audio data, it is possible to conduct in-depth analysis of teacher's work conditions. However, the quality of these data varies greatly, with the majority being collected spontaneously by schools and remaining unlabeled and uncleaned. Although the unlabeled data contains rich emotional information, it cannot be directly used for training deep neural network models. The application of deep neural networks in the field of speech emotion recognition can significantly improve the emotion recognition rate. The reason why deep learning technology exhibits powerful performance is that it requires a large amount of labeled data to train deep learning models. However, obtaining enough labeled data is often expensive and time-consuming.

© The Author(s), under exclusive license to Springer Nature Singapore Pte Ltd. 2024
W. Hong and G. Kanaparan (Eds.): ICCSE 2023, CCIS 2023, pp. 202–213, 2024.
https://doi.org/10.1007/978-981-97-0730-0_19

It has been shown that transfer learning as an effective solution to address the issue of data sparsity in the target domain by utilizing the abundant labeled samples in the source domain. The key to the success of a transfer learning model lies in learning a discriminative model that reduces the distribution discrepancy between the two domains. Traditional methods reweight the samples in the source domain [2] or seek explicit feature transformations that align the source and target domain samples into the same feature space [3]. With the rapid development of deep learning, adversarial learning can be embedded into deep networks to minimize the distribution discrepancy between the source and target domains [4]. Most transfer learning models align the target distribution of the source domain by learning a single domain discriminator [5], or focus on multiple discriminators to align the target distributions of subdomains [6]. However, in practical applications, the global and local distributions between domains often contribute differently.

When two domains are dissimilar, according to Fig. 1, such as (a) and (b) in Fig. 1, the global distribution becomes more important. However, when the two domains are highly similar, like (a) and (c) in Fig. 1, the attention should be focused more on the local distribution. Both distributions are beneficial for the adversarial training of the model, aiding in the learning of domain-invariant features. Therefore, it is a pressing issue in transfer learning to adaptively evaluate the relative importance of the global and local distributions.

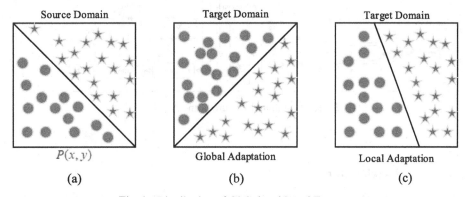

Fig. 1. Distribution of Global and Local Features

To address the afore mentioned issue, we propose an adaptive adversarial transfer network (AATN) model for cross-domain teacher's speech emotion recognition from other domains to the domain of teacher instruction. First, a Bidirectional Gated Recurrent Unit (BiGRU) network is employed to extract advanced features from both source and target domain data. These features are then fed into an adversarial network for adversarial training to learn domain-invariant characteristics. Second, an adaptive adversarial module is utilized to dynamically evaluate the relative importance of the global and local distributions and automatically allocate weights to the global and local distributions. Finally, a shared feature representation of the source and target domains is obtained, facilitating cross-domain teacher speech emotion recognition in the context of teacher instruction.

2   Method

2.1   Problem Definition

The labeled dataset from the source domain, denoted as $D_s = \{x_i^s, y_i^s\}^{n_s}$, where x_i^s represents the data samples from the source domain, y_i^s represents the corresponding labels, and n_s represents the number of data samples in the source domain. Given a unlabeled data from the target domain, denoted as $D_t = \{x_j^t\}^{n_t}$, where x_j^t represents the data samples from the target domain and n_t represents the number of data samples in the target domain. D_s and D_t have the same label space, $x_i, x_j \in i^d$, where d represents the dimension of the data. The distributions between the two domains are different, $P_s(x_x) \neq P_t(x_t)$, the objective of cross-domain teacher's emotion recognition is to design a deep learning network that can reduce the distribution discrepancy between the two domains, thereby extracting more domain-invariant features.

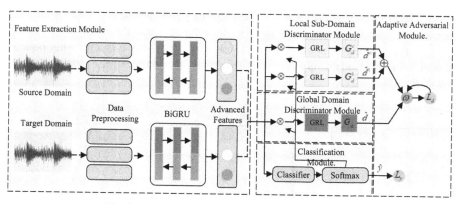

Fig. 2.   The overall architecture of the AATN model.

2.2   Overall Architecture

The proposed AATN model, as shown in Fig. 2, is composed of several modules: feature extraction module, local sub-domain discriminator module, global domain discriminator module, adaptive adversarial module, and classification module. AATN model is built upon mature Generative Adversarial Networks (GANs) with the aim of learning domain-invariant features through adversarial training. The speech data undergo preprocessing steps such as sampling quantization, framing, windowing, and endpoint detection. Then, the preprocessed data is fed into the feature extraction module where BiGRU models are employed to capture the temporal dependencies of speech sequences and extract advanced features from both source and target domains. The global domain discriminator module and local sub-domain discriminator module capture the global and local distributions, respectively, and measure the distribution discrepancy between the two domains. The adaptive adversarial module dynamically and adaptively evaluates the importance of these two distributions using an adaptive adversarial factor ω. The adaptive adversarial module uses adaptive adversarial factor ω to evaluate the importance of these two distributions dynamically and adaptively. By calculating the loss function of the global domain discrimination module and the local subdomain discrimination module, the Gradient Reversal Layer (GRL) is used to effectively train other parameters of the model.

Feature Extraction Module

The labeled data in the source domain is denoted as $D_s = \{x_i^s, y_i^s\}_{i=1}^{n_s}$, and in a teaching scenario, teacher's speech data without emotion labels is denoted as $D_t = \{x_j^t\}_{i=1}^{n_t}$. Here, x_i represents the data samples corresponding to various domains of speech, n_s, n_t represent the total number of samples, and y_i represents the emotion labels of samples in the source domain. Firstly, data preprocessing, such as sampling quantification, framing, windowing, and endpoint detection, is applied to both the source domain and the target domain, which is the teacher's speech data in this case. Subsequently, frame-level speech features are extracted from the preprocessed speech data. Then, the processed speech data is fed into a BiGRU for training, enabling the capture of advanced emotional characteristics, including contextual information before and after the speech feature. If the current input speech feature is denoted as e_s, the hidden state of the forward GRU can be represented as $\vec{h}_t$, as indicated by Eq. (1):

$$\vec{h}_t = GRU(e_s, \vec{h}_{t-1}) \tag{1}$$

Similarly, it can be deduced that the output hidden state of the backward GRU is denoted as $\overleftarrow{h}_t$, as expressed in Eq. (2):

$$\overleftarrow{h}_t = GRU(e_s, \overleftarrow{h}_{t-1}) \tag{2}$$

By concatenating the hidden memory information from both the forward and backward GRUs, one can obtain the overall hidden state h of the BiGRU, which represents the advanced features of the speech. This calculation can be expressed as shown in Eq. (3):

$$h = [\vec{h}_t, \overleftarrow{h}_t] \tag{3}$$

Local Sub-domain Discriminator Module

Adaptive adversarial learning draws inspiration from the concept of Generative Adversarial Learning [7] to aid in learning domain-invariant features. Adversarial learning can be likened to a two-player game, where one player is the well-trained domain discriminator module G_d, tasked with distinguishing the source domain from the target domain. The second player is the feature extraction module G_f, which endeavors to confuse the discriminator module G_d by extracting domain-invariant features. These two players are trained adversarially: the parameters of the feature extraction module G_f with parameters θ_f are learned by maximizing the loss of the domain discriminator module G_d. Conversely, the parameters of the domain discriminator module θ_d are trained by minimizing the loss of the domain discriminator module itself. Additionally, the loss of the label classification module G_y is also minimized. The loss function for adaptive adversarial learning can be formalized as shown in Eq. (4):

$$L(\theta_f, \theta_y, \theta_d) = \frac{1}{n_s} \sum_{x_i \in D_s} L_y(G_y(G_f x_i)), y_i) - \frac{\lambda}{n_s + n_t} \sum_{x_i \in (D_s \cup D_t)} L_d(G_d(G_f(x_i)), d_i)$$

(4)

where λ represents the weighting parameter; L_y and L_d respectively denote the loss functions for the classification module and the domain discriminator module. Since the target domain lacks emotion labels, d_i is a pseudo-label that signifies the domain label of the input samples. If a sample originates from the source domain, d_i is set to 0, and if it comes from the target domain, d_i is set to 1.

The role of the local subdomain discriminator module is to align the local distributions between the source domain and the target domain. In comparison to the global domain discriminator module, the local subdomain discriminator module can align the structures with both distributions, enabling finer-grained domain adaptation. Specifically, the local subdomain discriminator module can be divided into C-class subdomain discriminators G_d^c, with each subdomain discriminator responsible for matching the source and target domain data relevant to its respective class. The loss function for the local subdomain discriminator module is represented as shown in Eq. (5):

$$L_l = \frac{1}{n_s + n_t} \sum_{c=1}^{C} \sum_{x_i \in (D_s \cup D_t)} L_d^c(G_d^c(\hat{y}_i^c G_f(x_i)), d_i)$$

(5)

where G_d^c represents C-class subdomain discriminators, L_d^c denotes the cross-entropy loss of C-class subdomain discriminators, G_f represents the advanced features extracted by the feature extraction module, $\hat{y}_i^c$ represents the predicted probability distribution of input samples x_i in C-class subdomain discriminators, and d_i represents the domain label of the input samples.

Global Domain Discriminator Module

The role of the global domain discriminator module is to align the global distributions between the source domain and the target domain. This module aims to learn and identify domain-invariant features between the source and target domains in conjunction with the local subdomain discriminator module. The computation of the loss function for the global domain discriminator module is as shown in Eq. (6).

$$L_g = \frac{1}{n_s + n_t} \sum_{x_i \in (D_s \cup D_t)} L_d(G_d(G_f(x_i)), d_i)$$

(6)

where L_d represents the cross-entropy loss function of the domain discriminator, G_f denotes the advanced features in the feature extraction module, and d_i represents the domain label of sample x_i.

Classification Module

The classifier in the classification module is the domain classifier, and it is used to train and distinguish input samples as either source domain or target domain samples. The objective of the domain classifier is to learn domain-invariant features between the source and target domains, aiming to minimize the feature distribution differences between the two domains. Since it receives source domain samples with labeled attributes as input, it can be trained with the supervision provided by the labeled data from the source domain D_s. In contrast, the softmax function acts as the emotion classifier, primarily focused on mining and recognizing emotional features within speech. It concentrates solely on the emotional content present in the speech and does not consider the origin domain of the input. It is trained using source domain data containing emotion labels and eventually outputs the emotions contained in unlabeled samples from the target domain. The training objective for the classification module is the cross-entropy loss, as specifically illustrated in Eq. (7).

$$L_y = -\frac{1}{n_s} \sum_{x_i \in D_s} \sum_{C=1}^{C} P_{x_i \to C} \log G_y(G_f(x_i)) \tag{7}$$

where C represents the number of classes, $P_{x_i \to C}$ denotes the probability that the input sample x_i belongs to class C, G_y represents the label classification module, and G_f represents the advanced features extracted by the feature extraction module.

Adaptive Adversarial Module

The role of the Adaptive Adversarial Module is to dynamically compute the relative importance of global and local distributions and automatically adjust the adversarial factor ω. In transfer learning, we can consider that the AATN model uses neural networks to learn the importance of global and local distributions. Therefore, the use of the adaptive adversarial factor ω allows for perceiving accurate information about the distributions.

The adaptive adversarial module can automatically update the value of the adaptive adversarial factor ω within the network. Firstly, it employs deep adversarial feature representation to learn and update ω instead of using shallow features, enhancing the robustness and accuracy of the AATN model. Secondly, the AATN model directly fine-tunes ω using the loss of the domain discriminator module, making it simpler and more efficient. The global $A - distance$[8] representation of the global domain discriminator module is defined as shown in Eq. (8):

$$d_{A,g}(D_s, D_t) = 2(1 - 2(L_g)) \tag{8}$$

The calculation equation for the local $A - distance$ of the local subdomain discriminator module is defined as shown in Eq. (9):

$$d_{A,l}(D_s^c, D_t^c) = 2(1 - 2(L_l^c)) \tag{9}$$

Ultimately, the calculation equation for the adaptive adversarial factor ω is represented as shown in Eq. (10):

$$\omega = \frac{d_{A,g}(D_s, D_t)}{d_{A,g}(D_s, D_t) + \frac{1}{C} \sum_{c=1}^{C} d_{A,l}(D_s^c, D_t^c)} \tag{10}$$

where D_s^c and D_t^c represent samples from C-class subdomains, L_g denotes the loss of the global discriminator, and L_l^c represents the loss of C-class local subdomain discriminators.

The adaptive adversarial module does not require the construction of additional classifiers to calculate the local $A - distance$. This module can utilize the global and local discriminators to compute the distances. Similarly, the adaptive adversarial module can calculate the adaptive adversarial factor ω in each iteration after obtaining the global $A - distance$. Ultimately, when training converges, the AATN model automatically acquires an adaptive adversarial factor ω.

Combining all the components, the learning objective of the AATN model is ultimately expressed as shown in Eq. (11).

$$L(\theta_f, \theta_y, \theta_d, \theta_d^c|_{c=1}^C) = L_y - \lambda((1 - \omega)L_g + \omega L_l) \tag{11}$$

where λ represents the weighting parameter, L_y represents the loss function of the classification module, L_g and L_l represent the loss functions of the global domain discriminator and local subdomain discriminator respectively, and ω represents the adaptive adversarial factor.

3 Experiments

3.1 Datasets

The datasets used in the experiments include CASIA [9], CHEAVD [10], MASC [11], and NNIME [12]. The above four datasets are all in Chinese language. Each dataset contains both labeled and unlabeled data and is employed as the source domain dataset for cross-domain teacher's speech emotion recognition. In addition to the existing teacher's speech datasets, a Teacher Emotional Speech Database (TESD) is established by reclassifying emotions. This database consists of recordings from 6 male and 6 female teachers and includes four different emotion categories: anger, surprise, neutral, and sadness, comprising a total of 3564 teacher emotional speech samples. Approximately 20% of the TESD dataset is set aside for testing, while the remainder is used for training. The basic characteristics of the dataset are summarized in Table 1.

Table 1. Introduction to the Speech Datasets.

Domain	Dataset	Language	Number	Emotion Category
Source Domain	CASIA	Chinese	7200	6
	CHEAVD	Chinese	4200	6
	MASC	Chinese	5000	5
	NINME	Chinese	7000	6
Target Domain	TESD	Chinese	3564	4

In the four source domain databases, we selected four fundamental emotions as the emotion categories, anger, surprise, neutral, and sadness from each dataset. For each of these basic emotions, 500 speech segments were chosen as labeled data, as illustrated in Table 2.

Table 2. Source Domain Dataset.

Dataset	CASIA	CHEAVD	MASC	NINME
Anger	500	500	500	500
Surprise	500	500	500	500
Neutral	500	500	500	500
Sadness	500	500	500	500
Unlabeled	5027	2139	2856	4084

The evaluation metric for the paper is classification accuracy, which is defined as the proportion of correctly classified instances to the total number of instances.

3.2 Parameter Configuration and Model Comparison

In the feature extraction module, the BiGRU has 128 hidden nodes, with a training batch size of 32, a learning rate of 1e-3, and a dropout rate of 0.5. Since the domain classifier is trained from scratch, its learning rate is set to be 10 times higher than the other layers, and stochastic gradient descent is used as the optimization method. In AATN, $\lambda = 1$, with a batch size of 32. To validate the effectiveness of the proposed model, we conducted comparative experiments with the following models: DDC [13], RTN [14], DANN [15], JAN [16], and MEDA.

3.3 Results and Analysis

To demonstrate the effectiveness of the AATN model in cross-domain teacher's emotion recognition tasks, the experimental section initially compared the accuracy of cross-domain teacher's emotion recognition models. As shown in Fig. 3, the experiments were divided into four cross-domain recognition tasks. These tasks involved using four Chinese speech emotion datasets as source domains and transferring emotion recognition to the teacher lecture speech emotion dataset, denoted as CA→T, CH→T, M→T, N→T. Here, CA, CH, M, N, and T represent the abbreviations for the CASIA, CHEAVD, MASC, NNIME, and TESD dataset, respectively. The → indicates the direction of cross-domain recognition between two datasets. For example, CA→T signifies transferring emotion information from the CASIA dataset, as the source domain, to the target domain TESD dataset, thereby utilizing emotion information from CASIA to aid teacher's emotion recognition in the TESD dataset.

Table 3 displays a comparison of the average accuracy between the AATN model and other models in the cross-domain teacher's speech emotion recognition task within the teacher lecture domain.

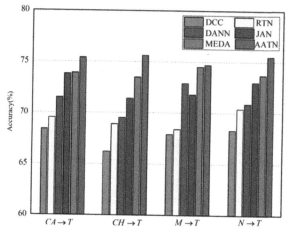

Fig. 3. The classification accuracy for cross-domain teacher's emotion recognition varies among different models.

Table 3. The average classification accuracy for cross-domain teacher's emotion recognition varies across different models.

Model	The average classification accuracy
DDC	67.7
RTN	69.8
DANN	71.2
JAN	72.5
MEDA	73.9
AATN	**75.3**

Comparing the experimental results between Fig. 3 and Table 3, it can be observed that the proposed AATN model performs the best in cross-domain teacher's emotion recognition tasks originating from different source domains. Its average accuracy is the highest, reaching 75.3%. Compared to the DDC model, the AATN model achieves a 7.6% improvement in average classification accuracy. This improvement is primarily attributed to the fact that the DDC model introduces only an adaptation layer and additional domain confusion loss to learn domain-invariant features, without using adversarial learning methods. This underscores the importance of adversarial learning in training cross-domain models. In comparison to the RTN model, the proposed model achieves a 5.5% improvement in average classification accuracy. This improvement can be attributed to the RTN model relying on several layers of residual functions for classifier adaptation, and its classification accuracy depends on the choice of domain-invariant features, making it less effective in learning domain-invariant features from source and target domains. Compared to the DANN model, the AATN model improves the average classification accuracy by 4.1%. This is because while the DANN model uses adversarial learning in training, its model structure for feature extraction in the domain-invariant part is relatively simple, which makes it challenging to improve recognition performance when there is a significant distribution gap between the source and target domains. The AATN model outperforms the JAN model by 2.8%. This improvement can be attributed to the fact that the joint adaptation network proposed by the JAN model can align the joint distribution of multiple domain layers, but it does not distinguish between the effects of global and local distributions, both of which play a crucial role in extracting domain-invariant features. Compared to the MEDA model, the AATN model achieves a 1.4% improvement in average classification accuracy. While the MEDA model shares structural similarities with the proposed AATN model and introduces an embedded distribution alignment method to calculate the weights for global and local distributions, it requires additional training of linear classifiers in each iteration, which is computationally intensive and time-consuming. It cannot adaptively allocate weights between the two distributions. In summary, the overall performance of the proposed AATN model surpasses that of the other comparative models.

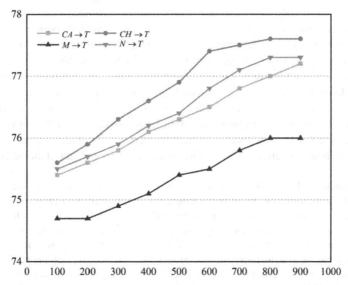

Fig. 4. The influence of the quantity of labeled source domain data on the teacher's emotion recognition performance of the model

To train the emotion recognition classifier, we utilize a pre-existing dataset with labeled data from the source domain. It is a common assumption that the target domain primarily consists of unlabeled data; however, in real-world scenarios, this dataset may not be entirely unlabeled. The target domain typically contains a small portion of already labeled data. Leveraging this labeled data from the target domain helps the classifier better capture the shared feature distribution between the two datasets. As depicted in Fig. 4, in the process of cross-domain teacher's emotion recognition in educational settings, the accuracy of the four classification tasks varies with different amounts of labeled data. Specifically, the performance of the AATN model can be enhanced with adding differently proportioned already labeled data to the target domain. Moreover, as the amount of labeled data increases, the model's performance gradually improves. When the proportion of labeled data in the target domain reaches 900 instances, the model's classification accuracy reaches its peak and stabilizes. This is because as the model has access to more labeled data from the target domain, it can extract more domain-invariant features.

4 Conclusions

In this paper, we exploit AATN for cross domain teacher's speech emotion recognition to address the problem of the lack of high-quality teacher's speech emotion dataset in educational scenarios. The model uses adversarial training to learn domain-invariant features in both the source and target domains, automatically adjusting the relative importance of global and local distributions to extract more domain-invariant features. It ultimately accomplishes cross-domain recognition tasks between the source and target domains. Firstly, the model extracts advanced speech features through data preprocessing and a BiGRU model. Secondly, it utilizes the global domain discriminator module and the local subdomain discriminator module to capture global and local distributions and calculate the distribution differences between the two domains. Thirdly, the adaptive adversarial module dynamically assigns weights to the global and local distributions, extracting more domain-invariant features. Finally, an emotion classifier identifies the emotion category of unlabeled data in the target domain. The paper employs datasets from different sources to conduct cross-domain teacher's speech emotion recognition in educational scenarios and compares the performance of the proposed AATN model with other transfer learning models. The results demonstrate that the AATN model outperforms others, effectively recognizing emotion categories in teacher's speech in unlabeled conditions.

Acknowledgments. This work is supported by National Natural Science Foundation of China (No. 62377007): Research on Intelligent Recognition and Explainable Evaluation on Teachers' Classroom Teaching Engagement, Chongqing Special Key Project for Technology Innovation and Application Development "R&D and Application of Key Technologies for Intelligent Education Evaluation" (Project No.: CSTC2021jscx−gksbX0059) and Chongqing Key Research Project for Higher Education Teaching Reform "Research and Exploration on Intelligent Evaluation of Students' Comprehensive Quality under the Background of Digital Education Transformation" (Project No.: 232073).

References

1. Ganin, Y., Ustinova, E., Ajakan, H., Germain, P., Larochelle, H., Laviolette, F., et al.: Domain-adversarial training of neural networks. J. Mach. Learn. Res. **17**(1), 2096–2030 (2016)
2. Chen, Y., Wang, J., Huang, M., Yu, H.: Cross-position activity recognition with stratified transfer learning. Pervasive Mob. Comput. **57**, 1–13 (2019)
3. Wang, J., Feng, W., Chen, Y., Yu, H., Huang, M., Yu, P.S.: Visual domain adaptation with manifold embedded distribution alignment. In: Proceedings of the 26th ACM International Conference on Multimedia, pp. 402–410 (2018)

4. Tzeng, E., Hoffman, J., Saenko, K., Darrell, T.: Adversarial discriminative domain adaptation. In: Proceedings of the IEEE Conference on Computer Vision and Pattern Recognition, pp. 7167–7176 (2017)
5. Ganin, Y., Lempitsky, V.: Unsupervised domain adaptation by backpropagation. In: International Conference on Machine Learning. PMLR, pp. 1180–1189 (2015)
6. Pei, Z., Cao, Z., Long, M., Wang, J.: Multi-adversarial domain adaptation. In: Proceedings of the AAAI Conference on Artificial Intelligence, vol. 32, no. 1 (2018)
7. Goodfellow, I., Pouget-Abadie, J., Mirza, M., Xu, B., Warde-Farley, D., Ozair, S., et al.: Generative adversarial networks. Commun. ACM **63**(11), 139–144 (2020)
8. Ben-David, S., Blitzer, J., Crammer, K., Pereira, F.: Analysis of representations for domain adaptation. In: Advances in Neural Information Processing Systems, vol. 19 (2006)
9. CASIA Homepage. http://www.chineseldc.org/resource_info.php?rid=76. Accessed 09 Oct 2010
10. Li, Y., Tao, J., Chao, L., Bao, W., Liu, Y.: CHEAVD: a Chinese natural emotional audio–visual database. J. Ambient. Intell. Humaniz. Comput. **8**, 913–924 (2017)
11. Yang, Y., Wu, T., Li, D., et al.: MASC@CCNT: a Chinese emotional speech database for speaker recognition. In: Proceedings of the 7th Phonetic Conference of China & International Forum on Phonetic Frontiers. Phonetics Division of the Chinese Language Society, pp. 131–137 (2006)
12. Chou, H.C., Lin, W.C., Chang, L.C., Li, C.C., Ma, H.P., Lee, C.C.: NNIME: the NTHU-NTUA Chinese interactive multimodal emotion corpus. In: 2017 Seventh International Conference on Affective Computing and Intelligent Interaction (ACII), pp. 292–298. IEEE (2017)
13. Tzeng, E., Hoffman, J., Zhang, N., Saenko, K., Darrell, T.: Deep domain confusion: maximizing for domain invariance. Speech Commun. **126**, 11–24 (2014)
14. Long, M., Zhu, H., Wang, J., Jordan, M.I.: Unsupervised domain adaptation with residual transfer networks. In: Advances in Neural Information Processing Systems, vol. 29 (2016)
15. Ganin, Y., Lempitsky, V.: Unsupervised domain adaptation by backpropagation. In: International Conference on Machine Learning, PMLR, pp. 1180–1189 (2015)
16. Long, M., Zhu, H., Wang, J., Jordan, M.I.: Deep transfer learning with joint adaptation networks. In: International Conference on Machine Learning, PMLR, pp. 2208–2217 (2017)

Personalized Programming Guidance Based on Deep Programming Learning Style Capturing

Yingfan Liu[1], Renyu Zhu[1,3], and Ming Gao[1,2(✉)]

[1] School of Data Science and Engineering,
East China Normal University, Shanghai, China
yfliu.ds@stu.ecnu.edu.cn, mgao@dase.ecnu.edu.cn
[2] KLATASDS-MOE in School of Statistics,
East China Normal University, Shanghai, China
[3] NetEase Fuxi AI Lab, Hangzhou, Zhejiang, China
zhurenyu@corp.netease.com

Abstract. With the rapid development of big data and AI technology, programming is in high demand and has become an essential skill for students. Meanwhile, researchers also focus on boosting the online judging system's guidance ability to reduce students' dropout rates. Previous studies mainly targeted at enhancing learner engagement on online platforms by providing personalized recommendations. However, two significant challenges still need to be addressed in programming: *C1*) how to recognize complex programming behaviors; *C2*) how to capture intrinsic learning patterns that align with the actual learning process. To fill these gaps, in this paper, we propose a novel model called **P**rogramming **E**xercise **R**ecommender with Learning **S**tyle (**PERS**), which simulates learners' intricate programming behaviors. Specifically, since programming is an iterative and trial-and-error process, we first introduce a positional encoding and a differentiating module to capture the changes of consecutive code submissions (which addresses *C1*). To better profile programming behaviors, we extend the Felder-Silverman learning style model, a classical pedagogical theory, to perceive intrinsic programming patterns. Based on this, we align three latent vectors to record and update programming ability, processing style, and understanding style, respectively (which addresses *C2*). We perform extensive experiments on two real-world datasets to verify the rationality of modeling programming learning styles and the effectiveness of PERS for personalized programming guidance.

Keywords: Programming Education · Sequential Recommendation · Learning Style

1 Introduction

The rapid advancement of AI technology has profoundly influenced on individuals of diverse backgrounds and skill levels. In this connection, online judge systems have emerged as an indispensable avenue for those seeking to boost their programming proficiency[1]. However, despite the growing popularity of this learning modality, high dropout rates have been observed, attributable to the inadequate provision of personalized instructions tailored to learners' unique learning preferences [22].

Recently, recommender systems have been widely applied in online education scenarios to facilitate personalized learning. There are various recommendation models, including CF(collaborative filtering)-based methods [20,31], content-based methods [1,13] and deep-learning-based methods [7,8]. These general models aim to provide personalized recommendations by capturing users' interests and needs through static preferences and individual interactions. In the context of programming, however, the learning process exhibits a dynamic and progressive nature. This represents an essential application of the sequential recommendation (SR) task, which predicts subsequent behavioral sequences based on historical records [12,27,29,32].

While extant SR models have yielded successful results in e-learning contexts, there remain significant gaps in directly deploying them to programming scenarios [18]. As illustrated by Fig. 1, programming learning differs from traditional learning in two crucial respects: i) it enables learners to make multiple attempts on the same exercise and edit their previous submissions based on the feedback received from the compiler and, ii) the platform can record fine-grained behavioral data related to programming, including code snippets, compilation time, and compilation status. Furthermore, current sequential models prioritize learners' patterns with little regard to their intrinsic behaviors, including learning styles. These styles reflect the ways in which learners process and comprehend information, and are thus factors that cannot be ignored.

Consequently, the study of SR in programming learning confronts two significant challenges. First, it is imperative to model distinctive and fine-grained patterns involved in programming, including code-related side features and iterative submission behavior (*C1*). Second, there is an urgent need to incorporate pedagogical theory into the model to bolster its interpretability with the actual learning process (*C2*).

To address the above challenges, we propose a new model named **P**rogramming **E**xercise **R**ecommender with Learning **S**tyle (PERS). To simulate the iterative process in programming, we employ a two-step approach. Firstly, we map programming exercises and code-related features (such as code snippets, execution time, and execution status) into embeddings using a representation module with positional encoding. Secondly, we formulate a differentiating module that calculates the changes between consecutive code submissions. This module can adeptly capture fine-grained learning patterns by effectively distinguishing between intra-exercise or inter-exercise attempts (for *C1*). To enhance the consistency between our proposed model and the actual learning process, we draw

---

[1] A theory proposed by Richard M. Felder and Linda K. Silverman to describe individuals' preferred ways of learning. Further details will be provided in the related work section.

inspiration from a pedagogical theory known as the Felder-Silverman Learning Style Model (FSLSM) [4], which is widely utilized in educational scenarios for mining learning patterns and delivering personalized guidance. Considering the processing and understanding dimensions in FSLSM, we present a formal definition and detailed descriptions of programming learning styles in this paper. On this foundation, we develop three latent vectors: programming ability, processing style, and understanding style, which are designed to track the learners' intrinsic behavioral patterns during the programming process (for $C2$). After obtaining the above vectors, our model employs a multilayer perceptron (MLP) to generate personalized predictions that align individuals' learning preferences. In summary, the main contributions of this paper are summarized as follows:

- Our study endeavors to furnish personalized programming guidance by emulating the iterative and trial-and-error programming learning process, thereby offering a novel vantage point on programming education.
- We have meaningfully incorporated the FSLSM pedagogical theory into our model, enabling us to effectively capturing the intrinsic behavioral patterns of students while also enhancing rationality and consistency.
- We conduct experiments on two real-world datasets to validate the efficacy and interpretability of our approach.

2   Related Works

2.1   Sequential Recommendation

Sequential recommendation models aim to incorporate users' personalized and contextual information based on their historical interactions [16] to predict the future behaviors.

In earlier studies, researchers considered Markov chains as a powerful method to model interaction processes and capture users' sequential patterns [2,9]. Later, the advent of recurrent neural networks (RNN) greatly has expanded the potential of recommender systems to process multi-type input data and understand complex item transitions. For example, [10] first adopt RNN on real-life session-based recommendations and then enhance the backbone with parallel RNN to leverage more rich features [11]. There are various techniques designed to improve the RNN-based models, such as data augmentation (GRU4Rec [29]), data reconstruction (SRGNN [32]), and unified module injection (SINE [28], CORE [12]). Recently, another line of works has seeked to use the Transformer module to capture global information, which RNN overlooks. For instance, BERT4Rec [27] utilize bidirectional self-attention with Cloze tasks during training to enhance the hidden representation.

2.2   Sequential Recommendation in E-Learning

Existing research on SR in e-learning typically focus on recommending the most appropriate resources, such as courses and exercises, to learners by capturing their static and dynamic characteristics through their past behavioral record [14]. For instance, [15] and [19] propose a cognitive diagnostic method to model students' proficiency on each exercises based on probabilistic matrix factorization and students' proficiency. [25] apply a knowledge tracing model with an enhanced self-attention to measures students' mastery states and assist model to recommend. These methods effectively capture students' preferences and mastery of knowledge points. However, they often overlook the impact of students' internal learning styles.

In the field of programming, some preliminary attempts have been made to explore the personalized recommendations. For example, [18] apply BERT [3] to encode students' source code and propose a knowledge tracing model to capture mastery of programming skills. However, the dynamic sequential patterns in existing works are not consistent with real programming process due to ignore the iterative process.

2.3 Learning Style Model

Learning styles refer to the way in which students prefer to obtain, process and retain information [5]. The most common theoretical models include Felder-Silverman Learning Style Model (FSLSM), Kolb's learning style [17] and VARK model [23]. Previous research has demonstrated that the FSLSM is more comprehensible and appropriate for identifying learning styles in online learning compared to other models [21]. This model describes learning styles from four dimensions: the perspective of perception (sensitive/intuitive), information input (visual/verbal), processing (active/reflective) and understanding (sequential/global) based on the learner's behavior patterns during learning process.

3 Preliminaries

3.1 Programming Learning Style Model

Inspired by the FSLSM, we define a programming learning style model (PLSM) centered around the problem-solving behavior observed in online judging systems.

As shown in Table 1, the PLSM delineates the inherent learning patterns during programming through two dimensions: processing and understanding. In terms of processing, learners can be classified as either active or reflective. When solving exercises, active learners tend to think through a complete answer before submitting their solution, while reflective learners prefer to attempt the same exercise multiple times and refine their previous submissions based on the compiler feedback. As for the dimension of understanding, learners can be labeled as sequential or global. Sequential learners tend to approach learning tasks in a progressive sequence, such as in numerical or knowledge concept order. In contrast, global learners tend to approach tasks in a non-linear fashion, such as by selecting tasks that they find most interesting or engaging. These distinct learning styles reflect learners' preferences and can significantly impact the trajectory of their problem-solving process.

Table 1. Programming Learning Style Model

Dimension	Label	Learning Characteristics
Processing	Active	Solving exercises by figuring out a complete answer before submitting
	Reflective	Solving exercises through multiple trials and errors
Understanding	Sequential	Solving step-by-step
	Global	Solving by leaps and bounds

3.2   Problem Definition

To foster learners' involvement and enhance their programming skills in online judge systems, we present a new task called programming exercise recommendation (PER). The definition of PER is as follows and an example of data model is depicted in Fig. 1.

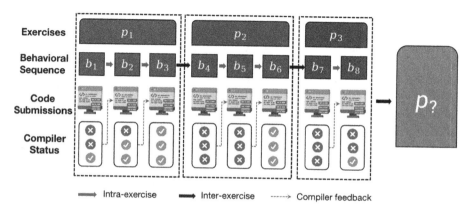

Fig. 1. Data model for PER task

Definition: Programming Exercise Recommendation. Suppose there are n online learning users $\mathcal{U} = \{u_1, u_2, \cdots, u_n\}$ with problem-solving behavior logs $\mathcal{B} = \{B_1, B_2, \cdots, B_n\}$ and m programming exercises $\mathcal{P} = \{p_1, p_2, \cdots, p_m\}$. Specifically, the i-th record $B_i = \{b_1, b_2, \cdots, b_{l_i}\}$ represents the interaction sequence of the i-th learner u_i, where l_i represents the length of the sequence. Each element b_j in the sequence is a triple $\langle p_{b_j}, c_{b_j}, r_{b_j} \rangle$ consisting of the problem p_{b_j}, the code c_{b_j} and the compilation result r_{b_j}. The ultimate goal of programming exercise recommendation is to predict learners' learning preferences in the future based on the past interaction behavior B_i between learners and exercises. that is, the next exercise $p_{b_{l_i}+1}$ that will be tried. Correspondingly, in machine learning methods, the optimization objective is:

$$l_i = \max_{\mathcal{A}} \prod_{(b_i, p_{b_{l_i}+1}) \in \mathcal{B} \cup \mathcal{B}^-} \log \mathcal{A}(p_{b_{l_i}+1}|B_i)^{y_i} (1 - \mathcal{A}(p_{b_{l_i}+1})|B_i)^{(1-y_i)}, \quad (1)$$

where $\mathcal{A}$ is a probabilistic prediction model, such as neural networks, whose output is to predict the probability of interacting with the next exercise $p_{b_{l_i}+1}$ based on the historical behavior sequence B_i. $\mathcal{B}^-$ is a set of negative samples, i.e., the exercises that learner u_i has not interacted with label $y_i = 1$ if and only if $(B_i, p_{b_{l_i}+1}) \in \mathcal{B}$, otherwise $y_i = 0$.

4   PERS Framework

In this section, we propose a deep learning framework, namely PERS, to solve programming exercise recommendation. As shown in Fig. 2, the architecture of PERS is mainly composed of four functional modules: representing, differentiating, updating and predicting. The details of the four modules are given in the following.

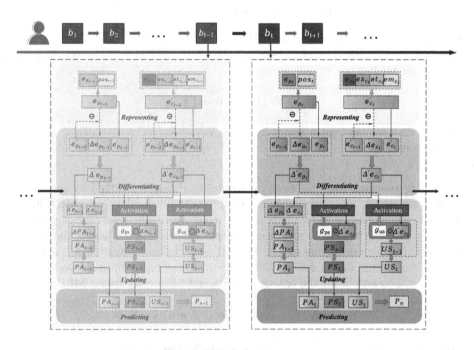

Fig. 2. PERS Architecture

4.1   Representing Module

The representing module mainly focuses on obtaining the embedding of the two inputs: exercises and codes.

Exercise Representation. As demonstrated in Fig. 1, learners typically attempt a programming exercise multiple times until they pass all test cases. Even when trying the same exercise, the compilation results for each attempt are distinct and progressive. Therefore, the exercise embedding and the positional embedding in the sequence are both critical. Suppose p_t denotes the programming exercise coded by the learners at time t. First, we use a projection matrix $\mathbf{E}_p \in \mathcal{R}^{(N+2) \times d_p}$ to represent each exercise by its id, where N is the total number of exercises and d_p is the dimension. The first dimension of the projection matrix here is $N + 2$ because two zero pads are added. Then the representation vector for the problem p_t can be obtained as $\mathbf{e}_{p_t} \in \mathcal{R}^{d_p}$. In addition, inspired by the work [30], we use the sinusoidal function to acquire the position embedding $\mathbf{pos}_t$ at time t:

$$\mathbf{pos}_{(t,2i)} = \sin(t/10000^{2i/d_{pos}}), \tag{2}$$

$$\mathbf{pos}_{(t,2i+1)} = \cos(t/10000^{2i/d_{pos}}). \tag{3}$$

where d_{pos} denotes the dimension. Based on the exercise embedding $\mathbf{e}_{p_t}$ and the position embedding $\mathbf{pos}_t$, we obtain the enhanced exercise embedding $\mathbf{e}'_{p_t}$ through an MLP:

$$\mathbf{e}'_{p_t} = \mathbf{W}_1^T[\mathbf{e}_{p_t} \oplus \mathbf{pos}_t] + \mathbf{b}_1, \tag{4}$$

where $\oplus$ denotes the vector concatenation, $\mathbf{W}_1 \in \mathcal{R}^{(d_p+d_{pos}) \times d_k}$, $\mathbf{b}_1 \in \mathcal{R}^{d_k}$ are learnable parameters.

Code Representation. Suppose c_t denotes the code submitted by the learners at time step t. First, we apply a code pre-training model CodeBERT [6] to obtain the initial embedding of code $\mathbf{e}_{c_t} \in \mathcal{R}^{d_c}$. Additionally, we employ different projection matrices to obtain the representation vectors of code-related side features: the execution time $\mathbf{et}_{c_t} \in \mathcal{R}^{d_{ct}}$, the execution memory $\mathbf{em}_{c_t} \in \mathcal{R}^{d_{cm}}$, and the execution status $\mathbf{es}_{c_t} \in \mathcal{R}^{d_{cs}}$. After all the representation vectors are generated, we can obtain the enhanced code embedding $\mathbf{e}'_{c_t}$ by an MLP:

$$\mathbf{e}'_{c_t} = \mathbf{W}_2^T[\mathbf{e}_{c_t} \oplus \mathbf{es}_{c_t} \oplus \mathbf{et}_{c_t} \oplus \mathbf{em}_{c_t}] + \mathbf{b}_2, \tag{5}$$

where $\mathbf{W}_2 \in \mathcal{R}^{(d_c+d_{cs}+d_{ct}+d_{cm}) \times d_k}$ is the weight matrix, $\mathbf{b}_2 \in \mathcal{R}^{d_k}$ is the bias term.

4.2 Differentiating Module

As the introduction highlights, one of the challenges in PER is to simulate the iterative and trial-and-error process of programming learning. In this paper, we develop a differentiating module to capture fine-grained learning patterns. To distinguish whether students are answering the same exercise or starting a new one, we first calculate the exercise difference embedding $\Delta\mathbf{e}_{p_t}$ between students' present exercise embedding $\mathbf{e}'_{p_t}$ and previous exercise embedding $\mathbf{e}'_{p_{t-1}}$ by subtraction. Then, we feed the above three embeddings into a multi-layer perceptron to output the final exercise difference embedding $\Delta'\mathbf{e}_{p_t}$:

$$\Delta\mathbf{e}_{p_t} = \mathbf{e}'_{p_t} - \mathbf{e}'_{p_{t-1}} \tag{6}$$

$$\Delta'\mathbf{e}_{p_t} = \mathbf{W}_3^T[\Delta\mathbf{e}_{p_t} \oplus \mathbf{e}'_{p_t} \oplus \mathbf{e}'_{p_{t-1}}] + \mathbf{b}_3, \tag{7}$$

For the same exercise, the codes students submit are different at each attempt, which can indicate their progress in the trial-and-error process. Therefore, we use students' present code embedding $\mathbf{e}'_{c_t}$, previous code embedding $\mathbf{e}'_{c_{t-1}}$ and the difference between them $\Delta\mathbf{e}_{c_t}$ to obtain the final code difference embedding $\Delta'\mathbf{e}_{c_t}$:

$$\Delta\mathbf{e}_{c_t} = \mathbf{e}'_{c_t} - \mathbf{e}'_{c_{t-1}}, \tag{8}$$

$$\Delta'\mathbf{e}_{c_t} = \mathbf{W}_4^T[\Delta\mathbf{e}_{c_t} \oplus \mathbf{e}'_{c_t} \oplus \mathbf{e}'_{c_{t-1}}] + \mathbf{b}_4, \tag{9}$$

where $\mathbf{W}_3, \mathbf{W}_4 \in \mathcal{R}^{3d_k \times d_k}$ is the weight matrix, $\mathbf{b}_3, \mathbf{b}_4 \in \mathcal{R}^{d_k}$ is the bias term.

4.3 Updating Module

The purpose of this module is to update the latent states that represent the learner's intrinsic learning style. Inspired by the classic learning style model FSLSM, we propose two hidden vectors, processing style $\mathbf{PS}_t$ and understanding style $\mathbf{US}_t$, to capture the programming learning style of learners. In addition, motivated by the programming knowledge tracing research [33], we introduce another hidden vector called programming ability $\mathbf{PA}_t$ to enhance the modeling of programming behavior.

First, we assume that all learners start with the same programming ability $\mathbf{PA}_0$, and their programming ability will gradually improve as they progress through exercises. The learners' programming ability $\mathbf{PA}_t$ at time step t depends on their performance in completing the current exercises as well as their previous programming ability $\mathbf{PA}_{t-1}$. The corresponding update process is as follows:

$$\Delta\mathbf{PA} = \mathbf{W}_5^T[\mathbf{e}'_{p_t} \oplus \mathbf{e}'_{c_t}] + \mathbf{b}_5, \tag{10}$$

$$\mathbf{PA}_t = \mathbf{W}_6^T[\Delta\mathbf{PA} \oplus \mathbf{PA}_{t-1}] + \mathbf{b}_6, \tag{11}$$

where $\mathbf{W}_5, \mathbf{W}_6 \in \mathcal{R}^{2d_k \times d_k}$ are weight matrices, $\mathbf{b}_5, \mathbf{b}_6 \in \mathcal{R}^{d_k}$ are bias terms. When $t = 0$, $\mathbf{PA}_0 \in \mathcal{R}^{d_k}$ is initialized as a vector of all zeros.

Similarly, the initial processing style $\mathbf{PS}_0 \in \mathcal{R}^{d_k}$ at time $t = 0$ is also initialized as a vector of all zeros. As shown in Table 1, the learner's processing style mainly manifests in their continuous trial-and-error behavior on the same exercise. Leveraging the difference of exercise $\Delta'\mathbf{e}_{p_t}$ and code $\Delta'\mathbf{e}_{c_t}$ generated from the difference module, we introduce a gating mechanism to update the learner's processing style vector $\mathbf{PS}_t$. We first calculate a selection gate $\mathbf{g}_{ps}$ using $\Delta'\mathbf{e}_{p_t}$, which determines whether the current exercise is identical to the previous one. Then $\mathbf{g}_{ps}$ is multiplied by $\Delta' \mathbf{e}_{c_t}$ to figure out how much semantic information should be learned from the code. Finally, we concatenate the result with the previous processing style $\mathbf{PS}_{t-1}$ and employ a multi-layer perception to fuse these vectors as follows:

$$\mathbf{g}_{ps} = \tanh(\mathbf{W}_7^T \Delta' \mathbf{e}_{p_t} + \mathbf{b}_7), \tag{12}$$

$$\mathbf{PS}_t = \mathbf{W}_8^T [\mathbf{PS}_{t-1} \oplus (\mathbf{g}_{ps} \odot \Delta' \mathbf{e}_{c_t})] + \mathbf{b}_8, \tag{13}$$

where tanh is the non-linear activation function, $\mathbf{W}_7 \in \mathcal{R}^{d_k \times d_k}$, $\mathbf{W}_8 \in \mathcal{R}^{2d_k \times d_k}$, $\mathbf{b}_7, \mathbf{b}_8 \in \mathcal{R}^{d_k}$ are trainable parameters, $\odot$ is the vector element-wise product operation.

Another latent vector is the understanding style $\mathbf{US}_t$, which indicates whether learners prefer to learn step-by-step or in leaps and bounds. It is derived from the learner's historical records. Thus, the initial understanding style $\mathbf{US}_0 \in \mathcal{R}^{d_k}$ is also initialized as a vector of zeros. Similar to the processing style, we also employ a gating mechanism to determine whether the learner is attempting the same exercise, and subsequently update the current understanding style $\mathbf{US}_t$ based on the previous one $\mathbf{US}_{t-1}$:

$$\mathbf{g}_{us} = \tanh(\mathbf{W}_9^T \Delta' \mathbf{e}_{p_t} + \mathbf{b}_9), \tag{14}$$

$$\mathbf{US}_t = \mathbf{US}_{t-1} + \mathbf{W}_{10}^T (\mathbf{g}_{us} \odot \mathbf{e}_{p_t}') \tag{15}$$

where $\mathbf{W}_9, \mathbf{W}_{10} \in \mathcal{R}^{d_k \times d_k}$ are weight matrices, $\mathbf{b}_9 \in \mathcal{R}^{d_k}$ is the bias term.

4.4 Predicting Module

After obtaining the learner's programming ability $\mathbf{PA}_t$, processing style $\mathbf{PS}_t$, and understanding style $\mathbf{US}_t$, we can predict the next exercise in the predicting module. First, the three intrinsic vectors are concatenated and then projected to the output layer using a fully connected network to get $\mathbf{Pre}_t$. After that, we encode $\mathbf{Pre}_t$ into an m-dimensional project matrix and obtain the final probability vector $\mathbf{p}_n$ of exercises being recommended at the next step.

$$\mathbf{Pre}_t = \mathbf{W}_{11}^T [\mathbf{PL}_t \oplus \mathbf{PS}_t \oplus \mathbf{US}_t] + \mathbf{b}_{11}, \tag{16}$$

$$\mathbf{p}_n = \mathbf{W}_{12}^T \mathbf{Pre}_t + \mathbf{b}_{12} \tag{17}$$

where $\mathbf{W}_{11} \in \mathcal{R}^{3d_k \times d_k}$ and $\mathbf{W}_{12} \in \mathcal{R}^{d_k \times d_n}$ are weight matrices, $\mathbf{b}_{11} \in \mathcal{R}^{d_k}$ and $\mathbf{b}_{12} \in \mathcal{R}^{d_m}$ is the bias term.

5 Experiments

In this section, we aim to evaluate the effectiveness of PERS on programming exercise recommendation through empirical evaluation and answer the following research questions:

- **RQ1**: How does PERS perform compared with state-of-the-art pedagogical methods and sequential methods on programming exercise recommendation?
- **RQ2**: What is the impact of different components on the performance of PERS ?
- **RQ3**: How do the primary hyperparameters influence the performance of our model?
- **RQ4**: Can the proposed method learn meaningful intrinsic representations of students during programming?

5.1   Experimental Settings

Datasets. We evaluate our proposed method PERS on two real-world datasets: BePKT [33]and CodeNet [24]. The two datasets are both collected from online judging systems, including problems, codes and rich contextual information such as problem descriptions and code compilation results. Due to the millions of behaviors and contextual data in CodeNet, memory overflow exists when processing contextual features such as code and problem descriptions. Therefore, we sample the CodeNet dataset based on sequence length and submit time, resulting in two smaller-scale datasets: CodeNet-len and CodeNet-time. A brief overview of each dataset is listed as follows:

- **BePKT:** collected from an online judging system[2] targeted at university education, with its users primarily being college students who start learning to program.
- **CodeNet:** collected and processed by IBM researchers from two large-scale online judgment systems AIZU[3] and AtCoder[4]. The dataset contains hundreds of thousands of programming learners from different domains.
- **CodeNet-len:** a subset of the CodeNet dataset, which only keeps learners' programming behavioral sequences with lengths between 500 and 600.
- **CodeNet-time:** a subset from the CodeNet dataset with submission timestamps between March and April 2020.

Table 2 presents detailed statistics for the above datasets. Specifically, the calculation formula of #Sparsity is as follows:

$$\#\text{Sparsity} = 1 - \frac{\#\text{Interactions}}{\#\text{Students} \times \#\text{Exercises}}, \qquad (18)$$

---

[2] https://judgefield.shuishan.net.cn/.
[3] https://onlinejudge.u-aizu.ac.jp/home.
[4] https://atcoder.jp/.

Table 2. Detailed statistics of all datasets in experiments, where #Learners denotes the number of learners, #Interactions denotes the number of interactions, #Exercises denotes the number of exercises, #Sparsity denotes the sparsity of the dataset, #Pass-Rate denotes the proportion of successful submissions in all submissions, and #APE(short for Avg-Attempts-Per-Exercise) denotes the average number of attempts on the same programming exercise.

Dataset	#Learners	#Interactions	#Exercises	#Sparsity	#Pass-Rate	#APE
BePKT	907	75,993	553	84.85%	32.03%	3.18
CodeNet	154,179	13,916,868	4,049	97.77%	53.61%	2.05
CodeNet-time	26,270	811,465	2,465	98.75%	53.42%	1.89
CodeNet-len	1,107	605,661	3,308	83.46%	56.88%	1.87

Baselines. We compare PERS with the following 8 comparable baselines, which can be grouped into two categories:

- **Pedagogical methods: ACKRec** [8] and **LPKT** [26] are two representative methods in e-learning recommendation. ACKRec constructs a heterogeneous information network to capture entity relationships. LPKT develops a model by simulating students' learning processes.
- **Sequential methods:** We introduce 6 state-of-the-art sequential models, which are 1) **GRU4Rec** [29] introduces data augmentation on recurrent neural network to improve model performance. 2) **GRU4Recf** [11] further integrates a parallel recurrent neural network to simultaneously represent clicks and feature vectors within interactions. 3) **BERT4Rec** [27] introduces a two-way self-attention mechanism based on BERT [3]. 4) **SRGNN** [32] converts user behavior sequences into graph-structured data and introduces a graph neural network to capture the relationship between items. 5) **SINE** [28] proposes a sparse interest network to adaptively generate dynamic preference. 6) **CORE** [12] designs a representation consistency model to pull the vectors into the same space.

Since all the above baselines do not incorporate code as the model input, for a fair comparison, we implement a degraded version of PERS:

- **ERS**: Remove the code feature input and all subsequent related modules in PERS.

Evaluation Metrics. To fairly compare different models, inspired by the previous [8], we choose the HR@10 (Hit Ratio), NDCG@10 (Normalized Discounted Cumulative Gain), and MRR@10 (Mean Reciprocal Rank) as the evaluation metrics.

Table 3. The overall performance on two full datasets and two sample datasets. OOM refers to out of memory.

Datasets	Metrics	Pedegogicals		Sequentials						Ours	
		LPKT	ACKRec	GRU4Rec	GRU4Recf	BERT4Rec	SRGNN	SINE	CORE	ERS	PERS
BePKT	HR@10	0.8762	0.8849	0.9172	0.9135	0.7369	0.9074	0.6419	0.9172	<u>0.9256</u>	**0.9288**
	MRR@10	0.6743	0.6838	0.7057	0.7053	0.5324	0.6870	0.4059	0.6923	<u>0.7104</u>	**0.7153**
	NDCG@10	0.7128	0.7269	0.7573	0.7560	0.5816	0.7408	0.4623	0.7466	<u>0.7645</u>	**0.7688**
CodeNet	HR@10	0.8423	0.8372	<u>0.8728</u>	OOM	0.6715	0.8700	0.7276	0.8566	**0.8803**	OOM
	MRR@10	0.6372	0.6305	<u>0.6927</u>	OOM	0.4205	0.6879	0.4643	0.5934	**0.7012**	OOM
	NDCG@10	0.6983	0.6847	<u>0.7374</u>	OOM	0.4811	0.7332	0.5285	0.6581	**0.7435**	OOM
CodeNet-len	HR@10	0.7539	0.7754	0.7812	0.7767	0.1157	0.7821	0.4602	0.7865	<u>0.7934</u>	**0.8010**
	MRR@10	0.5816	0.5938	0.6189	0.6143	0.0453	0.6073	0.2411	0.5251	<u>0.6235</u>	**0.6322**
	NDCG@10	0.6043	0.6139	0.6590	0.6545	0.0614	0.6504	0.2934	0.5850	<u>0.6631</u>	**0.6704**
CodeNet-time	HR@10	0.8532	0.8425	0.8993	0.8991	0.7517	0.8989	0.7742	0.8962	<u>0.9058</u>	**0.9167**
	MRR@10	0.6931	0.6852	0.7309	0.7316	0.6473	0.7236	0.5458	0.6060	<u>0.7422</u>	**0.7574**
	NDCG@10	0.7348	0.7233	0.7731	0.7735	0.5978	0.7675	0.6016	0.6775	<u>0.7841</u>	**0.7923**

Training Details. For pedagogical methods, we use the original codes released by their authors[5,6]. Additionally, we implement the PERS model and other baseline models using PyTorch and the RecBole library[7]. We run all the experiments on a server with 64 G memory and two NVIDIA Tesla V100 GPUs. For all models, we set the max sequence length to 50, the batch size of the training set to 2048 and the test set to 4096, and the optimizer to Adam. For the PERS model, we set the exercise and code representation embedding dimensions to 128. We perform the hyper-parameter tuning for the learning rate $\{0.1, 0.01, 0.001\}$, the layer number $\{1, 2, 3\}$, and the dropout rate $\{0.1, 0.3, 0.5\}$. For all methods, we fine-tune the hyperparameters to achieve the best performance and run experiments three times to report the average results.

5.2   RQ1: Overall Performance

Table 3 summarizes the performance results. We evaluate the methods on four datasets under three evaluation metrics. The best results are highlighted in bold and the best baselines are underlined. From results in the Table 3, we make the following observations:

- Our proposed models, PERS and ERS, demonstrate state-of-the-art performance on large-scale programming learning datasets. For instance, in the case of the CodeNet dataset, our models exhibit a significant improvement of 1.41% on HR@10, 1.30% on MRR@10, 1.12% on NDCG@10 over the best baseline.
- Code features can significantly improve the performance of the model. In the BePKT, CodeNet-len, and CodeNet-time datasets, the PERS model with

---

[5] https://github.com/JockWang/ACKRec.

[6] https://github.com/bigdata-ustc/EduKTM/tree/main/EduKTM.

[7] https://recbole.io/.

code features outperforms the ERS model This finding highlights that code-related features contribute to modeling students' programming learning preferences.

- RNN-based sequential models exhibit superior capabilities in capturing learning behaviors. Our PERS and ERS, which extends recurrent neural networks, achieve the best performance. Additionally, the GRU4Rec and GRU4Recf models, designed based on recurrent neural networks, outperform all other sequential methods. This observation suggests that RNNs are particularly adept at capturing sequential programming behaviors.

5.3   RQ2: Ablation Study

We conduct an ablation study on PERS to understand the importance of the primary components. We obtain five variants: 1) **PERS-ep**, which removes the exercise position encoding; 2) **PERS-cr**, which removes the code representation; 3) **PERS-pa**, 4) **PERS-ps**, and 5) **PERS-us** are another three variants that remove PA_t, PS_t and US_t, respectively. Figure 3 displays the results of the PERS model and the its variants on the CodeNet-len and CodeNet-time datasets. From the figure, we can observe:

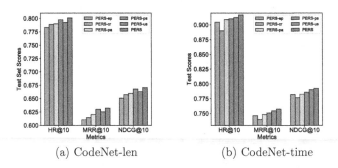

(a) CodeNet-len   (b) CodeNet-time

Fig. 3. Ablation Study Results on CodeNet-len(left) and CodeNet-time(right)

- Both the representating and updating modules play a crucial role in capturing programming behaviour. As can be observed, the removal of any component of the PERS adversely affects its performance, which emphasizes the rationality and effectiveness of the proposed methods.
- The impact of different components varies across different stages of learning. Specifically, in the CodeNet-len dataset, the performance is significantly affected when removing the position encoding of exercises (PERS-ep variant). On the other hand, in the CodeNet-time dataset, the performance sharply declines when the code representation (PERS-cr variant) is removed. This is because the CodeNet-len dataset comprises the latter part of students'

behavioral sequences, where students have developed a fixed behavioral pattern. Consequently, the representation of the exercises significantly impacts the model's performance. Similarly, removing different intrinsic latent vectors leads to different degrees of performance decline. The finding indicates that processing style is more critical in the initial learning stages while the understanding style are more influential as the learning pattern becomes more fixed.

5.4   RQ3: Sensitivity Analysis of Hyperparameters

We conduct a sensitivity analysis on the hyperparameter of PERS with two datasets: CodeNet-len and Code-time. In particular, we study three main hyperparameters: 1) sequence length $\lambda \in \{50, 100, 150, 200\}$, 2) dimension of exercise embedding $d_p \in \{32, 64, 128, 256\}$, and 3) dimension of code embedding $d_c \in \{32, 64, 128, 256\}$. In our experiments, we vary one parameter each time with others fixed. Figure 4 illustrates the impacts of each hyperparameter and we can obtain the following observations:

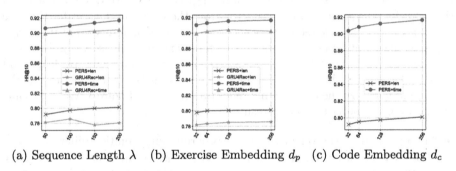

(a) Sequence Length λ (b) Exercise Embedding d_p (c) Code Embedding d_c

Fig. 4. Influence of three key hyperparameters on the performance of the PERS.

- Our model is capable of capturing long sequence dependencies. In Fig. 4(a), PERS performs better as the sequence length increases, while the results of GRU4Rec remain unchanged or even decline.
- As shown in Fig. 4(b), the performance of both PERS and GRU4Rec initially improves and then declines as the dimension of exercise embedding increases. The optimal performance is achieved at approximately $d_p = 128$.
- As the dimension of code embedding increases, the performance of PERS in Fig. 4(c) shows a consistent enhancement, highlighting the significance of code features in capturing programming learning patterns.

5.5   RQ4: Case Study on Visualization Analysis

To demonstrate the interpretability of our approach, we conduct a visualization analysis of three latent vectors involved in the PERS, i.e., programming ability

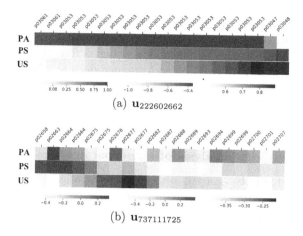

Fig. 5. Case study on latent vectors visualization

$\mathbf{PA}_t$, processing style $\mathbf{PA}_t$ and understanding style $\mathbf{US}_t$. We randomly selected the behavioral sequences of two students from the CodeNet dataset for the case study. From the exercise sequence of each student, we can observe that $\mathbf{u}_{222602662}$ tends to make multiple attempts at the same exercise and solve problems in a systematic manner, while $\mathbf{u}_{737111725}$ prefers solving problems by leaps and bound. We extract these three instinct vectors from the last time step of the model and visualize the dimensional reduction results in Figure 5. We note some observations in the visualization results:

- The extent of variation in students' programming abilities differs between inter-exercise and intra-exercise. Taking $\mathbf{u}_{222602662}$ as an example, as he made multiple attempts on $\mathbf{p}_{03053}$, his programming ability continuously improved. However, when he attempted the next exercise, his $\mathbf{PA}_t$ showed a noticeable decline. Therefore, fine-grained modeling of inter-exercise contributes to better capturing students' learning state.
- The changing patterns of learning styles among different students is consistent with their learning process. For $\mathbf{u}_{222602662}$, the value of $\mathbf{PS}_t$ and $\mathbf{US}_t$ gradually approach 1 during the programming learning process, suggesting a reflective and sequential learning style. As for $\mathbf{u}_{737111725}$, his corresponding latent vectors exhibit a gradual tendency towards -1, indicating an active and global learning style. This shows that the latent vectors can learn valuable information, thereby validating the rationality of our model.

6   Conclusions

In this paper, we study programming exercise recommendation (PER) to enhance engagement on online programming learning platforms. To solve PER, we propose a novel model called PERS based on simulating learners' intricate programming behaviors. First, we extend the Felder-Silverman learning style model to the programming learning domain and present the programming learning style. After that, based on the programming learning style, we construct latent vectors to model learner's states, including programming ability, processing style, and understanding style. In particular, we introduce a differentiating module to update the states based on enhanced context, which are positions for exercises and compilation results for codes, respectively. Finally, the updated states at the last time step are sent to predict. Extensive experiments on two real-world datasets demonstrate the effectiveness and interpretability of our approach. In future work, we will explore incorporating the difference of structural features from students' submitted code to further enhance the performance of the model.

Acknowledgement. This work has been supported by the National Natural Science Foundation of China under Grant No. U1911203, and the National Natural Science Foundation of China under Grant No. 62377012.

References

1. Bagher, R.C., Hassanpour, H., Mashayekhi, H.: User trends modeling for a content-based recommender system. Expert Syst. Appl. **87**, 209–219 (2017)
2. Cai, C., He, R., McAuley, J.J.: SPMC: socially-aware personalized Markov chains for sparse sequential recommendation. In: Sierra, C. (ed.) Proceedings of the Twenty-Sixth International Joint Conference on Artificial Intelligence, IJCAI 2017, Melbourne, Australia, 19–25 August 2017, pp. 1476–1482. ijcai.org (2017)
3. Devlin, J., Chang, M., Lee, K., Toutanova, K.: BERT: pre-training of deep bidirectional transformers for language understanding. In: Proceedings of the 2019 Conference of the North American Chapter of the Association for Computational Linguistics: Human Language Technologies, pp. 4171–4186 (2019)
4. Felder, R.M., Silverman, L.K., et al.: Learning and teaching styles in engineering education. Eng. Educ. **78**(7), 674–681 (1988)
5. Felder, R.M., Spurlin, J.: Applications, reliability and validity of the index of learning styles. Int. J. Eng. Educ. **21**(1), 103–112 (2005)
6. Feng, Z., et al.: CodeBERT: a pre-trained model for programming and natural languages. In: Cohn, T., He, Y., Liu, Y. (eds.) Findings of the Association for Computational Linguistics: EMNLP 2020, Online Event, 16–20 November 2020. Findings of ACL, vol. EMNLP 2020, pp. 1536–1547. Association for Computational Linguistics (2020)
7. Gong, J., et al.: Reinforced MOOCs concept recommendation in heterogeneous information networks. CoRR abs/2203.11011 (2022)
8. Gong, J., Wang, S., Wang, J., Feng, W., Peng, H., Tang, J., Yu, P.S.: Attentional graph convolutional networks for knowledge concept recommendation in MOOCs in a heterogeneous view. In: Huang, J.X., Chang, Y., Cheng, X., Kamps, J., Murdock, V., Wen, J., Liu, Y. (eds.) Proceedings of the 43rd International ACM SIGIR conference on research and development in Information Retrieval, SIGIR 2020, Virtual Event, China, 25–30 July 2020, pp. 79–88. ACM (2020)
9. He, R., McAuley, J.J.: Fusing similarity models with Markov chains for sparse sequential recommendation. In: Bonchi, F., Domingo-Ferrer, J., Baeza-Yates, R.,

Zhou, Z., Wu, X. (eds.) IEEE 16th International Conference on Data Mining, ICDM 2016, 12–15 December 2016, Barcelona, Spain, pp. 191–200. IEEE Computer Society (2016)

10. Hidasi, B., Karatzoglou, A., Baltrunas, L., Tikk, D.: Session-based recommendations with recurrent neural networks. In: Bengio, Y., LeCun, Y. (eds.) 4th International Conference on Learning Representations, ICLR 2016, San Juan, Puerto Rico, 2–4 May 2016, Conference Track Proceedings (2016)

11. Hidasi, B., Quadrana, M., Karatzoglou, A., Tikk, D.: Parallel recurrent neural network architectures for feature-rich session-based recommendations. In: Sen, S., Geyer, W., Freyne, J., Castells, P. (eds.) Proceedings of the 10th ACM Conference on Recommender Systems, Boston, MA, USA, 15–19 September 2016, pp. 241–248. ACM (2016)

12. Hou, Y., Hu, B., Zhang, Z., Zhao, W.X.: CORE: simple and effective session-based recommendation within consistent representation space. In: Amigó, E., Castells, P., Gonzalo, J., Carterette, B., Culpepper, J.S., Kazai, G. (eds.) SIGIR '22: The 45th International ACM SIGIR Conference on Research and Development in Information Retrieval, Madrid, Spain, 11–15 July 2022, pp. 1796–1801. ACM (2022)

13. Huang, R., Lu, R.: Research on content-based MOOC recommender model. In: 5th International Conference on Systems and Informatics, ICSAI 2018, Nanjing, China, 10–12 November 2018, pp. 676–681. IEEE (2018)

14. Jiang, L., et al.: Eduhawkes: a neural Hawkes process approach for online study behavior modeling. In: Demeniconi, C., Davidson, I. (eds.) Proceedings of the 2021 SIAM International Conference on Data Mining, SDM 2021, Virtual Event, 29 April–1 May 2021, pp. 567–575. SIAM (2021)

15. Jiang, L., Zhang, W., Wang, Y., Luo, N., Yue, L.: Augmenting personalized question recommendation with hierarchical information for online test platform. In: Li, B., et al. (eds.) ADMA 2022, Part I. Lecture Notes in Computer Science, vol. 13087, pp. 103–117. Springer, Cham (2021). https://doi.org/10.1007/978-3-030-95405-5_8

16. Kang, W., McAuley, J.J.: Self-attentive sequential recommendation. In: IEEE International Conference on Data Mining, ICDM 2018, Singapore, 17–20 November 2018, pp. 197–206. IEEE Computer Society (2018)

17. Kolb, D.A.: Learning style inventory (1999)

18. Li, R., et al.: PST: measuring skill proficiency in programming exercise process via programming skill tracing. In: Amigó, E., Castells, P., Gonzalo, J., Carterette, B., Culpepper, J.S., Kazai, G. (eds.) SIGIR '22: The 45th International ACM SIGIR Conference on Research and Development in Information Retrieval, Madrid, Spain, 11–15 July 2022, pp. 2601–2606. ACM (2022)

19. Ma, H., Huang, Z., Tang, W., Zhang, X.: Exercise recommendation based on cognitive diagnosis and neutrosophic set. In: 25th IEEE International Conference on Computer Supported Cooperative Work in Design, CSCWD 2022, Hangzhou, China, 4–6 May 2022, pp. 1467–1472. IEEE (2022)

20. Mao, K., et al.: Simplex: a simple and strong baseline for collaborative filtering. In: Demartini, G., Zuccon, G., Culpepper, J.S., Huang, Z., Tong, H. (eds.) CIKM '21: The 30th ACM International Conference on Information and Knowledge Management, Virtual Event, Queensland, Australia, 1–5 November 2021, pp. 1243–1252. ACM (2021)

21. Muhammad, B.A., Qi, C., Wu, Z., Ahmad, H.K.: GRL-LS: a learning style detection in online education using graph representation learning. Expert Syst. Appl. **201**, 117138 (2022)

22. Pereira, F.D., et al.: Early dropout prediction for programming courses supported by online judges. In: Isotani, S., Millán, E., Ogan, A., Hastings, P., McLaren, B., Luckin, R. (eds.) AIED 2019. LNCS (LNAI), vol. 11626, pp. 67–72. Springer, Cham (2019). https://doi.org/10.1007/978-3-030-23207-8_13

23. Prithishkumar, I.J., Michael, S.A., et al.: Understanding your student: using the Vark model. J. Postgrad. Med. **60**(2), 183 (2014)

24. Puri, R., et al.: Codenet: a large-scale AI for code dataset for learning a diversity of coding tasks. In: Vanschoren, J., Yeung, S. (eds.) Proceedings of the Neural Information Processing Systems Track on Datasets and Benchmarks 1, NeurIPS Datasets and Benchmarks 2021, December 2021, Virtual (2021)

25. Ren, Y., Liang, K., Shang, Y., Zhang, Y.: Muloer-san: 2-layer multi-objective framework for exercise recommendation with self-attention networks. Knowl. Based Syst. **260**, 110117 (2023)

26. Shen, S., et al.: Learning process-consistent knowledge tracing. In: Zhu, F., Ooi, B.C., Miao, C. (eds.) KDD '21: The 27th ACM SIGKDD Conference on Knowledge Discovery and Data Mining, Virtual Event, Singapore, 14–18 August 2021, pp. 1452–1460. ACM (2021)

27. Sun, F., et al.: BERT4rec: sequential recommendation with bidirectional encoder representations from transformer. In: Zhu, W., et al. (eds.) Proceedings of the 28th ACM International Conference on Information and Knowledge Management, CIKM 2019, Beijing, China, 3–7 November 2019, pp. 1441–1450. ACM (2019)

28. Tan, Q., et al.: Sparse-interest network for sequential recommendation. In: Lewin-Eytan, L., Carmel, D., Yom-Tov, E., Agichtein, E., Gabrilovich, E. (eds.) WSDM '21, The Fourteenth ACM International Conference on Web Search and Data Mining, Virtual Event, Israel, 8–12 March 2021, pp. 598–606. ACM (2021)

29. Tan, Y.K., Xu, X., Liu, Y.: Improved recurrent neural networks for session-based recommendations. In: Karatzoglou, A., et al. (eds.) Proceedings of the 1st Workshop on Deep Learning for Recommender Systems, DLRS@RecSys 2016, Boston, MA, USA, 15 September 2016, pp. 17–22. ACM (2016)

30. Vaswani, A., et al.: Attention is all you need. In: Guyon, I., et al. (eds.) Advances in Neural Information Processing Systems 30: Annual Conference on Neural Information Processing Systems 2017, 4–9 December 2017, Long Beach, CA, USA, pp. 5998–6008 (2017)

31. Wu, J., et al.: Self-supervised graph learning for recommendation. In: Diaz, F., Shah, C., Suel, T., Castells, P., Jones, R., Sakai, T. (eds.) SIGIR '21: The 44th International ACM SIGIR Conference on Research and Development in Information Retrieval, Virtual Event, Canada, 11–15 July 2021, pp. 726–735. ACM (2021)

32. Wu, S., Tang, Y., Zhu, Y., Wang, L., Xie, X., Tan, T.: Session-based recommendation with graph neural networks. In: The Thirty-Third AAAI Conference on Artificial Intelligence, AAAI 2019, The Thirty-First Innovative Applications of Artificial Intelligence Conference, IAAI 2019, The Ninth AAAI Symposium on Educational Advances in Artificial Intelligence, EAAI 2019, Honolulu, Hawaii, USA, 27 January–1 February 2019, pp. 346–353. AAAI Press (2019)

33. Zhu, R., et al.: Programming knowledge tracing: a comprehensive dataset and A new model. In: Candan, K.S., Dinh, T.N., Thai, M.T., Washio, T. (eds.) IEEE International Conference on Data Mining Workshops, ICDM 2022 - Workshops, Orlando, FL, USA, 28 November–1 December 2022, pp. 298–307. IEEE (2022)

Design Intelligent Manufacturing Teaching Experiments with Machine Learning

Feng Zhu[✉], Zhen Chen, Wu Zeng, Jun-jian Zhang, and Shuang-shou Li

Fundamental Industry Training Center, Tsinghua University, Beijing, China
fengzhu@tsinghua.edu.cn

Abstract. One of the key industrial technologies used in large-scale integrated circuit board production in electronic information manufacturing industry is SMT (surface mount technology). The application of information technology represented by AR (augmented reality) and AI (artificial intelligence) has produced considerable economic benefits and social impact in the production and manufacturing of SMT, which is a typical intelligent manufacturing application scenario. The SMT experimental teaching platform designed and developed based on AR and AI technology can analyze and compare product quality detection results at the experimental level by applying various machine learning algorithms through the three-layer structure of equipment physical layer, information system layer and experimental layer, and trace product defects in the production process at the information system layer, so that students can understand the key technologies in intelligent manufacturing in practice. Cultivate innovation and scientific research ability. The teaching satisfaction rate of this set of experimental teaching platform has increased by 10% points compared with the traditional experimental teaching platform.

Keywords: Machine Learning · AI (Artificial intelligence) · SMT (surface mount technology) · intelligent manufacturing · AR (augmented reality) · CPS (information physical system)

1 Introduction

1.1 Background

Intelligent manufacturing is an industrial technology that integrates new generation information technology and artificial intelligence technology with advanced manufacturing technology, and has become the core technology and core driving force of Industry 4.0 [1, 2]. The main application technologies of intelligent manufacturing include CPS (information physical system) developed by AR (augmented reality) technology, and AI (artificial intelligence) technology such as deep learning algorithms applied in computer vision. Combining the application scenarios of the actual manufacturing industry and integrating advanced information technology to carry out relevant practical teaching is an important demand for intelligent manufacturing talent training [3]. SMT (Surface Mounted Technology), one of the main technologies of integrated circuit board

W. Hong and G. Kanaparan (Eds.): ICCSE 2023, CCIS 2023, pp. 232–242, 2024.
https://doi.org/10.1007/978-981-97-0730-0_21

production, has an urgent demand for talents [4, 5]. SMT technology has become an important part of electronic technology practice courses in colleges and universities, and an important carrier of engineering practice education in the new era [6].

1.2 Challenge in Teaching Intelligent Manufacturing Practice

The difficulty of intelligent manufacturing practice teaching lies in how to integrate a number of key technologies of intelligent manufacturing, such as AR and AI, into the manufacturing scene to establish relevant platforms and carry out experiments. Based on the SMT production line, this paper first develops CPS (information physical system) based on AR technology, including two layers of equipment physical layer and information system layer, and then establishes a third experimental layer on the basis of the two-layer structure of CPS to run AI experimental algorithms and comparative analysis, and drives students to master the knowledge and related skills of intelligent manufacturing on the experimental platform with actual application scenarios.

In recent years, some domestic colleges and universities have also introduced AR technology to help experimental teaching and management [7–9]. For example, Zhejiang University and Ningbo University have designed virtual assembly teaching experiment platform for engineering graphics teaching by using AR technology. Beijing University of Chemical Technology uses AR technology to carry out safety education and training of chemical laboratories. Internationally, for example, the Fraunhofer Institute, a well-known industrial institution in Germany, has used AR technology to carry out non-destructive testing and maintenance of large-scale precision equipment such as helicopters [10]. Imperial College London in the United Kingdom uses AR technology to carry out operational training and experimental work of large-scale medical equipment CT machine [11]. In terms of AI experiment and practice, domestic universities have also carried out relevant work [12, 13], but there are still few literatures on the application of AI technology to experimental design in the manufacturing industry [14], and the open literature on the intelligent manufacturing teaching platform that combines AR and AI technologies to do experiments together in the manufacturing industry has not been found for the time being.

2 Experiment Teaching Platform

2.1 SMT Production and Teaching Experiment Platform

SMT production line involves more production equipment, as shown in Fig. 1, its main components include loading machine, printing machine, SPI (solder paste testing equipment), Chip placement machine 1 (Chip placement machine), chip placement machine 2 (IC placement machine), reflow welding, AOI (optical inspection) after the furnace, X-ray(X-ray) testing equipment and plate off machine. The whole SMT production line length contains different equipment, its operation mode, parameter adjustment method, operation phenomenon expression are different, involving the specific process technology more points, including screen printing, dispensing, mounting, curing, reflow welding, cleaning, testing and repair and other elements.

The teaching method of SMT is mainly to understand the process and production mode of each equipment one by one from front end to back end according to the production process of SMT production line under the guidance of teachers. Although this mode can allow students to understand each equipment and the overall processing links, but because of the lack of practical operation links and the application of advanced information technology to experiment links, it is difficult to reflect the practice teaching advocated by the "learn to do, do to learn" concept, as well as understand the relevant knowledge of intelligent manufacturing.

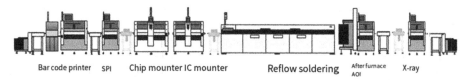

Bar code printer   SPI   Chip mounter IC mounter   Reflow soldering   After furnace AOI   X-ray

Fig. 1. Schematic diagram of SMT production line

The experimental platform designed in this paper will allow students to use AR technology to interactively learn the operating principle of each production equipment setting in the SMT production line and the corresponding CPS (information physics system). The post-furnace AOI (Optical inspection) link in Fig. 1 is an important quality assurance equipment for manual inspection of circuit board solder joint defects. In this equipment link, AI machine learning algorithm experiments will be designed so that students can master how to apply deep learning and other technologies to replace manual inspection. Through the AR technology and interaction in the CPS system, the experiment platform can trace the corresponding production equipment link of the circuit board products with defects found in the AI machine learning algorithm, so that students can further master the SMT production process.

2.2 Intelligent Manufacturing Teaching Experiment Process and Practical Teaching Platform Design

Firstly, on the basis of SMT production line, the related digital twin system platform is developed based on AR technology. On this platform, students can freely move and control the digital model of SMT production line equipment and get the relevant digital information, and compare the results of relevant experiments and analysis performance so as to have a better teaching effect (Fig. 2).

The digital platform of AR not only allows students to independently learn the relevant knowledge points of each device, but also is uniquely conducive to the learning of machine algorithms related to AI technology. For example, the digital platform established by AR technology allows more students to remotely detect the production quality, observe the running status of the production line and analyze the possible impact on quality, and to process and analyze the detection image data of multiple time periods through the cloud database, so as to achieve the data analysis and processing effect across time and space, and more conducive to the development and analysis of students' experiments. As shown in Fig. 3, the whole experiment system is divided into 3 layers, L1 the

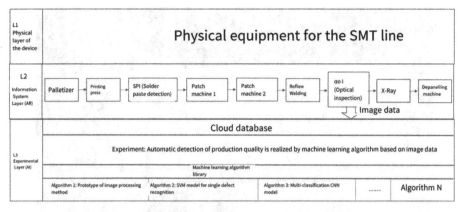

Fig. 2. Experimental platform structure based on AR + AI

first layer is the physical layer of the SMT production line including the devices as shown in Fig. 1, L2 the second layer is based on AR technology to model the physical layer of each device (digital twin) system layer, L3 the third layer is the experiment layer: Based on the data collected by the second layer of AR technology to apply machine learning algorithm to do experiments, the whole system constitutes CPS (information physical system) – an important basic concept in intelligent manufacturing technology.

The quality inspection of traditional electronic production line is to rely on artificial eyes to judge the quality of solder joints, and computer vision must be used to judge the quality of multiple solder joints of multiple circuit boards on the high-speed assembly line. AOI equipment is the welding production encountered in the common defects detection equipment, its own color light source irradiates the circuit board to be detected to form a related color light image. We use the color image obtained by AOI image optical imaging to carry out the experiment of AI algorithm.

2.3 SMT Intelligent Manufacturing Practice Teaching System and Machine Learning Algorithm Principle

The SMT production line practice teaching system based on AR technology is composed of seven parts: actual production line, virtual contour line, perspective structure, MES (Manufacturing Execution System) data table, connection track, equipment principle animation demonstration and equipment suspension introduction, as shown in Fig. 3.

In the teaching process, through the virtual contour line of the developed AR teaching system, students will see the appearance, overall structure and operation panel of the SMT mounter that is positioned to the real space faster; Through the virtual modeling of the perspective structure to understand the internal structure of the machine, so as to understand the processing principle of the equipment; Through the MES (Manufacturing Execution System) data display area and the connection track (the track that transmits the mount product), understand the relationship between each equipment and the overall production state, so as to understand the information processing mechanism in SMT manufacturing. At the same time, the interactive operation further increases the interest and autonomy of learning. The introduction of equipment principle animation and

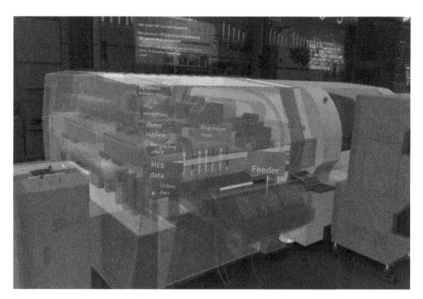

Fig. 3. AR interactive interface of SMT production line mounting unit.

equipment suspension will be expanded with students' clicks, and the parts that students don't understand or want to study deeply will be further answered by animation or text, which is very helpful for students' personalized learning.

3 Machine Learning Experiment in Teaching Design

3.1 Workflow of Defect Detection in Soldering

The system layer developed based on AR technology lays the foundation for the subsequent development of AI algorithms for data collection and analysis, especially in the integration of physical model and digital model analysis. As shown in Fig. 4, there are two types of SMT solder spot detection images, one is the image obtained by AOI equipment, and the other is the visible light image. The two types of images are respectively input into the algorithm processing model for solder spot defect detection to ensure the robustness of the algorithm recognition. There are 3 experimental teaching cases of AI algorithm developed on this system, the first is a typical computer image processing method, CC algorithm, the second is a SVM support vector machine method, which belongs to the traditional machine learning algorithm, and the third is a deep learning algorithm of AI, the teaching method of CNN (Convolutional neural network). Through these three algorithms for SMT production line solder joint defects analysis and discrimination, students can master from classic to cutting-edge AI methods in the actual production of the application and value.

The experimental process is arranged as follows:

a. Check the circuit board that has been processed before, the batch of circuit board contains solder joint defects and no solder joint defects, do manual record and mark

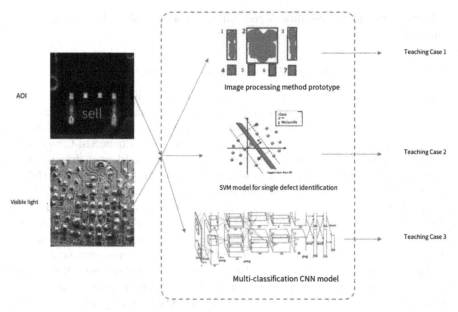

Fig. 4. Work flow of solder joint defect detection

in the experiment system, each circuit board has ID in the database and whether there is a solder joint defect mark; In this step to understand the typical circuit board with solder joint defects and no solder joint defects of the circuit board, and form the experimental database, the batch of circuit board in the database is divided into learning (training) sample set and test sample set two batches.

b. According to Fig. 1, batch of unprocessed circuit boards are placed on the upper board machine for SMT patch production. Corresponding to the physical layer operation of L1 in Fig. 2, understand the operation of the physical process in SMT production.

c. According to the process of L2 layer in Fig. 2, wear AR glasses to enter the space to observe the digital model space of the SMT production line, pay special attention to the detection image of AOI part, and understand the operation principle of each device and the reasons and environment that may affect the quality of the solder joints of the circuit board

d. According to the process of layer 3 in Fig. 2, the new relevant machine learning algorithm model and initial parameter configuration are called. The step is divided into two stages, the learning (training) stage and the test stage:

• Training stage: Step a is called to form the training image sample set of the database, and relevant machine learning algorithms are trained and parameter debugging is carried out. If the training results meet the requirements, it will enter the test stage

• Test stage: Get the test image sample set formed by step a of the database, test the machine learning algorithm model, make statistics on the test results, and analyze

e. Record the test data performance results of the current algorithm model and return to step b until the 3 machine algorithm models are called.

f. Perform performance comparison and analysis of the three machine learning algorithms

Through the above test flow, three different machine algorithm models can be compared.

3.2 Application of Prototype of Image Processing Method

From the experimental point of view, we first need to establish a logical and intuitive discrimination model. Using the method used to construct the rapid prototype, taking the welding defects as an example, we first use the pure image processing method to identify. After the AOI image is segmented, we use CC (Connected-Components) detection algorithm to extract the Connected domain. Connected domain detection From the teaching case 1 in Fig. 4, it can be seen that through the arrangement analysis (labeled "4", "5", "6", "7"), the connected domain forms a neat horizontal arrangement, and the corresponding solder joints are only 3, and the solder joints matching "5" and "6" are linked together, corresponding to the connected domain "2" and the comparison of the area characteristics of the connected domain. Construction of rule-based welding detection algorithm pure image processing method can detect some specific categories of defects. The algorithm is intuitive and explainable. The disadvantage is that the rule-based detection method is difficult to maintain and has poor anti-noise and anti-distortion performance. It is suitable for students to do experiments when they are getting started.

3.3 SVM Model for Single Defect Type Recognition

SVM (Support vector machine), as a classic machine learning algorithm, has developed rapidly since the 1990s and derived a series of improved and extended algorithms. It is widely used in pattern recognition problems such as portrait recognition and text classification, and its construction is relatively simple. The training and parameter tuning of the model are intuitive, which is suitable for application in teaching practice. SVM is usually used to deal with binary classification problems, and in general, the samples are required to be linearly separable.

In the teaching process, we use the labeled training data, where. $\{x_i, y_i\}i = 1, 2, \cdots, N, y_i \in \{-1, +1\}, x_i \in R^n$ Suppose we have a "divisible hyperplane" that separates both positive and negative labeled data samples. x The point is located on the hyperplane, where it is perpendicular to the hyperplane, the vertical distance from the hyperplane to the origin, and is the Euclidean norm. $w^T x + b w |b|/\|w\|_2 \|w\|_2 w$ Ream and are the shortest distances from the separated hyperplane to the nearest positive and negative data samples, respectively, so the distance between the separated hyperplanes can be defined as. $d_+ d_- d_+ + d_-$ The goal of the SVM is set to find the separation hyperplane with the largest edge. $d_+ + d_-$ To do this, all data vectors need to meet the following conditions

$$w^T x_i + b \geq +1, y_i = +1 \tag{1}$$

$$w^T x_i + b \leq +1, y_i = -1 \tag{2}$$

The above two conditions can be summed as a set of inequality constraints

$$y_i(w^T x_i + b) \geq 0, i = 1, \cdots, N \tag{3}$$

Satisfy that the hyperplane and corresponding sum in the above formula are respectively. $H_1 H_2 d_+ d_- d_+ = d_- = |2|/\|w\|_2$ Therefore, the hyperplane pair given the maximum margin can be minimized under constraints, i.e. $(H_1, H_2) \frac{1}{2} \|w\|_2^2$

$$\min_{w,b} \frac{1}{2} \|w\|_2^2 \tag{4}$$

$$s.t. y_i(w^T x_i + b) \geq 0, i = 1, \cdots, N \tag{5}$$

For the above equality constraints, the Lagrange multiplier method is used to give the following unconstrained original optimization problems

$$\min_{w,b,\alpha} \mathcal{L}_P(w, b, \alpha) = \frac{1}{2} \|w\|_2^2 - \sum_{i=1}^{N} \alpha_i y_i(w^T x_i + b) + \sum_{i=1}^{N} \alpha_i \tag{6}$$

where, the non-negative Lagrange multiplier. $\alpha_i \geq 0, i = 1, 2, \cdots, N$ Finally, the solution of such a set of optimization parameters is obtained by optimizing the conditions, and the SVM classifier is obtained [15].

By using this method, some nonlinear separable problems can be transformed into linear separable problems. Aiming at more than ten kinds of defects defined in advance, we set up a binary classification model for each kind of defects by using segmentation image and edge image as input, and finally successfully judge the welding defects. For the design of teaching cases, we first adopt SVM model as the benchmark, which can achieve relatively stable classification results on small and medium-sized sample sets. The single defect identification model based on SVM can also be used for semi-automatic and automatic labeling of large-scale samples.

3.4 Multi-classification CNN Model

The multi-classification model can uniformly deal with the visual identification problem of multi-class solder joint defect detection. The optimization scheme of the model is selected in the technical direction of deep learning. The popular image classification architecture adopted in the course is Convolutional neural network (CNN) -- the method of sending images into the CNN network, and then the network classificates the image data, starting from the input of "scanner", such as input of an image of size, without the need for $n \times n$ a network layer with nodes. $n \times n$ Instead, you just create a scanning input layer of size $m \times m$, scan the first pixel of the image, and then $m \times m$ move the scanner one pixel to the right to scan the next pixel $m \times m$. This is the sliding window. The input 2×2 data is fed into the convolutional layer instead of the normal layer. Each node only needs to process its closest neighbors, and the convolution layer also tends to shrink as the scan gets deeper. In addition to the convolutional layer, there will usually be a pooling layer. Pooling is a way to filter details, and a common pooling technique is maximum pooling, which passes the pixels with the most specific properties as a matrix of size. The convolutional layer is the core of CNN, and the relevant mathematical model needs to be established in the experiment.

Let the AOI image or visible light image in Fig. 4 be. The experiment task is to design a two-dimensional filter where and. $X = \begin{bmatrix} x_1, & \cdots & x_p \end{bmatrix} \in R^{n \times p} \Phi = \begin{bmatrix} \Phi_1, & \cdots & \Phi_q \end{bmatrix} \in R^{d \times q} x_j = \begin{bmatrix} x_j(1) & \cdots & x_j(n) \end{bmatrix}^T \in R^n, j = 1, \cdots, p \Phi_i = \begin{bmatrix} \varnothing_i(1) & \cdots & \varnothing_i(n) \end{bmatrix}^T \in R^d, i = 1, \cdots, q$ Thus, the $\varnothing$ **2-D convolution** of the filter and image X is

$$(X * \Phi)_{m,k} = \sum_{i=1}^{d} \sum_{j=1}^{q} x_{m+i-1,k+j-1} \varnothing_{i,j} \tag{7}$$

where; $m = 1, 2, \cdots, n = d + 1; k = 1, 2, \cdots, p + q - 1$ Can also be represented by a matrix two-dimensional convolution formula is

$$Y = (X * \Phi) = \begin{bmatrix} H(x_1)\Phi_1 & \cdots & H(x_1)\Phi_q \\ \vdots & & \vdots \\ H(x_p)\Phi_1 & \cdots & H(x_p)\Phi_q \end{bmatrix} = H_{d,q}(X)\Phi \tag{8}$$

Formula Medium

$$Y = \begin{bmatrix} y_1 & \cdots & y_p \end{bmatrix} = \begin{bmatrix} y_1(1) & \cdots & y_{p+q-1}(1) \\ \vdots & & \vdots \\ y_1(n-d+1) & \cdots & y_{p+q-1}(n-d+1) \end{bmatrix} \tag{9}$$

$$H_{d,q}(X) = \begin{bmatrix} H(x_1) \\ \vdots \\ H(x_p) \end{bmatrix} \tag{10}$$

$$H(x_j) = \begin{bmatrix} x_j(1) & x_j(2) & \cdots & x_j(d) \\ x_j(2) & x_j(3) & \cdots x_j(d+1) \\ \vdots & \vdots & \ddots & \vdots \\ x_j(d+1) & & & \\ x_j(n-d+1) & x_j(n-d+2) & \cdots & x_j(n) \end{bmatrix} \tag{11}$$

where j and is the i-th element of the j-th input channel. $= 1, 2, \cdots, p, x_j(i)$ According to the above formula, the convolutional layer calculation is constructed, and then the subsequent training, analysis and calculation are carried out. The trained CNN convolutional neural network can be used to identify the circuit board with solder joint defects.

4 Experimental Performance and Teaching Effect

Based on the intelligent manufacturing experiment platform, students can compare the AI algorithms in the three teaching cases in the previous chapter, choose to adjust the relevant parameters, and quickly and comprehensively understand the impact of the parameters of the algorithm on the overall performance. Using the AR based operation practice to understand the actual physical process of SMT production, students can better understand the manufacturing process problems corresponding to the wrong judgment in the AI algorithm, so as to partially solve the black box problem in the AI algorithm, and realize the unity of the mathematical meaning of the algorithm and the physical process of actual manufacturing.

Students use this set of experimental platform system to learn the SMT production line AR operation practice and AI algorithm experiment, the feedback effect is very good. At present, this set of experimental platform system has been put into use and experiment in many courses such as undergraduates, postgraduates and engineering doctors in University, and a total of more than 500 students have carried out practical work with this set of experimental platform. According to the sample survey of the students who have used the platform, 90% of the students are satisfied with this new experimental platform, compared with 80% satisfaction rate of the traditional SMT teaching platform in the past. The students "strongly agree" or "somewhat agree" that the SMT teaching platform can help them understand the integration of manufacturing technology and information technology in intelligent manufacturing industry, and believe that intelligent manufacturing is the future direction of manufacturing industry development.

5 Conclusion

Intelligent manufacturing technology is the integration of digital twin, CPS, AR and AI and other advanced information technology with traditional manufacturing technology. The AR-based CPS system developed on the SMT production line allows students to conduct interactive and operational learning and enhance learning interest with personalized learning tools, and master the concept of digital twins. The digital twin system layer developed based on AR technology is the application basis of the algorithm layer of AI technology, which can undertake the simulation operation and comparison of various AI algorithms, find the cause of the formation of solder joint defects, and realize the reduction cognition from mathematical model to physical phenomenon, so as to better let students master the related applications of intelligent manufacturing technology. Compared with the traditional SMT experimental teaching platform, the SMT experimental teaching platform designed and developed based on AR and AI technology has achieved significant improvement in teaching effect.

References

1. Zhou, J.: Introduction to Intelligent Manufacturing. Higher Education Press (2021)
2. Zang, J.: Research on intelligent manufacturing technology meeting and roadmap towards 2035. Chin. J. Mech. Eng. **58**(4), 285–307 (2022)
3. Steering Committee for the Teaching of Mechanical Majors in Institutions of higher Education, Ministry of Education. Intelligent Manufacturing Engineering Course. Higher Education Press (2022)
4. Liu, Y.: Construction of SMT digital production line for military electronic products. Electron. Process Technol. **43**(1), 1–3 (2022)
5. Ge, J.: Research on construction technology of surface mount digital production line for aerospace electronic products. Aerosp. Manuf. Technol. (1), 19–22, 44 (2021)
6. Wang, T.: Ten years of sharpening a sword and concentrating on Innovation road – exploration and practice of mechanism innovation in engineering practice laboratory. Exp. Technol. Manag. **31**(8), 16–19, 31 (2014). (in Chinese)
7. Zhao, X.: Design of engineering graphics assembly guided immersive teaching experimental platform based on augmented reality. Exp. Technol. Manag. **39**(3), 195–199, 213 (2022)

8. Wang, Y., et al.: Experimental teaching system design of mechanical principle based on augmented reality technology. Exp. Technol. Manag. **36**(11), 109–112 (2019)

9. Huang, X.: Application of virtual reality and augmented reality in laboratory safety education. Exp. Technol. Manag. **36**(1), 174–176, 179 (2019)

10. Rehbein, J.: 3D-visualization of ultrasonic NDT data using mixed reality. J. Nondestr. Eval. **41**(1), 26–41 (2022)

11. Amiras, D.: Augmented reality simulator for CT-guided interventions. Eur. Radiol. **31**, 8897–8902 (2021)

12. Wu, X.: Planning and construction of university artificial intelligence laboratory. Exp. Technol. Manag. **37**(10), 244–250 (2020). (in Chinese)

13. Wang, X.: Innovation and exploration of artificial intelligence practical teaching. Educ. Teach. Forum **4**, 73–77 (2021)

14. Luo, L.: Design of whole process control system of mechanical manufacturing based on artificial intelligence technology. Mod. Electron. Technol. **45**(15), 182–186

15. Zhang, X.: Matrix Algebra Methods for Artificial Intelligence. Higher Education Press (2021)

Privacy-Preserving Educational Credentials Management Based on Decentralized Identity and Zero-Knowledge Proof

Tianmin Xiong, Zhao Zhang[✉], and Cheqin Jing

School of Data Science and Engineering,
East China Normal University, Shanghai, China
tianminxiong@stu.ecnu.edu.cn, {zhzhang,cqjin}@dase.ecnu.edu.cn

Abstract. Educational credentials are an important part of the education ecosystem. However, these credentials often exist in the form of traditional paper documents, which are issued slowly, susceptible to forgery, and entail high verification costs. Moreover, electronic educational credentials stored on centralized servers may not adequately ensure their authenticity and can potentially expose sensitive student information. Historical educational credentials lacked a standardized formats, impeding efficient sharing and verification between parties. Additionally, conventional encryption schemes only safeguarded credential privacy during storage, posing challenges in protecting privacy while presenting the credentials. We propose a privacy-preserving educational credential management scheme based on decentralized identity and zero-knowledge proof. The scheme incorporates a decentralized identity authentication model utilizing blockchain technology, enabling flexible issuance and point-to-point sharing of educational credentials. Furthermore, by employing privacy-preserving credentials designed with zero-knowledge proofs, we can eliminate potential privacy breaches when students present their credentials. We also have developed a system prototype and conducted performance evaluations, thereby validating the correctness and practicality of our scheme.

Keywords: Educational Credential · Privacy Preservation · Decentralized Identity · Zero-Knowledge Proof · Blockchain

1 Introduction

In the field of education, students constitute the largest group and possess numerous educational credentials, including transcripts, recommendation letters, and various credentials such as diplomas, degrees, internships, and training records. These credentials are typically issued by universities, educational institutions, or authoritative institutions, carrying legal validity and reputation assurance. The secure sharing of these educational credentials is essential for the functioning of the education ecosystem and for facilitating the recruitment process in companies.

© The Author(s), under exclusive license to Springer Nature Singapore Pte Ltd. 2024
W. Hong and G. Kanaparan (Eds.): ICCSE 2023, CCIS 2023, pp. 243–255, 2024.
https://doi.org/10.1007/978-981-97-0730-0_22

Currently, many educational institutions employ centralized servers to store electronic education credentials. However, these credentials are often based on paper documents, resulting in slow issuance times, high verification costs. Moreover, traditional centralized server systems are vulnerable to credential tampering, thereby compromising the authenticity of student credentials. Additionally, there is also a risk of sensitive information leakage such as student birthdays, ID numbers, and course scores. For instance, during the scholarship review process, it is necessary for the committee to manually verify each student's course scores, credentials, and honors against their information in the student information system, which could lead to unauthorized access to their confidential details.

Blockchain is a distributed database that is decentralized, tamper-proof, traceable, and jointly maintained [1]. Researchers have leveraged this technology to develop robust, transparent, and trustworthy educational sharing platforms. For instance, studies [2–4] have utilized blockchain technology to create secure and tamper-proof platforms for students to store and share their educational credentials with external institutions. Additionally, recording students' course credit records on the blockchain enables credit sharing between different educational institutions, enhancing educational mobility for students [3,5]. However, while blockchain ensures the integrity and authenticity of educational credentials, it remains susceptible to sensitive information leakage due to its public and reviewable nature. To address this issue, some studies [6,7] suggest encrypting credentials, but delegating identity and keys to a single issuer lacks the ability to achieve autonomous security.

Moreover, when presenting credentials, sharing complete plain-text credentials can still expose students' sensitive information. Although verification schemes based on zero-knowledge proofs facilitate the validation of predicate proofs concerning credentials, they do not offer a means to authenticate the origin of the credential. Furthermore, users can easily forge credentials that meet the verification conditions. To address these limitations, zk-creds [8] introduced the LinkG16 protocol, which employs blinding and linking techniques to combine multiple zero-knowledge proofs. This ensures that all individual proofs originate from the same credential.

To address the above challenges, we have designed a privacy-preserving educational credentials management scheme based on decentralized identity and zero-knowledge proof. This scheme introduces a decentralized identity authentication model based on blockchain, allowing educational credentials to be flexibly issued and peer-to-peer shared. Additionally, by employing a privacy-preserving credential design based on zero-knowledge proof, potential privacy breaches during credential presentation can be mitigated. We have designed a concise Merkle Tree to maintain an on-chain issuance list to prove the source of the credentials. Finally, we have implemented a system prototype based on the CITA [9] consortium chain and analyzed its performance to validate the correctness and practicality of the privacy-preserving credentials.

The remainder of this paper is structured as follows. Section 2 provides related work on decentralized identity and zero-knowledge proof. Section 3 explains the proposed system model. Implementation and experimental results are presented in Sect. 4. Finally, Sect. 5 concludes the paper.

2 Relate Work

2.1 Blockchain and Decentralized Identity

Blockchain is a revolutionary technological framework that combines distributed data storage, peer-to-peer (P2P) protocols, consensus mechanisms, asymmetric encryption, and other computer technologies. It serves as a decentralized and tamper-proof database. The stored data remains immutable and transparent, allowing for enhanced traceability and other essential characteristics. Blockchain technology leverages chain data structures for data verification and storage, distributed node consensus algorithms for data generation and updates, cryptographic techniques to ensure secure data transmission and access, and smart contracts comprising automated script codes for data programming and manipulation.

The Merkle tree, a binary tree data structure extensively employed in the blockchain domain, serves as a fundamental method for validating the integrity and authenticity of large-scale data sets. Constructing a Merkle tree involves segmenting the data into fixed-size blocks, which are then hashed to establish the hierarchical tree structure. Each internal node's hash value is computed based on the hashes of its child nodes, while the root node's hash value provides verification for the entire dataset. The Merkle tree's verification path comprises the hash values of all non-leaf nodes traversed from the data block to the root node. By scrutinizing this path, one can ascertain the inclusion of a specific data block within the corresponding Merkle tree and promptly identify any potential data tampering.

Blockchain-based decentralized identity is a solution for decentralized identity authentication and management. It leverages the blockchain's decentralization features and non-tamperability to ensure secure storage, verification, and authorization management of identity information. By doing so, it addresses issues encountered in traditional identity verification methods, such as single points of failure, account switching, and data leakage. The decentralized identity authentication model utilizes smart contracts to execute identity authentication and management processes. Each user possesses a unique decentralized identity identifier(DID) [10], generated through an asymmetric key, ensuring its immutability and uniqueness.

The W3C Credentials Community Group has spearheaded the development of a series of standardized solutions for decentralized identity. These solutions are built upon blockchain-based distributed ledger technology and the DID protocol. The protocol primarily encompasses two key components: the decentralized identity identifier and the Verifiable Credential (VC) [11]. The VC consists of a declaration file containing holder identity attributes and issuer information, which is presented to the verifier during the authentication process. Figure 1 illustrates the general structure of the DID authentication model, involving three main entities: the Holder, the Issuer, and the Verifier. The Holder is responsible for storing and managing personal identity information along with related verifiable credentials. The Issuer, on the other hand, verifies the holder's identity, manages the schema, issues verifiable credentials based on the schema, and provides trust endorsement. Lastly, the Verifier verifies the holder's identity and examines the verifiable credentials information.

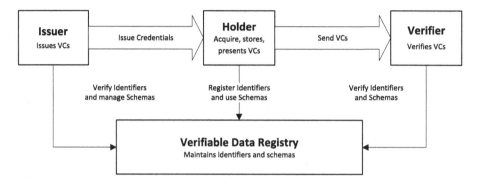

Fig. 1. W3C Decentralized Identity Authentication Model

2.2   Zero-Knowledge Proof

Zero-Knowledge Proof, initially proposed by Goldwasser, Micali, and Rackoff, is a cryptographic protocol that involves two parties: the prover and the verifier [12]. It serves the purpose of proving membership or knowledge in a secure manner. Zero-knowledge proof possesses three fundamental properties:

(1) Completeness: This property verifies the correctness of the protocol itself. If the prover possesses valid evidence for a statement and both parties (prover and verifier) honestly execute the protocol, the prover can convince the verifier that the statement is indeed correct.
(2) Soundness: Soundness protects honest verifiers from being deceived by malicious provers. It ensures that an incorrect statement cannot be proven as true by an untrusted party.
(3) Zero knowledge: The concept of zero knowledge implies that the prover can prove the validity of a statement to the verifier without revealing any additional information apart from its correctness. This property safeguards privacy during the proof process.

Zero-knowledge proof offers trust establishment and privacy protection through these properties, making it highly versatile and applicable in various domains. It finds application not only in classical cryptography, such as public key encryption, digital signatures, and identity authentication but also in blockchain technology, privacy computing, and other emerging fields. Current mainstream zero-knowledge proof protocols, including Zero-Knowledge Succinct Non-Interactive Arguments of Knowledge(zk-SNARK) [13], Zero-Knowledge Scalable Transparent Arguments of Knowledge(zk-STARK) [14], and Bulletproof [15], have shown practicality in specific scenarios.

3   System Model

3.1   Overview

We propose a privacy-preserving educational credentials management scheme based on decentralized identity and zero-knowledge proof. The scheme enables secure issuance, sharing, and verification of students' educational credentials. The system involves four entities: students, verifiers, educational institutions, and the blockchain. An overview of the system is presented in Fig. 2, with the roles and main processes described below:

- **Educational institution** provide students with the plain-text of educational credentials and construct the commitments of the credentials. They then upload these commitments to the issuance list on the blockchain, that is, creating leaves in the Merkle tree.
- **Student** can register a DID and use the DID to access any educational institution. All educational credentials received by the student will be bound to his DID. In the stage of presenting credentials, students need to construct multiple zero-knowledge proofs individually and link them into *link proof*: 1) *pred proof*: the credential satisfies certain predicate; 2) *memb proof*: the credential is a member of the Merkle tree of the issuance list.
- **Verifier** is any potential user, such as other students, companies, etc. The verifier performs verification on the linked zero-knowledge proof: 1) verifies the *pred proof*; 2) verifies the *memb proof*; 3) verifies the *link proof*, that is, all individual proofs are originate from the same credential.
- **Blockchain** stores DID and credential schema based on smart contracts, and maintains an issuance list for each educational institution, providing specified commitment verification path and tree root.

3.2   Architecture

The architecture of the system is depicted in Fig. 3, comprising of several layers: the business layer, API layer, service layer, blockchain service layer, and data layer. Within the blockchain service layer, a smart contract management module has been engineered to facilitate the deployment, updating, and invocation of contracts for DID (Decentralized Identifiers), VCS (Verifiable Credential Schema), Auth (Authentication), and Issuance List. Furthermore, the service layer encapsulates the following functionalities:

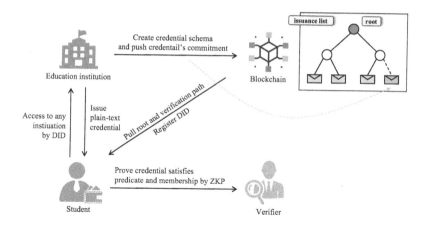

Fig. 2. Overview

- **DID Management.** This involves the creation, updating, and verification of DID identifiers on the blockchain.
- **Verifiable Credential Management.** This encompasses the management of verifiable credential schemas, issuance of verifiable credentials, and their verification.
- **Authority Management.** This includes the granting and revocation of issuing authorities, as well as their verification.
- **zk-SNARK.** This involves defining and compiling predicate circuits (*pred circuits*) and membership circuits (*memb circuits*), setting up Common Reference Strings (CRS), constructing zero-knowledge proofs, and their verification.

3.3   Smart Contract

Smart contracts enable the implementation of complex logic and real-world applications on the blockchain. However, once a smart contract is deployed, it operates independently and repetitively across all blockchain nodes. As such, it is generally considered that only businesses requiring consensus and reusable logic should implement smart contracts on-chain. Moreover, if issues arise or business logic changes after the release of a smart contract, they cannot be resolved simply by modifying and re-releasing the original contract. Consequently, we have implemented a contract layering and update mechanism in this system. As depicted in Fig. 4.(a), we have divided the contract into three tiers: role management, controller, and data. In the event of a contract upgrade, we only need to update the controller contract address in the role management contract, thereby significantly enhancing the system's scalability. The smart contract of this system primarily comprises five components:

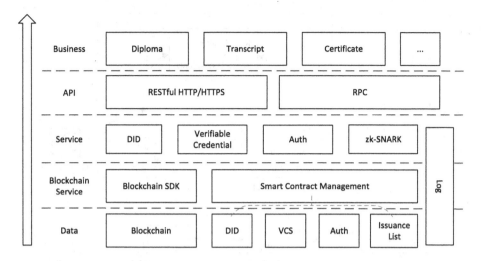

Fig. 3. Architecture

- **DID contract** is responsible for the establishment of the ID structure on the chain, including the generation, reading and updating of DID and DID Document.
- **Verifiable credential schema contract** maintains a key-value pair $<VCSId, VCS>$ mapping table, manages verifiable credential templates, and supports query, addition and update.
- **Role controller contract** is responsible for defining, operating and controlling the authority of DID roles on the chain.
- **Authority contract** is responsible for managing and storing information related to the issuing authority, and supports operations such as checking, adding, deleting, authorizing and revoking the authority institutions.
- **Issuance list contract** maintains a Merkle tree to store commitments with verifiable credentials. Returns the root and verification path for the specified commitments.

The DID contract necessitates the definition of the storage structure and the methods for reading and writing the DID Document. A DID Document is a dataset that describes a DID subject and can be utilized by the DID subject to authenticate itself and demonstrate its association with the DID. The structure of the DID Document is relatively straightforward, comprising a list of disclosed passwords, Authentication, and Service Endpoint. However, with the rapid influx of users, the number of DID will increase significantly. Consequently, designing a large and comprehensive mapping table is impractical due to the immense addressing overhead it would entail. To address this issue, We have implemented the Linked-Event [16] mechanism.

The main idea is to implement the linked list data structure to store and access DID documents, and trigger update events when the documents are modified. In a blockchain network running on Ethereum Virtual Machine (EVM),

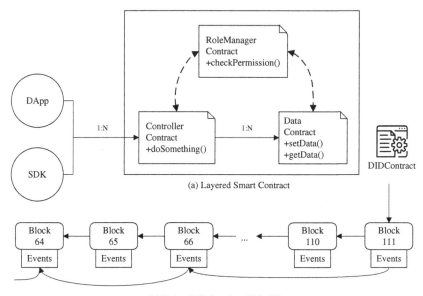

(a) Layered Smart Contract

(b) Update DID based on Linked-Event

Fig. 4. Smart Contract Framework

every block contains a designated area for storing events related to that block, which are eventually added to the event log. Therefore, when a DID document is updated, an update event can be triggered and stored in the current block's event storage. Additionally, each update event is indexed using the current block height, as depicted in Fig. 4.(b). To retrieve the complete DID document, the corresponding block's events can be traversed in reverse order based on the index.

We have designed the issuance list as a contract that stores all the commitments for credentials. The authorities are required to append leaf nodes to the Merkle tree in order to prove the issuance of the credentials. This enables any external auditor to download the complete list, reconstruct a local copy of the Merkle Tree, and validate the authenticity of the issued credentials. Our design utilizes a simplified Merkle tree structure. The contract status section solely maintains a string array for storing the credential commitments, without preserving the structural information of the tree. During the creation and verification process of the verification path, we calculate the parent-child relationship between nodes by utilizing the node's index in the list and the height of the tree. The specific procedure is outlined in Algorithm 1. The addition of -1 to $path$ indicates the left and right positions of the current node in relation to its parent node. This design effectively reduces the storage overhead of the contract while ensuring efficient construction and verification of the verification path.

Algorithm 1: Get verification path for target node

Input: Merkle tree *leaves*, target leaf *node*
Output: Merkle tree verification *path*

1 *path* ← null
2 *index* ← leaves.indexOf(*node*)
3 **if** *index* = −1 **then**
4 | **return** *path*
5 **end**
6 *level* ← leaves
7 *siblingIndex* ← (*index* % 2 = 0) ? *index* + 1 : *index* − 1
8 **while** *level.size*() > 1 **do**
9 | *siblingIndex* ← (*siblingIndex* = level.size()) ? *siblingIndex* − 1 : *siblingIndex*
10 | **if** *siblingIndex* % 2 = 0 **then**
11 | | *path*.add(*level*[*siblingIndex*])
12 | | *path*.add(-1)
13 | **end**
14 | **else**
15 | | *path*.add(-1)
16 | | *path*.add(*level*[*siblingIndex*])
17 | **end**
18 | *level* ← getNextLevel(*level*)
19 | *nextLevelIndex* ← *siblingIndex* / 2
20 | *siblingIndex* ← (*nextLevelIndex* % 2 = 0) ? *nextLevelIndex* + 1 : *nextLevelIndex* − 1
21 **end**
22 **return** *path*

---

4 Experiment

4.1 Implementation

We implemented the prototype of the system based on 9.3k lines of Java code and 1.1k lines of Solidity code. The relevant smart contracts are deployed on an open source alliance chain CITA. The code for communication with CITA relies on CITA-Java-SDK. We implemented a common prove and verify interface based on the Groth16 and LinkG16 [8] protocols and encapsulated it as a zk-SNARK module. Groth16 requires a one-time trusted setup to generate a set of parameters called a CRS for each statement (a.k.a., circuit). Once this CRS is generated, it can be used throughout the lifetime of the system to prove different instances of the statement.

4.2   Evaluation

All tests were performed on a server with an Intel Xeon Gold 6330 CPU with physical cores, 42.00 MB cache and 64 GiB memory, running Ubuntu 18.04 with kernel 5.4.0-139-generic. Each figure and table shows the median running time for 100 executions. In addition, the height of the Merkle Tree in our simulated issuance list contract is 32.

We assume a scholarship review scenario. Students need to prove to the review committee that the scores s_i in each subjects on their transcripts are greater than 60 points in order to be eligible for review. Concretely, the access predicate is:

$$\forall i, s_i \geq 60 \wedge expriy > today, 1 \leq i \leq n \tag{1}$$

where n is the number of subjects, and $expriy$ is the validity period of the credential.

For each system role in Fig. 2, we tested their running time for each operation in this scenario, as shown in Table 1. Among them, the operations of educational institutions pushing credential's commitment and students registering did take significantly more than 3 s. This is because both operations include the time to wait for the receipt of the transaction on the chain, and CITA's block time interval is exactly 3 s. Second. It takes a long time for students to prove credential by generate zk proof, which involves multiple operations in the zk-SNARK module, as shown in Table 2. We now further elaborate on these data and the reasons that influence them.

Before students construct a *link proof*, they must first construct *memb proof* to prove that the transcript credential exists in the on-chain issuance list. In this process, an important parameter that affects the proving time and proof size is the depth of the Merkle Tree, as shown in Fig. 5(a).

Secondly, students need to construct *pred proof* to prove that the individual subject scores in the transcript is greater than 60 points. The number of subjects in the transcript and the data type of the scores (such as integer or float) are different, which will affect the proving time and proof size. According to the characteristics of zk-SNARK, the more complex the proving logic is, the more gates exist in the circuit, and the larger the proving time and proof size are. We use the MultiAND circuit as an illustrative example. By progressively augmenting the number of inputs within the circuit, the total number of constraints in the circuit can be expanded. The evaluation results are presented in Fig. 5(b). As the number of circuit constraints increases, there is a corresponding escalation in compile time, Tau time, and prove time. However, owing to the succinct nature of zk-SNARK, both proof size and verification time are consistently maintained at a low level.

We assessed the influence of the quantity of DIDs on the registration and updating time of DIDs. Illustrated in Fig. 6(a), the utilization of Linked-Event technology ensures that, even with a continual rise in the number of DIDs within the system, the registration and update time of DIDs remains consistently around 3.2 s. It is noteworthy that the block interval of CITA is set at 3 s. Additionally, we investigated the impact of the number of DID events on query time, as depicted in Fig. 6(b). A linear relationship is observed, where an increase in the number of events necessitates the system to query more blocks to acquire comprehensive data. It is essential to highlight that, in practical applications, the frequency of updates to DIDs is generally minimal, thereby having an insignificant impact on the user's query experience.

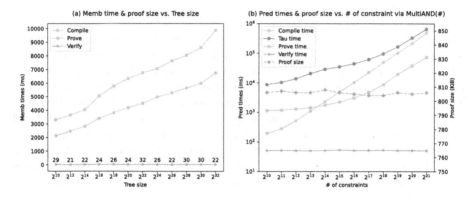

Fig. 5. Circuit Evaluation

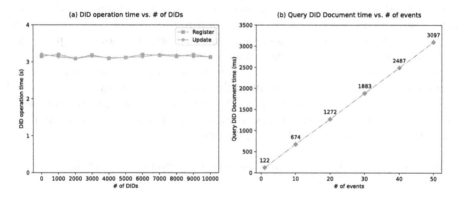

Fig. 6. DID Evaluation

Table 1. Time cost of each operation in scholarship review

Role	Operation	Cost Time (ms)
Education institution	create credential schema	107.02
	issue plaint-text credential	63.21
	push credential's commitment	3095.11
Student	register DID	3186.53
	prove credential by generate *link proof*	11290.35
Verifier	verify *link proof*	73.36
Blockchain	generate root and verification path	154.73

Table 2. zk-SNARK module performance

memb circuit and CRS	memb proof	pred circuit and CRS	pred proof	link proofs
7.35 s	10.13 s	801 ms	1.16 s	162.34 ms

5 Conclusion

This paper introduces a privacy-preserving educational credentials management scheme that leverages decentralized identifier and zero-knowledge proof. The scheme allows educational institutions to issue versatile educational credentials in an efficient manner by standardizing and managing credential templates. These credentials are structured as commitments, tied to specific decentralized identifiers, and stored on a blockchain. Students simply register a DID and can share their educational credentials directly with any supported educational institution or verifier. Building on this, by integrating zero-knowledge proofs with Merkle tree membership proofs, it can be demonstrated that the attributes of the blockchain-stored educational credential satisfy certain predicates. The verifier can cross-check the Merkle tree root and verification path provided by the student against the blockchain to ensure authenticity. We have implemented and deployed a prototype system of this scheme on a consortium blockchain, and have evaluated its performance. Experimental results indicate that the privacy-preserving educational management system based on zero-knowledge proofs has significant practicality and application potential. In future work, we aim to develop a secure credential backup mechanism to maintain data integrity in case of an identity wallet failure. Additionally, we plan to employ more advanced cryptographic primitives to optimize the performance of the zero-knowledge proof module, balancing proof size, computational cost, and verification cost for broader applicability in educational contexts.

Acknowledgment. This work was supported by National Natural Science Foundation of China (No.61972152).

References

1. Qifeng, S., Cheqing, J., Zhao, Z., et al.: Blockchain technology: architecture and progress. J. Comput. Sci. **41**(5), 969–988 (2018)
2. Arenas, R., Fernandez, P.: CredenceLedger: a permissioned blockchain for verifiable academic credentials. In: 2018 IEEE International Conference on Engineering, Technology and Innovation (ICE/ITMC), pp. 1-6. IEEE (2018). https://doi.org/10.1109/ICE.2018.8436324
3. Arndt, T., Guercio, A.: Blockchain-based transcripts for mobile higher-education. Int. J. Inf. Educ. Technol. **10**(2), 84–89 (2020)
4. Han, M., Li, Z., He, J., et al.: A novel blockchain-based education records verification solution. In: Proceedings of the 19th Annual SIG Conference on Information Technology Education, pp. 178–183 (2018). https://doi.org/10.1145/3241815.3241870

5. Turkanovic, M., Holbl, M., Kosic, K., et al.: EduCTX: a blockchain-based higher education credit platform. IEEE Access **6**, 5112–5127 (2018). https://doi.org/10.1109/ACCESS.2018.2789929

6. Mishra, R.A., Kalla, A., Braeken, A., et al.: Privacy protected blockchain based architecture and implementation for sharing of students credentials. Inf. Process. Manag. **58**(3), 102512 (2021). https://doi.org/10.1016/j.ipm.2021.102512

7. Du, R., Ma, C., Li, M.: Privacy-preserving searchable encryption scheme based on public and private blockchains. Tsinghua Sci. Technol. **28**(1), 13–26 (2022). https://doi.org/10.26599/TST.2021.9010070

8. Rosenberg, M., White, J., Garman, C., et al.: zk-creds: Flexible anonymous credentials from zk-SNARKs and existing identity infrastructure. In: S&P, pp. 1882–1900 (2023). https://doi.org/10.1109/SP46215.2023.10179430

9. CITAHub: CITA: Cryptape Inter-enterprise Trust Automation (2021). https://docs.citahub.com/zh-CN/0.25.0/cita/cita-intro

10. Sporny, M., Longley, D., Sabadello, M., et al.: Decentralized Identifiers (DIDs) v1.0 (2021). https://w3c.github.io/did-core/

11. Sporny, M., Longley, D., Chadwick, D.: Verifiable credentials data model v1.1 (2022). https://www.w3.org/TR/vc-data-model/

12. Goldwasser, S., Micali, S., Rackoff, C.: The knowledge complexity of interactive proof-systems (extended bstract). In: Proceedings of the Seventeenth Annual ACM Symposium on Theory of Computing (STOC), pp. 291–304. ACM (1985). https://doi.org/10.1145/3335741.3335750

13. Bitansky, N., Canetti, R., Chiesa, A., et al.: From extractable collision resistance to succinct non-interactive arguments of knowledge, and back again. In: Proceedings of the 3rd Innovations in Theoretical Computer Science Conference, pp. 326–349 (2012). https://doi.org/10.1145/2090236.2090263

14. Groth, J.: On the size of pairing-based non-interactive arguments. In: Fischlin, M., Coron, J.-S. (eds.) EUROCRYPT 2016, Part II. LNCS, vol. 9666, pp. 305–326. Springer, Heidelberg (2016). https://doi.org/10.1007/978-3-662-49896-5_11

15. Bunz, B., Bootle, J., Boneh, D., et al.: Bulletproofs: short proofs for confidential transactions and more. In: 2018 IEEE Symposium on Security and Privacy (SP), pp. 315–334. IEEE (2018). https://doi.org/10.1109/SP.2018.00020

16. WeBank: WeIdentity Document (2021). https://weidentity.readthedocs.io/zh-cn/latest/docs/weidentity-contract-design.html

Sentiment Analysis of Teaching Evaluation Based on Complex Semantic Analysis

Lina Chen[1]($\boxtimes$), Xianzhi Huang[2], Hongjie Guo[1], Fangyao Shen[1], and Hong Gao[1]

[1] School of Computer Science and Technology, Zhejiang Normal University, Jinhua, China
chenlina@zjnu.cn
[2] College of Physics and Electronic Information Engineering, Zhejiang Normal University, Jinhua, China

Abstract. In the era of digital education, student evaluations of teachers constitute a crucial component of digital education. They serve as a driving force for promoting teaching reforms and are the fundamental basis for enhancing the quality of education and teaching. The digitalization of education reform provides students with more opportunities and avenues for evaluating teachers, including classroom teaching evaluations, online network teaching evaluations, and periodic assessments. Effectively utilizing this evaluation data to identify student needs and discover teaching issues is one of the effective ways to implement student-centered educational reforms. Through analysis, it has been found that existing student evaluation data exhibits characteristics such as implicit expression and complex emotional semantics, posing significant challenges for data analysis. This paper addresses these challenges by constructing a sentiment lexicon in the educational evaluation domain and employing complex semantic analysis to more accurately analyze the underlying emotional states within the evaluation data. The methodology involves the expansion of a general sentiment lexicon. Using active learning algorithms, sentiment seed words are selected from the evaluation data. Based on these seed words, an educational domain sentiment vocabulary is generated using the SO-PMI algorithm. The normalized educational domain sentiment vocabulary is then merged with the expanded general sentiment lexicon, resulting in the construction of the educational evaluation domain sentiment lexicon. During the evaluation phase, complex semantic analysis is applied to the evaluation data, and the educational evaluation domain sentiment lexicon is used for data analysis. Experimental results indicate that the proposed method achieves consistency with the actual data ranking in terms of sentiment classification and evaluation scores (MAE = 1.06, RMSE = 1.28). The F1 values for positive and negative teaching comments increased by 7.3% and 34.9%, respectively, compared to a general sentiment lexicon. Furthermore, when compared with common supervised learning algorithms, the proposed algorithm demonstrates superior sentiment classification performance.

Keywords: Student Evaluation of Teaching · Sentiment Analysis · Teaching Evaluation Domain Lexicon · Active Learning

W. Hong and G. Kanaparan (Eds.): ICCSE 2023, CCIS 2023, pp. 256–264, 2024.
https://doi.org/10.1007/978-981-97-0730-0_23

1   Introduction

In the realm of digital education, Student Evaluations of Teaching (SET) are crucial for educational reform but face challenges due to the lack of domain-specific sentiment lexicons. The complex nature of teaching comments leads to discrepancies between evaluation outcomes and actual performance, hindering the evaluation process. SET involves collecting student feedback on course instruction to enhance teaching quality [1]. Text Sentiment Analysis (SA) in education has been explored by various researchers, such as Balahadia et al. [2], who used sentiments from evaluations to develop a performance evaluation system. Lin et al. [3] applied machine learning to extract sentiment from SET, and Wang et al. [4] used sentiment lexicons for emotional analysis in educational news. However, relying on general sentiment lexicons poses challenges to uncover deeper information [5].

Some studies address this limitation using different approaches. Hatzivassiloglou et al. [6] demonstrated the reliability of polarity relationships in English text, while Huang et al. [7] used conjunctions and emotional polarity constraints. Liu et al. [8] expanded HowNet to create an emotional lexicon, and Yang et al. [9] utilized HowNet and NTUSD for emotional tendency analysis. Zhou et al. [10] adopted cross-lingual techniques to extract semantic elements from HowNet.

Knowledge-based methods, like those employed by Zhang et al. [11] and Cai et al. [12], offer versatility but may lack domain specificity. Bollegala et al. [13] annotated word polarity using PMI, while Wawer [14] used search engines for sentiment seed words. Yang et al. [15] determined sentiment polarity using Baidu search results, and Gao et al. [16] enhanced a general sentiment lexicon with specialized lexicons for sentiment analysis of user reviews.

In conclusion, sentiment analysis in SET faces challenges, especially with implicit and complex language. Various approaches, including machine learning and knowledge-based methods, are employed to address these challenges, each with its strengths and limitations.

This paper addresses the mentioned issues by introducing a Sentiment Lexicon for Teaching Evaluation (SL-TeaE [17]) and proposing a method called SL-TeaE(CSA) based on this lexicon. The key contributions are:

1. Generation of a sentiment lexicon for evaluating teaching. Sentiment seed words are chosen using an active algorithm to create a domain-specific sentiment lexicon for teaching, employing the SO-PMI algorithm. This enhances the model's generalizability and sentiment classification accuracy. Varying weights, determined by a gradient descent formula, are assigned to different intensity adverbs, forming an adverbs of degree list. Additionally, a negative word list is constructed based on negation words. The incorporation of the adverbs of degree list and negative word list into the general sentiment lexicon enables a more precise emotional analysis of teaching comments, expanding the sentiment lexicon for teaching evaluation. Integration of domain-specific sentiment words into the expanded general sentiment lexicon improves the performance of the generated teaching evaluation domain sentiment lexicon in sentiment analysis of teaching evaluations.

2. Complex Semantic Analysis. Complex semantic analysis is applied to teaching evaluation data to more accurately extract semantic features from the evaluation comments.

2 SL-TeaE(CSA) Model Diagram

The model diagram of SL-TeaE(CSA) is shown in Fig. 1.

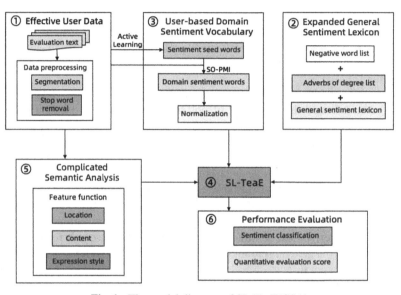

Fig. 1. The model diagram of SL-TeaE(CSA)

The teaching evaluation sentiment analysis model based on semantic analysis is divided into six sections:

1. Teaching Evaluation Data Preprocessing. The evaluation text undergoes preprocessing operations, including tokenization and stop-word removal, to enhance data quality. This step involves breaking down the text into individual words (tokenization) and eliminating common stop words, contributing to improved data quality.
2. The expansion process involves selecting a foundational sentiment lexicon, constructing a list of negation words, and creating a list of adverbs denoting intensity. These steps collectively contribute to enlarging the general sentiment lexicon, providing a more comprehensive set of words for sentiment analysis.
3. Generation of Teaching Evaluation Domain Sentiment Words.
   a. Generation of Sentiment Seed Words. An active learning algorithm is used to select sentiment seed words from preprocessed teaching evaluation data. These seed words are used to generate domain-specific sentiment words. The active learning algorithm selects words with maximum coverage for annotation. The TextRank algorithm [18], combined with the K-Means clustering algorithm, is used to generate sentiment seed words.

    b. Domain-Specific Sentiment Words Generation: Utilizing the selected sentiment seed words, the SO-PMI algorithm identifies necessary domain-specific sentiment words from teaching evaluation data, determining their sentiment polarity and tendency values.

    c. Normalization of Sentiment Inclination Values: Aligning the sentiment intensity of domain-specific sentiment words with the general foundational sentiment lexicon ensures a consistent scale for SA.

4. Generation of SL-TeaE. The normalized domain-specific sentiment words merge with the expanded general sentiment lexicon, forming the teaching evaluation domain sentiment lexicon.

5. Complex Semantic Analysis. Semantic analysis is conducted on the evaluation data to extract emotional central sentences representing the overall viewpoint of the reviewer as sentences representing the overall viewpoint of the reviewer.

6. Performance Evaluation. This section comprises sentiment classification and quantitative evaluation scores analysis. It involves evaluating the performance of general sentiment lexicon expansion, domain-specific sentiment word enrichment, and complex semantic analysis by comparing their performance on teaching evaluation data in terms of SA and sentiment computing.

3 Complex Semantic Analysis

3.1 Sentiment Center Sentences

Usually, the semantics in Student Evaluations of Teaching (SET) comments are more complex, expressions are more implicit, and emotions are more subtle. When a student writes a SET comment, they typically do not express negative emotions directly but rather use relatively implicit expressions. For example, phrases like "Compared to Professor Wang, Professor Li's teaching could be improved" or "It would be better if this instructor had a teaching assistant" are common. Due to the complex nature of these comments, it is challenging to extract emotional features from SET comments.

    Typically, the sentiment polarity in SET comments is determined by the most critical opinions of the reviewers rather than minor details. Therefore, it is essential to focus on extracting sentences that represent the overall opinions of the reviewers from SET comments. Here, we refer to the sentences that can represent the overall opinions of the reviewers as "sentiment center sentences". We evaluate SET comments' sentiment center sentences from three angles: the position angle, the content angle, and the expression style angle.

    Firstly, from the position angle, in a SET comment, sentences at the beginning and end of the comment are more likely to become sentiment center sentences. Therefore, the position feature function should assign higher scores to sentences at the beginning and end. Experimental results show that a negative Gaussian function can be used as the position feature function. Thus, given a sentence "s", the position feature function is determined as shown in Eq. (1):

$$f_1(s) = -\frac{1}{\sqrt{2\pi}\sigma}e^{-\frac{(s-\mu)^2}{2\sigma^2}}, 1 \leq s \leq len \tag{1}$$

In Eq. (1), μ represents the mean, σ represents the standard deviation, and *len* represents the length (the number of sentences in one comment). In the subsequent experiments, μ is set to $len/2$, and σ is set to 1.

From a content perspective, sentiment center sentences not only exhibit strong emotional intensity, but the sentiment polarity should also be unambiguous. Therefore, the definition of the content feature function is as shown in Eq. (2):

$$f_2(s) = \frac{\sum_{t \in s} l(t)}{\sum_{t \in s} |l(t)|} \tag{2}$$

In Eq. (2), $l(t)$ represents that the word "t" is a sentiment word and indicates its sentiment polarity. When 't' is a positive word, $l(t) = 1$; conversely, when 't' is a negative word, $l(t) = -1$. From the content feature function, it can be observed that only sentences containing sentiment words with the same polarity receive higher scores, while sentences with no sentiment words or a mixture of negative and positive sentiment words receive lower scores.

From an expression style perspective, sentiment center sentences often include summarizing words or phrases like "In conclusion" and "All in all ". Therefore, the definition of the expression style function is as shown in Eq. (3)

$$f_3(s) = \sum_{t \in s} conclusive\_Expressions(t) \tag{3}$$

In Eq. (1), $conclusive\_Expressions(t)$ represents that "t" is a summarizing expression. If a sentence contains summarizing words or phrases, the score of that sentence will be higher.

Taking into consideration the three feature functions of sentiment center sentences, the summation of feature functions in Eq. (1), (2), and (3) is performed. The top N sentences with the highest scores are selected (typically N is set to 1 or 2) as sentiment center sentences. If the total number of sentences in a text is less than N, all sentences are considered sentiment center sentences.

After conducting complex semantic analysis on the SET data following data preprocessing, sentiment center sentences from each SET comment are subjected to sentiment classification using SL-TeaE. This approach is referred to as SL-TeaE (CSA).

Input the SET comments after data preprocessing.

Perform complex semantic analysis on the SET comments, and output the sentiment center sentence for each SET comment.

4 Experimental Results Analysis

4.1 SET Data

The data originated from the SET data in our university's teaching system, including end-of-semester total evaluation data, mid-teaching phase data and online course real-time data. In total, there are 519 pieces of evaluation data from 4 teachers, and after data preprocessing, 508 pieces of valid data remain as corpus.

4.2   Experimental Metrics

We utilize standard evaluation metrics commonly employed in sentiment analysis models, including precision (P), recall (R), and F1 score (F1), and utilize the Mean Absolute Error (MAE) and Root Mean Squared Error (RMSE) as evaluation metrics for the quantitative scoring experiments in course evaluations.

4.3   Performance Comparison

Comparison of Sentiment Classification Performance. Teaching comments encompass both Positive Teaching Comments (PTC) and Negative Teaching Comments (NTC). By conducting comparisons with a General Sentiment Lexicon (GSL) and an Expanded General Sentiment Lexicon (EGSL), this study validates the effectiveness of the proposed domain-specific sentiment lexicon construction. Simultaneously, comparative experiments were carried out with common supervised learning algorithms such as K-Nearest Neighbors (KNN), Naïve Bayes algorithm, Maximum Entropy model (ME), and Support Vector Machine (SVM). The results of the comparative experiments on PTC and NTC are illustrated in Fig. 2 and Fig. 3.

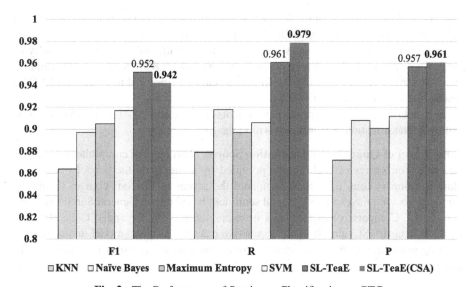

Fig. 2. The Performance of Sentiment Classification on PTC

From Fig. 2 and Fig. 3, the following conclusions can be drawn: 1) SL-TeaE(CSA) Improvement over SL-TeaE: SL-TeaE(CSA), which incorporates complex semantic analysis into SL-TeaE, demonstrates enhanced sentiment classification performance. Specifically, for negative teaching comments, SL-TeaE(CSA) outperforms SL-TeaE with notable improvements in precision, recall, and F1 score by 11.4%, 4.4%, and 7.6%, respectively. For PTC, while precision slightly decreases by 1%, both recall and F1 score show improvement. 2) Comparison with Common Supervised Learning

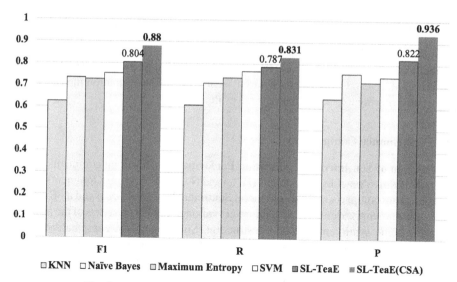

Fig. 3. The Performance of Sentiment Classification on NTC

Algorithms: Compared to common supervised learning algorithms such as KNN, Naïve Bayes, Maximum Entropy, and SVM, SL-TeaE(CSA) exhibits superior sentiment classification performance. It achieves better precision, recall, and F1 score, especially in positive teaching comments where precision increases by 7.8%, recall by 10.0%, and F1 score by 8.9%. For NTC, the highest improvements are observed in precision (19.4%), recall (34.0%), and F1 score (34.9%).

In conclusion, the comparative experiments indicate that SL-TeaE(CSA) excels in sentiment classification performance within the SET domain.

Comparison of Quantitative Evaluation Scores. Through the comprehensive teaching evaluation scores of each course provided by students on the school's academic administration system, this study compared the scores of the four courses taught by four teachers with the extended general sentiment based on the General Sentiment Lexicon (GSL). Comparative experiments were conducted with Expanded General Sentiment Lexicon (EGSL) and SL-TeaE to verify the accuracy of this model in quantitative teaching evaluation scores. The specific comparison results are shown in Table 1 and Table 2.

Table 1. Comparison of quantitative scores calculation performance

Teacher	GSL	EGSL	SL-TeaE	SL-TeaE(CSA)	Actual scores
Teacher1	73.54	73.96	94.49	**96.34**	97.54
Teacher2	82.70	83.92	96.56	**98.19**	98.77
Teacher3	81.73	82.09	93.38	**94.27**	96.45
Teacher4	83.59	85.45	96.15	**97.84**	98.10

Table 2. Quantitative scores calculation error comparison

Sentiment computing methods	MAE	RMSE
GSL	17.32	17.76
EGSL	16.36	16.90
SL-TeaE	2.57	2.62
SL-TeaE(CSA)	**1.06**	**1.28**

Analysis of Table 1 and Table 2 reveals notable disparities in the course composite assessment scores derived from the GSL when compared to the actual course assessment scores. Notably, these calculated scores exhibit a significant deviation from the correct relative order, displaying the largest mean absolute and root mean square errors. While the course composite assessment scores generated by the EGSL show a relative improvement compared to those derived from the general sentiment lexicon, they still exhibit inaccuracies in their ordering. Conversely, the course composite assessment scores obtained through SL-TeaE and SL-TeaE(CSA) are closer to the actual scores and follow the correct order. Specifically, SL-TeaE(CSA) demonstrates even greater proximity to the true values, boasting the smallest MAE and RMSE of 1.06 and 1.28, respectively.

5 Conclusion

In conclusion, this study explores a specialized emotion lexicon in the field of teaching, enhancing the generalization of the model. By combining complex semantic analysis, the emotional analysis performance of the model has significantly improved. Compared to a general emotion lexicon, the F1 values for positive and negative teaching comments have increased by 7.3% and 34.9%, respectively. The emotional classification performance is also superior to common supervised learning algorithms. Additionally, SL-TeaE(CSA) demonstrates greater accuracy in quantifying evaluation scores, with minimal error in comprehensive course evaluation scores. The model's scores closely align with actual course evaluations, exhibiting consistent ranking with the actual scores. The effectiveness of SL-TeaE(CSA) has been demonstrated.

The experimental results of this article have practical significance for the evaluation of teachers' teaching level, which can help teachers carry out personalized teaching evaluation analysis, such as comparing the teaching levels of different teachers, different courses, and different periods horizontally, and vertically discovering the teaching transitions of teachers in different periods, including the upward period, the teaching pause period, or the teaching decline period. In order to promote teacher teaching reform through student evaluation and improve teaching quality through teaching reform.

Acknowledgements. This study was supported by the Key Project of Regional Innovation and Development Joint Fund of National Natural Science Foundation of China (Grant No. U22A2025).

References

1. Wang, B.: Research on sentiment analysis of student evaluations of teaching based on deep learning. Chongqing University of Posts and Telecommunications (2021)
2. Balahadia, F.F., Fernando, M., Juanatas, I.C.: Teacher's performance evaluation tool using opinion mining with sentiment analysis. In: Region 10 Symposium. IEEE (2016)
3. Lin, Q., Zhu, Y., Zang, S., et al.: Lexical based automated teaching evaluation via students' short reviews. Comput. Appl. Eng. Educ. **27**(1), 194–205 (2019)
4. Wang, B., Gao, L., An, T., et al.: A Method of Educational News Classification Based on Emotional Dictionary. In: 2018 Chinese Control and Decision Conference, pp. 1–5. IEEE Press, Shenyang, China (2018)
5. Taboada, M., Brooke, J., Tofiloski, M., et al.: Lexicon-based methods for sentiment analysis. Comput. Linguist. **37**(2), 267–307 (2011)
6. Hatzivassiloglou, V., Mckeown, K.R.: Predicting the semantic orientation of adjectives. In: Proceedings of the ACL (2002)
7. Huang, S., Niu, Z., Shi, C.: Automatic construction of domain-specific sentiment lexicon based on constrained label propagation. Knowl.-Based Syst. **56**(Jan.), 191–200 (2014)
8. Liu, W., Zhu, Y., Li, C., et al.: Research on building Chinese basic semantic lexicon. J. Comput. Appl. **29**(10), 2875–2877 (2009)
9. Yang, C., Feng, S., Wang, D., et al.: Analysis on web public opinion orientation based on extending sentiment lexicon. J. Chin. Comput. Syst. **31**(4), 691–695 (2010)
10. Zhou, Y., Yang, J., Yang, A.: A method on building Chinese sentiment lexicon for text sentiment analysis. J. Shandong Univ. (Eng. Sci.) (6), 27–33 (2013)
11. Zhang, J., Ning, J., Li, Y.: Data analysis of students' subjective evaluation of teaching based on cluster analysis and its application. China Educ. Light Ind. **25**(2), 21–28 (2022)
12. Cai, Y., Yang, K., Zhou, Z., et al.: A hybrid model for opinion mining based on domain sentiment dictionary. Int. J. Mach. Learn. Cybern. **10**(8), 2131–2142 (2019)
13. Bollegala, D., Weir, D., Carroll, J.: Using multiple sources to construct a sentiment sensitive thesaurus for cross-domain sentiment classification. In: 49th Annual Meeting of the Association for Computational Linguistics 2011, vol. 1, pp. 132–141. Association for Computational Linguistics (2011)
14. Wawer, A.: Mining co-occurrence matrices for SO-PMI paradigm word candidates. In: 13th Conference of the European Chapter of the Association for Computational Linguistics 2012 (EACL 2012), pp. 74–80. Association for Computational Linguistics (2012)
15. Yang, A., Lin, J., Zhou, Y.: Method on building Chinese text sentiment lexicon. J. Front. Comput. Sci. Technol. **11**, 1033–1039 (2013)
16. Gao, H., Zhang, J.: Sentiment analysis and visualization of hotel reviews based on sentiment dictionary. Comput. Eng. Softw. **42**(01), 45–47 (2021)
17. Huang, X., Chen, L., Zheng, Y., Guo, H., Shen, F., Gao, H.: SL-TeaE: an efficient method for improving the precision of teaching evaluation. In: Yang, X., et al. (eds.) ADMA 2023. LNCS, vol. 14179, pp. 3–17. Springer, Cham (2023). https://doi.org/10.1007/978-3-031-466 74-8_1
18. Liu, Q., Shen, W.: Research of keyword extraction of political news based on Word2Vec and TextRank. Inf. Res. **6**, 22–27 (2018)

An Intelligent Scheduling System for Large-Scale Online Judging

En Zhang, Fan Wu, and Xuesong Lu[✉]

School of Data Science and Engineering,
East China Normal University, Shanghai, China
{zhangen,wufan_01}@stu.ecnu.edu.cn, xslu@dase.ecnu.ednu.cn

Abstract. Online judge (OJ) systems have been widely used for programming skill evaluation in various fields, including programming education, programming competition and talent recruitment. Existing OJ systems put the codes into a judge queue according to the order of user submission, and use the judge server to evaluate the correctness of the codes in turn. With the surge in the number of code submissions, this scheduling method causes the rapid increase of average response time for judge requests, resulting in a decline in user experience. To alleviate the problem, we develop an intelligent scheduling system, which consists of two modules. In the first module, we employ a deep representation learning model to predict the running time of the codes in the judge queue; in the second module, the judge queue is divided into fixed-size windows. The codes in each window are sorted according to their predicted running time in ascending order, and are scheduled to the judge server using the shortest job first algorithm. The experimental results show that, 1) the constructed prediction model predicts the running time of the codes accurately; 2) compared with the scheduling algorithm of existing OJ systems, the proposed scheduling algorithm can effectively reduce the average response time for large-scale online judging. Furthermore, by varying the code running time distribution and window size in the judge queue, we demonstrate the performance improvements of the proposed intelligent scheduling system under different settings, compared with the existing systems.

Keywords: online judge · intelligent scheduling · running time prediction · shortest job first · deep representation learning model

1 Introduction

Online Judge (OJ) [26] systems automatically assess the correctness of codes by running them with the pre-defined use cases and comparing the output with the standard results. Because of the convenience, OJ systems have been widely used in programming education [7], programming competitions [27], and talent recruitment[1,2]. For example, the China Computer Federation (CCF) uses an

---

[1] https://www.hackerrank.com/.

[2] https://www.qualified.io/.

© The Author(s), under exclusive license to Springer Nature Singapore Pte Ltd. 2024
W. Hong and G. Kanaparan (Eds.): ICCSE 2023, CCIS 2023, pp. 265–279, 2024.
https://doi.org/10.1007/978-981-97-0730-0_24

OJ system to organize a series of programming exams for "Software Professional Certification", usually with more than 10,000 examinees in a single exam [25]. For another example, on Chinese University MOOC[3], there might be up to 100,000 students who take the same programming course and practice programming in the built-in OJ system at the same time. In a typical OJ system, the codes submitted by users are inserted into a queue according to the submission order, and the judge server runs the codes in the queue based on the "First Come First Serve (FCFS)" scheduling algorithm, determining their correctness and returning the results to the corresponding users. As the amount of users and the number of code submissions grow, this scheduling method causes the rapid increase of the average response time for judging requests, i.e., the time between a code submission and the return of the evaluation results, thereby seriously affecting users' programming experience. Figure 1 shows the experimental results of average response time according to the FCFS scheduling algorithm, where the average running time of the experimented codes is only 96($\pm$84) ms. However, when the number of codes in the queue grows from 100 to 1,000, the average response time of the judging request rapidly increases from less than 5 s to more than 80 s.

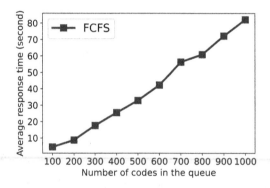

Fig. 1. Average response time vs. number of codes in the queue

In order to improve user experience, especially to reduce the anxiety of waiting for assessment results during competitions or exams, how to reduce the average response time in large-scale online judging scenarios is worth investigating. Some related works have proposed to build scalable OJ systems from a system architecture perspective to alleviate the load pressure caused by a single system. For example, Wang et al. [25] develop the MetaOJ system, which reduces the response time under high loads by building a distributed OJ system. Nerantzis et al. [19] develop the MI-OPJ system based on the micro-service architecture, which utilize Kubernetes to orchestrate the container services and realize the elastic scaling of the services of the OJ system.

---

[3] https://www.icourse163.org/.

Unlike the above work, we investigate how to improve the responsiveness of a single system in the face of large-scale judging loads, and the proposed method can be easily integrated into any existing OJ system, including those based on the distributed and micro-service architectures mentioned above. Specifically, we build an intelligent scheduling system that reduces the average response time of judging requests by prioritizing the judgements of codes in the queue with a shorter running time. The entire scheduling system is divided into two modules. First, in order to predict the running time of the codes in the queue, we employ a deep representation learning model to predict the code running time. In particular, we select three code representation models, i.e., graph2vec [18], ASTNN [29], and CodeBERT [8], to construct the prediction model and evaluate the performance. Through comparison, the ASTNN-based model is finally selected to predict the code running time. Second, we modify the FCFS scheduling algorithm to "Shortest Job First (SJF)" scheduling algorithm to prioritize the judgments of codes with a shorter predicted running time. In order to prevent the codes with a long running time from being unable to be judged for a long period of time, we divide the code queue into fixed-size windows, and in each window, the codes are sorted in ascending order according to their predicted running time and judged using the SJF scheduling algorithm. At the window level, the FCFS scheduling algorithm is still used to ensure that the codes with a long running time can be judged in the windows where they are inserted.

It is worth mentioning that in traditional CPU architectures, predicting code running time incurs considerable additional overhead, which greatly diminishes the judging response improvement brought by the above scheduling system. Fortunately, today's CPU-GPU heterogeneous architecture makes this overhead negligible: predicting a code's running time using GPUs is much faster than judging its correctness in the judge server, which is typically run on CPUs. As a result, except for the prediction and sorting time of the codes in the first window of the judge queue, which needs to be factored into the response time, the rest of the codes can complete the running time prediction and sorting during the waiting time for judgement, thus having no impact on the response time. The experimental results show that the model constructed in this paper can accurately predict the running time of the code, and the proposed SJF scheduling algorithm can effectively reduce the average response time of the judging requests. In addition, we vary the distribution of code running time in the dataset, and demonstrate how the proposed intelligent scheduling system reduces the average response time compared to the FCFS scheduling under different distributions. Finally, we vary the size of the window in the judge queue and demonstrate how the proposed system reduces the average response time under different combinations of queue length and window size.

In summary, we contribute in this work on the following three aspects:

- We propose to improve the responsiveness of a stand-alone OJ system for large-scale online judging by changing the scheduling algorithm of the judge server from FCFS to window-based SJF. To the best of our knowledge, this paper is the first to propose such an approach.

- In order to adopt the SJF scheduling algorithm, we construct a deep learning model to predict the running time of the codes, as a basis of the SJF scheduling algorithm. The experimental results show that the constructed model can accurately predict the code running time.
- We conduct experiments to demonstrate that the proposed intelligent scheduling system can effectively reduce the average response time of an OJ system under large-scale online judging. We vary the code running time distribution and the queue/window size to demonstrate the performance improvement over the traditional scheduling system under different settings.

2   Related Work

The intelligent scheduling system proposed in this paper contains two main parts: code running time prediction and code judging based on SJF scheduling algorithm. The former part belongs to the research category of running time prediction and the latter part belongs to the category of improving OJ systems. This section presents the related work in the two areas respectively.

2.1   Code Running Time Prediction

Predicting code running time has important applications in both industry and education. In industry, accurate prediction of code running time ensures that specific tasks in real-time systems do not exceed a preset time, guaranteeing system stability. In education, predicting code running time can give students real-time feedback and motivate them to write more efficient code.

Puschner and Koza [21] propose to split a complete code into different components, such as sequential, looping, branching, etc., and estimate the maximum running time of each component, and finally add them together to get the estimation of the maximum running time of the complete code. Park [20] combines the static analysis based on simple timing diagrams and the dynamic analysis based on execution paths to obtain tighter upper bounds on the running times of sequential programs. Benz and Bringmann [4] point out that accurate static code analysis relies heavily on loop boundaries, control flow constraints, and other program flow facts that need to be labeled by the user, and is difficult to apply in real-time systems. They improve code running time prediction using a scene-aware analysis based on the mode of operation, application-related program flow facts, and image resolution.

Another research area closely related to code running time prediction is code complexity prediction. Although the goals of the two prediction problems are slightly different, the way the code features are extracted in the proposed methods can be cross-referenced. For example, Gulwani et al. [10] propose both control flow refinement and progress invariant methods and combine them to estimate the complexity of codes with nested and multi-path loop structures. Chatterjee et al. [5,6] use sorting functions and linear programming to compute worst-case upper bounds for non-polynomials in codes. There is also a body of work that focuses on the problem of predicting code complexity in recursive functions. For example, Albert et al. [1] use "evaluation trees" to mine recursive relationships and derive complexity bounds for subsumption and sorting based on the mining results. Ishimwe et al. [14] use pattern matching to learn recursive relations in recursive programs, and represent asymptotic complexity bounds for recursive programs by obtaining closed-form schemes. With the public availability of huge amounts of code data and the widespread use of neural networks, deep learning-based approaches have emerged. For example, Sikka et al. [22] propose a deep learning-based code complexity prediction method, which uses graph2vec [18] to represent the code, and constructs a multi-classification model to predict the complexity of the code.

Due to the significant differences in the structural features of different codes, traditional prediction methods do not generalize well. Therefore, in this paper, we collect a large amount of codes and train a deep learning model to predict the code running time.

2.2 Improving OJ Systems

As OJ systems are widely used, researchers propose various improvement methods to cope with the application of OJ systems in different scenarios. For example, in order to adapt the OJ system to educational scenarios, Sun et al. [23] design the YOJ platform for classroom teaching scenarios by focusing on the curriculum, and develop modules such as course management, problem discussion, function evaluation, offline assignments, and online tests to facilitate teaching and learning. Francisco and Ambrosio [9] develop an automatic question grouping system based on the difficulty classification of questions to assist in the design of assignments and tests, with the goal of improving the ease of use of OJ systems. They also develop a student reporting system based on behavioral data to provide feedback to students on their learning performance. Hou et al. [13] utilize the error reporting information from compilation tools and judging servers to give feedback to users, in order to improve their programming training and testing efficiency. Wang et al. [25] build a stand-alone OJ system to alleviate the service response latency problem caused by large-scale cross-region online programming testing, by building a distributed OJ system and deploying it on the cloud. In order to cope with the load pressure caused by large-scale online training during the Covid-19 epidemic, Nerantzis et al. [19] follow the micro-service architecture to reconstruct an OJ system, which can be massively scaled using software such as Kubernetes, Apache Kafka, and NextJS. Other improvement works of OJ systems include [28, 30] and so on.

Among them, the works in [25] and [19] have the closet goals to our work, that is, improving the responsiveness of the OJ system to deal with large-scale online judging by improving the back-end structure. The difference is that these two works propose distributed and micro-service architectures, respectively, to rebuild the existing stand-alone OJ system, while we try to improve the system responsiveness by improving the intrinsic judging scheduling mechanism in existing OJ systems. The approach proposed in this paper is orthogonal to the approaches in [25] and [19], which is more lightweight and can be flexibly adapted to any existing OJ system.

3   The Intelligent Scheduling System for Online Judging

The overall architecture of the intelligent scheduling system proposed in this paper is shown in Fig. 2. The code submitted by OJ users is first put into an judging queue according to the submission order, and the system divides the queue into fixed-size windows. In each window, the system predicts the running times of the codes, and sorts the codes in ascending order according to the predicted running time. Subsequently, the system combines all the windows into a queue again following the original window order, and judges the codes in the queue sequentially. The whole system is divided into two key modules: code running time prediction and judging scheduling based on running time prediction.

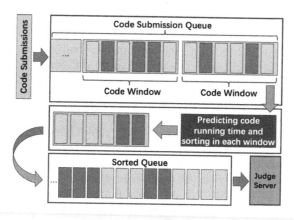

Fig. 2. The overall architecture of the proposed intelligent scheduling system

3.1   Code Running Time Prediction Based on Deep Representation Models

In recent years, code representation models based on deep learning have been applied to various tasks in the field of software engineering, including program classification [3], clone detection [2], code repair [12], etc., and have achieved the performance far beyond that of traditional algorithms. Therefore, in this paper we also predict the running time of code using deep representation learning models, since accurate prediction is very important to the subsequent scheduling algorithm.

We select three representative deep code representation learning models. The first model is graph2vec [18], which has been used to build models for predicting code complexity [22], and thus is closely related to our work. Graph2vec borrows the idea from word2vec [17] and doc2vec [16] to train graph representations by

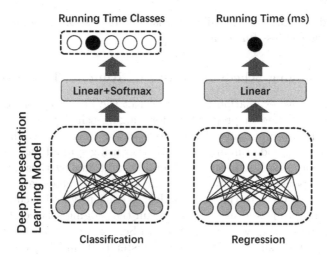

Fig. 3. The classification and regression model for evaluating the predictive performance of code representation learning models.

maximizing the probability of occurrence of the associated subgraphs of each node in the graph. When applied to code representation learning in this paper, we first convert the code into Abstract Syntax Tree (AST) intermediate representation, and consider the AST as a graph. Then we input the ASTs into Graph Attention Networks (GAT) [24] and train the code representation by applying the graph2vec algorithm. The second model is ASTNN [29], which performs prominently well among small-scale code representation models [11]. ASTNN splits the AST of a code into a set of statement subtrees, each of which corresponds to a complete statement, and then inputs the encoded sequence of subtrees into the bi-directional GRU, and finally performs max pooling over the hidden states of all time steps to obtain the representation of the entire code. The third model is CodeBERT [8], which is the first programming language pre-training model with strong code representation capability. The input of CodeBERT is a piece of code text and its natural language comments. Two pre-training tasks are designed to learn the code representation, which are masked token prediction and replaced token detection. After training, the encoding of the [CLS] token can be used to represent the input code. In order to evaluate the performance of the above three representation learning models, we construct both classification and regression models to predict the code running time, as shown in Fig. 3. In the classification task, we categorize the code running time into 5 classes, which are 0–50 ms, 50–100 ms, 100–200 ms, 200–500 ms, and 500–1000 ms, according to the distribution of actual code running time in the dataset. We add a linear layer with the Softmax activation on top of the code representation model to predict the classes and employ cross-entropy as the loss function. In the regression task, we similarly add a linear layer on top of the representation model, outputting a single value, which is finally converted into a value between 0–1000, representing the predicted running time in milliseconds. The regression model uses the mean square error as the loss function.

3.2   Code Judging Scheduling Based on Running Time Prediction

Based on the above evaluation tasks, we select the best deep model to predict the code running time in preparation for judging scheduling. Specifically, we first predict the running time of each code in the queue. In traditional architectures, predicting code running time, whether using symbol-based or machine-learning-based approaches, incurs considerable additional overhead, which affects the judging response time. However, in the GPU-CPU heterogeneous architecture, we can use a GPU to run deep models to efficiently and accurately predict the code running time and use a CPU to run the judging service of the OJ system, without interfering with each other. In Sect. 4, we will see that predicting code running time using a GPU is much faster than judging the code in the OJ's judge server. As such, the prediction overhead does almost not increase the response time of the code judging.

Algorithm 1: Average response time for judging code using the SJF scheduling.

Input: Code queue Q formed according to user submission time, window size w
Output: Average response time for judging codes in Q: rt_{avg}.

1 divide Q into disjoint windows of size w;
2 **foreach** *window W in Q* **do**
3   **foreach** *code c in window* **do**
4          $prt = predictRunTime(c)$ /* Predicting the running time prt of code c using a GPU */
5   **end**
6   sort the codes in W according to their prt in the ascending order
7      $RT_w = judgeAndCalRspTime(W)$ /* Feed W to the judge server and calculate the response time for each code */
8 **end**
9 calculate rt_{avg} using RT_w of all the windows in Q
10 return rt_{avg}

To implement the SJF scheduling algorithm, the codes in the queue need to be sorted in ascending order of predicted running time from shortest to longest and then fed to the judge server. A straightforward approach is to sort the entire queue, which may minimize the average response time. However, this approach makes the codes with long predicted running time unable to be judged for a quite long time, which affects the programming experience of the corresponding users. Therefore, we adopt a window-based SJF scheduling approach. Specifically, we divide the entire queue into windows of fixed size, sort the codes according to the predicted running time and use the SJF scheduling inside each window. On the other hand, different windows still maintain the order in the initial queue, and are sent to the judge server in turn, i.e., the FCFS scheduling is still used at the window level. Finally, we obtain the judging response time of each code and compute the average time for the entire queue. The complete procedure for calculating the average judging response time is shown in Algorithm 1.

It is worth noting that although Algorithm 1 is a serial pseudo-code written according to the judging process, in practice, the GPU predicting the code running time and the CPU running the judging service work in parallel.

4   Performance Evaluation

In this section, we empirically evaluate the proposed intelligent scheduling system. First, we evaluate the accuracy of the models in predicting the code running time. Then, we evaluate the effectiveness of the SJF scheduling algorithm based on the predicted running time for reducing the average response time. Our code is written in Python and PyTorch, and all experiments are conducted on a machine with 4 cpu-cores and 16 GB memory, equipped with a Tesla V100.

4.1   The Dataset

The code dataset used for the experiments is collected from 242 programming exercises of our OJ system, and a total of 63,355 C codes are collected. The running time distribution of these codes on the experimental machine is shown in Table 1.

Table 1. The distribution of the actual running time of the code in the data set.

Running Time	Number of Codes
0–50 ms	35854
50–100 ms	5977
100–200 ms	5611
200–500 ms	5550
500–1000 ms	10363
Total	63355

We can see that more than half of the code running times are smaller than 50 ms, and only about 16% of the running times are larger than 500 ms. We divide the entire dataset into training set, validation set and test set with proportion 6:2:2, and train the deep learning models to predict the code running time.

In the code judging scheduling experiment, we randomly select N codes from the test set to form the judging queue, and then slice the queue into fixed-size windows. Within each window, we use the ASTNN-based model to predict the code running time, and sort the codes in ascending order according to the predicted results. Finally, the codes in each window are fed into the judge server in turn.

4.2   Evaluation Metrics

In the running time prediction experiment, we treat the prediction task as a classification and regression task, respectively, and use Accuracy and Mean Absolute Error (MAE) as the evaluation metrics. In the classification task, the classes are the five classes in Table 1. In the regression task, the models directly predict the running time of the code.

In the code judging scheduling experiment, we compute the average response time of the codes in the judging queue. We randomly assign a submission time to each code and ensure that all codes in a queue are submitted within one second. The response time for each code is the time that the judge server returns the result subtracting the submission time. Finally, the average of the response times of all codes in the queue is calculated.

4.3   Hyperparameter Settings

When encoding the codes, the lengths of both the input embedding vector and the output token vector are set to 128. The length of the hidden layer vector for both graph2vec and ASTNN is set to 256, and the number of heads in the graph attention module of graph2vec is set to 4. The batch size for training is 64, and the maximum epoch is set to 20. We use adaMax [15] as the optimizer, and set the learning rate to 0.002. We use the default settings of CodeBERT.

In the judging scheduling experiments, the window size for dividing the queue is fixed to 50.

4.4   The Results

Code Running Time Prediction. Table 2 demonstrates the performance of the three running time prediction models. Table 3 demonstrates the performance in different running time classes.

From the two tables, we observe that ASTNN achieves the best performance in both the classification and regression task. ASTNN extracts from the AST the statement subtrees of the corresponding independent components in the code, which may make it capture better the execution structure of the code, and thus be more accurate at predicting the running time. Graph2vec focuses on the subgraph structure associated with each node, which does not necessarily represent a complete piece of code when applied to ASTs, making it worse at capturing the

Table 2. Predictive performance comparison of the three code representation models

code representation model	Accuracy	MAE
graph2vec[8]	0.872	20.64
ASTNN[9]	**0.946**	**15.26**
CodeBERT[10]	0.923	18.71

Table 3. Predictive performance comparison of the three code representation models for different classes of running time (ms)

Models	Accuracy					MAE				
	$\leq$50	50–100	100–200	200–500	>500	$\leq$50	50–100	100–200	200–500	>500
graph2vec	0.884	0.803	0.852	0.824	0.912	7.41	15.70	18.10	31.88	55.69
ASTNN	**0.961**	**0.917**	**0.926**	0.896	**0.956**	**3.21**	**10.91**	**15.73**	**24.82**	**38.04**
CodeBERT	0.953	0.899	0.867	**0.916**	0.909	4.46	13.91	22.73	30.64	42.26

execution structure of the code. CodeBERT does not use C codes in pre-training and does not learn structural features from intermediate representations such as ASTs and control flow graphs. Therefore it performs a bit worse than ASTNN. In order to achieve higher accuracy, in the future, pre-trained models that incorporate structural features such as GraphCodeBERT can be considered to train the prediction model [26].

Code Judging Scheduling. The ASTNN-based model is the most accurate among the three prediction models, so we use it to predict the running time of the code in the judging scheduling experiment. Based on the prediction results, we sort the codes in each window and prioritize the codes with shorter predicted running time. We refer to this scheduling algorithm as "SJF based on predicted running time". For comparison, we additionally implement "SJF based on cyclomatic complexity". Cyclomatic complexity is commonly used to measure the static complexity of a code and represents the number of linearly independent paths in the code, which is usually calculated as the number of closed paths in the control flow graph. The SJF algorithm based on cyclomatic complexity prioritizes codes with lower complexity for judging. Finally, in order to obtain the upper bound on the performance of the SJF scheduling algorithm, we sort and judge the codes based on their actual running time. We refer to this algorithm as "SJF based on actual running time". For each algorithm, we vary the number of codes in the judging queue from 100 to 1000 with increments 100, and compute the corresponding average response time of code judging.

Figure 4 shows the results. First, we can see that compared to FCFS scheduling, both SJF based on predicted running time and SJF based on cyclomatic complexity scheduling algorithms reduce the average response time. With the increase of the number of codes in the queue, the average response time is reduced more. This proves that the SJF scheduling algorithm can effectively improve the judging efficiency for large-scale online judging. Second, SJF based on predicted running time can reduce more average response time than SJF based on circle complexity, which indicates that the code running time is more suitable for the SJF scheduling algorithm and the constructed model can predict the running time accurately. Finally, SJF based on actual running time further reduces the average response time than SJF based on predicted running time, indicating that the scheduling performance of the current system can be further promoted by improving the accuracy of code running time prediction.

It is worth mentioning that in our experiments we can predict the running times of 30 codes per second using a Tesla V100 GPU, i.e., predicting the running time of the codes in a window of size 50 takes a bit more than 1 s. On the other hand, judging the codes in the window takes about 5 s. In other words, predict and sorting the codes in each window is much faster than judging them in the judge server. The overhead of code running time prediction does almost not increase the average judging response time when using a GPU as a standalone prediction module.

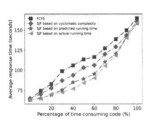

Fig. 4. The average response time of the four scheduling algorithms when the queue length increases.

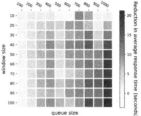

Fig. 5. Average response time for different distributions of code running time

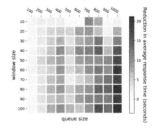

Fig. 6. The reduction in average response time under different combinations of queue length and window size, SJF vs. FCFS.

Impact of Code Running Time Distribution. The SJF scheduling algorithm is effective because the running times of the codes in the queue are quite different. In this section, we vary the distribution of code running times in the queue and observe the impact of the SJF scheduling algorithm on the average response time. Based on the collected dataset, we define codes with running time below 500 ms as "non-time-consuming code" and codes with running time above 500 ms as "time-consuming code". We increase the percentage of time-consuming codes from 0% to 100% with increments 10%, and randomly select 1,000 codes from the test set under each percentage control to calculate the average response time of code judging. Figure 5 shows the results. We can see that when the percentage of time-consuming codes is small or large, the SJF scheduling has a small reduction on the average response time over the FCFS scheduling, because the running times of all codes are more converged. The SJF scheduling algorithm based on predicted running times reduces the average response time the most when there are 50% time-consuming codes. This is instructive for designing code judging queues in OJ systems: one can group codes with different complexities into a queue, and use the scheduling system proposed in this paper to improve the average response time of the whole OJ system.

The Impact of Window Size in the Queue. In order to avoid the situation that codes with long running time are not able to be judged for a long time, we propose to divide the code queue into windows of fixed size, and use the SJF scheduling algorithm for the codes in each window, while different windows still follow the FCFS scheduling algorithm. Therefore, the window size has an impact on the overall performance of the scheduling system. We vary the code queue length from 100 to 1000 with increments 100, and for each queue length, we vary the window size from 10 to 100 with increments 10. Therefore, we obtain a 10×10 matrix, where each element of the matrix represents the average response time reduction of the SJF algorithm based on predicted running time over the FCFS algorithm, for the corresponding combination of queue length and window size. We visualize this matrix using a heat map. The more we reduce the average response time, the darker the color of the corresponding element in the matrix.

Figure 6 illustrates the experimental results. We can observe that the matrix gets progressively darker from the top left to the bottom right, i.e., overall the longer the queue and the larger the window, the more the average response time is reduced by using the SJF scheduling algorithm. The results are as expected, again demonstrating the accuracy of the running time prediction and the effectiveness of the SJF scheduling algorithm. In real systems, the length of the judging queue is usually determined by the system cache, and the administrator can dynamically adjust the window size according to the actual judging load, in order to meet the dynamic balance between the average response time of the codes with a long running time and the average response time of all codes.

5   Conclusion

In this paper, we address the problem of rapidly growing judging response time of OJ systems for large-scale online judging. We propose to reduce the average response time by improving the scheduling mechanism of the judging service, and construct a corresponding scheduling system. The system consists of two modules: the prediction module predicts the running times of the codes using a deep model, and the scheduling module judges the codes using a window-based SJF scheduling algorithm according to the predicted running time. Experimental results demonstrate that by accurately predicting the code running time, the scheduling algorithm proposed in this paper can effectively reduce the average judging response time of OJ systems. Importantly, the constructed intelligent scheduling system can be integrated into any existing OJ system.

In the future, we will continue to improve the scheduling system on two aspects. First, the experimental results prove that the response time using the predicted running time scheduling is still much larger than the response time using the actual running time scheduling. Therefore, we will investigate how to further improve the accuracy of code running time prediction. Second, we currently utilize a GPU for real-time prediction of code running time. For servers not equipped with a GPU, the benefit of intelligent scheduling will be affected by the prediction time. Therefore, we consider to predict and store the running times of a huge amount of codes offline. For online judging, we will design a retrieval algorithm to obtain the predicted running time of each submitted code, so as to improve the prediction efficiency on CPU-only machines.

Acknowledgement. This work is supported by the grant from the National Natural Science Foundation of China (Grant No. 62277017).

References

1. Albert, E., Arenas, P., Genaim, S., Puebla, G.: Automatic inference of upper bounds for recurrence relations in cost analysis. In: Alpuente, M., Vidal, G. (eds.) SAS 2008. LNCS, vol. 5079, pp. 221–237. Springer, Heidelberg (2008). https://doi.org/10.1007/978-3-540-69166-2_15
2. Alon, U., Brody, S., Levy, O., Yahav, E.: Code2Seq: generating sequences from structured representations of code. arXiv preprint arXiv:1808.01400 (2018)
3. Alon, U., Zilberstein, M., Levy, O., Yahav, E.: Code2Vec: learning distributed representations of code. Proc. ACM Program. Lang. **3**(POPL), 1–29 (2019)
4. Benz, J., Bringmann, O.: Scenario-aware program specialization for timing predictability. ACM Trans. Archit. Code Optim. (TACO) **18**(4), 1–26 (2021)
5. Chatterjee, K., Fu, H., Goharshady, A.K.: Termination analysis of probabilistic programs through Positivstellensatz's. In: Chaudhuri, S., Farzan, A. (eds.) CAV 2016. LNCS, vol. 9779, pp. 3–22. Springer, Cham (2016). https://doi.org/10.1007/978-3-319-41528-4_1
6. Chatterjee, K., Fu, H., Goharshady, A.K.: Non-polynomial worst-case analysis of recursive programs. ACM Trans. Program. Lang. Syst. (TOPLAS) **41**(4), 1–52 (2019)
7. Dong, Yu., Hou, J., Lu, X.: An intelligent online judge system for programming training. In: Nah, Y., Cui, B., Lee, S.-W., Yu, J.X., Moon, Y.-S., Whang, S.E. (eds.) DASFAA 2020. LNCS, vol. 12114, pp. 785–789. Springer, Cham (2020). https://doi.org/10.1007/978-3-030-59419-0_57
8. Feng, Z., et al.: CodebERT: a pre-trained model for programming and natural languages. arXiv preprint arXiv:2002.08155 (2020)
9. Francisco, R.E., Ambrosio, A.P.: Mining an online judge system to support introductory computer programming teaching. In: EDM (Workshops). Citeseer (2015)
10. Gulwani, S., Jain, S., Koskinen, E.: Control-flow refinement and progress invariants for bound analysis. ACM SIGPLAN Not. **44**(6), 375–385 (2009)
11. Han, S., Wang, D., Li, W., Lu, X.: A comparison of code embeddings and beyond. arXiv preprint arXiv:2109.07173 (2021)
12. Han, S., Wang, Y., Lu, X.: Errorclr: Semantic error classification, localization and repair for introductory programming assignments. In: Proceedings of the 46th International ACM SIGIR Conference on Research and Development in Information Retrieval, pp. 1345–1354 (2023)
13. Hou, D., Ma, J., Yin, L.: A framework of online judge systems for assessing programming skills. Int. J. Des. Anal. Tools Integr. Circuits Syst. **8**(1), 45–46 (2019)
14. Ishimwe, D., Nguyen, K.H., Nguyen, T.V.: DynAplex: analyzing program complexity using dynamically inferred recurrence relations. Proc. ACM Program. Lang. **5**(OOPSLA), 1–23 (2021)
15. Kingma, D.P., Ba, J.: Adam: a method for stochastic optimization. arXiv preprint arXiv:1412.6980 (2014)

16. Le, Q., Mikolov, T.: Distributed representations of sentences and documents. In: International Conference on Machine Learning, pp. 1188–1196. PMLR (2014)
17. Mikolov, T., Chen, K., Corrado, G., Dean, J.: Efficient estimation of word representations in vector space. arXiv preprint arXiv:1301.3781 (2013)
18. Narayanan, A., Chandramohan, M., Venkatesan, R., Chen, L., Liu, Y., Jaiswal, S.: Graph2Vec: learning distributed representations of graphs. arxiv 2017. arXiv preprint arXiv:1707.05005
19. Nerantzis, O.R., Tselios, A., Karakasidis, A.: Mi-OPJ: a microservices-based online programming judge. In: 2021 IEEE International Conference on Big Data (Big Data), pp. 5969–5971. IEEE (2021)
20. Park, C.Y.: Predicting program execution times by analyzing static and dynamic program paths. Real-Time Syst. 5(1), 31–62 (1993)
21. Puschner, P., Koza, Ch.: Calculating the maximum execution time of real-time programs. Real-Time Syst. 1(2), 159–176 (1989)
22. Sikka, J., Satya, K., Kumar, Y., Uppal, S., Shah, R.R., Zimmermann, R.: Learning based methods for code runtime complexity prediction. In: Jose, J.M., et al. (eds.) ECIR 2020. LNCS, vol. 12035, pp. 313–325. Springer, Cham (2020). https://doi.org/10.1007/978-3-030-45439-5_21
23. Sun, H., Li, B., Jiao, M.: YoJ: an online judge system designed for programming courses. In: 2014 9th International Conference on Computer Science and Education, pp. 812–816. IEEE (2014)
24. Veličković, P., Cucurull, G., Casanova, A., Romero, A., Lio, P., Bengio, Y.: Graph attention networks. arXiv preprint arXiv:1710.10903 (2017)
25. Wang, M., Han, W., Chen, W.: Metaoj: a massive distributed online judge system. Tsinghua Sci. Technol. 26(4), 548–557 (2021)
26. Wasik, S., Antczak, M., Badura, J., Laskowski, A., Sternal, T.: A survey on online judge systems and their applications. ACM Comput. Surv. (CSUR) 51(1), 1–34 (2018)
27. Watanobe, Y., Rahman, Md.M., Matsumoto, T., Rage, U.K., Ravikumar, P.: Online judge system: requirements, architecture, and experiences. Int. J. Softw. Eng. Knowl. Eng. 32(06), 917–946 (2022)
28. Xia, M., et al.: PeerLens: peer-inspired interactive learning path planning in online question pool. In: Proceedings of the 2019 CHI Conference on Human Factors in Computing Systems, pp. 1–12 (2019)
29. Zhang, J., Wang, X., Zhang, H., Sun, H., Wang, K., Liu, X.: A novel neural source code representation based on abstract syntax tree. In: 2019 IEEE/ACM 41st International Conference on Software Engineering (ICSE), pp. 783–794. IEEE (2019)
30. Zhou, W., Pan, Y., Zhou, Y., Sun, G.: The framework of a new online judge system for programming education. In: Proceedings of ACM Turing Celebration Conference-china, pp. 9–14 (2018)

Large Language Model

Automated Comment Generation Based on the Large Language Model

Kaiwei Cai[ORCID], Junsheng Zhou[✉], Li Kong, Dandan Liang, and Xianzhuo Li

Nanjing Normal University, Nanjing 210023, JS, China
zhoujs@njnu.edu.cn, {kongli,xli}@nnu.edu.cn

Abstract. Automated essay comment generation is important for writing in education, as it can reduce the burden on teachers while providing students with rapid feedback to improve their writing. When writing, students tend to take writing thought ideas in several excellent essays as references, which inspire them to be more creative in writing. For teachers, they can refer to them to make suggestions on how to improve the quality of essays. Inspired by this behaviour of writing psychology, we guide the Large Language Model (LLM) to also imitate this behaviour. In this paper, we apply the essay comment generation task in application, which aims to generate comments on how to amplify the writing thought ideas for the given English expository essay. To tackle this task, we propose the two-stage comment generation framework, in which we first search for some cases of the chain of writing thought ideas, and then use them as evidence to guide the LLM to learn from these references and generate more concrete comments. What's more, we manually collect some English expository essays to build the knowledge base and some essay-comment pairs (The source code is available at https://github. com/CarryCKW/EssayComGen). Extensive experiments show that our method outperforms strong baselines significantly.

Keywords: Automated essay comment generation · Large language model · Writing psychology · Knowledge base

1 Introduction

Automated essay evaluation is to evaluate the writing quality of the essay with the help of computer technologies. As a useful educational application of natural language processing (NLP), automated essay comment generation has significant social value for education. In particular, the generation of reasonable comments can reduce teachers' workload and improve teaching efficiency. What's more, students can also receive timely feedback and improve their writing skills.

Recent research [2,13,15] has demonstrated the strong performance of the Large Language Model (LLM) in NLP tasks that generate answers to user's questions without any additional fine-tuning operations, also known as

LLMprompting [8]. We can utilize the strong performance of LLM in text generation and local reasoning to further advance the task of automated essay comment generation. For example, in the actual application scenario, the user will fill in the content of the essay in the following template as input to the LLM: "Please now, as an English writing tutor, make some suggestions on how to improve the quality of the essay from the perspectives of amplifying writing thought ideas. The essay: the specific content of the essay", and then the LLM will return some texts of suggestions.

However, on the one hand, a better performance of LLM always requires a higher expensive deployment cost, depending on the model parameter scales, which is not conducive to the practical generalization of LLM. On the other hand, the output of the amiable parameter of LLM might be outdated, incomplete and incorrect, and they generate factually wrong answers, called *hallucination* [9,12].

In this work, we first make a study of automated comment generation for English expository essays, which requires commenting in natural language on how to improve a given essay, because expository essay writing ideas are more structured and diverse. The challenges of this work mainly lie in the following two folds: (1) Overcoming the problem of generating incorrect answers due to the weak performance of LLM with fewer parameters, and fine-tuning the model to update the knowledge is often expensive [5], how to introduce corrective steps to inject new knowledge to improve the accuracy of answers and the reasoning performance of the model. (2) How to guide LLMs to make specific suggestions for amplifying the writing thought ideas in given essay. Overcoming these challenges can lead to the generation of better quality comments, making this research and application more valuable in practice.

When writing, students tend to learn and associate writing thought ideas from several excellent essays as a way of inspiring themselves to produce a more polished and fulfilling piece of writing. This exercise of creativity by imitating ideas of good essays can be seen as a form of inspiration and stimulation for writing, helping them to improve their writing skills and expressive abilities, and is often referred to as "mimicry" in the psychology of writing [3,4].

To tackle the above problems, inspired by the "mimicry", we propose a two-stage comment generation framework based on the search and prompting. This framework consists of two components. Specifically, the first component mimics the behaviour that students will be inspired by the writing thought ideas of high-quality essays when they are writing and expand their own writing content by associating several cases of excellent writing ideas. Here are the more granular steps. In searching, we first parse out some of the ideas of the input essay by LLM, and the obtain multiple writing cases as references by utilizing topic-aware retrieval algorithms in the back-end knowledge base, where the cases are great writing thought ideas under the relevant topics for the given essay. Furthermore, the second component is to integrate the writing cases and the input essay, as the input to LLM and guide it to learn new writing cases and generate more informative and diverse comments, which can be implemented by the well-designed prompting templates.

On the one hand, using the retrieval algorithm to get the writing cases from the knowledge base can better guide the model to learn writing habits in a human way of thinking, and can also update the content of the knowledge base in real time. On the other hand, the integration of high-quality writing thought cases with background knowledge into user questions can be more targeted to students' writing improvement, generating higher quality and more relevant improvement comments.

To support the evaluation of our task, we additionally construct a knowledge base of writing cases and collect a number of essay-comment pairs to evaluate the effectiveness of this approach by the paradigm of zero-shot. The experimental results demonstrate the effectiveness of our approach, allowing the model to achieve higher performance in terms of correctness and diversity of comment generation.

In summary, our paper makes the following contributions:

- We propose a two-stage comment generation framework for the task of automated essay comment generation. It mimics the behaviour of students in the psychology of writing, which is beneficial in higher quality and diversity of the generated comments.
- We construct a knowledge base containing about five hundred writing cases of high-quality essays, and we collect over one hundred essay-comment pairs as our open source data.
- Our model improves significantly on both BLUE and Distinct scores, indicating the effectiveness of this framework.

2 Related Work

2.1 Automated Essay Evaluation

There have been wide explorations for automatic essay evaluation. Attali et al. [1] build an essay scoring system, known as the E-rater, which uses some hand-crafted features such as grammar. With the development of deep neural networks (DNN), several studies have utilized pre-trained language models (PLM) and well-designed algorithms to predict essay scores. LLM further advances the task of essay comment generation. The Linggle Write system [14] is capable of analyzing essays by focusing on grammatical and rhetorical perspectives. In a recent study, Zhang et al. [18] generate essay comments in the Chinese narrative essays, focusing on essay comments related to analysing rhetorical and descriptive writing skills.

2.2 LLM Prompting

Recently, the semantic understanding and reasoning capabilities of pre-trained language models have been significantly improved by scaling improvements with larger datasets and model sizes. The results show that large language models can be adapted to downstream tasks by inference alone [6], without parameter updates. Subsequent research has further improved the performance of in-context learning. Researchers have proposed advanced prompt formats from a variety of downstream tasks.

What's more, LLM has demonstrated strong ability in in-context learning and reasoning. With the few-shot prompting strategy, LLM is able to perform much better on the specific in-context learning and reasoning problems. Wei et al. [16] propose the Chain-of-Thought prompting, which appends several reasoning steps before the input question. To leverage the power of demonstrative examples and reduce manual effort, Zhang et al. [19] propose Auto-CoT, which automatically obtains k examples by clustering the given input and allows the model to generate rationales for the selected examples.

3   Method

The task of essay comment generation can be formulated as follows: given an essay $X = (x_1, x_2, ..., x_N)$ with N words, the method should generate a comment Y containing several words. In this work, we make a study of automated comment generation on English expository essays, in which the comments paraphrase how to improve the quality of essay on writing thought ideas.

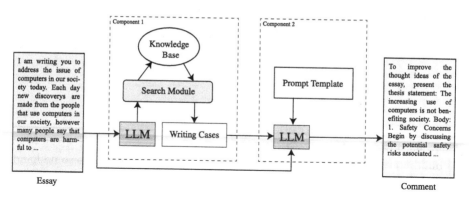

Fig. 1. An overview of our framework. The two components correspond to the ordered generation stage.

3.1   Comment Definition

Writing thought ideas in an essay are important indicators of the quality of essay. The comments generated by our method mainly contain the suggestions on how to improve the quality from the view of amplifying the writing thought ideas. Specifically, here are some of the elements to consider when manually evaluating essays: (1) Clarity of thought ideas. The ideas in an essay should present a clear, logical and well-structured line of thought. If not, we can suggest on how to amplify it by providing more explanations. (2) Coherence and cohesion. The ideas presented in the essay should be interconnected and form a coherent and cohesive narrative. If not, we can suggest on how to add or delete some ideas. (3) Evidence and examples. We can suggest that they include more examples to support their claims. Therefore, we aim to guide the model to generate more informative and diverse comments according to the above elements.

3.2 Two-Stage Comment Generation

As shown in Fig. 1, we propose a two-stage comment generation framework, in which the LLM first learns several examples of writing cases in excellent essays and then uses the template to improve the comment generation. Furthermore, in the processing of finding excellent writing cases, we first find the writing thought ideas within the input essay by parsing the essay though applying the LLM, then we design the specific search algorithm to match several examples in criteria of similar topics with the writing ideas. Moreover, in the comment generation stage, the well-designed template will integrate the previous cases and the input essay, which will be treated as a whole as the input to the LLM.

3.3 Writing Cases Searching

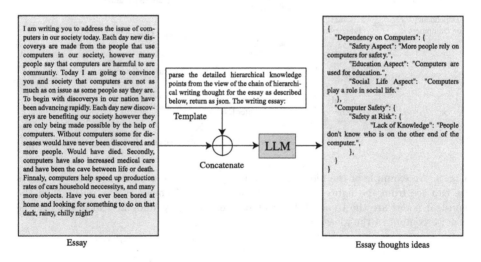

Fig. 2. The flow of parsing the given essay to the writing thought ideas. Taking advantage of the ability of LLM to follow instructions, we can directly use the LLM to generate the text containing the hierarchical writing thought ideas of the given essay, which can be easily extracted and saved in a *json* file. The writing thought idea consists of two parts, namely, the idea topic and the idea content. For example, the key in the *json* file is the idea topic, and the corresponding value is the idea content.

Parse Out the Writing Thought Ideas. Writing thought ideas are important to inspire and motivate writing and can assist in the use of attractive skills and diverse expression in writing. In essence, students tend to connect in the mind for the writing cases with related topics, learning their commonalities. Therefore, we first need a powerful tool to parse out the content of the input essay for related topics, which has good in-context learning capabilities to understand the textual content. Fortunately, the LLM itself has this capability. Hence, we utilize the LLM to parse out the essay, in which we can implement this step by *LLMprompting*. As shown in Fig. 2, we can see the flow of this parse and get part of the thought ideas of the essay. The *ideas*:

$$ideas = LLM(X, P) \tag{1}$$

where the X is the input essay and the P is the text template in parsing stage.

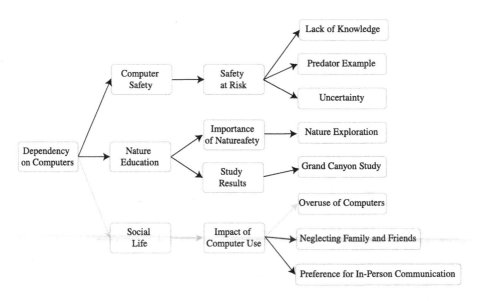

Fig. 3. An example of the hierarchical writing thought ideas in an excellent essay. As we can see from the figure, the root of the tree is the theme of the essay, then the non-leaf nodes are the topic of different part of the essay, and the leaf nodes are the concise content of the ideas in essay.

Knowledge Base. The challenge here is to express the structure of the thought ideas in an essay, which is hierarchical, structured and related between several writing thought ideas. Recent studies have shown that every document has its own structure [11,17], and the thought ideas in most essays can be illustrated through a tree structure. As shown in Fig. 3, each node in tree represents a thought idea in the essay, which has a lead from the previous idea and may branch to several other ideas, thus making the content of the whole essay grow up. Furthermore, we can see from the Fig. 3, the thought idea in the blue chain, called "Impact of Computer Use", can be led from "Social Life" in the topic of "Dependency on Computers" and has some actual impact in real life. What's more, because each essay can be transformed in this way, we can use this app-roach to build a content-rich knowledge base that includes several high-quality essays from a variety of topics, while using convenient data structures that help with subsequent searches. Intuitively, this type of data can be easily stored using JSON files.

Search Algorithm. The chain of writing thought ideas can provide students with the whole reasoning steps between several ideas. In this step, we need to search some excellent cases of the chain of writing thought ideas, since we have parsed out the writing thought ideas within the input essay. To do this, we design a searching-based algorithm, where the core idea is to find the $top - K$ chains containing the parsed writing ideas as much as possible. Specifically, every chain will be selected if itself contains the idea in the set of parsed writing thought ideas of the input essay. Then, we sort each chain according to the number of target ideas it contains, and finally select the $top - K$ chains. The pseudo-code is shown below:

Algorithm 1. Search Algorithm

Input: K, *ideas*, Knowledge Base, similarity threshold t
Output: the $top - K$ chains of the writing thought ideas S
 1: **Set** total = {}
 2: **Set** S={}
 3: **for** *idea* in *iedas* **do**
 4:     **for** every *tree* in Knowledge Base **do**
 5:         **for** every *node* in *tree* **do**
 6:             **if** *node.idea* is similar to *idea* **then**
 7:                 total.append(*node*)
 8:                 p_{node} = find_parent_node(*node*)
 9:                 c_{node} = find_children_node(*node*)
10:                 *chain* = construct_chain(p_{node}, *node*, c_{node})
11:                 S.append(*chain*)
12:             **end if**
13:         **end for**
14:     **end for**
15: **end for**
16: **String** $chain_{in}$ = construct_chain(*ideas*)
17: S = filter_top_K(K, $chain_{in}$, S)

Writing Case. The several cases of writing thought ideas can be used as evi-dences to inspire writing with authenticity, completeness, and diversity. We can use a formal format to illustrate this chain relationship, and the most basic method is to use arrows ↔ to represent progressive relationships. If extension is required, we can also design more specific relationship representations as needed. This demonstrates the adaptability and scalability of this method. As shown in the Table 1, these are some examples.

Table 1. Some examples of the case of the writing thought ideas. There is progressivity between nodes within each chain of the writing thought ideas, indicating the relevance, coherence and clarity in the contextual ideas.

Examples	
Id	Chain Content
1	Nature Education ↔ Importance of Nature safety ↔ Nature Exploration
2	Nature Education ↔ Study Results ↔ Grand Canyon Study
3	Social Life ↔ Impact of Computer Use ↔ Neglecting Family and Friends

3.4 Comment Generation

In the comment generation stage, we focus on how to guide LLM to learn some cases of writing thought ideas in order to improve the quality of the generated comments on the given essay. Specifically, a template have been carefully designed, which is used to integrate the writing thought cases and the essay. Finally, the whole text will be as an input to the LLM to generate comments on how to improve the essay. The *comments*:

$$comments = LLM(X, S, P) \tag{2}$$

where the X is the input essay, S is the writing cases from the output of the first component and the P is the text template in the comment generation stage.

4 Experiments

4.1 Dataset

Our task is to automatically generate comments for English expository essays on how to improve the quality of the essay, especially to amplify the writing thought ideas. As there is no dataset available for our task, we manually collect a English dataset to evaluate our model. Specifically, for the knowledge base, we collect about 500 expository essays with the corresponding writing thought ideas. For the evaluation, we collect over 100 expository essays with the corresponding annotated comment. For the process of annotation, we use the API of the ChatGLM-Pro model[1] to generate the preliminary comment and then perform manual secondary verification and supplementation, with the aim of obtaining comments as rich as possible.

---

[1] https://open.bigmodel.cn/.

4.2   Baseline

We use the llama2-13B of the chat version[2] as our backbone LLM, which is a collection of pre-trained and fine-tuned generative text models with 13B scale parameters and optimised for dialogue use cases. This LLM can directly generate comments on the input essay with the user query.

4.3   Experiment Settings

In the writing thought ideas parsing and comments generation stages, we use top-p sampling with $p = 0.95$ combined with beam search (number of beam is 1) while the parameter of *temperature* is 0.01. The fixed value of the parameter makes it easier for the LLM to generate a consistent context for multiple times. To improve the inference speed, we deploy our model on two GPU-3090Ti, the average cost of comment generation for an essay is 5.6 s.

4.4   Evaluation Metrics

The following automatic metrics will be adopt for the evaluation of comment generation.

BLEU (B-n). We use $n = 1$, 2 to evaluate the n-gram overlap between generated comments and ground truth comments [10]. BLUE is an algorithm for evaluating the quality of text between the output of a machine and that of a human.

Distinct (D-n). We use $n = 2$, 3, 4 to measure the generation diversity by the ratio of distinct n-grams to all the generated n-grams [7]. The distinct is a metric used to measure the degree of diversity in the content of machine-generated text.

4.5   Results

Table 2. Automatic evaluation results. All result values are multiplied by 100. The best performance is highlighted in **bold**.

Models	B-1	B-2	D-2	D-3	D-4
Llama2	35.39	**11.65**	10.74	29.76	43.86
Our Model	**42.58**	11.06	**11.47**	**31.61**	**46.13**
GroundTruth	100	100	16.25	41.18	58.75

Table 2 shows the automated evaluation results. Compared with the results of the **Llama2**, our method improves significantly on both BLUE and Distinct scores, indicating higher quality and diversity of the generated comments.

---

[2] https://huggingface.co/meta-llama/Llama-2-13b-chat-hf.

4.6 Analysis

As for the comparison of the results, we can draw the following analysis: (1) For the fact that the BLUE scores are generally not high, intuitively because the given ground truth comments may not cover all aspects, so that some of the correct answers generated by the model are not reflected in the labelled comments. (2) The first component, which searches for some cases of the writing thought ideas in excellent essays, has a positive effect on diversity, suggesting that the model may tend to benefit from learning some examples and generate more diverse comments.

5 Examples

An example of the generated comment for the given essay is shown below.

The Essay:
I believe that computers are very helpful for many people by searching for information or talking to friends. Although many children should spend time outdoors, computers are an environment that takes up enough space to help children learn and interact with others. I think children should have the right to stay on the computer for as long as they want. Nevertheless, they should still make time to go out and play, play with friends, and so on. Computers are fun, but it's always important to go out and enjoy nature. Another reason why students should not spend all their time on computers is because of their health. Many children grow up to engage in computer production or programming. Some children receive education online or go to teach others. Computers are an uninterrupted foundation of intelligence that can help people learn, play, and discover. Many people dream of one day being able to build a computer or create new programs. All students should have the right to spend time on computers, but also the right to save time outdoors and spending time with friends. Everyone has their own ideas and whether staying on the computer all day is a good thing. I think children should not do this because it may affect their health and the opinions of others towards them.

Search Output:
Example 1: computers are helpful ↔ learning and social interaction ↔ balanced approach; Example 2: programming and design ↔ education online ↔ education and career development; Example 3: time cost ↔ physical and mental health ↔ balance between screen and activities

Comment:
Here are some suggestions for improving the essay you provided.
Thesis Statement: Start your essay with a clear and concise thesis statement that reflects your main argument. In your case, it might be something like: "While computers offer numerous benefits, it is essential for kids to strike a balance between screen time and outdoor activities to ensure a healthy and well-rounded upbringing." Introduction: Begin with an engaging hook that grabs the reader's

attention. It could be a relevant statistic, a question, or a thought-provoking statement about the influence of computers on children. Introduce the topic and your thesis statement.

Body Paragraphs: Provide evidence and examples to support your claims. For instance, you can discuss the benefits of computer use for learning and interaction with peers.

6 Conclusion

We present a two-stage comment generation framework, where the LLM first learns several examples of excellent essay writing cases and then uses the template to improve the comment generation. Furthermore, when searching for writing cases, we start by parsing out the ideas of the input essay. Then, we design a search algorithm to find several cases of the chain of the writing ideas. In the comment generation stage, we use a carefully designed template that combines the previous cases and the input essay and treats it as input to LLM to generate comments on how to improve the quality of the essay from the perspective of extending contextual ideas. We manually collect some English expository essays to construct the knowledge base and some essay-comment pairs. Extensive experiments demonstrate the effectiveness of our method in the real application. In future work, we will add more technology to make the performance better. We expect that our work will contribute to further research on this application and research and benefit both teachers and students.

Acknowledgement. This work is supported by the Postgraduate Research & Practice Innovation Program of Jiangsu Province (KYCX23_1775) under Grant 181200003023202. The project name is the "Research and Implementation of Automated Essay Scoring".

References

1. Attali, Y., Burstein, J.: Automated essay scoring with e-rater® v. 2. J. Technol. Learn. Assess. **4**(3) (2006)
2. Chowdhery, A., et al.: Palm: scaling language modeling with pathways. arXiv preprint arXiv:2204.02311 (2022)
3. Deumert, A.: Mimesis and mimicry in language–creativity and aesthetics as the performance of (dis-) semblances (2018)
4. Guéguen, N., Martin, A., Meineri, S.: Mimicry and helping behavior: an evaluation of mimicry on explicit helping request. J. Soc. Psychol. **151**(1), 1–4 (2011)
5. He, J., Zhou, C., Ma, X., Berg-Kirkpatrick, T., Neubig, G.: Towards a unified view of parameter-efficient transfer learning. arXiv preprint arXiv:2110.04366 (2021)
6. Houlsby, N., et al.: Parameter-efficient transfer learning for NLP. In: International Conference on Machine Learning, pp. 2790–2799. PMLR (2019)
7. Li, J., Galley, M., Brockett, C., Gao, J., Dolan, B.: A diversity-promoting objective function for neural conversation models. arXiv preprint arXiv:1510.03055 (2015)

8. Liu, P., Yuan, W., Fu, J., Jiang, Z., Hayashi, H., Neubig, G.: Pre-train, prompt, and predict: a systematic survey of prompting methods in natural language processing. ACM Comput. Surv. **55**(9), 1–35 (2023)
9. Manakul, P., Liusie, A., Gales, M.J.: Selfcheckgpt: zero-resource black-box hallucination detection for generative large language models. arXiv preprint arXiv:2303.08896 (2023)
10. Papineni, K., Roukos, S., Ward, T., Zhu, W.J.: BleU: a method for automatic evaluation of machine translation. In: Proceedings of the 40th Annual Meeting of the Association for Computational Linguistics, pp. 311–318 (2002)
11. Power, R., Scott, D., Bouayad-Agha, N.: Document structure. Comput. Linguist. **29**(2), 211–260 (2003)
12. Rohrbach, A., Hendricks, L.A., Burns, K., Darrell, T., Saenko, K.: Object hallucination in image captioning. arXiv preprint arXiv:1809.02156 (2018)
13. Thoppilan, R., et al.: Lamda: language models for dialog applications. arXiv preprint arXiv:2201.08239 (2022)
14. Tsai, C.T., Chen, J.J., Yang, C.Y., Chang, J.S.: Lingglewrite: a coaching system for essay writing. In: Proceedings of the 58th Annual Meeting of the Association for Computational Linguistics: System Demonstrations, pp. 127–133 (2020)
15. Wang, B., et al.: Towards understanding chain-of-thought prompting: an empirical study of what matters. arXiv preprint arXiv:2212.10001 (2022)
16. Wei, J., et al.: Chain-of-thought prompting elicits reasoning in large language models. In: Advances in Neural Information Processing Systems, vol. 35, pp. 24824–24837 (2022)
17. Zhang, Y., Yu, X., Cui, Z., Wu, S., Wen, Z., Wang, L.: Every document owns its structure: inductive text classification via graph neural networks. arXiv preprint arXiv:2004.13826 (2020)
18. Zhang, Z., Guan, J., Xu, G., Tian, Y., Huang, M.: Automatic comment generation for Chinese student narrative essays. In: Proceedings of the 2022 Conference on Empirical Methods in Natural Language Processing: System Demonstrations, pp. 214–223 (2022)
19. Zhang, Z., Zhang, A., Li, M., Smola, A.: Automatic chain of thought prompting in large language models. arXiv preprint arXiv:2210.03493 (2022)

Enhancing Database Principles Teaching with ChatGPT-Like Language Models

Junwen Duan, Fei Guo$^{(\boxtimes)}$, Jin Liu, and Hongdong Li

School of Computer Science and Engineering, Central South University,
Changsha 410083, China
{jwduan,guofei,liujin06,hongdong}@csu.edu.cn

Abstract. This paper introduces a cutting-edge framework for Database Principles teaching, leveraging a ChatGPT-like language model to enhance learning experiences. It surpasses traditional teaching methods by offering tailored learning paths, real-time question-and-answer sessions, and smart content suggestions. The framework's potential lies in boosting student engagement, learning outcomes, and access to quality educational resources. It covers the concept, architecture, teaching strategies, and evaluation methods of the framework, highlighting its strengths and challenges. The conclusion reflects on the broader implications of AI in education.

Keywords: Database Principles · Personalized Learning · Blended Teaching Model

1 Introduction

Databases are crucial in computer and information sciences, serving as the foundation for systems needing organized storage, efficient data retrieval, and analysis [6]. Teaching Database Principles is more than imparting knowledge about data manipulation and query syntax; it involves developing skills in logical structuring and strategic data organization, vital in today's information era [2]. Traditional teaching methods, although fundamental, struggle to adapt to evolving educational needs, failing to customize instruction or fully utilize technological advancements in education. They often adopt a generic approach, neglecting the varied skills and learning paces of students.

Existing supplementary teaching systems attempt to overcome these limitations by integrating technology, but many lack the depth needed to foster critical thinking and contextual understanding. Furthermore, they often fall short

This work is supported by the Central South University Education and Teaching Reform Research Project (Grant No. 2023jy139), Central South University Graduate Education and Teaching Reform Research Project (No. 2023JGB102, 2022JGB113), Central South University Innovation and Entrepreneurship Education Teaching Reform Research Project (No. 2022–15).

in providing the personalized feedback and adaptive learning pathways essential in complex subjects like Database Principles [4]. The emergence of advanced technologies like large language models opens new possibilities.

ChatGPT-like models, with their exceptional natural language processing abilities, offer significant benefits. They enable personalized interaction, instant feedback, and content customization, aligning with personalized learning and supporting self-regulated learning [1,3,5]. This paper proposes a new framework for teaching Database Principles, combining a ChatGPT-like language model with traditional teaching methods to create an immersive learning environment. It aims to provide personalized learning pathways, real-time Q&A sessions, and intelligent content recommendations to enhance student understanding. Our framework's significance extends beyond improving engagement and learning outcomes; it also seeks to provide broader access to quality educational resources and streamline Database Principles education.

The following sections discuss the framework's concept, practical applications, potential architecture, and teaching methods, both traditional and modern. It also outlines teaching strategies, their educational impact, and concludes by suggesting evaluation methods for the framework, identifying expected strengths and challenges. Lastly, it contemplates the wider implications of AI in education and its prospects for further research.

2   System Design Concept

2.1   ChatGPT-Like Model-Based Auxiliary Teaching System

System Architecture. The architecture centers around the ChatGPT-like model, leveraging its AI capabilities (Figure. 1). This setup aims to cater to diverse student learning processes. The model excels in simulating intricate, human-like interactions, fostering an engaging and responsive learning environment. The architecture includes four main modules: a user-friendly front-end interface, a robust back-end for data processing, a comprehensive learning resource repository, and an intelligent analysis unit. The front-end acts as a portal for student interactions, collecting queries and feedback. The back-end processes student inputs through the ChatGPT-like model to generate relevant and intelligent responses. A resource library offers various educational materials, and the intelligent analysis module uses machine learning to analyze student data, enabling personalized educational experiences.

Natural Language Interaction Function. The model's natural language understanding (NLU) and generation (NLG) capabilities are critical, enabling it to grasp complex student inquiries and produce coherent, accurate responses. Its technological backbone includes deep learning models trained on diverse datasets, ensuring a comprehensive grasp of database concepts and pedagogy.

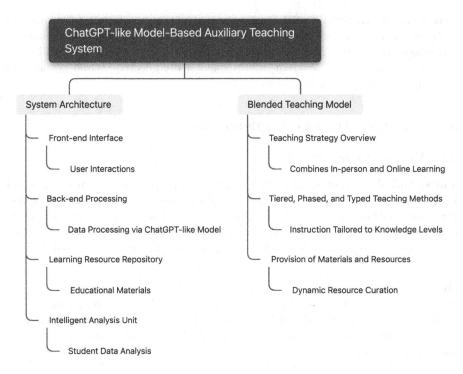

Fig. 1. The architecture of the proposed system.

Personalized Teaching Services. The system's goal is to create an adaptive learning environment that respects individual learner differences. It uses data mining techniques and machine learning algorithms to analyze student performance, learning habits, and feedback. These insights help the system design personalized learning paths, recommend tailored resources, and adjust teaching strategies in real-time to suit different learning speeds and styles.

2.2   Blended Teaching Model

Teaching Strategy Overview. The blended teaching model combines traditional in-person teaching with online learning methods. It incorporates the ChatGPT-like auxiliary system to enhance classroom interactions and resource use, making education more dynamic and efficient.

Tiered, Phased, and Typed Teaching Methods. The design employs a tiered instruction approach, aligned with students' existing knowledge. It progresses through phased educational content, in line with the curriculum, and offers various types of resources, such as visual aids and practical exercises, to suit different learning preferences. This tiered method ensures that materials are not one-size-fits-all but resonate with each learner's stage and style.

Provision of Materials and Resources. The system offers a wide range of materials and resources, including foundational texts, supplementary readings, and interactive tools. These resources, dynamically curated and updated by the system, remain relevant, current, and pedagogically effective, based on ongoing teaching feedback and performance analytics.

3   Teaching Strategy Implementation

3.1   Pre-class Preparation

Video and PPT Explanations. For pre-class preparation, we use video and PPT explanations to cater to various learning styles. These materials, designed with the ChatGPT-like model, are informative and logically structured. Technologies like video editing software, content management systems, and AI-based text-to-speech engines are utilized to optimize engagement and accessibility.

Online Tests. Online tests assess students' understanding of pre-class materials, guiding personalized teaching. These tests, administered through web-based platforms, offer immediate scoring and analytics. Machine learning algorithms analyze results, suggesting learning pathway adjustments based on individual student performance.

3.2   Application of the Auxiliary Teaching System

Personalized Exercises and Q&A. In class, our module provides tailored exercises and Q&A sessions, ensuring a suitable learning pace. The ChatGPT-like model-powered adaptive learning platform processes student inputs, evaluates their knowledge, and generates real-time questions and exercises. This dynamic adjustment employs NLU, NLG, and adaptive learning algorithms.

Real-Time Feedback and Assessment. Real-time feedback and assessment create a responsive learning environment. This functionality uses real-time analytics and educational data mining to process student inputs, offering instant feedback and navigating learning challenges.

3.3   Post-class Practice and Extension

Individualized Homework and Projects. Post-class, the system continues personalized learning with homework and projects tailored to each student's path. This approach reinforces classroom learning through practical application. Project management tools and educational platforms help track progress and adapt project difficulty and scope to student abilities. AI assists in aligning project briefs with learning objectives.

Group Discussions and Peer Learning. Group discussions and peer learning are encouraged for collaborative understanding.

Collaboration technologies include online forums, chat rooms, and peer review systems within the teaching system. AI may guide discussions, stimulate deeper inquiries, and ensure a constructive, inclusive learning atmosphere.

4   Effectiveness Assessment and Analysis

We aim to thoroughly evaluate the auxiliary teaching system, focusing on its impact on learning. Our approach considers various dimensions of educational outcomes to gauge the system's real-world effectiveness. We plan to use advanced data analytics, statistical software, and educational technology assessment tools for precise and comprehensive evaluation.

4.1   Evaluation Methodologies

Quantitative Performance Analytics. We may use quantitative metrics like grades, test scores, and usage statistics for evaluation. Learning analytics platforms could aggregate and analyze this data, offering a data-driven perspective on the system's influence on student performance.

Student Surveys and Feedback. Custom-designed surveys and feedback mechanisms could gather subjective data on student satisfaction, engagement, and perceived learning gains. These surveys might use advanced scaling and branching techniques to capture detailed student responses.

Comparative Studies. Comparative studies could contrast classes using the auxiliary system with traditional methods. These studies would use experimental design techniques to ensure fair comparisons and attribute results confidently to the system's impact.

4.2   Analysis of Course Application Effects

We plan to analyze the system's effects on student engagement, understanding of Database Principles, and skill acquisition, potentially involving:

- Monitoring time-on-task and interaction metrics for engagement.
- Administering pre- and post-tests for conceptual understanding.
- Evaluating portfolios and projects for skill development.

5 Future Directions

Future development of the system includes:

- Enhanced Personalization: Refining adaptive algorithms and incorporating real-time feedback for a more tailored learning experience.
- Collaborative Learning Tools: Introducing tools for group projects and discussions to foster community and enhance learning outcomes.
- Continuous Assessment and Feedback: Implementing mechanisms for ongoing insights into student progress, guiding immediate improvements in learning.

The future of the system involves continuous improvement, innovation, and adaptability, aiming to provide an exceptional educational experience.

6 Conclusion

This paper presented a novel auxiliary teaching system for Database Principles, integrating a ChatGPT-like model to address educational challenges. It detailed the system's architecture, strategies, and evaluation methods, showing potential for enhanced learning outcomes and efficiency. Despite limitations and areas for further research, the findings indicate significant potential in applying AI to elevate educational quality. Future work will explore deeper AI integration in education and further refine personalized teaching systems.

References

1. Gill, S.S., et al.: Transformative effects of ChatGPT on modern education: Emerging era of AI chatbots. Internet Things and Cyber-Phys. Syst. **4**, 19–23 (2024)
2. Ishaq, M., et al.: Advances in database systems education: Methods, tools, curricula, and way forward. Educ. Inf. Technol. **28**(3), 2681–2725 (2023)
3. Jeon, J., Lee, S.: Large language models in education: a focus on the complementary relationship between human teachers and ChatGPT. Education and Information Technologies, pp. 1–20 (2023)
4. Tetzlaff, L., Schmiedek, F., Brod, G.: Developing personalized education: a dynamic framework. Educ. Psychol. Rev. **33**, 863–882 (2021)
5. Villasenor, J.: How chatgpt can improve education, not threaten it. Scientific American. https://www.scientificamerican.com/article/how-chatgpt-can-improve-education-not-threaten-it. Accessed 6 (2023)
6. Zheng, Y., Dong, J.: Teaching reform and practice of database principles. In: 2011 6th International Conference on Computer Science and Education (ICCSE), pp. 1460–1462. IEEE (2011)

Assistant Teaching System for Computer Hardware Courses Based on Large Language Model

Dongdong Zhang[1,2(✉)], Qian Cao[1], Yuchen Guo[1,2], and Lisheng Wang[1,2]

[1] College of Electronics and Information Engineering, Tongji University,
Shanghai, China
`ddzhang@tongji.edu.cn`

[2] National Computer and Information Technology Experiment Teaching
Demonstration Center, Tongji University, Shanghai, China

Abstract. Recently, Large Language Models (LLMs), represented by ch1ChatGPT, have garnered significant attention in the field of education due to its impressive capabilities in text generation, comprehension, logical reasoning, and conversational abilities. We incorporate LLMs into the theoretical and experiment teaching of our Digital Logic and Computer Organization courses to enhance the teaching process. Specifically, we propose and implement an assistant teaching system consisting of a knowledge-based Question and Answer (Q&A) system and an assistant debugging and checking system. For the theoretical teaching session, the Q&A system utilizes historical Q&A records and ChatGPT to answer students' questions. This system reduces the repetitive workload for teachers by answering similar questions, and allows students to receive answers in time. For the Field-Programmable Gate Array (FPGA)-based experiment teaching session, the assistant debugging and checking system employ debug assistance module to explain error messages for students. Furthermore, a LLM-generated code checking module assists teachers in detecting academic misconduct among students' code submissions.

Keywords: Computer Science · Hardware Courses · Assistant Teaching System · Large Language Models · FPGA

1 Introduction

Digital Logic and Computer Organization Principles are fundamental courses in computer science education, significantly influencing students' comprehension of the underlying principles of computer. In addition to theoretical teaching in the fundamental concepts and principles of digital circuits and computer architecture, we have introduced experiment courses to culture students' practical skills [1]. These experiments require students to apply Hardware Description Languages (HDLs) like Verilog [2] to implement functional modules on Xilinx

W. Hong and G. Kanaparan (Eds.): ICCSE 2023, CCIS 2023, pp. 301–313, 2024.
https://doi.org/10.1007/978-981-97-0730-0_27

Nexys 4 FPGA development boards [3]. In the Digital Logic course, students engage in the implementation of basic modules of digital circuits, including basic gate circuits, data selector and distributor, encoders and decoders, barrel shifter, data comparator, trigger, PC register, RAM, ALU and so on. In the Computer Organization Principles course, students progress beyond these foundational modules to tackle more advanced experiments, such as multiplier, divider, interrupt handling experiments, ultimately culminating in the design of a MIPS CPU. Previously, we have meticulously crafted a comprehensive teaching strategy [1] and developed an automatic testing system for HDL practice teaching [4–6].

During our teaching practice, we have encountered several challenges in the Digital Logic and Computer Organization courses. These courses are distinguished by their extensive content, high complexity, and inherent concept abstraction. Both in theoretical teaching and laboratory exercises, students frequently encounter difficulties and experience delays in obtaining answers to their inquiries. Many of these difficulties are recurrent and shared among students, placing additional burden on educators to repeatedly address similar questions. Furthermore, a significant portion of these challenges is concentrated in the FPGA practical process of the courses. HDLs differ substantially from the software programming languages that students have previously encountered, and the error messages generated by Integrated Development Environments (IDEs) such as Vivado [7] and ModelSim [8] are often challenging to understand. These obstacles hinder the learning process, especially for novice learners.

Recent advancements in Large Language Models (LLMs), including ChatGPT [9], ChatGLM [10], and Llama [11], have garnered significant attention for their exceptional capabilities in text generation, comprehension, logical reasoning, and dialogue engagement. This growing interest extends to their potential applications in the field of education [12–15]. In this paper, we integrate LLMs into our computer hardware course teaching and propose an assistant teaching system, consisting of two main components: a question and answer (Q&A) system and an assistant debugging and checking system. The Q&A system first utilizes historical records and ChatGPT to promptly respond to questions submitted by students. Teacher intervention is reserved solely for new questions that cannot be resolved by the system, thereby reducing the redundancy in teacher workload. The Q&A system continuously updates and accumulates language data through the Q&A module, improving its response capabilities over time. Furthermore, we develop an assistant debugging and checking system for experiment courses. On the one hand, debug assistance module utilizes ChatGPT to explain error messages of the Verilog programs, aiding students in debugging. On the other hand, considering that the advent of LLMs also introduces potential academic integrity risks, a LLM-generated code checking module is introduced to check whether students' submitted code is generated by GPT. In summary, our assistant teaching system aims to enhance teaching efficiency, improve students' understanding of course content, and mitigate potential academic integrity risks in our computer hardware courses.

2 Related Technical Methods

Recently, LLMs usch as BERT [16], GPT3 [17], GPT4 [18] have emerged as a groundbreaking technology in the field of Natural Language Processing (NLP). Through extensive pre-training on vast text corpora and fine-tuning with specific instructions, they have exhibited remarkable performance in language generation and comprehension tasks. One common application scenario for LLMs is Q&A systems, such as ChatGPT [9], ChatGLM [10], claude [19], and LLaMA2Chat [11]. While LLMs showcase impressive capabilities in general domains, their limitations become evident when applied to specialized fields. As LLMs are pretrained on general corpora, they may lack domain-specific expertise in specialized fields. To address this issue, two primary approaches are considered. The first approach involves fine-tuning of pre-trained LLM on a domain-specific dataset, such as ChatDoctor [20], ChatLaw [21], EduChat [13]. This method allows LLMs to acquire specific domain knowledge and communicate effectively within a particular knowledge context. However, this fine-tuning approach requires a substantial amount of domain-specific data and significant GPU computing resources. The second approach utilizes embedding technology [22–24]. It involves computing vectors for specific knowledge using embedding models and then storing these vectors, along with their corresponding content, in a database. During the query phase, similarity queries are performed to match relevant top K results. At present, there is not enough corpus available to fine-tune large models to create a specialized LLM for hardware course teaching. We have opted the second approach to construct a Q&A system that responds to students' questions based on existing QA records within our courses.

As widely recognized, compiler error messages often pose a significant obstacle to beginners when learning programming. Previous studies have harnessed LLMs to generate explanations of error messages in programming education in languages such as C [15] and Python [14], making them easier to understand. Our course includes practical exercises where students write Verilog HDL code and deploy it onto FPGA. We have previously proposed an automatic testing system for Verilog HDL programs [5,6]. This testing system categorizes errors into two types. The first, Compile Error (CE), indicates compilation errors and returns error messages from ModelSim. The second, Wrong Answer (WA), indicates that the code compiles but produces incorrect simulation and returns a comparison report between simulation result and standard one. While this testing system can correctly assess the correctness of submitted code, it often fails to provide helpful guidance due to the incomprehensible error messages. Therefore, inspired by methods [14,15], we introduce a debug assistance module to enhance students' understanding of error messages.

Measure of Software Similarity (MoSS) [25] is widely used as a code plagiarism detection tool in programming courses, coding competitions, and research. MoSS's primary function is to identify similarity between two or more source code files, and it also supports HDLs like Verilog and VHDL. To counteract the possibility of specific students utilizing ChatGPT to generate code for their assignments, we introduce an LLM-generated code checking system based on code similarity.

3 Proposed Assistant Teaching System

3.1 Q&A System

We construct a question-and-answer(Q&A) system based on LLM. The workflow is shown as Fig. 1.

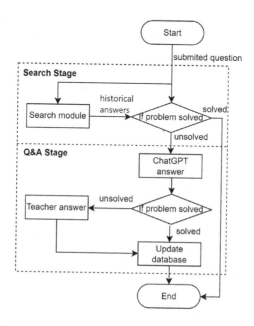

Fig. 1. Flow chart of Q&A system.

When a student submits a query, the system follows a 2-stage process to address the question. Search Stage: The system initially employs a search module to query the knowledge base for relevant historical question-and-answer pairs. This step aims to provide the student with immediate access to existing solutions to similar queries from the past. Q&A Stage: If the student's question remains unanswered after the search module's results, the system proceeds to the Q&A stage. First, it connects to the OpenAI API, utilizing ChatGPT to attempt to answer the student's question. ChatGPT engages in a conversation with the student, providing responses. Questions that cannot be solved by the GPT are then answered by the teacher. Once the question is resolved, whether by ChatGPT or a teacher, the system logs this Q&A interaction into the knowledge base. This ensures that the newly answered question becomes part of the knowledge repository for future reference, helping other students with similar queries. In addition, the embedding-based search module can find the most relevant content with greater accuracy and efficiency.

3.2 Assistant Debugging and Checking System

The emergence of LLM brings new changes in teaching and learning. Through experimental testing, we have observed that when design objectives, desired functionalities, and well-defined input-output interfaces are explicitly described within the prompt, ChatGPT is capable to generate Verilog code and successfully pass our automatic testing procedures. This signifies that ChatGPT has the potential to assist the learning of the HDL verilog in the practical course. However, it also raises the concern that students may resort to direct copying the Verilog code generated by ChatGPT.

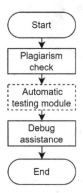

Fig. 2. Flow chart of assistant debugging and checking system.

In previous work, we have implemented an automatic detection system (dotted line parts in Fig. 2). To harness the potential of LLMs in educational assistance while mitigating the risk of academic misconduct, We propose an assistant debugging and checking system. Considering that students often encounter challenges during the practical phase of writing Verilog code, we propose a debug assistance module to utilize ChatGPT for interpreting error messages, thus assisting students in the debugging process. To avoid the risks that students may cheat by directly utilizing ChatGPT to generate Verilog code, we introduce a LLM-generated code checking module.

4 System Implementation

4.1 Q&A System Implementation

For the scheme above, we develop a Q&A website for a concrete implementation, as shown in Fig. 3. The entire system consisting of a front-end pages and a back-end server is implemented based on the Python Flask framework. The front-end serves as an interfacial interaction for students to submit questions and query results, and allows teachers to provide answers to unresolved inquiries.

The backend consists of two distinct modules. The Q&A module collaborates with ChatGPT and the teacher to answer the student's question and inserts the solved quastion-answer records into the database. The search module retrieves relevant Q&A records from the existing records in the database as references for students.

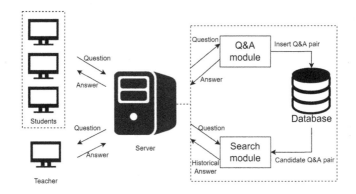

Fig. 3. Q&A system framework.

During the early stages of system operation, the primary focus is on knowledge accumulation through the Q&A module. Given that ChatGPT may not always provide satisfactory answers, teacher involvement is often required. After the system has been running for a while, the Q&A module has accumulated a sufficient number of question-and-answer records in the database. At this point, relying solely on the historical records returned by the search module is sufficient to address the majority of issues. Only when new questions arise that cannot be answered by the existing knowledge, is the Q&A module and the perhaps involvement of teachers required to further supplement the database.

Embedding-Based Search Module. The embedding-based search module evaluates similarity with the feature embeddings of question sentence and returns the top K most relevant QA records. The user's input question sentence is first vectorized into an embedding with the OpenAI's API text-embedding-ada-002. Afterwards, vector similarity is measured using cosine similarity based on the embeddings, and the system searches the database to retrieve the top K questions that are most similar to the submitted question.

For traditional relational databases, the specific process is as illustrated in Fig. 4. The query module first retrieves two columns, the question IDs and question embeddings from the database. After calculating the cosine similarity between the submitted question's embedding and all existing embeddings, the top K most similar records are selected. Finally, the complete Q&A records are retrieved according to the selected question IDs from the database and sent to the

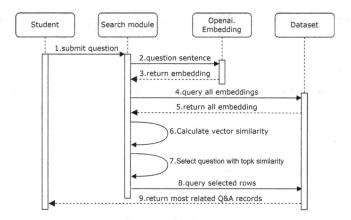

Fig. 4. UML of search module with relational database.

student's terminal. Embeddings are typically high-dimensional vectors. Specifically, OpenAI's text-embedding-ada-002 embeds text into a 1536-dimensional vector. In traditional relational databases, the need to extract entire embedding columns results in a significant amount of read and write operations, which can be time-consuming. Additionally, similarity computation for all rows also imposes a large computational effort. These limitations indeed restrict the scale of databases.

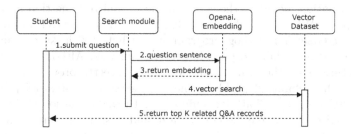

Fig. 5. UML of search module with vector database.

Vector databases are specifically designed for the storage and processing of vector data, offering efficient vector retrieval capabilities. The workflow as shown in Fig. 5, involves the creation of embedding, subsequently querying the database for similar vectors, and directly returning the corresponding content associated with these vectors. The core functionality of vector databases lies in similarity search, accomplished by calculating the distance between a vector and all other vectors to identify the most similar ones. Most vector databases provide efficient similarity measurement methods, such as cosine similarity, and are optimized to accelerate these queries. Vector databases align seamlessly with our solution.

Specifically, we chose Milvus [26] vector database to implement efficient similarity search.

Q&A Module. The Q&A module is responsible for addressing questions that cannot be answered by the historical records. It consists of two stages.

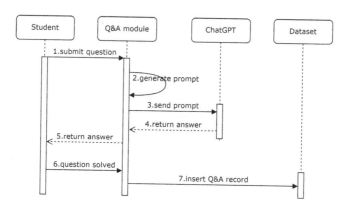

Fig. 6. UML of Q&A stage 1.

In the first stage, the Q&A module begins by attempting to address inquiries using ChatGPT as shown in Fig. 6. This module generates prompts by incorporating information including the course name, submitted question into a predefined template. When applied to specialized vertical domains such as knowledge within the course and Verilog programming, ChatGPT lacks domain-specific knowledge and often fails to provide effective answers. Although the historical records returned by the search module cannot directly provide a satisfactory solution to the submitted problem, they can serve as contextual prompts for ChatGPT to reference. ChatGPT suffers from the hallucination problem, where the generated response may be not truthful and mislead students. Therefore, it is essential to emphasize this point in the prompt. The prompt template example is as follows:

You are an expert in digital circuit and computer architecture. And you will help students study ¡course name¿.

I face the following problems ¡submitted question¿, please answer them.

Here are some historical records that might help ¡related Q&A¿

If you don't know the answer just say you don't know. DO NOT try to make up an answer.

The module sends the generated prompts via an HTTP API call to OpenAI's gpt-3.5-turbo, and then forwards the answers to the student's terminal. If the student feedback that the question has been resolved, the question is marked as resolved, and both the question and answer records are inserted into the database.

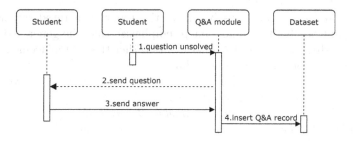

Fig. 7. UML of Q&A stage 2.

Otherwise, it proceeds to the second stage, where the teacher takes responsibility for answering as shown in Fig. 7. The question is marked as unsolved and sent to the teacher's terminal. Once the teacher answers it, both the question and answer records are inserted into the database.

4.2 Assistant Debugging and Checking System Implementation

Debug Assistance Module. In order to help students debug, the debug assistance module leverages ChatGPT to provide more comprehensible explanations for errors occurring during the compilation and simulation procedures of Verilog code. The specific workflow is as shown in Fig. 8.

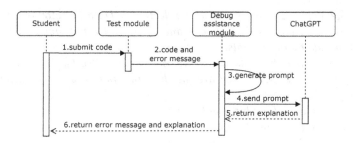

Fig. 8. UML of debug assistance module.

It first generates a prompt based on the information from the testing module. The prompt is then transmitted to ChatGPT through an API call, seeking explanations for the error message. Ultimately, the ChatGPT-generated error explanations are appended to the test report and delivered to the students' terminals.

The prompt is generated with a predefined template. It begins by outlining the objectives of the code, including functional description and interface definitions, just as in the previous section. Next, it incorporates the submitted design code along with the testbench code from the server. Finally, it populates the error types and error messages based on the report generated by the testing module. Additionally, it is important to emphasize that the generated feedback serves as an educational tool to aid students rather than a replacement for their efforts. The prompt template is as follows:

You are a tutor helping a student to explain the error in verilog program. Do not fix the program. Do not provide code.

I want to implement a module.: <module description>.

This is my Verilog design code: <submitted source code>.

This is my Verilog testbench code: <testbench code>.

An error occurred during the <error types>, help me understand this error message: <error reports>.

Remember, you are tutor helping a student. Do not write code for the student.

LLM-Generated Code Checking Module. Current LLMs have the capability to generate accurate Verilog code and pass the automatic testing. However, this also means that students can potentially plagiarize from LLMs, which is a situation we want to avoid. To address this concern, we propose a LLM-generated code checking scheme.

Before the module is put into operation, we need to utilize current leading LLMs such as ChatGPT and Claude to generate reference code as a basis for LLM-generated code checking. To enable LLMs to generate effective Verilog code, the prompt necessitates the inclusion of the functional descriptions, along with explicit input/output(I/O) interface definitions. Here is a prompt example of a data selector:

Write the Verilogg code for the data selector. A Data Selector is a fundamental logic circuit that is used to choose one of several input signals based on the state of input switching signals.

The interface is defined as: the switching is controlled by the encoding of two control signals s0 and s1, c0~c3 are the data inputs and z is the output.

selector41(

input [3:0] iC0, //four-bit input signal c0

input [3:0] iC1, //four-bit input signal c1

input [3:0] iC2, //four-bit input signal c2

input [3:0] iC3, //four-bit input signal c3

input iS1, //selection signal s1

input iS0, //selection signal s0

output [3:0] oZ //four-bit output signal z

);

The workflow of this plagiarism detection module is shown in Fig. 9. When a student submits a code for a particular assignment, the detection module will perform a similarity check between the submitted code and the reference code generated by the LLMs for that specific experiment. Specifically, we utilize the MoSS [25] provided by stanford to implement code similarity checks and obtain detection reports. If the similarity is too high, it raises suspicion of using LLM-generated content. It's important to note that code similarity doesn't certainly

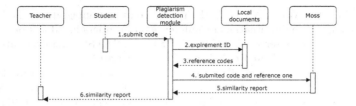

Fig. 9. UML of LLM-generated code checking module.

indicate plagiarism, but this module flags it and provides a report for administrators and teachers to review. This module serves only as an aid, and the final judgment is made by the teacher.

5   Conclusion

In this paper, we propose an assistant teaching system based on large language models for our courses in digital logic and computer organization. This system effectively improves teaching efficiency in both theoretical and experiment courses, enhances student understanding of course content, and reduces potential academic integrity risks. In the practical application of teaching, this system can greatly facilitate both students and teachers. The Q&A system can swiftly answer students' questions, helping them quickly resolve uncertainties in their learning process and providing real-time support. By storing historical Q&A records, a knowledge base can be built, thereby accumulating and disseminating knowledge. The search module utilizes LLM to extract semantics and matches relevant Q&A records based on feature embeddings, enabling the system to answer similar questions more effectively in subsequent queries. By utilising knowledge base and ChatGPT, Q&A systems can address a significant portion of questions, thereby substantially reducing the burden on teachers. In experiment teaching, using ChatGPT to assist students in debugging can expedite issue identification and resolution, thereby boosting efficiency in students' programming and experimental learning. Finally, the LLM-generated code checking system helps mitigate potential academic integrity risks.

References

1. Wang, L., Huang, R.: A comprehensive experiment scheme for computer science and technology. In: Proceedings of the International Conference on Frontiers in Education: Computer Science and Computer Engineering (FECS), p. 1. The Steering Committee of The World Congress in Computer Science, Computer(2012)
2. Thomas, D., Moorby, P.: The Verilog® Hardware Description Language. Springer, Heidelberg (2008). https://doi.org/10.1007/978-0-387-85344-4
3. Berg, M., Poivey, C., Petrick, D., Espinosa, D., Lesea, A., LaBel, K.A., Friendlich, M., Kim, H., Phan, A.: Effectiveness of internal versus external seu scrubbing mitigation strategies in a xilinx fpga: Design, test, and analysis. IEEE Trans. Nucl. Sci. **55**(4), 2259–2266 (2008)

4. Lu, S., Li, G., Wang, Y.: CPU design for computer integrated experiment. In: Proceedings of the International Conference on Frontiers in Education: Computer Science and Computer Engineering (FECS), p. 1. The Steering Committee of The World Congress in Computer Science, Computer (2012)

5. Wang, L., Zhou, H., Zhang, D.: Automatic testing scheme of hardware description language programs for practice teaching. In: 2017 12th International Conference on Computer Science and Education (ICCSE), pp. 659–662. IEEE (2017)

6. Wang, L., Ruan, J., Zhang, D.: MIPS CPU test system for practice teaching. In: 2017 12th International Conference on Computer Science and Education (ICCSE), pp. 663–666. IEEE (2017)

7. Feist, T.: Vivado design suite. White Paper 5, 30 (2012)

8. Ha, J., Jeong, H.: Modelsim simulation for real-time stereo matching using DP algorithm. In: 2012 International Conference for Internet Technology and Secured Transactions, pp. 244–248. IEEE (2012)

9. Chatgpt: Optimizing language models for dialogue. https://chat.openai.com/

10. Du, Z., et al.: GLM: general language model pretraining with autoregressive blank infilling. arXiv preprint arXiv:2103.10360 (2021)

11. Touvron, H., et al.: Llama: open and efficient foundation language models. arXiv preprint arXiv:2302.13971 (2023)

12. Baladn, A., Sastre, I., Chiruzzo, L., Ros, A.: Retuyt-inco at bea 2023 shared task: tuning open-source llms for generating teacher responses. In: Proceedings of the 18th Workshop on Innovative Use of NLP for Building Educational Applications (BEA 2023), pp. 756–765 (2023)

13. Dan, Y., et al.: Educhat: a large-scale language model-based chatbot system for intelligent education. arXiv preprint arXiv:2308.02773 (2023)

14. Leinonen, J., Hellas, A., Sarsa, S., Reeves, B., Denny, P., Prather, J., Becker, B.A.: Using large language models to enhance programming error messages. In: Proceedings of the 54th ACM Technical Symposium on Computer Science Education, vol. 1, pp. 563–569 (2023)

15. Taylor, A., Vassar, A., Renzella, J., Pearce, H.: Integrating large language models into the debugging c compiler for generating contextual error explanations. arXiv preprint arXiv:2308.11873 (2023)

16. Devlin, J., Chang, M.W., Lee, K., Toutanova, K.: Bert: pre-training of deep bidirectional transformers for language understanding. arXiv preprint arXiv:1810.04805 (2018)

17. Brown, T., et al.: Language models are few-shot learners. Adv. Neural. Inf. Process. Syst. 33, 1877–1901 (2020)

18. Gpt-4 technical report. https://cdn.openai.com/papers/gpt-4.pdf

19. Claude 2. https://www.anthropic.com/index/claude-2

20. Li, Y., Li, Z., Zhang, K., Dan, R., Jiang, S., Zhang, Y.: Chatdoctor: a medical chat model fine-tuned on a large language model meta-ai (llama) using medical domain knowledge. Cureus 15(6) (2023)

21. Cui, J., Li, Z., Yan, Y., Chen, B., Yuan, L.: Chatlaw: open-source legal large language model with integrated external knowledge bases. arXiv preprint arXiv:2306.16092 (2023)

22. Ma, X., Zhu, Q., Zhou, Y., Li, X.: Improving question generation with sentence-level semantic matching and answer position inferring. In: Proceedings of the AAAI Conference on Artificial Intelligence, vol. 34, pp. 8464–8471 (2020)

23. Reimers, N., Gurevych, I.: Sentence-bert: sentence embeddings using siamese bert-networks. arXiv preprint arXiv:1908.10084 (2019)

24. Muennighoff, N.: SGPT: GPT sentence embeddings for semantic search. arXiv preprint arXiv:2202.08904 (2022)
25. A system for detecting software similarity. http://theory.stanford.edu/~aiken/moss/
26. Vector database built for scalable similarity search. https://milvus.io/

Automatic Generation of Multiple-Choice Questions for CS0 and CS1 Curricula Using Large Language Models

Tian Song$^{(\boxtimes)}$, Qinqin Tian, Yijia Xiao, and Shuting Liu

Beijing Institute of Technology, Beijing 100081, China
songtian@bit.edu.cn

Abstract. In the context of increasing attention to formative assessment in universities, Multiple Choice Question (MCQ) has become a vital assessment form for CS0 and CS1 courses due to its advantages of rapid assessment, which has brought about a significant demand for MCQ exercises. However, creating many MCQs takes time and effort for teachers. A practical method is to use large language models (LLMs) to generate MCQs automatically, but when dealing with specific domain problems, the model results may need to be more reliable. This article designs a set of prompt chains to improve the performance of LLM in education. Based on this design, we developed EduCS, which is based on GPT-3.5 and can automatically generate complete MCQs according to the CS0/CS1 course outline. To evaluate the quality of MCQs generated by EduCS, we established a set of evaluation metrics from four aspects about the three components of MCQ and the complete MCQ, and based on this, we utilized expert scoring. The experimental results indicate that while the generated questions require teacher verification before being delivered to students, they show great potential in terms of quality. The EduCS system demonstrates the ability to generate complete MCQs that can complement formative and summative assessments for students at different levels. The EduCS has great promise value in the formative assessment of CS education.

Keywords: Large Language Models · GPT-3.5 · MCQs · automatic generation · CS education

1 Introduction

CS0 and CS1 are widely offered courses in computer science majors in universities, and teaching and evaluation are inseparable. MCQs have become the most common forms of assessment due to their advantages of rapid evaluation. Nowadays, universities are increasingly focusing on formative evaluation, which has brought about a significant demand for MCQs. However, manual preparation of MCQs is time-consuming and expensive. All these have prompted researchers and educators to develop a multiple-choice question bank, but outdated question banks may soon not match teachers' curriculum goals. We have seen that

W. Hong and G. Kanaparan (Eds.): ICCSE 2023, CCIS 2023, pp. 314–324, 2024.
https://doi.org/10.1007/978-981-97-0730-0_28

efficiently generating MCQs for CS0 and CS1 courses has become a significant development demand in CS education.

The latest progress in artificial intelligence has led to the emergence of large language models (LLMs) with excellent performance. These models have shown enormous application potential in education, medical diagnosis, social media management, and public opinion analysis, especially in computer education. For example, they have demonstrated near-human level in programming exercises [1], code generation [2], and code interpretation [3]. However, LLMs require domain-specific knowledge, and results cannot guarantee accuracy. Can we use them to generate high-quality MCQ for CS0/CS1 courses, thereby greatly supplementing formative and summative tests for different student levels? Regarding this, some scholars have initially attempted the possibility of using GPT to create multiple-choice questions for CS courses [4]. However, the existing problems include: 1) Automation still needs to be implemented; 2) Unable to generate a complete MCQ. Just extract the stem from the current question bank and generate distractors and correct answers based on the existing stem;3) There is no discussion on effectively applying LLMs in CS education.

While automating the generation of complete multiple-choice questions for CS0/CS1 courses, this study focuses on how to make LLMs perform well in CS education. The main contributions include:

1) We proposed an EduCS based on GPT-3.5, which can automatically generate multiple-choice questions based on the CS0/CS1 curriculum outline, which has a significant potential impact on the education field and can significantly reduce the workload of formative evaluation in the teaching process.
2) Design a set of prompt chains to enable LLMs to perform well in CS education.
3) Introducing user input to match the learning level of learners can generate different difficulty levels of MCQs for students at different levels, promoting personalized teaching.

2   Related Work

2.1   Multiple Choice Questions Generation

The generation of MCQ includes three parts: Stem Generation (SG), Answer Generation (AG), and Distractors Generation (DG). The paradigms of these studies have gone through rule-based [5], neural networks [6], transformers [7], and now large language models. Macaw [8] can execute SG, AG, and DG step by step. Dijkstra [9] et al. proposed an end-to-end quiz generator, EduQuiz, using GPT-3, which can generate complete multiple-choice questions and answers for reading comprehension tasks. Gabajiwala [10] et al. generated different types of questions based on keywords extracted by NLP. Experiments showed that about 60% of the questions generated by this model could not be correctly identified by survey participants. Andrew Tran and others used GPT3 and GPT4 to generate complete isomorphic multiple-choice questions using manual human-computer interaction. As far as we know, there is no work before this work that can be a one-stop solution, that is, simultaneously associate SG, AG, and DG to generate complete multiple-choice questions and simultaneously be dedicated to the research of automatic generation of high-quality questions.

2.2 Quality Evaluation Metrics

Most quality assessments of automatically generated multiple-choice questions typically rely on human evaluators. There is currently no gold metric that is applicable to the general field. MCQ consists of three components, and researchers have defined different metrics for assessing the quality of individual components. Literature [11] summarizes the existing evaluation metrics.

Evaluation of the Stem and Answer. Common ones include sentence format, sentence length, sentence simplicity, difficulty, usefulness for learning, answerability, sufficient context, question difficulty, field-related, too much information, insufficient information, correctness, etc.

Evaluation of the Distractors. The methods and criteria used to evaluate the quality of distractors (interference items) in different research works are: Mitkov et al. [12]. Proposed to use difficulty, discrimination and usefulness to evaluate the quality of distractors. To determine whether distractors were relevant and grammatical to the original text, Pino, Heilman, and Eskenazi [13] used grammatical and semantic criteria to measure the grammaticality and collocation of sentences. Readability measure, to assess whether distractors affect the clarity of a question, Agarwal and Mannem [14] asked evaluators to replace the distractors in the white space to check readability and semantics in sentences. To help determine whether a distraction is appropriate, Bhatia, Kirti, and Saha use intimacy values to evaluate distractions. If the distractor is close to the answer, it can be considered "good". Araki et al. [15] proposed a three-point scale to measure the quality of distractors. This scale evaluates the quality of distractors based on whether they are confusing and easily identifiable as incorrect answers.

2.3 Prompting Engineering

LLMS are very few learners who are able to answer the questions without additional fine-tuning. Finding the best tips for a specific task is a challenge. Some research focuses on hint engineering used in LLMs [16]. In the field of programming education, Reeves et al. [17] found that small changes in prompts have a significant impact on Codex performance, and the impact varies across different types of questions. Denny et al. [2] explored how to improve Copilot's performance in CS1 exercises through hints. Research shows that hint engineering can significantly improve Copilot's performance on CS1 problems. However, research has also found that too lengthy and detailed prompts may lead to reduced model performance. In the study of MCQs generation, Andrew Tran et al. summarized three effective tips through manual interaction with the GPT interactive interface. Since LLMs do not always produce optimal results on the first try, some research considers multi-round hint engineering to improve the output. Some studies adopt supervised methods to solve this problem [18]. However, they may require large amounts of training data or expensive human annotation, so some studies have designed improved methods without requiring extensive supervision. Shi et al. proposed a three-round iterative prompt including task instructions, keyword constraint prompts and length constraint prompts for food effect research summary in the biomedical field.

3 Methodology

3.1 Multiple Choice Questions

MCQ consists of three components: Stem, Correct Answer, and Distractors. The question stem is the central part of the multiple-choice question, which presents the problem or situation to be solved. Correct answer matches the question or situation in the stem and is the only correct option. Distractors are incorrect answer options that are designed to lead students into making mistakes or confuse them. They may look similar to the correct answer but are wrong. The purpose of distractors is to test students' discrimination skills to ensure they can identify the correct answer and avoid confusion. The example is as follows:

The programming language that can be directly executed by computer is ().

A. C language
B. BASIC language
C. assembly language
D. machine language

The stem of this MCQ is "The programming language that can be directly executed by a computer is?". It could be presented in question form: "What programming language can be directly executed by a computer?". Four choices are given in the question. Among these, the correct answer is 'machine language'. The rest three choices are the distractors.

3.2 The Framework of EduCS

The workflow of EduCS is shown in Figure 1. It mainly consists of three parts: input, generation, and output. Our research focuses on the first two parts, and we will introduce the main content in the first two parts below.

We know that LLMs need to improve in solving domain-specific problems, and research shows that prompt engineering can be practical for this problem. A prompt is a set of instructions provided to an LLM that programs the LLM by customizing it and enhancing or refining its capabilities. It is essential to mulate effective prompts that drive informative conversation. In general, finding the best prompt for a specific task is challenging. To improve the quality of MCQs, we focused on designing prompt chains.

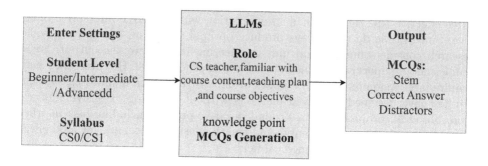

Fig. 1. The workflow of EduCS.

System User Input. CS0/CS1 syllabus, student level (beginner, intermediate, advanced). On the one hand, the input of the syllabus tells LLMs course information, and on the other hand, it is utilized by CS teachers to select knowledge points. The student-level option facilitates users to generate MCQs that match students' knowledge state.

Self-review. We introduce self-review that requires LLM to improve its previously generated results. Self-review can guide LLM self-correction. We feed the MCQs and reviews generated in the previous round into LLM and tell it to use these to regenerate the MCQs. Self-review design is crucial as it enables LLMS to look more closely at the generated MCQs from multiple perspectives.

Role-Playing. Telling LLMs its role in the dialogue, is used to guide LLMs to complete the responsibilities of the corresponding position. As we all know, in actual teaching environment scenarios, teachers of different subjects have different professional knowledge. Inspired by this situation, EduCS tells LLMs to play the role of CS teacher in the dialogue and what ability this role has, which is used to guide LLMs to complete the responsibilities of its position. Role-playing can limit the generated MCQs to a certain extent related to specific topics or fields. Making it professional helps improve quality.

4   Experimental Evaluation

In this section, our objectives revolve around validating the efficacy of EduCS through a series of experiments conducted using GPT-3.5. Firstly, we input various learner proficiency levels to assess whether the difficulty of the generated MCQs aligns with expectations. Secondly, We investigated whether EduCS has the ability to generate different types of MCQs. Lastly, we evaluate the quality of MCQs based on the proposed evaluation metrics.

4.1   Student Level

Study 1. We entered three student proficiency levels sequentially into EduCS: beginner, intermediate, and advanced. We evaluate whether the generated questions can adapt to different students by observing their difficulty levels.

Results. Figure 2 shows an example of MCQs generated by EduCS based on three different student levels for the same knowledge point. For MCQs for junior students, Correct Answers are almost included in the stem, which can help beginners build basic knowledge. Questions for intermediate students require a more careful comparison of options to choose. Encourage students to expand their breadth of knowledge, which can help students build self-confidence. Questions for advanced students require students to deepen their understanding of knowledge. It can be seen that EduCS can generate MCQs of different difficulty levels according to the student level. It can promote personalized learning and is of great significance.

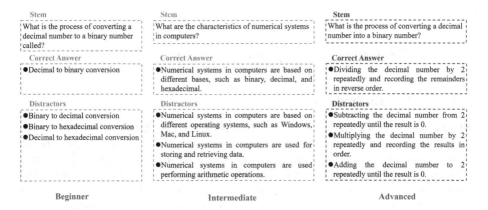

Fig. 2. An example of MCQs generated by EduCS from easy to difficult to the same knowledge point according to varying student levels.

4.2   The Different Types of MCQs

Study 2. We input the teaching outline of the Introduction to Computer Science into EduCS. Other settings remain unchanged. We investigated whether EduCS has the ability to generate different types of MCQs. The type here refers to declarative MCQs and questioning MCQs. Furthermore, conceptual MCQs, numerical MCQs.

Results. Figure 3 shows the two expression forms of MCQs generated by EduCS, with the description form on the left and the question form on the right. Figure 4 shows the MCQs generated by EduCS for two types of assessment content, with conceptual knowledge assessed on the left and numerical operation-related ability evaluated on the right. It can be seen that EduCS can generate different types of MCQs.

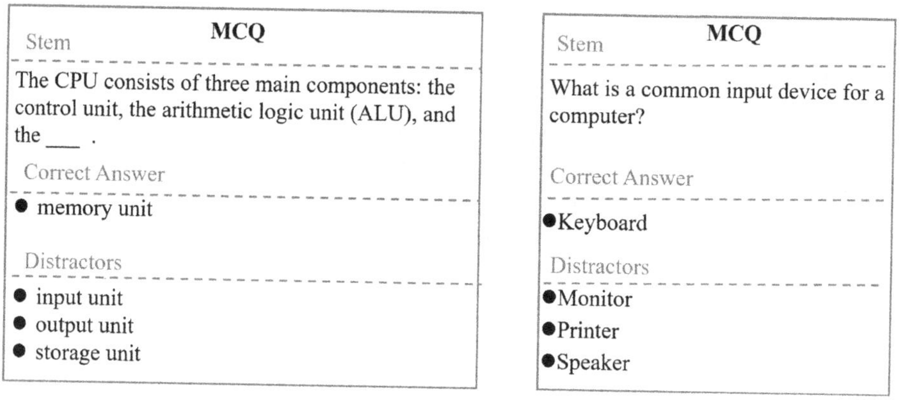

| **MCQ** |
| Stem |
| The CPU consists of three main components: the control unit, the arithmetic logic unit (ALU), and the ___ . |
| Correct Answer |
| ● memory unit |
| Distractors |
| ● input unit
● output unit
● storage unit |

a) Declarative

| **MCQ** |
| Stem |
| What is a common input device for a computer? |
| Correct Answer |
| ●Keyboard |
| Distractors |
| ●Monitor
●Printer
●Speaker |

b) Dnterrogative

Fig. 3. MCQs for two expression forms generated by EduCS.

4.3 Quality Evaluation

Study 3. To verify the quality of MCQs generated by EduCS. We will design quality evaluation metrics based on the characteristics and educational needs of each part of the MCQs. An MCQ consists of three distinct parts, each with its own unique features. Accordingly, different metrics are defined to assess the quality of individual components. The metrics and their definitions are presented in Table 1. All metrics are measured on a scale of 0 to 10, where 0 indicates that the criteria are not met at all, and 10 signifies complete satisfaction of the criteria.

We utilize EduCS to generate 50 intermediate-level MCQs for computer introduction course. Concurrently, we select 50 MCQs that have been used in previous years for this course at the Beijing Institute of Technology. Subsequently, we subject these 100 MCQs to expert evaluation. Two experts are invited to participate in the assessment: one is a computer teacher with extensive teaching experience, and the other is a professor from the Department of Computer Science at the Beijing Institute of Technology. Finally, we analyze the data to demonstrate the quality of the MCQs.

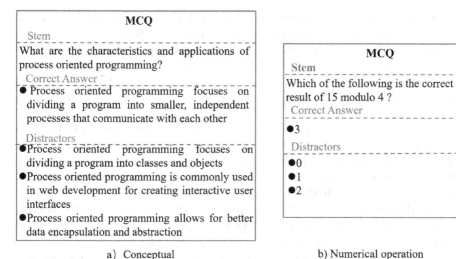

a) Conceptual   b) Numerical operation

Fig. 4. Two types of MCQs generated by EduCS,one of which assesses conceptual knowledge, while the other focuses on numerical calculations.

Table 1. Quality evaluation metrics

Metrics for the Stem	Definition
answerableness	the ease or suitability of a question being answered
relevance to knowledge	knowledge-point relevance
adequate context	to effectively understand, interpret, or assess a stem
Metrics for the Correct Answer	**Definition**
semantic correctness	the accuracy of the meaning conveyed by the statement
Metrics for the Distractors	**Definition**
discriminating power	Confusing and disruptive to others
closeness	at least one is close to the true answer
Metrics for the overall	**Definition**
guidance for learning	helpful for learning
moderate difficulty	the difficulty level of the question
grammatical correctness	syntactically correc
clearness	at least one is close to true answer

Results. Based on the statistical analysis conducted on the scoring results of human-generated MCQs and EduCS-generated MCQs, we obtained Fig. 5. In this figure, the left bar represents the EduCS-generated MCQs, while the right bar represents the human-generated MCQs.

From the graph, we observe that the MCQs generated by EduCS achieved scores exceeding 8 points on the five metrics: relevance to knowledge, adequate context, semantic correctness, grammatical correctness, and clearness. Particularly, the metrics of relevance to knowledge and grammatical correctness were close to the scores of human-generated MCQs. This indicates that MCQs generated using EduCS have great potential in terms of quality.

There is a significant difference in the scores for discriminating power and closeness compared to the metrics scores of human-generated MCQs. This suggests that generating distractors is more challenging than constructing the stem and correct answers. The moderate difficulty score was 7.9, which is close to the level set for intermediate students.

Overall, the trend in the metrics scores of EduCS-generated MCQs aligns with that of human-generated MCQs. This demonstrates the powerful capability of EduCS in generating MCQs. However, it is important to note that even though EduCS has automatic generation capabilities, it is still recommended to manually review and correct the MCQs before delivering them to students. This is because automated systems may not always capture subtle nuances or context-specific details accurately. Manual review allows for human expertise and judgment to ensure the quality and appropriateness of the questions.

By combining the automatic generation capability of EduCS with manual review, educators can benefit from the efficiency of generating a large number of MCQs while still ensuring the accuracy, relevance, and educational value of the questions.

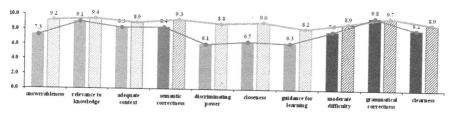

Fig. 5. Comparison of average scores of quality metrics between human-generated MCQs and EduCS-generated MCQs. The left bar corresponds to the EduCS-generated MCQs and the right bar corresponds to the human-generated MCQs.

5   Conclusion

In this study, we designed a set of prompt chains to optimize the performance of LLMs in CS education. Subsequently, we have developed and implemented EduCS, a system based on GPT-3.5, which is capable of automatically generating MCQs aligned with the CS0/CS1 course outline. Based on the experimental results, we made the following observations: 1) EduCS has the ability to generate MCQs of varying difficulty levels based on individual student proficiency. This personalized teaching approach is highly significant in education; 2) Although the generated questions require teacher verification before being delivered to students, they demonstrate great potential in terms of quality. 3) EduCS exhibits the ability to generate complete and diverse types of MCQs, which can be used for both formative and summative assessments. Automating the process of generating MCQs, significantly reduces the workload associated with formative evaluation in the teaching process. EduCS holds excellent value for formative assessment in CS education.

Acknowledgement. This work was supported by the grants of the following program: National Natural Science Foundation of China (NSFC, No. 62077004, 62177005)

References

1. Finnie-Ansley, J., Denny, P., Becker, B.A., Luxton-Reilly, A., Prather, J.: The robots are coming: exploring the implications of openai codex on introductory programming. In: Proceedings of the 24th Australasian Computing Education Conference, pp. 10–19 (2022)
2. Denny, P., Kumar, V., Giacaman, N.: Conversing with copilot: exploring prompt engineering for solving cs1 problems using natural language. In: Proceedings of the 54th ACM Technical Symposium on Computer Science Education, vol. 1, pp. 1136–1142 (2023)
3. MacNeil, S., et al.: Experiences from using code explanations generated by large language models in a web software development e-book. In: Proceedings of the 54th ACM Technical Symposium on Computer Science Education, vol. 1. pp. 931–937 (2023)
4. Tran, A., Angelikas, K., Rama, E., Okechukwu, C., Smith IV, D.H., MacNeil, S.: Generating multiple choice questions for computing courses using large language models
5. Heilman, M., Smith, N.A.: Good question! statistical ranking for question generation. In: Human Language Technologies: The 2010 Annual Conference of the North American Chapter of the Association for Computational Linguistics, pp. 609–617 (2010)
6. Du, X., Shao, J., Cardie, C.: Learning to ask: neural question generation for reading comprehension. arXiv preprint arXiv:1705.00106 (2017)
7. Vaswani, A., et al.: Attention is all you need. In: Advances in Neural Information Processing Systems, vol. 30 (2017)
8. Tafjord, O., Clark, P.: General-purpose question-answering with macaw. arXiv preprint arXiv:2109.02593 (2021)
9. Dijkstra, R., Genç, Z., Kayal, S., Kamps, J., et al.: Reading comprehension quiz generation using generative pre-trained transformers (2022)
10. Gabajiwala, E., Mehta, P., Singh, R., Koshy, R.: Quiz maker: automatic quiz generation from text using NLP. In: Singh, P.K., Wierzchoń, S.T., Chhabra, J.K., Tanwar, S. (eds.) Futuristic Trends in Networks and Computing Technologies, pp. 523–533. Springer, Singapore (2022). https://doi.org/10.1007/978-981-19-5037-7_37
11. Ch, D.R., Saha, S.K.: Automatic multiple choice question generation from text: a survey. IEEE Trans. Learn. Technol. **13**(1), 14–25 (2018)
12. Mitkov, R., Varga, A., Rello, L., et al.: Semantic similarity of distractors in multiple-choice tests: extrinsic evaluation. In: Proceedings of the Workshop on Geometrical Models of Natural Language Semantics, pp. 49–56 (2009)
13. Patra, R., Saha, S.K.: A hybrid approach for automatic generation of named entity distractors for multiple choice questions. Educ. Inf. Technol. **24**, 973–993 (2019)
14. Agarwal, M., Mannem, P.: Automatic gap-fill question generation from text books. In: Proceedings of the Sixth Workshop on Innovative Use of NLP for Building Educational Applications, pp. 56–64 (2011)

15. Araki, J., Rajagopal, D., Sankaranarayanan, S., Holm, S., Yamakawa, Y., Mitamura, T.: Generating questions and multiple-choice answers using semantic analysis of texts. In: Proceedings of COLING 2016, the 26th International Conference on Computational Linguistics: Technical Papers, pp. 1125–1136 (2016)
16. Reynolds, L., McDonell, K.: Prompt programming for large language models: Beyond the few-shot paradigm. In: Extended Abstracts of the 2021 CHI Conference on Human Factors in Computing Systems, pp. 1–7 (2021)
17. Reeves, B., et al.: Evaluating the performance of code generation models for solving parsons problems with small prompt variations. In: Proceedings of the 2023 Conference on Innovation and Technology in Computer Science Education, vol. 1, pp. 299–305 (2023)
18. Liu, M., Rus, V., Liu, L.: Automatic Chinese multiple choice question generation using mixed similarity strategy. IEEE Trans. Learn. Technol. 11(2), 193–202 (2017)

Data Mining in Social Science

Research of Virtual Simulation Experiment System for Geomorphologic Evolution of Taiwan Strait

Jiang Huixian[1,2(✉)], Chen Xin[3], and Chen Yian[1]

[1] Institute of Geograph, Fujian Normal University, Fuzhou, China
jhx155@163.com
[2] Provincial Engineering Research Center for Monitoring and Assessing Terrestrial Disasters, Fuzhou, China
[3] Disaster Reduction Center of Fujian Province, Fuzhou, China

Abstract. Geography is a highly practical subject which internship activities are an important part of geography teaching. However, due to the limitations of spatiotemporal dynamics, it is impossible to obtain the effect of situational learning in depth. To supplement the on-site experiment teaching of geography, this paper studies the coastal landform evolution in the Taiwan Strait. A data model to simulate the coastal landform evolution process and 3D game engine technology were adopted to build a virtual reality experiment system. The established system enables geography majors to empirically experience the formation and evolution of the coastal landforms and have a rational cognition. It also realizes the 3D simulation of the coastal landform evolution in the Taiwan Strait, displays the historic evolution process of the coastal landforms dynamically, and helps students explore the geographical space, geographical process, and geographical mechanism of the coastal landform in both virtual and real environment. By interning at the virtual reality experiment system, students therefore can have a better understanding of the formation and evolution process of the coastal landforms.

Keyword: The Taiwan Strait · Coastal Morphology · Virtual Simulation Experiment System · Geography Practice Teaching · Virtual Reality Environment

1 Introduction

With the characteristics of being intuitive, practical, comprehensive and innovative, experiment teaching of geography is an important link that connects theory and practice and the main way for teachers to cultivate students' geographical literacy, practical ability, and the ability to solve geographical problems. However, geographical experiments only show the current geographical environment, as a result, students cannot experience the internal factors that lead to the changes in the geographic elements such as the spatio-temporal environment and climate change process (e.g. the coastal landform evolution process). Many geologic and geomorphological sections were covered or damaged, leading to poor teaching quality due to the difficulty in finding some typical

W. Hong and G. Kanaparan (Eds.): ICCSE 2023, CCIS 2023, pp. 327–338, 2024.
https://doi.org/10.1007/978-981-97-0730-0_29

geologic and geomorphological phenomena. The geographical evolution in the Taiwan Strait since late Quaternary period is a typical example, especially since Last Glacial Maximum. The alternation of glacial and interglacial periods resulted in huge fluctuations in sea level and great impacts on coastal landforms. It is a pity that students can only imagine this abstract and irreversible geographical process based on the lecture and the description in related historical documents. Virtual reality experiment teaching has become an integral part of the informatization construction of college education and scientific research, demonstrating that information technology has been applied to disciplines in colleges and universities. Virtual reality experiment teaching has been gradually applied and promoted in college education and scientific research. For example, Prof. Lin Hui suggests that a more comprehensive and integrated research mode should be developed for geographical practice after analyzing the tasks of geo-science experiments and current issues. To construct a virtual geographic environment, greater emphasis should be put on the geo-science analysis and experiment auxiliary functions. Through the analysis, comprehensive and collaborative geographic experiments should be carried by combining "virtual and real environment" [1]. Peng Yuhui analyzed the current status of field practice in Mountain Lushan by investigation, and constructed a targeted platform for field practice in Lushan by using 3D geographic information technology, virtual reality technology and LBS spatial positioning services, to improve the informatization level of field practice [2].

To supplement the on-site experiment based on the supporting conditions, a comprehensive and collaborative geographic experiment environment that integrates both "real and virtual environment" is built, and a virtual geographic experiment simulation system is developed according to the teaching objectives and needs of experiment teaching of geomorphology, so as to simulate the real geographic environment and its evolution process as real as possible and lead students to explore the unknown geographical world. Geography is characterized by multidimensional temporal and spatial scales. In comprehensive consideration of the such feature and the regional characteristics of geological and geomorphological experiments in colleges and universities, a virtual reality experiment teaching system designed for geography is built to simulate the costal landform evolution process in the Taiwan Strait since Last Glacial Maximum. The established system enables the 3D simulation of the coastal landform evolution process in the experiment site since Last Glacial Maximum, and offers a vivid and intuitive display of the evolution process, thereby helping students to understand the formation and evolution of coastal landforms through virtual reality experiment teaching system, and master how to analyze specific geographical elements as well as how to carry out regional and comprehensive investigation and analysis. It is aimed to develop their comprehensive observation and experimental skills of geographical elements, and the ability to analyze the spatial variation law of geographical elements by using modern geographic spatial analysis techniques.

2 Scenario Setting for the Virtual Reality Experiment of Coastal Landform Evolution in the Taiwan Strait

The experiment area in the Taiwan Strait is located between Fujian Province and Taiwan Province, and belongs to the southeast coast of China. It is adjacent to the East China Sea in the north and the South China Sea in the south, the major channel for the two seas. The strait is distributed in a northeast-southwest direction. Huangqi Peninsula in Lianjiang County is the northwest corner, Fugui Cape in Taiwan is the northeast corner, Aojiao in Shandao Island, Fujian is the southwest corner and Maubitou Cape in the south of Taiwan is the southeast corner. The Taiwan Strait becomes narrowest between Pingtan Island, Fuzhou and Hsinchu, Taiwan. The strait is located on the continental shelf of the East China Sea, with an average water depth of about 60m. The landform of the experiment area is bumpy and different from place to place. For a long time, the seabed in the Taiwan Strait has been significantly impacted by the development and changes of the Asian mainland plate and the paleoclimate changes in the Quaternary. Last Glacial Maximum was the largest glacial period. The global climate turned cold, the sea level of China's border seas dropped, and most of the Taiwan Strait was exposed. It was the last time when Taiwan and Fujian were not separated, and the strait became the channel for the plants and animals on both sides to migrate. When the world entered the post-glacial period when Last Glacial Maximum ended, the climate became warmer and the sea level gradually rose. The continental shelf that was originally exposed as the sea level was low in the glacial period was almost completely submerged by sea water. After that, the sea level experienced several small oscillations. The rise and fall of the sea level in the Taiwan Strait plays an important role in the geographical environment evolution, climate change and biological migration and distribution.

The virtual simulation of the coastal landform evolution process in the Taiwan Strait makes the description of theoretical knowledge and related historical data contextualized and intuitive, thus facilitating the experiment teaching quality and providing students with deeper insights into the terrain characteristics and geological structures of the Taiwan Strait and both sides, sea level evolution and archaeology. The system is built based on the Taiwan Strait. When students enter the virtual reality experiment system, they can see the virtual 3D scene of the entire Taiwan Strait personally, explore the real topography of the Taiwan Strait, waves on the sea, and the distribution of major islands in the Taiwan Strait by zooming in and out the scene and roaming with the mouse and keyboard. By dragging the time axis in the system with the mouse to lift or drop the sea level, they can observe how the land and sea in the Taiwan Strait changed since Last Glacial Maximum from different angles and different perspectives, figure out the sea level altitude of each area in the Taiwan Strait at different geographical time nodes, and determine the specific location of the coastline in each geographical period. The established system is an important tool for analyzing the causes and evolution laws of coastal erosion and accumulation landforms in geomorphological experiments.

3 Simulation of Coastal Landform Evolution Process in Taiwan Strait

3.1 Reproduce Sea Level Evolution Process Based on Sedimentological Method

Since Last Glacial Maximum, the global climate had undergone substantial changes during glacial-interglacial cycles, and the sea level rose and dropped sharply. Sea level evolution directly affects the distribution of land and sea in the Taiwan Strait, and plays a vital role in the paleogeographical environment evolution, paleoclimate changes, and paleontological migration and distribution. Researchers have proposed a variety of methods to reproduce the sea level evolution but failed to reach a consensus because of the complicated driving factors of sea level evolution. In this regard, this paper aims to reproduce the sea level evolution in the Taiwan Strait based on relevant historical documents and data by using the stratigraphic data directly from sedimentological perspective. The sedimentological method is a traditional way to reproduce sea level evolution. Sea level markers can be used to quantitatively identify the location of paleo-sea level based on their dating. Sea level markers are the material basis for reproducing paleo-sea level altitude. They are the only evidence that can restore the history of sea level evolution and verify the inference of sea level evolution. Geomorphic marker is a kind of sea level markers, which mainly includes sea stacks, sea cliffs, sea erosion platforms, sea erosion troughs and other landforms [3]. Carbon-14 dating method, the most common dating method using sea level markers, can be used to quantitatively infer the year when animals and plants survived based on the radioactivity of Carbon-14 isotopes. This method can be applied to organic matter as early as 50,000 years ago [4].

3.2 Processing of Sea Level Change Data

The Taiwan Strait is located in the East China Sea. The sedimentation since Last Glacial Maximum can be learned from the well-developed continental shelf strata of the East China Sea during Last Glacial Maximum. For this sake, a large number of researchers have done a lot of work on the sedimentary records in this area, laying the foundation for the high-resolution sedimentary records since Last Glacial Maximum. Since the sea level markers usually experience a variety of internal and external forces of transformation over time, their elevation is mainly impacted by the compaction of sediments, the isostatic settlement of the location of sea level markers, and the geotectonic movement, etc.[5]. As a result, the elevation of the existing paleo-sea level markers is often not the original elevation when they formed. Therefore, the corrected paleo-sea level altitude data and corresponding Carbon-14 dating data retrieved from the sea level markers and transitional facies sediments found in some drill holes in the Taiwan Strait and its adjacent areas since Last Glacial Maximum were collected. The relatively unreasonable paleo-sea level altitude data in the samples were eliminated, the elevation of 13 key points of sea level markers in the Taiwan Strait is shown in Table 1.

Table 1. C-14 dating and elevation of sea level markers

Place	^{14}C dating (a,BP)	Corrected elevation (m)
Hole CK1 in Dianxia Town, Fuding	26,318 ± 1,140	-24.17
Hole DK1 in Licheng Village, Xiapu County	34,300 ± 950	-21.07
Oyster Shell in Intertidal Belt, Kenyuan Town, Lianjiang	833 ± 103	+ 0.04
Hole MN5 in Shangyang Village, Fuzhou	4,045 ± 75	-0.17
Beach Rock in Humian Bay, Pinghai Town, Putian	2,310 ± 85	+ 2.54
Large Remains of Plants on Beach of Shenhu Bay in Jinjiang	7,750 ± 120	-3.05
Hole CK48 in Xitoushe Community, Xiamen	27,849	-3.55
River Jiulongjiang in Longhai	4,184	-1.66
Oyster Shell in Xulintou, Longhai	3,330 ± 150	+ 0.5
Oyster Shell in Gaobiantou, Longhai	3,150 ± 150	+ 0.5
Beach Peat Moss on the East Coast of Taiwan	5,340 ± 260	-1.3
Seashells in Hengchun Peninsula, Taiwan	2,920 ± 180	-2.3
Penghu Coral Reef, Taiwan	4,700	2.4

3.3 Fitting the Sea Level Change Curve

According to the approximate start time of Last Glacial Maximum, the sea level altitude data extracted from historical data and previous research results were mapped into a unified time axis. The sea level altitude data in different periods was processed and analyzed by using statistical methods. The stages where sea level altitude changed on the time axis were identified, the range of sea level evolution in each stage was examined and verified to eliminate obvious outliers. With the measured age of the sediments by using Carbon-14 as the abscissa, the paleo-sea level altitude retrieved from the sediments

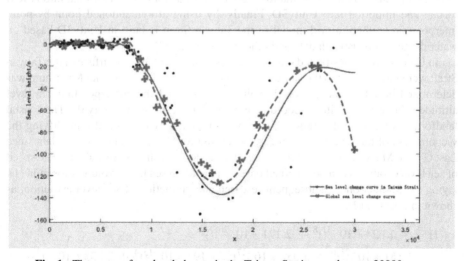

Fig. 1. The curve of sea level change in the Taiwan Strait over the past 30000 years

as the ordinate, a more reliable sea level evolution curve since Last Glacial Maximum was fitted, as shown in Fig. 1

According to the fitted curve of sea level evolution in the Taiwan Strait since 30,000 years ago, it can be inferred that the last and largest glacial period began around 26,000 years ago. The global climate became colder, and the sea level in the Taiwan Strait dropped significantly. It reached its lowest point, about 135m below the current sea level, around 17,000 years ago. After that, the last glacial period of the Quaternary period ended and the world entered the post-glacial period when the global climate became warmer. This resulted in a sharp rise of the sea level in the Taiwan Strait, with an increase of about 120–130m. The transgression reached its peak around 6,000–7,000 years ago. Since then, the sea level has been fluctuating above and below the current sea level with an amplitude of no more than 4m.

3.4 Dynamic Simulation of Coastal Landform Evolution

The coastal landform evolution in the Taiwan Strait since Last Glacial Maximum was virtually simulated. According to research findings [6], the sea level in the Taiwan Strait reached the lowest level in Last Glacial Maximum, about 130m lower than the present level. Therefore, the continental shelf where the seawater depth is less than 200 m is the best research object to show the coastal landform evolution. A real seabed terrain model is a must to reveal the evolution process. Irregular triangular mesh model [7], characterized by high modeling accuracy and applicability to complex terrain construction, was used to connect the discrete water depth points into a triangular grid that did not intersect or overlap each other according to certain rules. In addition, Unity3D game engine was used to visualize the terrain at the bottom of the Taiwan Strait. OGR library under the Geospatial Data Abstraction Library, an open source spatial data transformation library, was adopted to read the water depth, isobath and other vector data in Unity3D, and important parameters and information were converted from the vector data into ASCII format and imported into Unity3D. Finally, by using aforementioned point-by-point interpolation method, a grid model of the Taiwan Strait is built in Unity3D based on water depth points, isobath data and other imported data.

In Unity3D, the constructed real seabed topography and 3D sea surface of the Taiwan Strait were integrated into the same scene. The start time of Last Glacial Maximum was determined based on the sea level evolution curve, and the corresponding sea level altitude value was the initial y-coordinate of the 3D sea surface in Unity3D. The coastal landform evolution in the Taiwan Strait was simulated by dynamically modifying the y-coordinate of the real 3D sea surface according to the sea level evolution data since Last Glacial Maximum derived from the fitted sea level evolution formula(1). The speed of sea level evolution can be obtained based on the fitted sea level evolution formula (1), laying the foundation for subsequent research and prediction of sea level evolution, as shown in formula (2).

$$H = -1.624 * 10^{-31}t^8 + 2.171 * 10^{-26}t^7 -$$
$$1.151 * 10^{-21}t^6 + 3.052 * 10^{-17}t^5 - 4.197 * 10^{-13}t^4 + 2.833 * 10^{-9}t^3 -$$
$$8.574 * 10^{-6}t^2 + 0.008784t \tag{1}$$

$$V = -1.2992 * 10^{-30}t^7 + 1.5197 * 10^{-25}t^6 -$$
$$6.906 * 10^{-21}t^5 + 1.526 * 10^{-16}t^4 -$$
$$1.6788 * 10^{-12}t^3 + 8.499 * 10^{-9}t^2 - 1.7148 * 10^{-5}t + 0.008784. \quad (2)$$

Three representative geographical periods were selected, the terrain status of specific areas and the position of paleo-coastlines in the Taiwan Strait in different geographical periods were analyzed based on paleoclimate knowledge. About 26,000 years ago, the world entered Last Glacial Maximum. According to the result calculated by using the sea level evolution model, the sea level was about 53m below the current sea level. Most of the southwestern Taiwan Strait, the Taiwan Shoal, and Taichung Shoal became land. The sea level dropped to its lowest point about 17,000 years ago. According to the result calculated by using the sea level evolution model, the sea level was about 136m below the current sea level. At this time, the entire Taiwan Strait was almost entirely exposed and had become land, with the entire strait in a continental sedimentary environment. It was the last time when Taiwan and Fujian were not separated by the Taiwan Strait. The coastline had extended to the east of Taiwan Island and the original coastal islands of Fujian and Taiwan Island had become hills, large and small. About 17,000 years ago, the last glacial period of the Quaternary ended, and the world entered the post-glacial period. Under the impact of global warming, the sea level in the Taiwan Strait rose sharply, with a rise of about 130m. The continental shelf exposed during the glacial period was almost completely submerged by seawater, hills in the coastal areas were separated by the sea water and became islands, and the coastal tombolo developed sufficiently. Islands connecting the mainland with underwater tombolo or other islands became peninsulas. Marine erosion and terraces had been completely preserved on the coasts of central and southern Fujian. The sea level had risen and fallen many times since around 7,000 years ago, showing an oscillating change above and below the current sea level, with a maximum amplitude no more than 4m. The sea level has been relatively stable since then.

4 System Integrated Design and Demonstrated Application

4.1 System Construction Goals

This paper aims to apply the virtual reality experiment system of geomorphology to the practical geomorphology experiment, break the limitation of the on-site experiment environment regarding spatio-temporal dynamics, and build a system based on the supporting conditions of the on-site experiment. To simulate the coastal evolution process in the Taiwan Strait since Last Glacial Maximum, a comprehensive practice support data model framework for geographic information exploration is established. With this framework, students are taught how to represent and analyze complicated, fuzzy, and diverse geographic spaces, geographic processes, and geographic mechanisms in a virtual framework. The coastal landform evolution process in the Taiwan Strait since Last Glacial Maximum is virtually simulated, the typical landform of the experiment site are displayed realistically and intuitively. And students are taught to contextualize and visualize the abstract yet difficult issues from geographical perspective. It is a new teaching approach for geographical practice.

4.2 Overall System Architecture

This system adopts the B/S (Browser/Server) mode for the overall system architecture, as shown in Fig. 2. It is mainly composed of data layer, service layer and application layer.

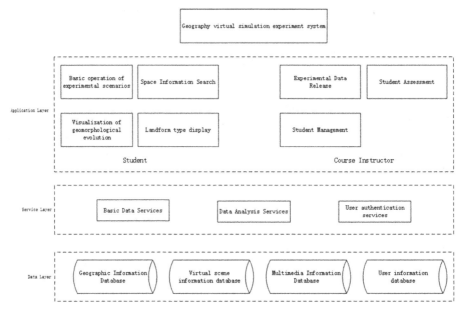

Fig. 2. System overall architecture diagram

The data layer provides the foundation for the efficient operation of the whole system, including a basic geographic information database, a virtual scene model database, a multimedia information database, and a user information database. The basic geographic information database is designed to store spatial data, including major places and addresses in the Taiwan Strait, experiment paths, soundings, depth contours, coastlines, DEMs, and remote sensing images. The virtual scene model database is responsible for retaining submarine terrain, sea surface, rocks, and other 3D modeling data. The multimedia information database stores text information related to the experiments, pictures of experiment site, audio/video materials and Flash animations introducing scenery spots and typical topography of the experiment site. Furthermore, the user information database is designed for personal information, login account and password, geomorphology experiment reports, and geomorphology experiment results. When the data layer receives a request from the user, it processes the SQL statement and delivers the result back to the service layer.

The service layer is the core of the entire system, acting as the intermediary between the user and the data ends. The user end relies on the service layer to invoke the business logic and achieve the corresponding functional response. The service layer mainly includes basic data service, comprehensive data analysis service and user authentication service. The basic data service is used to send a request to the data layer, which will then invoke the relevant data stored in the database and send the result to the user end browser for use. In terms of the data analysis service, specific data in the data layer will be invoked according to the user's individual needs, such as calculating the location information of the experiment site, analyzing the sea level altitude, and evaluating the learning outcomes of the students. The user authentication service is mainly designed to protect the user's personal information and improve the security and reliability of the system.

The application layer is a user-oriented browser-side application mainly intended for students and teachers, and a tool to complement to on-site experiment teaching of geomorphology. It enables a range of functions such as basic operations of virtual experimental scenes, spatial information query, visualization of landform evolution, and displaying different types of landforms, facilitating the teaching effect of geomorphology experiments.

4.3   Display of Typical Modules of System Functions

(1) Display of different types of landforms

A three-dimensional model is adopted to locate and display eolian plains, ancient volcanoes, headlands, bays, granite eggs and other typical landforms at the experimental site, as shown in Fig. 3. Based on audio introduction and text descriptions, students can learn more about landforms, including the morphological characteristics, causes, distribution and developmental laws.

(2) Display of landform evolution

In this module, students are able to control the sea level by dragging the time axis in the system with the mouse, observe how the landform of the Taiwan Strait evolved since Last Glacial Maximum from different angles and different positions, and master the sea level altitude of various regions in the Taiwan Strait at different geographical time nodes, and determine the specific location of the coastline in each geographical period. As shown in Fig. 4, corresponding text descriptions and related theoretical illustrations will pop up at special geographical time nodes such as the beginning of Last Glacial Maximum, the specific point in time when the sea level altitude fell to the lowest point, and the sea level altitude rose to the current height in the post glacial period, to impress the students relevant theoretical knowledge and facilitate their understanding.

(3) Experiment assessment

This module is mainly used to understand how much the students know about related theoretical knowledge after the geomorphology experiment. Students are required to take online examinations and write experimental reports. Teachers can review and score the electronic test papers and experimental reports submitted by students through this system, so as to fully understand each student's learning process.

(a) Aeolian plain

(b) Paleovolcano

(c) Cape

Fig. 3. Typical geomorphic

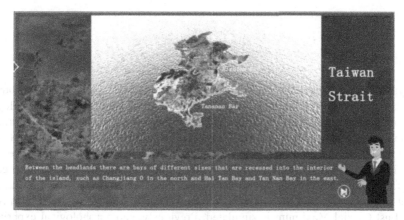

(d) Gulf

Fig. 3. (*continued*)

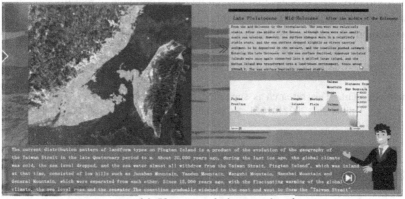

(a) 53 meters below sea level

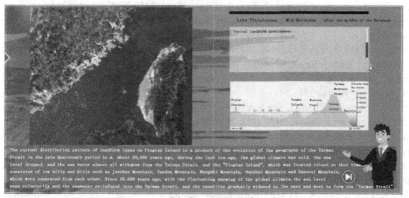

(b) Current sea level

Fig. 4. Geomorphic evolution display

5 Conclusion

Geography is characterized by multidimensional temporal and spatial scales. In comprehensive consideration of the such feature and the regional characteristics of geological and geomorphological experiments in colleges and universities, a virtual reality practice system designed for geography is built, to solve the problem that students cannot experience the landform evolution process in real life during geomorphology practice. This paper is a case study on the Taiwan Strait. By using the system built, the real seabed topography of the Taiwan Strait is 3D visualized, the 3D sea surface of the Taiwan Strait is real-time rendered and the coastal landform evolution process in the Taiwan Strait since Last Glacial Maximum is simulated. Previously, geomorphological experiment teaching was based on static description, focused on outcomes research and abstract theory. The virtual reality experiment system designed for geomorphology changed all that. It enables 3D dynamic stimulation, process recovery and Web-based simulation of landform evolution process that we can hardly experience in real life, and meets the needs of remote sharing and virtual teaching. This paper aims to help students understand the topographical and geomorphological evolution process as well as the geographical concepts, principles and laws involved, and to provide a reference for the development of virtual reality experiment system of geography in colleges and universities.

Acknowledgment. This research is supported by the Natural Science Foundation of Fujian Province of China(No. 2022J01621); Socially useful program of Fujian Province (No. 2021R1002006) .

References

1. Lin, H., Zhang, C., Chen, M., etal.: On virtual geographic environments for geographic knowledge representation and sharing. J. Remote Sens.2016,20(5):1290–1298
2. Peng, Y., The design of lushan geograohy field practice assistant platform. Jiangxi Normal Univ. 2019
3. Wang, S., Yang, J., Zeng, C., et al.: Sea Ievel changes since late pleistocene along fujian coast. J. Oceanogr. Taiwan Strait, 1994(02):166–175
4. Zhang, W., Huang, Z.: Environmental archaeology of taiwn sincelate pleistocwne .tropical geography, 1996(04):291–298
5. Zhao, X., Geng X., Zhang J. Sea level chances of the eastern china during the past 20000 years, Acta Oceanologica Sinica, 1979,1(2): 269–281
6. Jia, J., Tan, J., Chen, C., et al.: Vertex resampling of sounding triangle. Hydrographic surveying and charting, 2017, 37(3): 63–65
7. Yan, X., Ma, D., Yu, Z., et al.: 3D visualization of sea floor topography based on CGAL and opengl. Mar. Inf. 2020, v.35;No.243(01):38–42
8. Zhu, Y., Li, C., Zeng C., et al.: On the lowest sea level of the east china sea continental shelf in the late pleistocene. Sci. Bull. 1979(07):317–320
9. Bruneton, E., Neyret, F., Holzschuch, N.: Real-time realistic ocean lighting using seamless transitions from geometry to BRDF. Comput. Graph. Forum **29**(2), 487–496 (2010)

Research on Traffic Flow Prediction Based on Spatio-Temporal Correlation Analysis

Siwei Wei[✉] and Wentao He

CCCC Second Highway Consultants Co., Ltd., Wuhan, China
weisw@cccc.com

Abstract. With the advancement of urbanization, people's living standards have significantly improved, but have also resulted in various challenges, particularly in the domain of transportation. Traffic congestion and low traffic efficiency have led to substantial wastage of people's travel time. Traffic flow prediction is vital to Intelligent Transportation Systems (ITS) as it centers on projecting the future condition of road networks using historical data and pertinent information. Accurate traffic flow prediction helps users take proactive measures and is essential for addressing traffic challenges. Yet, the intricate nonlinear temporal and spatial correlations within traffic flow data pose notable challenges. To address the intricate correlations within traffic flow data, this study separately investigates the temporal and spatio-temporal correlations. Firstly, a model based on time correlation is developed, followed by the construction of a new network model that integrates time and space to extract complex spatio-temporal correlations from traffic flow data. The key research focuses are as follows: the analysis of time correlation in traffic data, the introduction of several commonly used neural network models for time sequences, and the incorporation of gating mechanisms into the TCN to create an enhanced gating TCN network structure model. This model aims to analyze the correlation between traffic data and time. The proposed gating mechanism TCN involves significant changes in network structure, with the integration of input and output gates akin to the LSTM structure. Furthermore, the convolutional correlation modules in each extended convolutional module are substituted by two internal parallel convolutional modules in the TCN. Forming an input gate and output gate structure. Furthermore, in order to reduce variance and simultaneously increase the input and output gates, Each parallel convolution component is enhanced by the addition of two identical parallel branches, resulting in the total output being the average of all the "gate" outputs. The performance of the proposed model is assessed using real traffic speed datasets. Demonstrating superior prediction accuracy and effectively capturing sudden changes in traffic speed while maintaining stable results.

Keyword: Intelligent Transportation · Traffic Flow Prediction · Time Convolution Network · Graph Space-time Model

© The Author(s), under exclusive license to Springer Nature Singapore Pte Ltd. 2024
W. Hong and G. Kanaparan (Eds.): ICCSE 2023, CCIS 2023, pp. 339–346, 2024.
https://doi.org/10.1007/978-981-97-0730-0_30

1 Introduction

As a widely studied project, traffic flow prediction has long been studied by many scholars at home and abroad using advanced models in other fields for reference. Given that traffic flow prediction models necessitate real-time performance, accuracy and reliability, the early traffic prediction models are all traditional statistical models. The main methods include AR, MA, ARMA, HA and Box-Cox transformation. With the progress of The Times, currently, both at home and abroad, there are five main types of theories for short-term traffic flow prediction based on specific methods. They are based on the combination of statistical theory nonlinear theory dynamic allocation knowledge discovery models, these methods in the traffic prediction has achieved good effect.

Statistical theory-based methods encompass parametric models, like the historical average model like the historical average model, Kalman filter model, and time series model. Stephanedes initially employed the historical average model in the UTCS in 1981 [1]. Additionally, non-parametric models, such as the KNN and the multiple regression model, have also been utilized.

Kalman filtering model was proposed by Okutani et al. in 1984.The time series models mainly include ARMR and its deformation, Autoregressive Integrated Moving Average model (ARIMA) and so on. In subsequent studies, many models based on ARMA have appeared.

Nonlinear theory-based methods primarily encompass the wavelet analysis model, fractal theory model, and chaos theory model. The wavelet theory model was used earlier in foreign countries, and the earliest one in China was the prediction model based on wavelet analysis and reconstruction proposed by He Guoguang et al. in 2002 [2], and the traffic prediction model based on non-parametric wavelet algorithm proposed by Wang Xiaoyuan et al. in 2005 [3]. Analytical theory was first proposed by Mandelbrot in the 1970s.Chaos theory model was first applied to traffic industry by Disbro and Frame in 1989.

Method based on dynamic traffic assignment, these a few years in the domestic research is more, for example, Hu Ting et al., Beijing Jiaotong University, 2010 [4], Sun Yu et al., Hunan University, 2016 [5], Chen Jianyu et al. 2017, [6] are studied, the dynamic traffic allocation theory proposed by Hu Ting et al. is different from several typical characteristics of static traffic prediction, a macro-urban dynamic network traffic flow allocation model proposed by Sun Yu and a model based on dynamic traffic flow allocation proposed by Chen Jianyu et al. are both analyzed on the influence of traffic on the road network of open blocks.

The methods mainly consist of SVM and ANN. Researchers such as Castro-neto et al. [7] and Jeong et al. [8] proposed effective SVM models for traffic flow prediction in 2008 and 2013, respectively. Zhu Zhengyu [9] and Yang Gang et al. In a study by [10], SVM has been integrated with other algorithms for traffic prediction research in China, where historical data was utilized in ANN to establish an approximate relationship by considering the deviation between the output and actual data.The ANN model requires a large number of training samples to achieve good adaptability without extensive prior knowledge. Early as 1994, Smith et al. [11] applied BP neural network to predict short-term traffic flow, and Jin Yuting et al. [12] In 2014, the successful integration of wavelet transform with neural network was employed to predict short-term traffic flow at intersections. Additionally, in 2017, Cheng Shanying introduced a prediction methodology based on fuzzy neural network, applying clustering techniques, which yielded commendable prediction outcomes [13].

This paper primarily focuses on researching a traffic flow prediction method based on a space-time graph network. Aiming at the problem that it is difficult to capture complex temporal and spatial states in traffic flow data, this paper combines sequential convolution and graph neural network, and introduces attention mechanism to study traffic prediction task. The specific research content is as follows: Aiming at the time correlation between data in traffic flow data set, a time series-based traffic flow prediction model is proposed. In this model, the time-series convolutional network (TCN), which deals with the time correlation of traffic data, introduces the structure of "gate", introducing input and output gates to the TCN network structure enables control over network input and output, so as to predict traffic flow. When compared with the original TCN model and several other time series models such as LSTM and gated recurrent unit (GRU), the prediction model is compared.

2   Traffic Flow Prediction Model Based on Gated TCN

2.1 Model Construction

The model for predicting traffic flow featuring gated TCN concentrates on effectively forecasting lane section flow potential and capturing spatio-temporal traffic flow characteristics. When the input sequence of traffic flow is provided, the time series $X = [x_{t-T}, x_{t-T+1}, \cdots, x_{t-2}, x_{t-1}]$ with the Time_step of T is adopted, and the time series $x_{t-T+1}, x_{t-T+2}, \cdots, x_{t-1}, x_t$ with the time step of $T + 1$ is predicted, namely the output sequence $\widehat{Y} = [\hat{y}_{t-T+1}, \hat{y}_{t-T+2}, \cdots, \hat{y}_{t-2}, \hat{y}_{t-1}]$. Figure 1 illustrates the time step T, which is also known as the backtracking time window.

The model depicted in Fig. 1 comprises four primary components: the input layer, convolution layer, fully connected layer, and output layer. The traffic flow time series X is described as a two-dimensional $M \times N$ matrix, where N represents the number of urban road sensors.

Before reaching the input layer of the model, the two-dimensional matrix must be converted into a three-dimensional matrix to align with the neural network's requirements. This transformation entails applying a sliding time window concept to segment a 2D matrix with dimensions $T \times N$ is generated at each 1 unit time step shift. The sequentially cut $T \times N$ matrices constitute the input, and a three-dimensional matrix of size $P \times T \times N$ is generated to accommodate the model's training sample division, assuming a batch size of P as the model's hyperparameter. This approach ensures that the sequence data X encompasses all original dataset information while enhancing temporal correlation.

After inputting the 3D matrix into the convolution layer, which comprises n time blocks in series, each time block's structure is depicted on the right side of Fig. 1. It shows an improved residual module as its internal structure. As the network deepens, The cavity coefficient (d) for the causal convolution within the time block will experience exponential increase ($d = 2^n$), the output from the residual connection link is employed

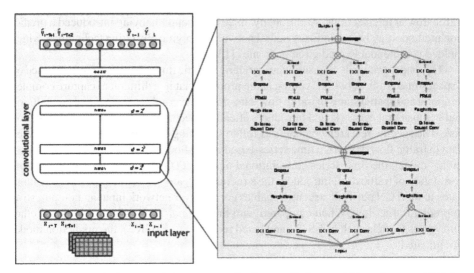

Fig. 1. Schematic diagram of short-term traffic flow prediction model based on gated TCN

as the input for the subsequent time block, completing the convolution operation. This leads to a 2D matrix with dimensions T × N. Afterward, the FC layer linearly reduces the matrix dimensionality, the output layer produce the prediction sequence $\hat{Y}$ with a dimension of N, effectively reducing the repetition rate to 0%.

2.2   Building a Gated TCN Network

In the time series-based traffic flow prediction model, for the time dependence of traffic data, the data is input into gated time convolution network for mining. The gated time convolution network here is inspired by LSTM and adds a new gating mechanism to the time convolution network TCN. In other words, in the expansion convolution module corresponding to each expansion factor, two gating mechanisms are added: one gate controls the input of internal information, and the other controls the processing and output of information.

As shown in Fig. 2, nonlinear gated activation is often used for sequence modeling, which helps the network establish complex interaction patterns. In ordinary TCN, in order to prevent deep network structure from causing gradient disappearance and other problems, a structure similar to residual block in ResNet is adopted to make TCN structure more capable of generalization.

Two gates are added to each one-dimensional convolution module, one of which contains two parallel input modules. The input module contains a 1 × 1 convolution layer, and a sigmoid function is added behind a 1 × 1 convolution layer of one of the input modules, whose range is (0,1), so the value of the input module belongs to (0,1). The output of two parallel input modules is then multiplied together to obtain the entire input gate, this is used to regulate the input of information. The other gate contains two output modules, which contain all the layers from the extended causal convolution to the output 1 × 1 convolution layer, and one of the output modules is followed by the

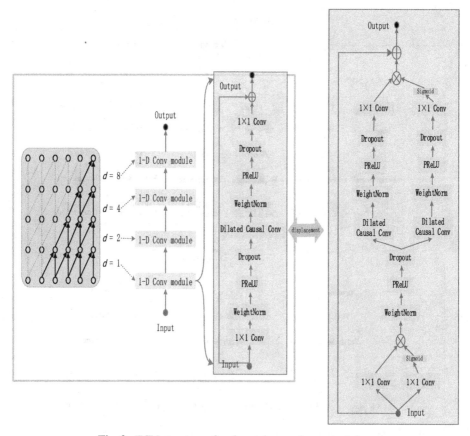

Fig. 2. TCN structure of an input door and an output door

sigmoid function, whose range is (0,1), so the output value belongs to (0,1), and then the outputs of the two parallel output modules are multiplied, the whole output gate is obtained, which is used to control information processing and output.

One prediction model's performance can be improved by integrating independent networks. The most common method is to average the models to reduce performance variance [20]. In Fig. 3, Module B introduces two parallel convolution components into each extended one-dimensional convolution module layer of the gated TCN, as shown in Fig. 2.The initial location is close to the input layer and consists of the 1×1 Conv layer, normalization layer, PReLU, and Dropout layer. Another location near the output encompasses all the remaining layers, such as the dilated causal convolution, PReLU, normalized layer, PReLU, Dropout, and 1x1 Conv layer. The final output of each parallel convolutional component is achieved by averaging the outputs of all unique branches. This integration at both levels aims to minimize the variability within each block.

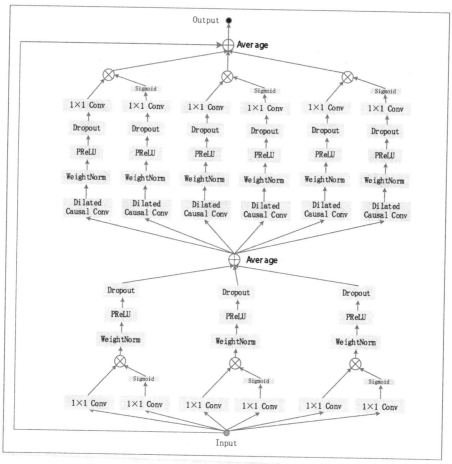

Fig. 3. Structure of a gated TCN with parallel inner convolution module

3 Experiment

In order to verify that the global iteration speed of the improved lightning connection process optimization algorithm combined with Levy's Flight strategy has indeed increased to a certain extent. This section tests the improved lightning search evolutionary algorithm through five classical benchmark functions. These five benchmark functions are unimodal functions. The basic attributes and formulas of the five unimodal functions are shown in Table 1 below. Because the prediction experiment studied in this paper only needs to find the minimum value. In this round of simulation function experiment, the experimental environment adopted is Win10 operating system, Intel Core i7 processor 2.66 Hz, 16 G memory, and the experimental environment is written in Python programming language.

Table 1. The basic properties and specific formulas of the five selected unimodal reference functions

Serial number	Function name	Search scope	Function	Minimum value
F1	Sphere	[0,100]	$f_1(x) = \sum_{i=1}^{n} x_i^2$	0
F2	Sum Different	[-100,100]	$f_2(x) = \sum_{i=1}^{n} \left(\sum_{j=1}^{i} x_j\right)^2$	0
F3	Schewel	[-10,10]	$f_3(x) = \sum_{i=1}^{n} |x_i| + \prod |x_i|$	0
F4	Booth	[-100,100]	$f_4(x) = \max\{|x_i|, 1 \le i \le n\}$	0
F5	Beale	[-30,30]	$f_5(x) = \sum_{i=1}^{n-1}[100\left(x_{i+1} - x_i^2\right)^2 + (x_i - 1)^2]$	0

The experiment compares the classical lightning connection process algorithm with the lightning connection algorithm combined utilizing Levy's flight, as suggested in this chapter. The experimental findings are detailed in the following Table 2.

The experimental results indicate that the optimization outcomes of the two algorithms are comparable in terms of the optimal value, average value and variance. Specifically, Levy-LAPO has a weak advantage in the four standard functions of F1, F2, F3 and F4, and the results of the two algorithms are close in the standard function of F5 and F9. It can be said that in the optimization search ability of unimodal function, the optimization performance of Levy-LAPO is similar to that of classical LAPO algorithm, and the gap between them is within the error range, but Levy-LAPO algorithm should have a better convergence speed.

Table 2. The basic properties and specific formulas of the five selected unimodal reference functions

Function serial number	Dimension	Algorithm	Optimal value	Average value	Variance
F1	2	LAPO	5.75E-25	2.54E-21	5.41E-21
		Levy-LAPO	2.69E-26	9.09E-23	1.34E-22
F2	2	LAPO	2.17E-12	6.02E-09	2.40E-08
		Levy-LAPO	1.70E-13	6.63E-10	1.83E-09
F3	2	LAPO	0.00490267	0.00179973	0.00347591
		Levy-LAPO	1.02E-07	0.002051	0.00173045
F4	2	LAPO	4.02E-13	3.96E-11	2.13E-10
		Levy-LAPO	7.23E-16	6.14E-12	1.61E-11
F5	2	LAPO	4.58E-06	1.28E-06	1.63E-06
		Levy-LAPO	3.76E-08	1.11E-06	1.49E-06

Acknowledgment. This work is funded by the National Natural Science Foundation of China under Grant No. 61772180, the Key R & D plan of Hubei Province (2020BHB004, 2020BAB012).

References

1. Stephanedes, Y.J., Michalopoulos, P.G., Plum, R.A.: Improved estimation of traffic flow for real-time control (discussion and losure). Transportation Research Record (1981)
2. He, G., Ma, S., Li, Y.: A short-term traffic flow prediction method based on wavelet decomposition and reconstruction. Syst. Eng. Theo. Pract. 09, 101–106+131 (2002)
3. Wang Xiaoyuan, W., Lei, Z.K., Jinglei, Z.: Nonparametric wavelet algorithm for traffic flow prediction. Syst. Eng. **10**, 44–47 (2005)
4. Hu, T., Yu, L., Zhao, N.: A review of dynamic traffic allocation theory. Traffic Standards **09**, 6–10 (2010)
5. Sun, Y.: Urban Dynamic Traffic Flow Allocation Model and Algorithm. Hunan University (2016)
6. Chen, J., Zhao, A., Li, H., et al.: Traffic analysis of road network based on dynamic traffic flow allocation model. China Science and Technology Paper Online Quality Paper, vol. 10, no. 19, pp. 2151–2162 (2017)
7. Castro-Neto, M., Jeong, Y.S., Jeong, M.K., et al.: Online-SVR for short-term traffic flow prediction under typical and atypical traffic conditions
8. Jeong, Y.S., Byon, Y.J., Castro-Neto, M.M., et al.: Supervised Weighting-Online Learning Algorithm for Short-Term Traffic Flow Prediction
9. Zhu, Z., Liu, L., Cui, M.: A short-time traffic flow prediction model combining SVM and kalman filter. Comp. Sci. **40**(10), 248–251+278 (2013)
10. Yang, G., Wang, L., Dai, L., Xu, F.: Adaptive particle swarm optimization weights LS - SVM traffic flow prediction [J]. Journal of control engineering **24**(9), 1838–1843 (2017). https://doi.org/10.14107/j.carolcarrollnkiKZGC.D5.0210
11. Smith, B.L., Demetsky, M.J.: Short-term traffic flow prediction: neural network approach
12. Jin, Y., Yu, L.: Short-term traffic flow prediction based on wavelet neural network. J. Transp. Sci. Technol. Econ. 01, 82–86 (2014). https://doi.org/10.19348/j.carolcarrollnkiissn1008-5696.2014.01.023
13. Cheng, S.: Short-term traffic flow prediction method based on fuzzy neural network study. Comp. Measure. Control **25**(8), 155–158 (2017). https://doi.org/10.16526/j.carolcarrollnki.11-4762/tp.2017.08.040

Hotspot Prediction Based on Temporal Characteristics

Qingwu Tong[✉], Jingjing Zheng, and Chongxi Zhao

Wuhan Fiberhome Technical Services Co., Ltd., Wuhan 430068, China
tongqw@fiberhome.com

Abstract. Nowadays, with the expanding population and city size, urban crime rate control will be a very important direction for the integration of artificial intelligence and urban police governance, and the prediction of the number of regional hotspots is an effective crime prevention method. Based on the real dataset of a city, we hope to improve the prediction effect of crime hotspots and make analysis and prediction feasibility judgments from the perspective of data analysis. First, the dataset was pre-processed and filtered, and then analyzed from the spatial and temporal perspectives to further judge the feasibility of prediction. From a non-spatial perspective, the effect of adding covariates on the prediction of urban crime hotspots was explored. First, a map was drawn based on the distribution of hotspots, the map was divided into a grid, and the grid information was classified into four categories by clustering, and then selected covariates were added to the model for experiments. This study extends the prediction range in terms of temporal characteristics. The differential integrated moving average autoregressive model (ARIMA) is commonly used for time series forecasting, but it is more suitable for dealing with linear data. The long short-term memory neural network (LSTM) has a strong advantage in dealing with nonlinear data. We construct a combined ARIMA-LSTM model. It can fully exploit the data information and improve prediction accuracy. The results show that the combined ARIMA-LSTM model can predict the property crime in a district of the city better than the single ARIMA model and LSTM model, and the combined model can better fit the actual trend of the cases.

Keywords: Hotspot Prediction · Machine Learning · temporal features · Data transfer

1 Introduction

The prediction of the number of regional hotspots is an effective crime prevention method and is a hotspot of concern for smart cities and smart policing [1], and good prevention can greatly enhance police resources and people's social stability. Crime prediction can use existing crime data records, using machine learning, to build a model that can make reasonable inferences and analysis of the number of upcoming crime incidents within a certain time frame in the future, so that the police can be deployed in advance to prevent and control deployment, to improve the efficiency of the police while safeguarding the social environment.

© The Author(s), under exclusive license to Springer Nature Singapore Pte Ltd. 2024
W. Hong and G. Kanaparan (Eds.): ICCSE 2023, CCIS 2023, pp. 347–356, 2024.
https://doi.org/10.1007/978-981-97-0730-0_31

Crime hotspot prediction is based on historical crime records to predict the number of hotspots or areas in the next period of time, is an application of data analysis in predictive policing, the earliest crime mapping software developed in the United States, CrimeStat, can be used to mark hotspot areas, the purpose is to help the police to fight crime. Nowadays, the technology of predicting crime hotspots in police forecasting is gradually moving closer to big data and artificial intelligence.

Data analysis is the further exploration and interpretation of data through existing data, with clear target groups, to turn the data into valid information. The difference between data mining and data analysis is that data mining is a discovery process that requires the use of algorithms in order to realise the hidden information value of the data. Nowadays, data analysis is of great value in the era of big data, not only in terms of its value but also as a decisive factor in the decision-making process [2, 3]. Data analysis in crime prediction involves a great deal of data pre-processing, the purpose of which is to normalise the data, use predictive models, provide the appropriate data results and follow up on the results. In the field of public security, the overall trend of future crime hotspots and recidivism populations can be predicted with the help of data analysis. This decision-making information can provide support for smart city management and is of great importance for social security management.

The growth of data volume is accompanied by the development of the information age. At this stage, research in the field of crime hotspot prediction is inseparable from the support of data analysis [4], machine learning and deep learning methods, etc. [5]. The research on crime hotspot prediction can make the predictive policing model largely applicable to the actual requirements of police work, and thus bring the value of data into play to prospectively control potential dangerous people, hotspot areas or case trends in the future. This allows for scientific guidance on the deployment of police operations, advance prevention and control, and optimises police effectiveness.

Considering that some of the crime data sets are collected and collated in a chronological order [6], the data sets have certain temporal characteristics, so there may be certain correlation between the data, and the analysis of temporal characteristics reveals that there is a regularity in the temporal characteristics of the cases and has proved that prediction from a temporal perspective is feasible. Therefore, in the process of analysing and modelling the dataset, the dataset can be considered as a time series, taking into account the fact that the occurrence of the number of crime hotspots is characterised by certain temporal characteristics [7].

2   The Algorithms

2.1   Algorithm Improvement - Construction of a Hybrid ARIMA-LSTM Model

The strength of the ARIMA model for time series processing lies in its ability to fit linear data, while the LSTM has advantages for non-linear time series prediction, and the LSTM can make up for the shortcomings of the ARIMA model. Therefore, by combining ARIMA and LSTM [17], the strengths of each model can be exploited to make full use of the data and thus greatly improve the prediction efficiency and accuracy. At this stage, some researchers have analysed the spatio-temporal analysis of crime in India by combining the kernel density and ARIMA models, and the final prediction results show that the combined model has a certain effect on the improvement of accuracy [16]. A number of researchers have purposefully attempted to combine linear and non-linear models and found that the resulting hybrid model not only retains the advantages of the linear model but also retains the advantages of the non-linear model and the prediction results even have substitutes, inferring that there is some feasibility in using a combination of models for prediction, so this section combines the ARIMA model with the LSTM model to investigate the prediction accuracy of the X district of H The change in the accuracy of the time series related predictions is used to explore the predictive effect of crime hotspots in H city X, thus providing scientific guidance for the predictive policing of H city from a chronological column perspective.

Building ARIMA-LSTM Hybrid Model Ideas
The steps in the construction of the hybrid model are shown in Fig. 1.

This section analyses the number of crimes in area X of city H in a temporal perspective in order to make predictions that will help to improve the efficiency of the use of police resources. The prediction of the number of crimes in the region can be done using time series to predict the next stage of development through its own trend, but for non-linear time series will be strained, for the non-linear part of the study, the LSTM model has good prediction results due to its own learning ability and the processing ability of non-linear data, and in turn, because of these advantages of LSTM, it has LSTM has been used by many researchers to deal with non-linear time series prediction problems. Therefore, LSTM can play a good complementary role to the weaknesses of time series. Therefore, this section proposes a hybrid approach to construct an ARIMA-LSTM model. The model diagram is shown in Fig. 2, which combines the respective strengths of the ARIMA model and the LSTM model to fully exploit the linear and non-linear parts of the fitted crime dataset of H city X, thus achieving an improvement in the prediction accuracy of the number of crimes in H city X. This is an improvement to the ARIMA model.

For this experiment, although the traditional combination model for the final model is weighted and superimposed, it is not applicable to the property case data of X district in H city, which has complex time series variation, so the traditional approach is differentiated and the hybrid model in this chapter is constructed as follows: Step 1: construct an ARIMA model based on the characteristics of the data and obtain the linear part of the data set through experimentation The first step is to construct an ARIMA model based on the characteristics of the data and experimentally obtain the predicted and residual values of the linear part of the data set; the second step is to construct an LSTM model using the characteristics of the obtained residual data to obtain the predicted values of the non-linear part; the third step is to use the predicted values obtained in the first two steps to explore the LSTM model and obtain the final predicted values.

2.2   Combined ARIMA-LSTM Model Modelling

ARIMA Model Modelling.
According to the construction process of ARIMA-LSTM model, the ARIMA model in ARIMA-LSTM model is constructed first.

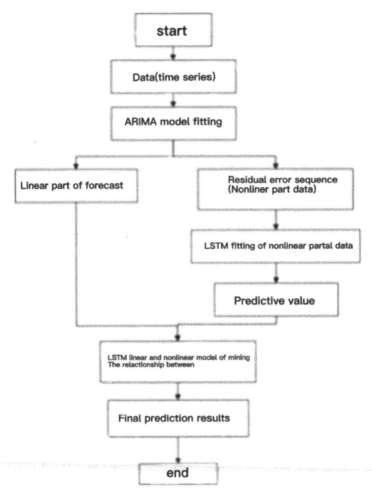

Fig. 1. Combined ARIMA-LSTM model construction

The principles of the RIMA model are combined with the actual situation of the data set for modelling. The modelling process of the ARIMA model is: step one: the series smoothness test, in order to determine the parameter d by differencing; step two: the model fixing order, in order to confirm the parameters p and q; step three: the parameters p, d and q are used in the model. The first two steps of modelling have basically identified the three parameters p, d and q needed for the model. The purpose of the third step is to assess the actual predictive effect of the model, if it passes the white noise test, then it means that the residuals of the series only have random values there is no potential linear relationship information to be mined, further explanation is that the model has been able to fit the original time series well and no subsequent mining is needed [18]. The modelling process of the ARIMA model is shown in Fig. 2.

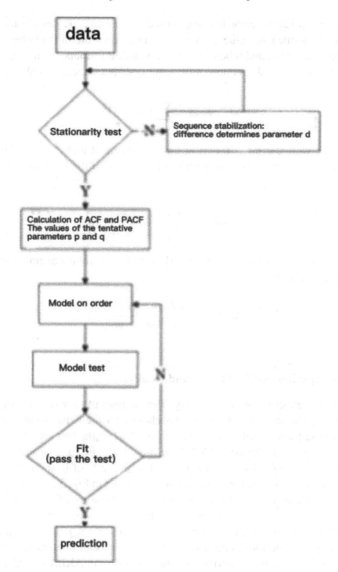

Fig. 2. ARIMA model construction process

3   Experiment

3.1   Evaluation Criteria

Among the evaluation criteria commonly used in the assessment of regression forecasts [26], the Root Mean Squared Error (RMSE), Mean Absolute Percentage Error (MAPE) and Mean Absolute Error (MAE) [27, 28] are chosen, where the predicted value is represented by x and the actual value is represented by y. These are described below.

The root mean square error is usually used to measure the deviation between the observed value and the true value, so it is an accurate measure of the unbiased nature of the measured time series, and is better for forecasting performance as its value is smaller, which can indicate a low dispersion of the error distribution, expressed as in Eq:

$$RMSE = \frac{1}{n} \sum_{i=1}^{n} (x_i - y_i)^2 \tag{1}$$

The mean absolute error is the most basic assessment metric commonly used and gives a good indication of the true picture of the error in the forecast values, with an expression such as Eq:

$$MAE = \frac{1}{n} \sum_{i=1}^{n} |x_i - y_i| \tag{2}$$

The mean absolute percentage error is designed to be robust against the mean with an expression such as Eq:

$$MAPE = \frac{100}{n} \sum_{i=1}^{n} |\frac{y_i - x_i}{y_i}| \tag{3}$$

3.2 Model Experimental Validation and Results

In this part of the experiment, the property crime dataset of City H, District X, selected after conducting the analytical process, was chosen for the experiment, using the data from 2018 as the training set and the data from 2019 as the test set. According to the construction diagram of the ARIMA-LSTM model, the first part was fitted using the ARIMA model, the ARIMA model was fitted to the test set in the dataset i.e. to the 2019 crime data in the dataset, and the results are shown in Fig. 3 in Figure a and Figure b. Figure a represents the fit of the training set where the red line represents the test set results, and Figure b represents the fit of the test set where the red represents the predicted results and the blue lines in both plots represent the real data situation.

By fitting, the prediction results shown are mainly concentrated in the smooth phase, and the fit for the peak is not perfect, mainly because the ARIMA model has certain advantages for the smooth series fitting. The residual series is obtained by subtracting the original series and the prediction results of ARIMA, and the visual display of the residual results is shown in Fig. 4.

By analysing the residuals of the model, it can be seen from Fig. 12 that the residuals have a similar distribution to the original series, which can indicate that the residuals have the potential to be further explored and analysed, and this result reflects the disadvantage of the ARIMA model from the side, i.e. the model has a weakness for non-linear data, i.e. the fit is not complete.

The parameters of the LSTM were selected with reference to the parameters of the LSTM modelling in the previous section, and the fit of the LSTM model to the residual series is shown in Fig. 5.

(a)   Training set fit

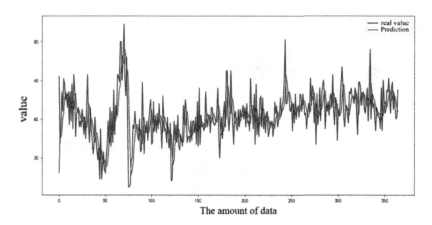

(b)   Test set fit

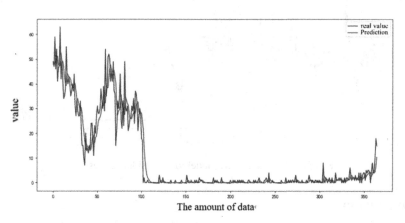

Fig. 3. Presentation of the data fit

The various coloured lines in Fig. 5 have their own meanings, indicating the true direction, the training results and the test results respectively. The visualisation of the data shows that the LSTM model is better than the ARIMA model for fitting the peaks, and the final results still need to be further processed with reference to the construction steps of the combined model.

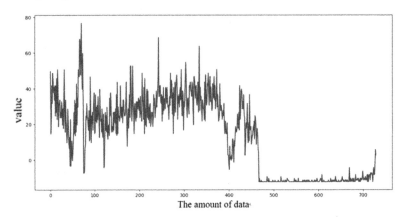

Fig. 4. Residuals between true and predicted values

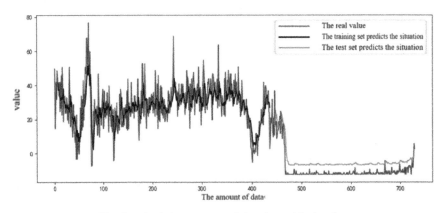

Fig. 5. Fit of the LSTM model to the residual series

4 Conclusion

In this chapter, the research perspective of forecasting starts from the temporal characteristics of the data, using the respective advantages of ARIMA and LSTM models and combining the characteristics of the data set to develop the description and experiments. The combination of the ARIMA model and the LSTM model is able to make full use of the linear and non-linear parts of the time series in the dataset to improve the prediction accuracy.

References

1. ToppiReddy, H.K.R., Saini, B., Mahajan, G.: Crime prediction & monitoring framework based on spatial analysis. Procedia Comput. Sci. **132**, 696–705 (2018)
2. Browning, C.R., Byron, R.A., Calder, C.A., et al.: Commercial density, residential concentration, and crime: land use patterns and violence in neighborhood context. J. Res. Crime Delinq.Delinq. **47**(3), 329–357 (2015)

3. Mohler, G.O., Short, M.B., Malinowski, S., et al.: Randomized controlled field trials of predictive policing. J. Am. Stat. Assoc. **110**(512), 00 (2015)
4. Priya, S.S., Gupta, L.: Predicting the future in time series using auto regressive linear regression modelling. In: Twelfth International Conference on Wireless and Optical Communications Networks, pp. 1–4 (2015)
5. Wang, Y., Ge, L., Li, S., Chang, F.: Deep temporal multi-graph convolutional network for crime prediction. In: Dobbie, G., Frank, U., Kappel, G., Liddle, S.W., Mayr, H.C. (eds.) ER 2020. LNCS, vol. 12400, pp. 525–538. Springer, Cham (2020). https://doi.org/10.1007/978-3-030-62522-1_39
6. Yi, F., Yu, Z., Zhuang, F., et al.: Neural network based continuous conditional random field for fine-grained crime prediction. In: IJCAI, pp. 4157–4163 (2019)
7. Dash, S.K., Safro, I., Srinivasamurthy, R.S.: Spatio-temporal prediction of crimes using network analytic approach. In: 2018 IEEE International Conference on Big Data (Big Data), pp. 1912–1917. IEEE (2018)
8. Lim, S., Kim, S.J., Park, Y.J., Kwon, N.: A deep learning-based time series model with missing value handling techniques to predict various types of liquid cargo traffic. Expert Syst. Appl. **184** (2021)
9. Manojkumar, G., Suresh Kumar, G.: Numerical investigations on a geothermal reservoir using fully coupled thermo-hydro-geomechanics with integrated RSM-machine learning and ARIMA models. Geothermics **96** (2021)
10. Im, C.-K., Youn, S.-K.: The generation of 3D trimmed elements for NURBS-based isogeometric analysis. Int. J. Comput. Methods **15**(7) (2018)
11. Desai Prathamesh, S.: News sentiment informed time-series analyzing AI (SITALA) to curb the spread of COVID-19 in Houston. Expert Syst. Appl. **180** (2021)
12. Lu, M., Xu, P., Chen, W., Yang, J., Zhao, X.: SRSF signal perception matrix based on auto-correlation function optimization method. J. Radio Sci. J. **4**(4), 539–546 (2021). https://doi.org/10.13443/j.carolcarrolljors.2020040805
13. Hemachandran, K., Shubham, T., Preetha, M.G., Parveen, S., Utku, K.: Bayesian Reasoning and Gaussian Processes for Machine Learning Applications. CRC Press, Hoboken, 01 Nov 2021
14. PérezSánchez, B., González, M., Perea, C., LópezEspín, J.J.: A new computational method for estimating simultaneous equations models using entropy as a parameter criteria. Mathematics **9**(7) (2021)
15. Zhang, X.: Research on improved GM (1, 1) Load forecasting model based on numerical analysis. Taiyuan University of Technology (2012)
16. Boppuru, P.R., Ramesha, K.: Spatio-temporal crime analysis using KDE and ARIMA models in the indian context. Int. J. Digit. Crime Forensics (IJDCF) **12**(4), 1–19 (2020)
17. Peng, Z., Dang, J., Unoki, M., Akagi, M.: Multi-resolution modulation-filtered cochleagram feature for LSTM-based dimensional emotion recognition from speech. Neural Netw. **140** (2021)
18. Víctor, S.: Computing the expected Markov reward rates with stationarity detection and relative error control. Methodol. Comput. Appl. Probab. **19**(2) (2017)
19. Ilham, U., Aina, M., Anny, K.S.: Optimization of ARIMA forecasting model using firefly algorithm. IJCCS (Indonesian J. Comput. Cybern. Syst. **13**(2) (2019)
20. Jones, H.F.: Comment on Solvable model of bound states in the continuum (BIC) in on dimension. Physica Scripta **96**(8) (2021)
21. Tibbs, J., et al.: KERA: analysis tool for multi-process, multi-state single-molecule data. Nucleic Acids Res. **49**(9) (2021)
22. Inthiyaz, S., Muzammil, P.M., Siva Kumar, M., Sri Sai Srija, J., Tarun, S.M., Amruth, V.V.: Facial expression recognition using KERAS. J. Phys. Conf. Ser. **1804**(1) (2021). Juan, M.,

Salvador, P.: An exact dynamic programming approach to segmented isotonic regression. Omega (2021, prepublish)

23. Arvind Kumar, T.: Deep Learning and Its Applications. Nova Science Publishers, Inc. (2021)
24. Kim, K.S., Choi, Y.S.: HyAdamC: a new Adam-based hybrid optimization algorithm for convolution neural networks. Sensors **21**(12) (2021)
25. Yijun, W., Pengyu, Z., Wenya, Z.: An optimization strategy based on hybrid algorithm of Adam and SGD. In: Proceedings of 2018 2nd International Conference on Electronic Information Technology and Computer Engineering (EITCE 2018), pp. 630–633 (2018)
26. Geng, X., Xu, W., Yin, Y.: Research on database parameters tuning method based on embedded device. J. Phys. Conf. Ser. **1873**(1) (2021)
27. Jing, X., Xu, J.: Improved protein model quality assessment by integrating sequential and pairwise features using deep learning. Bioinformatics (Oxford, England) (2020)
28. Laura, M.S., Tessa, L.J.: models to examine the validity of cluster-level factor structure using individual-level data. Adv. Methods Pract. Psychol. Sci. **2**(3) (2019)
29. Gu, C., et al.: Transformer bushing temperature measurement model based on infrared temperature measurement. In: Proceedings of 2019 2nd International Conference on Intelligent Systems Research and Mechatronics Engineering (ISRME 2019), pp. 24–30. Francis Academic Press (2019)
30. Stavelin, A.K., Madhu, B., Balasubramanian, S., Sahana, C.: A review on the comparison of box Jenkins ARIMA and LSTM of deep learning. J. Trend Sci. Res. Dev. **5**(3) (2021)

Governance Framework and Legal Regulation of Data Security

Yuzhuo Zou[1] and Weizhao Yang[2(✉)]

[1] Law School, Institute of Law and Economic Development, Guangdong University of Finance and Economics, Guangzhou, China
[2] Bank of Jiangsu Co., Ltd., Hangzhou Branch, Nanjing, China
weizhaoyang@qq.com

Abstract. Under the appearance of the vigorous development of the current data industry, there is a chaotic development pattern. The difficulty of exercising the right of individual data, the internal and external hidden dangers of digital platform and the problem between sharing and protection of public data are hindering its further development. Explore the causes of data security problems in China from the data dimension, individual dimension, platform dimension and technical dimension, build a data security governance framework with the combination of protection and sharing, and give suggestions on legal regulation. The model of cooperative governance, hierarchical network structure, public data pool, combination of public interest litigation and class action, and industrial regulation is adopted to realize the protection of personal information, promote data sharing, broaden relief channels and benign development of the industry.

Keywords: Personal Data · Data Security · Data Sharing

1 Question Raised

In early 2020, covid-19 pneumonia was spreading globally, the world economy was facing deep recession, the trend of "anti globalization" was surging, trade protectionism was rising, and the process of economic globalization was obviously blocked. Compared with commodities and capital, global flows are blocked. The new round of globalization driven by digitization maintains high-speed growth and reshapes the world pattern. The Fifth Plenary Session of the 19th CPC Central Committee proposed to "accelerate digital development. Develop the digital economy, promote digital industrialization and industrial digitization, promote the deep integration of the digital economy and the real economy, and create a digital industrial cluster with international competitiveness. Strengthen the construction of digital society and digital government, and improve the digital intelligence level of public services and social governance". The outline of the 14th

This paper is part of 2023 Foshan Philosophy and Social Science Planning Project: Xi Jinping's Rule of Law Thought on the Basic Essentials and Practice of the Trial Management System (2023-GJ070).

five year plan further proposes to accelerate digital development and build a digital China. Accelerate the construction of digital economy, digital society and digital government, and drive the transformation of production mode, lifestyle and governance mode with digital transformation as a whole. Based on this, this paper intends to take data security protection as the research object, discuss the current situation of the development of data industry, summarize the problems of data security, explore the approach of data protection, put forward the Legal Countermeasures of data security governance, and try to complete the thinking on the issues of data development and security protection.

2 Data Development and Current Situation of Date Security Protection

2.1 The Current Situation of Data Development: Vigorous and Disordered

China's data industry is at the forefront of the world in scale and growth. Even among the low economic situation of the new epidemic, China's digital economy industry will still maintain a vigorous development trend in 2020, reaching 3.92 billion yuan, an increase of 3.3 trillion yuan compared with the previous year, accounting for 38.6% of GDP, and the growth rate of digital economy is more than three times of that of the same period. Compared with the development of foreign data industry, China's data industry started late, but it came back and forth. The digital economy grew rapidly and China ranked the top ten in the world. Data industry has been integrated into all aspects of social politics, economy and culture development, and is closely related to our life. In politics, we should build digital government, promote intelligent operation, and the development of data industry will promote the modernization of national governance system and governance capability. During the epidemic prevention and control, the application of health code, travel code and other information technology greatly promoted the improvement of administrative management ability. Big data, cloud computing, artificial intelligence and Internet of things are widely used in epidemic trend research and judgment, real-time analysis of human flow, risk personnel identification, anti epidemic material allocation, virus gene detection and other fields, and in the construction of people's health protection network, It plays an irreplaceable role in coordinating epidemic prevention and control and economic and social development. In the aspect of economic development, data becomes the basic element in all fields. The production structure optimization is realized through data analysis and adjustment of production factors input in enterprises, and the development strategy is improved by external analysis of market change trend. In the development of culture, data analysis provides a lot of material and immediate feedback for cultural industry, and the development of data industry promotes the spread of culture.

Behind the booming development of data industry, it is the development mode of spontaneous flow of production factors under market allocation. It fully promotes economic growth, and disorderly and wilful development also brings many problems. In terms of data collection, the "overlord clause" and the act of over power collection without personal consent or compulsory authorization violate the citizens' information rights, privacy and right to know, and the use of the collected data and the further direction of data are unclear. In terms of data storage and use, there is no strict supervision and unified standards to commercialize personal data. Personal data used as feedback and improvement samples for product use are sold as commodities directly, (Stacy-Ann[1])Internet fraud and telecommunication fraud are caused. In the stage of data industry development exploration, when the data rights are not clear, enterprises and platforms actively promote the scale and progress of data industry development in order to collect, analyze and use data for their own development, and play a positive role. But the development volume of data industry has reached a certain scale, and the control of data by enterprises and platforms has seriously hindered the further development of data industry. Between the platform and consumers, the platform limits the basic rights of citizens, the independent decision-making rights of consumers and the individual rights and competitive interests of consumers in three stages: information collection, specific push and individual pricing, respectively, by means of data deviation, selection restriction and price discrimination (Li[2]).

2.2 Data Security Protection Status

Traditional data security refers to the static risk of data security, which mainly shows that the integrity, confidentiality and availability of data content are destroyed by using network system vulnerabilities. Since the human society entered the digital economy era, the maximization of data value often depends on the collection, flow, processing and analysis of a large number of diverse data. The flow data intensive activities involve more diverse governance subjects, more diverse interests demands, more rich governance issues, and the connotation and extension of data security concepts are constantly expanding Extension.

The continuous development of data technology and its application intensifies the difficulty of defining data and its security. The current data security supervision and management system is not clear, the data security legislation is not perfect, and the legal responsibility provisions, implementation rules and supporting systems are not perfect, which is not conducive to the definition of legal responsibility and the implementation of legal responsibility, and it is difficult to effectively resolve data security risks. On the other hand, the lack of operability of data security protection rules makes government law enforcement and enterprise law-abiding in a realistic dilemma. There are 12386 relevant cases searched on the "magic weapon of Peking University" only with the "crime of infringing on citizens' personal information" as the cause of action, while infringing on citizens' personal information is only the tip of the iceberg of data security. Data security also involves intellectual property rights, unfair competition, fraud, extortion and other issues (Fig. 1).

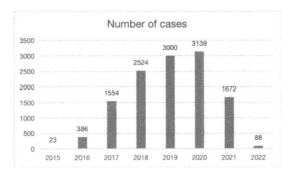

Fig. 1. Number of cases

3   Summary of Data Security Problems in China

3.1   Exercise Dilemma of Individual Data

Formalization of "informed consent" in individual data collection. The informed consent rule in the personal information protection law, also known as the "informed consent rule", means that any organization and individual should inform the information subject, that is, the natural person whose personal information is processed, and can carry out corresponding personal information processing activities after obtaining consent, otherwise such processing behavior is illegal, unless otherwise provided by law (Wang[3]) However, even if the personal information processor (application developer) makes an obvious prompt on the authorization consent interface, consumers will not read the authorization instructions carefully and are unable to interpret them professionally due to their indifference to personal rights and legal knowledge reserve. This leads to the situation that the form complies with the "informed consent rules", and in essence, consumers are not aware of the content of the authorized consent, the scope and object of the collected data, and the purpose of use. The information processor has made a detailed announcement, and in contrast, consumers have only vague and general authorization consciousness. The reason for this phenomenon lies in the failure of personal information processors to write a notice in a simple and easy way, or it may be that personal information processing intends to set up obstacles for consumers to fully understand the authorization. However, the majority of the reasons are that consumers' awareness of rights is indifferent and the convenience of using it at the cost of knowing is the most important reason. In addition, app will use authorization as a precondition for the use of this situation.

3.2   The Internal and External Hidden Dangers of Digital Platform

The data platform collects large amount of data based on user authorization, and the platform has its own technical advantages. Platform operators steal data for profit, which is very hidden and harmful. The platform operators' infringement on users mainly includes the arbitrary use of data, unclear direction of use and algorithm discrimination. As mentioned above, the arbitrary use of data is focused on collecting user personal data without the consent of the data subject or beyond the scope of the subject consent, and requesting permission beyond the necessary limit of application to obtain more personal data for some reason. The algorithm discrimination of users is embodied in the personalized pricing form represented by "big data discriminatory pricing", Through the precise "user portrait" of big data and algorithm, the economic benefits can be maximized in a hidden way. The damage to Individual users is small but the comprehensive benefit volume of the platform is huge. The number of platform practitioners in China is large, and the proportion of labor force is high. However, compared with the protection of the interests of traditional industry workers, the interests of the large emerging platform practitioners are ignored. Due to the particularity of platform employment, the existing labor law and judicial practice are difficult to provide effective protection for platform practitioners (Xie[4]) The operator's infringement of platform practitioners' interests is in a state of continuous deepening.

As a typical organization form and business model of digital economy, digital platform has not been supervised and managed in the process of rapid development and rapid expansion, which has resulted in serious competition problems and monopoly trend. Some of the digital platforms which were established earlier and have strong strength have accumulated the technical advantages, data volume and capital advantages far beyond the competitors, and threaten the market competition order through obvious network effect.

3.3   The Dilemma Between Sharing and Protecting Public Data

The public authority has a huge amount of data. Its public attribute determines that the security protection of data needs to seek a best balance between information sharing and privacy protection. It can not only ensure that the privacy of individuals, enterprises and government secrets are not leaked, but also promote social and economic development through the opening and opening of data.

4   Governance Framework and Legal Regulation of Data Security

4.1   Building a Governance Framework for Data Security: Protection and Sharing Go Hand in Hand

For the personal control mode of personal information data, there are some problems such as the limitation of consent mechanism and the lack of right relief. It can not realize the protection of information data well, but it has gradually alienated into absolute control crisis. As a response to this problem, there is a new personal information protection idea in academic circles, namely privacy by design (product regulation theory).The theory of product regulation can make up for the deficiency of personal control and has practical feasibility, but it still faces some challenges in theory and practice. In the era of big data and information, the protection of information data has become a public problem. As a technology design which will have a profound impact on society, it should be made by public decision-making rather than private rights design. From the main level, in the blank area of legal regulation, the rules of products have been set as the law of the Internet world to some extent, and the data platform is obviously not comparable with the legislature. The cooperative governance model can integrate the advantages of both, and advocate the common use of formal and informal systems, and mainly by consultation. In the cooperative governance model, in addition to order and control, the government is also responsible for forming linkage mechanism with other social departments, and participating in the cooperative governance mode combining non-governmental organizations and civil forces.

4.2 Information Data Sharing: Public Data Pool

The public data pool needs to be built step by step. Firstly, the primary data sharing platform should be built in the people's government and public security law systems to realize smooth data exchange among departments and integrate departmental data; Secondly, the sub data sharing platform is built to realize the cross departmental data sharing and exchange among regions, integrates the data information held by the public authority in the region, and develops the data in depth guided by regional development; Finally, the joint region will build the ultimate data sharing platform to realize national data sharing. The construction of regional level three-level data sharing platform is not one-way construction but three-dimensional data sharing platform. The hierarchical network construction mode can significantly reduce the technical difficulty of platform construction, and also build security protection system according to the level. Each platform is relatively unified and independent, and unified from data sharing independent of security protection, integrating departments. It is feasible to construct regional forces and effectively disperse the risk of out of control.

4.3 Class Action System

For the legal regulation of cooperative governance mode, when the public interest litigation mechanism for personal information protection has not been fully implemented, the class action system can be used as its supplementary mechanism to give full play to the power of social subjects (lawyers) to exercise right relief. In the United States, class action has developed to protect vulnerable individuals who lack equality between the parties to the contract. Class action often appears in disputes based on consumer contract. Under the class action system led by law firms, it can not only deter the data platform from huge compensation, but also implement the compensation for victims. Law firms actively advocate that in the case of class action, the data platform will spontaneously strengthen the protection of information data in order to avoid high compensation.

5   Conclusion

Data security is a macro concept, and the protection and utilization of data is also a complex dynamic process. In essence, the diversity of the stakeholders involved and the complexity of the specific interest forms are the real reasons for the difficulty of data security protection. On the one hand, the scope and form of data utilization are expanding with the development of technology, and the scene of data application is also constantly enriched, which makes the original connotation of data protection expand. On the other hand, frequent data security issues awaken people's awareness of data security, and the separation of worry consciousness and reality will aggravate people's irrational thinking about data security. To solve the problem of data security, we should expand the channels of data legal access and utilization, regulate the illegal use of data, and promote the development of data industry while protecting data security.

References

1. Elvy, S.-A.: Commodifying Consumer Data in the Era of the Internet of Things, 59 B.C. L. REV. **423** (2018); In: CONFERENCE 2016, LNCS, vol. 9999, pp. 1–13. Springer, Heidelberg (2016)
2. Li, D.: Algorithm discrimination against consumers: behavior mechanism, profit and loss definition and coordination mechanism. J. Shanghai Univ. Finance Econ. (2) (2021)
3. Wang, L., Cheng, X., Zhu, H.: Interpretation of personality rights in the civil code of the people's Republic of China. China Legal Publishing House (2020)
4. Xie, Z.: Legislative approach to the protection of labor rights and interests of platform employment. Chin. Foreign Law (1) (2022)

Design of Urban Smart Parking Management System Based on Credit System

Ruoxi Wang[✉] and Jingjing Zheng

Wuhan Fiberhome Technical Services Co., Ltd., Wuhan 430205, China
{rxwang,jjzheng}@fiberhome.com

Abstract. With the rapid development of national economy, the increase of the number of vehicles and the shortage of parking resources has become the main contradiction of urban parking in China, and the problem of "difficult parking" in cities is becoming more and more serious. Under the joint action of "Internet plus" and sharing economy, "shared parking" comes into being. Shared parking is a solution to the problem of "difficult parking" in cities with multi-party participation and win-win situation, rather than a "single-player game". This paper designed a set of urban intelligent parking management system based on credit system, through the upgrade of the parking lot, parking spaces comprehensive sharing as core business applications, solves the contradiction of large gap of parking spaces, the high vacancy rate of parking spaces,, low utilization rate of resources in advanced technical means to achieve the parking spaces of fine management, achieve the purpose of the urban parking level resource sharing.

Keywords: Credit System · Smart Parking · Shared Parking

1 Introduction

With the rapid development of national economy, vehicle ownership is rising in China. It has become the main contradiction of urban parking in China between the increasing number of vehicles and the shortage of parking resources, and this contradiction is worsening, becoming a pain point of many cities [2]. The problem of "difficult parking" in cities is becoming more and more serious. Increasing the supply of parking spaces is the most direct way to solve the parking problem. The parking gap rate in China is more than 50%, and the average vacancy rate is 51.3%. Existing parking Spaces are not fully utilized, resulting in a serious waste of resources.

How to improve the use efficiency of parking resources to alleviate the problem of "parking difficulty" has become a hot research direction. "Internet+" city smart parking mode is, in the era of "Internet+" through the internet related technologies applied to the traditional parking scenario, to integrate urban parking resources relying on mobile internet, big data, cloud computing and other advanced technology to enhance the level of parking information service, and maximize the parking resource utilization, improve the owner parking experiences and services. Under the joint action of "Internet plus" and sharing economy, "shared parking" comes into being. Shared parking is a solution to the problem of "difficult parking" in cities with multi-party participation and win-win situation, rather than a "single-player game". At the same time, smart parking is an important aspect of the construction of smart city.

This paper designs a set of urban intelligent parking management system based on the credit system, integrating the parking resources of the city's closed parking areas such as government parking lots, enterprises and institutions parking lots, commercial parking lots, residential parking lots and so on. Through the transformation and upgrading of parking lots, the basic data information is collected uniformly, and the data of parking berth resources in the whole city are managed uniformly. The comprehensive sharing of parking space is the core of business application, and the contradiction of large parking space gap, high parking space vacancy rate and low resource utilization rate is solved. The refined management of parking space is realized by advanced technical means, and the goal of city-level parking resource sharing is achieved.

2 Design of Urban Credit System

Shared parking system Based on parking resources in enclosed parking areas such as government, enterprises and institutions, commercial area, and community, The biggest difficulty is how to ensure that parked vehicles in accordance with the rules of orderly parking, not overtime, not disorderly parking, does not affect the normal operation of the unit. In order to solve this problem, we designed a set of credit system, based on the shared parking behavior of urban residents, to regulate residents' parking behavior.

The credit system was initially widely applied in the financial field, and later extended to other fields such as government affairs and social services, which is the necessary foundation for the development of social commerce. In order to ensure that shared parking behavior does not affect the daily work of each unit, the credit system should not be too complicated.

We simplify the credit system and design a set of credit system suitable for shared parking, which is only linked to residents' shared parking behaviors, and standardizes people's parking behaviors through credit scores to achieve the purpose of management. The credit system does not conflict with the city-level/national-level credit system, nor is it linked with it for the time being. It is only used within the urban shared parking. In the future, with the development and classification of urban credit system, it can be considered to connect to the platform of urban credit system.

The credit system is only linked to the daily activities of shared parking, not economic activities. The system is only available to resident residents of the city who participate in shared parking activities, and rewards and punishments will be given based on whether or not they park in accordance with regulations. Aliens and vehicles are not allowed to participate in shared parking activities [5] (Fig. 1).

The design of the credit system is as follows:

a) Only local residents have the qualification to register an account, and people outside the city cannot register and enjoy the shared parking service;

b) Only registered users can use the shared parking service with their real names.

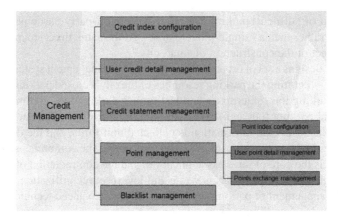

Fig. 1. Subsystem of Urban Credit System

c) The personal information required for real-name authentication includes: name, ID number (photo uploading), phone number (SMS verification), license plate number (driving license), home address (house ownership certificate) and other relevant information.

d) In principle, only locally licensed vehicles will be considered to provide convenience services and welfare policies for people living and residing locally. Local residents shall provide id cards, and non-local permanent residents shall provide property ownership certificates. The unit may collect personal information and issue a certificate collectively to the resident who works locally and does not own a local house [3] (Table 1).

Table 1. Design form of Credit System

Authentication level	Basic materials	Identity Card Requirements	License plate Number (vehicle license)	Other
Registered user	Name & telephone number	/	/	/
Authenticated user	Name & telephone number	ID card	Local license plate & driving license	/
Advanced User (Local resident)	Name & telephone number	Local ID card	Local license plate & driving license	/
Advanced Users (non-resident residents)	Name & telephone number	ID card	Local license plate & driving license	property ownership certificate
Advanced Users (Enterprise collective registration)	Name & telephone number	ID card	Local license plate & driving license	Enterprise collective register table

Different parking scenarios have different safety requirements for parking management. The system will establish the certification level system, according to the commercial area, community, enterprises and institutions to improve the level in turn. See the following table for details (Table 2):

Table 2. Design form of Certification Level System

Scenario	Certification Level Requirements	certification requirement	certification materials	Overdue/blacklisted vehicles
commercial area parking lot	registered user	register	telephone number	information cue
community parking lot	Authenticated user (Local License plate)	real name authentication	Id card, driving license and registration, telephone number, property ownership certificate	information cue
Government or enterprise parking lot	Advanced users (Local License plate & Local Resident)	real name authentication	Id card, driving license and registration, telephone number, property ownership certificate, Enterprise collective register table	No Entrance

a) Users can register and improve the certification materials to improve the certification level.
b) If the parking time exceeds, the owner of the community or the staff of the unit will be affected to park normally, the first contact to move the car;
c) If the user refuses to move the car or the car is parked for a serious time, corresponding restrictions and punishment measures will be taken: deduct the platform credit points (percentage system) of the reservation application owner, and the user and the vehicle will be added to the system blacklist.
d) After the vehicle is locked on the blacklist, it will not be able to enjoy shared parking service for a period of time (3 months). After the penalty period expires, they can use the service again, and if they do it again, they can never use the shared parking service.
e) Provide account points for punctual car owners, increase account points and redeem coupons later.

The parking behavior of all vehicles will be retained in the system in the form of points and credit points, which will affect the service level of vehicle and personnel parking sharing.

For specific point management, please refer to the following Table 3: [1, 4, 6].

Table 3. Parking behavior credit system design form

Scene Classification	Notifications	Punitive Measure	Remark
punctual visitors	/	/	Account points plus 1 point
15 min before finish	WeChat, Application	/	/
Overtime less than 30 min	WeChat, Application and short message	Minus 10 credit points	Credit Score Below 60 to join the blacklist
Overtime less than 2 h	WeChat, Application and telephone	Minus 20 credit points	Credit Score Below 60 to join the blacklist
Overtime less than 6 h	WeChat, Application and telephone	Minus 40 credit points	Credit Score Below 60 to join the blacklist
Overtime more than 6 h	WeChat, Application and telephone	Drop the credit score to zero	Drop the credit score to zero and join the blacklist

3 Key Module Design of System

3.1 Overall Architecture

The overall architecture of the whole system is divided into five areas, which are successively from bottom to top: in-road parking data collection area, off-road parking data collection area, urban parking application service area, car owners' public service area and data exchange service area [5]. In addition, it reserves with illegal stop evidence capture system, urban traffic guidance system, charging parking integration system (Fig. 2).

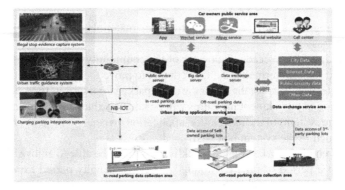

Fig. 2. The overall architecture of the whole system

3.2 Shared Parking Process Design

Shared parking requires car owners to register and verify their vehicle and personnel information in the mobile APP in advance, and complete the real-name authentication.

Free parking Spaces will be provided on "first come, first served" during shared parking hours. Car owners can also navigate by looking for free parking Spaces on their mobile apps. After parking, you can pay by yourself in the mobile APP or set it to automatic deduction. The exit camera recognizes the license plate and automatically clears (Fig. 3).

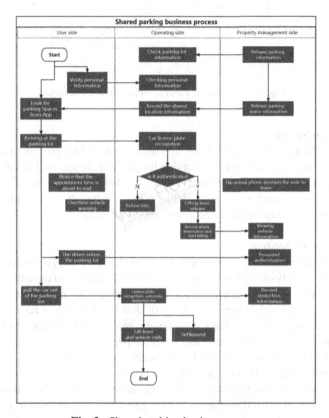

Fig. 3. Shared parking business process

3.3   Design of Main Business Functions

As shown in the figure, the urban shared parking system is divided into six subsystems and eight functional modules. Among them, the core subsystems used in the shared parking scenario based on the parking lot of enterprises and institutions are parking sharing network operation system, public service system, big data analysis system, and the core functional modules are resource management, user service, etc. (Fig. 4).

Parking Sharing Network Operation System
The system manages shared parking services, including management of shared parking Spaces and shared time, shared parking management and records, shared parking statistics and analysis, etc.

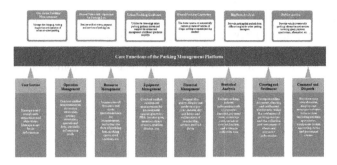

Fig. 4. Structure of Parking Management Platform

Public Service System
The system includes user APP and Wechat public account, which provides parking public information service and value-added service for parking owners and the general public through road guidance system, mobile APP and Wechat public account. Car owners can use the public service system for registration, real-name authentication, shared parking, online payment, route navigation and other related services.

Big Data Analysis System
Parking big data analysis system is business data storage and processing results, data mining, refining, analysis of the main body, according to the size of the data, the accuracy, completeness, value factors such as the hierarchy of all data logically from coarse to fine is divided into three levels, namely the basis of data layer, business layer, data analysis and mining. Among them, the basic data layer mainly saves all kinds of basic data in different formats. These basic data come from the public basic data of roadside parking services, such as car owners, vehicles, berths, accounts, members and other data systems, which are summarized and stored through the cloud as the bottom support data of parking business. The business data layer mainly manages the operation and maintenance process and platform configuration data, such as parking records, payment records and recharge records generated in the parking process. After data association analysis of basic data and business data, part of the result data will be stored in the data analysis and mining layer, so as to form operational indicator data, and further calculation and processing of report data.

Resource Management System
Intelligent transformation of parking lot, the combination of license plate video recognition technology and high-speed video image shooting, storage and comparison, to achieve accurate real-time management and monitoring of every parking space based on intelligent image recognition. It is of precise management and authorization of parking behavior of vehicles with different identities. For example, for the firefighting truck, police car and other special vehicles to be managed as the white list, so that they can enter all the shared parking lot; For licensed vehicles, conduct behavior analysis through big data, and directly send alarms when encountering vehicles suspected of licensed vehicles, and confirm through manual analysis; For the control of vehicles, the strategy

of "allowing in and not allowing out" is adopted. As long as the car is detected by the system, the system will send alarms and notify the public security, traffic management and other relevant units.

Fully integrate all the berths, including in-road berths, parking berths and social berths, realize the management of all the berths and provide various parking services for the whole city.

User Service System

User service system includes vehicle information management, user authentication, and financial management, including user credit system and user point system. There are three modules, specific functions as follows:

- Vehicle & user management: data statistical analysis, user management, vehicle management, financial management, complaint management, system management;
- User credit system: user behavior analysis, credit index setting, connection with credit investigation system, user credit details;
- User point system: point index configuration, point system design, point details.

3.4 Shared Parking Safety Design

Parking sharing platform needs to share the original private parking resources of business circles, communities and enterprises and institutions. The internal safety of parking lots and the safety of owners and vehicles is an issue that we have to consider carefully. In view of safety problems, it is suggested to adopt high-level and strict safety audit scheme in the early stage of shared parking operation to improve the public's awareness of the safety of shared parking.

For parking lots connected to the parking sharing platform, related management units can choose the number of shared parking resources based on their own actual situation and management system, and participate in the parking resource sharing service to the maximum extent on the premise of ensuring safety and not affecting their daily operation.

We solve security problems through the integrated management of user authentication, integral system and credit management. After the operation of shared parking has been gradually accepted by the public for a period of time, it can be considered to shorten the audit time for some high-quality users and improve efficiency. Wait for conditions to mature, and then fully open.

Commercial Area Parking Lot Safety Design

As a public place, the management of vehicles in and out of the business area is relatively loose. The commercial demand should also attract passenger flow and improve the convenience of car owners. The monitoring equipment construction of commercial area is relatively complete, and the management personnel are specially equipped. Therefore, the certification requirements for car owners are low. Register with a valid mobile phone number in APP or Wechat public account to obtain verification code for login. Register by mobile phone number, also can contact users in time.

Community Parking Lot Safety Design

The community is generally only open to owners, and for safety and management reasons, outside vehicles need to be strictly controlled. Therefore, for car owners who need to share parking, real-name authentication must be required, and the correct license plate number must be bound to ensure that the user's vehicle information is true. Car owners need to upload information on the mobile APP, pass the platform's review and complete the "human-vehicle certification", and become certified users before they can use the parking sharing function. Discredited car owners and blacklisted vehicles will be restricted from sharing parking services.

Government, Enterprises and Institutions Parking Lot Safety Design

As is known, for government, enterprises and institutions, With the exception of external departments, these areas, having the highest safety requirements, usually only allow internal vehicles to enter and are not open to the outside world. Therefore, only advanced users who have completed real-name authentication can obtain the shared parking resources. This strategy limits the number of people entering and leaving from the source and reduces the difficulty of management. In addition, need to increase the two-dimensional code scanning equipment in the duty room or pedestrian passage, car owners in and out of the parking lots need to show the mobile phone two-dimensional code scanning code verification, and reserve to increase face recognition function. Dishonest car owners and blacklisted vehicles are not allowed to use shared parking in government, enterprises and public institutions.

4 Conclusions

Through the design of credit system based on shared parking behavior, the daily parking behavior of shared parking users is standardized, the efficiency of parking resources is improved, the parking cost of citizens is reduced, and the social harmony is promoted. However, the credit system only considers the sharing of parking this small scene, the overall limitation is very large. In the future, other daily behaviors of citizens can be included in the credit system, expand the scope of application of the credit system, and urge everyone to abide by the convention and norms of daily behavior.

References

1. Li, X.: Research on Revenue Distribution of Shared Berth Based on Game Theory. Chongqing Jiaotong University, Chongqing (2018)
2. Liu, Y.-H., Luo, X., Hu, J.-P.: Dynamic allocation method for shared berth considering immediate and reservation demands. J. Transp. Syst. Eng. Inf. Technol. 22(1), 171–181 (2022)
3. Jia, F.-Q., Li, Y.-Z., Yang, X.-F., Ma, C.-X., Dai, C.-J.: Shared parking behavior analysis under government encouragement based on evolutionary game method. J. Transp. Syst. Eng. Inf. Technol. 22(1), 163–170 (2022)
4. Ardeshiri, A., Safarighouzhdic, F., Rashidi, T.H.: Measuring willingness to pay for shared parking. Transportation Research Part A: Policy and Practice 152, 186–202 (2021)

5. Liu, W., Zhang, F., Yang, H.: Modeling and managing the joint equilibrium of destination and parking choices under hybrid supply of curbside and shared parking. Transp. Res. Part C: Emerging Technol. **130**, 103301 (2021)
6. Wang, C., Wang, R., Su, Z.: Design of temporary vehicle parking management system of residential area based on credit system. In: 2020 15th International Conference on Computer Science & Education (ICCSE). IEEE (2020)

Research on Short-Term Traffic Flow Forecast Based on Improved Cuckoo Search Algorithm

Ruoxi Wang[1]([✉]), Jingjing Zheng[1], and Zaoning Wang[2]

[1] Wuhan Fiberhome Technical Services Co., Ltd., Wuhan 430205, China
{rxwang,jjzheng}@fiberhome.com
[2] School of Computer Science, Hubei University of Technology, Wuhan 430205, China
101910734@hbut.edu.cn

Abstract. In recent years, the traffic flow in big cities has increased significantly, and the development of intelligent transportation systems (ITS) has become the general trend. Most of the traditional traffic flow prediction models are highly dependent on experienced experts and lack the ability to learn independently. Since the traffic flow depends on various factors such as weather, road conditions, and whether there are major events, it's influenced by multi-factors and huge amounts of data. It is difficult to fit and process traffic flow data well, so traditional traffic forecasting models are no longer suitable for the analysis and prediction of current and even next-generation traffic flow. Now artificial neural networks are widely used in traffic flow forecasting due to their strong robustness and fault tolerance, high operating efficiency, ability to process massive data, strong nonlinear mapping capabilities, and strong learning and adaptive capabilities. To tackle the problem of random initial weights and thresholds of the traditional model for the neural network, we proposes an improved cuckoo search algorithm, and uses the improved algorithm to optimize the initial threshold in the long short-term memory neural network, and applies the improved model to the research on traffic flow prediction, in order to improve traffic planning and save people's travel time and fuel costs laid the groundwork.

Keywords: Traffic Flow Prediction · CS Search Algorithm · Weighted Traction Component · Long Short-Term Memory Neural Network

1 Introduction

In recent years, people's economic conditions improved significantly, and speed up the pace of urban life, more and more people choose to drive or take a taxi, thus significantly increased traffic in big cities. According to the statistics of relevant departments, by 2021, the national motor vehicle population is up to 395 million. While private cars bring convenience to people's travel, urban traffic problems are becoming more and more serious. Therefore, the construction of smart city has attracted more and more attention [1].

Since 1980s, there have been researches on short-time traffic flow prediction technology for Intelligent Transportation System (ITS) [2]. Up to now, researchers have put

© The Author(s), under exclusive license to Springer Nature Singapore Pte Ltd. 2024
W. Hong and G. Kanaparan (Eds.): ICCSE 2023, CCIS 2023, pp. 374–383, 2024.
https://doi.org/10.1007/978-981-97-0730-0_34

forward about dozens of different short-time traffic flow prediction methods. The famous short-time traffic flow prediction methods can be divided into non-parametric technology and parametric technology. Among non-parametric techniques, the well-known Neural Network methods include Back Propagation (BP) Neural Network [3], Generalized Regression Neural Network, GRNN) [4] and Wavelet Neural Network (WNN) [5]. Technology with parameters includes linear regression, nonlinear regression, historical average algorithm, smoothing technology, etc. According to the prediction method, it can be divided into traditional traffic flow prediction and traffic flow prediction based on deep learning.

In the early stage, scholars established traffic flow prediction models by using mathematical thinking or physical thinking and their combination, including ARMA [6], ARIMA [7] and HAM [8]. Shekhar S and Williams BM et al. proposed the application of Kalman filter model to short-term traffic flow prediction for the first time in the 19th century [9], and traffic flow prediction made a big step forward. This model can deal with stable and fluctuating data, but it cannot deal with randomness and nonlinear situations, so it has certain limitations in practical production and life.

Huang W et al. first proposed the introduction of Deep learning technology into traffic flow prediction in 2014 [10]. In 2015, Koesdwiady et al. used DBN to predict the traffic data set PeMS [11], which was a major breakthrough in the field of traffic flow prediction. In 2016, Ma et al. used long short-term memory neural network (LSTM) and microwave detector data to predict Beijing traffic speed [12]. LSTM was used to overcome error attenuation caused by back propagation through memory blocks, and showed superior performance in long-term dependent time series prediction. In a 2018 research paper, Zhuo et al. proposed a new traffic prediction model based on LSTM [13] and verified that the model had better performance.

In this paper, by comparing various intelligent optimization algorithms and combining the characteristics of each optimization algorithm, the improved cuckoo optimization algorithm is selected to optimize the random initialization parameters of the traditional neural network. Finally, the optimized network model is applied to short-term traffic flow prediction, and the original data set is preprocessed accordingly. The improved cuckoo search algorithm is compared with the standard cuckoo search algorithm to judge the optimization performance of each algorithm to the benchmark test function. The main research contents of this paper are as follows:

(1) Aiming at the problem that the step size factor of the standard cuckoo optimization algorithm is artificially set, which leads to low optimization efficiency, this paper proposes an adaptive step size factor based on logarithm function to improve it. In order to improve the accuracy of the algorithm, gaussian perturbation is used to guide the local search of bird's nest position. The weight traction component is also proposed to increase the relationship between individuals in the algorithm and strengthen population diversity.

(2) Explore the methods of data preprocessing, analyze in detail the methods of outlier processing, data dimension reduction, feature extraction and other preprocessing, and finally preprocess PeMS04 data set through the above methods.

(3) In view of the defect that LSTM model parameters need to be set manually, this paper uses the improved CS algorithm to optimize LSTM by taking advantage of cuckoo

optimization algorithm's strong global search characteristics, and then applies the optimized LSTM model to short-term traffic flow prediction. The original LSTM model and other common time series prediction models are compared to predict the same data set, to verify the prediction accuracy of the optimized LSTM.

2 Short-Term Traffic Flow Prediction Based on AWCS-LSTM Model

This chapter mainly introduces the optimization of traditional LSTM hyper-parameters based on improved CS algorithm, and applies the optimized model to traffic flow prediction. First introduced the circulation principle of neural network and its derivative network LSTM, then using improved CS algorithm (AWCS) to optimize the LSTM model, the number of iterations and the number of hidden layer neuron network, and train the prediction model. Finally, validate the improved model in PeMS04 data set; compared with the model accuracy and other evaluation indexes before and after the improvement, the experimental verification shows that the improved model has more advantages in traffic flow prediction.

2.1 Construction of Neural Network Model Based on AWCS-LSTM

Principles and Steps of LSTM Optimization by Cuckoo Optimization Algorithm
Artificial neural network model with animal neural network is simulated for inspiration, make it has the ability of learning and memory, including LSTM improved the long-term dependence of RNN defects, therefore has been widely applied in the field, the time-series data of forecasting and prediction accuracy of the model is closely related to neural network initialization parameter setting, super parameter selection directly influences the performance of the model. In general, the initial weights and thresholds of neural networks in traditional models are set manually, so they are random and not conducive to model training. Therefore, cuckoo search algorithm is introduced and improved to optimize the initial threshold in LSTM.

The flow chart of traditional LSTM model for data prediction is shown in Fig. 1:

Cuckoo optimization algorithm in the search for the optimal parameters showed better performance, thus introducing the LSTM, optimize the traditional LSTM model, the main idea is to the LSTM vector network, the number of iterations and the number of nodes in the hidden layer as a cuckoo search algorithm of the bird's nest, to verify that the collection of mean square error (MSE) as the fitness value, The optimization principle of CS algorithm is used to find the optimal initial value of the model, so as to improve the fitting accuracy of LSTM model in the direction of traffic flow prediction and obtain the optimal LSTM model.

When optimizing the model, the fitness value is calculated by Eq. (1):

$$\text{fitness} = \text{MSE} = \frac{1}{N}\sum\nolimits_{i=1}^{N}(f_i - y_i)^2 \tag{1}$$

f_i is the predicted value, y_i is the actual value, N is the number of samples, MSE is the mean square error, the greater the variance, the greater the dispersion, that is, the greater the error.

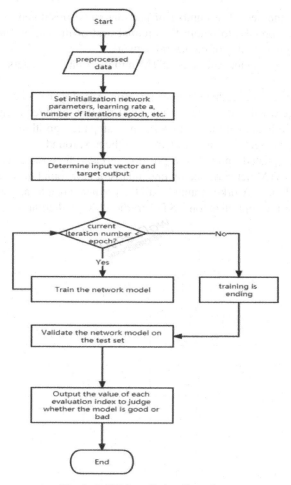

Fig. 1. LSTM prediction flow chart

The steps of the improved cuckoo search algorithm to improve LSTM and predict traffic flow data are as follows:

Input: preprocessed PeMS04 training set and test set.

Output: the value of traffic flow at a certain time.

Step 1: Parameter setting and group initialization: Randomly generate N initial nests as required and determine their positions. Set the initialization parameters: population size N, number of parameters to be searched corresponding to dimension D, discovery probability Pa, boundary values a and B of each optimization parameter, maximum iteration times itermax and current iteration times i, etc. In this paper, dimension D = 4 is set, optimization parameters are learning rate α, network iteration times epoch, hidden layer node number N1 and n2.

Step 2: The nests generated by the cuckoo search algorithm are decoded as parameters of each layer of the neural network, and the number of parameters corresponds to the dimension D of the nest. The number of parameters is substituted into the improved AWCS algorithm process to obtain the optimal nest of the current iteration number, namely, the parameter value of the neural network.

Step 3: Take parameter values as LSTM initialization parameters to predict traffic flow data;

Step 4: Substitute the predicted value into formula (4–1) to calculate the fitness value;

Step 5: Judge whether the fitness value meets the threshold requirements or reaches the maximum number of iterations. If I ≥ itermax, stop the algorithm; Otherwise, update the nest position and get the parameter value of the next round;

Step 6: The updated optimal nest position of each dimension corresponds to the initial value of LSTM network one by one, that is, a new round of training parameters are obtained and the network is trained until the predicted results are output.

AWCS algorithm optimization LSTM traffic flow prediction process is shown in Fig. 2:

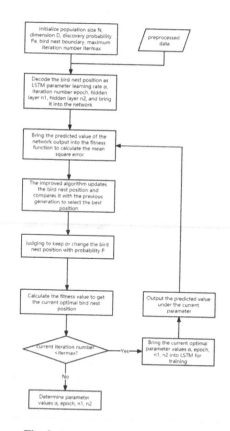

Fig. 2. Improved CS optimized LSTM

Model parameter setting.

Parameter Settings of the above training process are shown in Table 1:

Table 1. AGCS/AWCS-LSTM parameter Settings

	Parameter	Range
AWCS	Population size N	20
	Dimension D	4
	Discovery probability Pa	0.25
	maximum iteration number itermax	25
LSTM	batch size	128
	learning rate α	[0.001,0.01]
	epoch	[10,100]
	The number of hidden layers of the network	2
	layer n1	[1,100]
	layer n2	[1,100]

The activation function of LSTM forgetting gate and output gate selects sigmoid function, whose value range is [0,1]. 0 means discarding information, and 1 means reserving all information, as shown in Formula (2):

$$\sigma(z) = \frac{1}{1 + e^{-z}} \tag{2}$$

Tanh function is selected to activate the input gate, and the value range is [−1,1], as shown in Formula (3):

$$tanh(x) = \frac{e^x - e^{-x}}{e^x + e^{-x}} \tag{3}$$

2.2 Experimental Results and Analysis

Evaluation Indicators
After the prediction results are obtained, the pros and cons of the model and the accuracy of the prediction can be determined by evaluating the generalization performance of the prediction model. Common evaluation indexes are mean absolute error (MAE), root mean square error (RMSE), Average absolute percentage error (MAPE) and determinant coefficient (R2).

Comparison of Models Before and After Optimization
In order to verify the practical application of AWCS-LSTM model in short-term traffic flow prediction, this paper selects the public traffic flow data set PeMS04 for verification, and the data set only contains the traffic flow of working days in the selected period.

The training set contains 8778 records as samples from 2016.01.01 to 2016.02.29, and the verification set contains 2033 records as samples from 2016.03.01 to 2016.03.16.

The test set selected 2480 records as test samples recorded in six days from 2016.03.17 to 2016.03.31 to verify the accuracy of the model.

In this paper, the traditional LSTM model was firstly verified, and the model training iteration times epoch was set as 10, 20, 30, 40, 50, 60, 70 and 80 respectively for comparative experiments. The evaluation index values predicted by LSTM for PeMS04 data set under different epochs are shown in Table 2:

Table 2. LSTM prediction effects under different epochs

Nos. of Network training	MAE	RMSE	MAPE	R2
epoch = 10	12.4145	15.9587	0.4438	0.8441
epoch = 20	10.2707	13.3600	0.3329	0.8907
epoch = 30	8.1528	10.5815	0.2226	0.9315
epoch = 40	7.4542	9.7490	0.1688	0.9418
epoch = 50	7.3278	9.5706	0.1601	0.9439
epoch = 60	7.2345	9.4787	0.1599	0.9450
epoch = 70	7.2062	9.4711	0.1632	0.9451
epoch = 80	7.73120	9.5824	0.1603	0.9437

It can be seen from the table above, with the increase of the number of iterations, all the indicators tend to be better, but when the number of iterations is set to 80, when the back phenomenon, predicted results as the number of iterations instead of 70, so when the number of iterations is too large, not only the extension of training time, can also cause a trained fitting, resulting in a loss prediction effect. In order to display the prediction results more intuitively, the prediction curves under different iterations are visualized. The prediction results are shown in Fig. 3:

The improved CS algorithm is used to optimize the hyper-parameters of the traditional LSTM model. The AWCS with improved adaptive step size and weight traction component are introduced into LSTM respectively. The CS-LSTM model optimized by traditional LSTM and standard CS and the improved AWCS-LSTM model are used to predict the obtained evaluation indexes on the selected data set, as shown in Table 3:

It can be seen from Table 3 that the model built by using the improved CS algorithm to optimize the hyper-parameters of the traditional LSTM network has better accuracy in predicting PeMS04. Compared with the model optimized by the traditional LSTM model and the standard CS algorithm, AWCS has better performance in optimizing the hyper-parameters of LSTM. The visualization results of prediction are shown in Fig. 4:

The parameters of traditional LSTM, CS-LSTM and AWCS-LSTM are shown in Table 4:

The learning rate, number of hidden layer neurons and iteration times of LSTM model are set manually, while the learning rate, number of hidden layer neurons and iteration times of CS-LSTM and AWCS-LSTM are optimized by corresponding algorithms.

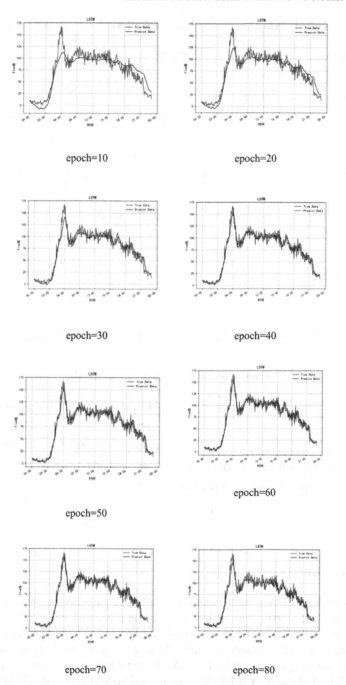

Fig. 3. LSTM prediction effect under different epochs

Table 3. Prediction effects of LSTM, CS-LSTM and AWCS-LSTM

Network Model	MAE	RMSE	MAPE	R2
LSTM	9.5913	12.9674	0.2043	0.8970
CS-LSTM	6.9455	9.1766	0.1706	0.9353
AWCS-LSTM	6.9389	9.1588	0.1615	0.9516

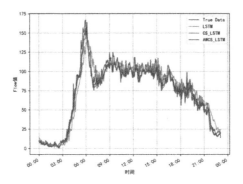

Fig. 4. Visualization of LSTM, CS-LSTM and AWCS-LSTM prediction

Table 4. Parameter Settings of each model

Model	LSTM	CS-LSTM	AWCS-LSTM
batch size	256	256	256
Learning rate	0.01	0.0036	0.0089
Number of neurons in the first hidden layer	20	57	73
Number of neurons in the second hidden layer	10	8	18
Dropout rate	0.2	0.2	0.2
iterations	70	72	75

3   Conclusion

Aiming at the problems of traditional traffic flow forecasting method, this paper proposes using the intelligent optimization algorithm of neural network parameters optimization of ideas, and set up a neural network based on improved cuckoo search algorithm and short - and long-term memory of traffic flow prediction model, using the improved algorithm used to optimize the LSTM AWCS random initial parameters of the model, LSTM, CS-LSTM and AWCS-LSTM were applied to the preprocessed PeMS04 data set respectively, and the effectiveness of the optimized model was verified by experiments.

Acknowledgments. This work is funded by the Key R&D plan of Hubei Province (2020BAB012).

References

1. Liu, Y.: Big data technology and its analysis of application in urban intelligent transportation system. In: 3rd International Conference on Intelligent Transportation, Big Data and Smart City, pp. 17–19 (2018)
2. Liao, H.: Intelligent transportation decision analysis system based on big data mining. In: International Conference on Computer Information Science and Application Technology - Big Data Search, Mining, and Visualization, vol. 1168, no. 3, pp. 1–5 (2019)
3. Mei, L.: Research on software reliability model based on improved BP neural network. In: 2018 International Conference on Smart Grid and Electrical Automation (ICSGEA), pp. 221–2232018https://doi.org/10.1109/ICSGEA.2018.00061
4. Kartal, S., Oral, M., Ozyildirim, B.M.: Pattern layer reduction for a generalized regression neural network by using a self-organizing map. Int. J. Appl. Math. Comput. Sci. 28(2), 411–424 (2018)
5. Liu, Z.: Research on face recognition based on the fusion of convolution and wavelet neural network. In: Proceedings of the 4th International Conference on Virtual Reality (ICVR 2018), New York, NY, USA, pp. 122–125. Association for Computing Machinery (2018)
6. Mikolov, T., Deoras, A., Povey, D., et al.: Strategies for training large scale neural network language models. In: Automatic Speech Recognition and Understanding, pp. 196–201. IEEE (2012)
7. Ahmed, M.S., Cook, A.R.: Analysis of freeway traffic time-series data by using Box-Jenkins techniques (1999)
8. Lee, S., Fambro, D.: Application of subset autoregressive integrated moving average model for short-term freeway traffic volume forecasting. Transp. Res. Rec. J. Transp. Res. Board 1678(1), 179–188 (1999)
9. Shekhar, S., Williams, B.M.: Adaptive seasonal time series models for forecasting short-term traffic flow. Transp. Res. Rec. 2024(1), 116–125 (2007)
10. Huang, W., Song, G., Hong, H., et al.: Deep architecture for traffic flow prediction: deep belief networks with multitask learning. IEEE Trans. Intell. Transp. Syst. 15(5), 2191–2201 (2014)
11. Koesdwiady, A., Soua, R., Karray, F.: Improving traffic flow prediction with weather information in connected cars: a deep learning approach. IEEE Trans. Veh. Technol. 65(12), 9508–9517 (2016)
12. Ma, X., Tao, Z., Wang, Y., et al.: Long short-term memory neural network for traffic speed prediction using remote microwave sensor data. Transp. Res. Part C Emerging Technol. 54, 187–197 (2015)
13. Zhuo, Q., Li, Q., Yan, H., Qi, Y.: Long short-term memory neural network for network traffic prediction. In: 2018 12th International Conference on Intelligent Systems and Knowledge Engineering (ISKE), pp. 1–6 (2018). https://doi.org/10.1109/ISKE.2017.8258815

Research on the Internet Access and Usage Gap in Rural Areas and Its Influencing Factors
—Empirical Analysis Based on Heckman's Two-Stage Model

Mingbo Ji[1], Rui Zhou[2], and Yaqin Fang[3(✉)]

[1] School of Economics, Sichuan University, Chengdu 610065, People's Republic of China
[2] School of Marxism, Sichuan University, Chengdu 610065, People's Republic of China
[3] School of Public Administration, Sichuan University, Chengdu 610065, People's Republic of China
294854375@qq.com

Abstract. With the implementation of the digital village development strategy, it is of great significance to explore the Internet access and usage divide and its influencing factors in rural areas of China to promote the rural revitalization strategy with high quality. Based on the data from the 2018 China Household Tracking Survey, this paper analyzes the Internet access and usage divide and its influencing factors in rural areas using the Heckman two-stage model. The empirical results show that people with higher education and better economic conditions are more likely to access the Internet, and men are more likely to access it through mobile Internet. Young people with higher levels of education and digital skills are more likely to use the Internet. Patterns of Internet use vary by gender, age, education level, occupation and geographic location. Young people are more likely to engage in e-commerce online activities, while older people are less likely to participate in online activities. The findings of this paper provide empirical evidence to analyze the digital divide in rural China and provide a basis for the government to formulate targeted telecommunications policies.

Keywords: rural · digital divide · digital access divide · digital usage divide · Heckman two-stage modeling

1 Introduction

Accessing and using the Internet can help residents gain digital advantages, such as obtaining valuable information, finding a job, consulting on health issues, or accessing public services. However, access to and use of the Internet presupposes access to technology and infrastructure, as well as the acquisition of skills to cope with innovations in the digital world [1], this difference in technology, facilities, and skills creates a digital divide, which primarily describes the differences between different countries in terms of technology, facilities, and skills. The digital divide primarily describes differences in Internet access and use by gender, income, and urban and rural residents [2]. Although China's Internet access facilities have achieved widespread coverage [3], but China's rural areas still face a serious digital divide problem. Therefore, this paper utilizes CFPS 2018 data to conduct a detailed analysis of the Internet diffusion in rural areas of China. The reason for choosing this database is that the CFPS database focuses on the economic and non-economic well-being of Chinese residents, as well as a number of research topics including economic activity, educational outcomes, health, and internet use, etc. It is a nationwide, large-scale, multidisciplinary social tracking survey project, with a sample covering 25 provinces/municipalities/autonomous regions. Data such as Internet use in the database allow us to determine the profile of Internet users and define various patterns of Internet use.

This paper contributes to the study of the digital divide in rural areas of developing countries in three ways. First, there are more existing studies on the urban digital divide, but relatively few on the rural digital divide. Secondly, by studying the rural digital divide through microeconomic data, this study can further clarify the status quo and reasons for the relative lagging behind of rural development under China's urban-rural dualistic system, especially in the presentation of "digital space". Third, this study provides solid empirical evidence for the Chinese government to formulate public policies, such as rural revitalization and common prosperity, aimed at increasing the benefits of adequate and effective handling of information technology (IT), including the Internet, and thus making it easier for a growing number of people living in rural areas of developing countries to access and use IT.

The structure of this article is as follows: the first part describes the significance of the study and leads to the research question. The literature review in Part II identifies the new characteristics of rural China in the new era, the digital divide, and the determinants of Internet access and use. The third part presents the CFPS survey data and the variables used in the econometric model. The fourth section includes regression results on Internet access, usage, and usage patterns in rural China. Finally, the conclusions, policy recommendations, and research deficiencies of this article are given.

2 Theoretical Analysis and Literature Review

2.1 New Characteristics of China's Rural Areas in the New Era

Since the reform and opening up for more than 40 years, China's rural society has undergone great changes, presenting the following main features: First, with the increasing urbanization rate, the number of villages in China shows an overall downward trend, and the rural space "gives way" to the urban space [4]; Secondly, rural population mobility has increased and heterogeneity has strengthened, especially the outflow of young and strong people, and the rural areas are mainly left with the elderly people, children, and women [5]; Thirdly, as population mobility reshapes the rural mechanism, there are also significant differences within rural China [6]. The new features presented in China's rural areas in the new era have led to non-agricultural activities in the countryside being strengthened, with more and more linkages between rural areas and towns, highlighting the multifunctional role of rural space [7].

In the context of the rural revitalization strategy, the Chinese government has put forward a digital rural development strategy, which attempts to modernize agriculture, rural areas and farmers through rural digital empowerment, and to crack the problem of unbalanced and insufficient development of agriculture, rural areas and farmers, in order to narrow the development gap between urban and rural areas, and to find the endogenous power for rural development as well as to provide a new momentum for the modernization of the rural society [8]. Information and communication technologies are naturally incorporated into the countryside as a key element of changes in the life of the country [9], which in turn makes rural and urban areas more connected.

Influenced by factors such as relative geographic isolation and low population density, digital access in rural areas falls behind the urban areas [8]. Although the Chinese government has dramatically improved the coverage of Internet access in rural areas through telecommunication policies such as "Village to Village", the lack of access devices [10], educational limitations [11] and other factors, resulting in the fact that there is still a large portion of rural residents without access to ICT products and services. Although mobile devices such as cell phones have improved rural residents' Internet access, most villagers have not yet been able to enjoy the digital dividends brought by the Internet due to the limitations of cell phone products and the generally low digital skills of the residents [12].

2.2 Digital Divide

The term "digital divide" originated in the United States in the 1990s and quickly became a topic of concern with the widespread use and penetration of ICT [13]. Existing research on the digital divide consists mainly of the Level 1 digital divide, where studies have focused on differences in Internet use and access [14]. The second-level digital divide, began to study the digital skills needed to use the Internet and differences in carrying out various types of activities online [15]. The third-level digital divide, which focuses on the types of inequalities that result from Internet use outcomes [16], suggesting that differences created through Internet use may exacerbate the social stratification in reality [17]. In addition, the current studies provide further details about differences in Internet use. For example, Internet use provides more opportunities and resources to improve their education, employment, professional life and social status [18]. Connected usage provides more insight into differences in devices, uses, skills and purposes of Internet use [19].

2.3 Literature Review: From Internet Access to Internet Use

Studies on Internet access and use have focused on both developed and developing countries. As far as China is concerned, some scholars point out that the digital divide exists, mainly manifested as the urban-rural divide [20] and the intergenerational divide [21], the essence of which is that the Matthew effect in the process of synergistic interaction between information and the social economy makes the digital society "replicate" the inequality of the real society, and even "create" new inequality. Research has shown that in the elderly people [22], low-income [23] and other groups in the digital divide, the choice of online activities is determined by the specific characteristics of each group, and the government needs to help these groups to Internet access and use through public decision-making.

The study found that the main factors affecting internet penetration between countries include income, education level, infrastructure [24]. Some scholars have found that income, telephone costs, and years of education are major determinants of online access [25]. Existing studies generally agree that the availability of Internet infrastructure in rural areas is in its infancy, which is largely determined by low population density and high network costs [26].

From a demand perspective, income disparities within countries hinder Internet diffusion [27]. Dohse and Cheng consider the important impact of geographic location on the digital divide [24]. This finding can be interpreted as a consequence of the lack of telecommunications infrastructure in rural and remote areas. Some studies have found that internet connections made by households are influenced by income, education level and number of children [28]. Some scholars have focused on the factors influencing the choice of Internet modes, arguing that the choice of online activities, such as communication, entertainment, social networking and e-commerce, is largely dependent on digital skills [29].

In contrast, the literature on the digital divide in China is less extensive and focuses mainly on comparative studies of urban-rural differences [30]. Regarding Internet diffusion, some scholars believe that in addition to traditional socio-economic factors determining Internet access, the factor of children in the family also plays an active role [31]. Scholars generally believe that education is still the biggest limitation for Chinese residents to use the Internet [32]. For the quality of Internet usage, it was found that economic income [33], education level, age [34], type of work [35] and digital skill [36] can affect Chinese residents' Internet use.

In the case of China, few studies have addressed the digital divide in the rural context by using microeconomic data. Some scholars have analyzed the disadvantages of rural areas in the digital divide through comparison between urban and rural areas [37], partly studying the impact of digital divide on income in rural areas [38], consumption structure [39], etc. There are also some studies focus on the impact of digital divide on youth [40], the Elderly people [41] and other special groups. However, existing studies have not comprehensively analyzed the situation of Internet access, use, and usage patterns (entertainment, social networking, e-commerce, study and work) in rural areas, as well as the factors influencing them. Therefore, this paper analyzes Internet access, usage and usage patterns in rural areas and their influencing factors based on differentiating Internet access (including mobile access and regular access) and usage patterns (entertainment, social networking, e-commerce, study and work).

3 Data Sources and Research Methodology

3.1 Data Sources

The data used in this paper come from the 2018 China Family Tracking Survey (CFPS) organized and implemented by the China Center for Social Science Research at Peking University. The CFPS observes and records China's characteristics and changes in social, economic, demographic, educational, and health aspects in an all-round way by tracking the data at the three levels of the individual, the family, and the community over a long period of time. A sample of 15,605 rural people aged 12 years and above in CFPS was selected for this study. The sample data contains socio-demographic information such as gender, age, education level and occupation. The main topic of the survey was Internet access (both in the form of regular Internet access, such as computers, and mobile Internet access, such as cell phones) and usage, and the respondents were asked about Internet access, frequency of use, online activities, digital skills, and so on.

The data shows the descriptive statistical information from the sample. In terms of gender, 51.84% of the respondents were male, which is basically in line with the percentage of male population (51.13%) in the China Statistical Yearbook 2019; 22.33% of the respondents were 32 years old or younger, which reflects the young population in rural areas. In terms of education, 45.11% were in elementary school and below, 32.40% in middle school, 12.41% in high school, and only 10.08% in college. This data reflects the reality of the low proportion of people with higher education typical of rural China, coupled with the fact that education is an important factor influencing the digital divide [42], which deepens the possibility of an internal digital divide in rural areas, exacerbating digital exclusion and educational backwardness of the rural population [8]. In terms of work, 59.14% of the respondents were mainly engaged in their own agricultural production and management, accounting for 35.71% of the employed. Interestingly, the western region has the highest percentage of farmers realizing Internet access at 39.99%, followed by the eastern and central regions respectively. As for digital connectivity in rural China, 35.53% of respondents realized Internet connectivity (either regular access or mobile access). Among them, the proportion of mobile Internet access (42.08%) has exceeded the proportion of regular Internet access (11.48%). A higher proportion of Internet users have accessed the Internet via mobile Internet. The proportion of rural users using the Internet is 34.27%, and the proportion of Internet users who fulfill the conditions for Internet use set in this paper is 96.45%.

3.2 Research Methodology

In order to determine the factors influencing Internet usage patterns in rural China, this paper identifies five usage patterns: entertainment, social networking, e-commerce, study and work. Overall, rural users in the sample used e-commerce activities and study and work activities relatively less. This also shows that rural residents' Internet applications are less used for value-creating activities such as work, study, and transactions, which is similar to the findings of the China Academy of Information and Communication Research Institute's "Research Report on China's Urban and Rural Digital Inclusive Development - Digitalization Helps Revitalize the Rural Areas and Shared Prosperity," which concluded that China's The proportion of rural residents using the Internet for learning and business activities is low [43]. First, we use a logistic regression model to estimate the determinants of Internet access. The dependent variable consists of two variables, regular access (regular) and mobile access (mobile), both of which are binary (1 indicates an Internet connection and 0 indicates no Internet connection). The independent variables are a set of socioeconomic and demographic characteristics at the household and individual level. Second, two equations were created to model Internet use decisions and usage patterns in rural areas. It is worth noting that the choice of usage pattern depends on the Internet usage decision. It is important to note that given the different demographic characteristics in the two models, Internet usage patterns are influenced by Internet usage decisions, meaning that the second equation may have a sample selection problem. Considering that the dependent variable of Internet use decision is a binary variable (1 means use, 0 means not applicable), according to the research of Shen Hongbo et al. [44], splitting the Heckman two-stage analysis so as to solve the sample selection bias problem and provide consistent and asymptotically valid estimates for the parameters.

3.2.1 Using Probabilistic Models to Estimate Whether Residents Use the Internet or Not

This view is based on the utility maximization model, which argues that the decision to use the Internet depends on a range of individual and household characteristics, reflecting differences in education, Internet use skills, financial status, social capital, and age [45]. For these reasons, the decision to use the Internet depends on the maximization of the utility of its use by each individual, which can be expressed as:

$$y_{io}^* = X_{io}\beta_0 + \varepsilon_{i0} \qquad (1)$$

where X_{io} represents a matrix of independent variables (such as socio-demographic characteristics, social capital and digital skills), β_0 represents a vector of coefficients, and ε_{i0} is a normally distributed random error term. Total utility is unobservable, but the decision to access the Internet is observable. Therefore, ε_{i0} is the result of a decision-making process that is influenced by the explanatory variables. Thus, $y_{io} = 1$ indicates an individual's decision to access the Internet (regular access or mobile access), $y_{io} = 0$ indicates not doing so.

3.2.2 Internet Usage Pattern Selection Model

After determining whether the residents use the Internet or not, the Internet usage pattern selection model is determined as shown in (2):

$$y_{ij} = X_{ij}\beta_j + \varepsilon_{ij} \qquad (2)$$

Among them, j (where $j = 1, ..., J$) represents the Internet usage pattern. y_{ij} measurement of Internet usage patterns, X_{ij} represents the matrix of independent variables and ε_{ij} denotes the normally distributed random error term. This section uses the Heckman two-stage method for regression analysis and assumes a binary normal distribution with zero mean and correlation. In applying this method, the presence of sample bias is indicated if the estimated Lambda coefficient is significant [46], and is suitable for use with sample selection models.

3.2.3 Variable Selection

This paper chooses five modes of use: entertainment, study, work, socialization, and e-commerce. In order to describe the use of rural residents on the Internet, this paper sets that as long as the frequency of use of any of the above five modes reaches at least once a month and above is deemed to have used the Internet. The independent variables in Internet use (Eq. 1) and Internet use pattern (Eq. 2) are divided into three categories, including the socioeconomic and demographic characteristics of the respondents, digital skills, and children.

The socio-economic variables include gender, age, education level, household economic status, and personal occupation. Regarding age, this paper refers to the study of Marlen et al., who identified three age ranges of 12–32, 33–64, and 65 and above [47]. Education level is measured using four categories: primary school and below (reference), middle school, high school/technical school/technical school/vocational high school, and university and above. Similarly, When dividing the work types of respondents, they are divided into own agricultural production and operation (reference), private enterprises/individual industrial and commercial households/other self-employment, agriculture work, employment, and non-agricultural casual workers. This paper chooses "net household income per capita" from the CFPS2018 database as a measure to reflect the living conditions of households. And we uses the questions "Do you send and receive emails?", "Online shopping expenses (yuan/year)?", "How many hours do you spend online in your spare time every week?" to measure. The number of children in the family are used to measure the impact of children in the family on Internet use. Finally, this article divides China into eastern, central and western to consider the Internet usage in different areas.

4 Empirical Results

4.1 Determinants of Internet Access

Table 1 shows the regression results of Internet access in rural areas of China. Our research results confirm that education level and family income are core influencing factors of Internet access, which means that residents with higher education and higher household income are more likely to have access to the Internet. This result is consistent with Chaudhuri et al. [48]. Possible reasons for this are that the level of education enhances a person's ability to receive information and learn, while mobile Internet access requires a certain level of learning ability, and the devices that enable mobile Internet access, etc., require a certain level of ability to pay for them. The significance of age and its squared term in relation to mobile Internet access suggests that older people are more likely to adopt mobile Internet access, but with decreasing marginal effects. However, it can be seen from the numerical value of the age coefficient that the impact of age on the mobile Internet is not very strong. Gender is another core factor affecting mobile access, with men (relative to women) more likely to have mobile Internet access, which may be related to the fact that men in rural areas are more likely to be valued in education. Residents who are 'private enterprise/self-employed/enterprise self-employed' and 'employed' are more likely to have both types of Internet access than those who have their own agricultural business. A possible reason why employed residents are more likely to have access to the Internet is that the organizations they work for have certain requirements for Internet use, which increases their opportunities and likelihood of joining the Internet. Geographically, residents in Western China (compared to Eastern China) are less likely to have access to the Internet (both regular and mobile), and residents in Central China (compared to Eastern China) are less likely to have mobile

Internet access. This reveals that Internet access in rural China may be closely linked to economic development across regions, suggesting that the digital divide in rural areas in the digital era is homogeneous with the development divide in the industrialized era Qiu Zeqi. Existing data do not confirm the relationship between household size, number of children and Internet access. In general, the group of farmers accessing the Internet has the following characteristics: better educated in the eastern part of the country, better family income, and men employed by an organization.

Table 1. Regression results of factors influencing rural Internet access

variant	Effects on Mobile (Std.Err)	Effects on Regula (Std.Err)	variant	Effects on Mobile (Std.Err)	Defects on Regula (Std.Err)
Gender (Female = 1)	0.113 (0.0701)	0.627*** (0.0830)	Non-farm labor	0.251 (0.1711)	0.214 (0.2577)
Age	0.047 (0.0244)	0.101* (0.0425)	Household income	0.279*** (0.0456)	0.384*** (0.0578)
Age squared	−0.002*** (0.0003)	−0.002*** (0.0001)	Family size	−0.013 (0.0117)	0.011 (0.0193)
Education	0.562*** (0.0538)	0.951*** (0.0457)	Number of children	−0.029 (0.0268)	−0.009 (0.0337)
Own Agricultural	reference	reference	Eastern	reference	reference
Private or self-employed	0.722*** (0.11355)	0.826*** (0.1560)	Central	0.015 (0.0942)	−0.206* (0.1009)
Working in agriculture	−0.468 (0.3706)	−1.287 (1.0945)	Western	−0.200** (0.6556)	−0.583*** (0.0977)
Employed	0.382*** (0.0835)	0.587*** (0.1241)	Observations	5970	5970

4.2 Determinants of Internet Use (First Stage)

Table 2 shows the results of the first stage regression of the Heckman two-stage estimation model. It shows that age, education level, digital skills, type of job, and household economic status are determinants of Internet adoption. Overall, the decision to use the Internet depends on the expected benefits of going online and the associated costs. The sample shows that young people in rural areas with a university degree or higher, higher digital skills, and better household economic circumstances are more likely to use the Internet. There is a clear disparity in terms of age: the younger the user, the more likely they are to use the Internet, suggesting that younger people are more willing to experiment with and adapt to new technologies, while older people are less comfortable with them. Residents with a university degree or higher are more likely to use the

Internet, which is consistent with existing research and confirms that the more educated users are more likely to use the Internet. This positive effect is still significant in rural areas. Residents in the "private enterprise/self-employed/enterprise self-employed" and "employed" categories are more likely to use the Internet than residents in their own agricultural operations, probably because they have a greater need to use the Internet at work.

Table 2. Regression results of factors influencing rural Internet use

Variables	Marginal Effects (Std.Err)	Variables	Marginal Effects (Std.Err)
Gender (Female = 1)	−0.077 (0.0975)	Employed	0.389** (0.1121)
Age (12-32 years)	0.460*** (0.1111)	Non-farm labor	0.074 (0.2212)
Age (13-64 years)	reference	Household economic status	0.230*** (0.0538)
Age (65 years and older)	−1.277 (0.3601)	Numerical Skills	4.577*** (0.1427)
Primary and below	reference	Number of children	0.038 (0.0378)
Secondary school	0.155 (0.1046)	Eastern	reference
High School	0.303 (0.1905)	Central	0.233 (0.1379)
University and above	1.250*** (0.2814)	Western	0.233* (0.1114)
Own Agricultural	reference	Log likelihood	−392.2732
Private or self-employed	0.601*** (0.1480)	Wald chi2	1204.82
Working in agriculture	−0.366 (0.5178)	Number of observations	5970

Access to wealth is crucial when using the Internet, as people of higher economic status are more likely to use the Internet, which is consistent with the findings of Kilenthong et al. [49]. As for digital skills, the likelihood of using the Internet is higher when a person has adequate work-study skills or business skills or recreational skills, this result is consistent with the findings of Hu Ying's study on Chinese rural residents [50], suggesting that digital skills are the main reason for promoting residents' Internet use.

Likewise, geographical location is crucial to Internet usage. Data shows that people living in rural areas of western China are more likely to use the Internet, which is an interesting phenomenon. Scholars generally believe that since the reform and opening up, China's economy has been doing better in the east and weaker in the central and western parts of the country. Information and communication technology (ICT) has been an important support for less developed regions to achieve "catch-up" development, but weak infrastructure and other factors have made Internet access and use in the west significantly less favorable than in the east [51]. However, our study found that residents of rural areas in the west are more likely to use the Internet, which may be related to China's western development and the "village-to-village" telecommunication policy, which encourages and supports more residents of rural areas in the west to use the Internet.

4.3 Determinants of Internet Use (Second Stage)

The Lambda coefficient of the treatment variable (Internet use) can be calculated based on the regression results of the first stage. After adding the Lambda coefficient, the regression results of the second stage of the two-stage estimation model can be calculated, as shown in Table 3. The Lambda coefficients of the five Internet usage patterns are all significant at the 0.001 level, Indicates that it is appropriate to use a sample selection model. The results show the regression results of the Heckman two-stage model on factors influencing Internet usage patterns (entertainment, social networking, e-commerce, learning, and work) in rural areas of China. Internet usage patterns vary by gender, age, education level, occupation and geographic location. In gender, women are more likely to use the Internet for social networking and electronic trading activities, while men are more likely to use the Internet to learn. It shows that Chinese rural women mainly use the Internet to maintain contact with family and friends, and these activities are related to the traditional role of Chinese rural women in the family. In terms of age, young people are more likely to use the Internet for entertainment, social networking, e-commerce, study and work, etc.; Except for the elderly people who did not show any significant relationship in learning, they are unlikely to carry out related activities through the Internet in other activities.

In education, those most likely to study and work via the Internet are those with university education and above, while those most likely to engage in e-commerce are those with high school education and above. It implies that rural users with higher levels of education are more likely to engage in value-added activities via the Internet. The conclusion is interesting. Residents with different education levels are relatively similar in their likelihood of using online entertainment. It is consistent with Hu Ying's (2022) study, currently, most residents use the Internet mainly for entertainment activities. This Internet usage pattern structure needs to be improved and adjusted urgently [52].

In terms of occupation, those residents who are "employed" and work in the private sector, for example, are more likely to participate in value-added online activities such as learning and working, while "agricultural wage earners" or "non-agricultural casual" users are less likely to participate in value-added online activities such as learning and working. "Working agricultural" or "non-farm casual" users are less likely to participate in such value-added activities, shows that a digital divide at the level of Internet use has formed in rural areas due to differences in occupational types.

Digital skills significantly increase the likelihood of engaging in entertainment, social networking, e-commerce and learning via the Internet, except for a non-significant effect

Table 3. Regression results of factors influencing rural Internet use

variant	Entertainment	Social networks	E-commerce	Learning	Working
	Marginal Effects (Std.Err)				
Gender (Female = 1)	0.009 (0.0085)	−0.016* (0.0070)	−0.056*** (0.0137)	0.038* (0.0147)	0.023 (0.0146)
Age (12–32 years)	0.060*** (0.0092)	0.040*** (0.0079)	0.161*** (0.0159)	0.055** (0.0162)	0.067*** (0.0162)
Age (33–64 years)	reference	reference	reference	reference	reference
Age (65 years and older)	−0.539*** (0.1112)	−0.329*** (0.0802)	−0.306*** (0.0552)	−0.109 (0.0670)	−0.133*** (0.0363)
Primary and below	reference	reference	reference	reference	reference
Secondary school	0.079*** (0.0127)	0.005 (0.0106)	0.154*** (0.0197)	0.172*** (0.0190)	0.128*** (0.0185)
High School	0.083*** (0.0138)	0.021 (0.0121)	0.264*** (0.0235)	0.338*** (0.0250)	0.300*** (0.0259)
University and above	0.064*** (0.0149)	0.037** (0.0111)	0.031*** (0.0231)	0.535*** (0.0246)	0.548*** (0.0242)
Own Agricultural	reference	reference	reference	reference	reference
Private or self-employed	0.050** (0.0158)	0.064*** (0.0134)	0.226*** (0.0255)	0.103*** (0.0270)	0.171*** (0.0271)
Working in agriculture	0.072*** (0.0173)	0.060*** (0.0130)	0.145 (0.1133)	−0.070 (0.1043)	−0.032 (0.1043)
Employed	0.054*** (0.0122)	0.050*** (0.0111)	0.175*** (0.0201)	0.080*** (0.0198)	0.185*** (0.0198)
Non-farm labor	0.069*** (0.0228)	0.027 (0.0235)	0.113* (0.0454)	−0.008 (0.0404)	−0.008 (0.0370)
Household Economic Status	0.044*** (0.0057)	0.020*** (0.0045)	0.051*** (0.0086)	0.023* (0.0095)	0.034*** (0.0094)
Number of children	−0.000 (0.0036)	0.001 (0.0027)	0.003 (0.0055)	0.012* (0.0060)	0.003 (0.0058)
digital skill	0.819*** (0.0748)	1.069*** (0.1239)	0.575*** (0.1497)	0.496*** (0.1055)	0.197 (0.1055)
Eastern	reference	reference	reference	reference	reference
Central	0.016 (0.0105)	0.019* (0.0097)	0.003 (0.0176)	0.021 (0.0191)	−0.006 (0.0194)

(*continued*)

Table 3. (*continued*)

variant	Entertainment	Social networks	E-commerce	Learning	Working
	Marginal Effects (Std.Err)				
Western	0.011 (0.0101)	0.042*** (0.0085)	0.008 (0.0164)	0.0861*** (0.0176)	0.008 (0.0178)
IMR	0.367*** (0.0063)	0.397*** (0.0078)	0.189*** (0.0091)	0.123*** (0.0079)	0.010*** (0.0095)
Cons	−0.479*** (0.0892)	−0.415** (0.1298)	−0.783* (0.1649)	−0.634*** (0.1330)	−0.464** (0.1448)
N	3860	3862	3859	3864	3471
R-sq	0.2427	0.296	0.2326	0.1878	0.274

on work patterns. It is broadly consistent with existing research, which generally agrees that people with higher digital skills are more likely to use different Internet modes [53].

Geographic location is crucial in explaining Internet usage patterns, and Table 5 illustrates the heterogeneity in Internet usage patterns across different rural areas in China. In rural China, users in the central region are more likely to use the Internet for social activities, and users in the western region are more likely to use the Internet for social and learning activities. It is inconsistent with existing research, as some scholars believe that residents in rural areas of western China are drowning in entertainment and other recreational "junk information". However, we feel that as China's western region continues to develop, the attitudes of rural residents towards the Internet have changed dramatically, and that the Internet may become an effective means of catching up by leaps and bounds in the western region. The higher the economic income, the higher the likelihood of using the Internet for entertainment, socializing, e-commerce, learning and work. Finally, users with more children in the household are more likely to use the Internet for learning, which may be related to the current promotion of online education and the importance that families place on their children's education.

5   Conclusions and Recommendations

This paper uses the Heckman two-stage model based on the China Family Tracking Survey (CFPS) 2018 data to study the influencing factors of Internet access, usage and usage patterns in rural China, which provides empirical evidence to prove the primary and secondary digital divide in rural China. This paper explains the influencing factors of rural residents' Internet access and usage behaviors at the micro level. It will help further enrich theoretical research on the digital divide. (1) It is found that the factors influencing Internet access, usage and usage patterns in rural China are similar to those observed in other developing countries at the early stage of Internet diffusion, mainly as follows: (1) We can infer the profile of Internet access user groups in rural areas of China: young and well-educated people with good economic income and digital skills; and there is a big gap in access methods in terms of Internet access. Mobile Internet access is significantly higher than conventional Internet access; (2) Age, education level, digital skills and family economic status are important factors affecting Internet use; (3) Internet use patterns (entertainment, social networking, e-commerce, learning, and geographic location and work) have significant differences in gender, age, education level, occupation and geographic location; and (4) rural users' Internet use is mainly dominated by non-value-creating activities such as entertainment and socializing. Accordingly, this paper puts forward the following policy recommendations:

Based on the conclusions drawn in this paper, the following countermeasures are proposed for Internet popularization and use in rural areas. First, it is necessary to comprehensively understand the evolution and trend of the digital divide in rural areas in practice, establish a sound digital policy in light of the fact that rural areas mainly rely on smartphones for Internet access, and increase the promotion of online services and applications related to employment, education, and public health, so that more people in rural areas of developing countries can enjoy the digital dividend. Secondly, continue to improve rural Internet access infrastructure to help more rural residents access the Internet through broadband; encourage communication companies to continuously strengthen smart phone products and related services so that mobile Internet access can obtain the same functions as conventional Internet access; establish a sound training system for rural users' Internet use skills, and realize the use of the Internet by improving the digital skills of rural users; and enhance the advantages brought by Internet use. Enhance the advantages and benefits brought by the use of the Internet. Once again, continuously improve e-commerce-related policies, provide policy support for rural young people to engage in e-commerce. And take e-commerce as an big way to solve the problem of young people's employment in rural areas; continuously improve young people's digital skills, and provide support to promote the sustainable and healthy development of e-commerce in rural areas. Finally, the government must pay attention to the problem of digital divide among rural elderly groups. On the one hand, we should use the community as a unit to improve the digital skills of the elderly people and minimize the digital divide among the elderly people; on the other hand, in various specific scenarios of grassroots governance (especially governance scenarios for the purpose of "intelligent"), focus on Taking into account the fact that the elderly people cannot use the Internet well reflects the temperature of grassroots governance.

It should be pointed out that this study only deals with the two levels of digital divide, Internet access and Internet use, and does not discuss the three levels of digital divide, such as the inequality brought by Internet use. This is also a breakthrough for future research, i.e., discussing the current situation of the three-level digital divide in rural areas and its influencing factors, so as to continue to enrich the research on the impact of Internet access and use on the life satisfaction of residents in rural areas in China and other developing countries.

References

1. Prieger, J.E.: The broadband digital divide and the economic benefits of mobile broadband for rural areas. Telecommun. Policy 37(2013), 483–502 (2013)
2. Cooper, M., Kimmelman, G.: The Digital Divide Confronts the Telecommunications Act of 1996: Economic Reality Versus Public Policy. Consumer Union, Washington, DC (1999)
3. Qiu, Z., Zhang, S., Liu, S., Xu, Y.: From digital divide to dividend difference - a perspective of internet capital. China Soc. Sci. (10), 93–115+203–204 (2016)
4. Gübli, G.A., Xue, D., Song, Y., Zhang, X., Yang, B.: Regional differences and factors influencing the evolution of the number of villages in China. China Agric. Resour. Zoning 42(11), 85–96 (2021)
5. Zhou, Z.: Hollowing out of China's rural population and its challenges. Popul. Stud. (02), 45–52 (2008)s
6. Li, Y., Wang, H.: Spatial distribution of hollow and solid villages of China's population-evidence from the administrative village sample of the third agricultural census. China Rural Econ. (04), 124–144 (2020)
7. Blumberg, R.: Alternative food networks and farmer livelihoods. A spatializing livelihoods perspective. Geoforum 88, 161–173 (2018)
8. Yang, R., Cao, Y.: On the tension between digital empowerment and digital divide in the countryside and its dissolution. J. Nanjing Agric. Univ. (Soc. Sci. Ed.) 21(05), 31–40 (2021)
9. De Grammont, H.: Hacia una ruralidad fragmentada. Nueva Soc. 262, 51–63 (2016). http://nuso.org/media/articles/downloads/2.TC_de_Grammont_262.pdf
10. Wang, D., Liu, Z.: Technological empowerment in rural areas: connotation, dynamics and boundaries. J. Huazhong Agric. Univ. (Soc. Sci. Ed.) (3), 138–148 (2020)
11. Zhang, J., Cheng, M., Gong, X.: Research on the characteristics and influencing factors of digital divide between urban and rural areas in China. Stat. Inf. Forum 36(12), 92–102 (2021)
12. Qiu, Z., Li, Y., Xu, W.: Digitalization and rural governance structure change. J. Xi'an Jiaotong Univ. (Soc. Sci. Ed.) 42(02), 74–84 (2022)
13. Erdiaw-Kwasie, M., Khorshed, A.: Towards understanding digital divide in rural partnerships and development: a framework and evidence from rural Australia. J. Rural. Stud. 43, 214–224 (2016)
14. Compaine, B.M. (ed.): The Digital Divide: Facing a Crisis or Creating a Myth? MIT Press, Cambridge (2001)
15. Büchi, M., Just, N., Latzer, M.: Modeling the second-level digital divide: a five-country study of social differences in Internet use. New Media Soc. 18(11), 2703–2722 (2016)
16. Van Deursen, A.J., Helsper, E.J.: The third-level digital divide: who benefits most from being online? Communication and information technologies annual, pp. 29–52. Emerald Group Publishing Limited (2015)
17. Van Dijk, J.A.G.M.: The Digital Divide. Polity Press, Cambridge (2019)
18. Van Deursen, A., Van Dijk, J.: The digital divide shifts to differences in usage. New Media Soc. 16(3), 507–526 (2014)
19. DiMaggio, P., Hargittai, E., Celeste, C., Shafer, S.: From unequal access to differentiated use: a literature review and agenda for research on digital inequality. In: Kathryn, N. (ed.) Social Inequality. Russell Sage Foundation, New York (2004)
20. Zhou, L., Feng, D., Yi, X.: Digital inclusive finance and urban-rural income gap: "digital dividend" or "digital divide". Economist (05), 99–108 (2020)
21. Huang, Y.: Causes and empowering governance of China's digital divide. Learn. Practic. (09), 23–33 (2022)
22. Liu, Y., Li, X.: How to cross the digital divide of the elderly people in the digital age? Southeast Acad. 05, 105–115 (2022)

23. Liu, W.: The effect of digital financial inclusion on residents' relative poverty. J. South China Agric. Univ. (Soc. Sci. Ed.) **20**(06), 65–77 (2021)
24. Dohse, D., Cheng, L.: Bad neighborhood and internet adoption in poor countries: what is behind the persistent digital gap? Growth Chang. **49**(1), 241–262 (2018)
25. Kiiski, S., Pohjola, M.: Cross-country diffusion of the internet. Inf. Econ. Policy **14**(2), 297–310 (2002)
26. Gwaka, L., May, J., Tucker, W.: Toward low-cost community networks in rural communities: the impact of context using the case study of Beitbridge, Zimbabwe. Electron. J. Inf. Syst. Dev. Ctries. **84**(3), 1–11 (2018)
27. Srinuan, C., Bohlin, E.: Analysis of fixed broadband access and use in Thailand: drivers and barriers. Telecommun. Policy **37**(8), 615–625 (2013)
28. Michailidis, A., Partalidou, M., Nastis, A., Papadaki-Klavdianou, A., Charatsari, C.: Who goes online? Evidence of internet use patterns from rural Greece. Telecommun. Policy **35**(4), 333–343 (2011)
29. Garín-Muñoz, T., López, R., Pérez-Amaral, T., Herguera, I., Valarezo, A.: Models for individual adoption of eCommerce, eBanking and eGovernment in Spain. Telecommun. Policy **43**(1), 110–111 (2019)
30. Cao, J., Mei, W.: The gap between urban and rural starting lines: an analysis of the digital divide in transitional China. Contemp. Commun. (02), 17–21+78 (2017)
31. Hong, J., Li, X.: WeChat's "feedback" diffusion in rural families: an examination based on Chen District village in Shanxi Province. Int. J. **41**(10), 50–74 (2019)
32. Wang, C., Li, J., Huang, Y.: Classification, impact and response of digital divide. Financ. Sci. (04), 75–81 (2022)
33. Fan, G., Zhang, X.: China's Information Economy in Global Perspective: Development and Challenges. Renmin University of China Press, Beijing (2003)
34. Cheng, M., Zhang, Z.: Internet development and consumption gap between urban and rural residents in the context of the new era. Res. Quant. Econ. Tech. Econ. (7), 22–41 (2019)
35. Song, H.: Digital divide or information empowerment? – a study on mobile phone usage of migrant workers in the Yangtze River Delta. Modern Commun. (J. Commun. Univ. China) **38**(06), 132–137 (2016)
36. Lu, J.H., Wei, X.D.: Analytical framework, concepts and path selection of digital divide governance for the elderly - based on the perspectives of digital divide and knowledge divide theory. Popul. Stud. **45**(03), 17–30 (2021)
37. Su, H.: Digital urban-rural construction: the road to urban-rural integration and common wealth. E-Government (10), 88–98 (2022)
38. Li, W., Zhou, D., Li, X.: Research on the impact of digital divide on rural household income and mechanisms - an empirical analysis based on China family tracking survey (CFPS) data. J. Southwest Univ. Natl. (Hum. Soc. Sci. Ed.) **43**(10), 116–127 (2022)
39. Huang, M., Dou, X.: Will the urban-rural digital divide hinder the upgrading of rural residents' consumption structure? – an analysis based on data from the China Family Tracking Survey (CFPS). Econ. Issues Explor. **09**, 47–64 (2022)
40. Wu, X., Wang, M.: A study of digital inequality among rural youth based on ethnographic futures research method. Libr. Constr. (03), 35–38+42 (2016)
41. Wang, M., Yan, H.: The value of social capital in the process of rural residents crossing the episodic digital divide - a report of a field survey in Jinghai, Tianjin. Chin. Libr. J. **39**(05), 39–49 (2013)
42. Huang, Y.: Causes and empowering governance of China's digital divide. Learn. Practic. (09), 23–33 (2022)

43. Research Report on China's Urban and Rural Digital Inclusive Development-Digitalization Boosts Rural Revitalization and Common Wealth. China Academy of Information and Communication Research Website. http://www.caict.ac.cn/kxyj/qwfb/ztbg/202112/t20211230_394812.htm

44. Shen, H., Yang, Y., Pan, F.: Political affiliation, securities violations and surplus quality of privately listed companies. Financ. Res. (01), 194–206 (2014)

45. Alderete, M.V.: Examining the drivers of Internet use among the poor: the case of Bahía Blanca city in Argentina. Technol. Soc. **59**, 42–58 (2019)

46. Wooldridge, J.M.: Econometric Analysis of Cross Section and Panel Data, 2nd edn. MIT Press, Cambridge (2010)

47. Martínez-Domínguez, M., Mora-Rivera, J.: Internet adoption and usage patterns in rural Mexico. Technol. Soc. (60), 101226 (2020)

48. Chaudhuri, A., Flamm, S., Horrigan, J.: An analysis of the determinants of internet access. Telecommun. Policy **29**(9–10), 731–755 (2005)

49. Kilenthong, T., Odton, P.: Access to ICT in rural and urban Thailand. Telecommun. Policy **38**(11), 1146–1159 (2014)

50. Hu, Y.: A review of the urban-rural digital divide in the context of rural revitalization. Res. Soc. Chin. Charact. (04), 60–69 (2022)

51. Wang, C.: Research on the innovation model generated in the process of digital economy development. Sci. Manag. Res. **41**(01), 74–79 (2023)

52. Hu, Y., Zhong, Y.: Digitalization helps rural revitalization and common wealth – the case of Maoming City, Guangdong Province. New Econ. (02), 47–53 (2023)

53. Ding, S., Liu, C.: Internet use, income improvement and skill premium of youth groups in the digital economy era - a perspective based on rural-urban differences. Contemp. Econ. Manag. **44**(08), 64–72 (2022)

Exploring the Causal Relationship Between Forgiveness and Sentencing Outcomes in Dangerous Driving Cases

Sibei Li[1] , Yang Weng[1] , Xianglong Wang[2] , and Xin Li[2(✉)]

[1] School of Mathematics, Sichuan University, Chengdu, China
wengyang@scu.edu.com
[2] Law School, Sichuan University, Chengdu, China
scufxy4010@163.com

Abstract. In the theoretical framework of criminal law in our country, the study of crime is primarily focused on the perpetrator, and criminal legislation is predominantly concerned with defining crimes from the perspective of the perpetrator. This has resulted in a relatively weak understanding of the behavior of victims in criminal studies. However, the crime of dangerous driving is a typical minor offense in our criminal punishment system and a common traffic safety crime, making the issue of sentencing in such cases a matter of concern. This article aims to explore the causal effect of whether the victim forgives the offender on the severity of sentencing in dangerous driving cases. Methods: Firstly, based on various statutory and discretionary sentencing factors, features are extracted from judicial documents using a combination of regular expressions and annotation. After determining the significance of these features, variable selection is performed. A sentencing prediction model is constructed using the Stacking method on the selected variables. Then, causal effects of forgiveness on the severity of sentencing are estimated using conditional outcome model, grouped conditional outcome model, inverse probability weighting, and doubly robust method. Finally, bootstrap sampling is used to provide interval estimates of causal effects under different models. Results: Our research results indicate that, on average, defendants who receive forgiveness from the victim are 32.7% more likely to receive lighter penalties. Quantifying the impact of forgiveness on sentencing outcomes through causal inference methods helps clarify the role of forgiveness in the sentencing system of criminal cases in our country. It also addresses the insufficient research on the post-crime factor of victim attitude in criminal and punishment theories, providing further data references for the standardization of judicial practices in our country.

Keywords: Causal effect · Dangerous driving crime · Forgiveness · Doubly robust estimator

This work was partly supported by National Key R&D Program of China under Grant 2020YFC0832400. This work was partly supported by Key R&D Program of Sichuan Province under Grant 2021YFS0397.

W. Hong and G. Kanaparan (Eds.): ICCSE 2023, CCIS 2023, pp. 400–414, 2024.
https://doi.org/10.1007/978-981-97-0730-0_36

1   Introduction

Dangerous driving offense refers to the crime of driving a motor vehicle on the road in a drunken state, or engaging in activities such as racing, severe overloading, illegal transportation of hazardous chemicals, which endangers public safety. This offense is a typical minor crime in China's criminal penalties and is a common traffic safety crime. The sentencing of this offense has attracted attention. The Supreme People's Court, the Supreme People's Procuratorate, and the Ministry of Public Security issued a notice titled 'Opinions on the Application of Laws in Handling Criminal Cases of Drunk Driving of Motor Vehicles,' which pointed out that the sentencing of the dangerous driving offense should comprehensively consider factors such as the defendant's level of intoxication, the type of motor vehicle, the road conditions, the driving speed, whether actual damage was caused, and the defendant's admission of guilt and remorse. However, the notice only provides general principles for sentencing and does not specify specific sentencing guidelines.

In the theory of criminal law in China, the study of crimes is primarily focused on the perpetrator, and criminal legislation is mainly based on the conduct of the perpetrator, which results in a relatively weak research on the behavior of the victims. Crimes directly harm the victims, and in the process of suffering from criminal acts, the victims have a firsthand experience and intuitive perception of the harm caused to them by the criminal acts. The court should listen to the opinions of the victims and consider them when sentencing. However, whether the forgiveness of the victim has a binding effect on the court cannot be generalized. In China's criminal law, victim behavior includes consent, fault, and forgiveness [17]. The forgiveness of the victim, as a criminal law principle that does not affect the nature of the crime based on post-crime matters, generally only affects the sentencing of the perpetrator's conduct and does not affect the qualification of the crime. In the existing statutory and discretionary circumstances of criminal cases, whether obtaining forgiveness from the victim is a factor related to the victim reflects the judiciary's emphasis on and concern for the victim. The forgiveness of the victim is manifested in the issuance of a criminal forgiveness document. The forgiveness document is generally completed during the process from prosecution to court testimony, and it has a mitigating effect in criminal law [4,8,17]. It means that the party or the victim has emotionally forgiven and indicated that they no longer pursue the matter, which has a certain reference for mitigating or exempting punishment in sentencing. In cases of dangerous driving involving traffic accidents and resulting in personal injury or property damage, whether obtaining forgiveness from the victim will affect the final sentencing outcome.

Currently, there is no clear definition of victim forgiveness in both the field of legal theory and judicial practice. Victim forgiveness can be understood as the expression of the victim's forgiveness towards the offender's actions. It refers to the victim, after understanding the relevant circumstances of the defendant, waiving the right to demand that judicial authorities prosecute the defendant's criminal responsibility or requesting leniency or reduced punishment for the defendant [4, 8, 17]. From an internal perspective, crime is not only a confrontation between the offender and the state but also primarily an infringement on the victim in cases involving victims. Therefore, while criminal law regulates the relationship between the offender and the state, it should also pay attention to the relationship between the victim and the defendant, focus on the interests of the victim, listen to the victim's opinions, and respect them.

However, in the actual trial of criminal cases, since forgiveness is a discretionary factor in sentencing, its significant impact on the severity of the sentence is still unknown. The standard for this factor in criminal law research and judicial practice is difficult to unify. Therefore, this paper considers quantifying the degree of impact of victim forgiveness on the severity of the sentence. We collecte relevant data on real-world dangerous driving cases and employ a combination of regular expression matching and manual annotation to extract sentencing factors from judicial documents. Furthermore, we integrate machine learning and causal inference methods to quantify the causal relationship between forgiveness and sentencing.

The rest of this paper is organized as follows: a review of relevant literature on the impact of victim forgiveness will be conducted in Sect. 2. Section 3 includes the experimental design and data collection. In Sect. 4, we summarize commonly used causal inference estimators, including conditional outcome model, grouped conditional outcome model, inverse probability weighting, and doubly robust methods. The models corresponding to different estimation methods and their predictive results will be presented and discussed in Sects. 5 and 6; and the conclusion will be presented in Sect. 7.

2   Literature Review

In China, there have been comprehensive studies on the sentencing factors of the offense of dangerous driving, most of which include the construction of sentencing prediction models. Due to the high proportion of cases related to drunk driving in dangerous driving offenses, a significant amount of research has focused on cases of drunk driving. One notable study by Chu Zhiyuan primarily examined cases of drunk driving and analyzed various sentencing factors using partial correlation coefficients and logistic regression models [2]. The study found that the most important influencing factor for the severity of sentencing in cases of drunk driving is blood alcohol content. Additionally, factors such as vehicle type, presence of other violations, voluntary surrender or confession, and the application of probation also have a significant impact on the duration of detention. Similarly, Wen Ji conducted research on cases of drunk driving and addressed issues related to the setting of dummy variables and the calculation of regression coefficients in earlier studies [15]. The conclusion drawn was that the most significant factor affecting the duration of detention is blood alcohol content. Su Caixia and Wang Nifa found that among all the considered factors, blood alcohol concentration has a decisive impact on sentencing, while aggravating circumstances and vehicle type only have significant effects on certain penalties, confirming the simplification feature of sentencing [14]. The aforementioned literature on sentencing analysis of dangerous driving cases is based on regression analysis in statistical methods and is divided into three parts: detention sentence, fine sentence, and probation, respectively. The analyzed factors can be primarily categorized into six types: road type, blood alcohol concentration, vehicle type, criminal outcome, aggravating circumstances, and mitigating circumstances.

In the sentencing of criminal cases in China, mitigating circumstances primarily revolve around the defendant. The forgiveness of the victim as a relevant factor related to the victim is considered in the sentencing determination and is an important aspect to study its impact on sentencing. In most cases, victim forgiveness is only considered as a mitigating factor for lenient punishment of the defendant and should not solely exempt the defendant from criminal responsibility or reduce their punishment. While victim forgiveness can influence the sentencing, its impact on the outcome of different types of litigation varies. Even within the same type of litigation, the influence of victim forgiveness on sentencing can differ depending on the nature of the case [4]. Han Junwen and Li Zhongyong explored the impact of victim forgiveness on sentencing and argued that courts should consider the opinions of victims as a sentencing factor when handling cases [4]. They discussed the relationship between victim forgiveness and the application of penalties based on grounds, limits, conditions, and supervision guarantees of victim forgiveness, proposing that considering victim forgiveness as a mitigating circumstance in sentencing contributes to social harmony and stability. Gao Tong examined the mechanism through which compensation and forgiveness affect the sentencing outcomes in cases of intentional injury [3]. It was found that compensation has a significant impact on the main sentencing outcome and the application of probation, and as the severity of the case increases, the influence of compensation on sentencing relatively decreases while the influence of forgiveness increases. Liu Xiaoyi studied the impact of victim forgiveness on sentencing in judicial practice [8]. By analyzing appellate court judgments that resulted in changed verdicts due to the presence of victim forgiveness during the second instance, it was found that in cases of intentional injury, whether the defendant obtains victim forgiveness affects whether the defendant is sentenced and also influences the length of the sentence. However, compared to legally prescribed mitigating circumstances such as voluntary confession and meritorious service, the influence of obtaining victim forgiveness as a mitigating factor on sentencing is less significant.

From the above studies, it can be inferred that in the current judicial practice in China, the focus of the trial process is primarily on the defendant, while the factors related to the victim are often overlooked. The victim's role is not given due attention during the trial, leading to difficulties in establishing unified standards for the factor of victim forgiveness in the research of criminal law and judicial practice. The existing system related to victim forgiveness requires urgent improvement.

The existing research on the impact of forgiveness on sentencing is mostly based on simple analysis and statistical methods. There is very little literature that quantitatively applies causal inference methods to analyze the impact of forgiveness on sentencing. The main reason for selecting causal inference methods combined with statistical methods in this study is that the presence of a correlation between data does not necessarily imply a causal relationship, but a causal relationship encompasses a correlation [5]. Correlation is a statistical relationship that indicates a statistical dependency between two variables and can help discover the connection between variables, but it does not provide a clear understanding of the underlying mechanism of influence between the two variables. When there are other confounding variables that are correlated with both variables, it may lead to statistically significant correlations between the two variables that do not have a causal relationship, which is known as a spurious causal relationship [5]. Causal inference, on the other hand, enables the analysis of causal relationships between variables, determines the direction of influence between variables, identifies and removes spurious causal relationships, and uncovers the genuine causal associations between phenomena.

In the research problem of this study, the presence of other legally prescribed and mitigating circumstances in the sentencing outcome as confounding variables can affect the accuracy of statistical analysis and calculations. By using causal inference methods, it is possible to eliminate the influence of these confounding factors and more accurately quantify the degree of impact of forgiveness on the sentencing outcome.

3   Experiment Design and Data Collection

To evaluate the impact of victim forgiveness on the sentencing outcomes of the defendants, we selected a total of 1,700 cases from 2019 to 2020 involving dangerous driving incidents resulting in vehicle damage or personal injury for analysis.

During the feature selection process, we categorized the features into three main groups: the defendants' personal demographic characteristics, factors influencing the sentencing outcomes, and the judgment results.

Firstly, the defendants' personal demographic characteristics included gender, age, education level, occupation, and the venue. For cases involving the offense of drunk driving, the sentencing outcomes were divided into two categories: non-criminal punishment and criminal punishment. Criminal punishment consisted of three types of judgments: imprisonment, suspended sentence, and fines. The factors influencing the sentencing outcomes included the blood alcohol concentration at the time of the offense, the type of vehicle driven, the type of road, whether actual personal or vehicle damage was caused and whether the defendant bore primary or full responsibility for the incident, traffic violations such as driving without a license, speeding, overloading, whether the defendant was a repeat offender, subjective factors including whether the defendant confessed voluntarily, attempted to escape, compensated the victim, or obtained victim forgiveness.

Among the factors influencing the sentencing outcomes, blood alcohol concentration was a continuous variable. The types of roads were categorized as ordinary roads, urban expressways, and highways. The types of vehicles driven were classified as motorcycles, tricycles, sedans, and trucks. Personal injury referred to the number of people injured or killed, while vehicle damage referred to the number of damaged vehicles. Primary or full responsibility, traffic violations, repeat offenses, escape, voluntary confession, compensation, and victim forgiveness were all binary variables indicating the presence or absence of these factors. Regarding the judgment results, this study primarily focused on the outcomes of imprisonment as a form of criminal punishment. The mean value of the imprisonment outcomes was used as a threshold to divide the cases into two categories: above the mean and below the mean. Cases with outcomes above the mean indicated heavier penalties, while those below the mean indicated lighter penalties.

The features were extracted from the court judgments using a combination of regular expressions and manual annotation. The factors influencing sentencing, such as the extent of personal injury or vehicle damage, were extracted through a combination of regular expression matching and manual annotation. The extraction of other factors influencing the sentencing outcomes, traffic violations, and subjective factors were performed using regular expressions. Table 1 gives the descriptive information of variables.

Based on the selected features mentioned above, we conducted hypothesis tests to assess the significance of each feature on the treatment variable A (whether forgiveness from the victim was obtained) and the outcome variable Y (sentencing outcome). For continuous variables, we used the Mann-Whitney U test, while for categorical variables, we used the chi-square test. According to the hypothesis testing results, all influencing factors were categorized as follows: the treatment variable A(1 - obtaining victim's forgiveness, 0 - not obtaining victim's forgiveness), confounding factor Z(including age, education level, occupation, blood alcohol content, type of vehicle driven, driving without license, assuming full responsibility, escape, vehicle damage, speeding, recidivism, self-surrender, compensation), the covariates X_Y associated with the outcome variable (gender, unlicensed driving, number of fatalities, overloading), and the covariates X_A associated with the treatment variable (recidivism, overcrowding).

4   Estimators for the Average Treatment Effect

We want to measure the causal effect of the treatment variable A (1-obtaining victim forgiveness, 0-not obtaining victim forgiveness) on the outcome variable Y (1-heavier sentencing, 0-lighter sentencing). According to the Neyman-Rubin causal model framework [13], we can define the potential outcomes as $Y_A : A = 1, 0$, representing the values of the outcome variable corresponding to obtaining forgiveness ($A = 1$) or not obtaining forgiveness ($A = 0$). The causal effect of the treatment variable on the outcome variable for an individual sample can be defined as $Y_1 - Y_0$. However, it is not possible to apply different treatments to the same sample to obtain the corresponding outcomes. Therefore, we can only define the causal treatment effect for the population [6]:

$$\tau = E[Y_1 - Y_0] = E[Y_1] - E[Y_0] \tag{1}$$

Table 1. Descriptive information of variables.

Variable	Description and Summary Statistics
Gender	Male (98.0%); Female (2.0%)
Age	Continuous (Mean 38.6, Max 76, Min 18, Standard deviation 10.8)
Education level	Illiterate (2%); Primary School (23.2%); Junior High School (48.7%); Vocational School (6.2%); High School (10.5%); Technical college degree (5.7%); Bachelor's degree (32.6%); Master's degree (0.2%)
Occupation	Unemployed (25.5%); Student (1.5%); Retired (0.6%); Farmer (34.5%); Worker (16.3%); Driver(0.6%); Freelancer (2.3%); Employee (10.6%); Self-employed (8.5%)
District	Northeast (46.3%); Southeast (31.4%); Northwest (12.9%); Southwest (9.5%)
Blood alcohol content	Continuous (Mean 178.9, Max 467.6, Min 0, Standard deviation 63.9)
Vehicle type	Motorcycle (34.9%); Tricycle(8.6%); Car (51.6%); Truck (5.0%)
Vehicle registration plate	0 (67.9%); 1 (32.0%)
Driving license	0 (66.7%); 1 (33.3%)
Responsible	0 (12.9%); 1 (87.1%)
Escape	0 (90.3%); 1 (9.7%)
Vehicle damage	0 (63.4%); 1 (3.0%); 2 (29.9%); 3 (3.26%); 4 (0.4%)
Injuries	0 (84.7%); 1 (6.0%); 2 (7.3%); 3 (1.4%); 4 (0.5%); 7 (0.1%)
Fatalities	0 (99.4%); 1 (0.4%); 3 (0.1%)
Roadway	0 (92.8%); 1 (7.2%)
Overloading (number of passengers)	0 (97.3%); 1 (2.7%)
Speeding	0 (92.5%); 1 (7.6%)
Overloading (exceeding the weight limit)	0 (99.7%); 1 (0.3%)
Repeat offender	0 (99.8%); 1 (0.2%)
Recidivism	0 (89.2%); 1 (10.8%)
Surrendering	0 (6.9%); 1 (93.1%)
Compensation	0 (31.6%); 1 (68.4%)
forgiveness	0 (44.7%); 1 (55.3%)

This is known as the average treatment effect (ATE), which can be interpreted as the average causal risk difference between obtaining forgiveness ($A = 1$) and not obtaining forgiveness ($A = 0$). If individuals can be randomly assigned to the forgiveness group and the non-forgiveness group in a randomized experiment, we can simply calculate the difference in the outcome variable between the treatment group and the control group to obtain an unbiased estimate of ATE [13]. However, in practical scenarios, we cannot manipulate whether each individual obtains forgiveness, and each individual is assigned to the treatment group or the control group based on whether they obtained forgiveness in the actual case.

For the selected data, the following relationships between variables can be obtained:

$$A = f_A(X_A, Z, \epsilon_A) \tag{2}$$

$$Y = f_Y(X_Y, Z, A, \epsilon_Y) \tag{3}$$

where ϵ_A and ϵ_Y are error terms; and f_A and f_Y denote the data generating process for A and Y, respectively. We implicitly assume that the forgiveness from the victim and the sentencing outcome of the defendant depend solely on the selected influencing factors, and we further assume that [13]:

$$\epsilon_Y \perp \epsilon_A | Z \tag{4}$$

This assumption implies that, given the demographic characteristics and factors influencing sentencing, the association between victim forgiveness and sentencing outcomes is due to the influence of forgiveness on the outcomes. Under this assumption, the causal effect ATE can be estimated using one of the following methods: conditional outcome estimator, grouped conditional outcome model, inverse probability weighting (IPW) estimator, or doubly robust estimator. In the subsequent subsections, we will describe each of these estimators in more detail.

4.1 Conditional Outcome Estimator

The conditional outcome estimator is proposed by Robins [10]:

$$\tau = E_{X,Z}[E[Y|A = 1, X_Y, Z] - E[Y|A = 0, X_Y, Z]] \tag{5}$$

where $E[Y|A, X, Z]$ is the conditional expectation of response function f_Y over the error term ϵ_Y, given A, X and Z. And importantly, in our case, the following holds true:

$$E[Y|A, X_Y, Z] = P(Y = 1 A, X_Y, Z) \tag{6}$$

So in order to estimate $E[Y|A, X_Y, Z]$, we just need to estimate $P(Y = 1|A, X_Y, Z]$. In the next section, we will describe how $P(Y = 1|A, X_Y, Z]$ may be estimated in practice. The conditional outcome model estimates the average causal effect for the entire sample by controlling for the influence of other covariates on the estimation of the effect of the treatment variable on the outcome variable. This approach considers the effect on the overall sample and aims to eliminate confounding factors from other variables.

Once we have proper estimations for $P(Y|A, X, Z)$, we can plug in $A = 1$ and $A = 0$ to generate predictive probabilities of the sentencing outcomes corresponding to whether each individual is granted leniency or not. The mean difference between corresponding counterfactuals, marginalized over all individuals and observations, yields an estimate for ATE:

$$\hat{\tau}_{CO} = \frac{1}{N} \sum_{n=1}^{N} \hat{P}(Y = 1 \, A = 1, X_Y = x_n, Z = z_n) - \hat{P}(Y = 1 \, A = 0, X_Y = x_n, Z = z_n)$$

(7)

where N denotes the number of individuals in the sample; x_n denotes the covariates of individual n; and z_n denotes the confounding factor of individual n. If the model $P(Y|A, X_Y, Z)$ is correctly specified, the conditional outcome estimator for ATE is consistent [5].

4.2   Grouped Conditional Outcome Estimator

The grouped conditional outcome is proposed by Kunzel [7]:

$$\tau = E_{X,Z}[E_{A=1}[Y|X_Y, Z] - E_{A=0}[Y|X_Y, Z]]$$

(8)

where $E_A[Y|X, Z]$ is the conditional expectation of response function f_Y over the error term ϵ_Y, given X and Z, while constraining the treatment variable A to be the same across observations.

Grouped conditional outcome models divide the sample into groups based on the values of the treatment variable and estimate conditional expectation within each group. For each individual, two predictive models predict their respective outcomes, and the difference between these predictions serves as the treatment variable's causal effect on the outcome variable for this individual. In this method, we also have:

$$E[Y|X_Y, Z] = P(Y = 1|X_Y, Z)$$

(9)

So the estimation of ATE is:

$$\hat{\tau}_{GCO} = \frac{1}{N} \sum_{n=1}^{N} \hat{P}_{A=1}(Y = 1|X_Y = x_n, Z = z_n) - \hat{P}_{A=0}(Y = 1|X_Y = x_n, Z = z_n)$$

(10)

4.3   Inverse Probability Weighting Estimator

The inverse probability weighting estimator is based on propensity scores [12]. Propensity scores represent the probability of an individual with a set of covariates receiving the treatment and are used to adjust for confounding factors and reduce bias in the estimation of causal effects due to differences in the distribution of confounding factors observed between the treatment and control groups. The IPW estimator is given by [5]:

$$\hat{\tau}_{IPW} = \frac{1}{N} \sum_{n=1}^{N} w_n y_n \tag{11}$$

$$w_n = \frac{I[a_n = 1]}{\hat{P}(A = 1 | Z = z_n, X_A = x_{an})} - \frac{I[a_n = 0]}{\hat{P}(A = 0 | Z = z_n, X_A = x_{an})} \tag{12}$$

where w_n is a weighting factor for individual n, y_n is observation of outcome variable for individual n, and I is an indicator function that equals one if the condition within the bracket is satisfied, and zero otherwise.

The inverse probability weighting estimator adjusts the weights of individuals in the sample based on the propensity scores to balance the distribution of confounding factors between the treatment and control groups. In other words, by reweighting each observed individual in the sample by the inverse of probability of treatment A, the IPW estimator creates a pseudo population where treatment A is no longer confounded with the observed covariates Z [11]. If the model $P(A|Z, X_A)$ is correctly specified, the IPW estimator for ATE is consistent [9].

4.4 Doubly Robust Estimator

A doubly robust estimator for ATE appropriately combines the estimate from the outcome model and the estimate from the treatment model. The doubly robust estimator is given by [5]:

$$\hat{\tau}_{DR} = \frac{1}{N} \sum_{n=1}^{N} (\frac{a_n(y_n - \hat{\mu}_1(x_n))}{\hat{P}(x_n)} + \hat{\mu}_1(x_n)) - \frac{1}{N} \sum_{n=1}^{N} (\frac{(1 - a_n)(y_n - \hat{\mu}_0(x_n))}{\hat{P}(x_n)} + \hat{\mu}_0(x_n)) \tag{13}$$

where $\hat{P}(x)$ is an estimation of the propensity score, $\hat{\mu}_1(x)$ is an estimation of $E[Y|A = 1, X_Y, Z]$, and $\hat{\mu}_0(x)$ is an estimation of $E[Y|A = 0, X_Y, Z]$. As long as either the treatment model or the outcome model is correctly specified, the estimated average treatment effect will be consistent [5].

5   Model Specification

To calculate the aforementioned estimators, we need to build two models: one is $P(A|X, Z)$, which is the predictive model for the treatment variable based on the covariates, and the other is $P(Y|A, X, Z)$, which is the predictive model for the outcome variable based on the covariates and treatment variable.

The commonly used estimation method for $P(A|X, Z)$ is the logistic regression model. However, research has shown that non-parametric machine learning methods perform better than traditional parametric models in balancing the distribution of covariates between the control and treatment groups [1]. There-fore, we selected Logistic regression, Adaboost, and XGBoost models to predict $P(A|X, Z)$ and chose the model that achieves the best balance in the distribution of covariates between the control and treatment groups to estimate the average causal effect. Here, we use the absolute standardized mean difference (ASMD) to measure the balance effect of the models on the distribution of covariates between the control and treatment groups [1]. The formula for ASMD is:

$$ASMD = \left| \frac{\overline{X}_1 - \overline{X}_0}{S} \right| \tag{14}$$

where $\overline{X}_1$ and $\overline{X}_0$ are the weighted sample means of the covariate X in the treat-ment and control groups, respectively, and s represents the standard deviation of the covariate after combining the treatment and control groups. A lower ASMD value indicates better balance of the covariates, and an ASMD less than or equal to 0.1 is typically considered acceptable [1]. We evaluate the balance effectiveness of the propensity score model by calculating the ASMD values for each covariate based on the propensity score weights estimated by different models.

$P(Y|A, X, Z)$ is the predictive model for the outcome variable based on the covariates and treatment variable, i.e., the sentencing outcome prediction model. Due to the numerous factors influencing the sentencing outcome, we choose the Stacking method [16], which is based on the ensemble learning approach, to con-struct the predictive model $P(Y|A, X, Z)$. The Stacking method aims to improve the accuracy and generalization ability of the overall prediction by first selecting a set of base models, each utilizing a different learning method. The predic-tions of the base models are then used as input data for the second-layer model (meta-learner), which is trained through cross-validation to generate the final ensemble prediction. Stacking leverages the predictions from different base learn-ers to learn and construct a meta-learner that captures patterns, relationships, and weights between the base learners. By combining the predictions of multiple learners, Stacking can enhance the overall prediction accuracy and generalization performance, demonstrating good performance in handling complex tasks and datasets. In this case, we select five models as our base learners: Naive Bayes, Logistic regression, Random Forest, XGBoost, and LightGBM. When training the second-layer model, we use the logistic regression model and employ the Lasso method to find the optimal linear combination of these five base models.

The training of each base model is based on minimizing the cross-entropy loss through 5-fold cross-validation, and then the logistic regression model is used to find the best linear combination of the five base models.

6   Estimation Results

6.1   Estimation of $P(A|X, Z)$

We chose the Logistic regression model, Adaboost model, and XGBoost model to predict $P(A|X, Z)$ and compared their balance effects on the distribution of covariates between the treatment and control groups using ASMD. We selected the model that achieved the best overall balance effect. The balance effects of each model are shown in the Table 2.

Table 2. Covariate balance results.

Model	Total ASMD	Number of Unbalanced Variables
Logistic regression	2.43	4
Adaboost	1.67	3
XGBoost	1.89	4

6.2   Estimation of $P(Y|A, X, Z)$

To improve the predictive accuracy of the model, we employed the Stacking ensemble method to predict $P(Y|A, X, Z)$, and compared the prediction results with those of individual base models (Naive Bayes, Logistic regression, Random Forest, XGBoost, and LightGBM). Through comparison, we found that using the Stacking ensemble method improved the generalization ability of the predictive model, resulting in a more accurate prediction.

6.3   Estimation of ATE

The estimation of the Average Treatment Effect (ATE) is based on the estimators from Sect. 4 and the predictive models $P(A|X, Z)$ and $P(Y|A, X, Z)$. By incorporating the predicted results of P(A|X,Z) and $P(Y|A, X, Z)$ into the four estimators for ATE, we obtained the average causal effect of victim forgiveness on sentencing outcomes. The point estimates of the average causal effect from the four estimators are as follows (Table 3):

Table 3. ATE estimate results.

Estimator	ATE estimate results
Conditional outcome estimator	0.254
Grouped conditional outcome estimator	0.158
Inverse probability weighting estimator	0.064
Doubly robust estimator	0.327

The average causal effect estimate based on doubly robust estimation is 0.327. This suggests that, on average, defendants who receive victim forgiveness are

32.7% more likely to receive a lighter sentence compared to those who do not receive forgiveness. There is a significant causal relationship between victim forgiveness and sentencing outcomes. In the estimation results, the causal effect value obtained by IPW estimation is the smallest, while the causal effect value obtained by doubly robust estimation is the largest.

The above results provide point estimates of the average causal effect. To perform statistical inference, since the true value of the average causal effect is unknown, we cannot assess the bias of the point estimates. Therefore, we consider using bootstrapping to obtain estimation intervals for each estimation method [6]. We randomly sample 1,700 cases to create a new sample set of the same size and calculate the average causal effect estimates using the same steps as before. Each sample generates a point estimate for ATE, and we repeat this process 50 times using bootstrap sampling to obtain estimation intervals for each method. By comparing the estimation intervals of different methods using box plots, we can visualize the 95% confidence intervals for various average causal effect estimates (see Fig. 1).

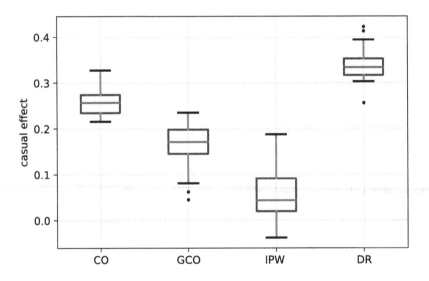

Fig. 1. The estimated intervals for ATE for different estimators.

From the box plots, we observe that the doubly robust estimation has smaller variance, yielding a more stable result. Additionally, apart from the inverse probability weighting method, the confidence intervals of other estimation methods indicate a significant causal relationship between victim forgiveness and sentencing outcomes.

7   Conclusion and Future Research

In this study, we investigated the causal effect of victim forgiveness on the severity of sentencing outcomes in cases of dangerous driving offenses. Based on a sample of 1700 dangerous driving cases, we employed four estimation methods: conditional regression modeling, stratified conditional outcome modeling, inverse probability weighting, and doubly robust method to estimate the average causal effect in the sample. Among these methods, doubly robust method combines the results from conditional regression modeling and inverse probability weighting, providing a doubly robust estimation. Therefore, we considered the doubly robust estimate as the estimation of the causal effect in this study. The results indicated a significant causal relationship between victim forgiveness and sentencing outcomes, with an estimated effect size of approximately 32.7%. This suggests that defendants who receive victim forgiveness are 32.7% more likely to receive a lighter sentence compared to those who do not receive forgiveness.

In the context of sentencing for dangerous driving cases, there are numerous confounding variables that can confound the causal relationship between forgiveness and sentencing. Analyzing the data using statistical methods alone may lead to conclusions that do not align with reality. Therefore, we chose causal inference methods to account for confounding factors and obtain more accurate and realistic conclusions. In constructing predictive models for sentencing in dangerous driving cases, we employed a stacking-based ensemble method to calculate the average causal effect. To provide estimation intervals for each method, we used bootstrap sampling to generate multiple samples of the same size and calculated the average causal effect estimates for each method. By comparing the estimation intervals using box plots, we visualized the 95% confidence intervals for the average causal effect estimates obtained from different methods. The results from the box plots indicated that the doubly robust estimate had a smaller variance. Meanwhile, apart from the inverse probability weighting method, the confidence intervals of other estimation methods indicate a significant causal relationship between victim forgiveness and sentencing outcomes.

It is worth noting that the interpretation of the estimated average causal effect should consider the limitations of this study. Firstly, the sample size used was relatively small, consisting of only 1700 cases. Due to the limitations of the feature extraction method used, this sample may not be representative and could introduce biases. To obtain a more accurate assessment of the causal effect, a larger and more representative sample should be employed. Secondly, our chosen causal inference methods were specifically designed for binary outcome variables. To analyze the severity of sentencing outcomes, we transformed the continuous variable of imprisonment duration into a binary variable, which could introduce some bias depending on the chosen threshold for the transformation. Moreover, the factors that influence the sentencing outcome are often binary variables, which affect the accuracy of the sentencing prediction model. Lastly, there might be unobserved confounding factors in our study that simultaneously influence victim forgiveness and sentencing outcomes, leading to biased estimates of the causal effect. These limitations will be further analyzed in our subsequent research.

References

1. Chang, T.H., Nguyen, T.Q., Lee, Y., Jackson, J.W., Stuart, E.A.: Flexible propensity score estimation strategies for clustered data in observational studies. Stat. Med. **41**(25), 5016–5032 (2022)
2. Chu, Z.: Research on the sentencing patterns of drunk driving offense. Politics Law **8**, 30–41 (2013)
3. Gao, T.: The mechanism of compensation impact on sentencing in intentional injury cases. Legal Res. 1 (2020)
4. Han, J., Li, Z.: The influence of victim forgiveness on sentencing. J. Yunnan Police Officer Acad. **6**, 73–77 (2011)
5. Hernán, M.A., Robins, J.M.: Causal inference (2010)
6. Kang, L., Vij, A., Hubbard, A., Shaw, D.: The unintended impact of helmet use on bicyclists' risk-taking behaviors. J. Safety Res. **79**, 135–147 (2021)
7. Künzel, S.R., Sekhon, J.S., Bickel, P.J., Yu, B.: Metalearners for estimating heterogeneous treatment effects using machine learning. Proc. Natl. Acad. Sci. **116**(10), 4156–4165 (2019)
8. Liu, X.: The Impact of Victim Forgiveness on Sentencing. Master's thesis, Jiangxi Normal University (2020)
9. Neugebauer, R., van der Laan, M.: Why prefer double robust estimators in causal inference? J. Stat. Plann. Inference **129**(1–2), 405–426 (2005)
10. Robins, J.: A new approach to causal inference in mortality studies with a sustained exposure period-application to control of the healthy worker survivor effect. Math. Modell. **7**(9–12), 1393–1512 (1986)
11. Robins, J.M.: Marginal structural models versus structural nested models as tools for causal inference. In: Statistical Models in Epidemiology, the Environment, and Clinical Trials, pp. 95–133. Springer, Cham (2000). https://doi.org/10.1007/978-1-4612-1284-3_2
12. Rosenbaum, P.R., Rubin, D.B.: The central role of the propensity score in observational studies for causal effects. Biometrika **70**(1), 41–55 (1983)
13. Sekhon, J.: The neyman-rubin model of causal inference and estimation via matching methods (2008)
14. Su, C., Wang, N.: Empirical study on the sentencing features and influencing factors of drunk driving offense: a case study in the central urban area of wuhan. J. South-Central Univ. Nationalities Humanities Soc. Sci. **38**(1), 140–146 (2018)
15. Wen, J.: Empirical study on the sentencing factors of drunk driving offense. Legal Res. 1, 165–186 (2016)
16. Wolpert, D.H.: Stacked generalization. Neural Networks **5**(2), 241–259 (1992)
17. Zhang, S.: Research on the Significance of Victim's Behavior in Criminal Law. Ph.D. thesis, East China University of Political Science and Law (2011)

Fourier-Based Instance Selective Whitening for Domain Generalized Lane Detection

Weiyan Xu[1,2], Shikui Wei[1,2(✉)], Sen Xu[1,2], Chuangchuang Tan[1,2], Shengli Zhang[1,2], and Yao Zhao[1,2]

[1] Institute of Information Science, Beijing Jiaotong University, Beijing, China
{21120310,shkwei,19112009,tanchuangchuang,victory_zhang,yzhao}@bjtu.edu.cn
[2] Beijing Key Laboratory of Advanced Information Science and Network Technology, Beijing, China

Abstract. Lane detection represents a fundamental task within autonomous driving. While deep learning has made remarkable advancements in the source domain, its ability to generalize to unseen target domains still poses a challenge. To address this issue, we present a Fourier-based instance selective whitening framework. This framework utilizes the distinct frequencies within the Fourier spectrum to decompose data style into environment and texture styles. Our method preserves semantic features by stabilizing the phase component, while also extending the style through perturbing and amalgamating the amplitude component. Further, we propose a standardized instance selective whitening strategy to analyze overall distributional changes, emphasizing general features and reducing domain-specific information. Our approach is validated through extensive experiments across multiple challenging datasets, such as Tusimple, CULane, and LLAMAS, which demonstrates significant effectiveness when compared to existing methods.

Keywords: Lane detection · Domain generalization · Fourier transform

1 Introduction

Lane detection is a key part of the autonomous driving task, and it is the front module of systems such as Lane Keeping Assist (LKA) and Lane Departure Warning (LDW). With the development of deep learning networks, lane detection methods have made great breakthroughs [36,41]. These methods have achieved satisfactory results in the source domain, but they perform very poorly when faced with unknown domains, especially those that we cannot access. This is due to the model degradation caused by the distribution shift between the source domain and the target domain. However, the source domain cannot contain all the data distribution, so it is particularly important to reduce the domain shift between the source domain and the target domain.

Domain Adaptation (DA) [2,8,15,34,38,40] extracts data information from the target domain to alleviate the difference in features or distributions between

W. Hong and G. Kanaparan (Eds.): ICCSE 2023, CCIS 2023, pp. 415–428, 2024.
https://doi.org/10.1007/978-981-97-0730-0_37

the source domain and the target domain. However, these approaches essentially rely on the availability of target domain data, limiting the generalization to unseen target domains. Additionally, there is no single ideal target domain that encompasses all possible distributions. In contrast, domain generalization (DG) focuses on acquiring generalized content features from the domain, preventing the model from overfitting to the unique style features of the source domain. It achieves the generalization of previously unseen target domains without requiring additional target data.

In recent researches [37,38], Fourier-based data augmentation has been proposed as a method for addressing the domain shift problem, showing remarkable performance improvements. The Fourier transformation has a particular advantage: the phase component retains high-level semantics, while the amplitude component encapsulates low-level statistics [13,22,23,27]. This property contributes to generate data that more closely aligns with the real data distribution. Nevertheless, learning basic features through gradient backward propagation remains challenging due to the difficulty networks face in distinguishing style differences. Concurrently, several studies [9,10,24,26,30,32,33] have explored the combination of instance normalization and instance whitening to constrain models by removing domain-specific style information from the data, enabling the learning of general domain content features. A recent study [6] has focused on the correlation between style and feature covariance matrices to identify style-sensitive elements within features for whitening. However, the single style of source domain and the random enhancement bring difficulties in distinguishing these sensitive elements. This approach leads to elements whitened, which contains critical semantic features. It also results in a decrease in performance when applied to an unseen target domain.

In this paper, we propose two modules: Fourier-based Style Extension (FSE) and Standardized Instance Selective Whitening (SISW). FSE utilizes different frequencies from the Fourier spectrum to decompose semantic features into environmental and texture features. Then the amplitude component is disturbed and mixed to extend the distribution of the source domain with diverse styles, as well as ensure the preservation of semantics by fixing the phase component. This effectively emphasizes domain-independent information. Based on FSE, SISW standardizes and analyzes the overall feature covariance matrices to identify elements responsible for domain shifts. Then whitening these elements to enhance the discrimination ability of essential features. Our method alleviates the lack of semantic information during style expansion and improves the accuracy in selecting style-sensitive elements. Unlike methods that let the network learn by itself, such as data augmentation, our approach explicitly guides the network to learn the domain-independent features. Thus, our method leads to effective generalization across various domains.

Our main contributions are as follows:

- We propose a novel domain generalization framework for lane segmentation, which extends the source styles with Fourier transform before catching and removing domain-specific information to learn content common features.

- The proposed domain-specific style whitening modules, FSE and SISW, are plug-and-play and convenient to migrate to different backbones. It effectively improves the generalization with ignorable time consumption.
- Our approach aims at the lane detection domain generalization. Through qualitative and quantitative evaluations, the proposed method shows state-of-the-art efficacy across different domains.

2   Relate Work

Semantic Segmentation on Lane Detection. Semantic segmentation is a task of pixel-level classification. Lane segmentation is an important application of it. With the development of deep learning, many advanced methods of lane segmentation have been proposed, such as [25] generalizes traditional deep convolutions to slice-by-slice convolutions on the four directions to enhance feature extraction, [35] adds an embedding model for pixel and combines binary segmentation to cluster lane instances, [14] proposes self-attention distillation to learn from itself from contextual information, [36] adopts multitask framework contains lane segmentation, road segmentation and object detection to mutual restraint. Although these methods are effective within the source domain, they perform poorly when tested on unseen target domains. As far as we know, there have been no existing methods to address domain generalization within lane segmentation.

Domain Generalization. Domain Generalization (DG) aims to acquire domain-independent common features to effectively generalize to unseen target domains. Unlike Domain Adaptation (DA), DG has no access to the target domain information during training, posing significant challenges to the task. Previous research in DG has been mainly focused on image classification tasks, such as meta-learning [3,17], adversarial training [18,28], auto encoder [11,18], metric learning [7,20], data augmentation [12,39,42]. There are a few recent studies on domain generalization for semantic segmentation, which research from two aspects: domain style diversity, normalization and whitening. The methods of domain style diversity adopt data augmentation and extension to enrich the data style of the source domain. [16] augments the source domain features to resemble wild styles and stylizes the data, subsequently enhancing the capability to distinguish category semantics within the feature space. The methods of normalization and whitening enhance the generalization ability of network by eliminating distribution noise and reducing feature redundancy. [33] proves instance normalization will reserve content information to avoid overfitting the data distribution. Further, [24] adds batch normalization to improve the feature discriminability. [26] combines IN with other whitening methods to learn essential features. [6] proposes an instance selective whitening to extract domain-specific features to normalize and whiten. These two aspects complement each other: domain style diversity highlights domain-independent general features, while normalization and whitening capture general features and eliminate redundant information. The effective combination of these two aspects opens up new possibilities for domain generalization, and our aim is to explore these possibilities to enhance model generalization ability.

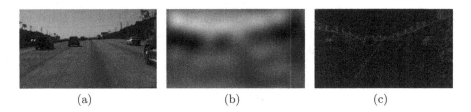

(a)   (b)   (c)

Fig. 1. Visualization of the low-frequency component and high-frequency component. (a) original image; (b) reconstructed image with low-frequency component; (c) reconstructed image with high-frequency component.

3   Methods

In this section, we apply the Fourier transform to break down the style of the data from the source domain into two different styles: environmental and textural. We extend the new data style by changing the amplitude component. Subsequently, we combine this process with standardized instance selective whitening to selectively remove domain-specific style information, thereby enhancing the generalization of model. The overall learning process is outlined in Fig. 3.

3.1   Fourier-Based Source Domain Style Extension

We consider that overfitting to the data style of the source domain is the primary factor leading to the decline in the generalization of model. While common data extension methods attempt to address this issue, they often present limitations. Moreover, the generated data does not consistently align with the real-world distribution, resulting in the loss of certain aspects of semantic information.

To address this challenge, we propose a Fourier-based data style extension method, which introduces random variations or mixes the amplitude information to extend the data styles. This method can diversify data styles while preserving semantic features, effectively alleviating incomplete semantic cases. Specifically, for a single-channel image, we obtain its Fourier transform:

$$\mathcal{F}(x)(u,v) = \sum_{h,w} x(h,w) e^{-j2\pi(\frac{h}{H}u + \frac{w}{W}v)} \tag{1}$$

$$\mathcal{F}^A(x)(u,v) = \left[R^2(x)(u,v) + I^2(x)(u,v)\right]^{1/2}$$
$$\mathcal{F}^P(x)(u,v) = \arctan\left[\frac{I(x)(u,v)}{R(x)(u,v)}\right] \tag{2}$$

where $R(x)$ and $I(x)$ represent the real and imaginary part of $\mathcal{F}(x)$, and $\mathcal{F}^{-1}(x)$ represents the inverse transform of Fourier, and the two processes can be efficiently calculated by [21].

Utilizing the diverse frequency ranges of the Fourier transform to represent various degrees of grayscale change, we attempt to break down the data style,

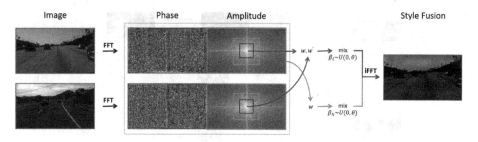

Fig. 2. Fourier-based style extension (FSE). We decompose the amplitude and phase components, dividing them into low-frequency and high-frequency regions. The semantic information in regions where they intersect is difficult to distinguish, so we don't address them here. Subsequently, we use different enhancement strategies for low-frequency and high-frequency amplitudes to extend styles.

as the Fig. 1. We consider the low-frequency signal in the Fourier domain as representing relatively smooth environmental features, while the high-frequency signal embodies the significantly changeable texture features. To represent these distinct types of signals separately, we define masks $M_{\beta_{low}}$ and $M_{\beta_{high}}$:

$$
\begin{aligned}
M_{\beta_l}(h, w) &= \mathbb{1}_{(h,w)\in[-\beta_l H:\beta_l H, -\beta_l W:\beta_l W]} \\
M_{\beta_h}(h, w) &= 1 - \mathbb{1}_{(h,w)\in[-\beta_h H:\beta_h H, -\beta_h W:\beta_h W]}
\end{aligned}
\tag{3}
$$

where $\mathbb{1}$ denotes value in the range is 1 and outside is 0. $\beta_l, \beta_h \in (0,1)$ and $\beta_l + \beta_h < 1$, as the Fig. 2.

In recent studies [13, 22, 23, 27], it has been proved that the Fourier phase component can effectively preserve semantic information. Based on this, we highlight the semantic feature by fixing the phase component of Fourier space. Then, we introduce random variations in the amplitude to extend the data styles. Inspired by [37, 38], for the low-frequency component, we engage in random linear interpolation of the amplitudes from two arbitrary images. Considering the similarity in style information from the source domain image, we randomly adjust the value of the amplitude component, either by enlarging or reducing it, before the linear interpolation of the amplitudes. Combined with the random transform, the extension of environmental styles can be expressed as:

$$
\mathcal{F}_{env}^A(x_i) = M_{\beta_l} \circ ((1-\lambda)w_i\mathcal{F}^A(x_i) + \lambda w_{i'}\mathcal{F}^A(x_{i'})) + (1 - M_{\beta_l}) \circ \mathcal{F}^A(x_i) \tag{4}
$$

where $\lambda \in (0,1)$ is the fusion factor, w_i and $w_{i'}$ are the disturbance factors of low frequency about different samples x_i and $x_{i'}$.

We attempted to apply a similar method to the high-frequency component, but it did not yield an improved outcome. This was primarily due to the high-frequency component containing a portion of semantic information. When combined with another image, the mix resulted in the destruction of semantic information. Consequently, we only and randomly reduce the amplitude, proportionally, in order to preserve the original semantics and prevent the loss of semantic details.

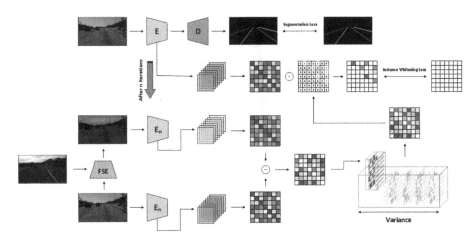

Fig. 3. The framework of the proposed FSW. E_n denotes our model is trained after n iterations. It stops training to generate a selective matrix, and then adds standardized instance selective whitening loss during subsequent training.

$$\mathcal{F}_{tex}^A(x_i) = M_{\beta_h} \circ b_i \mathcal{F}^A(x_i) + (1 - M_{\beta_h}) \circ \mathcal{F}^A(x_i) \tag{5}$$

where b_i is the disturbance factor of high frequency. Thus, for the source domain image x_i and arbitrary sample $x_{i'}$. We extend environmental features and texture features in turn. The style extension can be formalized as:

$$(\mathcal{F}_{env}^A(x_i), \mathcal{F}_{tex}^A(x_i)) \rightarrow \hat{\mathcal{F}}^A(x_i) \tag{6}$$

$$x_{ext} = \mathcal{F}^{-1}([\hat{\mathcal{F}}^A(x_i), \mathcal{F}^P(x_i)]) \tag{7}$$

where $\mathcal{F}_{env}^A(x_i)$ and $\mathcal{F}_{tex}^A(x_i)$ are two relatively independent processes that need to be executed sequentially, with no strict order between them.

3.2   Standardized Instance Selective Whitening

The previously mentioned Fourier-based style extension method enriches the data distribution of the source domain. However, merely constraining the model through the comparison loss results in the model overfitting the new distribution. This approach makes it challenging to learn domain-generalized content features. Recent studies [9,10] have highlighted the relationship between style and feature statistics. The adjustment of feature statistics using the IN layer proves beneficial in enhancing feature diversity. Inspired by [6], we propose standardized instance selective whitening, a method that standardizes the covariance matrix and selects the style-sensitive feature elements for whitening. We determine the feature sensitivity to style through overall distribution changes in covariance matrices. This enables us to improve the discernment of domain-specific features and accurately remove redundant style information.

Following [6,24], we add the instance standardization layer [33] into shallow networks. Initially, we train n epochs without containing whitening loss to enable the networks to learn basic semantic features. Subsequently, we infer both the original image and its stylistically extended image, calculating the covariance matrix for each:

$$\mu = \tfrac{1}{HW} X \cdot 1 \in \mathbb{R}^{C \times 1} \tag{8}$$

$$\Sigma = \tfrac{1}{HW}(X - \mu \cdot 1^\top)(X - \mu \cdot 1^\top)^\top \in \mathbb{R}^{C \times C} \tag{9}$$

where $X \in \mathbb{R}^{C \times HW}$ denotes the feature map with the dimensions of C, H and W, expanded along the channel dimension. $1 \in \mathbb{R}^{HW}$ is a column vector of ones, and μ and Σ are the mean vector and the covariance matrix.

[6] uses the mean of instance variance to describe the style sensitivity of feature elements. Nevertheless, the variance of individual instances has limitations. We consider the changes in the overall distribution might provide more accurate representations. As there are inherent differences among the feature covariance matrices of distinct images, our method standardizes covariance matrices initially. Then, we represent the style sensitivity of feature elements by the variance of overall distribution, thereby obtaining the variance matrix:

$$V = \frac{1}{N} \sum_{i=1}^{N} \sigma_i^2 \tag{10}$$

$$\mu_\Sigma = \frac{1}{2N} \sum_{i=1}^{N} (\Sigma_s(x_i) + \Sigma_s(\tau(x_i)) - 2\Sigma_{sta}(x_i)) \tag{11}$$

$$\sigma_i^2 = \frac{1}{2}((\Sigma_s(x_i) - \Sigma_{sta}(x_i) - \mu_\Sigma)^2 + (\Sigma_s(\tau(x_i)) - \Sigma_{sta}(x_i) - \mu_\Sigma)^2) \tag{12}$$

where N is the number of samples, x_i is the i-th image sample, τ is the Fourier-based style extension, and $\Sigma_{sta}(\cdot)$ denotes the regularized covariance matrix, here we simply use the covariance matrix of the original image, $\Sigma_{sta}(\cdot) = \Sigma_s(\cdot)$.

The above studies [9,10] indicate that the feature covariance of a model with poor generalization is sensitive to style shifts. The variance matrix V accurately reflects this sensitivity. Consequently, we assume that the elements with higher variance in the covariance matrix may contain more domain-specific styles. To select these elements, we follow the method of [6], utilizing k-means clustering to assign the elements $V_{i,j}(i < j)$ into k clusters. Subsequently, we select the elements in clusters with the top m high variance values as G_{high}. We can get the mask matrix M from G_{high}:

$$M_{i,j} = \begin{cases} 1, & if\ V_{i,j} \in G_{high} \\ 0, & \text{otherwise} \end{cases} \tag{13}$$

The mask represents the domain-specific style elements within the features. Consequently, we propose standardized instance selective whitening (SISW) loss and implement it within the instance normalization layer to optimize the network:

$$\mathcal{L}_{\text{FISW}} = E\left[\left\|\Sigma_{\text{s}} \odot \text{M}\right\|_1\right] \tag{14}$$

Combining with lane segmentation tasks, our total loss can be described as

$$\mathcal{L} = \mathcal{L}_{\text{seg}} + \mathcal{L}_{\text{exist}} + \frac{1}{L}\sum_{i}^{L} \mathcal{L}_{\text{FISW}}^{i} \tag{15}$$

where $\mathcal{L}_{\text{seg}}$ is the cross-entropy loss for lane segmentation, $\mathcal{L}_{\text{exist}}$ is the lane exist loss, i and L denotes separately the layer and the total number which applies SISW.

4 Experiments

In this section, we conduct many experiments between simple and complex scenes to prove the efficiency of our method. Besides, we compare our method with multiple representative methods of feature normalization and whitening in the field of domain generalization for semantic segmentation.

4.1 Dataset

We focus on the domain generalization of lane detection and design two standard benchmark settings: "Tusimple to CULane" and "Tusimple to LLAMAS". These aim to verify the generalization ability of models from a single scene to a complex scene.

Tusimple [1] is a small-scale dataset containing urban driving scene images with the resolution of 1280×720. The images are collected from high-speed roads. It provides 3626 training and 2782 testing images.

CULane [25] is a large-scale dataset for lane detection with the resolution of 1680×590. It collects more than 55 h videos and extract 133235 frames. The dataset is split into 88880 training, 9675 validation and 34680 testing images. The test set contains normal class and 8 challenging classes.

LLAMAS [4] is a large-scale and high-quality dataset for lane detection. It contains 100042 labeled images with the resolution of 1276×717. Since the label of testset is not public, we use the validation set for evaluation.

4.2 Experimental Setup

We conducted training on the Tusimple dataset and evaluated the performance of the model on the CULane and LLAMAS datasets to assess its generalization ability across a range of scenarios, from simple scenes to complex ones. In our comparison with other normalization methods, we re-implemented IBN-Net [24], IW [19], GIW [5], and ISW [6] on our baseline models. Metrics were consistently measured using the same evaluation standards for all approaches. To ensure fair comparisons, models were selected and trained on the last epoch.

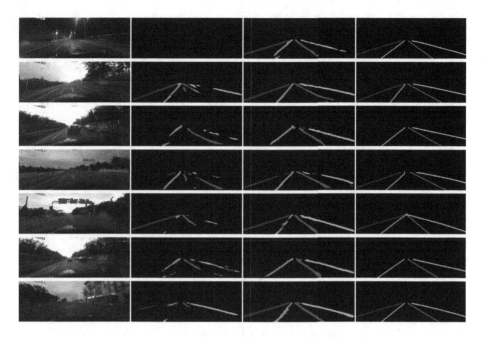

Fig. 4. Visualization results on CULane. From left to right are (a) Input image, (b) Baseline, (c) Ours (FSW) and (d) Groundtruth.

4.3   Implementation Details

We adopt ERFNet [29] pre-trained on ImageNet [31] as the network backbone. We use SGD optimizer with a momentum of 0.9 and weight decay of 1e-4. The initial learning rate is set to 1e-2 and is decreased using the polynomial policy with a power of 0.9. We train a model for 12 epochs with a batch size of 16. Before training, all datasets are preprocessed to contain a maximum of four categories (ranging from two lanes on each side), and all images are resized to 976×208.

We implement our method on PyTorch and use a single NVIDIA RTX 3090 GPU for our experiments. Following lane detection works, we use F1-score as the evaluation metric.

4.4   Comparison with DG Methods

We construct a simple to complex adaptation scenario to verify the effectiveness of FSW. We compare our results with other representative normalization methods: IBN-Net [24], IW [19], GIW [5] and ISW [6]. Table 1 shows the generalization performance test on CULane dataset. Note that all the methods use ERFNet [29] as the network backbone. We select the model from the last epoch of training to test for each method. FSW outperforms other methods on all challenging classes of CULane except the Crossroad. In addition, for styles that do

Table 1. Quantitative comparison on "TuSimple to CULane". *: For cross, it only shows FP.

Methods	Normal	Crowded	Dazzle	Shadow	No line	Arrow	Curve	Cross*	Night	F1@50
Baseline [29]	32.26	13.12	8.09	6.29	7.37	20.82	20.76	9656	4.70	16.82
IBN [24]	36.07	13.73	7.59	7.07	6.82	23.66	25.18	8597	8.54	18.48
IW [26]	38.07	14.70	10.95	6.39	7.82	26.61	26.31	8249	8.06	19.62
GIW [5]	39.25	16.05	12.48	8.94	9.11	27.91	28.09	**8180**	10.88	21.11
ISW [6]	40.10	17.59	10.62	8.32	8.43	28.93	28.49	9075	12.37	21.69
Ours	**41.84**	**19.65**	**13.20**	**10.00**	**10.09**	**30.30**	**29.35**	8802	**15.27**	**23.69**

Table 2. Quantitative comparison over multiple domains.

Methods	→CULane	→LLAMAS
Baseline [24]	16.83	66.17
IBN [24]	18.48	**69.95**
IW [26]	19.62	65.19
GIW [5]	21.11	65.66
ISW [6]	21.69	65.17
Ours	**23.69**	68.99

not exist in the source domain, such as dazzle and night, our method has significant improvements compared with other methods. To prove the generalization ability over multiple domains, we use the same model to verify the performance on CULane and LLAMAS datasets. Given in Table 2, our approach also achieves significant results, only slightly lower than IBN on the LLAMAS dataset, but we are much higher than it on the more complex CULane dataset. The visualization results are shown in Fig. 4.

Table 3. Ablation analysis of FSE and SISW.

Methods	FSE	SISW	F1@50
Baseline [24]			16.83
+ISW			21.69
+ISW	✓		22.98
+ISW	✓	✓	**23.69**

4.5 Ablation Studies

In order to further analyze the effectiveness of FSE and SISW, we extend experiments on the domain generalization scene from Tusimple to CULane. We evaluate the effectiveness through method stacking. As shown in Table 3, the baseline model, trained only with FSE module, achieves an F1-score of 22.98% with +6.15% improvement. This shows that style extensions with more semantic information will contribute to selecting elements that are sensitive to domain shift more accurately. Further, we adopt SISW module to achieve an F1-score of 23.69%. This shows the distribution of global covariance based on standardization is better for representing the sensitivity of features to domain shift.

5 Conclusions

This paper proposes a novel Fourier-based standardized instance selective whitening framework, which contains two modules: Fourier-based Style Extension (FSE) and Standardized Instance Selective Whitening (SISW). FSE focuses on preserving semantic information through the Fourier spectral phase while extending the amplitude to diversify the style. SISW selectively removes the domain-specific information to enhance common feature learning. The collaboration between the two modules, SISW and FSE, proves to be complementary. SISW encourages networks to learn style-independent essential features while FSE contributes to improving the discrimination of style-sensitive feature elements. Extensive experiments confirm its effectiveness in generalizing from simpler to more complex scenes. However, challenges remain in extending styles not present in the source domain, such as shadow and night scenes, this leads to a considerable performance gap between the source and target domains. Addressing these challenges will be a primary focus of our future work.

References

1. Tusimple. Tusimple benchmark (2017)
2. Araslanov, N., Roth, S.: Self-supervised augmentation consistency for adapting semantic segmentation. In: Proceedings of the IEEE/CVF Conference on Computer Vision and Pattern Recognition, pp. 15384–15394 (2021)
3. Balaji, Y., Sankaranarayanan, S., Chellappa, R.: Metareg: towards domain generalization using meta-regularization. Advances in neural information processing systems 31 (2018)
4. Behrendt, K., Soussan, R.: Unsupervised labeled lane markers using maps. In: Proceedings of the IEEE/CVF International Conference on Computer Vision Workshops (2019)
5. Cho, W., Choi, S., Park, D.K., Shin, I., Choo, J.: Image-to-image translation via group-wise deep whitening-and-coloring transformation. In: Proceedings of the IEEE/CVF Conference on Computer Vision and Pattern Recognition, pp. 10639–10647 (2019)

6. Choi, S., Jung, S., Yun, H., Kim, J.T., Kim, S., Choo, J.: Robustnet: Improving domain generalization in urban-scene segmentation via instance selective whitening. In: Proceedings of the IEEE/CVF Conference on Computer Vision and Pattern Recognition, pp. 11580–11590 (2021)

7. Dou, Q., Coelho de Castro, D., Kamnitsas, K., Glocker, B.: Domain generalization via model-agnostic learning of semantic features. Advances in neural information processing systems 32 (2019)

8. Ganin, Y., et al.: Domain-adversarial training of neural networks. J. Mach. Learn. Res. **17**(1), 2096–2030 (2016)

9. Gatys, L., Ecker, A.S., Bethge, M.: Texture synthesis using convolutional neural networks. Advances in neural information processing systems 28 (2015)

10. Gatys, L.A., Ecker, A.S., Bethge, M.: Image style transfer using convolutional neural networks. In: Proceedings of the IEEE Conference on Computer Vision and Pattern Recognition, pp. 2414–2423 (2016)

11. Ghifary, M., Kleijn, W.B., Zhang, M., Balduzzi, D.: Domain generalization for object recognition with multi-task autoencoders. In: Proceedings of the IEEE International Conference on Computer Vision, pp. 2551–2559 (2015)

12. Gong, R., Li, W., Chen, Y., Gool, L.V.: Dlow: domain flow for adaptation and generalization. In: Proceedings of the IEEE/CVF Conference on Computer Vision and Pattern Recognition, pp. 2477–2486 (2019)

13. Hansen, B.C., Hess, R.F.: Structural sparseness and spatial phase alignment in natural scenes. JOSA A **24**(7), 1873–1885 (2007)

14. Hou, Y., Ma, Z., Liu, C., Loy, C.C.: Learning lightweight lane detection CNNs by self attention distillation. In: Proceedings of the IEEE/CVF International Conference on Computer Vision, pp. 1013–1021 (2019)

15. Hoyer, L., Dai, D., Van Gool, L.: Daformer: improving network architectures and training strategies for domain-adaptive semantic segmentation. In: Proceedings of the IEEE/CVF Conference on Computer Vision and Pattern Recognition, pp. 9924–9935 (2022)

16. Lee, S., Seong, H., Lee, S., Kim, E.: Wildnet: Learning domain generalized semantic segmentation from the wild. In: Proceedings of the IEEE/CVF Conference on Computer Vision and Pattern Recognition. pp. 9936–9946 (2022)

17. Li, D., Yang, Y., Song, Y.Z., Hospedales, T.: Learning to generalize: Meta-learning for domain generalization. In: Proceedings of the AAAI Conference on Artificial Intelligence, vol. 32 (2018)

18. Li, H., Pan, S.J., Wang, S., Kot, A.C.: Domain generalization with adversarial feature learning. In: Proceedings of the IEEE Conference on Computer Vision and Pattern Recognition, pp. 5400–5409 (2018)

19. Li, Y., Fang, C., Yang, J., Wang, Z., Lu, X., Yang, M.H.: Universal style transfer via feature transforms. Advances in neural information processing systems 30 (2017)

20. Motiian, S., Piccirilli, M., Adjeroh, D.A., Doretto, G.: Unified deep supervised domain adaptation and generalization. In: Proceedings of the IEEE International Conference on Computer Vision, pp. 5715–5725 (2017)

21. Nussbaumer, H.J., Nussbaumer, H.J.: The fast Fourier transform. Springer (1982)

22. Oppenheim, A., Lim, J., Kopec, G., Pohlig, S.: Phase in speech and pictures. In: ICASSP'79. IEEE International Conference on Acoustics, Speech, and Signal Processing, vol. 4, pp. 632–637. IEEE (1979)

23. Oppenheim, A.V., Lim, J.S.: The importance of phase in signals. Proc. IEEE **69**(5), 529–541 (1981)

24. Pan, X., Luo, P., Shi, J., Tang, X.: Two at once: enhancing learning and generalization capacities via ibn-net. In: Proceedings of the European Conference on Computer Vision (ECCV), pp. 464–479 (2018)

25. Pan, X., Shi, J., Luo, P., Wang, X., Tang, X.: Spatial as deep: spatial CNN for traffic scene understanding. In: Proceedings of the AAAI Conference on Artificial Intelligence, vol. 32 (2018)

26. Pan, X., Zhan, X., Shi, J., Tang, X., Luo, P.: Switchable whitening for deep representation learning. In: Proceedings of the IEEE/CVF International Conference on Computer Vision, pp. 1863–1871 (2019)

27. Piotrowski, L.N., Campbell, F.W.: A demonstration of the visual importance and flexibility of spatial-frequency amplitude and phase. Perception **11**(3), 337–346 (1982)

28. Rahman, M.M., Fookes, C., Baktashmotlagh, M., Sridharan, S.: Correlation-aware adversarial domain adaptation and generalization. Pattern Recogn. **100**, 107124 (2020)

29. Romera, E., Alvarez, J.M., Bergasa, L.M., Arroyo, R.: Erfnet: efficient residual factorized convnet for real-time semantic segmentation. IEEE Trans. Intell. Transp. Syst. **19**(1), 263–272 (2017)

30. Roy, S., Siarohin, A., Sangineto, E., Bulo, S.R., Sebe, N., Ricci, E.: Unsupervised domain adaptation using feature-whitening and consensus loss. In: Proceedings of the IEEE/CVF Conference on Computer Vision and Pattern Recognition, pp. 9471–9480 (2019)

31. Russakovsky, O., et al.: Imagenet large scale visual recognition challenge. Int. J. Comput. Vision **115**, 211–252 (2015)

32. Siarohin, A., Sangineto, E., Sebe, N.: Whitening and coloring batch transform for gans. arXiv preprint arXiv:1806.00420 (2018)

33. Ulyanov, D., Vedaldi, A., Lempitsky, V.: Instance normalization: The missing ingredient for fast stylization. arXiv preprint arXiv:1607.08022 (2016)

34. Vu, T.H., Jain, H., Bucher, M., Cord, M., Pérez, P.: Advent: adversarial entropy minimization for domain adaptation in semantic segmentation. In: Proceedings of the IEEE/CVF Conference on Computer Vision and Pattern Recognition, pp. 2517–2526 (2019)

35. Wang, Z., Ren, W., Qiu, Q.: Lanenet: real-time lane detection networks for autonomous driving. arXiv preprint arXiv:1807.01726 (2018)

36. Wu, D., et al.: Yolop: you only look once for panoptic driving perception. Mach. Intell. Res. **19**(6), 550–562 (2022)

37. Xu, Q., Zhang, R., Zhang, Y., Wang, Y., Tian, Q.: A fourier-based framework for domain generalization. In: Proceedings of the IEEE/CVF Conference on Computer Vision and Pattern Recognition, pp. 14383–14392 (2021)

38. Yang, Y., Soatto, S.: Fda: fourier domain adaptation for semantic segmentation. In: Proceedings of the IEEE/CVF Conference on Computer Vision and Pattern Recognition, pp. 4085–4095 (2020)

39. Yue, X., Zhang, Y., Zhao, S., Sangiovanni-Vincentelli, A., Keutzer, K., Gong, B.: Domain randomization and pyramid consistency: simulation-to-real generalization without accessing target domain data. In: Proceedings of the IEEE/CVF International Conference on Computer Vision, pp. 2100–2110 (2019)

40. Zhang, P., Zhang, B., Zhang, T., Chen, D., Wang, Y., Wen, F.: Prototypical pseudo label denoising and target structure learning for domain adaptive semantic segmentation. In: Proceedings of the IEEE/CVF Conference on Computer Vision and Pattern Recognition, pp. 12414–12424 (2021)

41. Zheng, T., et al.: Clrnet: cross layer refinement network for lane detection. In: Proceedings of the IEEE/CVF Conference on Computer Vision and Pattern Recognition, pp. 898–907 (2022)
42. Zhou, K., Yang, Y., Hospedales, T., Xiang, T.: Learning to generate novel domains for domain generalization. In: Computer Vision-ECCV 2020: 16th European Conference, Glasgow, UK, August 23–28, 2020, Proceedings, Part XVI 16, pp. 561–578. Springer (2020)

Research on Traceability of Atmospheric Particulate Pollutants Based on Particle Size Data

Haonan Yu[1], Yunbao Zhou[1], Yuhuan Jia[2], Jingjin Ma[2], Benfeng Pan[2], Wei Zhou[1(✉)], and Yang Chen[1]

[1] Key Laboratory of Big Data and Artificial Intelligence in Transportation, Ministry of Education, School of Computer and Information Technology, Beijing Jiaotong University, Beijing 100044, China
wzhou@bjtu.edu.cn

[2] Hebei Sailhero Environmental Protection High-Tech Co. Ltd., Shijiazhuang 050035, Hebei, China

Abstract. Particle pollution is one of the important sources of air pollution. With the maturity and portability of domestic particle size monitoring equipment, a large amount of air particle size monitoring data has been generated. How to use these data to analyze pollution sources and propose corresponding prevention measures is currently an urgent problem to be solved. Firstly, this study analyzed particle size data and determined the distribution characteristics of particle size in different pollution sources; Secondly, a traceability model based on random forest and factor analysis was constructed to achieve the problem of analyzing air pollution sources using particle size spectrum data; Finally, through experimental comparison, case analysis, and expert experience, the model was verified its effectiveness in the actual situation. This study is the first to use pollutant particle size monitoring data, which achieves high-resolution pollutant traceability compared to traditional chemical composition methods. This study introduces machine learning methods into traditional factor analysis method to improve processing efficiency and accuracy, providing a reference basis for air pollution control.

Keywords: Random Forest · Factor Analysis · Particle Size Data · Pollutant Traceability

1 Introduction

1.1 Research Background

Air quality is related to people's well-being. Quickly identifying the location, time, and category of atmospheric pollution sources has important research value for the formulation of prevention and control measures. At present, pollutant traceability methods are mainly carried out through chemical component analysis. These methods have high recognition, but the detection instruments are expensive, the timeliness is poor, and the

W. Hong and G. Kanaparan (Eds.): ICCSE 2023, CCIS 2023, pp. 429–441, 2024.
https://doi.org/10.1007/978-981-97-0730-0_38

time resolution is low. In recent years, some companies have developed fine-grained particle size monitoring equipment and piloted it in some regions, aiming to analyze pollution sources through atmospheric particle size data. Therefore, this study conducts research on pollutant traceability based on particle size monitoring data.

The physical and chemical properties of particles mainly depend on their particle size [1]. We are familiar with air particle pollutants such as PM2.5 and PM10, in which 2.5 and 10 refer to particle size. The properties and sources of particles with different particle sizes may also be different. From Fig. 1, it can be seen that the transformation relationships between them are complex.

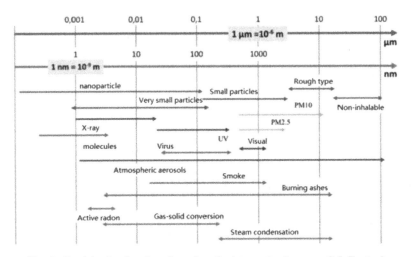

Fig. 1. Particle size fractionation of particulate matter [source: © J. Fontan].

Qualitatively or quantitatively identifying the source of atmospheric particulate pollutants in an environmental receptor through chemical, physical, and mathematical methods is called traceability of particulate pollutants [2, 3]. How to design a reliable and effective method for the traceability through particle size to achieve the purpose of environmental monitoring is a meaningful work at present.

1.2 Related Studies

Currently, there is less research literature on particulate matter, and higher resolution particle size spectrum monitoring data are difficult to obtain publicly in large quantities. Moreover, most of the current particle size data have fewer features, there are no more comprehensive datasets of particle size, and most of the time periods are relatively short.

Traditional air particulate pollutants traceability methods [4, 5] mainly include the source inventory method, source diffusion model method, and receptor model method, and there are fewer studies on traceability based on particulate particle size data.

The source inventory method refers to the real-time and accurate monitoring of the pollution emissions of each pollution source, and then the pollution traceability according to the emissions of each source. This method requires the monitoring of the specific emissions of each pollution source in the study area, so it requires a lot of financial and human resources and is difficult to implement.

The source diffusion model method [6] is a mathematical modeling approach to simulate the processes of diffusion, transmission, and deposition of pollutants, which fully considers external influences such as meteorology and topography. The disadvantages of the diffusion model method mainly include errors in the simulation process of the meteorological field.

The receptor model method refers to the sampling of discrete sampling points in the study area, and then analyzing the pollutant composition of the sampling points by physical or chemical methods, so as to obtain the proportion of the contribution of each pollution source to the points. Common methods for source analysis based on receptor models include chemical mass balance (CMB), probabilistic matrix factorization (PMF), principal component analysis (PCA), factor analysis (FA), and multi-source linear analysis (UNMIX), etc.

The study of traceability of particulate pollutants means analyzing the contribution proportion of pollutants by mathematical or physicochemical methods. Huang et al. [7] summarized the receptor model methods in the field of pollution source tracing and introduced the commonly used receptor models and development overviews at domestically and abroad. With the improvement of technology in recent years, Zheng et al. [8] introduced the source analysis methods for PM2.5 in China and proposed the future development direction of particulate matter source analysis research, which is an important scientific reference and reference value for future PM2.5 source analysis work. Wang [9] carried out a source analysis of atmospheric VOCs and used a factor analysis model to obtain the contribution ratio of each component.

Zhang et al. [10] used a positive definite factor model to analyze the source of winter road particulate matter particle size distribution in Tianjin and obtained three main sources of road dust, tire wear, and motor vehicle tailpipe emission aging. Huang et al. [11] analyzed the heavy metal pollution sources in agricultural soil at different scales and established a soil heavy metal pollution source analysis method adapted to different scales on the basis of the traditional source analysis work.

Chen et al. [12] used machine learning methods to study the source analysis of air pollution in Shanghai, using GBRT and Random Forest algorithm to establish a source analysis model and put forward some suggestions and measures for the prevention and control of air pollution in Shanghai. Chen et al. [13] compared hour-by-hour PM2.5 concentration prediction using multiple machine learning models, and XGBoost model, LightGBM model and random forest model were comparatively analyzed.

For the traceability of particulate pollutants, there are relatively few studies domestically and abroad, and most of them are based on the methods of factor analysis. While the existing factor analysis analytical methods have low temporal resolution, consume computational resources and require experts' experience, etc. Therefore, this study will explore the problem of pollution traceability from two technical routes factor analysis and machine learning.

1.3 Purpose

This study aims to quickly obtain the proportion of pollutants and achieve traceability through particle size data, based on factor analysis and machine learning methods. This study has two originalities: it is the first to use pollutant particle size data, which achieves high-resolution pollutant traceability compared to traditional chemical composition methods; it introduces machine learning methods into traditional factor analysis methods to improve processing efficiency and accuracy, providing a reference basis for air pollution control.

Traditional air pollution source methods are seldom analyzed by using particle size spectrum data, so this study has some practical significance in engineering; due to less research on machine learning in this field [14], this study has some theoretical research significance.

2 Data Analysis

2.1 Particle Size Data Description

The data used in this study were collected by particle size monitoring equipment developed by Hebei Advanced Environmental Protection Industry Innovation Center Co. The equipment is designed based on the principle of high-precision light scattering particle counting. The core element of the equipment is an optical particle sensor, which analyzes the Lorenz-Mie scattered light of individual particles in order to determine the particle size. During the measurement, individual particles will pass through an optically differentiated measurement space that is uniformly illuminated using a multi-colored LED light source. Each particle generates scattered light pulses detected at an angle of $85°$-$95°$, and the number of particles is determined based on the number of scattered light pulses, with the level of the measured scattered light pulses being the level of the particle size.

All particle size data captured by the equipment have 2 types of attributes: mass concentration (mass of particles per unit volume, $\mu g/m^3$) and number concentration (number of particles per unit volume, $count/m^3$) respectively. Because single type cannot fully capture the particle size distribution, the two attributes are used in the study.

The particle size data for this study includes two categories:

1. Pollution source spectrum data: about 20,000 items from seven types of pollution sources (categories are shown in Fig. 2), including 83 dimensions (11 mass concentration attributes and 72 number concentration attributes), collected in several places and specific pollution source situation.
2. Particle size monitoring data: about 30,000 items from Baoding City by continues monitoring every second from April 1st to 30th in 2023, which contains 83 dimensions of particle size data. During the period, there is an obvious dust weather event started at 21:00 on April 10th, with a PM10 concentration of $459\ \mu g/m^3$, peaked at $2084\ \mu g/m^3$ at 02:00 on the 11th, and ended at 19:00 on the 11th, with a PM10 concentration of $166\ \mu g/m^3$.

Fig. 2. Seven types of pollution sources

2.2 Characterization of Pollution Sources Based on Pollution Source Spectrum Data

Through the preliminary analysis of the pollution source spectrum data, it can be plotted to characterize the spectrum of different pollution sources, Fig. 3 is the distribution of the mass concentration attribute of different 7 pollution sources. It can be seen that the mass concentration distribution of different pollution sources has different feature, for example, construction dust has lower concentrations in small particle size segments and higher concentrations of PM7-10 in large particle size segments; road dust also has lower concentrations in small particle size segments and higher concentrations in large particle size segments, but the highest concentration occurs in PM2.5-4.

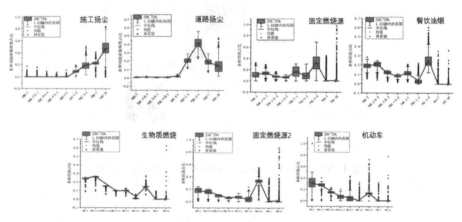

Fig. 3. Distribution of mass concentration from 7 pollution sources (Top (from left to right): 1. Construction dust, 2. Road dust, 3. Fixed combustion source, 4. Catering fumes. Bottom: 5. Biomass burning, 6. Fixed combustion source 2, 7. Motor vehicle)

2.3 Correlation Analysis of Particle Size Monitoring Data

Correlation analysis is one of the important statistical methods to study the correlation between attributes. The correlation coefficient can be used to describe the relationship between variables (attributes) and the degree of linear correlation between two variables by calculating the Pearson correlation coefficient, which takes a value between -1 and 1. Negative values indicate a negative correlation, positive values indicate a positive correlation, and absolute values closer to 1 indicate a stronger correlation, while values closer to 0 indicate a weaker correlation.

According to the formula of Pearson correlation coefficient, it can be calculated to obtain the correlation coefficient matrix, which was plotted as a heat map as shown in Fig. 4. It can be observed that there is a positive correlation among all particle sizes. Some particle size monitoring data exhibit strong correlations with each other. For instance, the correlation coefficients between PM0.2, PM0.2-0.3, and PM0.3-0.4 are 0.68, 0.67, and 1.00, respectively. The correlation coefficient between PM1-2.5 and PM2.5-4 is 0.88, while the correlation coefficient between PM10-15 and PM15-20 is 0.92, indicating a strong correlation. On the other hand, there is relatively weak correlation between large particle pollutants and small particle pollutants.

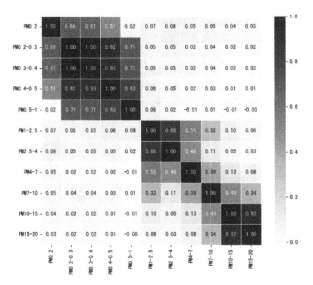

Fig. 4. Schematic diagram of correlation coefficient matrix

2.4   Similarity Analysis of Particle Size Monitoring Data

By analyzing the data feature between adjacent rows, we can gain insight into the similarity relationships between adjacent time data. To measure the similarity between adjacent data items, we calculate the Manhattan distance as a metric. Due to the large dataset, we applied this method to a dataset consisting of 2880 min-level data related to dust weather events (see Sect. 2.1). The calculated similarity relationships are presented in Fig. 5.

The lighter the color means the closer the data, and the higher the similarity, while the darker the color means the farther the data and the lower the similarity. It shows that the color between the data of adjacent time is very light, while the color turns very dark, especially April 10th 21: 00 to 11th 2: 00, means it enters the dusty time.

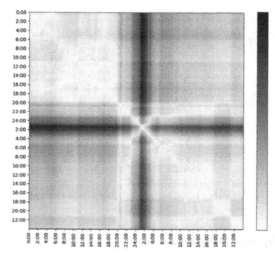

Fig. 5. Similarity analysis graph of dust event (from April 10th to 11th)

3 Research on Traceability Model for Particulate Pollutants

3.1 Overall Design

Factor analysis is one of the commonly used methods in pollutant traceability, it can be used to statistically identify underlying structures or "factors" that explain the correlation between variables. It can be reduced a large number of influences to a few key factors, which helps to improve the efficiency and interpretability of subsequent analyses. Machine Learning (ML) is an algorithmic approach that allows computers to learn laws and patterns from data and can be applied to a variety of prediction and classification tasks. For example, ML model (Random Forest) is used to classify the particle size spectrum data into different pollution sources.

Therefore, the purpose of the traceability of atmospheric particulate pollutants will be performed by two technical methods, factor analysis and machine learning, as shown in Fig. 6, and validated by comparative experiment, case study and expert's experience.

3.2 Classification Model Based on Random Forest

Random Forest (RF) [15–17] is an extension of Bagging [18] (a parallel integrated learning method), which fixes the base learner as a decision tree. In the process of constructing a random forest, the training set is first randomly sampled several times, and each time a sample set is obtained. Then, each sampling set is used to train a decision tree, and each tree randomly selects a portion of sample features at nodes and divides the left and right subtrees according to the optimal values of these features [19]. The main advantages of the random forest algorithm include high parallelization, advantageous training speed for large samples in the big data era, and insensitivity to some missing features [20]. Therefore, the random forest is used in this study for classifying 7 pollution sources by using the particle size spectrum data. Compared to other methods such as SVM, Naive Bayes, RF has the highest accuracy 95%.

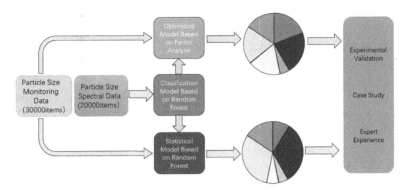

Fig. 6. Solution for the traceability of particulate pollutants

3.3 Method 1: Optimized Model Based on Factor Analysis

Factor Analysis Methods. Factor analysis is a method of multivariate statistical analysis that reduces a number of variables with intricate relationships to a few unrelated new composite factors. By grouping several variables that are more closely related in the same category, each category becomes a factor. Receptor models (in Sect. 1.2) are widely used in pollution source analysis, including positive definite matrix factorization (PMF), principal component analysis (PCA), and chemical mass balance (CMB), etc. PMF is a kind of factor analysis, which has non-negative constraints on the sources, so it can decompose the natural sources better. PMF often used to resolve pollution sources by chemical composition of particulate matter (water-soluble ions, organic fractions, carbon fractions, and metal elements). In the study method 1 is inspired by the PMF.

The PMF model first calculates the errors of different factors in the input data, and then finds the optimal source and contribution matrices by the least squares method. Input data matrix X can be defined as:

$$X = S \times F + E \tag{1}$$

The input data matrix is divided into S factor contribution matrix and F factor spectrum matrix. The Factor Contribution Matrix shows the average contribution of different factors to each component. The Factor Spectrum Matrix shows the percentage and concentration of different components in each factor.

Contribution Analysis of Pollution Sources Based on Random Forest. Firstly, the input data are processed in one hour time, by using factor analysis each hour will return the corresponding two matrices S and F, and the obtained S matrix size is 3600*7. Then, it will be averaged to get the percentage of each pollution source. However, since each pollution source does not correspond to the specific class of pollution source it belongs to, so it is necessary to judge its specific pollution source category. Obtained data on the percentage of pollution sources is input into the random forest model (in Sect. 3.2) to judge which specific category belongs to which pollution source. Finally, the obtained F matrix can be used to get the percentage of contribution of the pollution source.

3.4 Method 2: Statistical Model Based on Random Forest

Random Forest Based Pollution Source Contribution Analysis. By using the existing pollution source spectrum data random forest model is well trained (in Sect. 3.2). Then using the trained model to discriminate the categories of the monitoring data by using statistical method, that is counting the number of each type of pollution source in a certain time interval, and then calculate the percentage of each type of source as the contribution of that type of source to the pollution at that moment.

Calculation Method of Pollution Source Contribution Based on Probability Statistics. Due to the proportion value of categories with smaller contributions is very small, this study conducted a square root operation on the preliminary results and normalized them to optimize the results. To further optimize the fitting of the model to the real situation, weight is assigned to the results of each data, which is the ratio of the sum of the mass concentrations of the data to the sum of all data mass concentrations over the entire time interval.

4 Experiments and Discussions

4.1 Experimental Setup and Evaluation Indicators

Computer hardware uses CPU of i5-8300 and memory of 16GB, software is based on Anaconda and Visual Studio Code, a Python environment configuration software that makes it easy to manage different Python development environments without conflicts.

Because there are no evaluation indicators for traceability models, this study considers that the changes in the contribution of particulate air pollution in adjacent time periods are correlated, and therefore introduces the concept of similarity to analyze the experimental results. The Manhattan distance between the experimental results of two neighboring data is calculated as a measure of their similarity. The Manhattan distance (Eq. 2) is a geometric term used in geometric metric space to label the sum of the absolute axial distances of two points on a standard coordinate system. The shorter the Manhattan distance, the better we consider the algorithm fitting.

$$d(i, j) = |x_i - x_j| + |y_i - y_j| \tag{2}$$

4.2 Comparative Experiment of the Two Methods

Comparative experiment between method 1 (in Sect. 3.3) and method 2 (in Sect. 3.4) are conducted. In Fig. 7, we can see that the results of the two pollutant traceability methods by randomly selecting a day are roughly the same. Fixed combustion sources and fixed combustion sources 2 account for a large proportion, while the rest of the pollution sources of biomass combustion, construction dust, road dust, motor vehicles, and catering fumes do not contribute significantly. The two methods are consistent in the overall results.

By calculating the Manhattan distance of neighboring samples of the results of the two methods, it can be found that the average distance of method 2 is 0.0012 and method

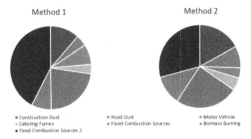

Fig. 7. Method1 (Optimized Model Based on Factor Analysis) vs. method2 (Statistical Model Based on Random Forest) (a day randomly selected)

1 is 0.0030, so the method 2 is a better fit for pollution over time in real data. Based on the expert experience for this period of data, it can be concluded that particulate pollutants were significantly affected by fixed combustion sources at that time. Therefore, we can believe that both methods have a certain degree of accuracy.

4.3 Case Study

In the particle size monitoring data during April 10th to 11th are typical dust weather. By using method 1, the experimental results are shown in Fig. 8. The contribution of road dust (green part) started to rise significantly from 20:00 on April 10th, which is in line with the weather observation results (the dust weather started at 21:00 on April 10th, with PM10 concentration of 459 $\mu g/m^3$, peaked at 2084 $\mu g/m^3$ at 2:00 on April 11th, and ended at 19:00 on April 11th with PM10 concentration dropping to 166 $\mu g/m^3$, and lasted for a total of 22h; then by the influence of sand and dust reflux, PM10 concentration exists to rise again.) The modeling of the PM10 concentration, which was carried out in the past, proved that the model has some feasibility.

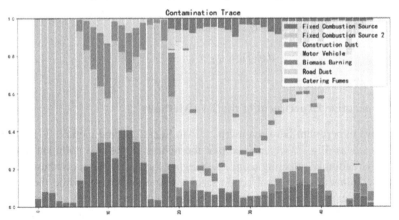

Fig. 8. Pile-up histogram of 7 pollution sources (from April 10th to 11th)

Figure 9 shows the contribution of various pollution sources in all April, the horizontal axis corresponds from April 1st to 30th, and the vertical axis is the contribution of pollution sources. The black box in the figure is the period when the dust weather is more serious, which is consistent with meteorological observations. The figure shows that the contribution of various pollution sources fluctuates greatly, and the model needs to be further optimized.

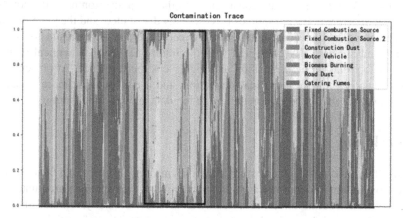

Fig. 9. Pile-up histogram of 7 pollution sources (from April 1st to 30th)

Analysis of the similarity: the results of calculating the Manhattan distance for the contribution results of the pollution sources are shown in Fig. 10, from which we can see that the overall similarity is consistent with the particle size spectral data, which indicates that the Random Forest-based particle pollutant traceability algorithm proposed in this study can fit the real dataset very well.

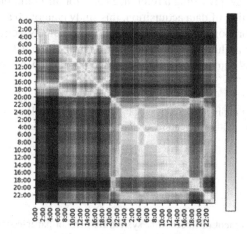

Fig. 10. Similarity analysis of the results of pollution source contribution

4.4 Expert Experience

Since the raw data could not provide accurate reference values for the contribution of pollution sources, this study also got confirmation and advices from experts in the field of environmental protection, who considered that the relevant experimental results were basically in line with the actual situation.

Through the case study on April 10, the experts believe that the conclusions of the model presented in this paper are consistent with the actual environment, the contribution ratio of different pollution sources is reasonably distributed, and the main pollution sources obtained are also consistent with the expert experience. The results of the proposed method are basically consistent with the traditional physicochemical methods, and our method has higher resolution and higher cost performance. At present, there is no particularly accurate numerical prediction, and it is hoped that more reasonable evaluation indicators can be explored through big data and machine learning.

5 Conclusion

By using of particle size data, this study combines machine learning and factor analysis methods to conduct in-depth research on traceability of atmospheric particulate pollutants, and the main contributions of this study are as follows: Firstly, this study analyzed particle size data and determined the distribution characteristics of particle size in different pollution sources; Secondly, a traceability model based on random forest and factor analysis was constructed to achieve the traceability of particulate pollutants using particle size data; Finally, through experimental comparison, case study and expert experience, the model was verified its effectiveness in the actual situation. This study is the first to use pollutant particle size data, which achieves high-resolution pollutant traceability compared to traditional chemical composition methods. This study introduces machine learning methods into traditional factor analysis method to improve processing efficiency and accuracy, providing a reference basis for air pollution control.

Due to the limitation of data acquisition, this study cannot obtain accurate pollution source contribution proportion data, so only pollution source spectrum data can be used for analysis, if many pollution source contribution proportion data can be obtained, the accuracy of the model can be further improved and the dependence on expert experience can be reduced.

Acknowledgements. Funding by Science and Technology Plan Project in Xinji City, Hebei Province: Development and Application of Particle Size Analysis Traceability and Decision Support System.

References

1. Yang, G.: Establishment of traceability system for aerosol particle size spectrometer. China University of Petroleum (Beijing), Master (2020)
2. Li, Y., et al.: Real-time chemical characterization of atmospheric particulate matter in China: a review. Atmos. Environ. **158**, 270–304 (2017)

3. Lv, M., Li, Y., Chen, L., Chen, T.: Air quality estimation by exploiting terrain features and multi-view transfer semi-supervised regression. Inf. Sci. **483**, 82–95 (2019)
4. Miao, Q., Jiang, N., Zhang, R., Zhao, X., Qi, J.: Characteristics and sources of atmospheric PM2.5 pollution in typical cities of the Central Plains Urban Agglomeration in fall and winter. Environ. Sci. **42**(01), 19–29 (2021)
5. Cao, J., Zhao, H.: Research on accurate enforcement of PM2.5 traceability in Beijing-Tianjin-Hebei region. Environ. Sustainable Dev. **44**(02), 57–61 (2019)
6. Zhu, S., Dong, W, Xu, J.: Characterization of PM2.5 pollution and its traceability and tracking in Urumqi. Environ. Protection Xinjiang **34**(03), 6–11 (2012)
7. Huang, S., Liu, F., Sheng, L., Cheng, L., Wulin, L.J.: Traceability of air pollution based on concomitant methods. Chin. Sci. Bull. **63**(16), 1594–1605 (2018)
8. Zheng, M., Zhang, Y., Yan, C., Zhu, G., James, J.S., Zhang, Y.: A review of source analysis methods for PM2.5 in China. Acta Scicentiarum Naturalum Universitis Pekinesis **50**(06), 1141–1154 (2014)
9. Wang, Q., et al.: Contribution of atmospheric VOCs to the generation of secondary organic aerosols and their sources in autumn in Shanghai. Environ. Sci. **34**(02), 424–433 (2013)
10. Zhang, G., Yin, B., Bai, W.: Particle size distribution and source analysis of roadway particles in Tianjin in winter. Environ. Sci. **43**(09), 4467–4474 (2022)
11. Huang, Y.: Research on the source analysis of heavy metal pollution in farmland soil at different scales. Zhejiang University, Master (2018)
12. Chen, Y.: Research on air pollution source analysis in Shanghai based on machine learning. East China Normal University, Master (2018)
13. Chen, J., Mou, F., Zhang, Y., Tian, T., Wang, J.: Comparison of hour-by-hour PM2.5 concentration prediction based on multiple machine learning models. J. Nanjing Forestry Univ. (Natural Science Edition) **46**(05), 152–160 (2022)
14. Wang, X., Huang, R., Zhang, W.: Ozone and PM2.5 pollution potential forecasting model based on machine learning method - a case study of Chengdu City. Journal of Acta Scicentiarum Naturalum Universitis Pekinesis **57**(05), 938–950 (2021)
15. Breiman: Random forests. Machine Learning **45**(1), 5–32 (2001)
16. JL Speiser, Michael, E., Miller, J.T., Edward Ip: A comparison of random forest variable selection methods for classification prediction modeling. Expert Systems with Applications **134**, 93–101 (2019)
17. Wang, Y., Xia, S.: A review of random forest algorithm for integrated learning. Inf. Commun. Technol. **12**(01), 49–55 (2018)
18. Sagi, O., Rokach, L.: Ensemble learning: a survey. Wiley Interdisciplinary Rev. Data Mining Knowl. Discovery **8**(5), e1249 (2018)
19. Cao, Z.: Optimization Research on Random Forest Algorithm. Capital University of Economics and Business, Master (2014)
20. Li, G., Li, J., Zhang, L.: A feature selection method fusing ant colony algorithm and random forest. Comput. Sci. **46**(S2), 212–215 (2019)
21. Chen, G., Li, S., Knibbs, L.D.: A machine learning method to estimate PM2.5 concentrations across China with remote sensing, meteorological and land use information. Sci. Total Environ. **636**, 52–60 (2018)
22. van Aaron, D., Martin Randall, V., Michael, B., Winker David, M.: global estimates of fine particulate matter using a combined geophysical-statistical method with information from satellites, models, and monitors. Environ. Sci. Technol. **50**(7), 3762–3772 (2016)

Analysis of Social Support Network on the Topic of "Smiling Depression" in Zhihu Online Community

Ji Li[1](✉), Xu Zou[2](✉), and Xueyan Tang[3]

[1] Department of Network and New Media, School of Journalism and Communication, Guangdong University of Foreign Studies, Guangzhou 510006, People's Republic of China
li-ji@gdufs.edu.cn
[2] School of Journalism and Communication, Guangdong University of Foreign Studies, Guangzhou 510006, People's Republic of China
424135983@qq.com
[3] Aosom International Development Co., Ltd., Zhejiang 315200, People's Republic of China

Abstract. In the era of social media, online communities such as Zhihu have become important platforms for vulnerable groups such as the people who suffer from smiling depression to communicate, learn, and provide or obtain social support from each other. Studying the structural characteristics of online social support network for the topic of "Smiling Depression" can provide an empirical basis for improving the level of social support. This paper takes the topic of "Smiling Depression" in Zhihu platform as the research object, uses Python crawler to collect the answers and comments of top 30 hot questions under this topic, and obtains 238 answers and 4048 comments as valid data. Then, according to the interaction relationship between the answers and commenters, the social support matrix is established. And network density, average degree and other indicators in the social network analysis method are further used to analyze the overall and individual characteristics of the social support network structure. Finally, combining the two indicators of degree centrality and betweenness centrality, core nodes are identified with the identity characteristics analyzed in the social support network.

Keywords: Social network analysis · Zhihu online community · Smiling Depression · Social support network

1 Introduction

According to the Chinese mental health survey, about 95 million people suffer from depression in China, and depression has become the hardest hit of the mental health problems [1]. People with depression have different patterns of illness response among which is "Smiling Depression" [2]. Relatively speaking, patients with smiling depression are more hidden and dangerous than ordinary depressed patients, because the society has less awareness of "Smiling Depression" and thus gives less support for it. The development of the Internet and social media has created social relationships online and brought new opportunities for online social support to vulnerable groups such as the people who suffer from smiling depression [3]. For example, Zhihu, the largest Q&A community in China, not only has a large number of users, but also has the advantages of detailed topic classification, convenient question retrieval, high content quality and much professionalism. In addition, it has a lower threshold for use, and provides users with a semi-closed circle which is more in line with the psychology of depressed patients. Many users carry out the activities of communication, emotional comfort and knowledge popularization and so on under the topic of "Smiling Depression". This topic in Zhihu has become an important way for users to provide or obtain social support of smiling depression, and also generated rich data for our research.

Virtual society formed by social support of users in social media has already been a new type of network different from traditional social relations [6]. Zhang and Zhou sorted out the types and effects of online support for depression [4]. Park and Lee showed that different structures of social network had different effectiveness [5]. Therefore, it is necessary to study the structural characteristics of the new social relationship network formed by online social support of "Smiling Depression" in Zhihu, analyze its role, and try to improve the social support to smiling depression and promote the recovery of patients.

This paper first uses Python to crawl top 30 questions with related data under the topic of "Smiling Depression" in Zhihu. The collected data is then processed to build a social support network based on the interaction between the answerers and commenters. The characteristics of the overall network and the individual network, and the key nodes with their identity characteristics are further analyzed. Finally, based on the results of the analysis, suggestions are made to improve social support of "Smiling Depression".

2 Related Work

Regarding "Smiling Depression", Cao and Lin studied the self-identity of the youth with smiling depression, and found that their self-presentation in daily life had typical performance characteristics [7]. Chen et al. showed that the factors for the formation of smiling depression included family, environment, individuality and so on, and found that nearly 70% of college students did not understand "Smiling Depression" at all by 2048 questionnaires [8]. Zhu took "false self" as the theoretical framework to study the psychological mechanism and evolution process of smiling depression among adolescents, and made suggestions for the prevention and recovery of smiling depression among adolescents [9].

MacGeorge et al. identified three main research perspectives on social support including social context, subjective cognition and action support [10]. From the perspective of social context, social support was considered to be the connection between an individual and other individuals in the social environment, and the researches based on this perspective usually used the method of social network analysis to analyze the important interpersonal structural characteristics of individuals [10]. This perspective provides a theoretical basis for this paper to study the structure of online social support network for "Smiling Depression" using social network analysis.

Yue believed that online social support was behavior and information flow of social support that occurred in the Internet field [11]. Sun and Kang analyzed the content of

1894 posts for the topic of "Depression" in Baidu Tieba, and the results showed that emotional needs were the most significant type which brought the most diverse and rich support supplies to the posters [12]. Aurora et al. used questionnaires to examine the impact of online social support on lifestyle, essential knowledge and skills for people over 65 years of age, and the results demonstrated that online social support was beneficial for the middle-aged and elderly people to integrate into the society, improve social skills and reduce loneliness [13]. Yan and Liu used the social network analysis method to analyze the structure of social support network for the super talk of "Depression" in Sina Weibo, and found that the overall network was highly discrete, the connection between users was weak, and the opinion leaders in the network structure had mobility [14].

In short, there is still room for progress in research on "Smiling Depression" and online social support. At present, the research methods of online social support to smiling depression are mostly traditional quantitative methods such as content analysis, structural equation model and questionnaire survey. The use of computational communication methods is insufficient such as social network analysis and data mining which are more suitable for the social media field. In this paper, we use Python to collect data, and analyze the structural characteristics of online social support network of "Smiling Depression" in Zhihu community by the social network analysis method.

3 Social Network Analysis

Social network analysis is a computational research method that treats society as a network containing nodes and relationships between nodes [15]. The social network analysis method mainly explores the characteristics of the structure and attributes of relational network. The attributes include the overall and individual ones. This paper analyzes network density, average distance, small world, and average degree among the overall attributes, and centrality and other characteristics among the individual attributes.

Density measures the closeness of the connection between actors and the degree of interaction where information is disseminated [20]. The computational formula in the undirected network is as follows [23]:

$$D = \frac{2L}{N(N-1)} \tag{1}$$

where L represents the number of edges that exist in the network, N represents total number of network nodes, and $N(N-1)$ represents the maximum number of possible edges in the undirected network.

Degree centrality measures the connection ability of the nodes themselves with the formula as follows [18]:

$$DC_i = \frac{K_i}{N-1} \tag{2}$$

where K_i represents the number of existing edges connected to the node i, and N is the total number of nodes in the network.

Betweenness centrality denotes the mediating ability of a node to convey information with the formula as follows [18]:

$$BC_i = \sum_{s \neq t \neq i} \frac{d_{st}^i}{g_{st}} \tag{3}$$

where d_{st}^i indicates the number of the shortest paths connecting two nodes s and t through the node i, and g_{st} indicates the number of the shortest paths connecting two nodes s and t.

4 Process of Experiment

The framework of this study is separated into five steps as shown in Fig. 1.

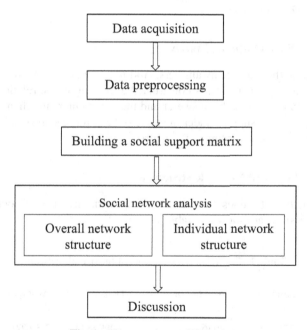

Fig. 1. The experimental flow chart

Step 1: Use Python to crawl the top 30 hot questions with answers, answerer IDs, comments and commenter IDs in the highlights section under the topic of "Smiling Depression" in Zhihu.

Step 2: Clean the data by deleting some invalid text.

Step 3: Build a social support matrix of users,and then use Pajek [22] to map the user's social support network.

Step 4: Analyze the overall and individual network characteristics.

5 Experiment and Discussion

5.1 Collecting Data

This paper uses Python to collect the top 30 hot questions in the highlights section under the topic of "Smiling Depression" in Zhihu as the samples. The collected data include questions, answerer IDs under the questions, answers, commenter IDs under the answers, and comments. A total of 30 questions, 1312 answers and 5319 comments are collected from April 15, 2015, to June 3, 2023.

5.2 Preprocessing Data

Invalid data are removed such as duplicated usernames, anonymous users, and answerer IDs with no comments. In the end, there are 238 answers and 4048 comments. After further deduplication of the collected answerer IDs and commenter IDs, a total of 3375 valid nodes of ID are obtained.

5.3 Building a Social Support Matrix

For each question, there are many answers. And for each answer, there are many comments. The social support matrix is constructed according to the relationship of commenting interaction between the answerer and the commenter, and then the undirected network graph of social support under the topic of "Smiling Depression" is established by making use of Pajek according to the matrix.

5.4 Analysis of Overall Network Structure

The related coefficient values for the overall network structure of social support to "Smiling Depression" are shown in Table 1.

Table 1. The related coefficients of the overall network

Coefficient name	Number of nodes	Number of edges		Density	Average degree	Average distance
Value	3375	4046		0.0006843	2.39769	5

Online social support network of "Smiling Depression" has a total of 3375 nodes and 4046 edges. The overall network structure presents a core-peripheral structure with a few nodes in the central area and sparse connections between the central nodes.

The density value of the overall network is between 0 and 1, and it is considered that the actors are more closely connected if the density exceeds 0.05. According to the calculation by Pajek, the overall density is 0.0006843, which is much less than 0.05, indicating that the overall interaction of the network is weak, the connection between the actors is loose, and most members only communicate with one of these nodes.

In addition, network density also depends on the size of the network. Therefore, the structural cohesion of a network needs to be measured by the average degree of all the vertices [15]. The results show that the average degree is 2.39762963, which once again proves the low overall density of the network and the loose connection between members.

Distance in the overall network refers to the length of the shortest path between nodes, and greater distance indicates less direct connections between nodes. The average distance is 5, which means that at least 5 nodes are needed to pass for any two actors which are not directly connected in the network to generate a connection. The *Small World* theory is one of the most well-known theories in the field of social network analysis, which states that any two strangers in the world can make a connection in up to 6 steps [21].An important measure of the small world is the average length of the shortest path connecting any two nodes. The average distance of the network is 5 indicating that a network relationship of small world has been formed between members under the topic of "Smiling Depression", but the accessibility of the network is poor, and the channels for information dissemination and social support circulation between nodes are weak.

That the overall network of the topic of "Smiling Depression" is loose may be due to the characteristics of Zhihu. The anonymity, equality, and sociability of Zhihu make numerous users come together to interact and connect with each other under a certain topic because of their interests. Users under the topic of "Smiling Depression" rely on such a network of weak relationship to interact. Although they are in the same topic network, each node has its own circle and small world. However, according to the research of Xu et al., the more decentralized the overall structure of social network is, the greater the scope of information diffusion is [20]. For the depression group, such a weak and scattered network structure is conducive to its own social support demands beyond the circle, breaking barriers, spreading to the larger Internet network, and bringing a wider range of social support.

5.5 Analysis of Individual Network Structure

Figure 2 shows the structure diagram of online social support network for "Smiling Depression" where the nodes whose usernames are marked in red are the top 10 users in degree centrality, and the nodes whose usernames are marked in blue are the top 10 users in betweenness centrality.

Degree centrality is an important basis for judging opinion leaders in social networks. The higher the degree centrality value of a node is, the more nodes it connects to, and the greater its influence and importance is. According to Pajek's calculations, there are 2830 users with degree centrality of 1, which means that about 84% of users are marginal in the network and have low engagement in the interactions of social support to "Smiling Depression". The top 10 users in degree centrality are shown in Table 2. They are active members in the social support network who answer questions related to smiling depression actively and drive social support interaction within the community. The user "Simple Psychology(简单心理)" has the largest degree centrality (851) in the entire network of 3375 nodes, which means that more than 25% of users have interacted with it for social support. And the degree centrality values of the other nine users are far from "Simple Psychology(简单心理)", which roughly form three descending gradients.

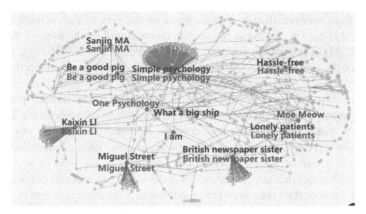

Fig. 2. Structure of social support network for "Smiling Depression"

Table 2. Top 10 users in degree centrality ranking

Rank	Degree centrality	Username
1	851	Simple Psychology(简单心理)
2	443	British Newspaper Sister(英国报姐)
3	422	Kaixin Li(李开心)
4	306	Miguel Street(米格尔街)
5	238	Sanjin Ma(马三金)
6	136	Be a Good Pig(做一只优秀的猪)
7	135	Hassle-Free(无忧)
8	100	Moe Meow(萌大喵)
9	94	One Psychology(壹心理)
10	88	Lonely Patients(孤独患者)

Betweenness centrality measures the control degree of nodes over resources in the network. The betweenness centrality value of nodes is positively correlated with the ability of controlling information flow. According to Pajek's calculation, the betweenness centrality values of 3105 users are 0. That is to say, more than 92% of users in the network do not have the ability of controlling other actors, and the flow of information resources is in the hands of 8% of users whose ability of controlling information is highly monopolized. The top 10 users in betweenness centrality are shown in Table 3. These user nodes have important bridge characteristics and play a key role in connecting other users to form an overall social support network. Bridge nodes also have greater power to control communication between members [13]. Many members must achieve social support interaction through the bridge nodes and have a large degree of dependence on them. By further analysis of the top 10 values, it is found that the polarization also occurs within the strong control circle. The user "Simple Psychology(简单心理)" is dominant in the support network, while the control ability of other nodes over resource is much weaker than that of it, which is similar to the characteristics of descending gradients in degree centrality.

Table 3. Top 10 users in betweenness centrality ranking

Order	Betweenness centrality	Username
1	0.467349312	Simple Psychology(简单心理)
2	0.223508729	British Newspaper Sister(英国报姐)
3	0.189499834	Kaixin Li(李开心)
4	0.149032097	Miguel Street(米格尔街)
5	0.147763651	I Am(我是)
6	0.069130595	Hassle-Free(无忧)
7	0.06799662	Lonely Patients(孤独患者)
8	0.067331516	Be a Good Pig(做一只优秀的猪)
9	0.058287106	Sanjin Ma(马三金)
10	0.051658738	What a Big Ship(好大的船)

5.6 Analysis of Core Node Features

Combining the two indicators of degree centrality and betweenness centrality, the core nodes and their identity attributes of the social support network for "Smiling Depression" are recognized as shown in Table 4. The users "Simple Psychology"(简单心理) and "Sanjin Ma(马三金)"are professional answerers in the field of psychology, releasing more popular science information such as depression identification and treatment, and providing psychological test and consultation. With its rich expertise, great influence, and active participation in answering, it is at the core of the social support network. Although "Miguel Street(米格尔街)" and "British Newspaper Sister"(英国报姐)are not professional in the field of depression, they are also core nodes because of their high-quality answers and large number of fans. These opinion leaders in other areas have played an important role in bringing wider social support to "Smiling Depression" beyond the circle. The four answerers "Kaixin Li(李开心)", "Be a good pig(做一只优秀的猪)", "Hassle-Free(无忧)", and "Lonely Patients(孤独患者)" are depression patients, and their posts mainly involved life sharing, symptom description of smiling depression, feelings, treatment experience, etc. As patients, they brought out the emotional resonance of other users with their personal experience of smiling depression and obtained more interaction. And the users also carried on the flow of social support such as emotion, information, and companionship in the interaction.

Table 4. The core users and their identity characteristics

Username	Identity	Influence
Simple Psychology (简单心理)	A psychological counseling institution	It is given the titles of Excellent Answerer and Annual New Knowledge Answerer. Zhihu includes its 141 answers and 88 articles in the sections of Editor's Choice, Zhihu Roundtable, Zhihu Weekly and Zhihu Daily. It has 1,290,589 approvals, 534,120 likes and 1,427,104 favorites. The number of its followers is 1095437
Sanjin Ma (马三金)	A psychological counselor	He is given the title of Zhihu Judge. Zhihu includes his 1 answer in the section of Editor's Choice. He has 7,325 approvals, 2,970 likes and 6,822 favorites. The Number of its followers is 30709
British Newspaper Sister (英国报姐)	An answerer in the field of overseas cultural	Zhihu includes her 2 answers and 2 articles in the sections of Editor's Choice, Zhihu Roundtable and Zhihu Daily. She has 1,826,251 approvals, 261,820 likes and 496,829 favorites. The Number of her followers is 364211
Miguel Street (米格尔街)	A blogger in the field of information and media	Zhihu includes his 1 answer and 3 articles in the sections of Editor's Choice and Zhihu Roundtable. He has 22,599 approvals, 1,456 likes and 10,240 favorites. The Number of its followers is 4518
Kaixin Li (李开心)	A depressed person	She has 4,034 approvals, 2,371 likes and 842 favorites. The Number of her followers is 2408
Hassle-Free (无忧)	A depressed person	She has 5,230 approvals, 1,718 likes and 1,121 favorites. The Number of her followers is 514
Be a Good Pig (做一只优秀的猪)	A depressed person	She has 2,161 approvals, 497 likes and 741 favorites. The Number of her followers is 149
Lonely Patients (孤独患者)	A depressed person	He has136 approvals, 36 likes and 33 favorites. The Number of his followers is 38

6 Discussion

This paper takes the topic of "Smiling Depression" in Zhihu online community as a sample to study the overall and local structural characteristics of its social support network. The results show that the social support network of "Smiling Depression" presents a core-peripheral structure which is loose in structure with weak connection between members and a large number of fringes nodes in the network. Although network technologies and social media have the vision of equal rights in discourse, in the practice of social support to "Smiling Depression", a few core nodes such as "Simple Psychology(简单心理)"and "British Newspaper Sister(英国报姐)"control the information flow, get more comments, likes and other forms of social capital, while other members rely on these opinion leaders for social support.

Based on the characteristics of the social network structure of "Smiling Depression", this paper puts forward the following suggestions to further promote the social support for "Smiling Depression" in the community.

Firstly, the core members are the bridge that transmits social support and connects other members in the social support network of "Smiling Depression". Our research has found that the lack of interaction between core members in the support network makes the network density lower. Topic administrators of "Smiling Depression" can strengthen the linkage between core members by various means such as building groups, organizing forums, and carrying out joint creation. Through the linkage between core nodes, the barriers between different small groups in the overall network are broken down, and social support is promoted to spread across more extensive circles. At the same time, the collision of ideas and joint creation of core nodes in different fields is expected to bring more forms of social support with higher quality to users.

Secondly, the depressed people themselves are also the core nodes of the social support network. Encouraging patients to actively participate in the interaction with other silent users is also the focus of promoting the flow of social support within the community. Administrators can regularly hold exchange meetings of patients, a variety of mutual assistance activities and so on to attract the participation of fringe users in the network to further promote the knowledge dissemination of "Smiling Depression", strengthen the emotional connection between users, and bring more social support to patients.

Finally, according to the classification of identity attributes of core members, it is found that there are relatively fewer types of core members including answerers in the field of psychology and patients with depression mainly. However, with the low popularity of the knowledge of "Smiling Depression", it is more necessary to enhance the dissemination of opinion leaders in various fields such as media and public figures with social influence, increase social attention, and improve social support for "Smiling Depression".

7 Conclusion and Future Work

This paper used Python to collect top 30 hot questions with related data under the topic of "Smiling Depression" in Zhihu online community, analyzed the overall and local characteristics of online social support network for "Smiling Depression" by the social network analysis method, and finally provided suggestions to improve social support according to the research results.

In the future, we will further explore the types of online social support to "Smiling Depression" in Zhihu community as well as emotional tendency of social support.

Acknowledgements. The research was supported by National Natural Science Foundation of China (Grant No.: 62077005), Guangzhou Urban Public Opinion Governance and International Image Communication Research Center (Guangzhou Philosophy and Social Science Development "the Fourteenth Five-year Plan" 2022 Joint Project, No.: 2022JDGJ02), School Project "School Innovation Team of Cross-culture Communication and International Communication" in the School of Journalism and communication, Guangdong University of Foreign Studies, P. R. China.

References

1. Homepage of Depressive disorder (depression) in the WHO website. https://www.who.int/news-room/fact-sheets/detail/depression. Accessed 11 June 2023
2. Rita, L.: Smiling depression. Psychology today (2014)
3. Xiao, Y.: "How Depression Arises": based on the perspective of neoliberal. Globalization Sociol. **36**(02), 191–214 (2016)
4. Zhang, L.: Zhou, Y: Research on the relationship between depression and social support among urban home-based elderly. Chin. J. Soc. Med. **39**(04), 412–415 (2022). (in Chinese)
5. Park, J., Lee, D.: When perceptions defy reality: the relationships between depression and actual and perceived Facebook social support. J. Affect. Disord.Disord. **200**, 37–44 (2016)
6. Liu, J., Chen, J.: Research on HIV/AIDS transmission path and prevention mechanism from the perspective of social network: an empirical analysis based on Zhihu question and answer. Northwest Population. **40**(06), 62–71 (2019). (in Chinese)
7. Cao, L., Lin, B.: Self-identity of "smiling depression" youth. J. Hebei Youth Manage. Cadre College **31**(03), 5–9 (2019). (in Chinese)
8. Chen, X., Feng, Q., Xiao, H., Liu, Y., Dai, J.: Factors, and interventions of "Smiling Depression" in college students. Psychol. Monthly **22**, 209–211 (2021). (in Chinese)
9. Zhu, Y.: The causes of smiling depression in adolescents: Based on the perspective of false self. Mental Health Education for Primary and Secondary Schools. (34):9–14.) (2022). (in Chinese)
10. McGeorge, E., Feng, B., Burleson, B.: Supportive communication. In: Knapp, M.L., Daly, J.A., (eds.) Handbook of Interpersonal Communication, pp. 317–354. Sage, Thousand Oaks (2011)
11. Yue, G.: Social support on the internet: current status and prospect of chinese and western research. Jiang Huai Forum. **03**, 185–191 (2010). (in Chinese)
12. Sun, S., Kang, J.: Health communication from a social support perspective: an empirical examination of patient communities. J. Shanxi Univ. (Philosophy and Social Sciences). **45**(01) (2022)
13. Aurora, G.C., Irene, G.C., María, M.A., Blanca, N.P., Beatriz, R.M.: Pilot testing the effectiveness of the Healthy Ageing Supported by Internet and Community program me for promoting healthy lifestyles for people over 65 years of age. Scandinavian Journal of Caring Sciences.**34**(3) (2020)
14. Yan, Q., Liu, Y.: Research on social support seeking of depressed groups on social media platforms: Based on the investigation of Weibo's "depression super talk". Press, No. 351(06), pp. 45–56+64 (2022). (in Chinese)

15. Liu, J.: Research and analysis of social network model. Sociological Res. No. **1**, 1–12 (2004). (in Chinese)
16. Li, J., Tang, X., Dong, D.: Identification of public opinion on COVID-19 in Microblogs. In: The 16th International Conference on Computer Science & Education (ICCSE), pp. 117–120 (2021)
17. Liu, X., Tian, X., Xiao, G.: Research on the application of social network analysis in microblog information dissemination. New Media Stud. **4**(5), 25–26 (2018). (in Chinese)
18. Burt, R.S., Kilduff, M., Tasselli, S.: Social network analysis: foundations and frontiers on advantage. Annu. Rev. Psychol.. Rev. Psychol. **64**(1), 527–547 (2013)
19. Li, J., Liang, Y.: Topic analysis of public welfare microblogs in the early period of the COVID-19 epidemic based on LDA model. In: Huang, DS., Jo, KH., Jing, J., Premaratne, P., Bevilacqua, V., Hussain, A. (eds) Intelligent Computing Methodologies. ICIC 2022. Lecture Notes in Computer Science, vol. 13395. Springer, Cham
20. https://doi.org/10.1007/978-3-031-13832-4-27 (2022)
21. Zhu, Q., Li, L.: Social Network Analysis Method and Its Application in Information Science. Intelligence Theory and Practice. (02): 179–183+174 (2008). (in Chinese)
22. Zhou, T., Bai, W., Wang, B., Zhou, Y.: Overview of Complex Network Research. Physics **01**, 31–36 (2005). (in Chinese)
23. Pajek Homepage. http://mrvar.fdv.uni-lj.si/pajek/. Accessed 13 Dec 2023
24. Smith, J.D., Thai, M.T.: Measuring edge sparsity on large social networks. In: International AAAI Conference on Web and Social Media, pp. 638–649 (2020)

A Study on the Physiological Effects of Pen Usage

For Application of EEG Measurement Technology to Information Science Education

Hironari Sugai[1]([✉]), Keisuke Tsukamoto[1], Hiroki Takada[1], Yasushi Komatsu[2], Shinichi Murakata[2], and Toshihide Kawasaki[2]

[1] Graduate School of Engineering, University of Fukui, Fukui, Japan
mf220141@g.u-fukui.ac.jp, takada@u-fukui.ac.jp
[2] PILOT CO., Ltd., 1-4-3, Nishiyawata, Hiratsuka, Kanagawa, Japan

Abstract. Recently, the proliferation of digital tools has extended into the field of writing instruments. However, the value of analog tools such as pens remains significant. Handwritten notes have been reported to enhance comprehension, aid in memory retention, and reduce stress. Human perception and values play a significant role in cognitive processes and may influence physiological responses. Moreover, interest in the use of subjective evaluations and physiological signal analysis for industrial applications through quantifying and utilizing the psychological responses of users to products is increasing. In this study, we explored the potential for industrial applications of physiological signal analysis to evaluate the psychological responses of users to writing instruments. We conducted a simple mental arithmetic task using two different pens and simultaneously performed brainwave measurements and subjective evaluations. The results suggest that users' sentiments toward pens, as reflected in subjective evaluations, may be mirrored in their brainwave patterns. Additionally, significant differences were observed in the brainwave analysis results for each pen, indicating the potential varying effects of different pens on the human body.

Keywords: EEG(Electroencephalography) · subjective evaluations · psychological responses

1 Introduction

Electroencephalography (EEG) records electrical variations that result from the generation and transmission of action potentials within the brain. The first human EEG measurements were performed in 1924 by Berger [1]. EEG indicates the synchronized vibrational activity of neuronal populations in the brain. What is measured is a small fraction, only 1%, that survives attenuation as it passes through the scalp, bones, meninges, and cerebrospinal fluid. Typically, EEG recordings are performed using electrodes placed on the scalp, with a reference electrode (RE) affixed to an area that is less susceptible to electrical brain activity. During this process, microvolt-level potential differences (voltages) on the order of tens of microvolts are generated. These voltages are continually and spontaneously present as background brainwaves (baseline brainwaves), as long as the individual is alive. Additionally, event-related potentials (ERPs) occur transiently in response to specific events, such as light, sound, and spontaneous movements, and are superimposed on background brainwaves. Some of the evoked potentials related to physical stimuli can be altered by psychological variables, such as the meaning of the stimulus and attention. Evoked potentials (EPs) also occur without any external stimuli. ERPs are frequently visualized by summing tens of them.

Over the years, research on the meaning of recorded waveforms and the development of convenient EEG measurement methods have advanced the field of neurophysiology. Human EEG is now an indispensable tool in various fields, including clinical medicine, basic science, and psychology. As mentioned earlier, the RE is attached to the earlobe, tip of the nose, or mastoid, or it is placed outside the head, connecting the electrodes on the upper spinal vertebrae and the joint between the right sternum and clavicle. Scalp electrodes are placed according to the international 10–20 system (Jasper, 1958) and its extensions (American Electroencephalographic Society, 1991). As mentioned earlier, the amplitude of brainwaves is extremely weak, and EEG measurements are performed only in electromagnetically shielded rooms (closed environments) to prevent noise contamination.

Recently, technological advancements have caused the proliferation of portable EEG devices, enabling brainwaves in daily environments to be recorded. This has expanded the application of EEG beyond the medical field to research human behavior based on changes in brainwaves as well as marketing activities such as neuromarketing research [2]. Additionally, EEG is used in brain–machine interfaces [3], which enable the operation of machinery and direct input to the brain without the use of sensory stimuli, such as cameras and audio.

Even in the domain of writing instruments, digital tools have been evolving and digitalization has become mainstream. However, the value of analog tools such as pens remains, and reports regarding the effectiveness of using writing tools have been published [4]. Nonetheless, individuals have their own preferences for perceptual cognitive processes that may influence physiological responses. Furthermore, interest in utilizing subjective evaluations and physiological signal analyses for industrial applications, such as product safety assessments, improvements, and excellent designs, is increasing. These approaches aim to quantify and utilize the psychological responses of users to products [5]. Psychological responses consist of unconscious responses that can be measured through physiological signals, such as brainwaves and electrocardiograms, and conscious responses that can be measured through subjective evaluations. The quantification of both is essential for industrial applications. Therefore, we explored the potential for industrial applications using physiological signal analysis to evaluate the psychological responses of users to writing instruments. We conducted a simple mental arithmetic task using two different pens and simultaneously performed brainwave measurements and subjective evaluations.

2   Nonlinear Analysis of Brain Waves

In previous studies, linear electro-magnetic dynamics were shown for mathematical modelling of the EEG [6]. Results in some cases has indicated that EEG signals exhibit nonlinear elements and cannot completely be described by linear stochastic models [7, 8]. In this study, we conducted a hypothesis test to determine whether the brainwave signals can be described by a linear stochastic differential equation in the pre-rest period (Pre)for the current experiment. For this purpose, surrogate data analysis was applied to the brainwave data of the healthy young during the Pre with their eyes closed.

Surrogate data analysis is a method for statistically examining the characteristics of data. Demonstrating the nonlinearity of a time series signal is often easier than showing that the signal is chaotic. For the nonlinear time series data, various null hypotheses can be considered, but it is natural to adopt a null hypothesis of the linear stochastic process. Typically, hypotheses presented for testing include that the measured time series are (1) temporally uncorrelated data, (2) data with linear temporal correlation, and (3) data obtained by observing time series with linear correlation through nonlinear transformation. In surrogate data analysis, surrogate data that follows the above null hypotheses is generated in large numbers, and the statistical properties of these data are tested for differences from the original data.

In this study, among various algorithms, surrogate data were generated using the Fourier Transform (FT) algorithm. We herein calculated the translation error between the generated surrogate data and the original brainwave data using the Double-Wayland algorithm.

Translation error is an indicator showing the determinism of the mathematical model of the generated time series data estimated from the Wayland algorithm [9, 10]. Translation error is represented as a positive value, and we can determine whether the mathematical model to generate time series data is deterministic or stochastic. When it takes a value greater than 0.25, it can be considered as stochastic. As an example, the translation error of the Brownian motion was estimated as 1.0.

The Double-Wayland algorithm reconstructs the attractor by taking the differential time series data from the original time series data [11]. The reconstructed attractor is then used to estimate the translation error with the Wayland algorithm. In the case of time series data generated by deterministic processes, the attractor reconstructed from the differential processes compared to the original attractor forms a smoothly regular trajectory. In the case of time series data generated by stochastic processes, the reconstructed attractor shows increased variability compared to the original attractor.

The graph below illustrates values of the translation error of the original signal for each embedding dimension (Fig. 1), which has indicated that the EEGs can be described by stochastic models. It was consistent with the previous study in which the optimal embedding dimension of the mathematical model describing the EEG was estimated to be 8 or more from the correlation dimension analysis for the observed data [12]. The value of the translation error at 10-dimensional embedding space was used in the reconstruction of the attractor for our nonlinear analysis of the EEGs.

A t-test was performed to compare estimated values of these translation errors with a significance level of 0.05. The results are presented below (Fig. 2).

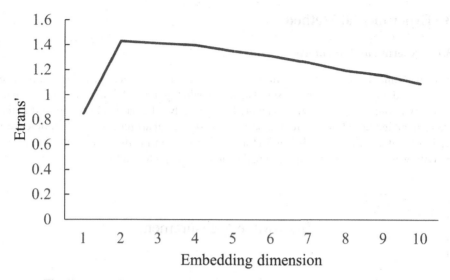

Fig. 1. Translation Error for Each Embedding Dimension of Brainwave Data

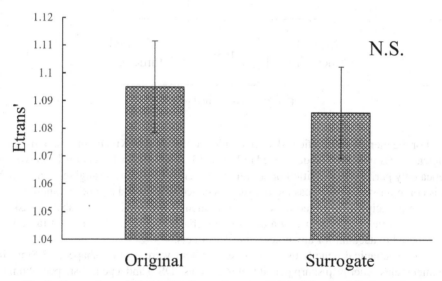

Fig. 2. Comparison of Translation Errors Between Original Data and Surrogate Data

As a result of the test, no significant difference was observed between the original data and surrogate data. Therefore, it can be concluded that the brainwave data obtained in this study was not generated by a nonlinear stochastic process. Consequently, assuming the brainwave data to be generated by a linear model, we analyzed it using Fast Fourier Transform (FFT) in this experiment.

3 Experimental Method

3.1 Experimental Variables

This experiment investigated the impact of selecting a mechanical pencil on brainwave activity and physiological responses. Thirteen healthy young adult males (mean ± standard deviation: 22.92 ± 0.79) participated in the study. The participants engaged in the experiment in the following order: a period of rest, mental arithmetic task 1, another rest period, mental arithmetic task 2, and a final rest period. During these intervals, brainwave activity was recorded. The experimental protocol is depicted in Fig. 3.

Brainwave Measurement				
180 s	180 s	180 s	180 s	180 s
rest	Mental Arithmetic Task 1	rest	Mental Arithmetic Task 2	rest

Fig. 3. Experimental protocol

For the mental arithmetic tasks, we employed the Uchida-Kraepelin Test, a psychological assessment method developed in Japan [13]. The Uchida-Kraepelin Test involves repeatedly performing addition operations on a series of numbers ranging from 1 to 9. It is commonly used to assess factors such as concentration and cognitive function.

The participants engaged in two separate mental arithmetic tasks, labeled Tasks 1 and 2, each involving the use of a different mechanical pencil. The order of tasks was considered to account for any potential order effects.

The mechanical pencils used in the experiment were a drum-shaped, 13.8mm in diameter elastomer grip sharp pencil (referred to as "DS") and a pencil-shaped, 9mm in diameter, plastic grip sharp pencil (referred to as "PS") (Fig. 4).

Brainwave activity during the experiment was recorded using MindbandSet, a simplified brainwave measurement device developed by Neurosky, which samples data at a frequency of 512 Hz.

Following the conclusion of the experiment, participants subjectively assessed the pens used. Visual analog scales (VASs) were used to gather these evaluations. Specifically, the participants were asked questions related to "fatigue resistance" and "ease of handling" to assess their subjective perceptions of the pen performance and comfort.

Figure 5 shows a photograph of the experimental setup.

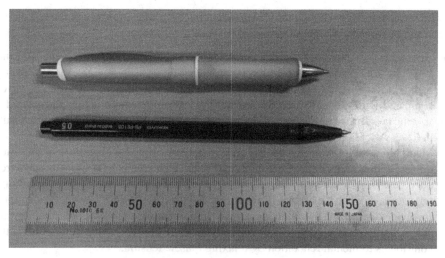

Fig. 4. Photograph of DS and PS

Fig. 5. Experimental setup

3.2 Data Analysis

In this study, we conducted a frequency analysis on the acquired brainwave data to calculate the power spectral density in the following frequency bands: low-α (7.5–9.25 Hz), high-α (10–11.75 Hz), low-β (13–16.75 Hz), and high-β (18–29.75 Hz). Additionally, we computed the β/α ratio, which represents the ratio of β waves to α waves.

Furthermore, we utilized two analysis metrics, Attention and Meditation, as output by MindbandSet. These metrics assess concentration and relaxation levels, respectively, on a scale from 0 to 100, with higher values indicating a stronger presence of the respective state and lower values suggesting a weaker focus or agitation.

- Attention: This metric signifies the intensity of concentration and attentiveness during tasks, such as focusing on a single point, engaging in deep thought, or performing mental arithmetic. Attention is calculated based on the relative change in β waves compared with other frequencies and is higher when attention is directed toward a specific task. In contrast, states of distraction, uncertainty, or scattered attention result in lower Attention values.
- Meditation: Meditation reflects the mental state associated with calmness and tranquility, with a focus on α waves and their relative change compared with other frequencies. High Meditation values are observed during moments of deep breathing, relaxation, or when the brain is in a state of rest with eyes closed. Conversely, scenarios involving distraction, agitation, or sensory stimuli can result in lower Meditation values. Although Meditation does not directly measure physical relaxation, it indirectly contributes to mental relaxation by relaxing muscle tension.

Both metrics are typically categorized as follows: 40–60 indicates a natural state, 60–80 represents a high state, and 80–100 signifies a very high level of the respective state.

We conducted statistical comparisons of Attention and Meditation during the use of each pen to assess any significant differences.

When reviewing the acquired brainwave data, we observed that data from two of the 13 participants were not recorded successfully. Consequently, data from 11 participants were used for subsequent brainwave analysis.

The Attention and Meditation data obtained for each pen were standardized using their respective medians and quartile deviations. Subsequently, we counted the number of high-scoring standardized values and conducted a two-way analysis of variance (ANOVA).

4 Results

Figure 4 depicts the average number of high Attention and Meditation scores recorded when the two different pens (Fig. 6).

For the PS pen, the average number of high Attention scores was approximately 19.4, and the number of high Meditation scores was approximately 18.7. For the DS pen, the number of high Attention scores was approximately 18.9, and the number of high Meditation scores was roughly 21.4.

The two-way ANOVA revealed a significant difference in meditation between the two pens.

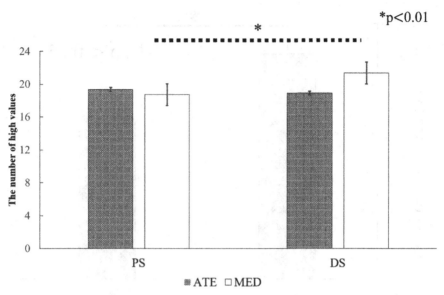

Fig. 6. Average number of high Attention and Meditation scores recorded when using two different pens.

5 Discussion

The results of the graphical analysis indicated a significant difference in Meditation, with no significant difference in attention.

These findings suggest that the unique features of pens, such as their thickness and grip, may have an impact on mental relaxation. Specifically, pen choice appeared to influence the level of relaxation experienced during the tasks.

Previous research has conducted subjective evaluations of the DS and PS pens, which corresponds with the results of this study. In a previous study, VAS assessments were performed with the addition of pen thickness and weight preferences. Before completing the VAS, the 86 participants were allowed to freely use both pens to assess comfort. The results of this preliminary study showed that DS was favored over PS in terms of causing less fatigue and being more comfortable to hold because it exhibited significantly higher scores (Figs. 7 and 8).

These results were consistent with the higher Meditation scores observed in this study. Notably, Attention exhibited minimal differences between the pens. This suggested that pen characteristics may not significantly affect the concentration levels.

Additionally, the measurement of brainwaves during the use of the pen in this experiment suggested the possibility of its application in educational settings. The ratio of alpha waves to beta waves among brainwaves is considered highly useful in understanding brain activity during human thinking, emotions, and the learning process. Specifically, it has been shown that the value of low beta waves to low alpha waves is the most indicative of task difficulty.

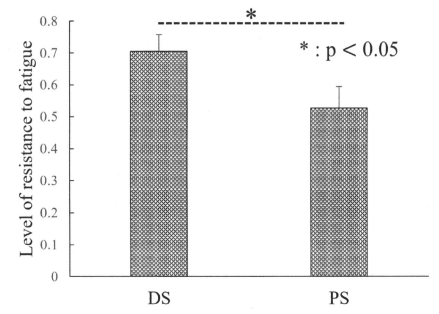

Fig. 7. Fatigue resistance in the VAS of previous research

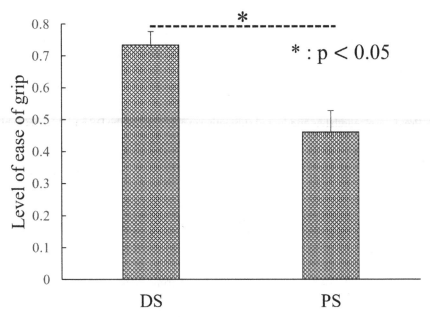

Fig. 8. Ease of grip in the VAS of previous research

Based on the results of this experiment and the implications thereof, we propose the application of similar studies to assess the efficient learning of information science subjects. As an example, we introduce a previous study aimed at capturing brain activity and psychological state fluctuations in the neural processing of problems with preferences for science and humanities [14].

Generally, humanities and social sciences are classified under the category of humanities, focusing on the study of human activities. On the other hand, natural sciences are classified under the category of science, focusing on the study of the natural world. The methods used for problem-solving often determine the classification, and science subjects, in particular, are often associated with a high affinity for mathematics. Therefore, there is a tendency to categorize discussions into the science group, which tends to prioritize numerical accuracy and objective evidence, and the humanities group, which excels in deeply understanding the meaning of words and interpreting the background and emotional aspects of things.

In this previous study, 17 young healthy individuals (16.1 ± 1.5 years) were engaged in solving problems with preferences for science and humanities, such as mathematics and classical Japanese. The rhythmic brainwaves during these activities were measured, and an example of the results is presented below (Fig. 9).

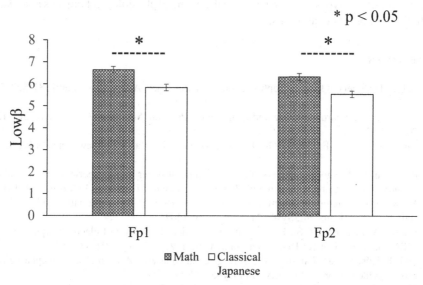

Fig. 9. Values of low beta (lowβ) during problem-solving in mathematics and classical Japanese for science-oriented subjects.

Values of low beta (lowβ), which are highly correlated with the thinking state, significantly increased during mathematics problem-solving compared to classical Japanese problem-solving for science-oriented subjects. The results of this experiment support the validity of brainwave measurements in research on education involving the use of writing instruments.

6 Conclusion

In this experiment, we explored the potential for industrial applications of physiological signal analysis to evaluate the psychological responses of users to writing instruments. We conducted a simple mental arithmetic task using two different pens and simultaneously performed brainwave measurements and subjective evaluations. We used Attention and Meditation scores obtained from brainwave data to assess the physiological effects of pen usage.

The results revealed that the number of high Meditation scores was significantly higher for the DS pen than for the PS pen. This outcome was consistent with previous research involving subjective evaluations, which suggests that different pen types may exert varying effects on the human body.

This experiment was conducted based on a previous study on beverage preference estimation using subjective evaluations and brainwave activity [5]. In this experiment, the estimation model using both subjective evaluations and brainwave activity showed higher predictive capability compared to the model using subjective evaluation alone. This supports that both psychological and physiological reactions influence the evaluation results, reflecting subjective values and preferences.

Although this study focused on PS and DS pens, future research should involve a wider range of pen types to further explore the nuanced physiological impacts associated with different product variations.

References

1. Berger, H.: Über das Elektrenkephalogramm des Menschen. Archiv f. Psychiatrie **87**, 527–570 (1929)
2. Sebastian, V.: Neuromarketing and neuroethics. Procedia Soc. Behav. Sci.Behav. Sci. **127**, 763–768 (2014)
3. Nicolas-Alonso, L.F., Gomez-Gil, J.: Brain computer interfaces a review. Sensors **12**, 1211–1279 (2012)
4. Hironobu, S., Kengo, O.: Understanding the value of paper in the paperless era - Cognitive science of reading and writing media. Industrial Efficiency University Publishing (2018)
5. Xu, K., et al.: Preference estimation of beverages based on subjective evaluation and brainwave activity. IEICE Trans. Inf. Syst. **121**(177), 31–36 (2021)
6. Darbas, M., Lohrengel, S.: Review on mathematical modelling of electroencephalography (EEG), Jahresbericht der Deutschen Mathematicer-Vereinigung **121**(1) (2018)
7. Fell, J., Röschke, J., Schäffner, C.: Surrogate data analysis of sleep electroencephalograms reveals evidence for nonlinearity. Biol Cybern (1996)
8. Mirzaei, P., Azemi, G., Japaridze, N., Boashash, B.: Surrogate data test for nonlinearity of EEG signals: a newborn EEG burst suppression case study. Digital Signal Process. **70**, 30–38 (2017)
9. Wayland, R., Bromley, D., Pickett, D., Passamante, A.: Recognizing determinism in a time series. Phys. Rev. Lett. **70**(5), 580–583 (1993)
10. Chen, J.Z., McCallum, R.W.: Clinical applications of electrogastrography. Am J Gastroenterology **88**(9), 1324–1336 (1993)
11. Yamazaki, T., Tsunashima, H., Takada, H., Yamada, I.: Study on the detection of heart disease using the double-Wayland algorithm. J. Japan Soc. Mech. Eng. (C edition) **73**(734), 9–14 (2007)

12. Yamaguchi, I.: Application of the method of surrogate data to human electroencephalogram (EEG). Res. J. Kobe Shoin Women's Univ. **39**, 106–125 (2006)
13. Hiroyuki, W., Katsunori, O.: The Influence of EEG and Handedness on Workload of the Kraepelin Test. Eng. Educ. **65**(6), 44–48 (2017)
14. Omine, A., Hirata, T., Takada, H.: Proceedings of the Form Science Symposium **8**(2), 7–8 (2023)

Development of Kanji Learning Materials
for Dysgraphia and EEG Measurement

Kenichiro Kutsuna[1]([✉]), Kunaj Somchanakit[1], Chowalert Teppradit[1],
Patcharaporn Nilaubol[1], Chaiyot Rongdech[1], and Hiroki Takada[2]

[1] Faculty of Humanities and Social Sciences, Thaksin University, Songkhla, Thailand
kenichiro.k@tsu.ac.th
[2] Graduate School of Engineering, University of Fukui, Fukui, Japan

Abstract. The primary aim of the research project is to develop instructional materials for Kanji learning, specifically targeting students facing difficulties or disabilities in writing. The effectiveness of traditional methods, emphasizing extensive reading and extensive handwriting to enhance brain working memory, has been questioned due to significant accumulations of fatigue and stress revealed in EEG results. To address these concerns, an innovative approach is proposed, focusing on the efficient development of a method to train the brain's working memory in Kanji learning, heightened by increased awareness of spatial cognition. This method is implemented in high schools and universities, with subsequent measurement of its effects. Iterative improvements is made based on the school feedback and the effectiveness assessments, including enlarging character size and enhancing spatial cognition skills associated with characters to optimize the efficacy of character learning. In this study, we introduce an evaluation of the proposed educational method by the measurement of rhythms in the Electroencephalograms (EEGs).

Keywords: Cognitive Science · Educational Technology · Japanese Language Education · Kanji · Teaching

1 Introduction

In the course of our research aimed at the scientific analysis of written characters and the development of efficient methods for learning them in Japan, we observed that many students are erroneously learning the forms of kanji characters. Traditional methods of teaching kanji involved repeatedly writing the same characters in notebooks, with students required to memorize them through iterations of 10 or 20 repetitions. If a student forgot a particular kanji, they were instructed to write it an additional 10 or 20 times until the character was firmly retained. From a neuroscientific perspective, it is understood that memory is not eternally enduring, and it is believed that reinforcing learning through repeated recall each time it is forgotten contributes to long-term retention. However, despite diligent efforts, accurate memorization is often elusive. Consequently, we have decided to develop instructional methods that facilitate the rapid and accurate memorization of kanji for orderly writing.

Research on pedagogical approaches to kanji acquisition is currently dominated by a culmination of past studies, with significant gaps in continuity. Various methods have been proposed, including those emphasizing extensive handwritten practice, teaching the origin of characters using brushes, and adopting an analytical approach to systematically learn kanji by breaking them down into constituent elements. While each method has its inherent limitations, resolving these challenges remains elusive.

Furthermore, in the field of Japanese language education for non-native speakers, there has been minimal attention given to the pedagogical nuances of kanji instruction. This oversight appears to stem from the perception that kanji learning is considered straightforward and simple compared to the time dedicated to grammar and conversation. Additionally, the scarcity of scholars specializing in kanji instruction within the field of Japanese language education contributes to this research gap.

To address this academic void, our research adopts three distinct strategies. The first focuses on strategies within special education, the second integrates the methodology of cognitive science, and the third explores strategies based on principles of neuroscience.

2 Experimental Method

2.1 Special Support Education Measures

Within the Japanese educational milieu, the historical focus of special support education has revolved around addressing the requirements of children with disabilities, thereby prompting the frequent proposition of inventive pedagogical methodologies. A notable exemplification is the Color Frame Notebook, delineated in Fig. 1, designed as an instructional tool to facilitate letter recognition for children with disabilities who may encounter challenges in discerning letter shapes (Akiko Wakiguchi et al., 2019).

In the capacity of a researcher specializing in Kanji education in Japan, the author has undertaken numerous experiments involving students requiring special support, as illustrated in Fig. 2. Substantive insights have emerged from these experiments.

Primarily, among students facing difficulties in memorizing letter shapes, the experiment disclosed their capacity to acquire such knowledge through a straightforward process involving connecting dots and drawing lines. For students contending with challenges in procedural memory, the hurdle lies in establishing associations and eliciting memory without overtly conveying the learning objective. It is noteworthy that a considerable number of students in mainstream educational settings grapple with concentration issues during learning, leading to compromised learning efficacy. Nevertheless, by integrating strategies informed by special needs education, there is an anticipatory enhancement in learning effectiveness.

2.2 Cognitive Science Measures

In order to comprehend strategies for memorizing kanji characters, an examination from the perspective of cognitive science is imperative. Firstly, according to a study conducted at Cornell University in 2011, when a list of words written in the alphabet was presented in various font sizes rather than in kanji, there was a reported increase in the ease of

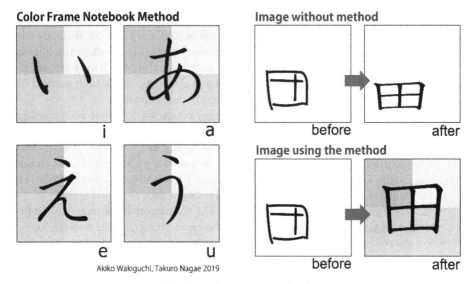

Fig. 1. Color Frame Notebook

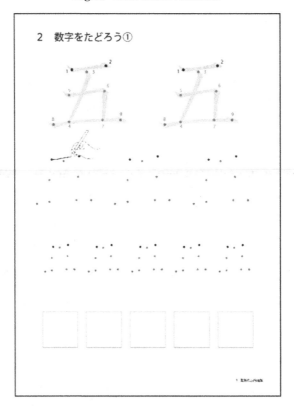

Fig. 2. Connect the dots character teaching materials.

memorization for words displayed in larger fonts. Additionally, research conducted at Princeton University and Indiana University indicated an improvement in the performance of participants who studied materials presented in difficult-to-read fonts. It is crucial to note, however, that this phenomenon is influenced by the fact that while the alphabet represents only sounds, kanji encompasses both meaning and sound.

To explore this aspect further, we conducted a preliminary experiment. Two sets of characters, one in 170 pt (5 cm) and the other in 18 pt (0.5 cm), were presented to students, and learning sessions comprising 10 characters each were conducted for 5 min. The results revealed that the accuracy rate for larger characters was approximately 60%, whereas for smaller characters, it was about 40% (Fig. 3). These findings suggest a tendency for a relatively higher learning effect with larger characters.

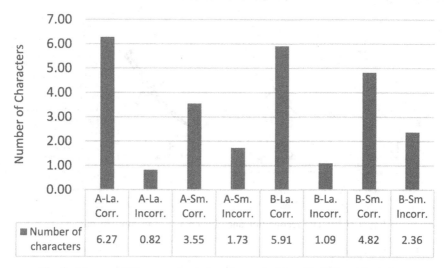

Fig. 3. Memory differences due to learning materials with different font sizes.

2.3 Neuroscientific Measures

The third consideration involves a neuroscientific analysis aimed at optimizing memory resources. Specifically, we focus on the association areas within the cerebral cortex responsible for short-term memory. This region demonstrates a close relationship with sensory inputs and other perceptual modalities, emphasizing its essential role in multisensory involvement in the learning process, including activities such as writing, reading, speaking, and listening—a concept akin to what is referred to as working memory in cognitive psychology.

We designate the approach depicted in Fig. 4 as the "Flexible Dimension Modification Learning Method." This learning method enables a concise explanation of complex cognitive processes, revealing that writing is a high-dimensional memory task. The method involves adjusting the dimensions of learning based on methods, preferences, and necessity.

The conventional method of learning kanji, involving the repetitive handwriting of the same character 20, 30, or even 100 times, is a highly intricate memorization method, and studies have shown that it is time-consuming for rote memorization. Additionally, memory tasks with three or more dimensions can lead to incorrect memories, accompanied by noise.

In contrast, the proposed learning method offers a one-dimensional memory model similar to single-task learning, particularly for children in their early years or those with learning disabilities. For high school students or adults, it provides a high-dimensional learning approach, allowing the utilization of rich memory resources tailored to individual characteristics and optimizing memory retention. While sensory memory inherently has limitations, this method aligns well with the goal of kanji learning, which focuses on acquiring the visual representation of characters.

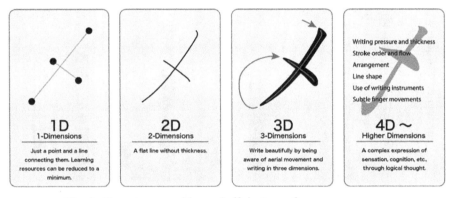

Fig. 4. Character recognition and efficient use of memory resources.

3   Method

To begin with, the creation of instructional materials for acquiring kanji through tracing or drawing lines with fingers is proposed. To mitigate the effects of the hot and humid environment, the materials are printed with pigment ink resistant to smudging from sweat, rain, or beverages. The target audience includes students ranging from elementary to university level in the southeastern region of Thailand, specifically in Songkhla, Hat Yai, and neighboring areas, with an estimated target group of around 100 individuals. The intended students are beginners and intermediate learners with limited exposure to the Japanese language, anticipating a proficiency level between 0% and 5%. Considering that the proficiency level for first-year university students in kanji learning ranges from 5% to 20%, the materials are designed to cater to this demographic.

These instructional materials cover an extensive range of kanji, accommodating 1006 characters for elementary school, 1110 for middle school, and 1026 for high school. Consequently, the materials can be adjusted to suit the desired proficiency level of Thai learners, spanning from an introductory level equivalent to Japanese first-grade students to a high school level. Although the Japanese Language Proficiency Test (JLPT) designates N5 as the proficiency level equivalent to middle school graduation, the materials also consider the utilization of kanji beyond that level. Additionally, these materials are crafted with consideration for students with developmental disorders in Japan. If successful, the implementation of a similar system is planned for Thai script instruction in elementary schools and kindergartens in the future, as well as for foreign language acquisition.

Following the utilization of the materials, surveys and quizzes are conducted, and subsequent analysis take place. The surveys are administered to both students and teachers. While integrating principles of cognitive science to create engaging materials that stimulate students' motivation, the surveys serve as an assessment tool to evaluate the on-site situation.

The quizzes focus on issues such as spelling errors and the structural composition of kanji, aiming to elucidate learning challenges. Following the implementation of the instructional materials, a comprehensive evaluation is conducted through surveys, quizzes, and subsequent analysis. Thorough scrutiny encompasses responses from both the survey and quiz results. The survey seeks input from both students and teachers, aligning with an educational approach that integrates insights from cognitive science to design engaging materials that stimulate students' interest in learning. Simultaneously, the survey functions as a tool to measure the effectiveness of the instructional materials under real-world conditions.

The assessment through quizzes aims to identify learning challenges, including spelling errors and structural composition of kanji. Through this analytical process, the intention is to gain valuable insights into the effectiveness of the developed materials and possibilities for improvement.

After the utilization of the instructional materials, a comprehensive survey and quiz are conducted, and the results is herein analyzed. The survey would gather responses from both students and teachers. While leveraging principles from cognitive science to create engaging materials that enhance students' learning motivation, the survey aims to understand the dynamics and perceptions in the field. The quizzes are specifically designed to focus on issues like spelling errors and the structural composition of kanji, aiming to reveal learning challenges.

4 Results

While instructing Japanese in Thailand, several challenges have been identified. The inherent complexity of Kanji characters, compounded by their vast quantity, renders comprehensive instruction challenging. Consequently, learners of Japanese in Thailand often exhibit low proficiency in recognizing correctly spelled characters.

In comparison to Thai characters, Japanese characters are notably larger and more intricate. The diminutive size of Japanese characters presents a significant impediment to character recognition during practice. Given the abundance of similar characters, the likelihood of misrecognition increases substantially if precise identification is not achieved (Fig. 5a).

In comparison to Thai characters, Japanese characters are notably larger and more intricate. The diminutive size of Japanese characters presents a significant impediment to character recognition during practice. Given the abundance of similar characters, the likelihood of misrecognition increases substantially if precise identification is not achieved (Fig. 5b).

We herein measured the Electroencephalograms (EEGs) to evaluate the abovementioned educational method and analyzed those rhythms in accordance with the Fast Fourie Transform (FFT) (Fig. 6).

(a)

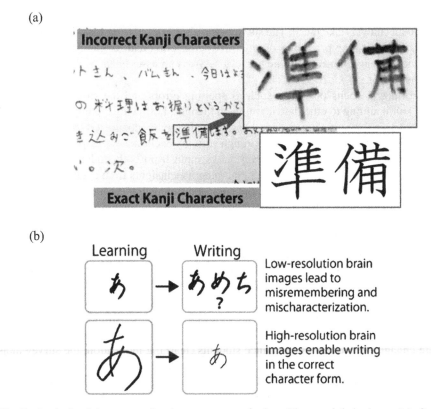

(b)

Fig. 5. Analysis of the reasons for the appearance of misspellings and their shapes (a), On the phenomenon of mistaking letters by writing them smaller and confusing them with similar letters (b).

5   Discussion

The objective is to design pioneering instructional materials for written character education. This involves the creation of an innovative letter teaching material integrating numerical and color elements to infuse an enjoyable element, thereby motivating students to discern the correct form of letters through perceptual augmentation. The strategic enlargement of letter size contributes to this perceptual enhancement. Additionally, the incorporation of colored dots serves to anchor spatial perception, thereby amplifying the overall efficacy of the learning experience.

(a)

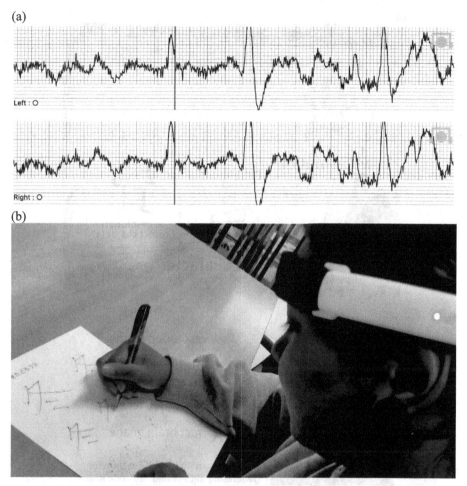

(b)

Fig. 6. Example of EEG when tracing text (a), An experiment in writing letters (b)

This developmental initiative was conceived and implemented within the educational landscape of Japan. Despite its successful implementation within the Japanese context, it has yet to be deployed in educational settings beyond the borders of Japan.

In our examination of the iPad utilization among students, it became apparent that a prevalent practice involves the use of scanned printed texts. The quality of the images is characterized by a coarse and low resolution, and the textual content is marred by inaccuracies. A marked distinction exists when comparing texts of high quality to those of low quality, significantly influencing the overall impression (Fig. 7a). It is noteworthy that even classrooms equipped with high-performance iPads encounter these issues.

The aforementioned trifecta of problems is poised to induce confusion and erode the learners' confidence, consequently leading to a substantial diminution in the efficacy of the learning process (Fig. 7b).

(a)

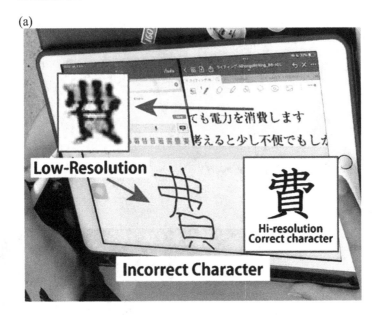

(b)

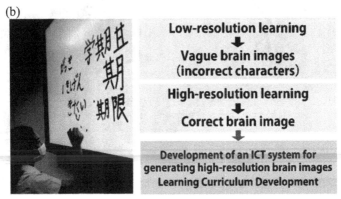

Fig. 7. Example of typographical errors caused by learning from scanned images of printed materials (a), Increasing resolution to help people notice typos and learn the correct letterforms (b).

Brain image creation is the most important factor in character learning [1]. Therefore, we analyzed the algorithm for creating brain images and examine how to apply it. Spatial cognition ability, visual resolution, and working memory in the brain are important for the creation of images in the brain. However, the importance of these factors has not been confirmed for Japanese language education today. In this study, we focused on the resolution in creating brain images.

The effect of learning about "fast reading aloud", reading aloud quickly, and the development of language skills when applied to Japanese language education were discussed [2]. Test results showed that students who practiced more greatly benefited from the learning effects of accent and inflection, acquired a reading style that made it easier to speak as a language rather than connecting words in isolation, and reduced reading time. However, the less-learned group was more exhausted, and tasks with more words lowered their performance. High-speed reading aloud was found to be a learning method with significant developmental potential from "reading" to language skills. The importance of short-term memory was confirmed for letter recognition. It is necessary to study the method of short-term memory development.

Kanji characters have an important position in Japanese language education [3]. This paper discusses the relationship between Kanji characters and language skills. Characters have changed their forms with the transition of typefaces to the present, but they still have a wide range of acceptable forms. This is because the development of characters is still continuing, which means that linguistic development has not stopped. In other words, the tolerance of Chinese characters should be considered as a margin adapted to the cultivation of language skills and the development of the ability to respond to the creation of new languages.

As a basis for designing type that can withstand aesthetic appreciation, a letterform evaluation method was examined [4]. Although typeface is basically composed of equally spaced margins, handwritten characters differ from part to part. Using Japanese language textbooks, we examined the relationship between letterforms and picture spacing, and found that there is a correlation between letterforms and picture spacing. If type is designed using this data, it was possible to give a dynamic expression to static type.

A study investigating the sensitivity of learning "Kanji" and "Kana" in non-Kanji speaking Thailand [5]. We investigated the influence of the characteristics of Thai characters on Kanji and Hiragana, and found that Thai characters, Kanji-Kana, and alphabets commonly approximate features such as writing pressure. In other words, the learning of the characters is strongly influenced by the native writing style of the characters. In Japan, this means that if the students still retain their usual writing habits, they did not change much even if they learn well-formed characters, and this has caused a stir in the teaching of character forms in Japan.

The development of language skills is a priority issue in the Courses of Study, and its application to the Japanese language subject "writing" and Japanese calligraphy is an urgent need [6]. Writing, as a written language, is directly related to the development of language skills, but classes have tended to focus on technique. Metacognition through writing deepens language expression, leads to language skills, and can greatly increase the use of strategies for language activities. Writing should be positioned as a more important basic academic skill, and instruction should be concentrated especially in the early grades.

Although many studies have been conducted on the center of gravity of letters, there is still no study that claims to have correctly captured the center of gravity [7]. Therefore, we experimentally examined the center of gravity of a letter by assuming the center of gravity to be the center of vertical writing. The results of the experiment showed that letters written using the superimposition method lacked balance between the upper and lower centers of gravity, which was unexpected. Those that were centered both vertically and horizontally were the most well rounded in the data, but did not appear to be correct. It was found that the weighting, i.e., placing the weight of the character at the lower right corner, may indicate that the characters appear stable in the superimposed method of writing.

A study was conducted on the posture of writing that is acquired during daily learning [8]. After analyzing the results separately for writing with a left tilt, middle, right tilt, and writing on the left, middle, and right sides of the body, we found that writing with a left tilt and writing on the left side of the body resulted in faster writing. However, it is more tiring and shorter in duration. The posture that has been considered the most correct is not faster writing, however, it is longer lasting. In other words, changing posture to write faster for homework or writing, etc., causes fatigue, breaks concentration, and reduces the effectiveness of learning. This shows the importance of posture instruction.

In order to understand the letter form structure from a cognitive scientific perspective, we developed a teaching material that uses "dot-connecting" instead of conventional "tracing" to connect the dots, and also allows students to enjoy learning the number of strokes by adding colors [9]. When we conducted experiments with special-needs children with handwriting disabilities, they were able to write the letter shapes correctly, no longer protrude from the frame, and no longer make mistakes in the number of horizontal strokes. Regular college students were also able to recognize the complex shapes of letters with simple dots, which made it easier for them to grasp the shapes and write the letters in the correct form.

It has been found that writing damage, in which the shape of the letter is severely damaged, is caused by problems in the way the writing utensil is used [10]. Poor use of writing utensils can lead to poor concentration and poor academic performance due to fatigue and pain. They may even dislike studying. From the standpoint of character instruction, we proposed a method of teaching learning using a touch panel monitor.

Recently, the existence of developmentally disabled children, especially those with dysgraphia, has become an issue in calligraphy education [11]. Although the name "disability" implies a disability, these children with dysgraphia are simply developmentally delayed, and with appropriate care, their functions can be quickly restored. However, in the field of school education, if instruction is tailored to these children, instruction for other children is delayed, and the appropriate care is not provided. Therefore, we discussed the teaching methods that are appropriate for the lower grades and include care for dysgraphia at the stage when students begin to learn letters in the lower grades.

In the past, it has been said that students should be taught to write fast writing in the running style, but in actual practice, fast writing in the block style is the main form of writing [12]. Therefore, we conducted a scientific investigation of hiragana in fast writing and examined a method of fast writing that does not compromise the form and alignment of the characters. As a result, we found that the most important thing is that the first stroke of the next character is smoothly entered. It was found that it is important to teach students to be aware of the classification of alpha and gamma letterforms.

Hiragana, created from the cursive form of Chinese characters, is a character characterized by its smooth movement [13]. We examined what kind of strokes should be drawn when writing hiragana horizontally at high speed. Experiments using a tablet showed that fast strokes with edges lead to damage of the characters. On the contrary, it was found that drawing smooth edges would also shape the letters.

This is a study on personal space of letters in cognitive psychology [14]. It teaches that the space between horizontal strokes should be equally divided, but there is nothing theoretical about this. So, we conducted a study: a statistical study of over 3000 samples showed that closed forms write smaller. Open shapes were found to be written smaller, and slanted lines and dots were found to be written largest. The study reaffirmed that visual perception has been universal for thousands of years with regard to Chinese characters.

Acknowledgment. This study was supported in part by the Whiterock Foundation and JSPS KAKENHI Grant Numbers 23H03678.

References

1. Kutsuna, K., Somchanakit, K., Honda, Y., Takada, H.: Brain image resolution during letter learning. In: Proceedings of 93rd Symposium Science Form, vol. 7, no. 2, pp. 47–48 (2022)
2. Kutsuna, K., Somchanakit, K., Honda, Y., Takada, H.: Learning effects of fast reading aloud and language ability. In: Proceedings of 87th Symposium on Science of Form, vol. 4, no. 1, pp. 33–34 (2019)
3. Honda, Y., Kutsuna, K.: Glyphs from revised joyo Kanji - cultivation of language ability. In: Proceedings of the 87th Symposium Science Form, vol. 4, no. 1, pp. 31–32 (2019)
4. Kutsuna, K., Takada, H.: Examination of evaluation of kanji glyphs as a basis for active type design. In: Proceedings of Symposium Science Form, vol. 3, no. 1, pp. 49–50 (2018)
5. Kutsuna, K.: On the trend of writing Kanji-kana in non-Kanji learners. In: Proceedings of Symposium Science Form, vol. 2, no. 1, pp. 15–16 (2017)
6. Kutsuna, K., Honda, Y.: Development of Japanese language course calligraphy focusing on the cultivation of language ability. Res. Calligraphy Calligraphy Educ. **28**, 21–30 (2014)
7. Kutsuna, K.: Analysis of the center of gravity of letters in vertical writing by vertical projection. Shizudai Kokugo **15&16**, 78–83 (2014)
8. Kutsuna, K.: Change of character shape by posture and holding style in calligraphy. Res. Report Faculty Educ. **44**, 169–176 (2015)
9. Kutsuna, K., Hirata, T.: Formation of a well-aligned writing image by the colored dot-connecting method. Bull. Soc. Sci. Form **28**(2), 148–149 (2013)
10. Kutsuna, K., Sugizaki, S.: Consideration of a desirable character shape teaching method as a response to character shape damage - using a touch panel monitor. Bull. Soc. Sci. Form **26**(3), 330–331 (2012)
11. Kutsuna, K.: The way of teaching calligraphy in the calligraphy education as a universal service. Bull. Soc. Sci. Form **26**(2), 255–256 (2011)
12. Kutsuna, K., Sugizaki, S.: A basic study on the instruction of how to hold writing instruments in writing horizontally. Res. Calligraphy Calligraphy Educ. **25**, 52–59 (2011)
13. Sugizaki, S., Kutsuna, K.: A basic study on the teaching of rapid writing of "hiragana" in horizontal writing. Shosha Shodo Kyoiku Kenkyu **24**, 63–72 (2010)
14. Kutsuna, K.: A proposal of classification between horizontal strokes in handwritten characters and its basic analysis. Univ. Calligraphy Res. **2**, 93–103 (2009)

Effects of Light-Dark Adaptation Processes on the Body as a Basic Study for Visually Induced Motion Sickness

Yasuyuki Matsuura[1,2], Mizuki Makino[2], Fumiya Kinoshita[3], and Hiroki Takada[2(✉)]

[1] Education and Research Center for Data-Driven Science, Gifu City Women's College, Gifu, Japan
[2] Graduate School of Engineering, University of Fukui, Fukui, Japan
takada@u-fukui.ac.jp
[3] Faculty of Engineering, Toyama Prefectural University, Toyama, Japan

Abstract. The use of stereoscopic images has become popular so that we might encounter numerous situations in which stereoscopic images can be viewed. As a side note, reports of people complaining symptoms of visually induced motion sickness (VIMS) such as headaches and vertigo have been observed. Furthermore, reports on the effects of the illuminance environment on biological reactions have been observed. However, the effects of the light/dark adaptation process on our bodies have not been investigated in detail when viewing stereoscopic images. Therefore, in this study, we conducted a basic study on the influence of differences in the light-dark adaptation process, which has not been well studied, on motion sickness when viewing 3D images.

Keywords: Visually induced motion sickness (VIMS) · Bio-signal · Light/Dark adaptation process · Hysteretic control · Body sway

1 Introduction

In recent years, with the improvement of shooting technology, it has become easier to shoot stereoscopic images (3D images), and new ways to present 3D images using 4K/8K television technology have been created, and various uses will be developed in the future. To go. On the other hand, the effects of motion sickness that occur when viewing 3D images remain unresolved. It has been reported that there are some influence of stereoscopic viewing on health, which causes unpleasant symptoms, such as visual fatigue, headache, and the vertigo [1, 2]. Severity of VIMS is not affected only by construction of the images but also by the viewing environment. It has also been reported that prolonged viewing of stereoscopic displays can cause several health hazards such as severe visual fatigue and headaches [3–5]. On the side notes, it has been reported that the elderly with the mild cognitive impairment (MCI) tends to have a strong interest in stimulation by stereoscopic images [6]. However, it is necessary to indicate further hygienic investigations because of little knowledge of the biological effects such as visual fatigue and the VIMS [7].

There are many unresolved issues regarding the relationship between 2D and 3D image viewing and biological reactions. Therefore, in this study, we conducted a basic investigation of the biological state during 2D/3D video viewing by measuring multiple biological signals. We also changed only the illuminance and examined changes in biological conditions due to changes in illuminance.

2 Method

2.1 Experiment 1

In this experiment, we measured eye movement, center of gravity sway, electroencephalogram, and electrocardiogram while viewing 2D and 3D images. Figure 1 shows the visible image. The video used in this experiment is a video showing a sphere, which moves proximally and distally with displacement left and right and up and down. The subjects were six healthy young men (mean ± standard deviation: 22.50 ± 0.50 years) with no history of ear or nervous system diseases. The experiment was fully explained to the subjects in advance and their consent was obtained in writing. The experiment was conducted in a dark room, and a 3D display 55UF8500 (LG) was placed at a viewing distance of 100 cm from the subject. 2D and 3D images were viewed in a random order for 60 s using peripheral viewing or central viewing, taking into account the order effect.

This experiment investigated the impact of selecting a mechanical pencil on brainwave activity and physiological responses. Thirteen healthy young adult males (mean ± standard deviation: 22.92 ± 0.79) participated in the study. The participants engaged in the experiment in the following order: a period of rest, mental arithmetic task 1, another rest period, mental arithmetic task 2, and a final rest period. During these intervals, brainwave activity was recorded. The experimental protocol is depicted in Fig. 1.

Eye mark recorder EMR-9 (Nac Image Technology) was used to measure eye movement, and the position of the eye at each sampling time during video viewing was recorded. Note that the sampling frequency was 60 Hz. Wii Balance Board (Nintendo) was used to measure center of gravity sway while standing in Romberg posture. The sampling frequency was 100 Hz, and resampling was performed at 20 Hz. A band-type telemetry electrode simple electroencephalograph (NeuroSky) was used for electroencephalogram and electrocardiogram measurements.

Regarding the analysis method, the center of gravity sway was measured at a sampling frequency of 100 Hz, and the data was resampled to 20 Hz, and the outer circumferential area and total trajectory length were calculated as analysis indicators. As with the center of gravity sway, the gaze movement was calculated using the peripheral area and total trajectory length as analysis indicators. The brain waves were obtained from two electrodes, Fp1 and Fp2, located in the prefrontal cortex, and were Fourier transformed, divided into frequency bands, and the power spectral density (hereinafter referred to as PSD) was calculated. Here, the calculated PSD is defined as δ waves below 4 Hz, θ waves between 4 and 8 Hz, alpha waves between 8 and 14 Hz, β waves between 14 and 30 Hz, and γ waves above 31 Hz. For the electrocardiogram, PSD was calculated from the R-R interval time series, and evaluation was performed using 0.05 to less than 0.15 Hz as the LF component and 0.15 to less than 0.40 Hz as the HF component. Differences in images and viewing methods were statistically compared using Wilcoxon signed rank sum test. The significance level was set at 0.05.

2.2 Experiment 2

In this experiment, we measured brain waves while changing the illuminance of the club room in stages. The subjects were eight healthy young men (mean ± standard deviation: 22.25 ± 1.20 years) with no history of ear or nervous system diseases. The experiment was fully explained to the subjects in advance and their consent was obtained in writing. A fixation point was placed at a viewing distance of 150 cm from the subject, and the illuminance of the room was set in 10 levels from 10 lx to 280 lx in 30 lx increments at the subject's eye position. Measurements were taken for 30 s at each level of illuminance, and measurements were taken for each subject under two conditions: an illuminance increasing process and an illuminance decreasing process. The two conditions were conducted in random order to account for order effects, and there was a 5-min rest period between the two conditions. A band-type telemetry two-electrode simple electroencephalograph (NeuroSky) was used for electroencephalogram measurement.

The electroencephalogram analysis method was the same as in Experiment 1. Regarding statistical analysis, comparisons were made using two-way analysis of variance (ANOVA). The significance level was set at 0.05.

3 Results and Discussion

3.1 Experiment 1

No significant trends were observed in the peripheral area and total trajectory length of center of gravity sway. Regarding gaze movements, significant differences were found in the total trajectory length and peripheral area between 2D peripheral viewing and 2D tracking viewing, and in the peripheral area between 3D peripheral viewing and 3D following viewing. In the fp1 of the brain waves, significant differences were observed between theta waves and alpha waves between 3D peripheral vision and 3D tracking vision, and between the beta and gamma waves between 2D peripheral vision and 3D peripheral vision. In the fp2 of the brain waves, significant differences were seen in alpha waves between 2D peripheral vision and 2D tracking vision, and between θ waves between 3D peripheral vision and 3D tracking vision. No significant difference was observed in the electrocardiogram.

These results suggest that 3D peripheral vision is most likely to induce motion sickness. On the other hand, the degree of relaxation during follow-up viewing was high, suggesting the possibility of reducing motion sickness when viewing 3D images.

3.2 Experiment 2

A two-way ANOVA using illuminance change and electroencephalogram as factors revealed no interaction. Regarding main effects, main effects were observed for fp1 on δ waves and θ waves, and for fp2 on δ waves, θ waves, β waves, and γ waves. Furthermore, the EGG Ratio was calculated by dividing the electroencephalogram value for each illuminance by the electroencephalogram value for 10 lx. The average value of the θ wave of fp1 is shown in Fig. 1 as an example of EGG Ratio. As a result of evaluating the time changes in the illuminance rising process and illuminance falling process using EGG Ratio, it was found that the illuminance rising process and the illuminance falling process do not follow the same process, and that the illuminance rising process and illuminance falling process are different from each other. It was suggested that hysteresis was involved.

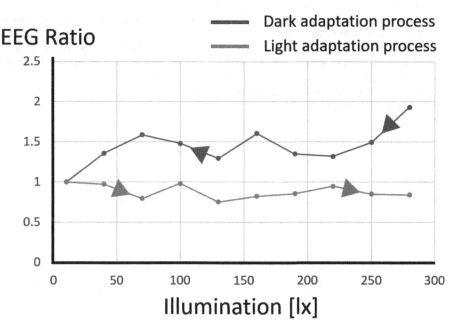

Fig. 1. An example of the average value of EGG Ratio (fp1, θ wave).

4 Conclusion

In this study, we focused on the biological state and light/dark adaptation process during 2D/3D video viewing, and evaluated it from multiple angles using biological signals. The results obtained this time provide important directions for future research development.

In the future, we will conduct a more detailed examination of the data obtained from this experiment, and at the same time examine the effects of illuminance, color temperature, and the adaptation process when viewing 3D images.

Acknowledgment. This study was supported in part by the Koshiyama Science & Technology Foundation, Whiterock Foundation, and JSPS KAKENHI Grant Numbers JP23H03678, 22K12141, 20K12528.

References

1. Reason, J.T., Brand, J.J.: Motion Sickness, Academic Press Inc. (1975)
2. Balaban, C.D., Porter, J.D.: Neuroanatomic substrates for vestibulo-autonomic interactions. J. Vestib. Res. **8**, 7–16 (1998)
3. Murata, K., Araki, S., Yokoyama, K., Yamashita, K., Okumatsu, Y., Sakoh, S.: Accumulation of VDT Work-related visual fatigue assessed by visual evoked potential, near point distance and critical flicker fusion. Ind. Health **34**, 61–69 (1996)
4. Hamagishi, G.: Ergonomics for 3D Displays and their standardization. The Tech. Rep. Inst. Image Inform. Telev. Eng. **33**(16), 9–12 (2009)
5. Nishimura, K., Iwata, T., Murata, K.: Effects of 3-dimensional video games on visual nervous function. Akita J. Med. **37**, 85–91 (2010)
6. Shibata, T., Kawai, T., Noro, K., Arimoto, A., Ohshima, T., Matsuoka, S.: A Study on the welfare application of stereoscopic 3D images for dementia patients. Ergonomics **36**(Suppl), 390–391 (2000)
7. Ministry of internal affairs and communications of Japan, final report of investigation committee for 3D television (2012)

Association Between Brain Activity of Dominant Ocular Mechanism and Visually Evoked Postural Responses

Akihiro Sugiura[1]([✉]), Saki Hayakawa[1], Yuta Umeda[1], Masahiro Suzuki[1], Akiko Ihori[1], Kunihiko Tanaka[1], Hiroki Takada[2], and Masami Niwa[1]

[1] Gifu University of Medical Science, Seki Gifu 501-3892, Japan
asugiura@u-gifu-ms.ac.jp
[2] University of Fukui, Fukui 910-8507, Japan

Abstract. This study investigates the association between ocular dominance and brain function using functional magnetic resonance imaging (fMRI), focusing on the dominant eye's role in processing visual information and its effect on visually evoked postural responses (VEPRs). The research involved participants with identified dominant eyes, using tasks designed to engage peripheral vision and evoke postural changes. The fMRI results revealed increased cerebral activity in the precuneus and occipital lobe regions during dominant eye viewing, suggesting these areas' significant role in processing ocular dominance mechanisms. This activity was asymmetric, predominantly occurring in the left hemisphere, supporting theories of contralateral visual processing in the brain. The study also explored the relationship between ocular dominance and VEPRs. However, no significant correlation was found between the dominant eye and postural changes, indicating a complex interplay of visual processing that may not directly influence postural control. These findings contribute to the understanding of ocular dominance in brain function, highlighting specific brain regions involved in processing visual information from the dominant eye and providing insights into the neural mechanisms underlying ocular dominance and visual perception.

Keywords: Dominant eye · Brain activity · Visually evoked postural responses (VEPRs) · Postural changes · fMRI

1 Introduction

The concept of a dominant eye, or "preferred eye," refers to the eye that plays a primary role in processing visual information and determining the position of objects when viewing scenes or objects with both eyes. The dominant eye handles the majority of visual input, playing a crucial role in activities such as distance assessment and tracking targets. Identifying the dominant eye requires a clear definition of what constitutes a "dominant eye," and it is generally understood to be the eye that exhibits functional dominance. A simple method for determining the dominant eye is as follows [1] (Fig. 1):

1. Create a small 'window' using both hands.

© The Author(s), under exclusive license to Springer Nature Singapore Pte Ltd. 2024
W. Hong and G. Kanaparan (Eds.): ICCSE 2023, CCIS 2023, pp. 483–494, 2024.
https://doi.org/10.1007/978-981-97-0730-0_43

2. Focus on a distant object in the room through the window formed by the hands.
3. While maintaining focus, slowly bring the hands closer to the face without diverting the eyes from the distant object, continuing to view it through the window.
4. The eye towards which the hands naturally move, and which maintains clear vision of the object, is considered the dominant eye.

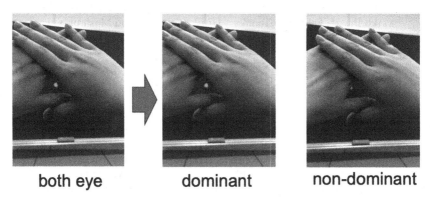

both eye   **dominant**   **non-dominant**

Fig. 1. A simple method for determining the dominant eye.

Interest in the dominant eye has been high historically, with extensive research conducted in various fields. For instance, studies have generally found no significant difference in sensitivity aspects such as vision between the dominant and non-dominant eyes [2], suggesting minimal functional differences between them as individual organs. In tasks involving eye tracking, such as following a moving object, no significant differences have been observed between the dominant and non-dominant eyes [3]. However, it has been established that the dominant eye processes visual stimuli 14 ms faster than the non-dominant eye [4].

Furthermore, the dominant eye plays a significant role in the development of a wide range of activities and skills. In sports performance, for instance, it is essential for accurately capturing targets and regulating movements. In reading and writing abilities, it enhances the recognition, understanding, and memory of letters and words. In driving skills, it contributes to the rapid and accurate processing of road information. In all these activities, the dominant eye enables precise and effective processing of visual information and fine-tuning of performance.

Information obtained through vision is integrated and processed along with information from other sensory organs. Notable examples of such integrated processing include the combination of visual, balance, and kinesthetic senses. Physical responses related to this processing include visually induced postural responses (VEPRs) [5] and visually induced self-motion perception (Vection) [6]. When viewing full-screen motion images, postural changes and sensations of self-motion occur due to the characteristics of the images or the observer. Experiments investigating VEPRs and Vection in the context of motion sickness suggest that these may be corrective responses to sensory discrepancies [7]. Figure 2 shows a scene from my previous study where the subject was watching a

3D movie with front-back directional motion. The subject's movements cycled in accordance with the global motion phase of the movie. This postural change is an example of a motile visually evoked postural response synchronized with the movement [8]. While research on the visual functions and activity factors related to the dominant eye has been conducted, sufficient investigation of the brain functions central to integrated understanding has not been extensive. Furthermore, there has been little verification of the relationship between the dominant eye and visually induced postural changes. Therefore, this study aims to provide a fundamental verification of the relationship between the dominant eye and brain functions. Using functional MRI (fMRI), a method of brain function imaging, we attempted to visualize brain activities related to the dominant eye mechanism and examine the relationship between the dominant eye and VEPRs.

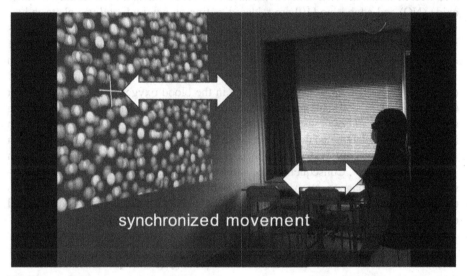

Fig. 2. Scene from my previous study where the subject was watching a 3D movie with front-back directional motion.

2   Methods

Gifu University of Medical Science Research Ethics Committee (Approval No. 2022-9) approved the participation of 14 individuals aged between 20 to 22 years old, comprising an equal number of males and females (7 each), who had no known issues with their vision or balance. Prior to the study, the dominant eye of each participant was determined using the Miles Method [1], revealing that 9 individuals had right eye dominance and 5 had left eye dominance. The study was rigorously carried out in strict accordance with the principles of research ethics and was conducted in conformity with the Declaration of Helsinki. The safety and rights of the participants were prioritized; comprehensive information was provided to all participants beforehand, and written consent was obtained. The research design was reviewed and approved by an independent ethics committee from an ethical standpoint prior to the commencement of the study. The privacy of the individuals was stringently protected, and the data was handled with confidentiality, being anonymized for the purpose of the study.

2.1 Experiments on the Visualization of Brain Activity

In the field of brain function imaging, instead of directly recording the activity of individual cells, the identification of functions is commonly based on the phenomenon of neurovascular coupling (NVC). NVC refers to the phenomenon where an increase in neuronal activity leads to a corresponding increase in local blood flow shown in Fig. 3 [9]. This response serves to meet the increased demand for energy metabolism associated with neuronal activity. When neurons are active, chemical mediators such as nitric oxide (NO) and adenosine [10] are released, acting on nearby blood vessels to induce vasodilation. Consequently, the increased blood flow through the dilated vessels supplies the necessary oxygen and nutrients to the neurons, thus supporting the maintenance of neural activity and meeting energy requirements. By tracing this sequence of actions in reverse, we can arrive at brain imaging, a prime example of which is functional MRI (fMRI). fMRI visualizes changes over time in the blood oxygenation level dependent (BOLD) signal [11, 12]. This signal is a magnetic resonance signal from protons, varying according to the ratio of oxyhemoglobin to deoxygenated hemoglobin in the blood. An increase in the BOLD signal does not signify a higher ratio of deoxygenated hemoglobin due to neuronal activity; instead, it reflects an excess of oxyhemoglobin resulting from increased blood flow. Consequently, the surplus of oxyhemoglobin, a diamagnetic substance, alters the magnetization state of the surrounding tissue. This alteration reduces the ratio of deoxygenated hemoglobin, thereby enhancing the magnetic resonance signal of protons.

Neuro-vascular coupling (NVC)

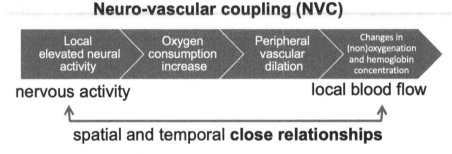

Regional brain activity can be captured through fluctuations in blood oxygen saturation.

Fig. 3. Diagram of neurovascular coupling (NVC)

Visual Presentation and Observation Method

Our visual stimulus consisted of a display filled with spheres randomly distributed across it. These spheres moved synchronously in a sinusoidal pattern on all axes at a frequency of 0.25 Hz, as depicted in Fig. 4. The observation setup involved positioning a mirror at approximately a 40° angle and at a distance of 15 cm from the participants' eyes, placed above the head coil. This arrangement enabled participants, lying reclined in the gantry, to see the screen positioned at the lower end of their visual field. A video was displayed on this screen, located near their feet (as outlined in Fig. 5 for an overview). Participants were instructed not to focus on any individual sphere but to view the entire array peripherally. Additionally, participants realized right eye, left eye, and binocular vision by covering one eye with an opaque cloth, thus enabling each visual condition to be tested in isolation.

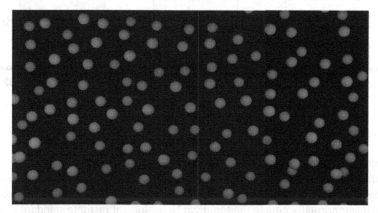

Fig. 4. Experimental movie as a visual stimulus.

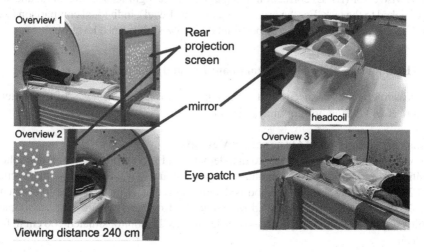

Fig. 5. Experimental setup

Experimental Design and Imaging Conditions
Participants were randomized to observe with the left eye, right eye, and both eyes in a predetermined sequence to mitigate any order effects. We employed a block design task, widely used in brain function imaging, which entailed alternating between periods of video stimulus observation (lasting 64 s) and rest phases with a black screen (lasting 32 s) over the course of three sets, as depicted in Fig. 6. The imaging protocol utilized a GRE-EPI sequence, specified by a TR of 4,000 ms, TE of 40 ms, 40 multislices, slice thickness of 3.8 mm, a matrix size of 128×128 pixels, and an FOV of 224 mm.

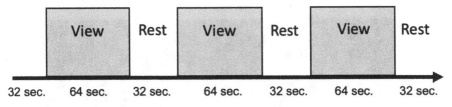

Fig. 6. Experimental task design

Analysis
The acquired brain function images were processed using the Statistical Parametric Mapping 12 (SPM 12) software [13]. This process included motion correction, linear and non-linear normalization to the Montreal Neurological Institute standard brain [14], and spatial smoothing. Significant activations were detected at the cluster level with a familywise error (FWE) correction, maintaining a 5% significance threshold, and were time-locked to the task. For the group analysis (2nd-Level), individual comparisons were compiled, and paired t-tests were performed at a 5% significance level.

2.2   Relationship Between the Dominant Eye and VEPRs

To measure visually induced postural changes, we assessed the sway of the center of posture (CoP) during upright image viewing.

Visual Presentation and Observation Method
The visual stimulus was identical to that depicted in Fig. 4, featuring numerous spheres positioned randomly, moving simultaneously in a sinusoidal pattern across all directions at 0.25 Hz. The observation method is detailed in the experimental setup presented in Fig. 7. Participants were instructed to maintain a Romberg posture on a stabilometer while peripherally observing images on a 42-inch LCD monitor situated 100 cm in front of them.

Experimental Design and Measurement
The experimental task design, as demonstrated in Fig. 8, entailed the use of an eye patch (supplied by Taiyo Pharmaceutical Co., Japan) to occlude one eye, thus permitting monocular viewing (left or right eye). Participants were randomly assigned to observe

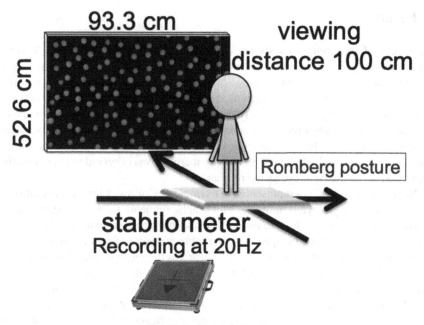

Fig. 7. Experimental setup.

with their left eye, right eye, and both eyes in sequence, with each viewing lasting 120 s. The CoP measurement device (provided by Takei Scientific Instruments Co., Japan) recorded the CoP continuously at 20 Hz during the image viewing.

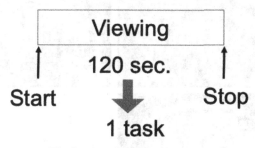

Fig. 8. Experimental task design.

Analysis

The analysis was confined to the left-right directional shifts in the CoP time series data over the initial 60 s. The standard deviation of the left-right CoP time series data was computed. Additionally, frequency analysis was conducted to determine the amplitude of the 0.25 Hz component, which was indicative of body sway. Task comparisons were made using the Wilcoxon signed-rank test, with a significance threshold of 5%.

3 Results

The results of the group analysis are depicted in Figs. 9 and 10. Figure 9 uses the non-dominant eye as a baseline for comparison, highlighting regions where activity significantly increased in the dominant eye ($p < 0.05$). Anatomically, significant increases in activity were noted in several regions, particularly in the precuneus and areas of the occipital lobe. This significant activity was asymmetrical, with a more pronounced distribution on the left side. Figure 10 displays the activity results for the right eye with the left eye serving as a reference. In these results, no significant increase in activity was detected. A similar lack of significant activity increase was observed when comparisons were made using the right eye as the reference.

Next, Fig. 11 includes a representative example of CoP sway for each condition (22-year-old female, right-eye dominant). The graphs sequentially wider extent the sway results for the left eye, right eye, and both eyes. It is apparent that the left-right sway trajectory is elongated in all graphs, with a notably wider extent in the conditions involving the right eye and both eyes. Figure 12 illustrates the mean standard deviation of the CoP's left-right directional data. While the results for the dominant eye were marginally higher, they did not reach significance. Lastly, Fig. 13 presents the amplitudes of the 0.25 Hz component ascertained through frequency analysis. Although the results for the non-dominant eye were somewhat greater, no significant differences were discerned. The same was true for binocular vision; no significant changes were detected.

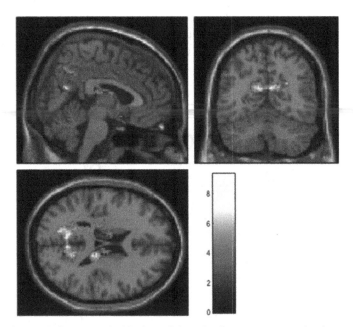

Fig. 9. Result for anatomical brain activity. (dominant eye vs non-dominant eye)

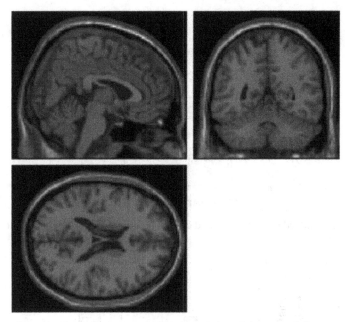

Fig. 10. Result for anatomical brain activity. (right eye vs left eye)

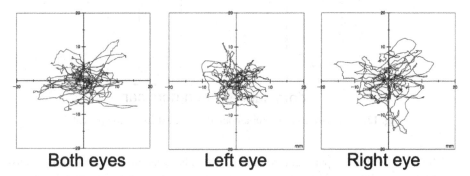

Fig. 11. Example of center of pressure sway (22-year-old female, right-eye dominant).

4 Discussion

In summary, the results of this study suggest the presence of specific brain regions that process peripheral visual information recognized through the dominant eye, with predominant activity in the precuneus and upper regions of the occipital lobe. The precuneus,

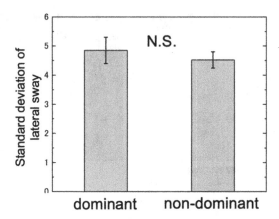

Fig. 12. Summarized result for standard deviation of the CoP's left-right directional data.

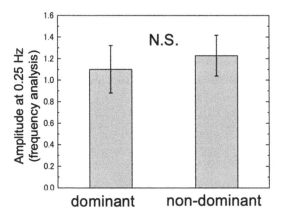

Fig. 13. Summarized result for amplitudes of the 0.25 Hz component.

which resides within the parietal lobe and is nestled between the cingulate and parieto-occipital sulci, plays a role in functions related to attention, cognition, and the spatial processing of visual information [15]. In this experiment, participants were exposed to images that generated a sense of depth through motion parallax during peripheral viewing, in alignment with the timing of the tasks. Peripheral viewing, as opposed to foveal viewing, tends to elicit a more potent spatial perception [16], indicating that the processing of visual information via the dominant eye was actively involved, considering the nature of the images and tasks presented.

The 2nd-Level analysis indicated an asymmetry in activity between the cerebral hemispheres, with a marked increase in the left hemisphere. This heightened activity is strongly believed to result from the brain's tendency to process visual information in the hemisphere opposite the eye receiving the input [17]. The transmission of visual information to the left hemisphere through the optic chiasm—and the prevalence of right-eye dominance in the study's participants—likely contributed to this finding. It is therefore postulated that processes such as object identification, motion detection, and color discrimination from the right eye occurred in the left occipital lobe. Hence, the amplified activity in the left occipital lobe in response to specific visual stimuli viewed by the right eye can be interpreted as a natural outcome of the brain's visual information processing mechanism.

In terms of the connection between the dominant eye and visually induced postural changes (VEPRs), no differences attributable to the dominant or non-dominant eye were noted. Although the underlying reasons for this result warrant further investigation, considering that VEPRs constitute a complex, coordinated reaction, it is conjectured that disparities in visual input are integrated during processing, thereby not impacting the manifestation of postural changes.

5 Conclusion

As a fundamental examination of the relationship between ocular dominance and brain function, we employed Functional Magnetic Resonance Imaging (fMRI), a technique for brain function imaging, to visualize the cerebral activities associated with the mechanism of ocular dominance. Additionally, we sought to investigate the correlation between ocular dominance and visually induced postural changes. The findings indicated an increase in activity in the precuneus and occipital lobe during the viewing with the dominant eye, hinting at the presence of specific brain regions involved in the processing of ocular dominance mechanisms. On the other hand, the assessment of the relationship between ocular dominance and visually induced postural changes did not reveal any significant associations.

Acknowledgment. We extend our deepest gratitude to all the participants who generously dedicated their time and effort to partake in this study. This work was supported by JSPS KAKENHI Grant Number 22K12710, 23H03678.

References

1. Miles, W.R.: Ocular dominance in human adults. J. Gen. Psychol. **3**, 412–430 (1930)
2. Mapp, A.P., Ono, H., Barbeito, R.: What does the dominant eye dominate? A brief and somewhat contentious review. Percept. Psychophys. **65**, 310–317 (2003)
3. Cui, Y., Hondzinski, J.M.: Gaze tracking accuracy in humans: two eyes are better than one. Neurosci. Lett. **396**, 257–262 (2006)
4. Coren, S., Porac, C.: Monocular asymmetries in visual latency as a function of sighting dominance. Am. J. Optom. Physiol. Opt. **59**, 987–990 (1982)
5. Bronstein, A.M.: Suppression of visually evoked postural responses. Exp. Brain Res. **63**, 655–658 (1986)

6. Fischer, M., Kornmüller, A.: Optokinetisch ausgelöste Bewegungswahrnehmung und optokinetischer Nystagmus. J. für Psychol. und Neurol. **41**, 273–308 (1930)
7. Sugiura, A., Tanaka, K., Wakatabe, S., Matsumoto, C., Miyao, M.: Temporal analysis of body sway during reciprocator motion movie viewing. Nihon Eiseigaku Zasshi. **71**, 19–29 (2016)
8. Sugiura, A., Tanaka, K., Takada, H., Kojima, T., Yamakawa, T., Miyao, M.: A temporal analysis of body sway caused by self-motion during stereoscopic viewing. In: Antona, M., Stephanidis, C. (eds.) UAHCI 2015. LNCS, vol. 9176, pp. 246–254. Springer, Cham (2015). https://doi.org/10.1007/978-3-319-20681-3_23
9. Donders, F.C.: Die Bewegungen des Gehirns und die Veränderungen der Gefässfüllung der Pia mater. Schmid's Fahrbucher. **69**, 16–20 (1851)
10. Hosford, P.S., Gourine, A.V.: What is the key mediator of the neurovascular coupling response? Neurosci. Biobehav. Rev. **96**, 174–181 (2019)
11. Ogawa, S., Lee, T.M., Nayak, A.S., Glynn, P.: Oxygenation-sensitive contrast in magnetic resonance image of rodent brain at high magnetic fields. Magn. Reson. Med. **14**, 68–78 (1990)
12. Logothetis, N.K., Pauls, J., Augath, M., Trinath, T., Oeltermann, A.: Neurophysiological investigation of the basis of the fMRI signal. Nature **412**, 150–157 (2001)
13. Ashburner, J.: SPM: a history. Neuroimage **62**, 791–800 (2012)
14. Evans, A.C., Collins, D.L., Milner, B.: An MRI-based stereotactic atlas from 250 young normal subjects. Soc. Neurosci. Abstr. **18**, 408 (1992)
15. Cavanna, A.E., Trimble, M.R.: The precuneus: a review of its functional anatomy and behavioural correlates. Brain **129**, 564–583 (2006)
16. Yamamoto, N., Philbeck, J.W.: Peripheral vision benefits spatial learning by guiding eye movements. Mem. Cognit. **41**, 109–121 (2013)
17. Diamant, E.: Unveiling the mystery of visual information processing in human brain. Res. **1225**, 171–178 (2008)

Author Index

© The Editor(s) (if applicable) and The Author(s), under exclusive license
to Springer Nature Singapore Pte Ltd. 2024
W. Hong and G. Kanaparan (Eds.): ICCSE 2023, CCIS 2023, pp. 495–499, 2024.
https://doi.org/10.1007/978-981-97-0730-0

Printed in the United States
by Baker & Taylor Publisher Services